COLLEGES WORTH YOUR MONEY

COLLEGES WORTH YOUR MONEY

A Guide to What America's Top Schools Can Do for You

Andrew Belasco, Dave Bergman, & Michael Trivette

ROWMAN & LITTLEFIELD
Lanham • Boulder • New York • London

Published by Rowman & Littlefield
An imprint of The Rowman & Littlefield Publishing Group, Inc.
4501 Forbes Boulevard, Suite 200, Lanham, Maryland 20706
www.rowman.com

6 Tinworth Street, London, SE11 5AL, United Kingdom

Distributed by NATIONAL BOOK NETWORK

British Library Cataloguing in Publication Information Available

Library of Congress Control Number: 2020932428

♾️™ The paper used in this publication meets the minimum requirements of American National Standard for Information Sciences—Permanence of Paper for Printed Library Materials, ANSI/NISO Z39.48-1992.

Contents

Before the birth of the modern internet, savvy teens seeking information on prospective colleges cracked open the latest Yellow Pages-thick college guidebook, eager to soak in school-specific admissions data that felt like classified information. Possessors of such guidebooks were the true insiders of the day, privy to admissions statistics that simply could not be found within the glossy brochures delivered to the masses via snail mail. By 2020, those oversized volumes have been rendered far less essential. Basic admissions data such as SAT ranges, grade point averages, tuition costs, and acceptance rates are available via fast and free Google searches. Everyone is now—at least in 1980s or '90s terms—an insider.

The formula for these annual editions is simple. Easy-to-find admissions and tuition data points are complemented by blocks of heavily anecdotal text designed to reveal something about the campus milieu: the quality of food, the architectural style of the buildings, the political leanings of the student body, and the subjective like. While these books all serve as useful starting points for your college search (we read them ourselves each year), they fail to acknowledge the seismic shift taking place in the national conversation about higher education—the idea that students should stop obsessing over gaining admission into the most prestigious schools that will accept them and instead ask, "What can a given college do for me?" If students/parents are going to pony up $200,000 or more in tuition alone, they should first demand to see outcomes data, return on investment (ROI) figures, and a statistically backed account of unique opportunities for undergraduates. That's where the college guide you're holding comes into play.

Why do I need this guide?

There are two main reasons:

(1) Given the absurd cost of a college education, finding a school that will provide an acceptable ROI has never been more challenging.

(2) Your prospective colleges are likely to be more selective than they were only a few years ago; greater information gathering/strategic planning will be required to successfully gain admission.

Let's begin with the issue of price. As we get older, it's easy to fall into a nostalgic trap on the subject of how much things cost. For example, "When I was a boy, you could feed a family of four for a Buffalo nickel." Yet when it comes to lamenting rising college expenses, there is actual data to back up the sticker shock. In 1950, the University of Pennsylvania charged $600 per year to attend—roughly $6,000 in 2020 money. Today, Penn's annual cost of attendance is over $77,000. By 1960, most private institutions charged an annual fee of $1,500–$2,000 that equates to $12,000–$16,000 today. In the current marketplace, a $50,000 annual tuition is considered "reasonable." This is hardly just a private school phenomenon. The University of North Carolina at Chapel Hill's in-state 2019–20 tuition cost of $9,018 is one of the best bargains in all of higher education. Of course, that pales in comparison to the in-state tuition of thirty years ago—only $504 per year. (No, that's *not* a typo).

Turning to the matter of increased selectivity, you don't need to look back to the '50s, '60s, or even '70s to find a college admissions landscape vastly different from today's hyper-competitive environment. In 1980, nearly half of all applicants were accepted into prestigious Swarthmore College while the Class of 2022 had a 9 percent acceptance rate. As recently as the 1990s, the University of Chicago accepted 60–70 percent of those who applied, but for applicants to the Class of 2022, only 7 percent were successful. Less drastic but still significant changes have proliferated as the overwhelming majority of desirable public and private schools have grown more selective in recent years. As of the publication of this book, many of the most prestigious schools in the country boast single-digit acceptance rates, including all the Ivy League schools (except Cornell University, which is a fraction over 10 percent) as well as Stanford University, Johns Hopkins University, Duke University, Northwestern University, Vanderbilt University, and the Massachusetts Institute of Technology. Other elite schools including Pomona College, Bowdoin College, Williams College, Amherst College, Rice University, and the University of Southern California all have inched closer to the single-digit club and will likely join it soon.

The reasons for this increased level of selectivity include an influx of highly-qualified foreign students applying to US colleges, the Common App making it easier for top students to apply to as many elite schools as they wish, and a greater number of applicants paying for services, such as private SAT tutors, that ultimately enhance their academic profiles.

How to use this guide:

We hope the above statistics have convinced you that the college selection and admissions process has never been more of a high-stakes game. Parents/students who are about to essentially take out another mortgage to finance their own or their teens' college education should, at the very least, first perform the equivalent of a home inspection. Just as it is easy to fall in love with a house based on a Zillow photo, many select a college based on surface observations such as the campus is pretty, the school colors would look nice on a bumper sticker, or you've heard good things from other parents in your social circle. Think of this guidebook as an inspection report with no crawlspace left unexplored.

Each profile includes six statistically rich narrative sections and two tables containing in excess of seventy additional data points. The following is a brief overview of the information included for each school and why it is important for prospective college students (and their parents) to know.

Inside the Classroom

We begin each profile by discussing what makes a given institution academically unique. Some schools have a core curriculum that dictates three semesters of study; others have an entirely open curriculum. Some mandate foreign language, physical education, a freshman seminar or two, and a senior thesis; others have no such requirements. Statistics on class size, undergraduate research opportunities, study abroad participation and — when possible — institutional survey data regarding professor availability and the quality of classroom instruction are included. In this section we also highlight particular programs/departments that have standout reputations as well as how seniors fare in landing nationally competitive postgraduate scholarships.

Outside the Classroom

Words such as "vibe," "feel," and "atmosphere" may sound like flaky reasons to pick one college over another, yet when formulating college lists, future applicants absolutely should be mindful of their fit at a given school. The key is to properly size up the vibe/feel/atmosphere through more than merely a brief and heavily sanitized campus tour.

Some traits of a given school are easy to spot, and the contrast between institutions can be stark. For example, attending a small liberal arts school is going to be a wholly different social experience than attending a flagship state university with ten times the enrollment. However, there are many small liberal arts schools with high percentages of student-athletes where Greek life dominates the social scene. While this section is certainly our most anecdotal, we use statistics to dig beyond mere generalizations wherever possible.

For instance, if — like at Wake Forest University — 85 percent of the student body participates in National Collegiate Athletic Association (NCAA), club, or intramural sports, and you hate sports, that information may help you cross the school off your list. If you are dead set on joining a fraternity or sorority, Bucknell University's 35-40 percent rate of participation in Greek life will be more attractive than the 4 percent pledge rate at Wesleyan University. If volunteer work is important to you, you may wish to target a school filled with kindred spirits, such as the College of William & Mary, where thousands perform community service every year. If a cappella is an essential creative outlet for you, a school such as Amherst, where one can barely count the number of established singing groups on two hands, may be appealing. Undoubtedly, any personality type can find at least a few like-minded souls at any of the 3,000 four-year colleges in the United States, but it's important that teens find schools where they can develop a true sense of belonging. Research has consistently demonstrated that college students who feel connected to their schools experience far greater academic success than those who do not.

Career Services

In an effort to entice applicants, college brochures are usually filled with group shots of smiling students on picturesque quads, amenities such as Olympic-size pools and rock-climbing walls, and dining halls that look like five-star restaurants. Those images are usually accompanied by some hollow catchphrase such as "Where leaders are born." Yet you likely won't find much (if any) information about the career services offerings—one of the most overlooked but important offices within a university. In reality, the professionals who provide individual career counseling, arrange internships, engage in corporate recruiting, and plan job fairs will do far more for your future than that towering rock climbing wall.

We answer the questions that students should ask when they evaluate their prospective colleges: What is the student-to-counselor ratio? What percent of students engage with career services? Does this happen in freshman year or does counseling only get utilized by seniors? We'll provide information on job fairs, networking events, corporate recruiting on campus, and how helpful staff are with arranging internships. In utilizing this section, you will discover which schools actually give rise to tomorrow's leaders vs. those whose public relations departments merely thought up an empty marketing slogan. And, yes, on occasion we will briefly note rock climbing walls or exceptionally delicious cuisine because, well, those things are nice to know as long as they aren't one of the top reasons you pick School A over School B.

Professional Outcomes

We'll look at how recent graduating classes are faring six months after graduation. In examining the list of companies that hire the most alumni, you'll see which schools serve as a pipeline to many of the nation's premier employers. Geographic information will allow you to see where the largest pockets of alumni settle—a factor that may assist your networking efforts. You'll also be able to identify which undergraduate institutions send large numbers of students to elite graduate and professional schools. Universities that have notable success preparing their students for admission into law and medical schools are highlighted.

Admissions

As wonderful as many high school guidance counselors are, even the best are pulled in a million different directions over the course of the day. To quantify that phenomenon, counselors in public high schools report spending only 22 percent of their time on college-related counseling while their private school counterparts spend a far healthier 55 percent. In either setting, given their breadth of responsibilities, even knowledgeable counselors may not be able to keep track of the latest admissions-related news at every one of the top postsecondary institutions in the country.

Given the aforementioned escalation in selectivity over the last few years, schools that may have been considered *safety schools* when you were a freshman may now be closer to *reach schools*. A multitude of applicants to the University of California's branch campuses discovered that reality the hard way in 2018. It's important to consider the way a given school is trending from a selectivity standpoint, which is why we include our unique "five-year admissions trend" metric that shows the degree to which the school has become more/less competitive in recent years. Further analysis of that number will reveal whether the decreasing acceptance rate is simply the result of an influx of borderline applicants or whether the profile of the average accepted student is actually shifting. We also will identify whether an admissions edge can be gained by applying early, the impact of legacy status, and the factors each admissions office values most.

Worth Your Money?

The worth of a college degree is almost always context-dependent. Plenty of students attend unspectacular universities and go on to incredible levels of success; conversely, plenty of young people have attended prestigious institutions and struggled in their careers. A school that may be an incredible value for an in-state electrical engineering major may be a terrible choice for out-of-state students concentrating in sociology.

The intent of this section is to (a) give you an overview of how generous (or stingy) particular schools are with financial aid; (b) inform you about cost of attendance, in-state vs. out-of-state tuition rates, and the amount of debt students graduate with; and (c) give an assessment of the circumstances in which one might want to be wary of paying the full sticker price for a given school. Think of this as an introductory counseling session that will get you thinking about whether a school's cost makes sense for *you*.

Data Tables

In addition to the data-heavy narrative section, each profile is accompanied by two tables brimming with useful and often underappreciated statistical information. The following data points are included:

Admissions Data

Admission Rate
The overall percentage of the total application pool that is offered admission.

Admission Rate (Men)
The overall percentage of male applicants that are offered admission.

Admission Rate (Women)
The overall percentage of the female applicants that are offered admission.

Early Action Admission Rate
The percentage of applicants admitted during the early action (EA) or single-choice early action (SCEA) rounds.

Early Decsion Admission Rate
The percentage of applicants admitted during the early decision (ED) round.

Admission Rate (five-year trend)
This is the percentage change in the acceptance rate from five years ago. For example, if a school's acceptance rate was 32 percent in 2013 and 27 percent in 2018, the five-year trend would be -5 percent.

Early Decision Admission Rate (five-year trend)
The percentage change in the early decision acceptance rate from five years ago.

Percent of Admits Attending (yield rate)
A school's yield rate is the percentage of accepted students who ultimately elect to enroll in the freshman class divided by the number of accepted applicants. For example, if 5,000 students were accepted and 1,000 chose to enroll, the yield rate would be 20 percent.

Transfer Admission Rate
The overall percentage of the total transfer application pool that is offered admission.

Number Offered Waitlist
The number of students offered a place on a school's waitlist.

Number Accepted Waitlist
The number of students who accepted a place on the waitlist.

Number Admitted Waitlist
The number of students who are admitted to the university from the waitlist.

SAT Math (middle 50 percent)
The 25th-and 75th-percentile SAT math scores for first-year students.

SAT Reading/Writing (middle 50 percent)
The 25th-and 75th-percentile reading/writing SAT scores for first-year students.

ACT Composite (middle 50 percent)
The 25th-and 75th-percentile composite ACT scores for first-year students.

Testing Policy
Whether the school requires the SAT/ACT or has a test-optional or test-flexible policy.

SAT Superscore
Whether the college will combine an applicant's highest scores by section across test administrations.

ACT Superscore
Whether the college will combine an applicant's highest scores by section across test administrations. (Note: More schools superscore the SAT than the ACT, and the policies are not always the same for both tests.)

Percent in Top 10 percent, 25 percent, and 50 percent of High School Class
Among enrolled freshmen who reported their class ranks, the percent that finished in the top tenth, quarter, and half of their graduating classes.

Enrollment Data

Total Undergraduate Enrollment
The number of undergraduate students attending the institution.

Percent Part-Time
The percentage of undergraduates taking fewer than twelve credits per semester.

Percent Male/Female
The percentage of males and percent of females that comprise the undergraduate student body.

Percent Out of State
The percentage of domestic (U.S.) students who are not residents of the state in which the college is located.

Percent Fraternity/Sorority
The percentage of undergraduates who are members of Greek organizations divided by the undergraduate population.

Percent on Campus (Freshmen)
The number of freshmen who live on campus divided by the number of freshmen.

Percent on Campus (All Undergraduates)
The number of undergraduates living on campus divided by the number of undergraduates.

Ethnic/Racial Demographics
The percentage of undergraduate students who identify as African American, Asian, Hispanic, and white.

Percent International
The number of foreign students enrolled at an American university who are studying through a temporary visa divided by the undergraduate population.

Percent Low-Income
The number of students who meet the US Department of Education standard for "low income" (for a family of four, that figure is $37,650 per year) divided by the undergraduate population.

Academics

Student-to-Faculty Ratio
The number of undergraduate students divided by the number of full-time faculty members.

Percent of Classes under Twenty Students
The number of undergraduate course sections with an enrollment under twenty divided by the number of undergraduate course sections.

Percent of Classes under Forty Students
The number of undergraduate course sections with an enrollment under forty divided by the number of undergraduate course sections.

Percent of Full-Time Faculty
The percentage of faculty members who are full-time professors at a given institution.

Percent of Full-Time Faculty with Terminal Degree
The percentage of full-time professors who possess the highest possible degree in their field (typically PhD).

Top Programs
This is not purely a list of the most popular majors by volume. While that is factored into our algorithm, so are other metrics including selectivity, student-to-faculty ratio, class size, peer assessment, graduate earnings (by major), and PhD productivity. (More details are included later in this section.)

Retention Rate
The percentage of freshmen who return to the same institution the following fall to begin their sophomore year.

Four-Year Graduation Rate
The percentage of enrolled undergraduate students who graduate in four years or fewer.

Six-Year Graduation Rate
The percentage of enrolled undergraduate students who graduate in six years or fewer.

Curricular Flexibility
Many colleges have a "core curriculum" and "distributional requirements" that dictate what specific courses and/or general categories of courses all undergraduates must complete in order to graduate. We awarded schools one of three grades: Very Flexible, Somewhat Flexible, or Less Flexible, depending on the extent and specificity of their curricular mandates.

<u>Academic Rating</u>
To construct an academic rating for each college, we rely on ten different indicators of academic quality, namely the average SAT/ACT composite of incoming students, the percentage of incoming students ranked in the top 10 percent of their high school class, student-to-faculty ratio, class size, the percentage of faculty who are full-time employees, the percentage of faculty with terminal degrees, mean faculty salary, freshman retention rate, six year-graduation rate, and graduation performance. This last variable compares an institution's actual graduation rate with its predicted graduation rate, after controlling for the high school class rank and SAT/ACT scores of incoming students as well as the percentage of undergraduates receiving a Pell Grant, a grant primarily given to low-income students.

After collecting data, we normalize and subsequently sum values across all ten indicators, assigning each institution a total score, and by extension, its academic rating. Academic ratings range from one to five stars (institutions receiving a rating of lower than three stars are not featured in this book), with a rating of five stars assigned to colleges and universities receiving the highest total scores. We opted to use a discrete variable (a "star" rating) instead of each college's total numerical score, because incorporating the latter would presume that our assessment is precise. It is not. An institution's academic environment and offerings can never be captured by a single number. That said, we do believe the ratings assigned can prove useful when comparing the academic climates and offerings of the colleges featured in this book.

Financial

<u>Institutional Type</u>
Indicates whether the school is a public or private institution.

<u>In-State Tuition</u>
For public schools, the annual cost of full-time tuition for one academic year charged to state residents. For private schools, we list the general tuition here.

<u>Out-of-State Tuition</u>
For public schools, the annual cost of full-time tuition for one academic year charged to state residents. For private schools, we list the general tuition here.

<u>Room & Board</u>
The annual cost for university-owned housing and meal plans.

<u>Required Fees</u>
Mandatory fees charged by the school for things such as technology, the library, athletics, laboratory experiences, and transportation.

<u>Books and Supplies</u>
The average figure students pay for one academic year's worth of books purchased through the university bookstore.

<u>Average Need-Based Scholarships</u>
Of students who qualified for need-based aid, the average dollar amount the institution awarded.

<u>Average Percent of Need Met</u>
Of students who qualified for need-based aid, the average percentage of the demonstrated need that the institution met.

<u>Average Merit-Based Scholarship</u>
Among those who received a non-need-based financial award, the average annual award that was granted.

Percent Receiving Merit-Based Scholarships
The percentage of undergraduates presently enrolled who received some degree of non-need-based aid.

Average Cumulative Debt
Among students who took out loans to pay for a given college, the average cumulative debt owed upon graduation.

Percentage of Students Borrowing
The percentage of students who are taking out loans in order to fund a portion of their educational expenses.

Career

Who Recruits
A list of high-profile companies that regularly recruit on campus.

Notable Internships
Collected from institutional data sources, this is a list of employers who regularly provide meaningful internships to undergraduate students.

Top Industries
A list of the sectors where the highest number of recent graduates find employment.

Top Employers
According to LinkedIn data, the companies/organizations that employ the largest number of graduates.

Where Alumni Work
According to LinkedIn data, the cities where the largest concentration of alumni currently live.

Earnings
In an effort to give you the most complete picture of alumni earning possible, we include three data points. They are as follows:

College Scorecard: This number is the median earnings of students who received federal financial aid ten years after entering a given college.

The Equality of Opportunity Project: The results of a Harvard economist's look at millions of anonymous tax records. The figures are median salary figures at age thirty-four. This ongoing research endeavor examined more than 30 million tax returns of individuals who were born between 1980 and 1991.

PayScale: The median salary of individuals with 10+ years of work experience based on millions of survey respondents. This figure tends to be higher than the other two because it includes professionals in mid-to-late career, when earnings are typically highest. Additionally, these salaries are self-reported, which makes them the least accurate of the bunch.

Rankings

Forbes Ranking
A college's ranking by *Forbes*, which is determined via the following formula: salary (20 percent), debt (20 percent), student experience (20 percent), American leaders list (15 percent), academic success (12.5 percent), and graduation rate (12.5 percent).

Money Ranking
A college's ranking by *Money*, which is determined via the following formula: six-year graduation rate (30 percent), value-added graduation rate (30 percent), peer quality (10 percent), instructor quality (10 percent), financial troubles (15 percent), and Pell Grant recipient outcomes (5 percent).

US News & World Report Ranking
A college's ranking by *US News & World Report (US News)*, which is determined via the following formula: outcomes (35 percent), faculty resources (20 percent), expert opinion (20 percent), financial resources (10 percent), student excellence (10 percent), and alumni giving (5 percent).

Wall Street Journal/Times Higher Education Ranking
A college's ranking by *The Wall Street Journal/Times Higher Education (THE)*, which is determined via the following formula: resources (30 percent), engagement (20 percent), outcomes (40 percent), and environment (10 percent).

Washington Monthly Ranking
A college's ranking by *Washington Monthly*, which is determined via the following formula: social mobility (33.3 percent), research (33.3 percent), and community and national service (33.3 percent).

Where did this data come from?

Admissions Data

Our primary source for SAT and ACT middle-50 percent ranges is the Common Data Set (CDS), a collaborative effort of data providers in the higher education community in which most institutions participate. We gathered superscoring policies from institutional websites and, in the many cases where nothing was listed publicly, from direct contact with admissions offices. We also gathered regular and early decision (ED) acceptance rates and waitlist statistics from a combination of the CDS and institutional websites.

Enrollment Data

We took enrollment and demographic data directly from each school's CDS. If the school did not publish a CDS, we collected that information from alternative institutional reports.

Academics Data

We pulled class sizes, student-to-faculty ratios, and graduation/retention rates from the CDS or other available institutional publications.

Top Programs Within Colleges

Our methodology for determining each college's top academic programs incorporated the following four factors:

1. Major Emphasis
Indicates the number of students at an institution studying a specific major. If a high percentage of students at a particular college are studying a major, it is likely that the major attracts a relatively large portion of the institution's resources. To measure major emphasis and we relied on data collected by the National Center for Education Statistics as reported by The Integrated Postsecondary Education Data System (IPEDS).

2. Student-to-Faculty Ratio and Class Size
Research consistently shows that class size as well as student–faculty interaction and collaboration leads to better learning and career-related outcomes. We collected data for these indicators from the US Department of Education, institutional websites, and surveys of college administrators.

3. Peer Assessment

To derive a peer assessment score, we relied on questionnaires distributed to both college admission experts (including school counselors, independent education consultants, and college admission officers) and higher education administrators, and then compared responses with "strong programs" data published by U.S. News & World Report, Niche, and other reputable sources that rank colleges within a specific discipline (e.g. *CSRankings.org* for Computer Science, *The Hollywood Reporter* for Film, *Foreign Policy* for International Relations, etc.) Alone, peer assessment surveys are subject to a fair amount of bias. However, when evaluated in sum and considered along with more objective data—such as that examining major emphasis and class size—they can provide more complete and corroborative insight into the strength of a particular program/major.

4. PhD Productivity

While most undergraduates have no intent to pursue a doctoral degree, the rate at which a department/program produces Ph.D. recipients arguably reflects how well the program promotes academic rigor and prepares students to tackle advanced coursework. When available, we used data provided by the National Science Foundation in order to assess which programs graduated the highest percentage of students who later completed a PhD degree.

Top Colleges for America's Top Majors

When choosing which majors to feature in section, we considered both professional prospects (i.e. which majors results in high salaries and ample job opportunities) and popularity of discipline (i.e. how many students pursue the major). In order to identify the top colleges for each major, we relied on the same variables used to select the top programs within each college, as well as three additional variables, namely those for institutional selectivity, major share, and graduate earnings (see descriptions of variables below). It is also important to note that for some areas of study (e.g. Actuarial Science, Information Systems), we list colleges that do not offer a formal major, but that possess offerings (within a minor or informal concentration) so strong that they warrant inclusion.

1. Institutional Selectivity

Though selectivity is not a perfect proxy for college or major/program quality, it is highly correlated with student ability/achievement and institutional expenditures per student, which both contribute significantly to the undergraduate learning experience. We looked to a college's freshman admission rate and average SAT/ACT score (as reported by each institution's CDS) to measure selectivity.

2. Major Share

If a college enrolls a relatively high percentage of all students in the United States studying a particular major, it is likely that the college has been identified by prospective students, employers, and other stakeholders as a leader in that subject area. Though this assumption may result in bias against smaller institutions or programs, it is important to account for the fact that larger programs often have the ability to attract more tuition revenue, meet fixed costs, and reinvest the major's offerings. To measure major share we relied on data collected by the National Center for Education Statistics as reported by IPEDS.

3. Graduate Earnings

To measure graduate earnings, we relied on salary data provided by College Score Card, PayScale, and the Equality of Opportunity Project, all of which indicate both early-career and mid-career wages of students by college. We analyzed both early-career and mid-career wages because the former is typically an indicator of how employers perceive the quality of a particular major/program, while the latter indicates how well a major/program may have prepared students for work.

In addition, when able, we used data indicating graduate earnings by field of study, as doing so provides a more accurate measure of the relationship between a specific academic program and graduate earnings. For example, PayScale provides salary data for a student attending Boston University and majoring in engineering, which is different from salary data for students attending Boston University and majoring in business.

Financial Data

Financial data is taken directly from each school's CDS. If the school did not publish a CDS, we collected this information from alternative institutional reports.

Career/Salary Data

There are two main sources for information related to the most popular industries and the companies at which alumni have the most representation. LinkedIn is an excellent resource for gathering data on how many alumni of all ages are working for a particular employer. Reports the colleges produce for each recent graduating class—often called "First Destination Surveys"—receive high response rates and offer a glimpse into where the Class of 2019 is headed. If your aim is to work at a relatively new mega-company such as SpaceX, Uber, or Airbnb, it may be more helpful to know where recent graduates have landed. Where possible, we included this data in the narrative sections of the profiles.

No one source of salary data is perfect, so we sought to give you as many data points as possible for each college. As previously mentioned, the salary figures provided in each data table come from College Scorecard, PayScale, and the Equality of Opportunity project. We also included First Destination Survey data in instances where reliable institutional data could be reported. This sometimes offers a glimpse at average or median starting salaries for a school's recent graduates; certain universities provide a breakdown of starting salary by major.

Rankings

Taken at face value, a school's rank in a given publication can be unhelpful or even misleading to your unique college search. For instance, the fact that the 2019 *US News & World Report* rankings list Emory University twenty-first and Tufts University is tied for twenty-seventh doesn't mean that one school is superior to the other; Emory and Tufts happen to be two of the finest schools in the country, and assigning any value to a fraction of a point in a ranking algorithm would just be plain silly. However, when considered in proper context and across several different rankings systems utilizing different algorithms, one can get a general idea of a school's reputation in the eyes of graduate schools and top employers. Collectively, we believe that these rankings can provide a degree of insight as you ponder your postsecondary future.

Why some colleges made the cut and others did not.

We wish to be fully transparent about an important issue: There is no definitive algorithm that would determine the dollar-for-dollar "best colleges for your money." Sure, you could base your rankings solely on return on investment figures and just list the top 150 schools in terms of median salaries. However, doing so would pretty much produce a list of the colleges that produce the greatest percentage of business, computer science, and engineering grads because those fields generally pay the best. You could also concoct a pseudoscientific formula with dozens of inputs that would spew out a concrete score that would serve as a defense as to why one school made the 150 and others were left out in the cold.

In truth, selecting these schools was as much art as science. In aiming to create a useful college guide, we drew on our collective experience of having guided thousands of students through the application process over the past decade. In seeking quantifiable evidence of value, we also examined every available report on earnings, social mobility, academic rankings, and school-specific outcomes. In the end, we were genuinely surprised by some of the lesser-known schools that stood out by those metrics and were equally surprised by some big-name schools that fared poorer than expected. Ultimately, we are extremely confident that every institution included in this book does admirable work on behalf of its undergraduates.

On the other hand, there are not only 150 schools that are, in our professional opinion, "Worth Your Money." So before alums or representatives from omitted schools start penning nasty emails to us, this book is not being intentionally exclusionary—150 is an arbitrary cutoff because—well—you have to have an arbitrary cutoff. Depending on one's circumstances, (again, all higher education value is context dependent), there may be 250-300 schools that could serve as fine postsecondary destinations from which to springboard into a successful career/life. Our hope is that this book will help give the tools and mindset to evaluate any prospective institution, whether or not you find that college in the pages that follow.

Final Thoughts

Before you turn to the profiles section of this book, consider the following startling facts:

- Barely half of current college students can provide an accurate estimate of their freshman year cost of attendance.
- Only 55 percent of undergraduates nationwide finish their degree within six years.
- For those who do graduate, the average debt load is roughly $30,000.
- Studies estimate that as many as 43 percent of college grads end up working in jobs that do not require a college degree.
- Fifty-one percent of college grads ultimately wish they had chosen a different school, degree program, or major.

If picking the right college was easy, the numbers above wouldn't be nearly so bleak. Selecting a school that will put you on the right side of those unfortunate statistics takes a great deal of hard work and planning. Applicants are often so swept up in the quest to gain admission into a given school that they fail to stop and consider exactly why their dream school became their dream in the first place.

A dream college—or to be less hyperbolic, a good-fit college—should check boxes in terms of the availability and quality of academic programs of interest, the extracurricular opportunities and aspects of campus life that will promote a sense of connectedness, the level of career services you will need to get on the path to the right career/graduate school, a demonstrated history of positive outcomes for graduates, and a school where you have a genuine chance of being accepted.

Whether you are a parent or high school student, rest assured that by carefully examining the profiles that follow you are about to become a more knowledgeable college consumer than your adult or teenage peers. Ideally, you will enter the pages that follow with an open mind and be willing to consider disconfirming data about a school you previously thought was perfect for you as well as new, unexpected information about a school you would never have considered before. While the college search and admissions process is rife with challenges and stressors, eschewing the cacophony of unhelpful voices in favor of data will result in increased confidence and focus as you make this extremely important life decision.

Enjoy the journey ahead!

America's Top Schools

American University

Washington, District of Columbia | Admissions Phone: 202-885-6000

ADMISSION
Admission Rate: 32%
Admission Rate - Men: 29%
Admission Rate - Women: 33%
EA Admission Rate: Not Offered
ED Admission Rate: 81%
Admission Rate (5-Year Trend): -12%
ED Admission Rate (5-Year Trend): +4%
% of Admits Attending (Yield): 29%
Transfer Admission Rate: 62%

\# Offered Wait List: 4,598
\# Accepted Wait List: 760
\# Admitted Wait List: 188

SAT Reading/Writing (Middle 50%): 630-700
SAT Math (Middle 50%): 590-680
ACT Composite (Middle 50%): 27-31
Testing Policy: Test Optional
SAT Superscore: Yes
ACT Superscore: Yes

% Graduated in Top 10% of HS Class: 31%
% Graduated in Top 25% of HS Class: 70%
% Graduated in Top 50% of HS Class: 93%

ENROLLMENT
Total Undergraduate Enrollment: 8,287
% Part-Time: 4%
% Male: 38%
% Female: 62%
% Out-of-State: 83%
% Fraternity: 9%
% Sorority: 11%
% On-Campus (Freshman): N/A
% On-Campus (All Undergraduate): N/A

% African-American: 7%
% Asian: 7%
% Hispanic: 12%
% White: 53%
% Other: 4%
% Race or Ethnicity Unknown: 4%
% International: 13%
% Low-Income: 19%

ACADEMICS
Student-to-Faculty Ratio: 12:1
% of Classes Under 20: 55%
% of Classes Under 40: 96%
% Full-Time Faculty: 54%
% Full-Time Faculty w/ Terminal Degree: 94%

Top Programs
Business Administration
Film and Media Arts
International Studies
Journalism
Political Science
Public Health
Public Relations & Strategic Communication

Retention Rate: 88%
4-Year Graduation Rate: 75%
6-Year Graduation Rate: 80%

Curricular Flexibility: Somewhat Flexible
Academic Rating: ★★★

Inside the Classroom

Located in the heart of our nation's capital, American University's highly desirable location and access to an abundance of government/corporate internships and networking opportunities has contributed to the university becoming far more selective than it was a decade ago. AU presently plays host to 8,100 undergraduate students as well as over 5,700 graduate and law students. Campus is a genuinely diverse place with an undergraduate population comprised 25 percent of underrepresented minorities and another 7 percent of international students. There are sixty-seven undergraduate degrees for students to choose from at AU across six undergraduate colleges: the College of Arts & Sciences, the Kogod School of Business, the School of Communication, the School of Education, the School of International Service, and the School of Public Affairs.

All undergrads are exposed to a recently-adopted core curriculum that focuses on enhancing students' meta-cognitive abilities. Requirements include more than thirty credits of study in courses such as Complex Problems, Quantitative Literacy, Ethical Reasoning, Creative-Aesthetic Inquiry, and Written Communication. As the school itself explains, the "AU Core general education program offers a four-year, inquiry-based liberal arts education, beginning with a Complex Problems seminar (small, nineteen-person seminars that include cocurricular experiences), bridging to essential habits of mind and integrating these skills and habits with the student's major, and culminating in a capstone." The American University Experience Program is designed to provide first-years with the advising and experiences that help students adjust to the academic rigors and social challenges that arise with the transition to college.

A low 12:1 student-to-faculty ratio allows roughly half of offered courses to be capped at nineteen students; the average undergraduate class size is twenty-three. Undergraduate research opportunities are taken advantage of by 50 percent of first-year students and 40 percent of seniors. For the last twelve years AU has hosted an Undergraduate Research Symposium at the end of each year where students can present their research. Students here are not afraid to hop on a plane and pursue a semester's worth of education in a foreign land. A substantial 55 percent of undergrads take a semester abroad with the most popular destination points being the United Kingdom, Italy, Spain, Kenya, and Belgium.

American's School of International Service (SIS) is one of the top-ranked programs in the country—its Public Affairs program also receives universally high marks. In terms of sheer popularity, the most commonly conferred degrees are in the social sciences (36 percent), business (17 percent), communication/journalism (11 percent), and the visual and performing arts (6 percent). Graduates fare quite well in securing service-oriented awards and scholarships. Among medium-sized universities, AU is the number one producer of Peace Corps volunteers in the country. It also boasts the most Boren Scholars, awarded to students who wish to study language for the purpose of national security. AU is also one of only seven schools to produce more than one Truman Scholar in 2017, and it saw thirty-seven undergraduates win Fulbright Scholarships from 2013-18.

Outside the Classroom

This ninety-acre campus receives accolades as one of the most beautiful urban campuses in the country. Off campus, Northwest DC is a happening place, containing a number of other large schools (Georgetown, GW, Howard, and UDC) and Capital One Arena, home to the Wizards, Capitals, and countless concerts. All of the dining, cultural, and museum experiences the District of Columbia offers can be accessed car-free via the Metro. For a flat fee, students receive a University Pass entitling them to unlimited Metro rides. The undergraduate population is 63 percent female, which certainly influences social life on campus. Fraternities attract 9 percent of men and sororities draw 11 percent of women. The Eagles play Division I sports in the Patriot League (except for wrestling) and boast six men's teams and eight women's teams. Another twenty-five club teams provide opportunities for athletic participation. For the less athletically inclined, 250 student organizations are available including student government, political clubs, charitable groups, and those dedicated purely to recreational pursuits. Facilities for student use include three gymnasiums, an aquatic center featuring two eight-lane pools, a two-mile fitness trail, and a beautiful outdoor athletic complex with basketball and tennis courts.

Career Services

The AU Career Center is staffed by thirty full-time professional employees who serve as career counselors, employer relations specialists, merit awards program coordinators, and alumni career coordinators. That works out to a phenomenal student-to-advisor ratio of 240:1, among the best of any midsize institution included in this book. It's no wonder that 99 percent of surveyed undergraduates are happy with the school's career advising services.

AU does an exceptional job hooking up students with internship opportunities; 91 percent of grads had such an experience. Being located in DC is a boon to internship opportunities as the leading host agencies include the Department of Education, State, Homeland Security, DC Public Schools, and the Public Defender Service for the District of Columbia. The Employer-in-Residence program brings organizations including Deloitte, the CIA, CNN, and Google on campus for one-one-one networking opportunities with undergrads. Student-Alumni

Networking Receptions in areas such as human security, public health, education, and energy, the environment, and sustainability allow current students to network with alumni working in their area of interest. In the 2018-19 academic year 504 employers recruited at AU, 238 hiring organizations attended career fairs, and 523 on-campus interviews were conducted. Among the employers that recruited on campus in that same time were the CIA, Politico, Booz Allen Hamilton, the Washington Nationals, the US Department of Defense, EY, Bloomberg, and Yelp.

Professional Outcomes

Within six months of graduation, 92 percent of AU grads have found employment, are enrolled in grad school, or both. There is a 60/40 split on landing jobs in the private sector versus finding employment in nonprofit/government arena. A healthy percentage of grads are attracted to public service in the form of Teach for America and the Peace Corps as both organizations are among the top five employers of recent grads. Ernst & Young, Deloitte, and the US Army round out the list. Across all graduating years, more than one hundred alumni presently work for the US House of Representatives, the US Department of State, Booz Allen Hamilton, Google, EY, IBM, PwC, and Accenture. With a heavy concentration of grads flowing into the public sector, starting salaries are not eye-popping—32 percent start above $50k, and 85 percent start above $40k. Predictably, graduates of the Kogod School of Business fare better than the average AU grad with 58 percent starting at over $50k. Many remain in DC but many others flock to New York City, Boston, San Francisco, Los Angeles, and Philly in substantial numbers.

Many of the most popular grad school destinations are only a Metro stop away. George Washington, Georgetown, Johns Hopkins, and American itself head the list. Seventeen percent of those who graduate from the School of Arts Sciences and the School of Public Affairs go straight into graduate school (including those working and going to grad school). Far lower concentrations of graduates from other schools within the university dive right into continuing their education. Fewer than fifty graduates apply to medical school each year, but some have had success in recent years gaining acceptance into schools including the Georgetown University School of Medicine, the University of Massachusetts Medical School, and Upstate Medical University. Recent grads pursuing a legal education have done so at the University of Pennsylvania, the University of Miami, Villanova University and, of course, American's own Washington College of Law.

Admission

American University had a 46 percent acceptance rate in 2014, hit an all-time low of 26 percent in 2016, and accepted 32 percent of applicants seeking a place in the Class of 2022. While acceptance rates have plummeted at AU in recent years, the profile of the average attending student hasn't changed commensurately. The ACT middle-50 percent range five years ago was 27-31, identical to the range today, and the SAT ranges have remained fairly constant as well. The average GPA for an entering member of the Class of 2022 was 3.6. While 40 percent possessed high school GPAs above a 3.75, 16 percent earned under a 3.25, giving hope to those with more B's than A's on their transcript.

Additionally, it is important to note that American is test-optional, having been one of the earlier competitive institutions to jettison test scores almost a decade ago. The strongest emphasis is placed on the rigor of one's course load, GPA and, most interestingly, applicant's interest. Since AU is a popular backup, the school very much wants to know if it is one of your top choices. This idea is supported by the school's early decision acceptance rate. In 2018, the school accepted 791 of 974 ED applicants, an overwhelming 81 percent. American is a quality institution situated in a city that is a highly desirable destination for young people. While a surface-level glance at its admissions data may suggest an increasingly competitive environment, AU is still accessible to good but not top-of-the-class students who view the school as their number one choice.

Worth Your Money?

Spending big money on tuition to attend American University can be a wise decision, but it really depends on your financial circumstances and academic area of interest. The annual cost of attendance is $64,769, but approximately 50 percent of undergraduates qualify for an average aid award of $29k. Unfortunately, American is not terribly generous with merit aid, awarding scholarships to only one-quarter of students. (The average award is $13k.) Yet, if you want a school that opens doors to jobs in politics, government, and major consulting firms, AU may be worth the expense.

FINANCIAL
Institutional Type: Private
In-State Tuition: $49,070
Out-of-State Tuition: $49,070
Room & Board: $14,880
Required Fees: $819
Books & Supplies: $800

Avg. Need-Based Aid: $29,118
Avg. % of Need Met: 87%

Avg. Merit-Based Aid: $13,347
% Receiving Merit-Based Aid: 25%

Avg. Cumulative Debt: $35,122
% of Students Borrowing: 63%

CAREER
Who Recruits
1. Central Intelligence Agency
2. Politico
3. Yelp
4. Government Accoutability Office
5. AARP

Notable Internships
1. United States Senate
2. Smithsonian
3. American Foreign Service Association

Top Industries
1. Business
2. Education
3. Media
4. Social Services
5. Operations

Top Employers
1. U.S. State Department
2. Deloitte
3. Booz Allen Hamilton
4. U.S. House of Representatives
5. IBM

Where Alumni Work
1. Washington, DC
2. New York City
3. Boston
4. Philadelphia
5. San Francisco

Median Earnings
College Scorecard (Early Career): $61,000
EOP (Early Career): $59,100
PayScale (Mid-Career): $102,900

RANKINGS
Forbes: 126
Money: 456
U.S. News: 77 (T), National Universities
Wall Street Journal/THE: 131
Washington Monthly: 255, National Universities

#CollegesWorthYourMoney

Amherst College

Amherst, Massachusetts | Admissions Phone: 413-542-2328

Inside the Classroom

One of the premier liberal arts colleges in the country—and one the most selective—Amherst College is an Ivy-equivalent institution that offers its brilliant student body a one-of-a-kind academic experience. A mere 1,850 undergraduates grace this picturesque rural campus located seventy-five miles west of Boston. Yet, a small town location is not at all indicative of an isolated existence. If the forty majors and 850 course offerings on campus aren't enough, Amherst belongs to the Five College Consortium that allows students to take any course offered at Mount Holyoke, Smith, Hampshire College, or UMass-Amherst.

Similar to Brown's "New Curriculum," Amherst operates its "Open Curriculum" that requires no specific courses or distribution of credits. Students have the flexibility to pursue their areas of passion and interest from the very start of their collegiate experience. With no burdensome requirements, double majoring is commonplace with over 30 percent of the student body electing to study at least one additional discipline. The college encourages students to "take full responsibility for their intellectual growth, in the same way they will take responsibility for important choices later in life."

If you crave facetime with your professors, Amherst delivers. A 7-to-1 student-to-faculty ratio allows for 71 percent of courses to have fewer than twenty students and 30 percent to have single-digit enrollments. That level of intimacy pays off with the forging of student-faculty relationships. By senior year, 98 percent of seniors report feeling close enough to a faculty member to ask for a letter of recommendation. The eight-to-ten-week Summer Science Undergraduate Research Program is available for students as are plenty of grants aimed at funding original student research projects. A sizable number of students study abroad, 43 percent to be precise, in just about any country you can name from Namibia to Trinidad. The school's student body has become increasingly diverse in recent years, now boasting double-digit percentages of African American, Latino, and first-generation students.

A true liberal arts college, Amherst possesses strong offerings across the board, most notably in economics, English, history, mathematics, and law (through its one-of-a-kind major in Law, Jurisprudence and Social Thought). Amherst also boasts one of the most esteemed (and highest paid) liberal arts faculties in the country. Students are always competitive for postgraduate awards and fellowships. The college has been recognized as one of the top producers of Fulbright Scholars for over a decade; it had eight winners in 2019 and had more Watson Fellows in 2017 than any other institution in the country.

Outside the Classroom

Amherst is the rare school where 98 percent of undergraduates reside in school-owned housing. There are no Greek organizations, but a colossal 37 percent of Amherst students are rostered on one of the college's twenty-seven NCAA Division III sports teams, which means that many are dedicating a good portion of their time to athletics. For everyone else, over 150 student organizations are operating on campus. The schools six a cappella groups and four-ensemble Choral Society play a notable enough role to have earned the school the nickname "The Singing College." Membership in the Five College Consortium opens the door to a variety of other clubs and activities within close proximity. However, it is important to note that the other four campuses are not adjoining—UMass and Hampshire are about a ten-minute drive, and Smith and Mount Holyoke take twenty minutes to reach by car. Guest speakers are regularly on campus. Each year, the Amherst Leads organization brings up to twenty-five well known athletes, business leaders, and writers/journalists to speak on campus. Dorms, food, and other amenities generally receive positive reviews. For students who want to be in touch with nature, a 500-acre wildlife preserve is located on campus, and it can be freely hiked and explored.

Career Services

Unlike at just about every other institution of higher education, the vast majority of the Amherst student body actually takes advantage of the Career Center's offerings. In fact, the Loeb Center for Career Exploration and Planning advises more than 1,400 students and alumni each year for a total of more than 6,000 sessions. That prodigious output comes from the office's thirteen full-time staff members who focus on either career advising or employer relations. Loeb's 142:1 student-to-advisor ratio is among the best of any school featured in this guide.

Amherst does a superb job recruiting companies to campus with more than 175 visiting per year and close to 450 interviews taking place on campus, which is roughly the size of the graduating class. There were fifty-nine days in the 2017-18 school year on which interviews were taking place on campus. Other programs, such as Career Treks, involve organized trips to Boston, New York City, and Los Angeles. Those trips allow students the chance to meet with alumni in the areas of finance, government, entertainment, education, and philanthropy. The Pathways program facilitates hundreds of additional mentoring relationships between alumni and current students each year. Nearly one-quarter of freshmen are enrolled in the Amherst Select Internship Program, which allows first-year students to jump directly into a hands-on learning opportunity.

E-mail: admissions@amherst.edu | Website: www.amherst.edu

Professional Outcomes

Whether you are interested in going directly into the workforce or continuing into graduate school, Amherst's reputation and connected alumni network will open doors. A few months after graduation, 98 percent of the Class of 2018 had already found its way into the world of employment, graduate school, or a volunteer organization. The highest number of recent grads went into finance (37 percent) with education (21 percent) and science/technology (11 percent) next in popularity. Recent graduates found jobs everywhere from Bain Capital to the United Talent Agency to the US Department of State. By sheer volume, the largest employers of Amherst grads is a high-end list including Google, Deloitte, Morgan Stanley, and Goldman Sachs. The average starting salary for Amherst graduates is around $60k, making them among the highest-paid liberal arts grads in the country. That is even more impressive when you consider that Amherst doesn't even have an engineering program, the profession that usually bolsters starting salary figures.

Amherst grads fare well at gaining acceptance to elite schools. It regularly sees 50 percent or more of applicants get into law schools like those at Georgetown, Columbia, Harvard, Berkeley, and Stanford, more than twice those schools' overall acceptance rates. In total, the schools where the highest number of Amherst grads can be found pursuing advanced degrees includes University of Cambridge (UK), MIT, Dartmouth, and the University of Pennsylvania. Fifty to sixty Amherst grads apply to medical school each year, and the acceptance rate hovers around 75-80 percent. As with law schools, students attend many of the finest medical institutions in the world. In order, the greatest number of alumni settle in New York City, Boston, San Francisco, and Washington, DC.

Admission

Amherst accepted under 13 percent of applicants to the Class of 2022. The average test score of admitted students was 33 on the ACT and 1492 on the SAT. That SAT number is twenty points higher than it was one year ago. However, Amherst has long been one of the most selective liberal arts schools in the country, so the landscape hasn't changed all that much. The college has had an acceptance rate of under 16 percent for more than a decade. Unsurprisingly, a high percentage of admitted students finished in the top 10 percent of their high school class—88 percent at last count. An impressive 20 percent of the Class of 2022 were valedictorians. This cohort has mid-50 percent standardized test score ranges of 1390-1540 on the SAT and 31-34 on the ACT.

The admissions office lists a whopping nine categories as having the highest level of influence on admissions decisions. That list includes talent/ability, character/personal qualities, recommendations, and first-generation status. While the process is holistic and genuinely committed to increasing the underrepresented minority and first-generation presence on campus, Amherst remains one of the most selective liberal arts colleges in the United States.

If Amherst is your top choice, applying ED can give you a slight edge; 38 percent of the 2018-19 freshman class were accepted via the ED round, versus 11.5 percent in the regular round; roughly 20 percent of those admitted via the early round were children of alumni. Many of Amherst's varsity athletes are also admitted early; the school claims that fewer than seventy admitted athletes per year are given preferential admissions treatment, a figure that equates to a sizable 15 percent of the class. Successful applicants will be near (or at) the top of their high school class, have earned standardized test scores in the top 1-2 percent, and possess unique gifts/intangibles that help separate them from a mass of similarly qualified peers.

Worth Your Money?

Close to half of Amherst students will pay the full $74,000 cost of attendance, a four-year sum of $296,000. This is because the college does not award merit aid, only need-based. For the 56 percent who qualify for financial aid, Amherst does meet 100 percent of their demonstrated need, which works out to an average of $59k per year, making the school quite affordable. The majority of the students paying full freight come from families in the top income percentiles, rendering the impact of the huge bill minimal. Amherst is an Ivy-level school that is worth attending for most as it will legitimately play a role in opening any and all employment or graduate schools dreams you could conjure up.

FINANCIAL
Institutional Type: Private
In-State Tuition: $55,520
Out-of-State Tuition: $55,520
Room & Board: $14,740
Required Fees: $906
Books & Supplies: $1,000

Avg. Need-Based Aid: $58,880
Avg. % of Need Met: 100%

Avg. Merit-Based Aid: $0
% Receiving Merit-Based Aid: 0%

Avg. Cumulative Debt: $13,710
% of Students Borrowing: 30%

CAREER
Who Recruits
1. Hulu
2. FiscalNote
3. T. Rowe Price
4. RBC Capital
5. Fox Sports

Notable Internships
1. National Center for Health Research
2. U.S. House of Representatives
3. NY State Division of Human Rights

Top Industries
1. Business
2. Education
3. Research
4. Media
5. Legal

Top Employers
1. Google
2. Goldman Sachs
3. JP Morgan
4. Massachusetts General Hospital
5. Citi

Where Alumni Work
1. New York City
2. Boston
3. San Francisco
4. Washington, DC
5. Springfield, MA

Median Earnings
College Scorecard (Early Career): $65,000
EOP (Early Career): $69,300
PayScale (Mid-Career): $116,500

RANKINGS
Forbes: 28
Money: 64
U.S. News: 2, Liberal Arts Colleges
Wall Street Journal/THE: 20
Washington Monthly: 3, Liberal Arts Colleges

#CollegesWorthYourMoney

Arizona State University

Tempe, Arizona | Admissions Phone: 480-965-7788

ADMISSION
Admission Rate: 85%
Admission Rate - Men: 83%
Admission Rate - Women: 87%
EA Admission Rate: Not Offered
ED Admission Rate: Not Offered
Admission Rate (5-Year Trend): +5%
ED Admission Rate (5-Year Trend): Not Offered
% of Admits Attending (Yield): 39%
Transfer Admission Rate: 84%

Offered Wait List: Not Offered
Accepted Wait List: Not Offered
Admitted Wait List: Not Offered

SAT Reading/Writing (Middle 50%): 570-670
SAT Math (Middle 50%): 560-690
ACT Composite (Middle 50%): 22-29
Testing Policy: ACT/SAT Required
SAT Superscore: No
ACT Superscore: No

% Graduated in Top 10% of HS Class: 33%
% Graduated in Top 25% of HS Class: 62%
% Graduated in Top 50% of HS Class: 89%

ENROLLMENT
Total Undergraduate Enrollment: 42,844
% Part-Time: 8%
% Male: 56%
% Female: 44%
% Out-of-State: 26%
% Fraternity: 10%
% Sorority: 16%
% On-Campus (Freshman): 76%
% On-Campus (All Undergraduate): 26%

% African-American: 4%
% Asian: 8%
% Hispanic: 21%
% White: 50%
% Other: 4%
% Race or Ethnicity Unknown: 0%
% International: 11%
% Low-Income: 29%

ACADEMICS
Student-to-Faculty Ratio: 20:1
% of Classes Under 20: 38%
% of Classes Under 40: 76%
% Full-Time Faculty: 79%
% Full-Time Faculty w/ Terminal Degree: 89%

Top Programs
Art
Business
Communication
Computer Science
Criminology and Criminal Justice
Earth and Space Exploration
Engineering
Psychology

Retention Rate: 88%
4-Year Graduation Rate: 52%
6-Year Graduation Rate: 69%

Curricular Flexibility: Somewhat Flexible
Academic Rating: ★★★

Inside the Classroom

It may be surprising to see one of the largest universities in the country—one which sports an 85 percent acceptance rate—included in this guidebook. Yet, Arizona State University has flourished across its five desert locations (including the ASU Colleges at Lake Havasu City), enhancing its offerings and academic quality in recent years. Serving over 42,000 students at its Tempe campus alone and close to 60,000 undergraduates overall, ASU offers a staggering 350 academic majors. The renowned Barrett Honors College enrolls an incredible 7,200 students compared to the average honors college size of 1,200. Barrett attracts a talented bunch, enrolling more National Merit Scholars than Duke, Stanford, or MIT.

All students must complete a minimum of twenty-nine credits in General Studies courses. Courses can be used to meet more than one requirement at a time but, ultimately, boxes must be checked in the areas of literacy and critical inquiry; mathematical studies; humanities, arts and design; social-behavioral sciences; and the natural sciences. Three "awareness areas" also must be satisfied: Cultural Diversity in the United States, Global Awareness, and Historical Awareness.

The faculty-to-student ratio is a fairly high 20:1, but not all classes call for stadium seating. In fact, 38 percent of course sections seat fewer than twenty students. You'll find classes of over fifty students 18 percent of the time, not unreasonable for a university of this unmatched size. There are plenty of opportunities for experiential learning as 60 percent of students engage in research, land an internship, or have a practicum experience as part of their academic program. The school also has above-average study abroad rates, ranking in the top ten in the nation by sending approximately 2,500 students to 250 programs in sixty-five countries each year.

Business is the concentration in which over one-quarter (27 percent) of total bachelor's degrees are conferred. Engineering (13 percent), the social sciences (9 percent), and biology (8 percent) are the next three most popular. The WP Carey School of Business offers many highly ranked programs as does the Fulton Schools of Engineering. In the last decade, the number of Sun Devils winning competitive national fellowships has skyrocketed. ASU produced an outstanding twenty-one Fulbright Scholars in 2019. It also is becoming a regular producer of Marshall, Gates-Cambridge, Truman, Goldwater, Udall, and Boren Scholarships. Over the past five years 117 graduates have been awarded National Science Foundation Graduate Research Fellowships.

Outside the Classroom

Young people don't typically come to ASU to live a hermetic existence. While the university has begun to shed its "party school" label in recent years, it remains a vibrant, extremely connected campus. Athletics are popular with ten NCCA Division I men's teams and fourteen women's teams. Sun Devil football stadium plays host to 71,000 raucous fans on game days. In addition, ASU fields forty club teams and at least 6,000 additional students take place in competitive intramural sports leagues. Greek life attracts 10 percent of men and 16 percent of women, giving it substantial influence on the social scene. There are more than 1,000 clubs operating across the five campuses with the ASU Outdoors Club and the school's seven identity-based student coalitions drawing large memberships. Interestingly, only 26 percent of the undergraduate student body lives on campus—however, 76 percent of freshmen do opt for that experience. Due to large numbers of students renting apartments/houses in surrounding neighborhoods, ASU hosts an Off-Campus Housing Fair and provides free advice to undergrads seeking a place to reside. In addition to living in the surrounding communities, Sun Devils like to get involved in volunteer work. Collectively, the student body contributes 1.8 million hours of community service each year. There is plenty to do in the cities of Phoenix, Tempe, Mesa, and Scottsdale, all a short drive from one another.

Career Services

ASU's Career and Professional Development Services (CPDS) has offices on its Tempe, Downtown, Polytechnic, and West locations. When you boast 59,000 undergraduate students across your four metropolitan campuses, things can only be so personalized, but ASU does a solid job making services available on a mass scale. Amazingly, it claims 95,000+ annual interactions with students through job fairs, workshops, and networking events.

Nearly 60,000 jobs are posted each year on Handshake, and the school has been selected as a top choice for recruiting talent by more than one hundred companies including Marriot International, Microsoft, General Mills, Charles Schwab, Geico, Ford, FedEx, and Yelp. For such a behemoth of an institution, ASU has a fairly impressive level of internship participation. Around 50 percent of undergraduates have at least one internship, and 44 percent of those are paid opportunities. In total, more than 13,000 internships are posted each year. Having an alumni base of over half a million Sun Devils is great for networking. It is an active and proud bunch that presently has over 100,000 members who donate annually to the university. Thanks to this strong alumni base, wealth of employer partnerships, and strong internship participation rate, the CPDS succeeds in helping the great majority of its graduates swiftly arrive at their next destination soon after receiving diplomas.

Arizona State University

E-mail: admissions@asu.edu | Website: www.asu.edu

Professional Outcomes

A healthy 92 percent of 2018 ASU graduates were employed or in graduate school within six months of earning their degrees. As you would expect from a large school offering 350 majors, the most prolific employers of Sun Devils represent a broad array of corporations and nonprofit entities. Among the school's top fifty employers are Amazon, Apple, Intel, The Vanguard Group, Walt Disney Company, a number of local school districts, and Arizona-based government organizations. In total, the five industries most frequently entered by alumni are banking and finance, technology and engineering, health care, and public and human services. Arizona also ranks thirteenth in the nation among large universities for graduates entering the Peace Corps. The average salary for a member of the Class of 2018 was $50,529. The majority (55 percent) of newly minted grads were working in Arizona with California (14 percent) next in popularity.

Approximately one-fifth of recent grads enrolled in graduate school. Similar to employment, the size and scope of the university leads to many graduate pathways. Many grads continue at ASU itself, but some continue at various prestigious institutions. For example, Yale Law School typically claims at least one ASU alum in its 1L class. From 2010-14, ASU sent 375 graduates to medical school; today, over 350 apply each year. The school's Mayo Medical Scholars program exclusively offered to Barrett Honors College students can open doors for future doctors. While the majority of ASU grads continuing their education do not enter prestigious graduate or professional programs, getting strong grades at ASU absolutely puts them in a position to be strong applicants at any university in the country, including the elites.

Admission

While ASU's reputation for academics has been climbing in recent years, the school is still only slightly selective, accepting 85 percent of those who apply. Considering that friendly acceptance rate, the academic profile of the typical Sun Devil may surprise you. The average freshman possessed a 1216 SAT score, a 3.54 GPA, and ranked within the top 23 percent of their high school class. One-third of Class of 2022 freshmen ranked in the top 10 percent of their high school class while 62 percent were in the top quartile, and 89 percent were in the top half. Among the students presently enrolled in the superb Barrett Honors College, the average SAT score was 1343 and the average GPA was a touch under 3.8. Only a decade ago, the 75th percentile SAT score was 1210, meaning that despite the high acceptance rate, ASU is attracting a more academically superior crop than in the past.

As you might expect at one of the nation's largest universities, admissions officers will not be agonizing over every detail of your application, carefully weighing the merits of your essay, recommendations, and extracurricular resume. In fact, none of those factors are even considered at ASU. Grades, class rank, and test scores are considered "most important," and the rigor of your secondary school record is "important." Conveniently for those entering the admissions process now, the university began accepting the Common Application in 2018. Getting into Arizona State is a straightforward proposition; those who bring a solid transcript and test scores to the table will be invited to join this thriving institution. Admission into the Honors College requires another level of achievement.

Worth Your Money?

Competitively priced for both in-state and out-of-state students, it's no wonder students from around the globe flock to Arizona State. Those from the Grand Canyon State pay less than $27,000 per year cost of attendance while nonresidents cough up $44,000, not that much more than the in-state rate for many public schools on the East Coast. Further, ASU awards merit aid to 43 percent of undergraduates; the average amount is $9k. Need-based aid is granted to 55 percent of full-time students with an average grant of $14k. Thanks to those extremely reasonable prices (we don't utter that phrase often without major qualifiers), this university produces graduates that carry a below-average debt load relative to their peers. Whether you're a local majoring in American Indian Studies or an out-of-stater learning cybersecurity, your tuition dollar goes far at ASU.

FINANCIAL
Institutional Type: Public
In-State Tuition: $10,104
Out-of-State Tuition: $27,618
Room & Board: $12,648
Required Fees: $718
Books & Supplies: $1,148

Avg. Need-Based Aid: $13,663
Avg. % of Need Met: 71%

Avg. Merit-Based Aid: $9,299
% Receiving Merit-Based Aid: 43%

Avg. Cumulative Debt: $23,731
% of Students Borrowing: 45%

CAREER
Who Recruits
1. Amazon
2. Aetna
3. ExxonMobil
4. Ticketmaster
5. General Motors

Notable Internships
1. Intel
2. Geico
3. Phoenix Suns

Top Industries
1. Business
2. Operations
3. Education
4. Sales
5. Engineering

Top Employers
1. Intel
2. Wells Fargo
3. Amazon
4. American Express
5. Apple

Where Alumni Work
1. Phoenix
2. Los Angeles
3. San Francisco
4. New York City
5. Seattle

Median Earnings
College Scorecard (Early Career): $47,700
EOP (Early Career): $46,300
PayScale (Mid-Career): $100,900

RANKINGS
Forbes: 186
Money: 247
U.S. News: 117, National Universities
Wall Street Journal/THE: 224 (T)
Washington Monthly: 46, National Universities

#CollegesWorthYourMoney

Babson College

Babson Park, Massachusetts | Admissions Phone: 781-239-5522

ADMISSION
Admission Rate: 24%
Admission Rate - Men: 19%
Admission Rate - Women: 34%
EA Admission Rate: 24%
ED Admission Rate: 39%
Admission Rate (5-Year Trend): -4%
ED Admission Rate (5-Year Trend): -5%
% of Admits Attending (Yield): 35%
Transfer Admission Rate: 36%

Offered Wait List: 1,852
Accepted Wait List: 746
Admitted Wait List: 5

SAT Reading/Writing (Middle 50%): 620-690
SAT Math (Middle 50%): 650-760
ACT Composite (Middle 50%): 28-32
Testing Policy: ACT/SAT Required
SAT Superscore: Yes
ACT Superscore: Yes

% Graduated in Top 10% of HS Class: 53%
% Graduated in Top 25% of HS Class: 84%
% Graduated in Top 50% of HS Class: 98%

ENROLLMENT
Total Undergraduate Enrollment: 2,361
% Part-Time: 0%
% Male: 52%
% Female: 48%
% Out-of-State: 71%
% Fraternity: 13%
% Sorority: 26%
% On-Campus (Freshman): 100%
% On-Campus (All Undergraduate): 82%

% African-American: 4%
% Asian: 12%
% Hispanic: 11%
% White: 36%
% Other: 2%
% Race or Ethnicity Unknown: 5%
% International: 28%
% Low-Income: 18%

ACADEMICS
Student-to-Faculty Ratio: 14:1
% of Classes Under 20: 18%
% of Classes Under 40: 81%
% Full-Time Faculty: 70%
% Full-Time Faculty w/ Terminal Degree: 88%

Top Programs
Accounting
Entrepreneurship
Finance
International Business
Management

Retention Rate: 95%
4-Year Graduation Rate: 89%
6-Year Graduation Rate: 91%

Curricular Flexibility: Somewhat Flexible
Academic Rating:

★★★★

Inside the Classroom

With an unmatched entrepreneurial ethos, tiny but powerful Babson College in Wellesley, Massachusetts, only has one offering on the menu, a BS in business administration, but it is expertly prepared. Instead of offering a smorgasbord of majors, Babson students pick from twenty-seven areas of concentration including business analytics, global business management, and statistical modeling that offer more curricular flexibility than a traditional major. Babson was an all-male college until 1969, but it has completely transformed as women now comprise close to 50 percent of the school's 2,300 undergraduate population. Of equal interest is the college's status as one the best schools for international students; over one-quarter of the population hails from outside the United States.

The Babson experience kicks off with a one-credit first-year seminar designed to help you "better understand your identity, your classmates' identities, and what it takes for all of you to be successful students in the diverse Babson community." While you'll unavoidably spend a good portion of your time swimming in business-related curriculum, roughly half of the courses you will take will be in the liberal arts on engaging subjects such as Art and Ecology; Imagining Nature, Imagining Ourselves; Sports and Literature; Literature and Philosophy of Madness; Constructing and Performing the Self; and Global Pop. One of the many unique experiences at Babson is Foundations of Management and Entrepreneurship, a freshman requirement. Students are given $3,000 in start-up money to launch and run an actual business. They concurrently take part in the Coaching for Teamwork and Leadership Program, working with staff and alumni coaches to enhance personal development, problem-solving skills, and ethical decision-making.

This school's exceptionally interactive and hands-on approach to undergraduate education is evident from the moment students step foot on campus. While a fair number of courses are large—half have more than thirty students—the nature of the instruction is highly interactive with professors and with peers. It is simply not possible to be an anonymous student at Babson. Around one-half of the undergraduate population spends time studying abroad in one of the college's 104 programs spread across forty-one countries. While Babson is more about doing than spending time in the ivory tower, students are encouraged to assist with faculty-led research or propose an independent research study of their own (for credit).

It's little surprise that a business school like Babson has done an excellent job of branding. It is regularly ranked at the top of any list of best colleges for entrepreneurship and business. Babson also ends up toward the top of any list that looks at return on investment as its graduates fare well on the job market. This institution usually produces one or two Fulbright Scholars per year, but the vast majority of graduates are champing at the bit to enter the workforce.

Outside the Classroom

Babson's classrooms are filled with entrepreneurial spirits, and that obsession doesn't disappear when students leave the academic setting. Of the one hundred or so clubs and activities at the college, a large number have the words "investment," "business," or "banking" somewhere in their titles. The school does run twenty-two varsity sports teams, but it does not offer athletic-based scholarships, so while its men's soccer and basketball teams have captured NCAA Division III titles in recent years, sports hardly dominate life at Babson. More than 20 percent of Babson students partake in Greek life, and the number of sorority and fraternity members has grown in recent years. Close to 80 percent of students live in one of the eighteen on-campus residence halls, and some socialize in the surrounding suburb of Wellesley, but with Boston a short T ride away, jaunts into town are commonplace. The campus vibe has a reputation as being somewhat preppy and conservative-leaning. However, the demographic makeup of the student body continues to grow more and more diverse as one-quarter of all students are international, coming from forty-three countries, and 45 percent of US students are nonwhite.

Career Services

The Career Development Services Center at Babson is dedicated solely to the college's undergraduates; a separate career services office exists for MBA students. With twelve full-time, professional staff members, Babson operates with a 190:1 student-to-advisor ratio, far better than the average school featured in this guide. The career center facilitates a number of corporate sponsorships with major companies including PEPSICO, Boston Scientific, EY, and PwC. Events sponsored by the office occur frequently, at least once per week, and are well attended by the student body. Those include regular Industry Spotlights where corporate guests present to and network with students as well as Career Expos.

A global alumni network of more than 40,000 graduates spread across 115 countries and all fifty US states and the Babson Connector, an online resource, help connect current students with alumni. As a result of this type of engagement, a staggering 89 percent of all Babson students embark on at least one internship during their four years of study. Further, thanks to the diligent, hands-on work of this career services office, less than 1 percent of graduates are still looking for employment/grad school within six months of graduating. Considering its well-staffed office and excellent track record for helping graduates find internships and high-paying employment options, Babson's career services is worthy of a great deal of praise.

Professional Outcomes

Babson students are a group of young people with exceptional drive and direction. Within six months of graduation, 99 percent are already employed or in graduate school. The largest numbers flock to finance, technology, and accounting with the highest concentration of recent graduates ending up at EY, PwC, Dell, and Wayfair. Many alumni also work at Fidelity Investment, IBM, Deloitte, Google, Amazon, Siemens, and Accenture. Keeping with the entrepreneurial philosophy of the college, 7 percent of Babson grads start their own businesses soon after graduation. Starting salaries are strong at approximately $58k. The highest average salaries await those entering the oil, financial services, and accounting industries while the lowest average salaries go to those in the sports/entertainment, staffing, and media/publishing fields. Even though only 16 percent of undergrads hail from Massachusetts, many put down roots nearby after graduation, and over 11,000 alumni are clustered in the Boston area.

While many pursue MBAs down the road, only 8 percent enter a program right out of undergrad. Babson students typically enter excellent institutions once they do decide to pursue a graduate or professional track. Recent grads have entered law school at the likes of Harvard, Tulane, Boston University, UVA, and UC-San Diego. Alumni going the MBA route have attended top programs including at the London Business School, Yale, Columbia, Boston College, USC, and Northwestern.

Admission

Babson is a school whose national and international reputation is on the rise, and with that has come shrinking acceptance rates. As recently as five years ago, 40 percent of applicants were accepted. For students entering in the 2018-19 academic year that number fell to an all-time low of 24 percent. Women fared better than men, gaining acceptance 34 percent of the time versus 19 percent for their male counterparts. The caliber of student admitted has risen with the school's selectivity. For those offered a place in the Class of 2022, the mid-50 percent SAT range was 1340-1480 and 29-33 on the ACT. Five years back, a 30 on the ACT would have placed you in the 75th percentile of attending students.

Successful Babson applicants do not have to have perfect grades, but they need to have performed at the B+/A- range within a rigorous high school program. Interviews are not required but are evaluative in nature and would be a good idea for any applicant with borderline statistics. The process is genuinely holistic as admissions staff want to see evidence of leadership and extracurricular involvement during your high school career. Writing ability is also highly valued as evidenced by the requirement of both a personal statement and writing supplement as part of your application. The committee also values recommendations, tests scores, class rank, extracurricular activity, and talent/ability. Those committing to Babson via early decision were admitted 39 percent of the time into the Class of 2022, making ED a wise choice, particularly for those on the admissions bubble. In general, Babson is undoubtedly getting more selective year by year, but students with excellent grades, strong standardized test scores, and a burning passion for business should still fare well in the application process.

Worth Your Money?

With business being the dominant area of focus in the classroom, the $72,000+ annual cost of attendance is not as terrifying as it might otherwise be. The school also offers students the chance to apply for various merit scholarships ranging from the Weissman Scholarship that covers full tuition to a Dean's Scholarship worth $5,000 per year. Babson does award need-based grants of $40k to qualifying students; however, only 40 percent of undergraduates qualify for any financial aid. Nevertheless, if you're committed to a career in business, Babson is worth your money thanks to its distinctive brand of education, industry connections, and solid starting salaries that would allow students to comfortably pay back some level of student loans.

FINANCIAL
Institutional Type: Private
In-State Tuition: $52,608
Out-of-State Tuition: $52,608
Room & Board: $16,776
Required Fees: $0
Books & Supplies: $1,144

Avg. Need-Based Aid: $39,582
Avg. % of Need Met: 100%

Avg. Merit-Based Aid: $21,920
% Receiving Merit-Based Aid: 10%

Avg. Cumulative Debt: $37,866
% of Students Borrowing: 40%

CAREER
Who Recruits
1. Boston Scientific
2. AXA Advisors
3. RxAdvance
4. Applause
5. PepsiCo

Notable Internships
1. Mid-Market Securities
2. CoreAxis Consulting
3. PepsiCo

Top Industries
1. Business
2. Finance
3. Operations
4. Sales
5. Marketing

Top Employers
1. Fidelity Investments
2. PwC
3. EY
4. Dell
5. IBM

Where Alumni Work
1. Boston
2. New York City
3. Sao Paulo, Brazil
4. San Francisco
5. United Kingdom

Median Earnings
College Scorecard (Early Career): $96,100
EOP (Early Career): $95,300
PayScale (Mid-Career): $133,800

RANKINGS
Forbes: 62
Money: 151
U.S. News: N/A
Wall Street Journal/THE: 120
Washington Monthly: N/A

#CollegesWorthYourMoney

Barnard College

ADMISSION
Admission Rate: 14%
Admission Rate - Men: 0%
Admission Rate - Women: 14%
EA Admission Rate: Not Offered
ED Admission Rate: 30%
Admission Rate (5-Year Trend): -7%
ED Admission Rate (5-Year Trend): -13%
% of Admits Attending (Yield): 55%
Transfer Admission Rate: 22%

Offered Wait List: 1,608
Accepted Wait List: N/A
Admitted Wait List: 11

SAT Reading/Writing (Middle 50%): 670-740
SAT Math (Middle 50%): 660-760
ACT Composite (Middle 50%): 30-33
Testing Policy: ACT/SAT Required
SAT Superscore: Yes
ACT Superscore: No

% Graduated in Top 10% of HS Class: 84%
% Graduated in Top 25% of HS Class: 97%
% Graduated in Top 50% of HS Class: 100%

ENROLLMENT
Total Undergraduate Enrollment: 2,562
% Part-Time: 2%
% Male: 0%
% Female: 100%
% Out-of-State: 72%
% Fraternity: Not Offered
% Sorority: 15%
% On-Campus (Freshman): 99%
% On-Campus (All Undergraduate): 91%

% African-American: 6%
% Asian: 15%
% Hispanic: 12%
% White: 51%
% Other: 6%
% Race or Ethnicity Unknown: 0%
% International: 10%
% Low-Income: 18%

ACADEMICS
Student-to-Faculty Ratio: 9:1
% of Classes Under 20: 75%
% of Classes Under 40: 90%
% Full-Time Faculty: 68%
% Full-Time Faculty w/ Terminal Degree: 98%

Top Programs
Area Studies
Art History
Dance
Economics
English
Neuroscience and Behavior
Political Science
Psychology

Retention Rate: 95%
4-Year Graduation Rate: 87%
6-Year Graduation Rate: 92%

Curricular Flexibility: Somewhat Flexible
Academic Rating: ★★★★↙

Inside the Classroom

Affiliated with Columbia University, this all-women's college serves 2,500-plus accomplished young women in the heart of Manhattan's Upper West Side. The institution's cosmopolitan locale is appropriately populated by a diverse student body—52 percent of attendees identify as women of color, and 22 percent are first-generation college students. Roughly fifty majors are offered, including crossover programs with Columbia such as the 3:2 engineering program or five-year programs that lead to a BA plus a Master of International Affairs or Master of Public Administration. Barnard also has partnerships with The Jewish Theological Seminary and the Julliard School.

The newly-adopted Foundations curriculum has refined an already rigorous educational tradition at the college. Freshmen must tackle a first-year writing course and a first-year seminar that emphasizes persuasive writing/speaking. In subsequent years, students must fulfill six Modes of Thinking courses that focus on local NYC history, global inquiry, social difference, historical perspective, quantitative and empirical knowledge, and technological thinking. Distributional requirements in a foreign language, arts/humanities, social sciences, and the hard sciences also must be fulfilled. Regardless of major, seniors must complete a semester or year-long thesis/project that is publicly presented or displayed.

All of this unfolds in an academic environment in which students will work closely with professors. Barnard has a 10:1 student-faculty ratio, and a sensational 75 percent of courses are capped at nineteen or fewer students; 26 percent have fewer than ten. Many get the chance to engage in research alongside a professor as 197 undergraduates were granted such an opportunity through the Summer Research Institute in 2018-19. Many students also take advantage of the more than 150 study abroad programs spread over sixty-five countries. Roughly one-third of students elect to take a semester in a foreign country.

Barnard's most popular majors, by number of degrees conferred, are economics, English, political science, history, psychology, biology, neuroscience, computer science, urban studies, and art history. The dance program is notably strong and often places near the top of national rankings. With a strong emphasis on global perspective and public service, it makes sense that the school produces a disproportionately high percentage of Fulbright and Truman Scholars. In 2019, four graduates won Fulbright Scholarships, and three students captured Critical Language Scholarships. Additionally, four Barnard grads were named National Science Foundation fellows in 2018.

Outside the Classroom

Outside the classroom is where Barnard's affiliation with Columbia really comes into play. The school doesn't have its own athletic teams, so Barnard students are recruited to play for Columbia's NCAA Division I teams. Barnard has seventy clubs of its own, mostly of a fairly serious nature (pre-professional and performance-oriented), but the bulk of opportunities for campus engagement come from Columbia's more than 500 student organizations that are open to Barnard students. Parts of dorm life are also a shared experience. For the 91 percent of students who decide to live on campus, two buildings serve as co-ed dorms where Barnard students are mixed with Columbia students, and meal plans for all dorm residents can be utilized at either school's cafeterias. Of course, being located in the heart of New York City, opportunities for fun and excitement are hardly limited to the Barnard and Columbia campuses. Within a single mile of their dorm rooms, students can enjoy multiple parks, theaters, music venues, diners, and countless other attractions.

Career Services

Barnard has ten professionals, a number of peer advisors, and a handful of administrative assistants working in the offices of Beyond Barnard, the recently reorganized/renamed career services center. In past years complaints about the lack of hands-on assistance from the career services office were voiced by the student government and school newspaper. The college responded by beefing up its offerings, and the work being done today is impressive by any quantifiable measure. Beyond Barnard's 256:1 student-to-advisor ratio is superior to many other colleges featured in this guide, and it puts that staffing to good use. In 2018-19, they conducted 4,424 one-on-one appointments, hosted 350+ events, and served 2,500 individuals in some capacity.

The school hosts career and internship fairs in the fall and spring. Fairs are attended by 1,000 students and approximately fifty employers including Brown Brothers Harriman, Uber, and Hearst Magazines. Those sessions also are open to Columbia students, and there is some degree of reciprocity with Barnard students being allowed to attend a good number of Columbia-hosted events. The New York Network mentoring program saw 140 alumni work in person with current students, and an additional seventy individuals participated in a Virtual Mentoring program. Beyond Barnard helps fund internships offering summer stipends of $4,000; it funded 425 internships last year alone. Students interned at exciting locations including the New York Times, the US House of Representatives, Comedy Central, and Christie's.

Barnard College

E-mail: admissions@barnard.edu | Website: www.barnard.edu

Professional Outcomes

Six months after graduation, 93 percent of 2018 Barnard grads had found employment or were enrolled in a graduate program. The school is known for producing women with a wide array of interests, so it makes sense that grads disperse into many different fields. Finance and banking led the way, albeit only representing 10-15 percent of graduates. JP Morgan, Goldman Sachs, Blackrock, Citibank, and Morgan Stanley all appear on the list of the top fifteen employers of Barnard alumni. Education, law, and technology sectors are next in popularity. Across all fields, companies employing twenty-five or more Barnard alums include the NYC Department of Education, Google, IBM, Accenture, and the Metropolitan Museum of Art. The median income for Barnard grads at age thirty-four is $56,000. For comparison, women graduating from Columbia have a median income of $64,000 at the same age. By leaps and bounds, New York City remains home to alumni with small clusters of graduates forming in San Francisco, Boston, Los Angeles, DC, and Philadelphia.

It is rare for a student to call it an academic career after finishing her bachelor's. Within ten years of graduation, over 80 percent of Barnard alums eventually enroll in graduate school. Those entering graduate school flock to a number of other nearby institutions with Columbia, Yeshiva, Rutgers, Fordham, NYU, and Hunter College (CUNY) among the ten most commonly attended schools. Boston University, Georgetown, and Harvard also have a strong representation of Barnard grads in their graduate/professional programs. Medical Schools where 2018 grads enrolled include St. Louis University School of Medicine, Icahn School of Medicine, and Jefferson College of Health. Barnard typically sports a medical school admissions rate of 60-75 percent.

Admission

The last five years have seen the admission rate at Barnard fall from 24 percent (2014) to an all-time low of 14 percent for those entering the Class of 2022. The middle-50 percent SAT range of attending students is 1350-1500; for the ACT it's 30-33. In 2014, the 25th percentile was a far friendlier 1240 SAT/28 ACT. Therefore, it is safe to conclude that Barnard is trending in a more selective direction.

The average weighted high school GPA of a Barnard student was over 4.0, and 84 percent finished in the top 10 percent of their high school class. That aligns with the school's stated beliefs that rigor of secondary record and GPA are among the admissions committees' strongest considerations. Also making this list are more holistic factors including the essay, recommendations, and character/personal qualities. The early decision acceptance rate is 30 percent compared to 12 percent in the regular round, so that may be an avenue worth exploring for those dead-set on attending this fine institution. Additionally, transfer students fare well at Barnard, especially relative to other highly selective liberal arts schools. In 2018, there were 166 applicants accepted as transfers—22 percent of the transfer applicant pool. As at many selective colleges, gaining acceptance into Barnard is more difficult than ever. Sterling grades, solid test scores, and winning personal attributes are the right combination to receive serious consideration at one of, if not the best women's college in existence.

Worth Your Money?

Forty-six percent of Barnard students come from families that fall in the top 5 percent of income-earners in the United States. Those individuals will almost always be asked to pay the full $78,000 cost of attendance as merit aid is nonexistent at this school. Those on the lower end of the income scale see 100 percent of their demonstrated need paid for by the college through an annual grant of $49k. Thanks to this equitable process, the average debt carried by a Barnard graduate is far less than the average college graduate. In addition to its generous financial aid, Barnard is worth the price for the incredible employment and graduate school networks it will open for you postgraduation.

FINANCIAL
Institutional Type: Private
In-State Tuition: $55,781
Out-of-State Tuition: $55,781
Room & Board: $17,856
Required Fees: $1,887
Books & Supplies: $1,150

Avg. Need-Based Aid: $48,845
Avg. % of Need Met: 100%

Avg. Merit-Based Aid: $0
% Receiving Merit-Based Aid: 0%

Avg. Cumulative Debt: $20,829
% of Students Borrowing: 43%

CAREER
Who Recruits
1. Harlem Arts Alliance
2. 826NYC
3. Bank of America
4. Mastercard
5. Hospital for Special Surgery

Notable Internships
1. U.S. Embassy
2. MacMillan Publishers
3. Prudential

Top Industries
1. Business
2. Education
3. Media
4. Social Services
5. Healthcare

Top Employers
1. NYC Department of Education
2. Google
3. JPMorgan Chase
4. Citi
5. IBM

Where Alumni Work
1. New York City
2. San Francisco
3. Boston
4. Los Angeles
5. Washington, DC

Median Earnings
College Scorecard (Early Career): $57,900
EOP (Early Career): $56,300
PayScale (Mid-Career): $109,800

RANKINGS
Forbes: 50
Money: 94
U.S. News: 25, Liberal Arts Colleges
Wall Street Journal/THE: 51
Washington Monthly: 20, Liberal Arts Colleges

#CollegesWorthYourMoney

Baruch College (CUNY)

New York, New York | Admissions Phone: 646-312-1400

Inside the Classroom

Locating a certifiable commuter school with a highly selective admissions process and an outstanding academic reputation sounds about as realistic as stumbling upon a unicorn on your way to the grocery store. Amazingly, there may be only one institution in the country that perfectly fits that description. Baruch College, a gem within the CUNY system, shines bright in the eyes of employers, even those New York City juggernauts with a taste for Ivy League grads. Of course, not every commuter school is situated in Midtown Manhattan, a primo location for high-level internships and flourishing corporate connections. Baruch students take full advantage; of the three undergraduate schools within the college, the Zicklin School of Business attracts a mind-boggling 75 percent of the student population.

All students at Baruch have to complete a forty-five-credit sequence of required courses, but there is some choice within the broad boxes that need to be checked. The nonnegotiable courses are Writing I & Writing II, Speech Communication, Mathematics, and Foreign Language. Students also need to choose classes that fulfill requirements in fine and performing arts, history, literature, philosophy, natural sciences, anthropology/sociology, economics, politics and government, and psychology. Those who are part of the Honors Program complete an honors thesis as a culminating academic experience during their senior year.

With an 18:1 student-to-faculty ratio and more part-time than full-time faculty, one-on-one bonding time with your professors is at a premium. Single-digit classes are a rarity, and only 20 percent of courses have twenty or fewer enrolled students. That being said, Baruch does offer many courses in the twenty- to thirty-student range; 39 percent of sections fall in that span. Tapping into undergraduate research projects is tough at a business-oriented commuter school. Procuring those opportunities requires initiative, but it can be accomplished through connecting with individual faculty members. Those who do make such a connection eventually share their research at the college's Creative Inquiry Day. Studying abroad is an option at any of the CUNY system's 166 programs in fifty-one countries.

Zicklin is not only a great business school for the money, it's a great business school period. Popular majors within this well-respected and well-connected institution include accounting, finance, marketing, and business communication and, as we will cover later, leading companies in those fields have a strong affection for Baruch graduates. With so many entering the job market postgraduation, prestigious scholarships and fellowships are an afterthought, but the school does produce an occasional Fulbright winner.

Outside the Classroom

Only 2 percent of undergraduate students live on campus, and no—that is not a typo—it is simply a reality for this school of 15,000 set on three Manhattan acres. Baruch is not going to provide a typical college campus experience, and for some that's not a bad thing, but it's just important to go in with the right expectations. The surrounding area is not a college town in any way, shape, or form. As a result, the typical student is there for one purpose—to earn a degree. This "nose to the grindstone" ethos shapes campus life. There are no Greek organizations, although there are thirteen NCAA Division III sports teams that play as the Bearcats. While most time spent on campus is time spent in the classrooms themselves, there are ways to get involved through 130+ clubs and activities. The weekly newspaper, The Ticker, and the student-run radio station, WBMB, have lengthy histories. Most clubs meet at specific times during the early afternoon while people are actually on campus, and most of those meetings are held in the Newman Vertical Campus, a seventeen-floor architectural wonder that was erected in 2003 for $327 million dollars. (For a CUNY school, Baruch has some very wealthy donors.)

Career Services

The Starr Career Development Center (SCDC) employs seven full-time professional staff as well as four part-time staff members. Full-timers play roles such as career counselor, internship coordinator, and employer relations director. The part-time staff assists with tasks like pre-law advising and alumni coordination. Baruch's 2,146:1 student-to-advisor ratio (only counting the full-time professionals) may be undesirable but, overall, the data on actual service delivery is far more promising.

More than eighty companies traveled to Baruch's campus for recruiting purposes in 2017-18 including KPMG, Amazon, Moody's, HarperCollins Publishers, and Colgate-Palmolive. In excess of 2,900 students attended those events. Overall, 46 percent of Baruch students land at least one internship; the average student who found employment within six months had 1.5 such experiences. Five or more 2018 graduates interned at each of KPMG, EY, Citi, Deloitte, and JP Morgan. The SCDC provided 3,480 career consultations in 2017-18; for perspective, that is similar to the number of total graduates annually. It also conducted over 2,700 resume reviews, posted 6,600+ jobs online, and facilitated 1,271 on-campus interviews with employers. The online system, cleverly named Starr Search, is utilized by 84 percent of the undergraduate student body, and it offers countless opportunities for those aggressive and motivated enough to follow leads. Additional staffing would likely be needed to ensure a personal connection with all 15,000+ undergrads.

Professional Outcomes

Within six months of graduation, 82 percent of the Class of 2018 were already employed or in full-time graduate programs. Given that over three-quarters of graduates possess business-related degrees, most first jobs are in the realms of accounting, finance, real estate, management, and marketing. Baruch is one of the few accessible public institutions that is a direct feeder to many of Wall Street's top banks. In fact, the top employers of Class of 2018 members were JP Morgan (33 grads), Morgan Stanley (18), EY (14), Citi (14), TD Bank (12), and Bank of America (10). Goldman Sachs, Moody's, Deloitte, and PwC were other companies scooping up eight or more 2018 graduates. The average salary for Arts & Sciences grads was $46,000 while Zicklin School of Business grads earned $53,000. Just about everyone graduating from this college remains in New York City, although some alumni head to Miami, DC, San Francisco, or Los Angeles, but only in dribs and drabs.

Graduate studies are not usually the immediate step after receiving one's diploma from Baruch—only 9 percent of those finishing their bachelor's go right into another degree program. There are few students majoring in the hard sciences at this school, so you don't see a ton on the premed path, but sophomores do have the option of applying for early admission to the Icahn School of Medicine at Mount Sinai through the FlexMed program. Of the alumni who decide to go the law school route, even if they do so years later, many attend local NYC schools like Pace or Brooklyn Law School, but a handful of recent grads have been welcomed to the law schools of the University of Michigan, Tufts, Fordham, and Cornell.

Admission

Baruch admitted 39 percent of the 21,469 students who applied for admission into the Class of 2022; that is significantly higher than the 23 percent acceptance rate the college registered a decade prior. Part of the change is that the school's enrollment has grown during that same period, increasing by a few thousand undergraduates even though admissions standards have become more rigid. Today, 50 percent of entering freshman are top 10 percent finishers at their respective high schools; in 2009, only 32 percent held that distinction. Further, the 75th percentile SAT score from ten years ago is close to the 25th percentile score today. The 2018-19 freshmen had a mid-50 percent range of 1220-1390 on the SAT, the test submitted 83 percent of the time by applicants.

The Baruch College Admissions Office considers GPA, standardized test scores, and rigor of curriculum above all else. Recommendation letters and essays sit alone in the next rung of important categories. This is a school that can be forgiving of a bad grade or two. In fact, the majority of freshmen earned under a 3.5 in high school, and 22 percent had under a 3.0. It's hard to find a school as exceptional as Baruch that is willing to accept late-bloomers and, in some cases, bright AP/honors kids who earned B's and C's throughout high school.

Worth Your Money?

New Yorkers pay under $7,000 in tuition for a school with an alumni network with deep ties to a number of major Wall Street players. This school is unequivocally worth every cent for Big Apple denizens. Outsiders pay a reasonable $18,600 per year in tuition—of course, there is the small matter of finding an affordable place to live. Once again, that's about as likely as spotting that unicorn.

FINANCIAL
Institutional Type: Public
In-State Tuition: $7,921
Out-of-State Tuition: $18,971
Room & Board: $15,499
Required Fees: N/A
Books & Supplies: $1,364

Avg. Need-Based Aid: $9,920
Avg. % of Need Met: 51%

Avg. Merit-Based Aid: $2,452
% Receiving Merit-Based Aid: 7%

Avg. Cumulative Debt: $9,182
% of Students Borrowing: 13%

CAREER
Who Recruits
1. BBC Worldwide Americas
2. FDM Group
3. Home Advisor
4. NYS Department of Civil Service
5. Yelp

Notable Internships
1. PwC
2. RBC Capital Markets
3. Atlantic Records

Top Industries
1. Business
2. Finance
3. Accounting
4. Operations
5. Sales

Top Employers
1. JPMorgan Chase
2. Citi
3. NYC Department of Education
4. Morgan Stanley
5. EY

Where Alumni Work
1. New York City
2. Miami
3. Washington, DC
4. Los Angeles
5. San Francisco

Median Earnings
College Scorecard (Early Career): $57,200
EOP (Early Career): $57,600
PayScale (Mid-Career): $107,100

RANKINGS
Forbes: 174
Money: 2
U.S. News: 16, Regional North
Wall Street Journal/THE: 232 (T)
Washington Monthly: N/A

#CollegesWorthYourMoney

Bates College

Lewiston, Maine | Admissions Phone: 207-786-6000

Inside the Classroom

The nation's second adopter (1984) of a test-optional admissions policy, Bates College has always prided itself on a commitment to egalitarian education—even back to its official founding in the middle of the Civil War when it proudly admitted students regardless of race, religion, or sex. Today, the school is once again on the cutting edge of higher education, advocating a curriculum that honors the liberal arts tradition but also prepares students for "purposeful work" that is both personally meaningful and societally relevant.

Toward those aims Bates students are required to complete (a) three "writing-attentive" courses; (b) three courses focused on scientific reasoning, lab experience, and quantitative literacy; and (c) two four-course concentrations revolving around a particular issue or area of inquiry. General education at Bates is intended to ensure "depth of knowledge" and a "comparative appreciation of how the several disciplines function and what they can teach us." Distinctive features include a mandatory first-year seminar, senior thesis requirement, and a Short Term at the end of the academic year that provides students the opportunity to focus exclusively on one course, field project, internship, or study abroad opportunity. For those wishing to save money and/or fast-track their undergraduate education, the college offers a three-year option that allows students to graduate in three years, provided they register for five courses (as opposed to four) each semester and one course during each Short Term.

Forty-one percent of courses at Bates have a single-digit enrollment, and 72 percent of classrooms contain nineteen or fewer students, allowing for this process to unfold in an intimate academic atmosphere. Additionally, the student-to-faculty ratio is 10:1, and not a single graduate student is present to vacuum up professorial attention. Students interested in research will find opportunities across all disciplines, many of which culminate with a presentation at the Mount David Summit, an annual campus-wide celebration of undergraduate research and creative works. Bates has one of the highest percentages of study abroad participation of any college in the country, typically sending over two-thirds of each class to one of 200+ global destinations.

Twenty-eight percent of all degrees earned at Bates are in the social sciences and biology (15 percent), psychology (8 percent), English (8 percent), and natural resources and conservation (7 percent) are next in popularity. Though strong across many disciplines, Bates boasts exemplary programs in political science, art, philosophy, economics, and psychology. The college has produced more than seventy Fulbright Scholars in the last five years and is recognized as a top recipient of prestigious academic fellowships, even among highly selective institutions. In 2018 alone, Bates produced twenty-three Fulbright Scholars, more than any other undergraduate-only liberal arts college in the United States.

Outside the Classroom

Outside the classroom Bates places a particularly strong emphasis on community and civic engagement, facilitating numerous volunteer and civic leadership opportunities, primarily through the Harward Center. More than half of all Bates students participate in community-engaged learning (for academic credit). Aside from community service, Bates offers more than 110 officially recognized student organizations, including a nationally ranked debate team and an active investment club. Athletic opportunities also abound at the Division III varsity level and within the college's extensive intramural program that encompasses club sports ranging from equestrian to rugby. There are no fraternities or sororities at Bates, and 95 percent of students live in one of the dorms or school-owned Victorian homes that accommodate ten to thirty students each. Lewistown is the state's second most populous city, yet that isn't saying much in Maine because Lewistown is a post-industrial town with only 60,000 residents. Portland, the state's largest city, can be reached in about forty minutes by car.

Career Services

The Bates Career Development Center (BDCD) features nine full-time staff and a student-to-advisor ratio of 204:1, a superior level of support when compared to most other institutions included in this book. Services offered by the center include career/interest assessment, interview preparation, and a guest lecture series. The BDCD hosts an annual graduate and professional school fair (with Bowdoin and Colby), as well as a number of its own networking events throughout the year, one example being a presentation from Google/Pinterest on tech careers for liberal arts majors. Organizations such as The Beacon Group, Analysis Group, Barclays, and the CIA have recruited on campus in recent years. Over 350 interviews are conducted on campus by sixty-five companies in a single academic year.

The Career Discovery Program in Practice, in existence since 1978, affords undergrads the opportunity to job shadow a Bates alum in a field of interest. Roughly 250 Bobcats take advantage of that program each year. The Purposeful Work Internship Program helps fund living expenses of students interning more than 300 summer hours. Despite Bates' location in Maine, internship opportunities are plentiful, particularly in Boston and smaller cities throughout the New England region. This past summer Bates students worked in over 130 companies/organizations throughout the United States and internationally, including at JP Morgan, the Institute of Infectious Diseases, the Conservation Law Foundation, Amazon, and the Sloan Kettering Cancer Center.

Professional Outcomes

Within six months of graduation 98 percent of the Class of 2018 were either employed, enrolled in graduate school, or otherwise meaningfully engaged in a fellowship or internship. The most frequently entered fields were education (21 percent), health care (17 percent), finance/banking (9 percent), and technology (7 percent). Popular employers included Accenture, Fidelity Investments, Google, Wayfair, and Liberty Mutual Insurance whereas common employment destinations of Bates graduates were concentrated primarily in the Northeast, namely Boston, New York, and Portland, Maine. However, sizable numbers of Bates alumni also can be found working in the Washington, DC, and San Francisco areas. Ten years after arriving in Lewiston, alumni are making a median salary of $59,200, a touch more than Colby grads and almost $6k less than Bowdoin alums.

According to the Bates Career Development Center, within ten years of graduation approximately 13 percent of Bates graduates are in, or have competed, law school whereas 7 percent enroll in medical school. In addition, Bates is currently among the top producers of graduates who eventually go on to enroll in PhD programs in the social sciences, especially economics and sociology. In the past three years Bates alumni have enrolled in several selective graduate programs including those at Harvard Law School, Washington University Medical School, and the Stanford Graduate School of Business. By midcareer Bates alumni are most frequently found working in the professional fields of business development, education, and community and social services.

Admission

From 2014 to 2018, Bates experienced a hefty 52 percent increase in applications and, during the same period, the school's acceptance rate fell from 24 percent to 18 percent. SAT scores were submitted by 46 percent of applicants, and 32 percent included ACT results as part of their application. The mid-50 percent ranges were 1290-1460 on the SAT and 29-32 on the ACT. Students typically ranked high in their graduating high school class with 55 percent in the top 10 percent and 89 percent in the top quartile. Those numbers are almost identical to those held by the freshman class of 2013-14, meaning that while the acceptance rate has declined, the profile of the typical accepted applicant has not changed much.

Aside from grades, class rank, and course rigor, Bates places significant emphasis on an applicant's essay, letters of recommendation, extracurricular profile, talent/ability, and character/personal qualities. Demonstrated interest also plays a considerable role. Of course, the ultimate declaration of love is the submission of an early decision application. Those who go the binding ED route enjoy an acceptance rate three times higher than those who apply in the regular cycle (45 percent vs. 15 percent). A massive 64 percent of the 2018-19 freshman class was admitted via early decision, making it a wise strategic maneuver for anyone serious about attending Bates.

Worth Your Money?

A sizable percentage of the undergraduate student body come from fairly wealthy homes—the median family income is $226,500—and over three-quarters come from families with incomes in the top 20 percent nationwide. Many families with hefty salaries will pay the full $73,238 annual cost of attendance. For the 42 percent of students who do qualify for need-based financial aid, Bates delivers in a big way. The college meets 100 percent of the demonstrated need for every qualifying student with grants averaging $44,644 each year. Not only do Bates grads generally find solid-paying jobs after graduation, they also have far less debt, on average, than their peers receiving diplomas from other institutions.

FINANCIAL
Institutional Type: Private
In-State Tuition: $55,683
Out-of-State Tuition: $55,683
Room & Board: $15,705
Required Fees: N/A
Books & Supplies: $900

Avg. Need-Based Aid: $44,644
Avg. % of Need Met: 100%

Avg. Merit-Based Aid: $0
% Receiving Merit-Based Aid: 0%

Avg. Cumulative Debt: $21,525
% of Students Borrowing: 35%

CAREER
Who Recruits
1. Chevron
2. Hulu
3. Oppenheimer & Co.
4. athenaHealth
5. Owl Cybersecurity

Notable Internships
1. CNN
2. United States Senate
3. Morgan Stanley

Top Industries
1. Business
2. Education
3. Operations
4. Social Services
5. Research

Top Employers
1. Fidelity Investments
2. Massachusetts General Hospital
3. Liberty Mutual Insurance
4. Google
5. Amazon

Where Alumni Work
1. Boston
2. New York City
3. Portland, ME
4. Lewiston, ME
5. Washington, DC

Median Earnings
College Scorecard (Early Career): $59,200
EOP (Early Career): $55,900
PayScale (Mid-Career): $111,900

RANKINGS
Forbes: 39
Money: 38
U.S. News: 21, Liberal Arts Colleges
Wall Street Journal/THE: 63 (T)
Washington Monthly: 17, Liberal Arts Colleges

#CollegesWorthYourMoney

Waltham, Massachusetts | Admissions Phone: 781-891-2244

ADMISSION
Admission Rate: 43%
Admission Rate - Men: 40%
Admission Rate - Women: 49%
EA Admission Rate: Not Offered
ED Admission Rate: 69%
Admission Rate (5-Year Trend): -1%
ED Admission Rate (5-Year Trend): Not Offered
% of Admits Attending (Yield): 28%
Transfer Admission Rate: 52%

\# Offered Wait List: 1,659
\# Accepted Wait List: 534
\# Admitted Wait List: 1

SAT Reading/Writing (Middle 50%): 600-680
SAT Math (Middle 50%): 640-730
ACT Composite (Middle 50%): 28-32
Testing Policy: ACT/SAT Required
SAT Superscore: Yes
ACT Superscore: Yes

% Graduated in Top 10% of HS Class: 50%
% Graduated in Top 25% of HS Class: 89%
% Graduated in Top 50% of HS Class: 98%

ENROLLMENT
Total Undergraduate Enrollment: 4,253
% Part-Time: 2%
% Male: 60%
% Female: 40%
% Out-of-State: 50%
% Fraternity: 4%
% Sorority: 7%
% On-Campus (Freshman): 97%
% On-Campus (All Undergraduate): 78%

% African-American: 4%
% Asian: 10%
% Hispanic: 8%
% White: 69%
% Other: 3%
% Race or Ethnicity Unknown: 5%
% International: 16%
% Low-Income: 14%

ACADEMICS
Student-to-Faculty Ratio: 11:1
% of Classes Under 20: 21%
% of Classes Under 40: 93%
% Full-Time Faculty: 63%
% Full-Time Faculty w/ Terminal Degree: 54%

Top Programs
Accounting
Data Analytics
Finance
Management
Managerial Economics
Marketing
Professional Sales

Retention Rate: 93%
4-Year Graduation Rate: 82%
6-Year Graduation Rate: 91%

Curricular Flexibility: Less Flexible
Academic Rating: ★★★⭑

Inside the Classroom
Situated just west of Boston, Bentley University is one of the premier business-focused institutions in the country. Rival Babson College is only ten miles away geographically, but the two schools used to be a much greater distance apart in reputation and prestige. That gap has closed quickly in recent years. The school's 4,200 undergraduate students traversing this attractive 163-acre Waltham, Massachusetts, campus are, somewhat surprisingly, exposed to a top-notch liberal arts education while working toward a BA or BS in a business-related field. Of the twenty-five majors and thirty-six minors to choose from, a handful are non-business concentrations such as English, philosophy, and history. These students typically supplement their education with a healthy number of business courses. The majority take the opposite path, majoring in business and supple-menting their studies with liberal arts courses. Always innovating, the school recently started three cutting-edge majors in data analytics, professional sales, and creative industries. Regardless of one's major, the core curriculum consisting of sixteen mandatory courses must be tackled. That includes a first-year seminar, information technology and computer system concepts, a sequence of two expository writing classes as well as courses in math, the hard sciences, government, and history.

Earning a Bentley degree is far from a passive experience. The average undergraduate class is comprised of twenty-six students, and academics are intense. Twenty percent of the student body is double majoring, tacking the liberal studies major on to their business concentration. Roughly half of Bentley students elect to study abroad in one of eighty programs spread across twenty-five countries. Just about everyone lands an internship; the majority of students complete two. Undergraduate research participation has increased in recent years as the school has joined The Council on Undergraduate Research. While not a focal point of the school, it is possible to land a position assisting a faculty member with a research project at some point during your four years on campus.

Bentley is a school on the rise. Having just celebrated its one-hundred-year anniversary, it has become a highly-respected name in the corporate world and possesses an international reach. The most popular majors are all within the business domain and include finance, business, management, marketing, accounting, and poetry—just kidding on that last one. Bentley is a one-trick pony, and that's not a bad thing when you examine the outcomes data for recent graduates (more ahead).

Outside the Classroom
A bastion for extraverts, 90 percent of Bentley undergrads belong to at least one student organization; one-third consider themselves "highly involved." Over one hundred clubs and activities are available with a multitude of options in the academic, cultural, religious, arts and media, and recreational realms. Participation in athletics is high. The Falcons compete in eleven men's and ten women's sports in NCAA Division II (men's ice hockey is the lone Division I team). Intramural and club sports are popular, including ultimate Frisbee, sailing, rugby, and equestrian. More than 1,700 students participate in an intramural sport each year. With 78 percent of students living in school-owned housing, most social events are centered on campus. Fraternity and sorority life attract a significant but not dominant 17 percent of undergraduates. Additionally, some students live in defined communities—residential housing for those passionate about areas such as women's leadership, social justice, or service learning. Waltham, also home to Brandeis University, is a historic and pretty New England town with plenty of bars, restaurants, and other attractions. The university is only thirteen miles from downtown Boston, and the school provides free public transportation to-and-from Harvard Square.

Career Services
The Career Services Office at Bentley has thirteen professional staff members who work with the college's undergraduates. That equates to a 323:1 student-to-advisor ratio, placing the university in the average range compared to other schools featured in this guide. Career services may be average in this category, but it is exceptional by just about every other metric. For example, the staff does an incredible job facilitating meaning-ful internships. Of the 92 percent of Bentley students who had an internship (71 percent complete more than one) as part of their undergraduate education, 37 percent landed their first job directly through this experience. On-campus recruiting events led another 18 percent of employed graduates to their first employment destina-tion, and a sizable number of students also found their way through alumni networking, school-organized career fairs, and referrals from the school. The school has developed close corporate partnerships with companies including Dell, Fidelity Investments, Liberty Mutual, and United Technologies, all of whom hire their fair share of graduates each year.

Offerings include career development seminars that begin freshman year; 97 percent of first-years sign up for the introductory class. Those seminars are part of the school's larger Hire Education Program that helps students formulate career goals, hone job-readiness skills, and build professional networks. The Mentor Marketplace is an online tool that helps connect current students with alumni who work in a relevant field to serve as a career resource. In addition to the full internships taken advantage of by the bulk of the student body, Bentley also offers micro-internships in which alumni can bring in undergraduates to work on short-term, impactful projects within their company. Taking into account the breadth and quality of its services as well as the stellar outcomes achieved by its graduates, Bentley has as high quality of a Career Services Office as you will find anywhere in the country.

Professional Outcomes

A superb 99 percent of 2018 Bentley grads were employed or in graduate school six months after receiving their diplomas. The financial services and technology sectors each account for 22 percent of new hires. Most job functions are in the areas of finance, sales, accounting, analytics, marketing, consulting, and operations/logistics. A hub of entrepreneurship, the school saw 7 percent of its graduating class start their own businesses right out of college. Companies employing the highest number of alumni include Fidelity Investments, PwC, EY, Dell EMC, and Wayfair. The median starting salary for graduates is $59,000, a strong figure compared to other universities of its ilk. By midcareer, Bentley grads have a median income similar to Harvard and Tufts alumni.

Bentley does not see a high number of graduates directly enter graduate school—roughly 10 percent in any given year. While many pursue MBAs or other advanced business degrees later in their careers, those in this field typically gain work experience prior to attending graduate school. Recent graduates have ended up in advanced degree programs at elite business schools like Wharton (Penn), Stern (NYU), Columbia Business School, Yale School of Management, Sloane School of Management (MIT), and the Tuck School of Business (Dartmouth). Whether entering graduate school or chasing their first job, the vast majority of Falcons stay in the Boston area. New York City and San Francisco are the next two most popular US destinations; there is also a large cluster of graduates settled in Brazil, a country from which the university attracts a large number of international students.

Admission

In the 2017-18 admissions cycle Bentley accepted 43 percent of the 9,252 who applied. Members of the Class of 2022 averaged 1321 on the SAT and 29 on the ACT. For perspective, in 2011 the acceptance rate was a nearly identical 46 percent, but the 75th percentile on the SAT was a 1300. The percent of students ranking in the top 10 percent (50 percent) and 25 percent (89 percent) of their high school classes has risen sharply in that same time. Therefore, we can deduce that while acceptance rates have stayed relatively similar at Bentley in recent years, the standardized test scores and grades needed to gain acceptance have risen significantly.

Test scores, grades (including an emphasis on senior year grades), two letters of recommendation, and an on-campus interview are all important components of the admissions process. While the interviews are not mandatory, they can be an excellent opportunity to highlight interpersonal skills and intangible attributes that a top business school like Bentley is seeking. With a relatively low yield of 28 percent, Bentley is competing with many other rival institutions for the same pool of students. Thus, it makes sense that the school accepts 69 percent of applicants through its binding early decision program. It locks down just short of one-quarter of its incoming freshman class via ED. Bentley is a competitive business school and is a notch easier to gain admission into than comparable Babson. Demonstrating interest and/or applying early is a strong strategic move for serious applicants.

Worth Your Money?

Forty-two percent of Bentley's 4,171 undergraduates qualify for financial aid, and 39 percent of that group sees 100 percent of their demonstrated need met by the university. The average annual grant is for just over $38k, helping to alleviate the pain of the $71,320 per year cost of attendance. To help lessen the cost, even for families who can pay, 20 percent of undergrads receive a merit-based award of roughly $9,000. Even at that high cost, Bentley is worth the money for most applicants. The school rates very well in terms of pure salary—both starting and midcareer—and it rates well for social mobility, allowing those from poor-to-modest backgrounds to climb the economic ladder.

FINANCIAL
Institutional Type: Private
In-State Tuition: $51,830
Out-of-State Tuition: $51,830
Room & Board: $16,960
Required Fees: N/A
Books & Supplies: $1,300

Avg. Need-Based Aid: $37,997
Avg. % of Need Met: 95%

Avg. Merit-Based Aid: 10,128
% Receiving Merit-Based Aid: 22%

Avg. Cumulative Debt: $30,997
% of Students Borrowing: 57%

CAREER
Who Recruits
1. Cognex Corporation
2. Boston Scientific
3. Grant Thornton LLP
4. P&G Gillette
5. Lincoln Financial Group

Notable Internships
1. Liberty Mutual Investments
2. KPMG
3. L'Oreal

Top Industries
1. Business
2. Finance
3. Accounting
4. Sales
5. Operations

Top Employers
1. Fidelity Investments
2. PwC
3. Liberty Mutual Insurance
4. EY
5. State Street

Where Alumni Work
1. Boston
2. New York City
3. Hartford
4. San Francisco
5. Providence

Median Earnings
College Scorecard (Early Career): $86,900
EOP (Early Career): $79,800
PayScale (Mid-Career): $116,600

RANKINGS
Forbes: 107
Money: 88
U.S. News: 2, Regional North
Wall Street Journal/THE: 134 (T)
Washington Monthly: N/A

#CollegesWorthYourMoney

Binghamton University (SUNY)

Binghamton, New York | Admissions Phone: 607-777-2171

Inside the Classroom

Created in the GI Bill era to accommodate the influx of returning soldiers entering college, SUNY Binghamton (a.k.a., Binghamton University) is the shining star of the State University System of New York. Considered a "Public Ivy," the nearly 14,000 undergraduates are an accomplished bunch (average SAT is 1350), and the excellence of the academic offerings is commensurate with the student body. It's no wonder that 92 percent of freshmen return to campus the next fall, a retention rate that is unparalleled among non-flagship public institutions.

The university offers over 130 areas of concentration across its five undergraduate schools: the Harpur College of Arts and Sciences, the College of Community and Public Affairs, the Decker School of Nursing, the School of Management, and the Thomas J. Watson School of Engineering and Applied Science. General education requirements include foreign language (except for engineering majors), creating a global vision, the liberal arts (aesthetics, humanities, laboratory sciences, social sciences, and mathematics), and a series of physical activity and wellness classes. Unlike many state universities there is no long list of required courses awaiting you. Rather, the mandated categories of coursework are broad enough that you'll have plenty of room for exploration.

The student-to-faculty ratio is on the high side at 19:1, but class sizes are reasonably small with 48 percent of sections containing fewer than twenty students. Only 13 percent of courses are held in large lecture halls with fifty+ students. Research opportunities are available with the Freshman Research Immersion program being one shining example. This program welcomes students to college with a year-long authentic research experience in the sciences and engineering. The Office of Undergraduate Research is adept at connecting students in all fields, not just STEM, to research opportunities alongside faculty members. The school's own undergraduate research journal, Alpenglow, gives students the chance to publish scholarly, as well as original creative works. Study abroad opportunities are available at over fifty worldwide locations, and roughly one-fifth of undergraduates spend a semester in a foreign country.

In the spring of 2018 Binghamton awarded the greatest number of degrees in the social sciences (17 percent), biology (16 percent), business (14 percent), engineering (9 percent), and psychology (8 percent). The School of Management is renowned for its accounting program and is well known by NYC-based companies. Programs in chemistry, psychology, and nursing are also well respected. The university's graduates are somewhat competitive in procuring prestigious postgraduate fellowships, and between 2017 and 2019 the school produced seventeen Fulbright Scholars.

Outside the Classroom

Just over half of undergrads reside on campus in dorms or in residential college communities designed for 200 to 1,000 students each, and all have their own distinct personalities. Most off-campus apartment dwellers reside in the city's West Side neighborhood, but some end up in small towns a ten- to twenty-minute drive away. With fifty-six fraternities and sororities and thousands of participants, you might think that Greek life would be a dominant presence, yet only 14 percent of men and 11 percent of women pledge, leaving the majority to carve out their own social scene. The Binghamton Bearcats field twenty-one varsity sports teams in NCCA Division I. However, with no football team, the university is not a sports-centered campus. There is much to do within the university's 930 acres of grounds that includes a 190-acre nature preserve, a 156,000-square-foot multipurpose center, two fully equipped gyms, two pools, twenty-six tennis courts, and a 1,200-seat theater for art/speaking/musical events. Over 2,000 students participate in forty-two recreational and club athletic teams, and another 3,000 play intramural sports. There are 300 other clubs and activities. From their high-achieving speech and debate squad to a plethora of political, cultural, academic, and religious clubs, all 14,000 undergrads can find some way to connect. There are also eighty-five organizations focused on community service and volunteer work. Green initiatives are popular on campus, including energy efficiency, local food sources, recycling, and the bike-share program.

Career Services

The Fleishman Center for Career and Professional Development is not your average state school career services office. Consisting of twenty-one professional employees and fifty peer assistants and interns, the 666:1 student-to-advisor ratio (only counting the professionals) is more supportive than it appears. In a single year Fleischman staff conducted 7,246 1:1 counseling sessions. The 740 career programs hosted by career services personnel drew 27,500 attendees. About 10,000 unique students connected directly with career services, a sizable portion of the undergraduate population.

Recruiting on campus is a regular occurrence with over 2,700 on-site interviews conducted each year. The hireBing platform (run by Handshake) sees 7,000 job and internship postings annually. SUNY Binghamton's Fall Job Fair attracts more than 120 corporate, government, and nonprofit employers including Teach for America, Geico, Wayfair, and Raytheon Company. The school's recently launched Washington, DC, Employer Site Visit Program complements its successful New York City Site Visits Program. Having increased its staffing, outreach, and technological capabilities in recent years, Binghamton's career services is on the rise.

Professional Outcomes

The Class of 2018 saw 77 percent of job-seeking graduates land their first professional job within six months of commencement. Those entering the technology/computing fields found homes at companies like Facebook, IBM, Apple, and Microsoft in large numbers. Graduates entering finance careers were successful in finding employment at firms like Morgan Stanley, JPMorgan, Goldman Sachs, and CitiGroup. In the accounting/consulting realm the most popular employers of Binghamton grads were EY, PwC, Deloitte, and KPMG. The average starting salary procured was nearly $57,425, well above the national average for college grads. Of course, it is important to note that figure does not include the 23 percent of job-seeking graduates who were still looking for jobs at the time of the survey. New York City is, by far, the most common landing spot for Binghamton graduates, but many also remain in Upstate New York or travel to Washington, DC; Boston; San Francisco; Philadelphia; and Los Angeles.

Of the Binghamton grads seeking to transition directly into graduate studies, 90 percent were already enrolled in a program six months after graduation. Many SUNY branch campuses were among the most popular graduate school destinations, but many prestigious universities also graced this list including Harvard, Dartmouth, Georgetown, Columbia, Stanford, Penn, and the University of Michigan. SUNY Binghamton's reputation also helped open the doors to law school as it enjoyed an 84 percent acceptance rate. The school's early admission med school program (during sophomore year) creates a pipeline into SUNY Upstate Medical University. In the 2018-19 academic year, 196 seniors applied to medical school and were accepted at a rate 14 percent higher than the national average.

Admission

SUNY Binghamton received 33,467 applications in 2018 and accepted 40 percent. That acceptance rate was similar to acceptance rates at this selective state university over the past decade, but the profile of the average enrolling freshman indicates that the school is becoming significantly more competitive. Entering freshmen in 2019-20 had solid grades with a mid-50 percent high school GPA of 3.7-3.9. The mid-50 percent range on the SAT for the previous year's freshmen was 1310-1440 and 28-32 for the ACT. Ten years ago, the SAT range was 1190-1350. Even with SAT score inflation, it is safe to say that the average student at this school today is a higher achiever than the average student of a decade ago.

The factors that are considered above all others in admissions decisions are grades, test scores, and rigor of secondary curriculum. Class rank, the essay, recommendations, and extracurricular activities make up the second tier of important considerations. With such a massive applicant pool, interviews are not offered. SUNY Binghamton is a special value, especially by the standards of today's higher education marketplace. With an annual in-state tuition of just over $7,000, this excellent public research university continues to draw more and more qualified applicants each year. The admission formula falls far short of rocket science. Strong test scores and solid grades in AP/honors classes rule the day.

Worth Your Money?

You simply won't find a better combination of quality and price anywhere on the East Coast than Binghamton University. With a total annual cost of attendance of $26,612 (much lower for those who commute) for an in-state student, this SUNY school is worth anyone's money, no matter your major or career path. More than half of students qualify for financial aid and receive an average grant package of almost $10k, making an already affordable school nothing less than a ridiculous bargain.

FINANCIAL
Institutional Type: Public
In-State Tuition: $6,870
Out-of-State Tuition: $23,710
Room & Board: $15,058
Required Fees: $2,934
Books & Supplies: $1,000

Avg. Need-Based Aid: $9,908
Avg. % of Need Met: 70%

Avg. Merit-Based Aid: $6,629
% Receiving Merit-Based Aid: 12%

Avg. Cumulative Debt: $27,470
% of Students Borrowing: 50%

CAREER
Who Recruits
1. AMETEK Aerospace and Defense
2. NYS Department of Transportation
3. Dick's Sporting Goods
4. AXA Advisors
5. Mirabito Energy Products

Notable Internships
1. United Health Services
2. Cushman & Wakefield
3. Deloitte

Top Industries
1. Business
2. Education
3. Engineering
4. Operations
5. Information Technology

Top Employers
1. IBM
2. EY
3. JPMorgan Chase
4. PwC
5. Morgan Stanley

Where Alumni Work
1. New York City
2. Ithaca, NY
3. Washington, DC
4. Boston
5. San Francisco

Median Earnings
College Scorecard (Early Career): $61,600
EOP (Early Career): $65,700
PayScale (Mid-Career): $109,600

RANKINGS
Forbes: 145
Money: 33
U.S. News: 79, National Universities
Wall Street Journal/THE: 153 (T)
Washington Monthly: 90, National Universities

#CollegesWorthYourMoney

Boston College

Chestnut Hill, Massachusetts | Admissions Phone: 617-552-3100

ADMISSION
Admission Rate: 28%
Admission Rate - Men: 31%
Admission Rate - Women: 26%
EA Admission Rate: 34%
ED Admission Rate: New in 2019
Admission Rate (5-Year Trend): -4%
ED Admission Rate (5-Year Trend): Previously Not Offered
% of Admits Attending (Yield): 28%
Transfer Admission Rate: 34%

Offered Wait List: 7,566
Accepted Wait List: 2,953
Admitted Wait List: 273

SAT Reading/Writing (Middle 50%): 650-720
SAT Math (Middle 50%): 670-770
ACT Composite (Middle 50%): 31-34
Testing Policy: ACT/SAT Required
SAT Superscore: Yes
ACT Superscore: Yes

% Graduated in Top 10% of HS Class: 78%
% Graduated in Top 25% of HS Class: 94%
% Graduated in Top 50% of HS Class: 98%

ENROLLMENT
Total Undergraduate Enrollment: 9,377
% Part-Time: 0%
% Male: 47%
% Female: 53%
% Out-of-State: 67%
% Fraternity: Not Offered
% Sorority: Not Offered
% On-Campus (Freshman): 100%
% On-Campus (All Undergraduate): 84%

% African-American: 4%
% Asian: 11%
% Hispanic: 12%
% White: 65%
% Other: 4%
% Race or Ethnicity Unknown: 4%
% International: 8%
% Low-Income: 14%

ACADEMICS
Student-to-Faculty Ratio: 12:1
% of Classes Under 20: 49%
% of Classes Under 40: 87%
% Full-Time Faculty: 50%
% Full-Time Faculty w/ Terminal Degree: 47%

Top Programs
Applied Psychology and Human Development
Chemistry
Communication
Economics
English
Finance
History
Nursing

Retention Rate: 95%
4-Year Graduation Rate: 88%
6-Year Graduation Rate: 93%

Curricular Flexibility: Less Flexible
Academic Rating: ★★★★✦

Inside the Classroom

Along with Notre Dame, Georgetown, and Villanova, Boston College, home to 9,300 undergrads and an additional 4,700 graduate students, is among the most academically renowned Catholic universities in the world. The college offers fifty-eight majors across four schools that award undergraduate degrees: the School of Management, the School of Education, the School of Nursing, and the Morrissey College of Arts & Sciences. Certain majors that one takes for granted as being offered at a large research institution, such as engineering, do not yet exist at BC. However, the school is breaking ground on a new $150 million science facility that will offer a full spectrum of engineering degrees in the not-too-distant future.

The core curriculum lays out an extensive series of academic requirements that includes two courses in the natural sciences, social sciences, history, philosophy, and theology as well as one course in the arts, cultural diversity, math, and writing. All told, the core curriculum accounts for three full semesters of coursework. The breadth of the requirements is far from accidental—BC's program is designed to expand students' intellectual horizons and build character at the same time.

This odyssey unfolds in a caring and personal atmosphere. Approximately half of the college's sections contain nineteen or fewer students; there are some larger lecture hall classes, but those are fairly rare. Working closely with their professors pays off for students. In their own self-assessment, 95 percent of graduates reported learning how to think critically at BC, and 93 percent said they learned how to write clearly and effectively. Fifty percent of BC grads pursued a semester abroad in one of 200+ locations around the globe, and 90 percent cited the experience as a source of personal growth.

BC offers highly respected programs in communications, psychology, and business through the renowned Carroll School of Management. Other popular and well-regarded majors include economics, biology, and chemistry. Graduates fare decently in procuring prestigious awards, especially in the realm of fellowships to study abroad. Sixteen members of the Class of 2018 won Fulbright Scholarships, and BC holds the distinction as one of the top twenty Fulbright-producing research universities over the past decade.

Outside the Classroom

Unlike at Boston University, BC is not located in the heart of its namesake city. Fortunately, downtown Boston is only six miles away and easily accessible from the Chestnut Hill section of Newton where BC's main campus is located. With 70 percent of students identifying as Catholic, it is little surprise that religion and spirituality are a big part of campus life. Clubs in this arena are well represented among the 273 student organizations on campus, but there are a multitude of pre-professional, special interest, performing arts, and political offerings as well. There are no Greek houses at BC, a void that is filled by tightly knit groups with common interests. One such galvanizing force is the school's athletic teams. The Eagles compete in thirty-one NCAA Division I and forty-four intramural sports. The men's ice hockey team is always in the national spotlight, regularly appearing in the Frozen Four. For those seeking charitable opportunity, the Volunteer & Service Learning Center connects students with a plethora of organizations all over the country. One of the most popular of those experiences is the Appalachia Volunteers Program that sends around 500 students each year on spring break to forty impoverished cities and towns in the United States.

Career Services

The Career Center is manned by sixteen professionals whose specialty areas include career counseling, exploration, and employer engagement. Not counting the five graduate assistants and nine peer coaches who also are available to work with undergraduate students, this calculates to a student-to-advisor ratio of 581:1, below average compared to the pool of institutions included in this book.

The better news is that the office is effective at what is most important—helping students achieve positive career and graduate school outcomes. In fact, five of the top six resources cited by job-holding recent grads as being most helpful in landing employment had to do with the Career Center—EagleLink interviews, BC career fairs, networking through BC, EagleLink listings, and internships. Over 200 companies recruit on campus each year with most offering in-person interviews. Career fairs occur throughout the year; some events are general while others cater to specific areas of interest including public accounting, government, and sports and entertainment. The Career Center regularly offers job shadowing opportunities, networking nights, Career Treks, workshops covering a host of topics, and the Eagle Intern Fellowship that provides a $3,500 stipend to selected students pursuing unpaid internships. The alumni network is 180,000 strong and is generally very active and willing to help current students.

Professional Outcomes

Within six months of graduation 96 percent of the Class of 2018 had landed at their next destination, whether that was employment, graduate school, a fellowship, or a volunteer position. The most favored industries were finance/accounting/real estate (23 percent), health care/science (15 percent), business/consulting (14 percent), and technology/engineering (11 percent). More than forty newly minted alumni found employment at both Ernst & Young and PricewaterhouseCoopers. Notable numbers also flocked to Oracle, Citi, Mass General, and KPMG. Across all graduating years, more than 150 alumni also work at Deloitte, Google, Morgan Stanley, and Goldman Sachs.

The median starting salary for a BC grad is $58,500. Those in the School of Education and A&S had a median salary of below $51k while those exiting the management and nursing schools enjoyed median starting incomes of $60k. By a wide margin, the locale where the must alumni settle is the university's home state of Massachusetts; New York City also draws a sizable number of BC grads.

Examining the last five years of graduate data, enrollment in graduate, medical, or law school is a choice made by 18-23 percent of graduates. Of that higher-education-minded cohort, the greatest number are pursuing master's degrees in education or business. Law school was next in popularity at 12 percent followed by a PhD or applied doctorate at 10 percent and medical school at 8 percent. Of the law school attendees, a dozen continued in BC's own program. BC was also, by far, the most common graduate choice for those pursuing advanced degrees in education and business. Tufts was the No. 1 target for medical school and the natural sciences. Graduates also enjoyed acceptances into other elite medical schools including Georgetown, Duke, and Boston University.

Admission

Boston College received more than 31,000 applications for the Class of 2022, a 9 percent increase from the previous year, but fewer than it received in 2012. The acceptance rate fell to 28 percent in 2018; it was 32 percent in 2017. However, this level of selectivity is nothing new for BC. A decade ago, acceptance rates were in the 26-27 percent range.

What is changing is the academic profile of the average student being offered a spot at this high-end Catholic university. The mid-50 percent SAT score for the Class of 2022 was 1320-1460; fifteen years ago that 1320 would have had you close to the 75th percentile. Almost four-fifths of freshmen in the 2018-19 academic year placed in the top decile of their high school graduating class, and 94 percent hailed from the top quartile. The early admission window plays a large role in shaping the freshman class at BC, but there hasn't been much of an admissions edge. BC accepted 33 percent of EA applicants compared to 26 percent during the regular round. Disparities between early and regular admission rates are expected to grow, however, as the school introduced an Early Decision admission plan this past fall.

No matter when you apply, BC places a high value on writing ability and requires completion of the Boston College Writing Supplement. There are no interviews as part of the admissions process. BC attracts some of the most gifted Catholic students in the country as well as a fair number of non-Catholics. SAT scores in the 1400s and A/A- grades in a rigorous curriculum will put applicants on solid footing.

Worth Your Money?

In 1990, Boston College had an annual cost of attendance of around $15,000. Today, you will owe $75,586 per year for the privilege of attending this fine institution. While this jump in price far outpaces the rate of inflation, so goes the entire higher education marketplace. The good news is that BC awards healthy amounts of financial aid to those unable to pay full freight, so 43 percent of undergraduates receive upwards of $45,000 per year, making the cost far more palatable. Many others do pay full price as recent tax return data estimates that approximately one-half of all BC students come from families who are in the top 5-to-10 percent of income earners. If you were in a situation where you had to take on massive loans to study at BC, it would likely be a good investment if you planned on going the finance or consulting route but less so if you planned to study education.

FINANCIAL
Institutional Type: Private
In-State Tuition: $53,346
Out-of-State Tuition: $53,346
Room & Board: $14,142
Required Fees: N/A
Books & Supplies: $1,250

Avg. Need-Based Aid: $45,393
Avg. % of Need Met: 100%

Avg. Merit-Based Aid: $53,346
% Receiving Merit-Based Aid: 1%

Avg. Cumulative Debt: $20,915
% of Students Borrowing: 47%

CAREER
Who Recruits
1. MullenLowe Mediahub
2. Oracle
3. Epsilon
4. Liberty Mutual
5. Accenture

Notable Internships
1. NBC Sports Boston
2. Pfizer
3. IBM

Top Industries
1. Business
2. Education
3. Finance
4. Operations
5. Sales

Top Employers
1. PwC
2. EY
3. Deloitte
4. Morgan Stanley
5. Citi

Where Alumni Work
1. Boston
2. New York City
3. Washington, DC
4. San Francisco
5. Los Angeles

Median Earnings
College Scorecard (Early Career): $72,500
EOP (Early Career): $71,800
PayScale (Mid-Career): $115,400

RANKINGS
Forbes: 41
Money: 151
U.S. News: 37, National Universities
Wall Street Journal/THE: 59 (T)
Washington Monthly: 67, National Universities

#CollegesWorthYourMoney

Boston University

Boston, Massachusetts | Admissions Phone: 617-353-2300

ADMISSION

Admission Rate: 22%
Admission Rate - Men: 23%
Admission Rate - Women: 22%
EA Admission Rate: Not Offered
ED Admission Rate: 28%
Admission Rate (5-Year Trend): -15%
ED Admission Rate (5-Year Trend): -12%
% of Admits Attending (Yield): 25%
Transfer Admission Rate: 43%

Offered Wait List: 5,441
Accepted Wait List: 3,446
Admitted Wait List: 1

SAT Reading/Writing (Middle 50%): 650-720
SAT Math (Middle 50%): 680-780
ACT Composite (Middle 50%): 30-33
Testing Policy: ACT/SAT Required
SAT Superscore: Yes
ACT Superscore: Yes

% Graduated in Top 10% of HS Class: 65%
% Graduated in Top 25% of HS Class: 93%
% Graduated in Top 50% of HS Class: 100%

ENROLLMENT

Total Undergraduate Enrollment: 18,515
% Part-Time: 6%
% Male: 40%
% Female: 60%
% Out-of-State: 72%
% Fraternity: 5%
% Sorority: 2%
% On-Campus (Freshman): 99%
% On-Campus (All Undergraduate): 75%

% African-American: 4%
% Asian: 15%
% Hispanic: 11%
% White: 37%
% Other: 4%
% Race or Ethnicity Unknown: 8%
% International: 21%
% Low-Income: 15%

ACADEMICS

Student-to-Faculty Ratio: 10:1
% of Classes Under 20: 62%
% of Classes Under 40: 83%
% Full-Time Faculty: 70%
% Full-Time Faculty w/ Terminal Degree: 90%

Top Programs
Biomedical Engineering
Business Administration and Management
Communication
Computer Science
Economics
Health Science
International Relations
Psychology

Retention Rate: 94%
4-Year Graduation Rate: 84%
6-Year Graduation Rate: 88%

Curricular Flexibility: Somewhat Flexible
Academic Rating: ★★★★

Inside the Classroom

Growing more selective each year, Boston University is a private research institution playing host to more than 18,000 undergrads as well as an additional 15,000 graduate students. It's hard to imagine a more dynamic locale than BU's sprawling campus that shares a neighborhood with Fenway Park, the Museum of Fine Arts, MIT, and countless culinary and cultural enticements. In total, the university offers more than 250 programs of study, about half of which are distinct undergraduate degrees spread across ten schools/colleges.

Unique programs include the Kilachand Honors College that welcomes 150 new students each year and offers a unique, original, integrated four-year curriculum thematically centered on global challenges and practical solutions. Not shockingly, it's tough to pin down course requirements with so many colleges within the larger university. College of Arts & Sciences students must satisfy basic requirements in foreign language, mathematics, and writing as part of their 128 credits. Engineering students, on the other hand, must complete sixteen credits in mathematics and twelve in the natural sciences. First-year experience courses are available but not required.

Many classes at BU are reasonably small—62 percent contain fewer than twenty students; only 12 percent contain more than fifty. The student-to-faculty ratio is 10:1, quite an achievement for a school of its size. BU's Undergraduate Research Opportunities Program (UROP) funded 650 students in 2018-19, and many additional students participate in BU's research for credit, volunteer, work study, and other independent opportunities. More than ninety study abroad sites in twenty-five countries are available for those seeking a global experience. Participation is relatively high—40 percent of arts and sciences students complete a semester on a foreign campus.

The greatest number of degrees are conferred in business/marketing (21 percent) communications and journalism (14 percent), social sciences (14 percent), biology (10 percent), engineering (9 percent), and health professions/related sciences (7 percent). The Questrom School of Business and the College of Engineering are highly regarded as well as the university's College of Communication and College of Health & Rehabilitation Services. Over the last five years, BU has produced at least five Fulbright Scholars annually. In 2019, grads took home ten Fulbright Scholarships, four Goldwater Scholarships, two Critical Language Scholarships, a Boren Scholarship, and a Truman Scholarship.

Outside the Classroom

Three-quarters of the undergraduate student body reside on campus. Greek life has a modest presence at BU—13 percent elect to pledge one of the school's eight frats and twelve sororities. Nicknamed the Terriers, BU is represented by twenty-three teams (13 women's, 10 men's) in NCAA Division I, highlighted by its perennially stellar men's ice hockey team. In an odd move for a school of its size, BU dissolved its football program in 1997. The basketball team makes an occasional appearance in March Madness. For those a bit less serious about/skilled at sports, 7,000 students participate in intramural athletics. With close to 500 student organizations and offerings from improv to synchronized swimming, just about everyone can find their niche. The student-run Daily Free Press is recognized as one of the tops in the country and claims the fourth highest circulation of any paper in Boston. Volunteer spirit runs rampant at BU—the Community Service Center has a volunteer base of over 1,500 students and contributes 75,000 hours of service to the Boston-area community each year. Being located in the heart of Boston, students have limitless choices for nightlife and culture and can conveniently hop aboard the Green Line to explore the farthest reaches of the city.

Career Services

Twenty counselors, recruiters, and outreach coordinators comprise the BU Center for Career Development (CCD). That equates to a student-to-advisor ratio of 925:1, well below average compared to the pool of institutions included in this book. Despite limited personnel for a school so large, the office is successful at working with those who engage with them. In fact, students who regularly utilized the career center reported 22 percent higher earnings than their peers. Last year, staff conducted 2,437 one-on-one advising sessions. Remarkably for a school of BU's size, the CCD helps 89 percent of students complete at least one internship over their four years of study.

Every spring and fall the CCD organizes an All-Majors Career Fair with over one-hundred guest employers; individual colleges within BU also host discipline-specific career fairs in business, engineering, nonprofit leadership, and public health. In total, 725 employers attended BU fairs, and 770 recruited on campus in 2018-19. That led to 600+ on-campus interviews being facilitated by the CCD. Freshmen are encouraged to attend a seminar called Career Directions: Starting Your Journey that gives tips on how to maximize one's educational experience with an eye on life beyond college. Through the Career Advisory Network, the CCD also works to connect students with over 6,000 participating alumni who are employed in a wide spectrum of fields. Even with a less-than-ideal number of counselors, BU's career services staff works hard to reach students through seminars, job fairs, and online resources.

Professional Outcomes

Six months after graduation, 96 percent of BU grads have found their way into the world of employment or full-time graduate study. A recent survey of corporate recruiters with international companies revealed that Boston University alums have the sixth highest employability ranking, directly behind the likes of MIT, Caltech, Harvard, and Stanford. Recent graduating classes have seen more than ten graduates join employers like EY, PwC, Deloitte, and TJX Companies. Healthy numbers of engineering grads found their way to Amazon, IBM, Lockheed Martin, and Pfizer. Across all graduating years, companies employing more than 250 BU alums include Google, Oracle, Accenture, and Wayfair. Starting salary data is highly dependent on which school within BU one attended. For the Class of 2018, grads of the Questrom School of Business earned a starting salary of roughly $63k, College of Engineering grads averaged $70k, and Arts & Sciences students came in just shy of $50k.

Respect for the BU degree comes from more than just the corporate world. Of the 19 percent of 2018 grads who moved directly into graduate school, many were welcomed onto the campuses of elite graduate programs. For example, engineering students found new academic homes at MIT, Stanford, Carnegie Mellon, and Columbia. Most top law schools have some level of representation from BU alumni including BU Law itself, a top twenty-five institution that accepts a significant number of its own undergraduates. Those aiming to become medical doctors can apply for the Seven-Year Liberal Arts/Medical Education Program that leads directly to study at the BU School of Medicine. Overall, the university saw almost 300 undergraduates apply to med school in 2018 alone, the eighth highest total in the nation. Whether attending grad school or starting their careers, the greatest number of BU grads remain in Boston with New York City, San Francisco, Los Angeles, DC, and Philadelphia next in popularity.

Admission

Over 64,000 applications rolled into BU for spots in the Class of 2022, and 22 percent gained acceptance. For historical context, 46 percent of applicants were accepted in 2012 and close to three quarters in 2005. The average member of the Class of 2022 finished with a 3.71 GPA and earned a 1421 SAT score. Back in 2012, the 75th percentile on the SAT was 1390, an indicator that gaining acceptance into BU is considerably more difficult than in the not-too-distant past. Most BU students finished in the upper echelon of their high school classes—65 percent were in the top 10 percent, and 93 percent were in the top 25 percent. On a 4.0 scale, 83 percent had GPAs of 3.5 or higher.

The only two admissions criteria rated as "very important" for all applicants are the rigor of one's high school course load and talent/ability. Factors in the second run of importance are class rank, GPA, standardized test scores, recommendations, essays, extracurricular activities, alumni relation (legacy), and the level of an applicant's interest. Those who demonstrate the most fervent interest and commitment by applying early decision receive a slight boost, gaining acceptance at a 28 percent clip. It is critical to remember that this isn't your mother's or father's BU—it's not even your older sibling's BU. Far more highly selective than even a few years ago, Boston University hopefuls need to bring top-tier credentials in order to be offered admission at this fine private research institution.

Worth Your Money?

At $72,000, Boston University has a hefty list price cost of attendance, a sum made slightly more manageable for the 16 percent of undergraduates who receive an annual merit-based award of $24k or some level of need-based financial aid. BU does award need-based aid to 41 percent of its undergraduates, but it fails to meet 100 percent of all demonstrated need for all students. Still, the average annual award to qualifying students is $45k, which cuts the overall costs considerably. Boston University graduates end up with an average debt load of $43,000, a figure that is higher than the national average. If you were in the position that attending BU would necessitate taking out large loans, your decision should come down to whether you intend to major in a field with a high enough starting salary so you could comfortably make monthly payments.

FINANCIAL
Institutional Type: Private
In-State Tuition: $52,816
Out-of-State Tuition: $52,816
Room & Board: $15,720
Required Fees: $1,132
Books & Supplies: $1,000

Avg. Need-Based Aid: $44,891
Avg. % of Need Met: 91%

Avg. Merit-Based Aid: $23,779
% Receiving Merit-Based Aid: 16%

Avg. Cumulative Debt: $42,976
% of Students Borrowing: 46%

CAREER
Who Recruits
1. Marriott
2. Turner Broadcasting System
3. TJX
4. General Electric
5. Bloomberg LP

Notable Internships
1. Amazon
2. Boston Scientific
3. BuzzFeed

Top Industries
1. Business
2. Education
3. Operations
4. Media
5. Information Technology

Top Employers
1. IBM
2. Google
3. Amazon
4. Microsoft
5. Oracle

Where Alumni Work
1. Boston
2. New York City
3. San Francisco
4. Los Angeles
5. Washington, DC

Median Earnings
College Scorecard (Early Career): $65,300
EOP (Early Career): $62,000
PayScale (Mid-Career): $113,600

RANKINGS
Forbes: 74
Money: 209
U.S. News: 40 (T), National Universities
Wall Street Journal/THE: 44 (T)
Washington Monthly: 126, National Universities

#CollegesWorthYourMoney

Bowdoin College

Brunswick, Maine | Admissions Phone: 207-725-3100

Inside the Classroom

Set on 215 lush acres in the quaint town of New Brunswick, Maine, Bowdoin College serves just over 1,800 undergraduate students. This quintessential, elite New England liberal arts college is steeped in history and tradition; its oldest buildings date to the late eighteenth century, and the curriculum is guided by a poem, "The Offer of College," penned by the school's president in 1906. Does it get any more New England liberal-artsy than that?

Among its core beliefs, Bowdoin offers a flexible and broad liberal arts education. Polar Bears can choose from one of thirty-three academic programs or get more creative through an interdisciplinary or student-designed major. One-size-fits-all requirements are minimal. All must take a freshman seminar in an area of interest such as Women of Color in Politics, Intro to Documentary Film Studies, or Food and Foodways in China: A Cultural History. Bowdoin students are required to take one course from each of five distribution areas: (1) mathematical, computational, or statistical reasoning; (2) inquiry in the natural sciences; (3) exploring social difference; (4) international perspectives; and (5) visual and performing arts.

Class sizes are small—70 percent contain fewer than twenty students—and more than one-quarter have fewer than ten students. The student-faculty ratio is 9:1, which leads to ample and meaningful interaction and guidance in and out of the classroom. More than half of Bowdoin undergrads report interacting with a professor outside of regular class time at least once per week. Professors have a reputation for being extremely dedicated to their teaching. Students also enjoy a plethora of study abroad opportunities with over 50 percent electing to spend a semester learning in a foreign locale.

The greatest percentage of degrees are conferred in the social sciences (30 percent), biology (13 percent), area/ethnic/gender studies (9 percent), and mathematics (7 percent). Economics and government and legal studies are two of the more popular majors within the social sciences. Bowdoin is one of the strongest in the country for those on a pre-med track. The school is also a prolific producer of fellowship/scholarship winners. In 2018 alone, twenty graduates were named Fulbright Scholars—the second highest total from any one school. Graduates also routinely win other prestigious awards including National Science Foundation Graduate Research Fellowships, Boren Scholarships, Watson Fellowships, and Critical Language Scholarships awarded by the US State Department.

Outside the Classroom

By sheer numbers, athletics are a driving force of life outside the classroom. An insanely high 43 percent of undergrads are varsity athletes who compete on one of thirty NCAA Division III teams. And that doesn't include those who play on one of the six club teams or participate in one of ten intramural sports, each of which has an A, B, and C level. Over one hundred non-sports clubs are also active, including the Outing Club, which boasts over 400 members and takes over 150 nature-themed excursions per year. Greek life was disbanded around the turn of the new millennium and replaced with a system of eight college houses that serve as the backbone of the campus residential experience. Each house has its own student government and hosts special events throughout the year. The dining halls are known to prepare extravagant meals that receive rave reviews across the board. Over 90 percent of students live on campus, and certain annual events like the Gala and Ivies concert bring together the whole student body. Among the most favored off-campus destinations is Portland, Maine's largest city, which is less than half an hour away.

Career Services

Bowdoin Career Planning is staffed by six full-time career counselors and one employer relations professional. That works out to a student-to-advisor ratio of 304:1, lower than the average institution included in this book. Students are always welcome to schedule a one-on-one counseling session or mock interview or drop by between noon and 2 p.m. each weekday, unannounced, with a quick question. In 2017-18, the office planned 204 programs with over 5,200 attendees, more than two-and-half times the size of the student body. Incredibly, the staff managed to work, in some capacity, with 80 percent of students and 99 percent of the senior class.

The school combines some events with Colby and Bates; the Graduate & Professional School Fair that is held every October, and the annual Maine Employers Career Fair are two examples. The school's outreach efforts pay off with additional companies recruiting on campus each year. In 2017, it added HSBC, Jefferies Group, Wayfair, and LogMeIn to an already long list. Bowdoin also distributes close to a quarter of a million dollars in grants to support unpaid internships each year. Two-thirds of graduates complete some type of internship. To provide further assistance in carving out career pathways, 200 alumni and parents of current students come to campus to help students with career exploration and networking.

E-mail: admissions@bowdoin.edu | Website: www.bowdoin.edu

Professional Outcomes

An examination of five years' worth of outcomes data (2012-2016) reveals that by the fall after graduation between 70 and 78 percent of recent grads have found full-time employment, and between 15 and 20 percent have gone directly into graduate school. Only 2-4 percent are still seeking employment. Prominent corporations across all sectors love Bowdoin grads. Recent alumni have found positions at Apple, IBM, Goldman Sachs, Google, HBO, and Microsoft. Other companies that employ more than a dozen alumni are Fidelity Investments, Morgan Stanley, Amazon, UBS, Facebook, and Barclays. At age thirty-four, Bowdoin grads have a median salary of $61k per year, placing them in the 73rd income percentile nationwide, slightly higher than nearby Bates or Colby. The cities attracting the greatest numbers of graduates are (in order) Boston; New York City; Portland, Maine; San Francisco; DC; and Los Angeles.

Of those entering graduate school, 20 percent were enrolled in PhD programs, 15 percent were in med school, 8 percent in law school, and 41 percent were in master's programs. The top twenty graduate schools attended, by volume, in the last five years make an exclusive list including six Ivies along with Duke, MIT, Johns Hopkins, Northwestern, and Stanford. Boston University is also one the largest recipients of Bowdoin grads. Those aiming for medical school fare exceptionally well with 90 percent typically earning acceptance into at least one institution. Recent grads are presently studying medicine at Tufts, Harvard, Boston University, NYU, and the University of Michigan.

Admission

Already a highly selective school, Bowdoin has become even more difficult to get into in recent years. The acceptance rate for applicants to the Class of 2022 was a paltry 10.3 percent compared to 13.6 percent the previous year and 20 percent back in 2012. The number of applicants increased by one-quarter since last year. An examination of the middle-50 percent ranges on standardized tests for attending students suggests there is little evidence that the school is accepting a higher caliber of student than it was five years ago. In 2013-14, Bowdoin freshmen scored 1360-1510 on the SAT and 30-33 on the ACT. In 2018-19, those SAT figures were slightly lower at 1300-1510 while the upper-end of the ACT range was slightly higher at 30-34. Bowdoin is famous for becoming the first test-optional school in the country (1969). Nevertheless, 60 percent of the Class of 2022 submitted SAT scores, and 46 percent shared ACT scores. Those numbers add up to more than 100 percent because a decent number of students submitted results from both tests, so it is fair to conclude that the vast majority of successful applicants elected to submit standardized test scores.

Being in the top 10 percent of your high school class is almost required—80 percent of freshmen held that distinction, and 96 percent were in the top 25 percent. The school also ranks essays, recommendations, talent/ability, personal qualities, and extracurricular activities as "very important" in the admissions process. Although Bowdoin is, technically, a test-optional school, it pays to have high SAT/ACTs. The acceptance rate may be shrinking, but the average student profile has held relatively steady. Those with the best chance of acceptance will be near the top of their high school class and possess standardized test scores above the 95th percentile. Applying early decision also will provide a great boost for your prospects; 23 percent of ED applicants are accepted compared to only 8.5 percent in the regular round.

Worth Your Money?

Bowdoin's annual cost of attendance is $73,800, and merit aid awards are not typically large enough to make any kind of a difference. Fortunately, the school is generous with need-based aid, meeting 100 percent of the demonstrated need for qualifying students. At present, 885 of the 1,824 undergraduates receive an average annual grant of $48,856. If you come from a family making an income in the top 5 percent nationwide—it is estimated that nearly half of all Bowdoin students do--you can expect to pay full price. In the end, the average graduate is in roughly $5,000 less debt than the average college student in the United States.

FINANCIAL
Institutional Type: Private
In-State Tuition: $55,822
Out-of-State Tuition: $55,822
Room & Board: $15,360
Required Fees: $528
Books & Supplies: $840

Avg. Need-Based Aid: $48,856
Avg. % of Need Met: 100%

Avg. Merit-Based Aid: $1,000
% Receiving Merit-Based Aid: 1%

Avg. Cumulative Debt: $25,482
% of Students Borrowing: 27%

CAREER
Who Recruits
1. Barclay's
2. Deutsche Bank
3. Prudential
4. Cornerstone Research
5. Teach for America

Notable Internships
1. Athena Global Advisors
2. eBay
3. CBS News

Top Industries
1. Business
2. Education
3. Research
4. Operations
5. Social Services

Top Employers
1. Unum
2. Fidelity Investments
3. Massachusetts General Hospital
4. Google
5. Morgan Stanley

Where Alumni Work
1. Boston
2. New York City
3. Portland, ME
4. San Francisco
5. Washington, DC

Median Earnings
College Scorecard (Early Career): $65,500
EOP (Early Career): $61,000
PayScale (Mid-Career): $112,000

RANKINGS
Forbes: 26
Money: 82
U.S. News: 6, Liberal Arts Colleges
Wall Street Journal/THE: 44 (T)
Washington Monthly: 5, Liberal Arts Colleges

#CollegesWorthYourMoney

Brandeis University

Waltham, Massachusetts | Admissions Phone: 781-736-3500

ADMISSION
Admission Rate: 31%
Admission Rate - Men: 29%
Admission Rate - Women: 32%
EA Admission Rate: Not Offered
ED Admission Rate: 39%
Admission Rate (5-Year Trend): -6%
ED Admission Rate (5-Year Trend): -6%
% of Admits Attending (Yield): 24%
Transfer Admission Rate: 25%

Offered Wait List: 1,844
Accepted Wait List: 721
Admitted Wait List: 1

SAT Reading/Writing (Middle 50%): 630-720
SAT Math (Middle 50%): 650-780
ACT Composite (Middle 50%): 29-33
Testing Policy: Test Optional
SAT Superscore: Yes
ACT Superscore: No

% Graduated in Top 10% of HS Class: 56%
% Graduated in Top 25% of HS Class: 91%
% Graduated in Top 50% of HS Class: 99%

ENROLLMENT
Total Undergraduate Enrollment: 3,639
% Part-Time: 1%
% Male: 39%
% Female: 61%
% Out-of-State: 70%
% Fraternity: Not Offered
% Sorority: Not Offered
% On-Campus (Freshman): 100%
% On-Campus (All Undergraduate): 76%

% African-American: 5%
% Asian: 14%
% Hispanic: 8%
% White: 46%
% Other: 3%
% Race or Ethnicity Unknown: 3%
% International: 20%
% Low-Income: 18%

ACADEMICS
Student-to-Faculty Ratio: 10:1
% of Classes Under 20: 57%
% of Classes Under 40: 85%
% Full-Time Faculty: 68%
% Full-Time Faculty w/ Terminal Degree: 94%

Top Programs
Biology
Chemistry
Economics
Health: Science, Society, and Policy
History
International Studies
Neuroscience
Sociology

Retention Rate: 92%
4-Year Graduation Rate: 80%
6-Year Graduation Rate: 88%

Curricular Flexibility: Somewhat Flexible
Academic Rating: ★★★★

Inside the Classroom

Unlike many other elite Boston-area universities, this institution does not have 300-400 years of history and tradition. Founded in 1948 by a group of Jewish donors only a few weeks before the modern State of Israel was established, Brandeis has been a nonsectarian university open to talented students of all backgrounds and faiths. Home to 3,600 undergraduates with a male-heavy split (60/40), Brandeis offers forty-four majors, the most popular of which are the social sciences (21 percent), biology (15 percent), business (9 percent), psychology (7 percent), and computer science (7 percent).

An ethos of high academic standards and intellectual curiosity permeates this Waltham, Massachusetts, campus. An awe-inspiring 54 percent of Brandeis undergraduates double major, and 40 percent elect to study abroad in one of over 350 approved programs across the globe. Core requirements for all students include a university writing seminar; one qualitative reasoning course; one diversity, equity, and inclusion course; one difference and justice in the world course; three semesters of a foreign language; and at least one class within each of the schools of humanities, science, social science, and creative arts.

Professors at Brandeis are committed to undergraduate education and will interact with you in close enough quarters that you can rest assured they will learn your name. The student-faculty ratio is 10:1, and 57 percent of courses contain fewer than nineteen students. Invitations to assist faculty members with academic research is common, even for undergraduates. In the Chemistry Department alone, 260 undergrads have coauthored and published papers with their professors in the last fifteen years. International experiences also abound, whether you are interacting with the 20 percent of the student body who are citizens of another country or decide to travel abroad for a semester, which 40 percent of undergraduates do.

Departments with a particularly strong national reputation include economics, international studies, and sociology as well as all of the traditional premed pathways including biology, chemistry, and the health: science, society, and policy program. More than 200 students work each year with the school's Office of Academic Fellowships to pursue sponsored opportunities to pursue their intellectual passions after graduation. Many have successfully landed Fulbright, Boren, and Critical Language Scholarships, among others.

Outside the Classroom

With over 260 student organizations, the club scene plays a prominent role at Brandeis. A cappella, Jewish groups, intramural sports, and theater are among the most popular. Opportunities to volunteer in the local community abound, and many take advantage; forty-four members of the Class of 2017 accrued more than 300 service hours over their four years. Fraternities and sororities do operate on campus and have a genuine presence, although they are unrecognized by the university. The Brandeis Judges (the school is named for famed Supreme Court Justice Louis Brandeis) compete in NCAA Division III and field nineteen teams (10 for women, 9 for men). The school also has nineteen club teams that include Brazilian Jiu-Jitsu, archery, and sailing. With a plethora of activities in which to participate and a generally active social scene, you don't need to venture off campus in order to fill your days with excitement. Of course, with Boston less than ten miles away, many do stray away from Waltham on the weekends. For the 76 percent of undergrads (and 100 percent of freshmen) who choose to live on campus, Brandeis' nineteen dorms are often ranked highly on lists of best collegiate housing.

Career Services

The Hiatt Career Center is staffed by fifteen professionals with expertise in career counseling, giving it a 240:1 student-to-advisor ratio, which is better than average compared to other schools featured in this guide. It deploys its resources effectively, connecting annually with over 50 percent of each class through counseling appointments, workshops, or job fairs. One-on-one counseling is available to all students as often as once per week, and the center encourages developing a relationship with one particular counselor over your four years of study. Specialized counseling is available for those considering pursuing an MD or other health-care-related position after undergrad. Walk-in hours are more generous than most universities and can be utilized for quick questions that require fifteen minutes or less of interaction. Career Services connects students with internship/employment opportunities by a variety of means. Industry Meetups bring Brandeis alumni to campus from a host of fields. Brandeis Networking Nights are held over winter break each year in Washington, DC, and New York City. It also hosts area-specific fairs for students concentrating in computer science, careers with a social impact, or volunteer and internship opportunities. On-site interviews are conducted at fall and spring career fairs. As an additional aid, 19,000 jobs and internships are posted each year on Handshake. This adds up to almost all graduates finding their next destination within months of leaving the university.

Brandeis University

E-mail: admissions@brandeis.edu | Website: www.brandeis.edu

Professional Outcomes

Within six months of graduation, 98 percent of the Class of 2018 had found their way to employment (59 percent), graduate school (33 percent), or another full-time activity like travel or volunteer work (6 percent). The most common industries entered by Brandeis grads are (in order) health care, scientific research, computer science, finance/banking, education, and consulting. Three of the four largest employers of recent grads are in the health-care sector: Boston Children's Hospital, Massachusetts General Hospital, and the Dana Farber Cancer Institute. Nonprofits such as Teach for America, City Year, and the Peace Corps are also well represented. The corporations employing the greatest number of recent graduates (classes of 2014-17) are Amazon, Goldman Sachs, and Walt Disney Parks & Resorts. By age thirty-four Brandeis graduates have a median income of $61k, putting them in the 72nd percentile for income nationally. The greatest number of graduates remains in Boston but many flock to New York City, DC, San Francisco, Los Angeles, and Philadelphia.

A large contingent of grads elect to continue at Brandeis for graduate school. The next most commonly attended graduate/professional schools from 2014-2017 were (in order) BU, Columbia, NYU, Harvard, and Tufts. That list is a good indication that Brandeis' reputation for academic excellence leads to positive outcomes for those applying to elite graduate schools. Those applying to medical school are remarkably successful, gaining acceptance between 65 and 75 percent annually, 20-30 points higher than the national average.

Admission

Brandeis is one of the rare, elite New England liberal arts schools that has not experienced an admissions rate freefall over the past decade. Typically, 33-35 percent of applicants find success, the same range as five years ago, although the Class of 2022 faced a slightly harsher 31 percent. The average SAT and ACT scores of accepted students has increased, but that is likely more a result of the school going test-optional in 2013 (lower scores no longer drag down the average) than an indicator that the applicant pool has become more competitive. We should note that Brandeis is test-optional, but with an asterisk. Students must submit one of the following: SAT/ACT scores; 3 AP/SAT Subject Tests, including a math/science and an English/social science discipline; or one graded analytical writing sample as well as an additional recommendation from an eleventh or twelfth grade course. Those who submitted traditional standardized test scores generally earned high scores. The middle 50 percent of Brandeis students earned a 1280-1500 on the SAT and a 29-33 on the ACT.

Excellent performance in the classroom is valued most strongly by the admissions committee with 90 percent of Brandeis undergrads in the top 25 percent of their high school class and 56 percent in the top 10 percent. The other categories that qualify as "very important" to the committee are class rank, character, personal qualities, and the rigor of one's high school curriculum. The rate of acceptance for early decision is only nine points higher than during the regular cycle (39 percent vs. 30 percent), which means that ED may only offer a slight admissions edge. The small gap between ED and RD acceptance rates could also mean that the ED applicant pool is not as strong, on average, as the RD applicant pool—a reasonable hypothesis given the large number of high-achieving applicants who apply to Brandeis but who do not have Brandeis at the top of their college list. Naturally, as a consequence, demonstrated interest is considered as important in the admission process.

Overall, Brandeis remains an accessible destination for students who are extremely strong in the classroom but who may not have aced the SAT. Those with straight A's in a rigorous high school curriculum and winning personal attributes will succeed as part of this holistic process.

Worth Your Money?

Given the annual cost of attendance of $76k you may be surprised to learn that, according to tax return data, Brandeis students come from homes with a significantly more modest median income, on average, than students at other comparable private schools. It is estimated that only about 55 percent come from families in the top 20 percent of income earners nationwide, a much lower percentage than many other prestigious institutions. What does that mean? Even though it does not meet 100 percent of demonstrated need for all undergraduates, Brandeis does prioritize enrolling an economically diverse student body, awarding need-based grants of close to $39,000 to 47 percent of its student population. Due to that generosity, many lower-to-middle income students have the opportunity to attend this school, and graduates hold less debt than the average college graduate in the United States. With solid financial aid offerings (as well as bit of merit aid) and positive graduate outcomes, Brandeis University is worth its net price.

FINANCIAL
Institutional Type: Private
In-State Tuition: $55,340
Out-of-State Tuition: $55,340
Room & Board: $16,080
Required Fees: $2,221
Books & Supplies: $1,000

Avg. Need-Based Aid: $38,944
Avg. % of Need Met: 94%

Avg. Merit-Based Aid: $12,912
% Receiving Merit-Based Aid: 21%

Avg. Cumulative Debt: $29,785
% of Students Borrowing: 46%

CAREER
Who Recruits
1. TIBCO
2. Analysis Group
3. John Hancock
4. Sun Life Financial
5. Kayak

Notable Internships
1. Uber
2. Symantec
3. Goldman Sachs

Top Industries
1. Business
2. Education
3. Research
4. Healthcare
5. Social Services

Top Employers
1. Dell
2. Google
3. IBM
4. Morgan Stanley
5. Amazon

Where Alumni Work
1. Boston
2. New York City
3. Washington, DC
4. San Francisco
5. Los Angeles

Median Earnings
College Scorecard (Early Career): $57,900
EOP (Early Career): $63,100
PayScale (Mid-Career): $113,200

RANKINGS
Forbes: 96
Money: 153
U.S. News: 40 (T), National Universities
Wall Street Journal/THE: 109
Washington Monthly: 106, National Universities

#CollegesWorthYourMoney

Brigham Young University

Provo, Utah | Admissions Phone: 801-422-2507

ADMISSION
Admission Rate: 64%
Admission Rate - Men: 62%
Admission Rate - Women: 67%
EA Admission Rate: Not Offered
ED Admission Rate: Not Offered
Admission Rate (5-Year Trend): +16%
ED Admission Rate (5-Year Trend): Not Offered
% of Admits Attending (Yield): 79%
Transfer Admission Rate: 57%

Offered Wait List: Not Offered
Accepted Wait List: Not Offered
Admitted Wait List: Not Offered

SAT Reading/Writing (Middle 50%): 600-710
SAT Math (Middle 50%): 590-710
ACT Composite (Middle 50%): 26-31
Testing Policy: ACT/SAT Required
SAT Superscore: No
ACT Superscore: No

% Graduated in Top 10% of HS Class: 54%
% Graduated in Top 25% of HS Class: 85%
% Graduated in Top 50% of HS Class: 98%

ENROLLMENT
Total Undergraduate Enrollment: 31,441
% Part-Time: 10%
% Male: 50%
% Female: 50%
% Out-of-State: 65%
% Fraternity: Not Offered
% Sorority: Not Offered
% On-Campus (Freshman): 73%
% On-Campus (All Undergraduate): 15%

% African-American: 1%
% Asian: 2%
% Hispanic: 6%
% White: 81%
% Other: 4%
% Race or Ethnicity Unknown: 1%
% International: 3%
% Low-Income: 16%

ACADEMICS
Student-to-Faculty Ratio: 20:1
% of Classes Under 20: 45%
% of Classes Under 40: 82%
% Full-Time Faculty: 67%
% Full-Time Faculty w/ Terminal Degree: 93%

Top Programs
Accounting
Entrepreneurial Management
Engineering
Excercise Science
International Relations
Public Health
Statistics

Retention Rate: 90%
4-Year Graduation Rate: 21%
6-Year Graduation Rate: 83%

Curricular Flexibility: Less Flexible
Academic Rating: ★★★

Inside the Classroom

An almost exclusively Mormon student body of more than 31,000 undergraduates occupy Brigham Young's high-altitude campus in the mountainous and breathtaking area of Provo, Utah. In addition to living by a strict honor code guided by the LDS Church (more on this later), students come to BYU for its more than 200 programs and reputation for academic excellence.

Required coursework for BYU undergraduates includes a number of courses in the Mormon faith including Teachings & Doctrine of the Book of Mormon, Christ and the Everlasting Gospel, Foundations of the Restoration, and The Eternal Family. Mandatory courses in American heritage, global and cultural awareness, first-year writing, advanced oral and written communication, foreign language, and the social, biological, and physical sciences are all part of the core curriculum that supports BYU's larger mission "to provide an education that is (1) spiritually strengthening, (2) intellectually enlarging, and (3) character building, leading to (4) lifelong learning and service."

A 20:1 student-to-faculty ratio translates to some undergraduate sections being a bit large. Roughly 12 percent of sections contain more than fifty students. However, those lecture hall courses are balanced with classes of more modest size; 45 percent of courses have nineteen or fewer students. Despite the size of the university and some classes, the school does an excellent job getting undergraduate students involved in hands-on research. In the Department of Chemistry and Biochemistry, 88 percent of students worked with a faculty mentor on a research project. Additionally, the school offers 206 approved study abroad programs in seventy-five countries, and 17 percent of undergrads participate.

The ten most popular majors at BYU are exercise science, elementary education, psychology, management, English, public health, computer science, family life (a major unique to BYU), chemical engineering, and communications. The programs with the strongest national reputations are those within the Marriott School of Business and, to a slightly lesser extent, the Ira A. Fulton College of Engineering. Brigham Young alumni do occasionally win highly competitive postgraduation recognition, but in 2017 the National Scholarships, Fellowships, and Programs office was shut down, and those duties now fall under the purview of the Honors College. Students can still apply, but this is certainly a program in transition.

Outside the Classroom

While not a requirement, most freshmen (73 percent) live in on-campus dorms. In total, only 15 percent live on campus, but over 23,000 students live in BYU-contracted housing in the immediate area. There is no Greek life; rather, the LDS Church is at the center of much of student life outside the classroom. The school is governed by an Honor Code that includes clauses about facial hair, foul language, chastity, and abstaining from the consumption of caffeinated beverages. A good number of recognized student organizations are related to religion, volunteer work, or professional associations. One of the more recognizable and typical elements of BYU college life is the passion displayed for the school's sports teams. The Cougars send twenty-one athletic squads into high-level competition in NCAA Division I and have seen ten NCAA titles, a Heisman Trophy winner, and over 1,000 All-Americans. Football games draw 56,000 fans to LaVell Edwards Stadium. Over 12,000 students participate in intramural sports each year on this extremely athletically-inclined campus. Outdoor activities are also emphasized and are aided by the overwhelming natural beauty surrounding the school's 550+ acre campus situated at the edge of the Rocky Mountains.

Career Services

Brigham Young's University Career Services Office employs seventeen professionals (not including office managers) who are responsible for career development and counseling. That works out to a counselor-to-student ratio of 1,837:1, one of the poorest figures of any college featured in this guide. BYU's Career Services staff believes that a career is more than just a job; it is a calling to which one is deeply dedicated. To help students find their path, the office offers free assessments such as the Myers-Briggs, the Strong Interest Inventory, and TypeFocus. The university even offers a credited course called Career Exploration intended to help undergrads learn their strengths, define their interests, and begin seriously thinking about a vocation.

The fall 2018 Career Fair was attended by 126 companies and 1,919 students. Fifteen of those employers conducted 189 interviews. A larger operation, the STEM Career Fair, also held in fall 2018, drew 246 companies to campus and was visited by 5,346 students. All students are able to utilize Handshake accounts that allow them to connect with potential employers for jobs and internships. One of the school's greatest career services strengths is the tightknit network of alumni who are always willing to help a fellow Cougar. While this office is understaffed, it does excel in the areas of graduate school placement and career development that is uniquely tailored to this mostly LDS-affiliated population.

Brigham Young University

E-mail: admissions@byu.edu | Website: www.byu.edu

Professional Outcomes

In 2018, the average age of a BYU graduate was nearly twenty-five, a result of the eighteen months to two years of missionary work members of the LDS Church are required to complete. The most popular fields entered are business management, education, operations, engineering, sales, and information technology. By a wide margin, the two largest employers of BYU alums are the university itself and the LDS Church. However, there are hundreds of Cougars working at major corporations including Adobe, Google, Microsoft, and Goldman Sachs. Average salaries for BYU grads are on the low end compared to alumni of other selective universities. Ten years after entering the school, alumni are earning a median salary of $59,700. Unsurprisingly, Provo and the Greater Salt Lake area see the highest concentrations of BYU alumni. Major cities outside of Utah with significant numbers of graduates include San Francisco, Phoenix, LA, and Seattle.

Brigham Young is in the same league with Berkeley, Cornell, the University of Michigan, and the University of Wisconsin in terms of producing future PhDs. Over the past decade, more than 3,000 alumni have gone on to earn doctoral degrees. Many grads pursuing advanced degrees do so at BYU, yet plenty of others relocate to pursue educational opportunities at institutions such as MIT, Harvard, and the University of North Carolina. (In 2005, two-thirds of the UNC PhD in accounting candidates were BYU alums.) Each year, approximately 500 BYU students apply to medical school; 67 percent are accepted, a far better mark than the national average. Those who attend law school flock to BYU's own well-regarded Rueben Clark Law School, but many attend other elite law schools. Harvard Law and Yale Law have BYU representation in just about every one of their entering 1L classes.

Admission

Despite a 64 percent acceptance rate, gaining admission to BYU requires a strong academic profile. The high rate of acceptance is attributable to the school's uniquely self-selecting applicant pool. Unless you are a member of the Church of Jesus Christ of Latter-day Saints, you likely aren't placing the university on your college wish list. Most students who apply favor the ACT over the SAT, and among 2018-19 freshmen, the middle-50 percent ACT range was 26-31. A narrow majority, 54 percent, also finished in the top 10 percent of their high school class; 85 percent placed in the top 25 percent. On a 4.0 scale, 81 percent had a GPA of 3.75 or higher.

Even with roughly 13,000 applicants per year, BYU employs a holistic review of each one. It values eleven factors as being "very important" in influencing admissions decisions. In addition to the usual factors of rigor of curriculum, grades, recommendations, essays, and test scores, the university also places great importance on religious affiliation, volunteer work, work experience, character/personal qualities, talent/ability, and extracurricular involvement. High-achieving LDS teenagers frequently see BYU as their top or, perhaps, even their only choice for postsecondary education. Those who fit the mold will gain acceptance. Only rarely do non-Mormon individuals attend BYU; they comprise less than 2 percent of the student body.

Worth Your Money?

Similar to an in-state and out-of-state rate, BYU charges different tuition to Latter-day Saints than it does to non-Latter-day Saints. Members of the LDS Church pay an annual tuition of only $5,790, an unheard amount in the third decade of the twenty-first century. The total annual cost of attendance is under $20k, and the majority also receive some type of merit aid with the average award being over $4,000. Close to half also receive need-based aid that averages out to the full price of tuition. For members of the LDS Church, BYU is an amazing fit and worth every penny. For the limited numbers of non-LDS members who apply, Brigham Young University is still an exceptional value, even at a higher cost.

FINANCIAL
Institutional Type: Private
In-State Tuition: $5,790 (LDS)
Out-of-State Tuition: $11,580 (non-LDS)
Room & Board: $7,766
Required Fees: $0
Books & Supplies: $872

Avg. Need-Based Aid: $5,378
Avg. % of Need Met: 30%

Avg. Merit-Based Aid: $4,341
% Receiving Merit-Based Aid: 57%

Avg. Cumulative Debt: $15,701
% of Students Borrowing: 24%

CAREER
Who Recruits
1. Podium
2. Qualtrics
3. Domo, Inc.
4. Pluralsight
5. Lucid

Notable Internships
1. Adobe
2. Bain Capital
3. Utah Jazz

Top Industries
1. Business
2. Education
3. Operations
4. Engineering
5. Sales

Top Employers
1. LDS Church
2. Intermountain Healthcare
3. Qualtrics
4. Adobe
5. Vivint Smart Home

Where Alumni Work
1. Provo, UT
2. Salt Lake City, UT
3. Phoenix
4. San Francisco
5. Los Angeles

Median Earnings
College Scorecard (Early Career): $59,700
EOP (Early Career): $32,600
PayScale (Mid-Career): $108,000

RANKINGS
Forbes: 95
Money: 147
U.S. News: 77 (T), National Universities
Wall Street Journal/THE: 143 (T)
Washington Monthly: 15, National Universities

#CollegesWorthYourMoney

Brown University

Providence, Rhode Island | Admissions Phone: 401-863-2378

ADMISSION
Admission Rate: 8%
Admission Rate - Men: 9%
Admission Rate - Women: 7%
EA Admission Rate: Not Offered
ED Admission Rate: 21%
Admission Rate (5-Year Trend): -2%
ED Admission Rate (5-Year Trend): +2%
% of Admits Attending (Yield): 61%
Transfer Admission Rate: 8%

Offered Wait List: N/A
Accepted Wait List: N/A
Admitted Wait List: 100

SAT Reading/Writing (Middle 50%): 700-760
SAT Math (Middle 50%): 720-790
ACT Composite (Middle 50%): 32-35
Testing Policy: ACT/SAT Required
SAT Superscore: Yes
ACT Superscore: Yes

% Graduated in Top 10% of HS Class: 96%
% Graduated in Top 25% of HS Class: 98%
% Graduated in Top 50% of HS Class: 100%

ENROLLMENT
Total Undergraduate Enrollment: 7,043
% Part-Time: 4%
% Male: 46%
% Female: 54%
% Out-of-State: 95%
% Fraternity: 14%
% Sorority: 10%
% On-Campus (Freshman): 100%
% On-Campus (All Undergraduate): 72%

% African-American: 6%
% Asian: 15%
% Hispanic: 11%
% White: 42%
% Other: 6%
% Race or Ethnicity Unknown: 7%
% International: 12%
% Low-Income: 17%

ACADEMICS
Student-to-Faculty Ratio: 6:1
% of Classes Under 20: 70%
% of Classes Under 40: 86%
% Full-Time Faculty: 84%
% Full-Time Faculty w/ Terminal Degree: 95%

Top Programs
Applied Mathematics
Computer Science
Economics
Engineering
English
Geology
History
Neuroscience

Retention Rate: 98%
4-Year Graduation Rate: 85%
6-Year Graduation Rate: 95%

Curricular Flexibility: Very Flexible
Academic Rating: ★★★★★

Inside the Classroom

Founded in 1764, Brown University holds the distinction as one of the oldest colleges in the United States and, of course, as a member of the vaunted Ivy League. Yet, much like its Rhode Island home, Brown possesses an uncommon blend of tradition and extraordinary commitment to the celebration of individuality. Toward that aim, Brown's Open Curriculum has long been the guiding academic force at the university, perfectly capturing its spirit and core values. The 7,000+ undergraduates who choose (and were chosen by) Brown fit the school's ethos and relish the chance to be the architects of their own educational journey.

Students must choose one "concentration program," but there are no required courses. In essence, the guiding philosophy is that students should take control of their learning, pursue knowledge in areas that they are truly passionate about, and learn to integrate and synthesize information across disciplines. Specialized programs include the Brown/RISD five-year Dual Degree program that leads to a bachelor's from Brown as well as a BFA from the famed Rhode Island School of Design. Teens committed to the medical field even before exiting high school can apply for entry into the program in Liberal Medical Education that allows students to graduate in eight years with an MD from Brown's Warren Alpert Medical School.

This one-of-a-kind experience transpires with a student-faculty ratio of only 7:1, and 100 percent of faculty members spend time teaching the undergraduate population of just under 7,000. Class sizes tend to be small—70 percent have fewer than twenty students—and 34 percent are comprised of nine or fewer students. Student surveys reveal an unsurpassed level of satisfaction with the quality of instruction and professor availability. Undergraduates give favorable reviews in those areas at an overwhelming 92-97 percent clip. Undergraduate research is a big part of the Brown experience for many students; 54 percent conduct research alongside a faculty member or work on an independent project with supervision. As is typical in the Ivy League, the majority of students stay grounded on (or near) campus for all four years. The number of students choosing to study abroad has declined in recent years and presently sits at approximately 500 per year.

Biology, economics, computer science, mathematics, and engineering are among the most popular areas of concentration at Brown; however, it is hard to distinguish any one program, because Brown possesses outstanding offerings across so many disciplines. Computer science is a growing department, conferring 10 percent of the school's degrees in 2018; applied math and English are notably strong. Graduates are a scholarly lot and experience high levels of success at procuring prestigious academic fellowships. In 2019 alone, the school produced thirty-eight Fulbright Scholars and, in 2018, graduates and alumni earned thirty National Science Foundation Graduate Research Fellowships. Brown has produced the seventh most Rhodes Scholars of any institution in history.

Outside the Classroom

The Main Green, surrounded by iconic buildings and located at the heart of campus, is almost always a lively hub of activity. There are more than 300 clubs and activities available to what tends to be a highly involved student body. Performance-based groups such as a cappella, improv, music, and theater draw large numbers of participants. A thriving student-run media scene includes the Brown Daily Herald, the nation's second oldest collegiate daily, and two award-winning campus radio stations. Brown fields an unusually large number of varsity athletic teams, thirty-eight, which compete in NCAA Division I. The Brown Bears claim twenty-one women's teams, the largest number of any school in the country. Greek life plays a moderate role on campus with about a 10 percent participation rate for women and a 14 percent rate for men. Seventy-two percent of students (100 percent of freshmen) live on campus in one of forty-nine residence halls as old as 1822 and as new as 2012. Off-campus housing and a multitude of cultural and entertainment options exist in Providence, including the bustling Thayer Street that runs through campus.

Career Services

The CareerLAB ("LAB" stands for Life After Brown) has twelve full-time staff members who focus on career advising, pre-professional advising, employer relations, marketing, and BrownConnect, which connects current students with alumni. The 587:1 student-to-advisor ratio is slightly higher than the ratio for other schools featured in this guide. However, the LAB is extremely effective at outreach and has a measurable impact on student success.

In the 2018-19 academic year career services staff counseled 3,237 students and brought 251 employers to campus, leading to 950 job interviews. Freshmen engaged at an extremely high rate, 68 percent, which has been an institutional goal. Keeping busy, Brown manages to put on more than one hundred career programs and one hundred employer information sessions per year. Its career fairs, alumni events, and workshops drew almost 13,000. If you can name a corporation, chances are it will be visiting Providence at some point this upcoming year. Help finding internships is always available as the school provides 600+ funded opportunities per year. The CareerLAB deploys its resources well in order to meet the needs of its talented population, and it receives high praise from our staff.

Professional Outcomes

Soon after receiving their Brown diplomas, 70 percent of graduates enter the world of employment. The university has placed significant numbers of recent graduates in the top companies within the following fields: the arts (CAA, Lincoln Center), consulting (every major firm), finance (every major investment house), government (United Nations, Federal Reserve Board), technology (Amazon, all major tech companies), and the list goes on and on. Companies employing the most Brown alums all time are Google, Microsoft, Facebook, Goldman Sachs, Amazon, Morgan Stanley, Apple, McKinsey & Company, and Bain & Company. New York, Boston, Providence, San Francisco, and DC are the five cities attracting the greatest number of Brown alumni. That makes sense given that the two most popular areas of employment are in technology and finance, and many such firms are based in those urban areas. At age thirty-four Brown graduates have a median income well above that of the average college grad, but it is the lowest among Ivy League schools.

The Class of 2017 saw one-fifth of graduates go directly into graduate/professional school. Right out of undergrad Brown boasted an exceptional 92 percent admission rate to med school (the national average was 43 percent) and a 91 percent admission rate to law school (national average was 75 percent). A decade after graduating, 80 percent of Brown alumni have earned an advanced degree. Frequently attended institutions include all of the Ivies plus Stanford, Duke, Carnegie Mellon, the London School of Economics, Oxford, Johns Hopkins, Berkeley, UCLA, and UVA. In sum, you can rest assured that if you do well at Brown, there are few graduate or professional schools on the planet that will not welcome you with open arms.

Admission

In 2018, Brown accepted only 7 percent of applicants, and 96 percent of those who went on to enroll were in the top 10 percent of their high school class. A decade earlier, the admit rate was just shy of 16 percent, but it has been in the single digits since 2014. Back in 2014, the middle 25th-75th percentile range for Brown freshmen was 1330-1550 compared to the current range of 1420-1570. Even with a degree of SAT score inflation, those numbers indicate that the university has become even more competitive in recent years. Over three-quarters of freshmen in the Class of 2022 scored better than 700 on their SAT reading section and over 80 percent scored better than 700 on the math section.

The admissions office lists eight areas that are considered most important in determining admission: rigor of courses, grades, class rank, recommendations, essays, test scores, talent/ability, and character/personal qualities. In a typical year, close to half of admitted students were either the valedictorian or salutatorian of their high school class. Those applying early are accepted at a much higher rate than in the regular round. The Class of 2022 saw 732 seats filled through ED with an acceptance rate of 21 percent compared to a 6 percent acceptance rate in the regular cycle. The 737 admits account for roughly 45 percent of the total class. In short, those looking to come to Providence should be individuals at the top of their class who are intellectually curious, open-minded, and who possess intangible qualities that would allow them to flourish in Brown's unique academic program.

Worth Your Money?

With a $77,490 annual cost of attendance, Brown University will cost a great deal for anyone who does not qualify for financial aid. For the 41 percent of current students who receive need-based grants, 100 percent of their demonstrated need will be covered. That equates to an average grant of almost $50,000 per year. Despite the cost, Brown is the type of school worth its hefty price tag. Not only will the Ivy League credentials benefit you in graduate/professional school admissions and the world of employment, but the quality of the educational experience, the flexibility of your coursework, and the chance to take many small, seminar-style classes with distinguished faculty are of incredible value.

FINANCIAL
Institutional Type: Private
In-State Tuition: $57,112
Out-of-State Tuition: $57,112
Room & Board: $15,332
Required Fees: $1,292
Books & Supplies: $1,632

Avg. Need-Based Aid: $49,256
Avg. % of Need Met: 100%

Avg. Merit-Based Aid: $10,000
% Receiving Merit-Based Aid: 0%

Avg. Cumulative Debt: $29,620
% of Students Borrowing: 35%

CAREER
Who Recruits
1. Boston Consulting Group
2. Oracle
3. Millenium Management
4. BlackRock
5. Teach for America

Notable Internships
1. Google
2. Etsy
3. Apple

Top Industries
1. Business
2. Education
3. Research
4. Media
5. Engineering

Top Employers
1. Google
2. Microsoft
3. Facebook
4. Goldman Sachs
5. Amazon

Where Alumni Work
1. New York City
2. Providence
3. Boston
4. San Francisco
5. Washington, DC

Median Earnings
College Scorecard (Early Career): $67,500
EOP (Early Career): $66,900
PayScale (Mid-Career): $127,600

RANKINGS
Forbes: 7
Money: 72
U.S. News: 14, National Universities
Wall Street Journal/THE: 7 (T)
Washington Monthly: 28, National Universities

#CollegesWorthYourMoney

Bryn Mawr College

Bryn Mawr, Pennsylvania | Admissions Phone: 610-526-5152

ADMISSION
Admission Rate: 34%
Admission Rate - Men: Not Offered
Admission Rate - Women: 34%
EA Admission Rate: Not Offered
ED Admission Rate: 53%
Admission Rate (5-Year Trend): -6%
ED Admission Rate (5-Year Trend): 0%
% of Admits Attending (Yield): 36%
Transfer Admission Rate: 15%

Offered Wait List: 450
Accepted Wait List: 244
Admitted Wait List: 0

SAT Reading/Writing (Middle 50%): 660-730
SAT Math (Middle 50%): 640-770
ACT Composite (Middle 50%): 28-33
Testing Policy: Test Optional
SAT Superscore: Yes
ACT Superscore: Yes

% Graduated in Top 10% of HS Class: 59%
% Graduated in Top 25% of HS Class: 91%
% Graduated in Top 50% of HS Class: 99%

ENROLLMENT
Total Undergraduate Enrollment: 1,360
% Part-Time: 1%
% Male: 0%
% Female: 100%
% Out-of-State: 85%
% Fraternity: Not Offered
% Sorority: Not Offered
% On-Campus (Freshman): 100%
% On-Campus (All Undergraduate): 91%

% African-American: 6%
% Asian: 13%
% Hispanic: 10%
% White: 39%
% Other: 6%
% Race or Ethnicity Unknown: 6%
% International: 22%
% Low-Income: 16%

ACADEMICS
Student-to-Faculty Ratio: 9:1
% of Classes Under 20: 71%
% of Classes Under 40: 95%
% Full-Time Faculty: 81%
% Full-Time Faculty w/ Terminal Degree: 97%

Top Programs
Biology
English
Growth and Structure of Cities
History of Art
Mathematics
Physics
Psychology

Retention Rate: 92%
4-Year Graduation Rate: 79%
6-Year Graduation Rate: 87%

Curricular Flexibility: Somewhat Flexible
Academic Rating: ★★★★

Inside the Classroom

Eleven miles west of Philadelphia and situated on the swanky Main Line rests an immaculate, 135-acre campus that serves as the educational home to more than 1,300 brilliant, politically active, and fiercely independent young women. Bryn Mawr College, still an all-female institution, used to serve as the sister school to Haverford College, which was all male until the late 1970s. The two schools still retain a degree of partnership. In fact, Bryn Mawr, Haverford, and Swarthmore (collectively known as the Tri-Co) all run on the same academic calendar so students can take courses at all three schools. Additionally, Bryn Mawr undergraduates can opt to take up to two courses at Penn each semester. There are more than 3,000 cross-registrations exercised each year.

On the home campus, undergraduates can choose from thirty-six majors and forty-six minors. A phenomenal 31 percent of the student body earns degrees in the natural sciences or mathematics, a figure four times the national average for women. However, as a true liberal arts school, all students must take courses in each of Bryn Mawr's four "approaches": critical interpretation, cross-cultural analysis, inquiry into the past, and scientific investigation. Additional courses in quantitative reasoning and a full year studying one of ten foreign languages round out the mandated coursework. The college does point out that "within this structure, variety abounds," noting that students averse to the hard sciences can fulfill their scientific investigation requirement through the likes of anthropology or psychology.

A 9:1 student-to-faculty ratio leads to small class sizes with 71 percent of sections having fewer than twenty students, and 23 percent of sections enrolling nine students or fewer. This type of academic setting leads to close mentoring from professors. Over 500 undergraduates collaborate on research and independent projects with faculty each year. Those electing to study abroad have more than seventy programs to choose from and, in recent years, students have spent a semester in thirty countries across six continents.

This elite liberal arts school offers a number of excellent academic programs that receive national recognition from employers and graduate schools. By volume, the most popular majors are mathematics, psychology, sociology, English, and biology. Nationally competitive fellowship/scholarship programs also look favorably upon Bryn Mawr alumni. Recent graduates have been successful in procuring Boren, Fulbright, and Watson Fellowships.

Outside the Classroom

Bryn Mawr's breathtakingly beautiful and historic campus is where 100 percent of freshmen and 91 percent of the overall student body reside. Sororities are not permitted at Bryn Mawr as the college prefers participation in the 150 nonexclusive student organizations presently active. Clubs in music/performing arts and community service are among the most popular. Student government is also strong as elected members are dedicated to carrying out the institution's Honor Code. This is a tradition-rich school with events such as Parade Night, Lantern Night, and May Day all taken seriously by the student population. The Owls participate in twelve NCAA Division III sports, and casual athletic participation is always an option as the school boasts a 50,000-square-foot gymnasium, Olympic-size swimming pool, and outdoor tennis courts. While there is plenty to do on campus, nearby Haverford College, Swarthmore, and Villanova University provide Bryn Mawr undergrads with additional social scenes to explore. The college's proximity to Philadelphia means that restaurants, concerts, sporting events, museums, and theater are only a short drive away.

Career Services

The Career Services Department at Bryn Mawr is housed within the Leadership, Innovation, and Liberal Arts Center (LILAC). The office is staffed by seven professionals who specialize in areas like career counseling, pre-law advising, and employer relations. With a 189:1 student-to-advisor ratio, Bryn Mawr rates well above average compared to other colleges featured in this guide. That provides undergraduates with ample opportunity to work closely with a career counselor on resume development, internship hunting, and networking.

In terms of employer relations, rather than hosting their own events the college tends to rely more on partnerships with other Seven Sisters schools and the Tri-College Consortium (TCC) with Haverford and Swarthmore. The Fall Policy & Government Career Fair is held at the University of Pennsylvania and is open to members of the TCC. Spring events held at Haverford College include the Tri-College STEM Recruiting Day and the Philadelphia Career Connection that attracts forty employers. Students can find internship and job opportunities online through Handshake or via the Selective Liberal Arts Consortium that can facilitate off-campus interviews. Bryn Mawr has a low student-to-counselor ratio and has an excellent track record for helping its students gain acceptance into top graduate schools. However, its alumni salary figures lag behind its peers, and its on-campus recruiting opportunities are somewhat limited.

Professional Outcomes

One year after receiving their diplomas, 57 percent of Bryn Mawr graduates have found employment, a robust 29 percent have already entered graduate school, and 5 percent are still in the job-hunting phase. Among those who are employed, the five most popular fields are business, education, health/medicine, science, and communications/media. With graduating classes of under 400 students there are no massive numbers of alumni clustered in particular companies as is the case at many larger institutions. Most of the organizations employing the greatest number of alumni are universities and hospital systems although Google, Accenture, JPMorgan Chase, and Vanguard do employ a fair number of Bryn Mawr graduates. Median salaries by age thirty-four are on the low side by elite college standards, in part due to the heavy concentration of students pursing lengthy graduate programs. The median salary figure at the start of midcareer is $47k, significantly lower than other highly selective Pennsylvania liberal arts schools like Franklin & Marshall, Haverford, and Swarthmore, which all sport median income figures of $56k and above.

Of those pursuing further education, 63 percent were in master's programs, 10 percent in medical school, 2 percent in law school, and 13 percent were already working on their PhD. Again, due to the minuscule class sizes, it's rare that multiple graduates flock to particular institutions for graduate school. However, to get a sense of the prestigious programs accepting Bryn Mawr alumni one can simply examine the higher education destinations of members of the Class of 2017. Those included a PhD in applied physics at Rice University, a PhD in machine learning at Carnegie Mellon, and a PhD in chemistry at Princeton. Other 2017 graduates were pursuing advanced degrees at Columbia, Tufts, Yale, University of Chicago, the London School of Economics, and UVA School of Medicine.

Admission

Bryn Mawr accepts 34 percent of those who apply, making it more selective than Mount Holyoke, comparable to Smith, and a touch less selective than Barnard and Wellesley. Freshmen at Bryn Mawr possessed middle-50 percent SAT scores of 1300-1500 and 28-33 on the ACT. A healthy 59 percent finished in the top 10 percent of their high school class; 91 percent were in the top quarter. In terms of class rank/GPA, the average accepted applicant looks similar to those from five years ago. Yet, the SAT scores of admitted applicants has risen rather dramatically. In 2013, the middle-SAT range for the freshman class was 1190-1420.

The admissions office places the greatest emphasis on the rigor of an applicant's high school curriculum and recommendation letters. Grades, essays, extracurricular activities, and character/personal qualities are next. While Bryn Mawr is a test-optional school, 61 percent submitted SAT results, and 34 percent submitted ACT scores, so tests do still play a role in shaping the overall admissions picture. Early decision is the right choice for those who have the school atop their college list. Bryn Mawr fills 45 percent of its freshman class in the early round and accepts 53 percent of those who apply.

A highly selective destination point for high-achieving young women, this member of the Seven-Sisters Colleges is tougher to get into than its acceptance rate would imply. Known as a supportive, collaborative, and academically excellent school, Bryn Mawr draws brilliant and accomplished applicants from around the globe. An impressive resume is needed, and applying early can give you an edge.

Worth Your Money?

Despite a list price above $73,000, Bryn Mawr is generous with aid, leading to graduates who possess lower-than-average debt. Unusual for a school of its ilk, 27 percent of current students receive an annual merit award averaging $16k in value. A healthy 53 percent of students are found eligible for need-based aid, and 100 percent of their demonstrated need is met by the college. The average annual value of these grants is close to $44,000, helping to make Bryn Mawr more accessible to those of varying socioeconomic backgrounds.

FINANCIAL
Institutional Type: Private
In-State Tuition: $53,180
Out-of-State Tuition: $53,180
Room & Board: $17,100
Required Fees: $1,260
Books & Supplies: $1,000

Avg. Need-Based Aid: $43,903
Avg. % of Need Met: 100%

Avg. Merit-Based Aid: $15,759
% Receiving Merit-Based Aid: 27%

Avg. Cumulative Debt: $25,682
% of Students Borrowing: 51%

CAREER
Who Recruits
1. FDIC
2. Moody's Corporation
3. Philadelphia Museum of Art
4. Vanguard
5. Northwestern Mutual

Notable Internships
1. Whitney Museum of Art
2. JetBlue
3. Citi

Top Industries
1. Education
2. Business
3. Healthcare
4. Social Services
5. Media

Top Employers
1. Penn Medicine
2. Children's Hospital of Philadelphia
3. Vanguard
4. Accenture
5. Google

Where Alumni Work
1. Philadelphia
2. New York City
3. Washington, DC
4. Boston
5. San Francisco

Median Earnings
College Scorecard (Early Career): $54,600
EOP (Early Career): $47,400
PayScale (Mid-Career): $95,300

RANKINGS
Forbes: 111
Money: 370
U.S. News: 27 (T), Liberal Arts Colleges
Wall Street Journal/THE: 53
Washington Monthly: 14, Liberal Arts Colleges

#CollegesWorthYourMoney

Bucknell University

Lewisburg, Pennsylvania | Admissions Phone: 570-577-3000

Inside the Classroom

Approximately 3,600 undergraduate students grace this gorgeous, 450-acre campus in bucolic Lewisburg, Pennsylvania. While technically a "university," the number of graduate students is nominal and, academically, the school functions more as a liberal arts college with a strong engineering program. Socially, with its focus on athletics and Greek life, the "university" label may start to feel more apt.

Over fifty majors and sixty-five minors are on tap across three undergraduate schools: the College of Arts & Sciences, Freeman College of Management, and the College of Engineering. Required core curriculum coursework for A&S and Freeman is identical and must include multiple classes under the umbrella categories of intellectual skills, disciplinary perspectives, tools for critical engagement, and a culminating experience that involves research and/or independent study. The College of Engineering keeps the vast majority of its requirements concentrated in the areas of math, science, and engineering. Before classes even commence, all first-year students attend a five-day new student orientation centered around scholarship and community. Further, all freshmen take a foundation seminar course, and that instructor serves as the faculty adviser until the student declares a major in the sophomore year. That supportive environment helps the school maintain a superb 93 percent retention rate.

Getting well-acquainted with your professors is easy with a 9:1 student-faculty ratio, and class sizes are reasonably small. Slightly more than half of courses at Bucknell unfold in a classroom of no more than nineteen students, and 85 percent of all sections enroll fewer than twenty-nine students. All of Bucknell's 350 full-time professors spend some of their time teaching undergraduates. Last year, 268 students took advantage of summer research opportunities on campus. An additional 175 typically engage in research for academic credit during the regular school year. Study abroad semesters are available at over 130 sites across six continents, and 45 percent of the student body takes advantage of that.

The greatest number of degrees are conferred in the areas of the social sciences (26 percent), engineering (16 percent), business (14 percent), biology (9 percent), and psychology (6 percent). The Freeman College of Management and College of Engineering have the most prominent national reputations, but Bucknell is a well-regarded institution across the board. With a career-focused student body, this is a not a college that produces a sizable number of postgraduate fellows or scholars, but two class of 2018 Bucknell grads were awarded Fulbright Scholarships, and the school has averaged one Goldwater Scholar per year over the last five years.

Outside the Classroom

The vast majority of the student body, 92 percent, reside in university housing on campus. Many join the school's thriving Greek life with 35 percent of men and 40 percent of women becoming members of one of the school's eight fraternity or ten sorority chapters. For a university of Bucknell's modest size, athletics are massive in scale. The school fields twenty-seven teams that play in the Patriot League of NCAA Division I. The Bison men's basketball squad has appeared in the most recent March Madness tourneys, and the swimming and lacrosse teams are also strong. On top of that, intramural and club sports attract a high level of participation. Over 150 student clubs run on campus and enjoy small but loyal followings, thanks to the energy pouring into fraternities and athletics. The most popular clubs include the Black Student Union, Bucknell Outing Club, Activities & Campus Events, French Club, and Catholic Campus Ministries. Many Bucknell students also make time for volunteer work; three-quarters perform some degree of community service over the course of their four years. With no major city within a quick driving distance, students seeking some semblance of nightlife settle for Main Street in quiet Lewisburg. Central Pennsylvania does offer limitless opportunity for those who love the great outdoors with camping, hiking, kayaking, and similar activities available in abundance.

Career Services

Manned by fifteen full-time professionals with expertise in career counseling, internship coordination, and company recruitment, the Career Development Center (CDC) offers a 225:1 student-to-advisor ratio, which is better than average compared to other schools featured in this guide. Each year the CDC hosts a fall Job Expo attended by up to one hundred employers and 750 students. Attendees include corporations like Deloitte, Coca Cola, and Hershey Entertainment & Resorts. Additionally, it organizes a separate internship/job fair in the spring, the Health & Law School Fair, Engineering Career Network Event, and several off-campus events in New York and DC to afford Bucknell students the chance to meet with additional companies in the finance and government realms. More than 200 employers attend school-sponsored career fairs each year.

Corporations, including the likes of ExxonMobil and Proctor & Gamble, appear regularly on campus to conduct job interviews. In fact, recent alums listed those opportunities as the number one factor in how they secured employment. In the 2017-18 school year 670 on-campus interviews were conducted with Bucknell seniors. Annually, the CDC helps over 500 students secure summer internships, which also was cited by grads as frequently leading to their maiden jobs. All told, 71 percent of Class of 2017 graduates completed at least one internship. With generous staffing and a track record of helping students, Bucknell's career services does a strong job preparing its undergraduates for the real world.

Professional Outcomes

Nine months after graduation, 96 percent of the Class of 2018 had launched their careers or entered graduate school. Business is the most common sector for Bucknell grads to enter, and 58 percent of graduates that head directly into the working world enter corporate life. The largest concentration of recent grads can be found working at Accenture, Sloan Kettering Cancer Center, PwC, Amazon Robotics, Yelp, and Axis Group. Across all graduating years more than fifty Bucknellians are presently working at Goldman Sachs, Google, Merck, JPMorgan Chase & Co., IBM, and Johnson & Johnson. Starting salaries for recent grads are solid but highly dependent on the field of study. The mean salary for a computer science major is $85k, an accounting and financial management major takes home $63k, and those who studied education have a mean starting income of only $39k. Across all disciplines, the mean salary for a Class of 2018 grad was $60k.

The Class of 2018 saw 17 percent of diploma recipients go directly into an advanced degree program. Bison alumni heading to graduate school predominantly pursue degrees in the medical field, social sciences, or engineering. Recent graduates have found their way into top med schools (e.g., Columbia, Duke, and Johns Hopkins) and to top engineering schools (e.g., Carnegie Mellon, Princeton, Stanford). Ten percent of this group decided to pursue a legal education. Law schools attended by members of the Class of 2018 included Boston University, George Washington, and the University of California, San Diego. Geographically, most Bucknell grads remain concentrated in Pennsylvania, New York, New Jersey, and the DC metro area.

Admission

Bucknell admitted 33 percent of more than 10,144 applicants into the Class of 2022. Surprisingly, the university received more applications three years prior and had a significantly lower acceptance rate of 24.8 percent. Admission into the well-regarded engineering programs is far more difficult (24 percent acceptance rate for the Class of 2021) than it is for the College of Arts & Humanities (43 percent acceptance rate for the Class of 2021). The middle 50 percent SAT range for the Class of 2022 was 1250-1420; the ACT range was 28-32. A hefty 58 percent finished in the top 10 percent of their high school class, and 85 percent were in the top quarter. The average GPA was a 3.56, and one-third of attending students earned better than a 3.75.

Rigor of classes, GPA, test scores, and essays headline the most important factors for acceptance into Bucknell. Admissions staff members have stated that they keep a six-minute timer on their desks while they examine each application as a team. Thus, we know that your measurable achievements need to be within range in order for your intangibles/outside-the-classroom activities to become serious factors in admission. Those who apply early decision enjoy a major edge; last year, 56 percent of ED applicants were accepted compared to 31 percent in the regular round. However, it is important to point out that recruited athletes make up a good number of those early-round success stories. Being a legacy also gives you an admissions boost. The school regularly hosts events for children (or grandchildren) of alumni, and legacy students comprise 7 percent of the average freshman cohort.

Worth Your Money?

A $75,400 list price cost of attendance is made slightly less onerous by the $18,000 (on average) annual merit aid package that goes to 19 percent of undergraduates as well as the $32,000 (on average) need-based aid package that is awarded to 38 percent of current students. However, Bucknell's clientele tends to include many—an estimated 60 percent of current undergraduates come from families in the top 20 percent income-wise. Those falling in between—not qualifying for aid but not well-off enough to pay full freight—will need to consider whether their intended major/future career is likely to make loan payments worth the cost. If you were on a budget and studying to be a teacher, Bucknell may not prove a wise choice. If you were in the same financial boat but studying engineering or business, attending this school absolutely could be worth your money.

FINANCIAL
Institutional Type: Private
In-State Tuition: $57,882
Out-of-State Tuition: $57,882
Room & Board: $14,174
Required Fees: $314
Books & Supplies: $900

Avg. Need-Based Aid: $32,000
Avg. % of Need Met: 92%

Avg. Merit-Based Aid: $18,017
% Receiving Merit-Based Aid: 19%

Avg. Cumulative Debt: $31,087
% of Students Borrowing: 46%

CAREER
Who Recruits
1. Exelon
2. Horizon Media
3. Nielsen
4. Ralph Lauren
5. Southwest Airlines

Notable Internships
1. NBCUniversal
2. CBRE
3. Bloomberg LP

Top Industries
1. Business
2. Education
3. Operations
4. Finance
5. Sales

Top Employers
1. PwC
2. Deloitte
3. Morgan Stanley
4. IBM
5. Merck

Where Alumni Work
1. New York City
2. Philadelphia
3. Washington, DC
4. Boston
5. Williamsport, PA

Median Earnings
College Scorecard (Early Career): $70,800
EOP (Early Career): $71,800
PayScale (Mid-Career): $122,900

RANKINGS
Forbes: 73
Money: 185
U.S. News: 35, Liberal Arts Colleges
Wall Street Journal/THE: 74
Washington Monthly: 44, Liberal Arts Colleges

#CollegesWorthYourMoney

California Institute of Technology

ADMISSION
Admission Rate: 7%
Admission Rate - Men: 4%
Admission Rate - Women: 12%
EA Admission Rate: N/A
ED Admission Rate: Not Offered
Admission Rate (5-Year Trend): -4%
ED Admission Rate (5-Year Trend): Not Offered
% of Admits Attending (Yield): 43%
Transfer Admission Rate: 2%

Offered Wait List: 634
Accepted Wait List: 512
Admitted Wait List: 6

SAT Reading/Writing (Middle 50%): 740-780
SAT Math (Middle 50%): 790-800
ACT Composite (Middle 50%): 35-36
Testing Policy: ACT/SAT Required
SAT Superscore: Yes
ACT Superscore: Yes

% Graduated in Top 10% of HS Class: 96%
% Graduated in Top 25% of HS Class: 100%
% Graduated in Top 50% of HS Class: 100%

ENROLLMENT
Total Undergraduate Enrollment: 948
% Part-Time: 0%
% Male: 55%
% Female: 45%
% Out-of-State: 63%
% Fraternity: Not Offered
% Sorority: Not Offered
% On-Campus (Freshman): 100%
% On-Campus (All Undergraduate): 86%

% African-American: 1%
% Asian: 40%
% Hispanic: 14%
% White: 27%
% Other: 8%
% Race or Ethnicity Unknown: 0%
% International: 10%
% Low-Income: 10%

ACADEMICS
Student-to-Faculty Ratio: 3:1
% of Classes Under 20: 68%
% of Classes Under 40: 89%
% Full-Time Faculty: 89%
% Full-Time Faculty w/ Terminal Degree: 98%

Top Programs
Biology
Chemistry
Computer Science
Engineering
Geological and Planetary Sciences
Physics
Mathematics

Retention Rate: 98%
4-Year Graduation Rate: 81%
6-Year Graduation Rate: 92%

Curricular Flexibility: Somewhat Flexible
Academic Rating: ★★★★★

Inside the Classroom

The setting of television's Big Bang Theory, the California Institute of Technology is, as suggested by the show's focus on a group of socially-awkward physicists, a collection of some of the most brilliant science and engineering minds in the world. Situated in gorgeous Pasadena, California, Caltech enrolls a mere 948 undergraduates, affectionately known as "Techers," very few of whom got a single question wrong on the math portion of the SAT. As tough as it is to gain admission, coursework at the school is perhaps an even more rigorous and consuming process.

The university's common core is, not surprisingly, STEM-heavy with requirements that includes Freshman Mathematics, Freshman Physics, Freshman Chemistry, and Freshman Biology. However, students also must conquer 36 units of the humanities and social sciences, nine units of physical education, and one course in scientific communication in which undergrads write a paper for submission to a peer-reviewed academic journal. There are six academic divisions: biology and biological engineering; chemistry and chemical engineering; engineering and applied science; geological and planetary sciences; the humanities and social sciences; and physics, mathematics, and astronomy, each with more options for specialized concentrations. Across all divisions, there are thirty-two distinct majors.

Possessing an absurdly favorable 3:1 student-to-faculty ratio, plenty of individualized attention is up for grabs. Class sizes are not quite as tiny as the student-to-faculty ratio might suggest, but 68 percent of courses enroll fewer than twenty students, and 30 percent enroll fewer than ten. Summer Undergraduate Research Fellowships (SURF) enjoy wide participation with 80 percent of undergraduates partaking, and 20 percent of that group going on to publish their results. Six approved study abroad programs are available at Cambridge University, University College London, University of Edinburgh, Copenhagen University, the University of Melbourne, and Ecole Polytechnique in France.

Engineering is the most popular major, accounting for 36 percent of all degrees conferred. Computer and information science (26 percent), the physical sciences (20 percent), and mathematics (11 percent) also have strong representation. Grads find a high level of success in obtaining prestigious scholarships for graduate study including Watson, Fulbright, and Hertz Fellowships. The school also sees an incredible number of students win National Science Foundation Fellowships (the head of the organization received her PhD from Caltech). An astounding twenty-seven 2018 graduates won NSF Graduate Research Fellowships.

Outside the Classroom

Given its small undergraduate population, campus is a spacious 124 acres, and 85 percent elect to live in one of the university's eleven residences; freshmen are required to do so. Greek life was long ago banished in favor of a coeducational residential house system. Each house has its own vibe and traditions, and students go through a two-week rotation period (in place of a pledging process) to find the best fit. On the athletics front, the Beavers field nine men's and nine women's teams to compete in intercollegiate sports, mostly at the NCAA Division III level, although they are more noted for insanely long losing streaks than anything else (the baseball team once lost 228 straight games). Four-fifths of undergrads participate in some kind of organized athletics, and the high rate of involvement isn't limited to sports. Roughly 65 percent of students also play a musical instrument, and many join one of the more than one hundred student-run organizations on campus. There are plenty of pre-professional and tech-oriented club options as well as groups like Magic: The Gathering Club or the Anime Society. While students generally report that academic pursuits plus a club or two generally take up 100 percent of their waking hours at Caltech, gorgeous Pasadena and nearby downtown Los Angeles provide limitless opportunities for those seeking some degree of socialization.

Career Services

The Caltech Career Development Center has five full-time professional staff members working on career counseling, internship coordination, and employer recruiting. That equates to a 189:1 student-to-advisor ratio, which is among the best of any university featured in this guide. Caltech hosts two large career fairs per year, one in October and one in January. Anywhere from 150-200 companies attend those fairs, which is a massive number when considering the school has fewer than 1,000 undergraduates. Small events take place pretty much weekly, and samples of those regular offerings include visits from the likes of Harvard Business School, Bain & Company, Yahoo, and the Google Women's Focus Group.

Caltech students have little trouble procuring summer internships in engineering, computer science, or business/finance. Unlike most schools where undergrads compete for internships at top companies, the top companies typically have to compete to attract Caltech students. (Its website offers advice for companies in that regard.) Similarly, on-campus recruiting is strong with companies constantly visiting campus to try to snag young talent. That list includes NASA, Facebook, Goldman Sachs, Oracle, and SpaceX. Based on its low student-to-counselor ratio, prodigious on-campus recruiting efforts, placement of more math/science PhD candidates than any university in the country, and unmatched starting salaries for graduates, Caltech's Career Development Center easily earns the highest praise from the College Transitions staff.

Professional Outcomes

Caltech is a rare school that sees six-figure average starting salaries for its graduates; the class of 2017 figure was $106,000. Over 60 percent of recent grads go directly into the workforce and find homes at tech giants such as Google, Intel, Microsoft, Apple, and Facebook. Engineering students are routinely courted by the likes of Boeing, Lockheed Martin, SpaceX, and Northrup Grumman. The school also has a strong alumni representation at NASA. Those who go the academic/research route ultimately end up on the faculty at schools such as Stanford, MIT, USC, and Caltech itself. Networking as a Caltech alum is a dream. The university has 22,000 alumni, many of whom are leaders in the tech world including seventeen living Nobel Prize winners and countless founders/execs of major corporations.

Not surprisingly, the largest number of alumni remain in California, settling into careers in Silicon Valley. A healthy 35 percent of those receiving their diplomas continue directly on the higher education path, immediately entering graduate school. Caltech is the number one producer of math/science PhDs in the country. Many continue their education at Caltech or other elite STEM graduate programs. After attaining graduate degrees, careers in research and higher education are popular pursuits. While engineering is where the largest number of grads eventually land, higher education is a close second.

Admission

With an acceptance rate of 6.6 percent, Caltech occupies the same uber-selective air as MIT. Sporting a middle 50 percent SAT range of 1530-1580 and near-perfect ACT range of 35-36, it is next to impossible to gain admission without acing your standardized tests. In fact, 95 percent of accepted applicants possess a 700 or higher on the reading section of the SAT; 99.4 percent have a 700 or higher on the math portion of the exam. SAT subject test scores are just as impeccable with mid-50 percent ranges of 770-800 for the physics and biology tests, 780-800 for the chemistry exam, and 800-800 (not a typo) on math. Ninety-six percent of enrolled freshmen placed in the top 10 percent of their high school class, and 100 percent were in the top quartile.

Directly from the admissions office, five factors carry the heaviest weight in the process: rigor of secondary curriculum, standardized test scores, essay, recommendations, and character/personal qualities. Caltech does not offer early decision, but its nonbinding early action round does offer better odds of gaining acceptance. In previous cycles the regular round saw 6 percent admitted, but 12 percent of those who applied by Nov. 1 found success. Caltech is among the most competitive universities in the world and is a top choice for many of the most brilliant young minds seeking to study computer science, the hard sciences, and engineering. Flawless standardized test scores are necessary but not sufficient for admissions consideration; those whose intangibles shine brightest gain an edge in this highly competitive process.

Worth Your Money?

Anything beyond a simple "Yes" here feels superfluous but, nevertheless, we'll offer a few statistics to back up the claim. While the school rarely offers merit aid, the majority of students do not pay anything close to the almost $75,000 annual cost of attendance. Need-based aid is awarded to 53 percent of the undergraduate population and carries a mean value of $46,749. Regardless of what you have to pay to attend this institution, it will be well worth the cost. As we highlighted previously in the profile, students' average starting salaries right out of Caltech are in the six figures.

FINANCIAL
Institutional Type: Private
In-State Tuition: $52,506
Out-of-State Tuition: $52,506
Room & Board: $16,644
Required Fees: $2,594
Books & Supplies: $1,428

Avg. Need-Based Aid: $46,749
Avg. % of Need Met: 100%

Avg. Merit-Based Aid: $0
% Receiving Merit-Based Aid: 0%

Avg. Cumulative Debt: $16,337
% of Students Borrowing: 31%

CAREER
Who Recruits
1. Goldman Sachs
2. Southern California Edison
3. Amazon
4. Facebook
5. Intel

Notable Internships
1. Facebook
2. Adobe
3. Apple

Top Industries
1. Engineering
2. Business
3. Research
4. Education
5. Information Technology

Top Employers
1. Northrop Grumman
2. Google
3. Boeing
4. NASA Jet Propulsion Laboratory
5. Apple

Where Alumni Work
1. Los Angeles
2. San Francisco
3. New York City
4. Boston
5. San Diego

Median Earnings
College Scorecard (Early Career): $85,900
EOP (Early Career): $83,000
PayScale (Mid-Career): $151,600

RANKINGS
Forbes: 8
Money: 16
U.S. News: 12, National Universities
Wall Street Journal/THE: 5 (T)
Washington Monthly: 73, National Universities

#CollegesWorthYourMoney

ADMISSION
Admission Rate: 30%
Admission Rate - Men: 26%
Admission Rate - Women: 35%
EA Admission Rate: Not Offered
ED Admission Rate: Not Offered
Admission Rate (5-Year Trend): -4%
ED Admission Rate (5-Year Trend): Not Offered
% of Admits Attending (Yield): 27%
Transfer Admission Rate: 16%

\# Offered Wait List: 6,643
\# Accepted Wait List: N/A
\# Admitted Wait List: 2,436

SAT Reading/Writing (Middle 50%): 620-700
SAT Math (Middle 50%): 620-730
ACT Composite (Middle 50%): 26-32
Testing Policy: ACT/SAT Required
SAT Superscore: Yes
ACT Superscore: Yes

% Graduated in Top 10% of HS Class: 59%
% Graduated in Top 25% of HS Class: 89%
% Graduated in Top 50% of HS Class: 99%

ENROLLMENT
Total Undergraduate Enrollment: 21,037
% Part-Time: 4%
% Male: 52%
% Female: 48%
% Out-of-State: 14%
% Fraternity: 7%
% Sorority: 11%
% On-Campus (Freshman): 91%
% On-Campus (All Undergraduate): 32%

% African-American: 1%
% Asian: 13%
% Hispanic: 17%
% White: 54%
% Other: 8%
% Race or Ethnicity Unknown: 4%
% International: 2%
% Low-Income: 19%

ACADEMICS
Student-to-Faculty Ratio: 19:1
% of Classes Under 20: 15%
% of Classes Under 40: 74%
% Full-Time Faculty: 64%
% Full-Time Faculty w/ Terminal Degree: 75%

Top Programs
Agricultural Business
Biological Sciences
Civil Engineering
Computer Science
Electrical Engineering
Industrial Engineering
Mechanical Engineering

Retention Rate: 94%
4-Year Graduation Rate: 48%
6-Year Graduation Rate: 82%

Curricular Flexibility: Less Flexible
Academic Rating: ★★★

Inside the Classroom
Nestled between San Francisco and Los Angeles, California Polytechnic State University-San Luis Obispo is the more competitive of the state's two public polytechnic schools, Pomona being the less selective branch. Home to more than 21,000 undergraduate students, Cal Poly churns out a jaw-dropping number of engineers each year, but it is far from a unidimensional university.

Cal Poly is comprised of six undergraduate schools: the College of Agriculture, Food & Environmental Sciences, College of Architecture & Environmental Design, College of Engineering, College of Liberal Arts, College of Science & Mathematics, and the Orfalea College of Business. Across all divisions there are sixty-three majors and eighty-four minors offered. While academic requirements vary by college and program, there are a number of general graduation must-haves that apply to all Mustangs. They include seventy-two units of general education, demonstration of writing competency, and the completion of a senior project.

You won't find many small, liberal-arts-style learning spaces—only 3 percent of classes have a single-digit enrollment. Yet you also won't find many classes that enroll one hundred or more students; only 4 percent do. The majority of courses, 59 percent, fall between twenty and forty students. Cal Poly's student-to-faculty ratio is a high 19:1, but such is the cost of an uber-affordable STEM degree from an excellent institution. Still, faculty receive extremely favorable reviews for their accessibility, and opportunities to work intimately with professors are built into the curriculum in many programs. For example, all students in the College of Science & Mathematics are required to participate in faculty-directed research and complete a senior project in order to graduate. More than 20 percent of students take advantage of the school's robust study abroad program that offers learning opportunities in over seventy-five countries.

The School of Engineering is the university's crown jewel. Over one-quarter of all degrees conferred (27 percent) are in engineering, and Cal Poly gets recognition in many specialty areas of the field including industrial engineering, mechanical engineering, aerospace engineering, computer engineering, and civil engineering. The Orfalea College of Business also receives strong national recognition and is recognized as one of the better ROI business degrees one can find; 13 percent of undergrads earn a business degree. Other popular majors include agriculture (12 percent), biology (6 percent), architecture (5 percent), and the social sciences (5 percent).

Outside the Classroom
While more students are living on campus than ever—the university has added 5,600 beds since 2003—only 32 percent of undergraduates presently reside on campus. Eleven percent of men and 8 percent of women sign up for Greek life. However, thirty-six of the school's sororities and fraternities were suspended in the spring of 2018 for racial insensitivity, leaving the future of Cal Poly Greek life in question. With twenty-one NCAA Division I sports on tap, there is always an opportunity to cheer on the Mustangs. Across all men's and women's sports, Cal Poly squads have captured fifty Big West Conference championships. Twenty-seven club sports, from rodeo to surfing, are available, and massive intramural program attracts 10,000 participants each year. There are an additional 300 student-run clubs, including a heavy dose of pre-professional organizations. San Luis Obispo is known as "The Happiest City in America" for a reason. Located on the coast, students have access to the beach and the natural beauty of Big Falls Trail. Outdoor concerts, an art museum, and the Thursday night farmer's market offer a taste of the effervescence of the surrounding town known as SLO Cal.

Career Services
The Cal Poly Career Services Office has eighteen full-time professional staff members working on career counseling, employer relations, and employer recruiting. That includes two counselors—the Freshman Focus Team—who are dedicated solely to first-year students. Overall, the school's 1,184:1 student-to-advisor ratio does not fare well against other colleges featured in this guide. In spite of the high student-to-counselor ratio, the office does accomplish impressive things on behalf of students. Each year Cal Poly hosts ten major career fairs, including three large, non-major-specific events in the fall, winter, and spring that draw 150+ employers each. Additional fairs cover fields that include teaching, architecture and environmental design, computing, and construction management.

A survey of recent graduates revealed that among those already employed, 43 percent attributed obtaining employment directly to the Career Services Office. An additional 22 percent cited MustangJOBS, the office's online database of employment opportunities, and 9 percent were offered employment after an internship experience while in undergrad. An impressive 97 percent of graduates ended up in jobs related to their major. Such success is not merely a byproduct of producing highly employable STEM graduates. Amazingly, the Freshman Focus Team engaged 100 percent of the 4,451 first-year students in over 6,000 counseling sessions. Further, the office has forged official employer/university partnerships with 334 companies, creating excellent networks for current undergrads to lean on while pursuing employment.

California Polytechnic State University, San Luis Obispo

E-mail: admissions@calpoly.edu | Website: www.calpoly.edu

Professional Outcomes

Within nine months of graduating, 99 percent of job-seeking Cal Poly grads have secured employment; 72 percent already have a job offer by the time they complete their degrees. Top employers of Cal Poly grads include many of the top tech/consulting/engineering/financial firms in the country such as Google, Deloitte, KPMG, Microsoft, Northrup Grumman, Adobe, EY, and Apple. Overall, grads enjoy an average starting salary of $62,000. Engineering majors lead the way at $72,000 while liberal arts grads bring in a median income of only $44,000. Given that the in-state tuition is under $10K per year, this makes the university one of the best ROI schools in the country. An overwhelming majority, 88 percent, remain in California upon graduation. Washington, Colorado, and Texas are next three most popular destinations.

Of the 15 percent of alumni who directly enter graduate school, the six most commonly attended schools are all in California. By far the greatest number continue their studies at Cal Poly. UC Davis, USC, UC San Diego, San Jose State, and Berkeley also draw more than a handful of graduates each year. Many graduates of the Orfalea College of Business pursue master's degrees in accounting. The highest number of engineering students pursued MBAs or master's degrees in specific branches of engineering. Pursuing a legal education is a frequent choice of liberal arts graduates, and the University of San Diego, USC, and UCLA are the most commonly attended law schools.

Admission

Cal Poly accepted 30 percent of the nearly 55,000 freshmen applicants and 16 percent of the almost 11,000 transfer students who applied in 2018. Like many California public universities, Cal Poly has become more competitive in recent years. While acceptance rates have remained steady, other indicators strongly suggest this trend. A startling 10,000 students with 4.0 GPAs (or higher) were denied entry to the Class of 2022. Mid-50 percent standardized test scores were 1240-1430 on the SAT and 26-32 on the ACT. Fifty-nine percent of freshmen entering in 2018-19 claimed a spot in the top 10 percent of their high school class, and 89 percent were in the top quartile. Five years ago, those numbers were all significantly lower.

Freshman applicants apply to one of six colleges within the university, and some are more competitive than others. For example, the acceptance rate into the College of Engineering is 23 percent, and the average SAT of an admitted student is 1481. Those aiming for the School of Agriculture, Food & Environmental Sciences enjoy a 44 percent acceptance rate and average a significantly lower 1325 on the SAT. No matter the college to which you apply, Cal Poly is mainly interested in three factors when making admissions decisions: the rigor of your secondary curriculum, GPA, and standardized test scores. Things like extracurricular activities, work experience, and first-generation status also carry a small amount of weight. Getting into Cal Poly is a straightforward, albeit increasingly challenging proposition. Candidates with a sparkling transcript and SATs north of 1350 should fare well. Those aiming to study engineering, business, or science and mathematics will need stronger credentials than those applying to other colleges.

Worth Your Money?

Annual in-state tuition and fees to attend Cal Poly remain below five figures, an astounding value in today's higher education marketplace. Including room, board, and all other expenses, the cost of attendance for California residents sits at $28,988. Out-of-staters pay an annual COA of under $43,000, not at all an unreasonable sum for the quality of education one will receive at this university. The school does not award large sums of need-based or merit-based aid; however, the net price most students pay still remains relatively low given the school's modest sticker price.

FINANCIAL
Institutional Type: Public
In-State Tuition: $5,742
Out-of-State Tuition: $17,622
Room & Board: $13,796
Required Fees: $4,074
Books & Supplies: $1,941

Avg. Need-Based Aid: $3,442
Avg. % of Need Met: 56%

Avg. Merit-Based Aid: $1,561
% Receiving Merit-Based Aid: 26%

Avg. Cumulative Debt: $22,298
% of Students Borrowing: 42%

CAREER
Who Recruits
1. Lockheed Martin
2. NBCUniversal
3. Greystar
4. The Raymond Group
5. Cushman & Wakefield

Notable Internships
1. Nike
2. EY
3. Oracle

Top Industries
1. Business
2. Engineering
3. Operations
4. Education
5. Sales

Top Employers
1. Apple
2. Google
3. Cisco
4. Oracle
5. Amazon

Where Alumni Work
1. San Francisco
2. San Luis Obispo, CA
3. Los Angeles
4. San Diego
5. Orange County, CA

Median Earnings
College Scorecard (Early Career): $66,900
EOP (Early Career): $55,100
PayScale (Mid-Career): $119,500

RANKINGS
Forbes: 115
Money: 75
U.S. News: 4, Regional West
Wall Street Journal/THE: 193 (T)
Washington Monthly: N/A

#CollegesWorthYourMoney

Carleton College

Northfield, Massachusetts | Admissions Phone: 507-222-4190

ADMISSION
Admission Rate: 20%
Admission Rate - Men: 19%
Admission Rate - Women: 20%
EA Admission Rate: Not Offered
ED Admission Rate: 26%
Admission Rate (5-Year Trend): -1%
ED Admission Rate (5-Year Trend): -4%
% of Admits Attending (Yield): 38%
Transfer Admission Rate: 10%

Offered Wait List: 1,486
Accepted Wait List: 556
Admitted Wait List: 34

SAT Reading/Writing (Middle 50%): 670-750
SAT Math (Middle 50%): 680-780
ACT Composite (Middle 50%): 31-34
Testing Policy: ACT/SAT Required
SAT Superscore: Yes
ACT Superscore: No

% Graduated in Top 10% of HS Class: 79%
% Graduated in Top 25% of HS Class: 96%
% Graduated in Top 50% of HS Class: 100%

ENROLLMENT
Total Undergraduate Enrollment: 2,097
% Part-Time: 1%
% Male: 50%
% Female: 50%
% Out-of-State: 84%
% Fraternity: Not Offered
% Sorority: Not Offered
% On-Campus (Freshman): 100%
% On-Campus (All Undergraduate): 96%

% African-American: 5%
% Asian: 8%
% Hispanic: 8%
% White: 58%
% Other: 7%
% Race or Ethnicity Unknown: 1%
% International: 11%
% Low-Income: 11%

ACADEMICS
Student-to-Faculty Ratio: 9:1
% of Classes Under 20: 70%
% of Classes Under 40: 99%
% Full-Time Faculty: 80%
% Full-Time Faculty w/ Terminal Degree: 97%

Top Programs
Biology
Chemistry
Computer Science
Economics
Geology
History
Mathematics
Political Science

Retention Rate: 97%
4-Year Graduation Rate: 88%
6-Year Graduation Rate: 93%

Curricular Flexibility: Somewhat Flexible
Academic Rating: ★★★★✓

Inside the Classroom

One of the top liberal arts schools (if not the top) in the Midwest, Carleton has the reputation as a destination point for studious young people who love to learn for learning's sake. Located in fairly remote Northfield, Minnesota, the college still manages to be a magnet for the academically gifted and intellectually curious from coast to coast. Carleton is a small institution of just over 2,100 undergraduate students. It offers thirty-four majors, the most popular of which are within the disciplines of the social sciences (29 percent), biology (15 percent), English (6 percent), and computer science (5 percent).

Mandated coursework is extensive and includes an argument and inquiry seminar for first-year students, a global citizenship requirement, a class in international studies as well as domestic studies, and three writing-intensive courses. Undergrads also must take a stroll through the usual liberal arts categories of humanistic inquiry, literary/artistic analysis, the arts, science, statistics, and social inquiry. All of this is done via three ten-week terms per academic year during which most students take only three courses per term.

Students work closely with their professors, and the college is routinely rated atop lists of best undergraduate teaching institutions. Small classes are the norm with the average being only sixteen students; in almost one-quarter of your classes you will be surrounded by no more than eight of your peers. Faculty-mentored research is embedded into many courses, independent study opportunities abound, and full-time supervised research is available during summer and winter break. Over three-quarters of the student body elect to study abroad in one of 130 programs offered in sixty countries. Furthermore, 100 percent of students in the Class of 2017 majoring in a foreign language, art history, dance, and photography spent a semester studying in another part of the globe.

All academic programs at this elite liberal arts school are well regarded, particularly by other universities where an exceptional percentage of Carleton grads later pursue doctoral degrees (more on this below). Consistently named a top producer of Fulbright Scholars, the college enjoyed ten award recipients in 2019. The Peace Corps also ranked Carleton thirteenth on its list of Top Volunteer-Producing (small) Colleges.

Outside the Classroom

With 92 percent of students living on campus and no Greek life at Carleton, the dorms take on the role as the preferred social setting. Fourteen theme houses also play a big role on campus, allowing people with aligned interests to live communally. Those include the WHOA House for campus activists, the Culinary House for those committed to gastronomic pursuits, and the Q&A House for the LBGTQA community. Over 200 student-run clubs offer a multitude of niche activities to suit this fairly eclectic student body. The Ravens' eighteen varsity athletic teams are split evenly between men and women, and they all compete in NCAA Division III. Club and intramural sports are popular with ultimate Frisbee in the lead by a wide margin. Northfield is a small town, but it has its share of social/cultural offerings as well as neighboring St. Olaf's College, which opens additional social opportunities. Those looking for more action than Northfield can provide will be pleased to find the bustle of Minneapolis and St. Paul, both less than fifty miles away. Students seeking natural beauty do not have to look any further than the on-campus Cowling Arboretum, a 900-acre wooded area perfect for hiking or cross-country skiing.

Career Services

The Career Center is staffed by ten full-time professionals, just about all of whom have director, assistant director, or manager in their title. However, at such a small school most of these individuals do work directly with students in some capacity, and that results in a student-to-advisor ratio of 210:1, significantly better than the average institution included in this book.

The major career/internship/graduate school fairs that are open to Carleton students are joint efforts with other Minnesota-based universities, yet many companies, nonprofits, and government entities do make the trip to Northfield to directly recruit this talented cohort of undergraduates. Those companies include Amazon, Ernst & Young, Facebook, Google, and Microsoft. The 30 Minutes Program brings current students face-to-face with alums who work in a field of interest for quick (hence the name) informational/networking sessions. Externships with alumni allow students to shadow alumni in their place of employment for one to three weeks. Alumni remain extremely engaged with the school as evidenced by an extremely high percentage who donate. The area in which the career services office truly excels is advising students on graduate school pathways, an area we will explore further in a moment.

Professional Outcomes

Carleton does not track the activities of every graduating class, but when it last administered a senior survey in 2016, nearly three-quarters of soon-to-be grads were headed into the workforce with the most common job functions being business analyst, project manager, research assistant/associate, software engineer, and medical scribe. There are thirty-five companies that employ more than ten Carleton alums. Many are prestigious academic institutions including the University of Chicago, the University of Michigan, Colombia, Stanford, Northwestern, and Penn; the University of Minnesota is the largest employer of Knights with over 160 alumni in its ranks. Target, Epic Systems, UnitedHealth Group, Wells Fargo, Amazon, 3M, and Facebook all employ more than twenty-five alumni. Geographically, the greatest number of students remain in the Minneapolis-St. Paul area, but many also head to New York City, San Francisco, Chicago, DC, Boston, Seattle, and Los Angeles.

Carleton is a breeding ground for future scholars as a ridiculously high number of graduates go on to earn PhDs. In fact, by percentage, Carleton is one of the top ten producers of any college or university in the country of PhDs in economics, math, political science, sociology, chemistry, physics, biology, and history. In recent years 20-25 percent of graduates immediately entered graduate school; within ten years, 75 percent of graduates have enrolled in or completed an advanced degree program. Such a focus on time-consuming scholarly pursuits helps explain why Carleton graduates have a median income of $52,000 at age thirty-four, a fairly low figure when measured against other elite colleges.

Admission

The 7,100 applications submitted for the Class of 2022 doesn't sound like an overwhelming number, but for tiny Carleton, that figure represented a 9 percent increase from the previous year. Only 20 percent of those applicants received an offer of admission. That was only a slight decrease from the admit rates of the previous five years. Those presently enrolled at Carleton almost exclusively finished near the top of their high school classes; 79 percent of those admitted into the 2018-19 freshman class were in the top 10 percent, and the school typically attracts around fifty National Merit Scholars each cycle. The 25th percentile SAT score was 1350, and the 75th percentile marker was 1530. A larger number of applicants submitted ACT scores to Carleton with a middle-50 percent range of 31-34. Many members of the Class of 2022 also were active in their high school communities; 58 percent played varsity sports, 43 percent studied music, and an overwhelming 83 percent participated in some type of volunteer work.

The college lists three factors as the most significant in the admissions process: rigor of secondary curriculum, GPA, and class rank. Yet, excellent standardized test scores seem to be a prerequisite as 83 percent of enrolling students possess an ACT above 30, and 70 percent scored better than a 700 on the math section of the SAT. With such a low number of applications, those from remote areas of the country may particularly benefit from the quest for geographic diversity; thirteen US states sent 0-1 student to Carleton in 2017. Early decision can also provide a major advantage to those targeting the college as their number one choice. With two rounds of early decision offered, in a typical year Carleton fills 43 percent of its incoming class via ED. Yet, the acceptance rate isn't all that encouraging, as they admitted only 27 percent of ED students in 2018. Carleton is among the most highly selective liberal arts colleges not located on the East or West coasts. Its remote location keeps application numbers in check, but the applicant pool tends to be self-selecting.

Worth Your Money?

With little merit aid and a $73,500 estimated annual cost of attendance, there are many Carleton students who will be paying $294,000 for their bachelor's degree. The good news is that current undergraduates with demonstrated financial need see 100 percent of that need met, which averages to a $44,774 grant. Fifty-five percent of the student body comes from families without need, and most of those families will pay the sticker price, as Carleton offers little in the way of merit aid. While Carleton's excellence isn't directly reflected in the early-to-mid career salaries of its graduates, the tiny classes, professor quality, extensive career services, and preparation for those aiming for prestigious graduate schools makes this school very much worth your money.

FINANCIAL
Institutional Type: Private
In-State Tuition: $56,778
Out-of-State Tuition: $56,778
Room & Board: $14,658
Required Fees: $333
Books & Supplies: $866

Avg. Need-Based Aid: $43,187
Avg. % of Need Met: 100%

Avg. Merit-Based Aid: $4,174
% Receiving Merit-Based Aid: 8%

Avg. Cumulative Debt: $21,020
% of Students Borrowing: 42%

CAREER
Who Recruits
1. U.S. Bank
2. Anderson Corporation
3. Lewin Group
4. SPS Commerce
5. UnitedHealth Group

Notable Internships
1. Moody's Analytics
2. Smithsonian
3. Federal Rserve Bank of St. Louis

Top Industries
1. Education
2. Business
3. Research
4. Social Services
5. Media

Top Employers
1. Google
2. Epic
3. UnitedHealth Group
4. Target
5. Wells Fargo

Where Alumni Work
1. Minneapolis
2. New York City
3. San Francisco
4. Chicago
5. Washington, DC

Median Earnings
College Scorecard (Early Career): $54,200
EOP (Early Career): $51,700
PayScale (Mid-Career): $109,900

RANKINGS
Forbes: 52
Money: 267
U.S. News: 7, Liberal Arts Colleges
Wall Street Journal/THE: 40
Washington Monthly: 24, Liberal Arts Colleges

#CollegesWorthYourMoney

Carnegie Mellon University

Pittsburgh, Pennsylvania | Admissions Phone: 412-268-2082

Inside the Classroom

Founded by steel baron Andrew Carnegie in 1900 as an eponymous technical school, CMU's rise to its present position as one of the best research universities in the country is as much a Horatio Alger story as that of its original namesake. Despite its humble roots and gradual ascension into a regional powerhouse, Carnegie Mellon today is home to 6,900 brilliant undergrads and an additional 7,600 graduate students who come from all over the world to reap the benefits of a top-notch educational experience.

Carnegie Mellon is unique in a number of ways; it is both highly segmented by area of study and, at the same time, interdisciplinary. Students are admitted to one of six colleges: the College of Engineering, College of Fine Arts, Dietrich College of Humanities and Social Science (which houses the popular information systems program), Mellon College of Science, Tepper School of Business, and the School of Computer Science. There are a combined ninety undergraduate majors available across the six schools, but young people simply do not come to CMU as "undecided." CMU students are expected to be well-rounded, and that philosophy is reflected in departmental requirements. For example, Dietrich students are required to take courses on data and computer science as freshmen, and students in the College of Engineering must take courses in writing and expression and foreign language.

Impressive, particularly for a school with more graduate students than undergrads and a good but less-than-tiny 13:1 student-to-faculty ratio. class sizes are small with 28 percent containing single digits and two-thirds having an enrollment of nineteen or fewer. In the 2018-19 school year 823 undergraduates conducted research through the University Research Office, and many others participated through various outside arrangements. Between 500-600 students study abroad for a semester each year in such countries as Japan, China, and Germany.

The most commonly conferred degrees are in engineering (25 percent), computer science (13 percent), business (10 percent), mathematics (10 percent), and visual and performing arts (10 percent). CMU boasts a number of programs that have a stellar worldwide reputation. In fact, it's hard to think of a university that accrues such high praise across such a broad spectrum of disciplines. The School of Computer Science is one of the best in the country, perennially ranked right next to (or above) the likes of MIT, Caltech, and Stanford. Also of note, it enrolls women at two or three times the national average. Tepper is recognized as one of the top undergraduate business schools by corporations around the globe. The drama program is a constant producer of top talent and, amazingly, in 2016 seven alumni were nominated for Tony Awards. The School of Engineering and the information technology program are also regulars in any top ten list. In the last five years CMU students also have captured thirty Fulbright Scholarships, six Goldwater Scholarships, and two Churchill Scholarships.

Outside the Classroom

CMU undergrads are known for being so consumed with academics that some might ask, "What life outside the classroom?" Yet, there is plenty of activity, both on campus and in the surrounding Oakland section of Pittsburgh. All freshmen, and 58 percent of the entire student body, live on campus. There are over 280 student organizations including the famed Scotch'n'Soda, one of the oldest student theater groups in the country. It regularly puts on professional quality plays and musicals. More than sixty of the clubs on campus are pre-professional in focus, such as the popular Society of Women Engineers, but there are plenty of options in the LGBTQ, spiritual, tech-hobby realms as well. Fraternities and sororities have twenty-three chapters on campus, and a substantial but not overwhelming 16 percent of men and 11 percent of women participate in Greek life. Star speakers from all walks of life can frequently be heard on CMU's campus. Attending sports events is not among the most favored CMU pastimes, but the Tartans do compete in eight men's and nine women's sports in NCAA Division III. Plenty of club sports are available as well including badminton, cricket, and Alpine skiing.

Career Services

The Career and Professional Development Center at Carnegie Mellon produces enviable results for its students. A fantastically high number of graduates find their first jobs through internships (26 percent), career fairs (14 percent), Handshake (12 percent), or directly through their career advisor (11 percent). The university pours ample resources into career services, employing twenty-seven full-time consultants, experiential learning coordinators, and employee relations specialists. That equates to a student-to-advisor ratio of 257:1, which is better than average when compared to the other institutions included in this book.

The office does a strong job of engaging with students, whether in person or virtually. Over three-quarters of undergrads login to Handshake to view the roughly 12,000 job and 5,000 internship postings. Many job search-related events focus on specific sectors such as the Civil & Environmental Engineering Career Fair, Energy Industry Career Fair, or Tepper Meetup (for business students). Those events have corporate partnerships with a number of top companies that recruit on campus including Google, Facebook, Uber, Microsoft, Apple, and Salesforce. Multiple members of each class intern at companies that include Amazon, Deloitte, and JP Morgan Chase. In 2018-19, an impressive 488 companies recruited at the university and conducted 5,900 on-campus interviews. Close to 80 percent of undergraduates complete at least one internship. Possessing a heavy arsenal of industry connections and hands-on offerings, CMU's Career and Professional Development Center provides exemplary service to its undergraduates.

Professional Outcomes

By the end of the calendar year in which they received their diplomas, 64 percent of grads were employed, and 23 percent were continuing to graduate school. The companies that have routinely scooped up CMU grads include Google, Facebook, Microsoft, Uber, Apple, Disney Research, McKinsey, and Deloitte as well as Pittsburgh-based PNC Bank. Starting salaries for CMU grads are exceptionally high, due in part, of course, to the high number of engineering and computer science diplomas it awards, yet all Tartans tend to do well financially. With an average starting salary of almost $85,000, CMU grads outpace the average starting salary for a college grad nationally ($51k) by a wide margin. Some majors offer even better remuneration, such as computer science ($114k), electrical and computer engineering ($107k), information systems ($90k), and business ($77k). While some do remain in Pittsburgh, graduates flock in large numbers to San Francisco, New York, and DC.

Of those pursuing graduate education, 20 percent enrolled immediately in PhD programs. A perusal of the schools where recent grads have decided to continue their education is a who's who of the Ivy League and includes MIT, Caltech, and Stanford as well as Carnegie Mellon itself (a popular choice). In 2018-19, there were fifty-nine CMU applicants to medical school. Recent grads have gone on to medical institutions at Harvard, Rutgers, Temple, UMass, and SUNY Downstate Medical Center. Those entering law school are currently studying at elite schools including UVA, Columbia, Penn, Yale, and Georgetown.

Admission

Carnegie Mellon received more than 24,000 applications in 2018, a 19 percent increase over the previous year and almost double the number that applied a decade ago. The overall acceptance rate for the Class of 2022 was 17 percent, however, since applicants apply to one of the six schools within the university, it's essential to examine a school-specific breakdown. Further, those applying to the College of Fine Arts (CFA) must indicate their intended area of study from six choices. Acceptance rates vary greatly from program to program. For example, in 2018-19 only 5 percent of applicants were accepted into the School of Computer Science (SCS) while 14 percent were accepted into the Dietrich College of Humanities and Social Sciences (DC). Within the DC, School of Architecture applicants enjoyed a robust 27 percent admit rate while among School of Drama applicants the percent admitted was an infinitesimal 4 percent. You can apply to more than one program at CMU, but you must fill out separate applications, pay the fee for each, and meet the unique requirements for every school you apply to.

The 50 percent SAT range for students admitted into the CFA was 1330-1510; for the SCS it as a markedly more competitive 1530-1580. The average GPA across all schools is 3.84 on a 4.0 scale. Successful applicants to CMU have taken the most rigorous high school schedules available to them, and the school also lists work experience, volunteer work, and extracurriculars among the most important factors for admission. Additionally, it is worth highlighting the fact that women fared much better than their male counterparts, being admitted at a 24 percent rate versus less than 13 percent for men. One almost needs a degree in applying to Carnegie Mellon in order to apply to Carnegie Mellon. It is a complicated process, and each program has highly specific requirements and greatly varying standards for admission, but excellent grades in honors and AP courses and excellent-to-near perfect SAT/ACT scores are pretty much prerequisites for consideration.

Worth Your Money?

A Carnegie Mellon education carries an annual cost of attendance of $74,000 that, for most attendees (except fine arts and many humanities students), will be less than their starting salary when they graduate. Rare for a school of its caliber, CMU does offer merit aid to 12 percent of the undergraduate population with the average award being $15k per year. While it does not meet 100 percent of the demonstrated financial aid for all qualifying students, the 39 percent of students who receive financial aid see grants averaging $43k. With few exceptions, a degree from Carnegie Mellon is worth taking on a bit of debt. The average amount owed by graduates is just shy of $28,000, slightly less than the average college debt nationwide.

FINANCIAL
Institutional Type: Private
In-State Tuition: $55,816
Out-of-State Tuition: $55,816
Room & Board: $14,972
Required Fees: $1,303
Books & Supplies: $2,400

Avg. Need-Based Aid: $43,090
Avg. % of Need Met: 97%

Avg. Merit-Based Aid: $15,308
% Receiving Merit-Based Aid: 12%

Avg. Cumulative Debt: $27,818
% of Students Borrowing: 59%

CAREER
Who Recruits
1. PNC
2. Uber
3. Epic
4. Google
5. Goldman Sachs

Notable Internships
1. GoDaddy
2. Microsoft
3. Chicago Trading Company

Top Industries
1. Engineering
2. Business
3. Education
4. Information Technology
5. Research

Top Employers
1. Google
2. Microsoft
3. Facebook
4. Amazon
5. Apple

Where Alumni Work
1. Pittsburgh
2. San Francisco
3. New York City
4. Washington, DC
5. Boston

Median Earnings
College Scorecard (Early Career): $83,600
EOP (Early Career): $78,400
PayScale (Mid-Career): $136,100

RANKINGS
Forbes: 37
Money: 120
U.S. News: 25, National Universities
Wall Street Journal/THE: 25 (T)
Washington Monthly: 89, National Universities

#CollegesWorthYourMoney

Case Western Reserve University

Cleveland, Ohio | Admissions Phone: 216-368-4450

ADMISSION
Admission Rate: 29%
Admission Rate - Men: 29%
Admission Rate - Women: 30%
EA Admission Rate: 36%
ED Admission Rate: 42%
Admission Rate (5-Year Trend): -13%
ED Admission Rate (5-Year Trend): Previously
Not Offered
% of Admits Attending (Yield): 18%
Transfer Admission Rate: 23%

Offered Wait List: 9,908
Accepted Wait List: N/A
Admitted Wait List: 0

SAT Reading/Writing (Middle 50%): 650-730
SAT Math (Middle 50%): 700-790
ACT Composite (Middle 50%): 30-34
Testing Policy: ACT/SAT Required
SAT Superscore: Yes
ACT Superscore: Yes

% Graduated in Top 10% of HS Class: 66%
% Graduated in Top 25% of HS Class: 92%
% Graduated in Top 50% of HS Class: 99%

ENROLLMENT
Total Undergraduate Enrollment: 5,262
% Part-Time: 3%
% Male: 55%
% Female: 45%
% Out-of-State: 72%
% Fraternity: 28%
% Sorority: 36%
% On-Campus (Freshman): 97%
% On-Campus (All Undergraduate): 80%

% African-American: 4%
% Asian: 21%
% Hispanic: 8%
% White: 47%
% Other: 5%
% Race or Ethnicity Unknown: 1%
% International: 14%
% Low-Income: 20%

ACADEMICS
Student-to-Faculty Ratio: 11:1
% of Classes Under 20: 59%
% of Classes Under 40: 83%
% Full-Time Faculty: 78%
% Full-Time Faculty w/ Terminal Degree: 92%

Top Programs
Accounting
Biochemistry
Biology
Biomedical Engineering
Business Management
Electrical Engineering
Nursing

Retention Rate: 94%
4-Year Graduation Rate: 65%
6-Year Graduation Rate: 85%

Curricular Flexibility: Somewhat Flexible
Academic Rating: ★★★★

Inside the Classroom

A private, midsize institution in Cleveland, Ohio, Case Western Reserve University (CWRU) is a school whose reputation and selectivity are among the fastest risers in the nation. Long an engineering powerhouse with a rich history of technical education, there has been a recent, sharp rise in the caliber of students clamoring to join this undergraduate student body of just over 5,100. In fact, the university granted acceptance to close to three-quarters of applicants a mere decade ago; today, that figure is sliding toward one-quarter.

Unlike many schools of its ilk, CWRU has a single-door admission policy. Those accepted into the broader university are free to pursue any of the nearly one hundred areas of concentration. All students must complete four seminars called SAGEs (one first-year seminar, two university seminars, and one in the major), and two semesters of physical education. From there, most requirements are school/major specific. In their final year students must conquer the senior capstone, which can take many forms, but it must be designed in consultation with a faculty member.

Sporting an 11:1 faculty-to-student ratio, the university does a nice job keeping classes on the small side with 59 percent of course sections capped at nineteen and only 15 percent of courses having fifty students or more. An exceptional 83 percent of students have the opportunity to participate in undergraduate research as the school places heavy emphasis on experiential learning. The same goes for international experiences. Case Western has a high rate of undergraduates who elect to study abroad; just under half spend a semester in a foreign land.

The Weatherhead School of Management and the Case School of Engineering have stellar reputations within the worlds of employment and academia. Engineering is the most commonly conferred undergraduate degree at 33 percent followed by biology (11 percent), business (10 percent), the social sciences (8 percent), and computer science (6 percent). In a typical year Case Western produces between two and four Fulbright Scholars as well as Churchill Scholars and NSF Fellowship recipients. The school counts sixteen Nobel Prize winners among its alumni and faculty, past and present.

Outside the Classroom

The main campus covers 155 acres, not including a verdant 389-acre, university-owned farm located only ten miles away. Freshmen and sophomores are required to live on campus and four-fifths of the overall undergraduate student body reside on the university's grounds. First-year students live in one of four residential colleges designed to foster a sense of community and belonging. Greek life is thriving with twenty-seven fraternities and sororities attracting 28 percent of men and 36 percent of women. An academically focused student body does not pay a ton of attention to the school's nineteen NCAA Division III sports teams. There are over 200 student-run groups, including plenty of opportunities for intramural athletics, volunteer work, and faith-based connections. CWRUbotix, the school's robotics team, has placed near the top of various national competitions in recent years. Case Western's proximity to downtown Cleveland makes off-campus excursions popular even though the immediate surroundings of East Cleveland are less than ideal. An endless array of restaurants, museums, concerts, and professional sporting events are easily within reach for those willing to take an occasional break from studying.

Career Services

The Career Center at CWRU includes twelve full-time staff members, equating to a student-to-advisor ratio of 420:1, a bit higher than the average institution included in this book. The office is guided by a Four-Phase Plan designed to cultivate career-oriented thinking from freshman through senior year. CWRU has implemented the Student Success Initiative in which each freshman is assigned to a "navigator," a single staff person who remains the student's contact throughout the student's time at the school. Workshops are regularly offered on basic topics such as resume development, internship search strategies, interviewing, and graduate school preparation. Two major career fairs take place each year: the University Career Fair held in October and the Get Experienced! Internship & Career Fair held in February.

Annually, more than 300 employers, from global corporations to start-ups, conduct on-campus interviews with undergraduates. Case Western has fifteen official career center partners including IBM Watson Health, GE, Progressive Insurance, and Yelp. A healthy 81 percent of those landing jobs did so in an area relevant to their college major. Thanks to a strong emphasis on hands-on education, 98 percent of graduates report having the opportunity to engage in some type of experiential learning. Those opportunities include both traditional internships and more structured 560-hour practicums. Three-fifths of students complete at least one internship during their undergraduate years. In a given year, more than a handful of Case Western students land internships at organizations including NASA, Proctor & Gamble, Amazon, and Deloitte.

Case Western Reserve University

E-mail: admission@case.edu | Website: www.case.edu

Professional Outcomes

Fifty-four percent of 2018 CWRU graduates head into the world of professional employment upon receiving their diplomas; only 6 percent were still looking for work six months after leaving the university. Members of the Class of 2018 enjoyed a median salary range of $55,000-$59,000 with engineering majors leading the way with a $65-$70K range, and arts and sciences grads earning the lowest salaries in the $35-40K range. The employers of the greatest number of graduates the previous year included the Cleveland Clinic (21), University Hospitals (20), Accenture (8), Microsoft (8), Deloitte (6), and Google (6). Many alumni also presently work for IBM, Medtronic, EY, and PwC. Nearly 40 percent work in the engineering field, 11 percent enter nursing, and 10 percent find employment in the research realm. A good number of alumni stay in the Cleveland area, but San Francisco and New York are other common destinations.

Of the 36 percent of graduates who decide to enroll in an advanced degree program after completing their undergraduate work, many are accepted by elite graduate schools. In 2017, an impressive number of grads were accepted to continue their studies at Columbia (12), Johns Hopkins (7), Cornell (6), Carnegie Mellon (5), Northwestern (5), and Penn (5). However, the most popular option is to continue studying at Case Western as 44 percent of those going on to graduate school elect to stay on the CMU campus. Of those going directly into graduate/professional studies, between 13 and 23 percent have gone on to medical school in recent years. Only 3 percent of those going to graduate school chose to pursue a law degree.

Admission

Case Western received a record 26,642 applications for admittance into its Class of 2022 and accepted an all-time low of 29 percent. For comparison, only a decade ago Case Western received a little over 7,300 applications and accepted 73 percent of those students. SAT/ACT scores in the 75th percentile for incoming freshmen back then would barely crack the 25th percentile now. Freshmen in 2018-19 boasted a middle-50 percent SAT of 1350-1520 and a 30-34 on the ACT, and roughly the same number of applicants submitted each standardized test. Nearly two-thirds of successful applicants finished in the top 10 percent of their high school classes and 92 percent placed in the top 25 percent.

This increasingly selective admissions committee ranks five factors as "very important": rigor of secondary school record, class rank, GPA, standardized test scores, and extracurricular activities. Essays, recommendation letters, interviews, volunteer work, ethnic status, talent/ability, and personal qualities comprise the second tier of considerations. Case Western offers an early action as well as ED I & ED II rounds. Those applying early find success at close to twice the rate of regular round applicants—42 percent versus 23 percent in applications for the Class of 2022. We often see schools make massive jumps in selectivity over the course of a generation where a warning of "This isn't your mother's/father's fill-in-the-blank university" would be apt. Yet, with CWSU, "This isn't your older sibling's Case Western" is a far more accurate statement. Exponential leaps in the profile of the average accepted student have created an extremely competitive environment, so applying prior to the regular cycle is a much-needed admissions edge.

Worth Your Money?

A Case Western degree will cost you $69k per year if you do not qualify for any need-based or merit aid. Fortunately, there aren't many students who fail to qualify for some sort of tuition reduction. Merit aid is awarded to 60 percent of current undergraduates, and the average award is a hefty $24,454. Need-based aid is awarded to 48 percent of students, and the average award is over $34k; the majority of those eligible see 100 percent of their demonstrated need met by the university. When all is said and done, graduates possess reasonable levels of postsecondary debt relative to the national average. Higher-than-average starting salaries make repaying those loans a doable task.

FINANCIAL
Institutional Type: Private
In-State Tuition: $50,450
Out-of-State Tuition: $50,450
Room & Board: $15,614
Required Fees: $1,029
Books & Supplies: $1,200

Avg. Need-Based Aid: $34,419
Avg. % of Need Met: 100%

Avg. Merit-Based Aid: $24,454
% Receiving Merit-Based Aid: 60%

Avg. Cumulative Debt: $31,820
% of Students Borrowing: 45%

CAREER
Who Recruits
1. Progressive Insurance
2. Lubrizol Corporation
3. Rockwell Automation
4. Amazon
5. The MetroHealth System

Notable Internships
1. Merck
2. Deloitte
3. MITRE

Top Industries
1. Business
2. Healthcare
3. Education
4. Engineering
5. Research

Top Employers
1. Cleveland Clinic
2. University Hospitals
3. Rockwell Automation
4. IBM
5. Microsoft

Where Alumni Work
1. Cleveland
2. New York City
3. San Francisco
4. Washington, DC
5. Chicago

Median Earnings
College Scorecard (Early Career): $74,600
EOP (Early Career): $73,400
PayScale (Mid-Career): $117,800

RANKINGS
Forbes: 100
Money: 320
U.S. News: 40 (T), National Universities
Wall Street Journal/THE: 52
Washington Monthly: 155, National Universities

#CollegesWorthYourMoney

Claremont McKenna College

Claremont, California | Admissions Phone: 909-621-8088

ADMISSION

Admission Rate: 9%
Admission Rate - Men: 10%
Admission Rate - Women: 9%
EA Admission Rate: Not Offered
ED Admission Rate: 25%
Admission Rate (5-Year Trend): -2%
ED Admission Rate (5-Year Trend): -6%
% of Admits Attending (Yield): 56%
Transfer Admission Rate: 6%

Offered Wait List: 1,037
Accepted Wait List: 651
Admitted Wait List: 25

SAT Reading/Writing (Middle 50%): 670-730
SAT Math (Middle 50%): 680-770
ACT Composite (Middle 50%): 31-34
Testing Policy: ACT/SAT Required
SAT Superscore: Yes
ACT Superscore: Yes

% Graduated in Top 10% of HS Class: 78%
% Graduated in Top 25% of HS Class: 93%
% Graduated in Top 50% of HS Class: 100%

ENROLLMENT

Total Undergraduate Enrollment: 1,324
% Part-Time: 0%
% Male: 52%
% Female: 48%
% Out-of-State: 54%
% Fraternity: Not Offered
% Sorority: Not Offered
% On-Campus (Freshman): 100%
% On-Campus (All Undergraduate): 96%

% African-American: 4%
% Asian: 11%
% Hispanic: 15%
% White: 41%
% Other: 6%
% Race or Ethnicity Unknown: 6%
% International: 16%
% Low-Income: 11%

ACADEMICS

Student-to-Faculty Ratio: 8:1
% of Classes Under 20: 81%
% of Classes Under 40: 97%
% Full-Time Faculty: 88%
% Full-Time Faculty w/ Terminal Degree: 99%

Top Programs

Accounting
Economics
Environment, Economics, and Politics (EEP)
Government
History
International Relations
Philosophy, Politics, and Economics
Psychology

Retention Rate: 96%
4-Year Graduation Rate: 82%
6-Year Graduation Rate: 93%

Curricular Flexibility: Very Flexible
Academic Rating: ★★★★★

Inside the Classroom

Start with your average elite liberal arts college in the Northeast, cut the size of the student body in half, replace stuffy Gothic edifices with a modern California feel, and physically connect the campus to four other elite schools whose premier offerings can all be shared communally. That's the recipe for Claremont McKenna College (CMC), a liberal arts school that is home to 1,324 bright and motivated undergraduates and is a founding member of the Claremont Consortium that is comprised of four additional undergraduate institutions: Pomona, Pitzer, Scripps, and Harvey Mudd.

CMC offers thirty-two majors and eleven "sequences," series of courses that can be completed across the neighboring schools in addition to one's major. Registering for courses in one or more of the other Claremont Colleges is a staple of academic life at CMC; 99 percent of undergrads do so. An academically focused group, 32 percent of the student population ends up completing a double major. No matter your academic pursuit, required courses will include a first-year writing seminar, a humanities seminar, multiple semesters of a foreign language, a laboratory science, a math or computer science course, physical education and—of most significance—a senior thesis.

The college boasts an average class size of eighteen, and 81 percent of course sections have fewer than twenty students. With an 8:1 student-to-faculty ratio and only one graduate program offered (an MA in finance), undergrads benefit from ample professor attention. In the 2018-19 school year an incredible 79 percent of CMC students had the chance to conduct research with a faculty member, and the school has eleven partner research institutes and centers that provide graduate-level research experiences. Studying abroad is another popular pursuit as CMC offers approved programs on each of the world's six populated continents. Forty-percent of undergrads spend time at one of 115 approved programs in forty countries.

Economics, government, international relations, and psychology are the most popular majors, and among the strongest. Interdisciplinary majors such as Environment, Economics, and Politics (EEP) and Philosophy, Politics and Economics (PPE) also carry outstanding reputations. Claremont graduates annually have representation of Fulbright, US Department of State Critical Language, and Luce Scholarships. Per capita, it is often among the top ten in Fulbright production, boasting five winners in 2019.

Outside the Classroom

Academically, students attending any of the Claremont Colleges are used to crossing campuses to take courses at one of the other schools. Those permeable borders apply to life outside the classroom as well. Pomona, Pitzer, Scripps, Harvey Mudd, and CMC are all located on the same 560-acre property, and many activities are joint efforts between members of the consortium. Even Claremont McKenna's twenty-one NCAA athletic teams are combined squads with Harvey Mudd and Scripps student-athletes; it has won over 300 conference championships since its founding in 1958. Not everything is a shared-venture; there are seventy CMC-exclusive student- run organizations of the academic, identity-based, service, sports, or music/arts nature. The Model UN team has won the world championship four of the last five years. An endless flow of public speakers grace the stage at the Marian Miner Cook Athenaeum that presents guest lectures four nights per week. With 96 percent of CMC students electing to live on campus and no fraternities or sororities, campus life is an open and vibrant experience. Most facilities are shared among the members of the consortium, including the eight-lane pool; Roberts Pavilion, which includes a 2,200 seat arena and a state-of-the-art fitness center; and the Collins Dining Hall, which garners solid culinary reviews. Situated thirty-five miles east of Los Angeles, all of the culture and excitement you could want is never more than a relatively quick car ride away. The SoCal beaches are about an hour drive as is Disneyland and Joshua Tree National Park.

Career Services

The Claremont McKenna Career Services Office has eight full-time professional staff members working on grad school/career advising and employer relations and internship procurement. That equates to a 166:1 student-to-advisor ratio, which is superior to just about every college featured in our guidebook. The college aims to provide individualized career coaching to all of its students and begins that process freshman year. It even has a counselor solely dedicated to the school's 350 first-year students, and that counselor met with 93 percent of the class that entered last year. Annual fall career expos attract representatives from more than one hundred top employers. Events like company information sessions, two-to-five-day networking treks, and job shadowing experiences take place frequently throughout the year.

In 2018, employers recruiting at CMC included Google, Deloitte, Bain, the CIA, NASA, Goldman Sachs, and the National Football League. A phenomenal 90 percent of students participate in at least one internship. Many of those are financially supported by the Sponsored Internship Experiences Program that provided between $500 and $8,000 grants for 340 students in 2018. Also in the 2018 school year, staff conducted 3,000 one-on-one counseling appointments, enticed forty-four employers into recruiting on campus, and facilitated 581 on-campus interviews, more than one per member of the senior class. Thanks to that focus on hands-on experience, strong employer relations, and ample resources (including personnel), Claremont McKenna's career services easily earns the highest praise from the College Transitions' staff.

Professional Outcomes

Eighty percent of graduates have found employment within six months of graduation, and only 4 percent are still looking for work. Financial services/accounting, consulting, and technology are the most frequently entered sectors. Companies employing the highest number of 2016 and 2017 graduates include Accenture, Ernst & Young, Goldman Sachs, Amazon, Deloitte, and JP Morgan. The average starting salary for a Claremont grad is $68,200, a particularly impressive figure for a liberal arts college. The highest average starting salaries are traditionally earned by those majoring in computer science ($94k) and economics ($70k), but those studying the humanities ($65k) or social sciences ($57k) fare well too.

Of the 2016/2017 graduating classes, 12 percent elected to continue their education rather than immediately enter the working world. You name the prestigious graduate/professional program and, chances are, a recent CMC grad (or two or three) is presently studying there. In the last four years students have been accepted to medical schools at Stanford, Emory, Harvard, Johns Hopkins, and Penn. Students also have enjoyed law school acceptances at institutions including Columbia, NYU, Berkeley, the University of Chicago, and Yale. The list of MBA and other graduate programs attended by alumni is similarly eye-popping. Ten years out, 15 percent of the total alumni have earned a law degree, 5 percent a PhD, 4 percent a medical degree, and 10 percent have completed an MBA.

Admission

Applications to CMC were actually down slightly in the race for a spot in the Class of 2022, but so was the acceptance rate, which fell to the lowest point yet—9.3 percent. (It fell even further, to 8.6 percent, for 2019-20 freshmen.) The mid-50 percent test scores of freshmen entering in 2018-19 were a 1350-1500 on the SAT and a 31-34 on the ACT. The vast majority, 78 percent, placed in the top 10 percent of their high school class, and 93 percent landed in the top quartile. Claremont McKenna has trended in the more selective direction in recent years. Five years ago, the acceptance rate was a slightly higher 12 percent, median test scores were 1410/31, and fewer students placed in the top 10 percent of their graduating classes.

The process is a holistic one with seven factors deemed "very important" by the admissions committee: rigor of secondary coursework, class rank, GPA, standardized test scores, recommendations, extracurricular activities, and character/personal qualities. First-generation status is listed as a factor that is merely "considered," yet 19 percent of the Class of 2022 met that criterion. Applying early decision is a worthwhile strategic maneuver as the ED acceptance rate tends to be up to four times that of the regular cycle; in 2018, it was 25 percent versus 7 percent in the regular round. To gain admission into CMC applicants should bring exceptional credentials, as expected at any highly selective liberal arts college. There are sometimes surprise decisions here. For example, in looking at the freshman class of 2017-18, 4 percent of accepted freshmen scored lower than 600 on the reading portion of the SAT, and a different 4 percent (presumably) finished outside the top 25 percent of their high school cohort. However, in general, students should be closer to the mean to have a genuine chance at being granted admission.

Worth Your Money?

Two-fifths of CMC undergrads qualify for need-based financial aid, taking home an annual grant averaging $55,880. Additionally, one-quarter of students receive merit aid awards that average over $13k, helping make the $73,775 sticker price a bit more manageable. Those who can pay full price at Claremont McKenna likely will, and there are plenty of students capable of handling the bill. Tax return data estimates that nearly 50 percent come from families with incomes in the top 5 percent nationally. Whether you're a full-paying student or the recipient of generous aid, CMC's strong academics, sterling reputation and incredible career service offerings will more than justify your investment in this top-notch liberal arts school.

FINANCIAL
Institutional Type: Private
In-State Tuition: $56,190
Out-of-State Tuition: $56,190
Room & Board: $17,300
Required Fees: $285
Books & Supplies: N/A

Avg. Need-Based Aid: $55,880
Avg. % of Need Met: 100%

Avg. Merit-Based Aid: $13,355
% Receiving Merit-Based Aid: 25%

Avg. Cumulative Debt: $19,355
% of Students Borrowing: 34%

CAREER
Who Recruits
1. Cloudfare, Inc.
2. United Talent Agency
3. Whittier Trust Company
4. Boston Pharmaceuticals
5. Morgan Stanley

Notable Internships
1. BlackRock
2. Adidas
3. House of Representatives

Top Industries
1. Business
2. Education
3. Finance
4. Operations
5. Research

Top Employers
1. Deloitte
2. Google
3. Microsoft
4. EY
5. Accenture

Where Alumni Work
1. Los Angeles
2. San Francisco
3. New York City
4. Seattle
5. Orange County, CA

Median Earnings
College Scorecard (Early Career): $72,900
EOP (Early Career): $69,600
PayScale (Mid-Career): $125,400

RANKINGS
Forbes: 29
Money: 101
U.S. News: 7, Liberal Arts Colleges
Wall Street Journal/THE: 38
Washington Monthly: 10, Liberal Arts Colleges

#CollegesWorthYourMoney

Clarkson University

Potsdam, New York | Admissions Phone: 315-268-6480

ADMISSION
Admission Rate: 71%
Admission Rate - Men: 73%
Admission Rate - Women: 69%
EA Admission Rate: Not Offered
ED Admission Rate: 78%
Admission Rate (5-Year Trend): +7%
ED Admission Rate (5-Year Trend): +18%
% of Admits Attending (Yield): 16%
Transfer Admission Rate: 68%

Offered Wait List: 55
Accepted Wait List: 2
Admitted Wait List: 0

SAT Reading/Writing (Middle 50%): 570-660
SAT Math (Middle 50%): 590-690
ACT Composite (Middle 50%): 25-29
Testing Policy: ACT/SAT Required
SAT Superscore: Yes
ACT Superscore: No

% Graduated in Top 10% of HS Class: 35%
% Graduated in Top 25% of HS Class: 69%
% Graduated in Top 50% of HS Class: 95%

ENROLLMENT
Total Undergraduate Enrollment: 3,091
% Part-Time: 2%
% Male: 69%
% Female: 31%
% Out-of-State: 29%
% Fraternity: 15%
% Sorority: 13%
% On-Campus (Freshman): 95%
% On-Campus (All Undergraduate): 80%

% African-American: 2%
% Asian: 4%
% Hispanic: 5%
% White: 80%
% Other: 3%
% Race or Ethnicity Unknown: 2%
% International: 4%
% Low-Income: 29%

ACADEMICS
Student-to-Faculty Ratio: 13:1
% of Classes Under 20: 52%
% of Classes Under 40: 77%
% Full-Time Faculty: 71%
% Full-Time Faculty w/ Terminal Degree: 85%

Top Programs
Biology
Civil Engineering
Environmental Engineering
Environmental Science and Policy
Global Supply Chain Management
Innovation and Entrepreneurship
Mechanical Engineering

Retention Rate: 89%
4-Year Graduation Rate: 60%
6-Year Graduation Rate: 76%

Curricular Flexibility: Somewhat Flexible
Academic Rating: ★★★

Inside the Classroom

Among the lesser-known of the Upstate New York schools, Clarkson University is even further north than Syracuse, Rochester, or Buffalo. For perspective, it would take a six-hour drive to reach Potsdam from New York City. The good news is that Clarkson's remote location makes getting in much easier than at comparable small, engineering-heavy schools like Lehigh University, Lafayette College, or Union College. The student body is comprised of 3,400+ undergraduate students pursuing more than fifty programs in engineering, business, the arts, education, and sciences and health professions.

All Golden Knights are required to complete the Common Experience Curriculum that includes a First-Year Experience course on adjustment to college life, the Clarkson Seminar, which is an introduction to college-level thinking and writing, and five courses that adequately cover the six broad areas of knowledge: cultures and societies; contemporary and global issues; imaginative arts; science, technology, and society; economics and organizations; and individual and group behavior. The four common threads in all of the introductory coursework are communication, diversity, ethics, and recognizing how technology can better serve humanity. Students in the business and engineering schools have a fairly rigid schedule of courses the first two years of study. For instance, all business students take Principles of Microeconomics their first semester and Principles of Macroeconomics second semester.

A student-to-faculty ratio of 11:1 translates to reasonable undergraduate class sizes. Forty percent of sections enroll fewer than twenty students, but there are a mix of fifty or more or even one hundred or more student sections for some introductory courses. Undergraduate research is embedded in the Honors Program that admits forty to fifty students each year. Everyone else can apply to programs like the Research Experience for Undergrads (REU) that offers a ten-week apprenticeship funded by the National Science Foundation. Within the Biology Department, for example, all students are strongly encouraged to engage in research during their four years via the REU program, departmental connection, or by completing a senior thesis and presenting the findings at the Clarkson Symposium for Undergraduate Research. The school also offers thirty-seven study abroad programs in twenty countries but, as at most engineering-focused schools, the participation is low, approaching 10 percent.

An overwhelming 55 percent of undergrads are studying in the Coulter School of Engineering, 20 percent in the business school, and 18 percent in the School of Arts and Sciences. Overshadowed in most ranking systems by large research institutions, the School of Engineering is, nevertheless, a stud whose quality is fully recognized by big-time employers well outside the region. The National Science Foundation awarded two engineering undergrads and one biology student their prestigious Graduate Research Fellowship in 2019.

Outside the Classroom

Clarkson students tend to be proud nerds. As the admissions office states, "If the idea of working all night on an animated video for physics class sounds more like fun than work, you'll fit right in at Clarkson." This school has a 70 percent male, 30 percent female student body, which impacts the make-up of the social scene. The presence of SUNY Potsdam and its 58 percent female student body does help even the town's gender divide a bit. Four in five undergrads live on campus in one of eight dorm buildings or in one of the four apartment complexes. Additional Living-Learning Communities bring together students with common interests in areas like robotics, gaming, or women in engineering/business. There are nine fraternities and four sororities that, together, attract 10-15 percent of students. The school's 225 intramural teams draw an incredible 80 percent of the student body into recreational athletics. NCCA Division I ice hockey is huge as this tiny powerhouse has produced approximately thirty NHL players in its history; the other ten teams participate in Division III. Overall, there are 250 student-run clubs and activities from which to choose. Like the woods? If so, you're in luck. Not only do you get to enjoy the 640 wooded acres on which the campus is set, but the grounds are adjacent to Adirondack Park that adds another six million acres (not a typo). Like to spend time in a major metropolitan area? You're not so lucky on that front—Ottawa and Montreal, Canada, are closer to Clarkson than any major American city.

Career Services

The Clarkson Career Center (CCC) is staffed by six professionals with expertise in career coaching, employer relations, and graduate school advising. That works out to a 515:1 student-to-advisor ratio, which is in the average range compared to other schools in the guidebook. Despite its distance from major American cities, the CCC still manages to entice companies to campus with regularity, and 200 come to the annual career fairs. Even more impressive are the office's efforts in arranging internship and co-op experiences; the rate of participation is near 100 percent, and many undergrads procure two or more placements. It's no wonder 95 percent of Clarkson grads end up finding a job directly related to their area of study.

Clarkson University

A proactive office, the Clarkson Career Center has a reputation for seeking to connect personally with every student. Whether you are a freshman or a senior, staffers are equally happy to have you stop by to take a personality assessment, discuss career options one-on-one, work on your resume, or arrange an employer site visit. Golden Knights have a powerful alumni base to tap when it comes time for the job hunt. According to the university, among its 42,000 alumni, "One in five is already a CEO, senior executive, or owner of a company." Thanks to a thriving internship/co-op network that leads to fantastic employment/salary results for grads, the CCC gets high marks as an efficient and effective career services office.

Professional Outcomes

Within eight months of graduation the Class of 2018 enjoyed a job/grad school placement rate of 96 percent and an average starting salary of just under $60,100. Annually, 170+ employers snatch up Clarkson seniors. Top employers of this graduating class included BAE Systems, Amazon, IBM, General Electric, Lockheed Martin, and Pratt & Whitney. Other companies that historically hire large numbers of Golden Knights include GlobalFoundries, Corning Incorporated, Xerox, Siemens, Accenture, and Intel. While a fair number of graduates stay in Upstate New York—Utica, Syracuse, Albany, and Rochester rank as the third through sixth most popular cities—the Greater New York and Boston areas are the most common alumni destinations.

Only 13 percent of Class of 2018 members were pursuing advanced degrees immediately after completing their undergraduate education. Students from that cohort were admitted into graduate school at institutions including Duke, Georgia Tech, the University of Rochester, and Rochester Polytechnic Institute. Medical school is usually the direction of choice for around ten graduates each year. Medical school-bound students often attend SUNY schools, including SUNY Upstate Medical University, SUNY Stonybrook Medical School, and SUNY Buffalo Medical School. Recent grads also have landed at Dartmouth, Johns Hopkins, and Penn State. Remaining at Clarkson for graduate study is an option many also pursue, and the school offers approximately forty advanced degree programs.

Admission

Clarkson sports acceptance rates that range from the high 60 percents to the low 70 percents, pretty nice considering that your average engineering school of this quality typically possesses an admit rate that is a mere fraction of those generous figures. Still, many top students choose Clarkson as 37 percent of freshmen hailed from the top decile of their high school class, and roughly three-quarters finished in the top 25 percent. The average high school GPA was 3.6, and the average test scores were 1240 on the SAT and 27 on the ACT. The admissions standards have toughened in recent years. Back in 2012, the university admitted 80 percent of those who applied, and the SAT range was 1100-1270, significantly lower than the 2018-19 freshman class, even when accounting for recent SAT inflation.

Two factors reign supreme in the minds of admissions officials—GPA and a rigorous high school curriculum. Factors on the next rung of importance include standardized test scores, class rank, extracurricular activities, recommendations, and volunteer work. The early decision acceptance rate is even friendlier than the regular round as 78 percent of ED applicants were admitted during the last cycle. A personal visit to Potsdam as well as a face-to-face informational interview with an admissions counselor is highly recommended. Clarkson remains a rare, strong engineering school that is open to B students with less-than-perfect test scores.

Worth Your Money?

The focus on engineering unsurprisingly raises starting salaries into a higher stratosphere than most schools of Clarkson's size. The list price of this university is $65,000, including room and board, but merit and need-based aid are distributed generously; nine of ten students receive financial aid. Middle-class families can expect to pay closer to $30-35k per year in total costs which, depending on one's academic track, can lead to a terrific return on investment.

FINANCIAL
Institutional Type: Private
In-State Tuition: $49,858
Out-of-State Tuition: $49,858
Room & Board: $15,340
Required Fees: $1,270
Books & Supplies: $1,446

Avg. Need-Based Aid: $37,012
Avg. % of Need Met: 90%

Avg. Merit-Based Aid: $30,928
% Receiving Merit-Based Aid: 29%

Avg. Cumulative Debt: $31,000
% of Students Borrowing: 81%

CAREER
Who Recruits
1. Procter & Gamble
2. General Dynamics
3. Tecnica Group
4. Whiting-Turner
5. Novelis

Notable Internships
1. Salesforce
2. Siemens
3. Hewlett Packard

Top Industries
1. Engineering
2. Operations
3. Business
4. Information Technology
5. Sales

Top Employers
1. IBM
2. Lockheed Martin
3. GLOBALFOUNDRIES
4. Corning Incorporated
5. GE

Where Alumni Work
1. New York City
2. Boston
3. Utica, NY
4. Albany, NY
5. Syracuse, NY

Median Earnings
College Scorecard (Early Career): $72,000
EOP (Early Career): $73,300
PayScale (Mid-Career): $130,100

RANKINGS
Forbes: 207
Money: 165
U.S. News: 117, National Universities
Wall Street Journal/THE: 205 (T)
Washington Monthly: 97, National Universities

#CollegesWorthYourMoney

Clemson University

Clemson, South Carolina | Admissions Phone: 864-656-2287

ADMISSION
Admission Rate: 47%
Admission Rate - Men: 47%
Admission Rate - Women: 48%
EA Admission Rate: Not Offered
ED Admission Rate: Not Offered
Admission Rate (5-Year Trend): -10%
ED Admission Rate (5-Year Trend): Not Offered
% of Admits Attending (Yield): 28%
Transfer Admission Rate: 67%

Offered Wait List: 2,715
Accepted Wait List: 1,153
Admitted Wait List: 449

SAT Reading/Writing (Middle 50%): 610-690
SAT Math (Middle 50%): 610-710
ACT Composite (Middle 50%): 27-32
Testing Policy: ACT/SAT Required
SAT Superscore: Yes
ACT Superscore: No

% Graduated in Top 10% of HS Class: 56%
% Graduated in Top 25% of HS Class: 87%
% Graduated in Top 50% of HS Class: 98%

ENROLLMENT
Total Undergraduate Enrollment: 19,669
% Part-Time: 4%
% Male: 51%
% Female: 49%
% Out-of-State: 34%
% Fraternity: 16%
% Sorority: 31%
% On-Campus (Freshman): 98%
% On-Campus (All Undergraduate): 41%

% African-American: 6%
% Asian: 3%
% Hispanic: 5%
% White: 81%
% Other: 3%
% Race or Ethnicity Unknown: 0%
% International: 1%
% Low-Income: 16%

ACADEMICS
Student-to-Faculty Ratio: 16:1
% of Classes Under 20: 55%
% of Classes Under 40: 75%
% Full-Time Faculty: 77%
% Full-Time Faculty w/ Terminal Degree: 87%

Top Programs
Agriculture
Architecture
Biosystems Engineering
Civil Engineering
Industrial Engineering
Management
Nursing

Retention Rate: 93%
4-Year Graduation Rate: 59%
6-Year Graduation Rate: 83%

Curricular Flexibility: Somewhat Flexible
Academic Rating: ★★★

Inside the Classroom

Championship-caliber sports teams, thriving Greek life, and a passionate and generally happy undergraduate population of close to 20,000 young people define the Clemson experience—not to leave out the strong academic reputation, which becomes more pronounced with each passing year. A highly selective school for out-of-staters, Clemson caters to those residing within its home state of South Carolina. Nearly two-thirds of the student body are South Carolina born and bred, and locals enjoy more relaxed entry requirements (not to mention one-third the tuition costs) of those from out of state.

There are seven undergraduate colleges within the larger university: the College of Forestry and Life Sciences; the College of Architecture, Arts, and Humanities; the College of Business; the College of Engineering, Computing and Applied Sciences; the College of Education; the College of Science; and the College of Behavioral, Social, and Health Sciences. All Tigers, regardless of their academic program, must tackle thirty-three hours of required coursework that includes six credits in communications, ten in mathematical, scientific, and technical literacy, six in arts and humanities, six in social science, three in cross-cultural awareness, and three in science and technology in society. Most degree programs also require coursework in a foreign language.

Class sizes are mixed, and many sections are smaller than you would expect for such a large university where the student-to-faculty ratio is 16:1. Seventeen percent of classes have single-digit enrollments, and 55 percent contain fewer than twenty students; 14 percent of courses are larger, playing host to fifty or more undergraduates. More than half of Clemson students participate in some type of undergraduate research, a strong percentage given the size of the school. Each year over 1,400 students elect to study abroad in one of Clemson's own programs or one offered by a third party.

Business and engineering are the two programs with the highest profiles, and the university's highly selective Calhoun Honors College regularly draws national attention and praise. Business and engineering also are the most popular majors with a 19 percent and 20 percent market share of diplomas, respectively. The next most frequently conferred degrees are in biology (10 percent), agriculture (7 percent), and psychology (6 percent). With such an emphasis on professional career tracks there is not a strong emphasis on winning prestigious postgraduate fellowships. In 2018, two graduates received Boren Fellowships and one captured a Fulbright; Clemson had four Fulbright Scholars in 2017.

Outside the Classroom

Only 41 percent of undergrads, mostly underclassmen, reside on Clemson's 1,400-acre campus. Yet, that figure is not indicative of a dull social scene. Athletics are a galvanizing force as the Tigers compete in eight men's and nine women's NCCA Division I sports. Over 81,000 pack Memorial Stadium, nicknamed "Death Valley," on Saturdays to watch their highly ranked football squad; Clemson won the national title in 2016 and again in 2019. Other sports draw large audiences as well. Greek life is almost as big a tradition here as 34 percent of women join a sorority and 16 percent of men are fraternity affiliated. As at many Greek-heavy institutions, there has been increased scrutiny of those organizations in the wake of some incidents of sexual assault and hazing. Other opportunities for involvement abound as Clemson has over 500 student-run organizations. The school's thirty-four club sports attract widespread participation as does the intramural program. The town of Clemson offers plenty of enjoyable bars and restaurants within walking distance. Hiking trails and botanical gardens offer nature lovers everything they could ask for. Greenville, only forty minutes away, provides a more exciting downtown feel.

Career Services

Clemson's Center for Career and Professional Development employs twenty-four full-time staff members who function as counselors, recruiters, and internship coordinators. That equates to a student-to-advisor ratio of 833:1, well above average compared to the other institutions included in this book. Despite a less-than-ideal ratio, Clemson's staff garners much-deserved praise for its dedication to student success through the sheer scope of their offerings. Fall and spring career fairs attract more than 600 employers and more than 5,500 students annually. The school's online database features up to 9,000 job and internship postings each year. The center has forged corporate partnerships with twenty-four large corporations including Home Depot, Vanguard, Bosch, and General Electric.

Even more impressively, the CCPD personally reaches a massive number of students, claiming more than 31,000 engagements in the 2017-18 school year. Fifty-five percent of those engagements were made at workshops, job fairs, and information sessions while the other 45 percent were made via one-on-one counseling sessions. An astonishing 99 percent of those attending information sessions or individualized career counseling rated the experience favorably. Staff also does an exceptional job hooking students up with hands-on learning experiences; 78 percent of graduates had one experiential learning opportunity and 64 percent partook in two.

Clemson University

E-mail: cuadmissions@clemson.edu | Website: www.clemson.edu

Just under 900 students participated in the University Professional Co-op/Internship Program with the school's 450 employer partners. An additional 1,400 participated in other co-op placements, and 92 percent reported being satisfied with the experience. As a result, 94 percent of those receiving diplomas believe their resumes demonstrate marketable skills.

Professional Outcomes

Within six months of graduation 96 percent of Clemson alumni have entered the working world or are pursuing a graduate degree. The top employers of Class of 2017 graduates included Michelin (8), Amazon (8), Vanguard (5), and Wells Fargo (4). Including all alumni, the most frequent employers include Bank of America, GE Power, Deloitte, IBM, and Microsoft. Graduates of the College of Engineering, Computing and Applied Sciences reported a median starting salary of $63,000. College of Business graduates enjoyed median earnings of $49,000. Graduates of the College of Architecture, Arts, and Humanities averaged $47k while those completing degrees in the College of Education brought in a university-low $37k per year. Forty-five percent of graduates remain in South Carolina, and most stay in the Southern United States with North Carolina, Georgia, Florida, and Virginia being the next most popular destinations.

Of the 21 percent of 2017 graduates directly entering graduate or professional school, the largest number retained their Tiger stripes by continuing their studies at Clemson. The next most frequently attended institutions were the Medical University of South Carolina (47), the University of South Carolina (33), UNC (12), the University of Georgia (11), and Wake Forest University (9). Clemson grads also enjoyed three or more acceptances to prestigious graduate schools including Duke, Penn, Emory, Vanderbilt, and the University of Virginia. Among all alumni pursuing advanced degrees, 15 percent were in PhD programs, and a robust 33 percent were pursuing professional degrees in law or medicine.

Admission

The number of applicants to Clemson has rapidly risen in the past decade as 28,845 students applied in 2018 compared with 15,542 in 2008. In that time the average SAT score of attending students has climbed from 1221 to 1302; the ACT mid-50 percent range was 27-32. Admitted applicants from South Carolina public schools averaged only a 1058 on the SAT in 2017. No matter where they hail from, most successful applicants— 87 percent—finished in the top 25 percent of their high school class, and 56 percent were in the top 10 percent. The average high school GPA for entering students was 4.43, and 90 percent earned a 3.75 or higher. Those applying to the Calhoun Honors College need to be even stronger. The average accepted Calhoun students have a 1480/32 and are ranked in the top 4 percent of their class.

A healthy 60 percent of first-year students accepted are from South Carolina, but including transfers, home-state students comprise an even larger percentage of the student body. Being a South Carolina resident is listed among the five most important criteria for admission along with rigor of secondary coursework, GPA, class rank, and standardized test scores. Soft factors like essays, recommendations, and extracurricular activities comprise a distant second tier. Legacy status is also considered at Clemson. There is no early admission round at Clemson, but those who apply by the priority deadline of December 1 will receive an answer by February 15. This desirable Southern public university is friendlier toward in-state applicants than outsiders. Applicants not from South Carolina will need to bring above average standardized test scores and strong grades in honors and AP courses to gain acceptance.

Worth Your Money?

The cost of attendance for South Carolina residents is under $30,000 per year, making Clemson a fantastic bargain for them. For nonresidents, the price is over $50k, not a fortune relative to the out-of-control higher education marketplace at large, but not the steal that it is for those from the Palmetto State. Almost 45 percent of current students are recipients of need-based aid awards that average $10,967 per year. For a state university, Clemson awards an usually high number of students some degree of merit aid. Currently, 78 percent of undergraduates receive an average annual amount of $6k. In-state, attending Clemson is worth your money no matter what you are studying. If you hail from outside the state, a little bit of financial aid can keep the university affordable and a strong educational investment.

FINANCIAL
Institutional Type: Public
In-State Tuition: $13,702
Out-of-State Tuition: $35,056
Room & Board: $10,832
Required Fees: $1,268
Books & Supplies: $1,392

Avg. Need-Based Aid: $10,967
Avg. % of Need Met: 55%

Avg. Merit-Based Aid: $5,979
% Receiving Merit-Based Aid: 78%

Avg. Cumulative Debt: $32,285
% of Students Borrowing: 47%

CAREER
Who Recruits
1. Bank of America
2. ScribeAmerica
3. Global Lending Services LLC
4. Insight Global
5. TD Bank

Notable Internships
1. BMW
2. Booz Allen Hamilton
3. Capital One

Top Industries
1. Business
2. Operations
3. Engineering
4. Education
5. Sales

Top Employers
1. Michelin
2. Fluor Corporation
3. Bank of America
4. Wells Fargo
5. Amazon

Where Alumni Work
1. Greenville, SC
2. Charlotte
3. Charleston, SC
4. Atlanta
5. Columbia, SC

Median Earnings
College Scorecard (Early Career): $52,400
EOP (Early Career): N/A
PayScale (Mid-Career): $106,700

RANKINGS
Forbes: 134
Money: 78
U.S. News: 70, National Universities
Wall Street Journal/THE: 188
Washington Monthly: 179, National Universities

#CollegesWorthYourMoney

Colby College

Waterville, Maine | Admissions Phone: 207-859-4828

Inside the Classroom

Situated within the natural splendor of Waterville, Maine, Colby College's location may be remote, but the alluring sheen of this liberal arts gem is spotted each year by a growing number of top students from around the globe. Over the past decade, applications to Colby have tripled, and the school has become commensurately more selective. The 1,917 undergraduates presently on campus are, by far, the highest-achieving group the school has seen in its 205 years.

Offering fifty-eight majors and thirty-five minors, Colby provides a classic liberal arts education with a high degree of flexibility and room for independent intellectual pursuits. Dual engineering degrees with Dartmouth and Columbia, independent majors of your own creation, and a strong premed track are among the bevy of options. Academic requirements for all Colby undergraduates include a freshman writing seminar, three semesters of a foreign language, two natural science courses (including one lab science), two courses dealing with diversity, and one course each in historical studies, literature, quantitative reasoning, history, and social sciences.

A 10:1 student-to-faculty ratio is put to good instructional use as 35 percent of courses have a single-digit enrollment, and 74 percent have fewer than nineteen students. The school's "Jan Plan" tacks on a truncated semester during which students can conduct research alongside faculty, pursue internships, or take an accelerated course; 90 percent of undergraduates participate. An exceptionally high 67 percent of students study abroad at some point during their four years at Colby. The college runs three of its own off-campus study programs and allows participation in hundreds of programs around the globe.

Being a true liberal arts school, Colby has strengths across many disciplines, but biology, economics, and global studies draw especially high praise. These programs, along with other strong programs in government and environmental science, attract the highest number of students as well. Unlike many of its elite Northeastern liberal arts counterparts, Colby does not produce a significant number of fellowship/scholarship winners, but in 2018 three graduates were named Fulbright Scholars. Bates and Bowdoin routinely produce in excess of twenty winners per year. In 2019, Colby also had a Davis Projects for Peace and Watson Fellowship winner.

Outside the Classroom

The vast majority of students—95 percent—live on campus with a smattering of undergraduates living off campus in the surrounding town of Waterville. Colby ditched fraternities and sororities in the 1980s, but underground Greek-like organizations still exist. The Colby Mules field thirty-two NCAA Division III athletic teams (16 men's, 15 women's, 1 co-ed) as well as extensive intramural and club sports programs. An incredible one-third of undergraduates are members of a varsity athletic team. Of the one hundred student-run clubs and activities, the Colby Outing Club has the largest membership, catering to an outdoorsy student body. Wildlife trails and a pond perfect for ice skating are only two of the many natural treasures found on the school's 714-acre campus. In fact, the outdoor life is impossible to avoid as all freshmen participate in an outdoor bonding experience prior to the start of the fall semester. Manmade features of note include three libraries, the Colby College Art Museum that features more than 6,000 works, and an Olympic-size pool. Getting to major cities from Colby will require the use of planes, trains, or automobiles. Portland, Maine, is seventy-eight miles from the college, Boston is 180 miles away, and New York City is a lengthy 390-mile trip.

Career Services

DavisConnects, the office that provides Colby students with career counseling, internship procurement, and facilitates employer recruiting features eight full-time professional staff members and a student-to-advisor ratio of 240:1. That figure is significantly better than average compared to the other institutions included in this book. Career services staff members do an excellent job of directly engaging the undergraduate population, reaching roughly 1,200 students per year in more than 3,300 counseling sessions. The office also runs a job shadowing program, hosts an interview boot camp, and the CampusTap program that hooks undergraduate students up with alumni-parent mentors in their fields of interest.

Due to its small size and remote location, Colby hosts an annual joint career fair with fellow elite Maine-based schools Bowdoin and Bates. However, many companies do host information sessions directly with Colby undergrads, and those employers include Google, Prudential, Epic, and Citigroup. DavisConnects has increased its number of credited internship opportunities in recent years, now facilitating close to 300 summer/winter experiences at Lockheed Martin, Goldman Sachs, Citigroup, Time, Massachusetts General Hospital, and others. Organizations that have formal partnerships with DavisConnects include PwC, Goldman Sachs, Accenture, Hearst Magazines, the US Department of State, and IBM. Overall, with strong graduate school advising, employer relations, and job placement rates, Colby's career services receive high marks from our staff.

E-mail: admissions@colby.edu | Website: www.colby.edu

Professional Outcomes

More than 55 percent of graduates have already secured gainful employment by the time they receive their diplomas. Within six months of graduation 95 percent have either obtained jobs or are enrolled full-time in a graduate program. Over one-quarter of graduates enter the financial industry, 19 percent start careers in education, with government/nonprofit, STEM, and health- care work next in popularity. Organizations hiring recent Colby grads were an eclectic bunch that included Teach for America, Barclays, Harvard Medical School, HBO, Deutsch Bank, and the United States Olympic Committee. The median income for a Colby graduate by age thirty-four is $59,000, which places it slightly behind Bowdoin and slightly ahead of Bates in the Maine liberal arts pecking order.

Medical school results have fluctuated over the past five years with acceptance rates between 48 percent and 81 percent. In that time multiple graduates have enrolled at prestigious medical schools including Tufts University School of Medicine, Emory University School of Medicine, Dartmouth Medical School, and University of Michigan Medical School. Overall, the five-year average for the medical school acceptance rate is double the national average. Over 80 percent of law school applicants also find success. Law schools where multiple recent alumni have studied include the University of Pennsylvania, Georgetown University, Boston College, and Cornell University.

Admission

In 2018, the number of applicants to Colby hit 12,313, a 10 percent increase over the previous year, and 2017 applications had seen a 14 percent spike from 2016. Such has been the pattern at Colby in recent years. A decade ago, Colby attracted fewer than 5,000 applicants and had an acceptance rate greater than 30 percent. The Class of 2014 enjoyed a 28 percent acceptance rate. In stark contrast, those seeking a place in the Class of 2022 were accepted at a paltry 13 percent clip. The average standardized test scores of this cohort were a 1490 SAT with a 33 ACT, and 90 percent of students graduated in the top 10 percent of their high school class. Just four years ago, a 1430 SAT/32 ACT would have placed you in the 75th percentile of attending students.

Among the factors rated as most important by the admissions committee are rigor of secondary curriculum, grades, recommendations, and character/personal qualities. In the fall of 2018 Colby announced it would become a test-optional institution. Serious applicants should strongly consider early decision as the ED rounds usually allow more generous acceptance rates, often more than three times as high as the regular round. The Class of 2022 was comprised of 51 percent ED-round applicants, and the acceptance rate was 38 percent versus 11 percent for those in the regular cycle.

Colby has become exponentially more competitive in recent years and shows no sign of slowing down. Applicants that would have been accepted a mere five years ago may quickly end up on the rejection pile. Those dead-set on Colby should apply early to gain a much-needed edge in this now hypercompetitive admissions process.

Worth Your Money?

While priced at the level one would expect for a premier New England liberal arts school—the current cost of attendance is $73,600—Colby College is generous when it comes to need-based financial aid. In fact, all undergraduates with demonstrated financial need—approximately 46 percent of Colby's student body-- have the full amount of their need met, with the annual grant averaging more than $53,000. Those grants are balanced by the many wealthy families who send their children to the college and pay full price for the pleasure. It is estimated that slightly more than half of the student body comes from families placing in the top 5 percent of incomes. That makes possible the school's new policy that says, "Families with a total household income of $60,000 or less and typical assets may expect a parent or guardian contribution of $0." Overall, given its excellent reputation and generous need-based aid, Colby proves a sound investment for most.

FINANCIAL
Institutional Type: Private
In-State Tuition: $54,870
Out-of-State Tuition: $54,870
Room & Board: $14,720
Required Fees: $2,410
Books & Supplies: $800

Avg. Need-Based Aid: $53,497
Avg. % of Need Met: 100%

Avg. Merit-Based Aid: $0
% Receiving Merit-Based Aid: 0%

Avg. Cumulative Debt: $24,437
% of Students Borrowing: 25%

CAREER
Who Recruits
1. CGI
2. Market Axess
3. Analysis Group
4. Ocean Spray
5. Boston Medical

Notable Internships
1. Morgan Stanley
2. Boston Red Sox
3. Vertex Pharaceuticals

Top Industries
1. Business
2. Education
3. Operations
4. Research
5. Social Services

Top Employers
1. Fidelity Investments
2. Morgan Stanley
3. Goldman Sachs
4. Massachusetts General Hospital
5. Google

Where Alumni Work
1. Boston
2. New York City
3. Lewiston, ME
4. Portland, ME
5. Washington, DC

Median Earnings
College Scorecard (Early Career): $58,100
EOP (Early Career): $59,200
PayScale (Mid-Career): $103,300

RANKINGS
Forbes: 75
Money: 124
U.S. News: 11, Liberal Arts Colleges
Wall Street Journal/THE: 71
Washington Monthly: 37, Liberal Arts Colleges

#CollegesWorthYourMoney

Colgate University

Hamilton, New York | Admissions Phone: 315-228-7401

ADMISSION
Admission Rate: 25%
Admission Rate - Men: 23%
Admission Rate - Women: 27%
EA Admission Rate: Not Offered
ED Admission Rate: 41%
Admission Rate (5-Year Trend): -2%
ED Admission Rate (5-Year Trend): -6%
% of Admits Attending (Yield): 34%
Transfer Admission Rate: 22%

Offered Wait List: 1,788
Accepted Wait List: 1,007
Admitted Wait List: 0

SAT Reading/Writing (Middle 50%): 650-730
SAT Math (Middle 50%): 670-780
ACT Composite (Middle 50%): 31-34
Testing Policy: ACT/SAT Required
SAT Superscore: Yes
ACT Superscore: Yes

% Graduated in Top 10% of HS Class: 77%
% Graduated in Top 25% of HS Class: 94%
% Graduated in Top 50% of HS Class: 100%

ENROLLMENT
Total Undergraduate Enrollment: 2,958
% Part-Time: 1%
% Male: 45%
% Female: 55%
% Out-of-State: 74%
% Fraternity: 11%
% Sorority: 19%
% On-Campus (Freshman): 100%
% On-Campus (All Undergraduate): 92%

% African-American: 5%
% Asian: 5%
% Hispanic: 9%
% White: 65%
% Other: 4%
% Race or Ethnicity Unknown: 4%
% International: 9%
% Low-Income: 12%

ACADEMICS
Student-to-Faculty Ratio: 9:1
% of Classes Under 20: 71%
% of Classes Under 40: N/A
% Full-Time Faculty: 94%
% Full-Time Faculty w/ Terminal Degree: 96%

Top Programs
Economics
English
Education Studies
History
International Relations
Neuroscience
Philosophy
Political Science

Retention Rate: 94%
4-Year Graduation Rate: 84%
6-Year Graduation Rate: 89%

Curricular Flexibility: Less Flexible
Academic Rating: ★★★★⅃

Inside the Classroom

When the sons of toothpaste/soap magnate William Colgate bailed out the penniless, struggling seminary/college known as Madison University in the late 1800s, the school had no idea that, from that point on, it would bear the family's name and rise to become one of the most respected liberal arts colleges in the country. Today, Colgate University is just that—one of the finest schools of its kind and home to approximately 2,900 high achievers in the rustic, hilly town of Hamilton, New York.

Fifty-six majors are on tap at Colgate, including all of the expected liberal arts concentrations. No matter your discipline, students must work through the extensive core curriculum. The requirements start with five classes that everyone must complete by the end of sophomore year: Legacies of the Ancient World, Challenges of Modernity, Communities and Identities, Scientific Perspectives on the World, and Global Engagements. An additional six courses from a range of the usual disciplines round out the mandated components of the curriculum as well as foreign language and physical education requirements.

With a student-faculty ratio of 9:1 and an average class size of seventeen, Colgate undergraduates work intimately with their instructors. Undoubtedly, the resulting connections help to explain the school's sterling 94-95 percent freshman retention rate. It is commonplace for Colgate students to research alongside professors. Each summer the school funds over 200 undergraduates who assist with research projects and, year-round, it maintains a useful database of professors who are seeking research across all disciplines. Raiders study abroad in overwhelming numbers with a 72 percent participation rate in one hundred programs that operate in fifty countries.

The social sciences account for 29 percent of all degrees conferred and, within that umbrella, economics, political science, and English are among the most popular and most well-regarded majors. International relations and neuroscience are also very strong. Other commonly issued degrees include biology (15 percent), psychology (7 percent), foreign languages (5 percent), and computer science (5 percent). Compared to other elite liberal arts schools, Colgate grads do not pursue competitive fellowships at a high rate. The university produces an occasional Fulbright, Gilman, Watson, Goldwater, or Critical Language Scholarship recipient, but not on the scale of many in its peer group.

Outside the Classroom

Rural Hamilton is not exactly a hotbed of activity, leading many to spend a great deal of time within the bubble of the university's grounds. Fortunately, those grounds happen to be a lush, 575-acre paradise that often receives accolades as one of the most beautiful colleges in the country. The university's eight Greek organizations, dating as far back as 1856, attract over 30 percent of the student body and play a leading role in defining the university milieu. Like many other colleges in frigid Central/Upstate New York, Colgate has, not unfairly, earned a "party school" label. The sports tradition at Colgate is rich as the Raiders field twenty-five teams that compete in NCAA Division I. The ice hockey team is particularly exceptional and has produced many NHL players. Also competing are club teams in forty sports including Aikido, juggling, and Nordic skiing. Including those who play in varsity, club, and intramural sports, a majority of undergraduates find themselves involved in some level of athletic competition. For everyone else, there are 190+ student-run organizations with a fair representation of environment-oriented clubs. That aligns with the university's status as one of the more eco-friendly campuses as it runs almost exclusively on hydroelectric power and places a strong emphasis on organic food, sustainable energy, and increasing the use of bicycles on campus.

Career Services

The Center for Career Services (CCS) is comprised of fourteen professionals with expertise in career advising, employer relations, and alumni engagement. That works out to a 206:1 student-to-advisor ratio, which is better than average compared to other schools featured in this guide. Further, this staff deploys its ample resources effectively, engaging with 90 percent of students each academic year, including 93 percent of seniors and 88 percent of freshmen.

In 2016-17, the CCS held over 10,800 individual meetings with more than 3,000 current students and recent alumni. On-campus workshops and programs attracted over 11,000 attendees. The office also excels in employer relations, having forged formal recruiting partnerships with 177 companies/hiring institutions, which leads to roughly 600 on-campus interviews per year (close to one per senior). Premier employers include many of the top banking, accounting, and consulting firms in the country. The university supplies generous funding to students who wish to take low-paying or nonpaying internships, financially supporting close to 200 students per year. Job shadowing opportunities with alumni were arranged for 322 students in 2016-17, and 4,500 jobs and internships were posted exclusively for Colgate students. Displaying proficiency in undergraduate engagement, recruiting, and generating positive graduate outcomes, Colgate's career services rates among the best anywhere in the country.

Colgate University

E-mail: admission@colgate.edu | Website: www.colgate.edu

Professional Outcomes

Nine months after graduation only a few Colgate alumni are still looking for work; in 2017, that group represented less than 1 percent of the graduating class. A substantial 84 percent had already landed full-time jobs. Business, education, sales, and finance are the most commonly entered sectors, in that order. Employers hiring the most Colgate grads included Bank of America Merrill Lynch, IBM, EY, Sloan Kettering Cancer Center, Massachusetts General Hospital, and the NIH. Including alumni of all ages, the strongest concentrations of Raiders can be found roaming the corporate offices of Google, Goldman Sachs, JPMorgan Chase & Co., Deloitte, Citi, UBS, PwC, and Amazon. At age thirty-four the alumni's median earnings were $71,500, comparable to other elite private universities such as Wake Forest, Bucknell, and Boston College. A sizable portion of alumni set up shop in the Greater New York City area. Boston and DC are the next most popular locales.

In 2017, a healthy 85 percent of law school applicants were accepted into one of their target institutions. The medical school numbers were even more impressive with 100 percent of graduating seniors (who were recommended by the school) gaining acceptance into at least one med school. The other most commonly pursued areas of graduate study are biology, business, engineering, public affairs and policy, and the social and behavioral sciences. Over the last four years the most frequently attended graduate schools were primarily elite institutions that included Boston College, Boston University, Columbia, Cornell, Georgetown, NYU, Northeastern, and the University of Pennsylvania.

Admission

Colgate hit an all-time high in the number of applications received in 2018. The 9,705 applicants represented a 13 percent increase over the previous year. The acceptance rate for a spot in the Class of 2022 was 25 percent, down from 28 percent the previous year. The average standardized test scores of enrolled students in the Class of 2022 were 1402 on the SAT and 32 on the ACT; and unusual for an East Coast school, two-thirds of applicants submitted ACT results. The average unweighted GPA was 3.72. Among freshmen in the 2018-19 school year, 77 percent finished in the top 10 percent of their high school class while 94 percent were in the top 25 percent.

The admissions office ranks only three factors as being "very important": rigor of coursework, GPA, and class rank. Standardized test scores are included in the next tier of factors, however students who gain acceptance tend to score well. Though Colgate claims that demonstrated interest is not a factor, 48 percent of the Class of 2022 was admitted through early decision, so the school does "want you to want them." Those who applied early in 2018 got in at a far more generous 41 percent acceptance rate than those who applied in the regular cycle (23 percent). Children of alumni, so-called legacies, obtained an even more favorable 47 percent. Over the past decade Colgate's admit rate has held fairly steady, but on the metrics of class rank and standardized tests scores, the average admitted student possesses superior credentials to Raiders of the recent past.

Worth Your Money?

Tax return data suggests that, along with schools such as Colorado College, Trinity College, and Washington University in St. Louis, Colgate enrolls the highest percentage of students from the "top 1 percent." It's no wonder the average amount of debt accrued by its graduates is lower than the national average. While the majority of students come from upper-income homes, those from less-fortunate backgrounds are showered with need-based aid. The 35 percent of undergraduates who qualify receive $55k per year, meeting 100 percent of their demonstrated need. One way or another, people are pleased with their decision to invest their time and money in Colgate University.

FINANCIAL
Institutional Type: Private
In-State Tuition: $57,695
Out-of-State Tuition: $57,695
Room & Board: $14,540
Required Fees: $350
Books & Supplies: $1,040

Avg. Need-Based Aid: $55,163
Avg. % of Need Met: 100%

Avg. Merit-Based Aid: $0
% Receiving Merit-Based Aid: 0%

Avg. Cumulative Debt: $24,243
% of Students Borrowing: 32%

CAREER
Who Recruits
1. NYU Langhorne Medical Center
2. Revlon
3. Guidepoint Global
4. AlphaSights
5. Zipcar

Notable Internships
1. ESPN
2. Wells Fargo
3. Barclay's

Top Industries
1. Business
2. Education
3. Operations
4. Finance
5. Sales

Top Employers
1. EY
2. Morgan Stanley
3. Google
4. Goldman Sachs
5. JPMorgan Chase

Where Alumni Work
1. New York City
2. Boston
3. Washington, DC
4. San Francisco
5. Syracuse, NY

Median Earnings
College Scorecard (Early Career): $63,600
EOP (Early Career): $71,500
PayScale (Mid-Career): $130,600

RANKINGS
Forbes: 46
Money: 54
U.S. News: 17 (T), Liberal Arts Colleges
Wall Street Journal/THE: 48
Washington Monthly: 18, Liberal Arts Colleges

#CollegesWorthYourMoney

ADMISSION
Admission Rate: 50%
Admission Rate - Men: 48%
Admission Rate - Women: 51%
EA Admission Rate: Not Offered
ED Admission Rate: 60%
Admission Rate (5-Year Trend): +7%
ED Admission Rate (5-Year Trend): -1%
% of Admits Attending (Yield): 23%
Transfer Admission Rate: 45%

Offered Wait List: 2,207
Accepted Wait List: 602
Admitted Wait List: 8

SAT Reading/Writing (Middle 50%): 580-670
SAT Math (Middle 50%): 580-680
ACT Composite (Middle 50%): 25-30
Testing Policy: ACT/SAT Required
SAT Superscore: Yes
ACT Superscore: Yes

% Graduated in Top 10% of HS Class: 37%
% Graduated in Top 25% of HS Class: 75%
% Graduated in Top 50% of HS Class: 97%

ENROLLMENT
Total Undergraduate Enrollment: 7,048
% Part-Time: 3%
% Male: 43%
% Female: 57%
% Out-of-State: 6%
% Fraternity: 15%
% Sorority: 13%
% On-Campus (Freshman): 90%
% On-Campus (All Undergraduate): 54%

% African-American: 6%
% Asian: 12%
% Hispanic: 13%
% White: 64%
% Other: 0%
% Race or Ethnicity Unknown: 4%
% International: 0%
% Low-Income: 19%

ACADEMICS
Student-to-Faculty Ratio: 13:1
% of Classes Under 20: 42%
% of Classes Under 40: 97%
% Full-Time Faculty: 43%
% Full-Time Faculty w/ Terminal Degree: 91%

Top Programs
Accounting
Business Administration
Biology
Criminology
Communication Studies
Elementary Education
Nursing

Retention Rate: 93%
4-Year Graduation Rate: 76%
6-Year Graduation Rate: 86%

Curricular Flexibility: Somewhat Flexible
Academic Rating: ★★★⯪

Inside the Classroom
Let's lead off with a telling factoid: The freshman-to-sophomore retention rate at the College of New Jersey is 94 percent, better than at the majority of selective private schools. As one of only six public colleges in the country to maintain a four-year graduation rate above 70 percent, the school is in the esteemed company of such institutions as UVA, Michigan, and UNC-Chapel Hill. Central Jersey may not draw a flood of applicants from the far reaches of the globe (only 6 percent of the student population comes from out of state), but the TCNJ, a midsize state school with 6,700+ undergraduate students, is simply one the best bargains you can find in the Northeastern United States.

There are more than fifty majors, but whether you're studying art history or computer science, there are an identical series of general requirements known as Liberal Learning awaiting you, beginning as a freshman. As part of the Intellectual and Scholarly Growth phase of your education, new arrivals participate in a First-Year Program, a seminar-style course centered on one of seventy engaging topics. Students also complete an online, not-for-credit course on Information Literacy. A second language requirement exists for the School of Humanities and Social Sciences and selected programs with the arts and sciences, business, and science schools. While you can test out of the introductory course, three writing-intensive classes are on the menu, including a senior capstone. Additionally, you must choose a collective eight courses that fulfill your breadth requirements in the areas of the arts and humanities, social sciences and history, and natural science and quantitative reasoning.

TCNJ sports a 13:1 student-to-faculty ratio, an average class size of twenty-one, and 81 percent of sections contain fewer than thirty students. While you won't find many seminar-style courses with single-digit enrollments, there are plenty of ways to personally connect with faculty thanks to the school's serious commitment to facilitating undergraduate research. In fact, the Council on Undergraduate Research awarded TCNJ its signature honor, the Campus-Wide Award for Undergraduate Research Accomplishment. In addition to plenty of research opportunities in the hard sciences, this school has invested in specialized facilities that include twenty psychology research labs, a digital humanities lab, and a fully equipped quantitative studies lab for criminology and sociology students. The College of New Jersey may not attract many from outside its state borders, but it certainly helps its own expand their global horizons as 30 percent of undergrads participate in one of 500 study abroad programs.

Twenty-percent of degrees conferred are in education as many attend TCNJ to become teachers. The School of Education is widely considered the finest in the state. Next in popularity are business/marketing (16 percent), psychology (9 percent), engineering (8 percent), the social sciences (7 percent) and biology (6 percent). Jersey- and New York-based employers think highly of the school that also has strong programs in biology, criminology, accounting, and nursing. Recent TCNJ students have won or placed as finalists for Fulbright, Marshall, Gates, and Truman awards. Two 2019 graduates won Goldwater Scholarships, and five 2018 graduates were awarded National Science Foundation Graduate Research Fellowships.

Outside the Classroom
While only 55 percent of the undergraduate student body reside on the 289-acre, well-maintained grounds of this suburban campus in Ewing, The College of New Jersey's fourteen residence halls do accommodate 95 percent of freshmen; housing is guaranteed for a student's first two years only. Greek life does have a noticeable presence on campus with 14 percent of men pledging fraternities and 11 percent of women entering sororities. Aikido, knitting, and broadcasting on WTSR 91.3 are only three of the diverse 150+ active clubs available. A strong Division III athletics program features nine men's and nine women's teams that, since 1979, have captured forty team and forty-nine individual NCAA championships. The Student Recreation Center features an indoor track, tennis courts, and a dance studio for those wanting to stay in shape, and there are plenty of intramural sports on tap at that same location. TCNJ is only five miles from the state capital of Trenton, ten miles from Princeton, and an hour's drive from Philly or New York City.

Career Services
A small office, the Career Center at the College of New Jersey employs only six full-time professional staff, not counting secretaries, office assistants, interns, or peer career educators who assist with things like resume reviews and career fair organization. The student-to-counselor ratio of 1,100:1 isn't terribly strong, but it's clearly enough staffing to make plenty of positive things happen for the school's undergraduates.

Over 400 employers recruit on campus, a phenomenal number given that there are only 6,600 undergrads. A solid 71.6 percent of surveyed graduates reported having at least one internship with 63.1 percent participating in an internship for two or more semesters, and 36.2 percent securing a paid position following their internship.

In large part due to the efforts of the Career Center, 30 percent of graduates say the school did an excellent job in preparing them for entering the workforce, 44 percent rate the center's efforts as "above average," and fewer than 5 percent of respondents gave a mark of "below average." The large presence of graduates, recent and otherwise, in the offices of many top companies and banks around the country speaks to the superb employer engagement efforts of this school.

Professional Outcomes

Checking in with TCNJ grads one year after receiving their degrees, a near-perfect 98.4 percent had entered the working world or started an advanced degree. The list of companies employing significant numbers of Class of 2017 alumni includes Johnson and Johnson (14), JP Morgan Chase & Co., (11), Bank of America (11), Bloomberg LP (8), AT&T (7), Emergency Medical Associates/EmCare (7), EY (6), and PricewaterhouseCoopers (6). Factoring in all alumni, the school also has a huge presence within Verizon, Merrill Lynch, Merck, and Bristol-Meyers Squibb. The starting salary after exiting the College of New Jersey was an impressive $56,200, more than 12 percent higher than the national average for college grads. School of Arts & Communication grads earned $47,350 while School of Business degree-holders took home $60,050. The most popular geographic destinations were New Jersey (65.5 percent), New York (18.1 percent), and Pennsylvania (5.7 percent).

The most frequently attended graduate schools by members of the Class of 2017 were TCNJ (59), Rutgers University (35), University of Pennsylvania (7), New York University (7), Columbia University (7), Penn State University (6), Monmouth University (5), and Johns Hopkins University (5). Class of 2017 graduates entered law schools including William & Mary, Hofstra, Penn State, and Rutgers. Members of the same cohort went on to attend an array of excellent medical schools including Johns Hopkins, the Icahn School of Medicine at Mt. Sanai, NYU, Drexel, and Penn State University. Many also attend Rutgers via the 7-Year Combined BS/MD Program with Rutgers New Jersey Medical School. Overall, undergraduates enjoy a 65 percent medical school acceptance rate, more than 20 points higher than the national average.

Admission

The College of New Jersey is a rare school that isn't terribly hard to get into—the acceptance rate for 2018-19 freshman was right at 50 percent—but it provides a superior and supportive academic experience to its undergraduates. Thirty-seven percent of the Class of 2022 placed in the top 10 percent of their high school class, three-quarters were in the top 25 percent, and 97 percent were in the top 50 percent. The mid-50 percent standardized test score ranges were 25-30 on the ACT and 1160-1350 on the SAT. In a higher education world where many schools have experienced massive spikes in selectivity in recent years, TCNJ remains fairly steady; the profile of an accepted student five years ago is similar to today's freshman.

At the top of the list of "very important" admissions factors sits participation in a rigorous course load, class rank, standardized test scores, extracurricular activities and, most interestingly, volunteer work. The essay, teacher recommendations, talent/ability, character/personal qualities, and state residency are all in the next tier of "important" factors. However, given that the overwhelming majority of TCNJ students come from inside New Jersey, out-of-state applicants should enjoy a slight advantage. This is reality is made more evident by the fact that TCNJ offers an application fee waiver to all students applying from out of state. Finally, applying Early Decision may also offer an edge--of the 686 submitting ED applications in 2018, three-fifths were accepted. Those accepted through early decision comprised 27 percent of the entire freshman class.

Worth Your Money?

Garden State residents will pay around $17,000 per year in tuition and fees, and while the school isn't as cheap as it used to be (what is?), TCNJ represents an exceptional bargain for an East Coast public school with a tremendously successful alumni base. Few out-of-state students seek out this college, but the price is not unreasonable, particularly for those wishing to study business or a STEM field.

FINANCIAL
Institutional Type: Public
In-State Tuition: $16,942
Out-of-State Tuition: $28,921
Room & Board: $13,964
Required Fees: N/A
Books & Supplies: N/A

Avg. Need-Based Aid: $11,889
Avg. % of Need Met: 40%

Avg. Merit-Based Aid: $5,648
% Receiving Merit-Based Aid: 38%

Avg. Cumulative Debt: $37,787
% of Students Borrowing: 62%

CAREER
Who Recruits
1. Target
2. withum
3. NJM Insurance Group
4. Cenlar
5. Johnson & Johnson

Notable Internships
1. U.S. Department of Education
2. Prudential Financial
3. Lockheed Martin

Top Industries
1. Education
2. Business
3. Operations
4. Healthcare
5. Sales

Top Employers
1. Johnson & Johnson
2. Merrill Lynch
3. Bristol-Myers Squibb
4. Merck
5. Prudential Financial

Where Alumni Work
1. New York City
2. Philadelphia
3. Washington, DC
4. Boston
5. Los Angeles

Median Earnings
College Scorecard (Early Career): $58,500
EOP (Early Career): $60,100
PayScale (Mid-Career): $101,800

RANKINGS
Forbes: 149
Money: 48
U.S. News: 4, Regional North
Wall Street Journal/THE: 266 (T)
Washington Monthly: N/A

#CollegesWorthYourMoney

College of the Holy Cross

Worcester, Massachusetts | Admissions Phone: 508-793-2443

ADMISSION
Admission Rate: 38%
Admission Rate - Men: 43%
Admission Rate - Women: 34%
EA Admission Rate: Not Offered
ED Admission Rate: 81%
Admission Rate (5-Year Trend): +5%
ED Admission Rate (5-Year Trend): +18%
% of Admits Attending (Yield): 32%
Transfer Admission Rate: 37%

Offered Wait List: 1,581
Accepted Wait List: 752
Admitted Wait List: 0

SAT Reading/Writing (Middle 50%): 640-710
SAT Math (Middle 50%): 640-710
ACT Composite (Middle 50%): 28-32
Testing Policy: Test Optional
SAT Superscore: Yes
ACT Superscore: Yes

% Graduated in Top 10% of HS Class: 58%
% Graduated in Top 25% of HS Class: 88%
% Graduated in Top 50% of HS Class: 100%

ENROLLMENT
Total Undergraduate Enrollment: 3,128
% Part-Time: 1%
% Male: 48%
% Female: 52%
% Out-of-State: 58%
% Fraternity: Not Offered
% Sorority: Not Offered
% On-Campus (Freshman): 99%
% On-Campus (All Undergraduate): 90%

% African-American: 4%
% Asian: 4%
% Hispanic: 10%
% White: 71%
% Other: 3%
% Race or Ethnicity Unknown: 4%
% International: 4%
% Low-Income: 15%

ACADEMICS
Student-to-Faculty Ratio: 10:1
% of Classes Under 20: 60%
% of Classes Under 40: 98%
% Full-Time Faculty: 88%
% Full-Time Faculty w/ Terminal Degree: 96%

Top Programs
Biology
Chemistry
Economics
English
History
Political Science
Psychology
Sociology

Retention Rate: 95%
4-Year Graduation Rate: 88%
6-Year Graduation Rate: 92%

Curricular Flexibility: Somewhat Flexible
Academic Rating: ★★★★✔

Inside the Classroom
The oldest Catholic college in all of New England, the College of the Holy Cross in Worcester, Massachusetts, offers an exceptional liberal arts education with a strong Jesuit influence that permeates the service-oriented undergraduate student body of just under 2,900. The college offers thirty traditional majors as well as additional subjects in which one can pursue a student-designed major. Hands-on learning, interdisciplinary connections, a genuine quest for meaning and value, and faculty guidance that extends beyond the classroom are all staples of academic life for all Crusaders.

So-called "common requirements" that must be fulfilled by all undergraduate students is a comprehensive but straightforward list. Mandatory areas of study include one course each in religion, philosophical studies, arts, literature, history, and cross-cultural studies. Two courses are required in language studies, social science, and natural and mathematical sciences. All freshmen complete a year-long seminar called Montserrat that is centered on an interdisciplinary topic and designed to help students "develop broad foundational skills, including critical thinking, strong writing, and effective communication."

The average class size is a manageable nineteen students, and 60 percent of courses have enrollments lower than that. An undergraduate-only institution, Holy Cross offers ample individualized attention and guidance from faculty. Each year one hundred students participate in the intensive Weiss Summer Research Program that offers STEM majors the opportunity for one-on-one mentorship from a professor. Across all disciplines, research apprenticeships are available to undergrads as early as the sophomore year. Study abroad figures are relatively modest as roughly 300 students travel each year to one of fifty approved locales.

There are no majors that undergrads flock to in overwhelming numbers, but the most popular are economics (14 percent), psychology (12 percent), political science (11 percent), history (7 percent), and English (7 percent). All of those popular departments also rank well nationally. Biology and chemistry are also very strong. Highly competitive postgraduate fellowships are frequently pursued by seniors. In fact, Holy Cross is one of the nation's top Fulbright producers with ninety-three such scholars named since 2005, and seven students and alums took home the award in 2019 alone.

Outside the Classroom
Thanks to a campus regularly voted as one of the country's most beautiful, few undergraduates wish to flee the grounds. Guaranteed housing is available for all four years in one of eleven residence halls, and 90 percent of students elect to live in college-owned housing. The nine campus eateries also receive acclaim and leave students with little reason to seek off-campus dining options. Those seeking the typical university experience of Greek parties and big-time athletics will find themselves batting .500. There are no fraternities or sororities on campus, but with twenty-seven Division I squads, twenty-two club teams, and eleven intramural sports on the menu it seems like most of the student body participates in some form of athletic competition. The Hart Center is replete with amenities including a six-lane swimming pool, ice rink, and a 2,800-square-foot facility dedicated to cardiovascular and strength training. There are 103 student organizations, including a healthy dose of clubs in the performing arts, service, and multicultural realms. While Worcester isn't a town that teems with alluring activities, the college is located only forty-four miles west of Boston and sixty-one miles northeast of Hartford.

Career Services
The Center for Career Development (CCD) is staffed by eight professional employees (not counting office assistants), resulting in a 377:1 student-to-advisor ratio that is in the average range when compared with other schools featured in this guide. The CCD believes in a "three-stage model of career development: self-assessment, exploration, and implementation." Individualized attention is available to undergraduates at each stage of their education, whether it involves discussing the results of an interest inventory, preparing a resume, engaging in a mock interview, or applying to graduate/professional school.

Fall and spring career fairs attract approximately sixty employers and 300 students. Well-known employers such as City Year, GE, EY, PepsiCo, and the FBI are regular attendees. The office excels in coordinating student internships as an impressive 73 percent of graduates end up with at least one such experience. In 2017-18, the school ponied up $209,000 to help defray costs of eighty-two undergrads completing unpaid summer internships. Students who completed internships enjoyed better job placement rates and higher starting salaries than those who did not. Through the Career Advisor Network current students can link up to alumni in fields of interest to arrange a job-shadowing experience or to receive career advice. Thanks to a high level of student engagement and strong employment/graduate school results (more on this in a moment), the Center for Career Development is performing admirably on behalf of its undergraduates.

Professional Outcomes

Seven months after moving their tassels to the left, 72 percent of the Class of 2018 were employed, 14 percent were in graduate school, 7 percent were engaged in volunteer work, and only 1 percent were still seeking full-time employment; the overall success rate was 97 percent. The industries drawing the most Holy Cross grads were health care (17 percent), financial services (16 percent), technology (8 percent), government/politics/law (7 percent), and accounting (7 percent). Organizations employing more than one recent graduate include Fidelity Investments, JP Morgan, Goldman Sachs, Massachusetts General Hospital, Deloitte, EY, PwC, Oracle, and Dell. Large numbers of alumni also can be found at State Street, Morgan Stanley, and the Dana Farber Cancer Institute. The median salary for graduates is $51,600 and varies greatly by industry. Those in finance enjoyed median starting salaries of $67,000 while those entering health care, government, or education took home $35-42k. New England is the most popular home, keeping 56 percent of grads in the area with the Mid-Atlantic region soaking up an additional 30 percent. Boston and New York City are the two most common destinations.

Among those enrolled in graduate school, 19 percent were in law school, 13 percent were pursuing degrees in a health profession, and 12 percent were in PhD programs. Boston College and Fordham are among the most frequently attended law schools. Recent graduates have earned spots in medical schools such as Tufts and acceptances into dental school at the University of Pennsylvania and Boston University. Overall, Holy Cross graduates enjoy 90 percent acceptance rates to both law and medical schools. Grads have been accepted into masters and doctoral programs at elite schools including Georgetown, Johns Hopkins, Princeton, Harvard, the University of Chicago, and Columbia.

Admission

A competitive pool of more than 7,000 applicants for a place in the Holy Cross Class of 2022 encountered a 38 percent acceptance rate. This is in the same ballpark as the acceptances rates over the last five years. Holy Cross is test-optional and, unlike many other highly selective test- optional schools, attending freshmen actually submitted test-free applications. Of the Class of 2022, only 46 percent submitted SAT scores, and 27 percent submitted ACT scores. Given that a fair number of applicants are likely to have submitted both, it is reasonable to assume that a healthy percentage of the class were admitted sans standardized tests scores. Among those that did submit scores, the mid-50 percent range on the SAT was 1280-1420 and 28-32 on the ACT. Crusaders finished in the top 10 percent of their high school class at a 58 percent clip, and 88 percent fell within the top quarter.

According to the admissions committee, six factors rise above the rest when evaluating applicants: rigor of secondary school record, GPA, essays, recommendations, the interview, and character/personal qualities. Extracurricular activities and talent/ability are the only other factors labeled as being "important." Those dead-set on attending this school shouldn't think twice about applying early decision as the ED acceptance rate climbed as high as 81 percent last cycle. (The regular round acceptance rate was 35 percent.) Early decision admits comprised 44 percent of the Class of 2022. The two most notable items related to admissions at the College of the Holy Cross are its test-optional admissions and incredibly generous ED acceptance rate. Serious applicants are advised to strongly consider the latter.

Worth Your Money?

Holy Cross helps to mitigate the impact of its $71,710 sticker price by meeting 100 percent of demonstrated need for every single student who qualifies for financial aid. All told, 53 percent of students qualify for an average grant of $36,173, making the overall cost sting a bit less. Merit aid is awarded to only 16 percent of the student body, so if you don't obtain need-based aid, you're likely to be paying a large portion of the 300k four-year bill. Holy Cross is an excellent school, but you won't get a huge income boost from attending (median salaries are right around average), so you may not want to go deep into debt to afford a full-price tab, especially if you're considering a lower-paying field.

FINANCIAL
Institutional Type: Private
In-State Tuition: $54,050
Out-of-State Tuition: $54,050
Room & Board: $15,070
Required Fees: $690
Books & Supplies: $1,000

Avg. Need-Based Aid: $36,173
Avg. % of Need Met: 100%

Avg. Merit-Based Aid: $15,200
% Receiving Merit-Based Aid: 16%

Avg. Cumulative Debt: $25,260
% of Students Borrowing: 60%

CAREER
Who Recruits
1. Dell
2. General Electric
3. Peace Corps
4. Wayfair
5. Deloitte

Notable Internships
1. National Football League
2. McCann
3. MetLife

Top Industries
1. Business
2. Education
3. Finance
4. Operations
5. Sales

Top Employers
1. Fidelity Investments
2. PwC
3. Deloitte
4. EY
5. Morgan Stanley

Where Alumni Work
1. Boston
2. New York City
3. India
4. Washington, DC
5. United Kingdom

Median Earnings
College Scorecard (Early Career): $71,000
EOP (Early Career): $71,900
PayScale (Mid-Career): $114,600

RANKINGS
Forbes: 77
Money: 43
U.S. News: 27 (T), Liberal Arts Colleges
Wall Street Journal/THE: 125
Washington Monthly: 13, Liberal Arts Colleges

#CollegesWorthYourMoney

ADMISSION

Admission Rate: 37%
Admission Rate - Men: 42%
Admission Rate - Women: 34%
EA Admission Rate: Not Offered
ED Admission Rate: 58%
Admission Rate (5-Year Trend): +4%
ED Admission Rate (5-Year Trend): +11%
% of Admits Attending (Yield): 29%
Transfer Admission Rate: 52%

Offered Wait List: 4,133
Accepted Wait List: 2,172
Admitted Wait List: 94

SAT Reading/Writing (Middle 50%): 660-730
SAT Math (Middle 50%): 650-760
ACT Composite (Middle 50%): 30-33
Testing Policy: ACT/SAT Required
SAT Superscore: Yes
ACT Superscore: Yes

% Graduated in Top 10% of HS Class: 77%
% Graduated in Top 25% of HS Class: 95%
% Graduated in Top 50% of HS Class: 99%

ENROLLMENT

Total Undergraduate Enrollment: 6,377
% Part-Time: 1%
% Male: 42%
% Female: 58%
% Out-of-State: 31%
% Fraternity: 28%
% Sorority: 29%
% On-Campus (Freshman): 100%
% On-Campus (All Undergraduate): 71%

% African-American: 7%
% Asian: 8%
% Hispanic: 9%
% White: 59%
% Other: 5%
% Race or Ethnicity Unknown: 6%
% International: 6%
% Low-Income: 11%

ACADEMICS

Student-to-Faculty Ratio: 12:1
% of Classes Under 20: 47%
% of Classes Under 40: 86%
% Full-Time Faculty: 70%
% Full-Time Faculty w/ Terminal Degree: 96%

Top Programs

Accounting
Business
Biology
Chemistry
Government
History
International Relations
Public Policy

Retention Rate: 95%
4-Year Graduation Rate: 85%
6-Year Graduation Rate: 91%

Curricular Flexibility: Somewhat Flexible
Academic Rating: ★★★★

Inside the Classroom

Brimming with tradition, the College of William & Mary is one of the oldest public institutions in the country (some contend the oldest), the alma mater of three US presidents, and a school that has long been a member of the "Public Ivy" club. Roughly two-thirds of the 6,300+ undergraduates on this spectacularly beautiful Williamsburg campus hail from in-state, and members of the student body known as "the Tribe" tend to be an intellectual and passionate lot who adore their school. Of W&M's nearly 100,000 living alumni, you'll rarely meet one who doesn't have a strong affinity for their school.

Forty undergraduate programs are available with the most popular being business, psychology, economics, biology, and government. All undergraduates must work through the College Curriculum, the school's liberal arts core including two first-year seminars, four COLL 200 courses covering a variety of topics, COLL 300 (that often involves studying abroad), and COLL 400 as a senior, which requires the production of original research. Additional requirements include taking courses in three "knowledge domains" and demonstrating proficiency in mathematics and foreign language.

William & Mary has an 11:1 student-to-faculty ratio. Class sizes are rarely tiny seminars, but close to 50 percent do enroll fewer than twenty students, and only 14 percent contain more than fifty. An extremely high percentage of undergrads study abroad for a semester; by graduation, roughly half of the class has done so, traveling to one of more than sixty countries. Undergraduate research opportunities are widely available. In the Chemistry Department, for example, 80-90 percent of students complete independent/professor-assisted research with many becoming coauthors of studies alongside faculty. Across the college an average 85 percent of undergraduates participate in research each year.

Among the college's most notable academic programs are (1) government and (2) international relations, both of which serve as pipelines to Washington, DC, employers. The Mason School of Business is highly regarded in the corporate world. With a notable service-minded ethos, William & Mary is the top producer of Peace Corps volunteers among midsize universities. In 2018, the college had thirteen Fulbright Scholarship winners, most in the state of Virginia. However, the school doesn't take home other prestigious scholarships in large numbers.

Outside the Classroom

The campus is large and lush with over 1,200 acres, including an amphitheater, Lake Matoaka, and College Woods, the latter two of which can be freely enjoyed by nature-loving students. William and Mary's grounds easily make any list of the most beautiful college campuses in the country. A touch under three-quarters of students live on campus, including a sizable number of Greek houses. Greek life first appeared at W&M in 1776, and the tradition is still alive and well today. Presently, 28 percent of undergrads participate with higher numbers in the school's sororities than fraternities. More than 450 student clubs in every area imaginable are available with volunteer organizations drawing large numbers—3,500+ each year. That spirit of involvement carries over into athletics as well with an 85 percent participation rate when including the school's twenty-three NCAA Division I teams and thriving intramural and club sports. Nightlife in the surrounding Williamsburg area is generally pretty tame unless you happen to be a colonial-era history buff. Most students enjoy a social life more centered around campus activities and dorm life.

Career Services

The Cohen Career Center (CCC) employs thirteen full-time staff members, not counting graduate assistants or administrative assistants, giving it a student-to-advisor ratio of 571:1, which is higher than the average school profiled in this guide. The CCC does arrange several well-attended job fairs each year including the Government & Nonprofit Career Expo that features ninety employers as well as large-scale career and internship fairs in the fall and spring that are attended by as many as 1,000 undergrads. All told, 397 employers attended William & Mary career fairs in 2018-19.

In a typical year the office conducts over 900 mock interviews, one hundred workshops, and information sessions with 125 employers. In the 2018-19 academic year 2,344 one-on-one counseling sessions were conducted with undergraduates. For those interested in graduate school, representatives from more than one hundred programs across the academic spectrum attend the annual Graduate & Professional Fair. Partnerships with Deloitte, PwC, KPMG, EY, and Accenture lead to on-campus recruiting and interviewing with those giants of the accounting and consulting fields. Close to 1,000 on-campus interviews are arranged each year with W&M seniors. A respectable 61 percent of grads participated in at least one internship, externship, or research project. The office does a solid job guiding undergraduates toward meaningful work as 88 percent found first jobs that aligned to some degree with their career goals.

Professional Outcomes

The Class of 2017 (the most recent class for which data is available) saw 60 percent of its cohort join the workforce, and 26 percent enter graduate school within six months of graduation. Over 500 employers snatched up at least one member of the Tribe. Companies hiring the highest number of grads were IBM (25), Deloitte (17), EY (12), Accenture (11), and Booz Allen Hamilton (11).

More than fifty alumni across all graduating years can be found in the corporate offices of Capital One, PwC, Microsoft, Google, Amazon, and Deloitte. Starting salaries varied significantly by industry. The average salary for those entering the world of IT/computing was over $78k, financial services was $69k, the sciences were $36k, and museums and libraries were $29k. The vast majority of alumni remain in the Mid-Atlantic region; the Northeast is a distant second.

Those opting for immediate entry into graduate school enrolled at 132 institutions. The greatest number of fresh alums stayed at their alma mater with 102 continuing their studies at William & Mary. The next most frequented universities were Virginia Commonwealth University (14), Georgetown (10), UVA (9), Eastern Virginia Medical School (8), Columbia (7), Emory (4), Virginia Tech (4), and Yale (4). Thirty-eight grads were pursuing PhDs, twenty-seven were studying to be MDs, and sixteen headed to law school. In previous years a greater number of alumni have entered JD or PhD programs. Most impressively, William & Mary graduates gain acceptance into medical school at a rate twice the national average.

Admission

Of the 14,644 applicants vying for a seat in W&M's Class of 2022, just over 5,400 received the proverbial thick envelope. That calculates to an acceptance rate of 37 percent. Like UNC-Chapel Hill, but not to nearly as extreme a degree, in-state applicants have an easier pathway to acceptance at William & Mary. The acceptance rate for out-of-state students typically runs under 30 percent while in-staters enjoy closer to a 45 percent acceptance rate. Of those who enrolled in the Class of 2022 the SAT middle-50 percent range was 1310-1490, and the ACT range was 30-33. (A far greater number of applicants submit SAT scores.) Over three-quarters of enrolled freshmen hail from the top 10 percent of their high school class, and 95 percent placed in the top quartile.

The admissions office ranks a dozen factors as being most important in the admissions process. In addition to the obvious factors of grades, test scores, and class rank, the college also prioritizes state residency status, volunteer work, work experience, character/personal qualities, and talent/ability. Applying early decision can work to your advantage as over 58 percent of ED applicants get positive results, and ED admits comprised 35 percent of the 2018-19 freshman class. The regular round acceptance rate is only 36 percent. William & Mary is a highly selective school, but even more so for non-Virginia residents. The school maintains a 65/35 split of in-state versus out-of-state students. Still, in 2018 the school accepted students from all fifty states as well as forty-eight foreign countries, so candidates with strong academic profiles can still find a home here.

Worth Your Money?

High-achieving residents of Virginia are lucky to have two Ivy-level public schools at their disposal. Like UVA, William & Mary comes at a bargain price for those living in Virginia. The cost of attendance is roughly $38,000 in state and $62,000 out of state. Almost one-fifth of the student population receives a merit aid award with an annual value of $13k. The 38 percent who receive need-based aid rarely see 100 percent of their need met, but the average grant amount of $19,108 certainly helps, particularly for those paying the in-state rate. The average amount of debt for a W&M graduate is slightly less than the national average. For in-state students attending this school is a no-brainer. Prospective out-of-state students have to factor in the amount of loans you would need and the starting salaries typical of the field you eventually wish to enter.

FINANCIAL
Institutional Type: Public
In-State Tuition: $17,434
Out-of-State Tuition: $40,089
Room & Board: $12,926
Required Fees: $6,194
Books & Supplies: $1,000

Avg. Need-Based Aid: $19,108
Avg. % of Need Met: 82%

Avg. Merit-Based Aid: $13,080
% Receiving Merit-Based Aid: 19%

Avg. Cumulative Debt: $25,409
% of Students Borrowing: 35%

CAREER
Who Recruits
1. Central Intelligence Agency
2. National Institutes of Health
3. The Carlyle Group
4. Aldi
5. Navigant Consulting

Notable Internships
1. Booz Allen Hamilton
2. Vanguard
3. NFL Films

Top Industries
1. Business
2. Education
3. Operations
4. Social Services
5. Research

Top Employers
1. Capital One
2. Booz Allen Hamilton
3. Deloitte
4. EY
5. IBM

Where Alumni Work
1. Washington, DC
2. Norfolk, VA
3. New York City
4. Richmond, VA
5. Boston

Median Earnings
College Scorecard (Early Career): $58,500
EOP (Early Career): $59,800
PayScale (Mid-Career): $108,900

RANKINGS
Forbes: 47
Money: 45
U.S. News: 40, National Universities
Wall Street Journal/THE: 79
Washington Monthly: 109, National Universities

#CollegesWorthYourMoney

Colorado College

Colorado Springs, Colorado | Admissions Phone: 719-389-6344

ADMISSION
Admission Rate: 15%
Admission Rate - Men: 16%
Admission Rate - Women: 14%
EA Admission Rate: 18%
ED Admission Rate: 27%
Admission Rate (5-Year Trend): -7%
ED Admission Rate (5-Year Trend): -6%
% of Admits Attending (Yield): 42%
Transfer Admission Rate: 11%

\# Offered Wait List: 851
\# Accepted Wait List: 244
\# Admitted Wait List: 60

SAT Reading/Writing (Middle 50%): 650-720
SAT Math (Middle 50%): 650-750
ACT Composite (Middle 50%): 29-33
Testing Policy: Test Optional
SAT Superscore: Yes
ACT Superscore: No

% Graduated in Top 10% of HS Class: 75%
% Graduated in Top 25% of HS Class: 97%
% Graduated in Top 50% of HS Class: 99%

ENROLLMENT
Total Undergraduate Enrollment: 2,114
% Part-Time: 1%
% Male: 45%
% Female: 55%
% Out-of-State: 83%
% Fraternity: 12%
% Sorority: 8%
% On-Campus (Freshman): 100%
% On-Campus (All Undergraduate): 80%

% African-American: 2%
% Asian: 5%
% Hispanic: 9%
% White: 65%
% Other: 8%
% Race or Ethnicity Unknown: 1%
% International: 9%
% Low-Income: 10%

ACADEMICS
Student-to-Faculty Ratio: 10:1
% of Classes Under 20: 73%
% of Classes Under 40: 100%
% Full-Time Faculty: 86%
% Full-Time Faculty w/ Terminal Degree: 99%

Top Programs
Art
Economics and Business
Environmental Studies
International Political Economy
Organismal Biology and Ecology
Political Science
Sociology

Retention Rate: 96%
4-Year Graduation Rate: 84%
6-Year Graduation Rate: 89%

Curricular Flexibility: Very Flexible
Academic Rating: ★★★★✦

Inside the Classroom

With the Rocky Mountains visible from Colorado College's ninety-acre campus, the school's 2,100 undergraduates find themselves in rarefied air—in more ways than one. A magnet for high-achieving, civic-minded, and generally liberally inclined young people, CC is ideally located seventy miles south of Denver and within a reasonable car ride of seven national parks and ten ski resorts. The student body is geographically diverse with about one-quarter hailing from the Northeast, one-quarter from the West Coast, and a sizable representation from the Midwest and the South.

Rather than the typical semester schedule, Colorado College operates on the "block plan," a series of eight three-and-half-week periods during which students take only one course. Requirements are broad, affording undergraduates the opportunity to chart their own course. That course, however, must stay within some boundaries that include a first-year seminar, a foreign language, as well as courses fitting under the umbrellas of global cultures, social inequality, quantitative reasoning, and scientific investigation of the natural world.

You won't find a more intimate liberal arts college than CC. Classes have a cap of twenty-five students, and no more than a handful of courses exceed that figure. The average class consists of sixteen students, and one-quarter of offerings have single-digit enrollments. Face time with your professors is a certainty as the school boasts a 10:1 student-faculty ratio. Although it does offer master's programs for teachers, this is a teaching college that focuses on undergraduate education. In faculty-wide surveys, the vast majority of professors report that quality of instruction is properly factored into their evaluations. Research opportunities are built in to the academic program as 20 percent of CC classes involve some degree of undergraduate research. Another 6 percent of students receive stipends to conduct research. Tigers appear unafraid to go into the world and immerse themselves in other cultures as a healthy 81 percent study abroad.

Regularly ranked among the top liberal arts schools in the country, Colorado College has an excellent reputation. Environmental studies, art, and sociology are considered very strong, but CC doesn't necessarily offer programs that clearly stand above the rest. In its own words, "The most popular majors at CC are those that are popular nationally." In terms of sheer volume, most degrees are conferred in the social sciences (30 percent), biology (13 percent), physical sciences (9 percent), natural resources and conservation (7 percent), and the visual and performing arts (7 percent). This institution is a regular producer of Watson and Fulbright Scholarship winners. It also ranks seventh in the nation for the number of Peace Corps volunteers produced, which is especially impressive given the modest size of each graduating class.

Outside the Classroom

Every freshman lives on Colorado College's campus, and 80 percent of the total undergraduate student body remains in school-owned housing. There is a Greek presence, but it in no way dominates the social scene. Only 12 percent of men join fraternities and 8 percent of women enter a sorority. More than 135 student clubs and organizations are available, the most popular being the Outdoor Recreation Committee. That makes sense given the natural splendor surrounding campus that is conducive to hiking, skiing, cycling, and the like. Students have the dual benefit of attending what is, technically, an urban campus situated in Colorado Springs that is, by area, the largest city in the state. Dorms, food, and campus facilities all receive generally favorable reviews from the student body. Community service projects are inclusive with an 80 percent undergraduate participation rate. While no one would mistake CC for a jock school, it does have sixteen total men's and women's sports teams competing in NCAA Division III, except for the highly competitive Division I ice hockey squad.

Career Services

The Career Center has eight full-time staff members who focus on either career advising or employer relations. Titles include career coach, health professions advisor, and pre-law advisor. The 262:1 student-to-advisor ratio is superior to many schools featured in this guide. The center puts its personnel to excellent use, having conducted a remarkable 1,700 one-on-one counseling sessions in the 2018-19 academic year.

Colorado College is a member of the nine-school Selective Liberal Arts Consortium that is comprised mostly of elite schools on the East Coast such as Vassar and Haverford College. This organization hosts off-campus interview days based in New York City and DC as well as video interviewing days with a host of high-caliber employers. The Career Center also arranges so-called "Tiger Treks" in which current students travel to a major city to meet with alumni in a variety of job settings. On-campus recruiting and interviewing is not a regular occurrence; only twenty-two companies recruited on campus last year. Internship opportunities are available, but assistance in landing one is limited. Roughly 57 percent of graduating seniors report having participated in at least one internship.

E-mail: admission@coloradocollege.edu | Website: www.coloradocollege.edu

Professional Outcomes

Being a small school, Colorado College does not send massive numbers of graduates to any one company or organization, but there are employers that have wrangled their fair share of Tigers. That list includes Microsoft, Wells Fargo, Amazon, Google, and Charles Schwab. The largest number of graduates who pursue employment end up in the fields of education, technology, health care, the arts, and government. Ten years after entering college, CC alumni have a median salary of about $45,000, lower than many schools of its ilk. Again, this is attributable to many graduates pursuing careers in nonprofit sectors and the relatively low number of STEM majors. Further, as we will discuss in a minute, seemingly all graduates of this school continue their educational journeys, a choice that typically delays financial rewards. Roughly one-quarter of grads stay in the state of Colorado while the majority migrate to major cities across the United States with San Francisco, New York, Seattle, and Los Angeles among the most popular destinations.

The bachelor's degree earned at Colorado College is unlikely to be the last degree a graduate will earn. Five years after graduation the typical cohort sees 70-90 percent of its members having either completed or finishing an advanced degree. Over half of that group are in PhD or professional programs with an average of 25 percent going to medical school. Recent graduates pursuing legal training have matriculated at a wide range of law schools including UVA, Columbia, NYU, Fordham, the University of Colorado, Temple, and Vermont Law School.

Admission

With an acceptance rate of only 15 percent, Colorado College unquestionably qualifies as a highly selective school. That figure has been sliced in half over the past five years as the number of applicants continues to soar. The good news is that the profile of the average admitted student has remained fairly steady. An SAT score in the mid-1300s (or an ACT around 30-31) will put you on solid ground if accompanied by a strong academic transcript. The mid-50 percent on standardized tests for those entering the Class of 2022 was 1300-1470 on the SAT and 29-33 on the ACT.

Colorado College's testing policy used to be as unique as its academic calendar. However, starting in 2020 the school made the shift from test-flexible to full-blown test-optional. Superb grades in a challenging high school curriculum are a must as "rigor of secondary school record" is the sole category rated by the admissions staff as "very important." The data suggests that the school means what it says: more than one-quarter of those attending finished in the top 1 percent of their graduating class; over three-quarters finished in the top 10 percent. Applying via early action or early decision can have a profound impact on your chances of gaining admission. Last year, those applying nonbinding early action were accepted 18 percent of the time, ED applicants 27 percent of the time, and regular applicants at only an 8.5 percent clip. Early decision applicants alone made up 57 percent of the incoming freshman class. In short, Colorado College is an institution with a low acceptance rate but a clear idea of what type of applicants it is looking for. While highly selective, those who performed at the top of their high school class can expect to be welcomed here, even if they didn't score perfectly on the SAT/ACT.

Worth Your Money?

The affluent make up a sizable portion of the undergraduate population at Colorado College, rendering the $73,600 annual cost of attendance of little concern to many considering the school. Tax return data estimates that almost one-quarter of students come from one-percenter households. For those who are concerned about the price tag, Colorado College awards minimal merit aid to 12 percent of its students, but it comes through strong for qualifying applicants, meeting 100 percent of demonstrated need for every financial aid recipient. The average annual value of those grants is roughly $50,000, helping make the school a worthy investment to students coming from more modest economic backgrounds. Students coming from families who make too much to qualify for significant need-based aid, but who make too little to comfortably cover CC's hefty price tag, are encouraged to consider their career and/or graduate school plans before committing.

FINANCIAL
Institutional Type: Private
In-State Tuition: $57,612
Out-of-State Tuition: $57,612
Room & Board: $12,956
Required Fees: $474
Books & Supplies: $1,240

Avg. Need-Based Aid: $50,108
Avg. % of Need Met: 100%

Avg. Merit-Based Aid: $8,036
% Receiving Merit-Based Aid: 12%

Avg. Cumulative Debt: $23,714
% of Students Borrowing: 42%

CAREER
Who Recruits
1. US Olympic Committee
2. El Pomar Foundation
3. Accenture
4. SunShare Community Solar
5. Amazon

Notable Internships
1. National Science Foundation
2. Late Show with Stephen Colbert
3. Accenture

Top Industries
1. Business
2. Education
3. Operations
4. Social Services
5. Media

Top Employers
1. Denver Public Schools
2. Microsoft
3. Amazon
4. Google
5. Charles Schwab

Where Alumni Work
1. Denver
2. Cororado Springs, CO
3. San Francisco
4. New York City
5. Seattle

Median Earnings
College Scorecard (Early Career): $45,400
EOP (Early Career): $43,600
PayScale (Mid-Career): $97,900

RANKINGS
Forbes: 92
Money: 345
U.S. News: 27 (T), Liberal Arts Colleges
Wall Street Journal/THE: 111 (T)
Washington Monthly: 66, Liberal Arts Colleges

#CollegesWorthYourMoney

Golden, Colorado | Admissions Phone: 303-273-3200

ADMISSION
Admission Rate: 49%
Admission Rate - Men: 45%
Admission Rate - Women: 59%
EA Admission Rate: Not Offered
ED Admission Rate: Not Offered
Admission Rate (5-Year Trend): +13%
ED Admission Rate (5-Year Trend): Not Offered
% of Admits Attending (Yield): 19%
Transfer Admission Rate: 47%

\# Offered Wait List: 1,280
\# Accepted Wait List: 426
\# Admitted Wait List: 16

SAT Reading/Writing (Middle 50%): 630-710
SAT Math (Middle 50%): 660-740
ACT Composite (Middle 50%): 28-33
Testing Policy: ACT/SAT Required
SAT Superscore: No
ACT Superscore: No

% Graduated in Top 10% of HS Class: 59%
% Graduated in Top 25% of HS Class: 85%
% Graduated in Top 50% of HS Class: 100%

ENROLLMENT
Total Undergraduate Enrollment: 4,954
% Part-Time: 5%
% Male: 70%
% Female: 30%
% Out-of-State: 41%
% Fraternity: 14%
% Sorority: 21%
% On-Campus (Freshman): 100%
% On-Campus (All Undergraduate): 11%

% African-American: 1%
% Asian: 4%
% Hispanic: 9%
% White: 72%
% Other: 6%
% Race or Ethnicity Unknown: 2%
% International: 6%
% Low-Income: 16%

ACADEMICS
Student-to-Faculty Ratio: 15:1
% of Classes Under 20: 29%
% of Classes Under 40: 66%
% Full-Time Faculty: 53%
% Full-Time Faculty w/ Terminal Degree: 92%

Top Programs
Computer Science
Civil Engineering
Engineering Physics
Environmental Engineering
Geological Engineering
Metallurgical and Materials Engineering
Petroleum Engineering

Retention Rate: 92%
4-Year Graduation Rate: 59%
6-Year Graduation Rate: 81%

Curricular Flexibility: Less Flexible
Academic Rating: ★★★

Inside the Classroom

Less than a half hour ride from Denver and a neighbor of the Coors factory, the Colorado School of Mines, commonly referred to as "Mines," is a public technical institute with an ever-increasing undergraduate enrollment of nearly 5,000, roughly 1,000 more students than a decade ago. The majority of students are Coloradans taking advantage of the reasonable $17,000 in-state tuition. However, the school is becoming more of a draw for out-of-staters and international students. Presently, there are representatives from all fifty states and eighty countries on campus.

There are sixteen bachelor of science degree options to choose from as well as additional areas of specialization. Close to 90 percent of undergraduates are pursuing engineering degrees in areas such as petroleum engineering, mining, mining engineering, geological engineering, mechanical engineering, and chemical engineering. In short, you don't come to Mines to read Tolstoy or intensively study Picasso's Blue Period. That being said, the university does demand that all undergrads complete its core curriculum that does include a smidgeon of work in the humanities and social sciences with an emphasis on "fundamental technical, mathematical, and writing skills."

Classes are rarely small as Mines possesses a student to faculty ratio of 16:1. The average class has thirty-four students, and only 29 percent of sections have an enrollment under twenty. Yet, that does not translate into a lack of hands-on opportunities. All Mines students must take a two-semester sequence of courses called EPICS (Engineering Practices Introductory Course Sequence) in which they tackle an open-ended design problem as part of a small team. Freshmen also take Cornerstone Design in which teams of students must solve real-world design problems. In the 2017-18 school year, 127 students were awarded Mines Undergraduate Research Fellowships and worked as research assistants on faculty-led projects.

The largest number of degrees are conferred in mechanical engineering and petroleum engineering. To be precise, 88 percent of all earned degrees are classified under the engineering umbrella. However, any degree from the Colorado School of Mines, thanks to its terrific academic reputation and extensive alumni base, will open doors in the world of industry. Eight percent major in computer science, 4 percent in math, 2 percent in the physical sciences, and 1 percent in the social sciences. Prestigious postgraduate fellowships are within reach even though they are not pursued in large numbers; four Mines graduates in 2018 were awarded National Science Foundation Graduate Research Fellowships.

Outside the Classroom

The 373-acre campus is populated by mostly modern, recently-renovated buildings, but only five residence halls that mostly house freshmen who are required to live on campus. Just about everyone else lives off campus in apartments in Golden, nearby Lakewood, or in Greek houses. Greek life is prevalent, but not overbearing, with seven fraternities and three sororities attracting 14 percent of men and 21 percent of women. The Orediggers compete in eighteen NCAA Division II sports and generally place well within the Rocky Mountain Athletic Conference. Club and intramural programs enjoy widespread participation. There are 220 registered student clubs and endless opportunities for outdoor recreation. The school's official Outdoor Recreation Center lends equipment for hiking, biking, or rock climbing. A practice rock climbing wall prepares students for organized climbing trips to the Rockies. "E-Days" are campus-uniting events held multiple times per year that feature activities like carnivals, boat races, concerts, and fireworks shows. Golden, Colorado, which many know only through beer commercials "brewed in Golden, Colorado"—is a place of natural beauty where the Great Plains meet the Rocky Mountains. In addition to natural splendor and ample outdoor recreational opportunities, Golden has a nice downtown replete with shops, restaurants, and cafes. Denver is only a quick fifteen-mile car ride away, making Mines' location anything but remote.

Career Services

The Colorado School of Mines Career Center has seven full-time professional staff members working on career counseling and employer relations. That equates to a 708:1 student-to-advisor ratio that is higher than many schools featured in this guide. Yet, that statistic is not at all telling of the level of career services the school provides. For a moderately sized institution, Mines' career fairs draw an exceptional number of companies to campus. In 2017, the Fall Career Day event drew 288 employers and the spring 2018 event attracted 249 hiring organizations. Combined, more than 5,300 Mines students attended. The 2017-18 school year saw 120 companies visit the school for information sessions as well as 2,912 job interviews take place with undergraduate students on campus.

One-on-one counseling was also dispensed at an excellent rate with more than 5,800 sessions taking place in the previous year (including graduate students). Over sixty small-group workshops were held on topics related to career skill acquisition and job and internship search strategies. A fantastic 83 percent of 2018 graduates had at least one hands-on internship or co-op experience. The school's online job database, DiggerNet, is well maintained and features postings from 790 employers.

Professional Outcomes

Members of the Class of 2018 landed industry jobs or full-time graduate school positions at a clip of 88 percent. However, it is important to note that the success rate varied greatly by major. Geology and geological engineering students were placed at a 100 percent rate while only 77 percent of chemical engineering grads quickly found their next home. Within two years 97 percent or more alumni have successfully launched their career or graduate school path. The largest number of students entered the oil and natural gas industry; construction, aerospace/defense/transportation, and information technology were next in line. Companies employing massive numbers of Mines' grads include Lockheed Martin, BP, ExxonMobil, Halliburton, Chevron, and Shell. Those finding employment enjoyed an average starting salary of $68,000. Petroleum engineering majors averaged $76k and had offers as high as $120k; computer science majors scored similar compensation. After graduating, 61 percent of Mines alumni remain in Colorado. Texas and California are the next most popular destinations.

One-fifth of freshly printed diploma-holders directly enter graduate school, and the most popular institution is Mines itself, which is the choice of 75 percent of those pursuing advanced degrees. Other universities attended by recent graduates include Baylor College of Medicine, Boston University, Carnegie Mellon, Columbia University, Imperial College London, Kyoto University, Rice University, and Worchester Polytechnic Institute.

Admission

Accepting 49 percent of the 12,661 who applied for a spot in the Class of 2022, Mines may not sound as highly selective as it actually is. Acceptance rates can fluctuate greatly at this school from year to year. Last year, it was friendlier—56 percent of applicants were admitted—but in 2015 only 38 percent were. Freshmen in 2018-19 sported ACT middle-50 percent ranges of 28-33 (72 percent of applicants submit ACT results) and 1290-1450 on the SAT. Sixty percent finished in the top 10 percent of their high school classes and 85 percent were in the top 25 percent. The profile of the average freshman today is similar to previous years, whether 56 percent or 38 percent of applicants were admitted.

There is nothing complicated about the admissions process at Mines. The committee considers four cut-and-dried factors to be "very important" in evaluating applicants: rigor of secondary school record, class rank, GPA, and standardized test scores. There are no factors considered "important." Criteria including recommendations, essays, and extracurricular activities are "considered." With 71 percent of the student body being male, being a qualified female applicant can yield a significant admissions edge. The acceptance rate for women is 59 percent compared to 45 percent for men. Almost three-fifths of the student body hail from the Rocky Mountain State, and being a resident can give you a slight boost. No early round is offered, but students should aim for the priority deadline of November 1 to maximize their chances. Mines uses about as straightforward a formula as you will find to make its admissions decisions. That makes self-assessment of one's chances for admission simple. Strong grades in rigorous courses + standardized test scores in the 90th percentile = probable acceptance.

Worth Your Money?

With the annual cost of attendance under $35,000 for Colorado residents and under $55,000 for out-of-staters, Mines is a good value for everyone, especially given that the average starting salary is close to $70k. The news only gets sunnier when you look at the fact that 80 percent of attendees also receive a merit aid award averaging $8,875. Another 48 percent of undergraduates receive an annual need-based grant with a mean value of $6,211. Whether you live in the Centennial State or not, the Colorado School of Mines is a wonderful place to study engineering or computer science. You will have no trouble finding well-compensated work after you earn your diploma.

FINANCIAL
Institutional Type: Public
In-State Tuition: $16,650
Out-of-State Tuition: $36,270
Room & Board: $13,169
Required Fees: $2,314
Books & Supplies: $1,500

Avg. Need-Based Aid: $6,211
Avg. % of Need Met: 62%

Avg. Merit-Based Aid: $8,875
% Receiving Merit-Based Aid: 80%

Avg. Cumulative Debt: $32,482
% of Students Borrowing: 53%

CAREER
Who Recruits
1. Rio Tinto
2. Chevron
3. Phillips 66
4. Procter & Gamble
5. Occidental Petroleum

Notable Internships
1. ExxonMobil
2. Cigna
3. Chevron

Top Industries
1. Engineering
2. Operations
3. Business
4. Research
5. Education

Top Employers
1. Lockheed Martin
2. Chevron
3. Aramco
4. BP
5. National Renewable Energy Laboratory

Where Alumni Work
1. Denver
2. Houston
3. San Francisco
4. Colorado Springs, CO
5. Dallas

Median Earnings
College Scorecard (Early Career): $84,900
EOP (Early Career): $81,500
PayScale (Mid-Career): $139,600

RANKINGS
Forbes: 94
Money: 121
U.S. News: 84, National Universities
Wall Street Journal/THE: 169
Washington Monthly: 117, National Universities

#CollegesWorthYourMoney

Columbia University

New York, New York | Admissions Phone: 212-854-2522

Inside the Classroom

Attending an Ivy League school that also happens to be located in Manhattan is, for many, an opportunity to have your cake and eat it too. It's no wonder that this particular "cake," Columbia University, is one of the most selective schools in the country. It's also one of the most rigorous in the classroom. The 6,323 exceptional students who make it through a treacherous admissions gauntlet are spread across two schools: Columbia College and the Fu Foundation School of Engineering & Applied Sciences. Combined, those schools offer ninety-six unique areas of study as well as a number of pre-professional and accelerated graduate programs.

The academic experience at Columbia is driven by the famed core curriculum that lays out an extensive to-do list that includes highly specified courses rather than categorical requirements. Those courses include Introduction to Contemporary Civilization in the West, Masterpieces of Western Art, Masterpieces of Western Literature & Philosophy, Frontiers of Science, University Writing, and Music Humanities. Additional science, global core, foreign language, and physical education mandates add seven courses to the core as well as two activities (for phys ed). School of Engineering & Applied Science students only tackle approximately half of the core curriculum (depending on your major). Columbia College students will spend roughly a year and a half slogging through this considerable scholarly workload.

Class sizes are small with more than 80 percent containing fewer than twenty students. The student-faculty ratio is 6:1, but you are likely to be instructed by a few graduate students as you work through the core. Fortunately, only full-time professors lead classes within each major. More than 500 students per year participate in the Columbia Overseas Program. A little over one-quarter of the students leave Manhattan for a foreign country during their four years of study. Undergraduate research is taken seriously by the university, which offers multiple avenues through which students can work side-by-side with faculty on their projects or pursue funding for their own original research ideas. Recent student projects included the following: "Analyzing Sediment Levels in New York Harbor to Examine Urban Growth" and "Examining Chemical Pathways in Stimulating Ovarian Follicle Stem Cell Renewal." Those who participate in a ten-week Summer Undergraduate Research Fellowship present their findings the following spring at a school-run symposium and can publish their work in a number of undergraduate academic journals affiliated with the university.

The largest number of degrees are conferred in political science, economics, history, computer science, and mechanical engineering. The Engineering School as a whole can be found near the top of most national rankings, along with nearly every other department and program. Fewer students pursue prestigious postgraduate fellowships at Columbia than at its Ivy-League brethren; Dartmouth produces double the number of Fulbright Scholars, Brown closer to triple. Yet, if earning a Clarendon, Gates Cambridge, Schwarzman, US State Department Critical Language, or Truman Scholarship is your aim, it can certainly be done at Columbia.

Outside the Classroom

Morningside Heights is a quiet, relatively safe section of New York City, and while Columbia is not situated in the traditional heart of the city like NYU, there are plenty of restaurants and cultural experiences within the immediate vicinity of campus. Unusual for an NYC university, 93 percent of the student body lives in college-owned housing. (Try to rent a place in Manhattan at your own risk—or your wallet's.) A decade ago, Greek life was flatlining with a minimal number of participants, but in recent years it has undergone a rebirth, and now nearly one in every five undergrads joins a fraternity or sorority. The Lions field thirty-one NCAA Division I teams and an additional forty+ club squads, including a number of recent strong performers. Columbia has won seventeen Ivy League titles in the last five years. A full cornucopia of opportunities await through the school's more than 500 student-run organizations. With thirteen a cappella groups, twenty-three dance troupes, thirty-one student run media outlets/publications, and forty political organizations, everyone can find a place to explore their passions at Columbia. The volunteer spirit is also strong with the Community Impact organization attracting more than 900 members who work in twenty-seven community service programs throughout New York City.

Career Services

The Columbia Center for Career Education (CCE) has twenty-six professional staff members who are dedicated to undergraduate counseling, employer relations, and other functions related to undergraduate career/graduate school exploration. That 243:1 student-to-advisor ratio is better than average compared to other schools featured in this guide. The CCE is a well-oiled machine that provides meaningful guidance and experiential opportunities from freshman year through graduation. In 2017, staff engaged in 8,473 one-on-one counseling sessions (98 percent of students reported those as helpful), facilitated 3,547 on-campus interviews, and posted more than 36,000 jobs and internships on the LionSHARE database. Hosting over 400 events that attracted 10,305 students, the CCE is dedicated to bringing a range of large-scale career fairs as well as industry showcases where students with targeted interests can learn from professionals in fields such as book publishing, fashion, sports marketing, and health-care technology.

Columbia does an excellent job with outreach, but its internship numbers are, perhaps, even more impressive. A staggering 85 percent of undergraduates complete at least one internship. In part, that phenomenal participation rate is due to Columbia's relationships with hundreds of major employers. Thanks to its high level of undergraduate engagement and superb employer relations efforts, the Center for Career Education receives high praise overall from our staff.

Professional Outcomes

Examining the most recent graduates from Columbia College and the Fu Foundation School of Engineering & Applied Science, 72 percent had found employment within six months, and 17 percent had entered graduate school. Financial services, engineering, and consulting were the three most favored industries. The companies hiring the largest number of Lions are among the most desirable employers in the world including IBM, Goldman Sachs, Morgan Stanley, Google, Citigroup, and Credit Suisse. The median starting salary for graduates of Columbia College/Columbia Engineering is $70,000. Six-figure salaries were reported by 13 percent of graduates, primarily those with engineering degrees, while 30 percent of grads earned less than $50k in their first year of full-time work.

Those moving on to graduate/professional school were welcomed in large numbers into other universities of Columbia's ilk. In addition to remaining at Columbia (the most popular choice), top ten institutions attended were Stanford, Harvard, NYU, Yale, Carnegie Mellon, Cambridge, Oxford, Icahn School of Medicine, and Cornell. A significant number of students from each graduating class also generally secure spots at elite law and medical schools that include the university's own top five law school and the esteemed Vagelos College of Physicians & Surgeons.

Admission

As with the rest of the Ivy League, Columbia received a record number of applications for entry into the Class of 2022. Of the 40,203 hopefuls, only 2,214 were offered admission, which works out to a 5.5 percent acceptance rate, on par with Princeton. Infinitesimal chances at admission is not a new phenomenon here—the acceptance rate hasn't been in the double-digits since 2011.

The profile of the average accepted student is impressive. Entering 2018-19 freshmen had a midde-50 percent SAT of 1450-1560, and the ACT range was 33-35. Over 90 percent were in the top 10 percent of their high school class. Straight from the admissions office, there are six main factors that are given primary importance as part of the university's holistic process: curriculum and grades, context (family circumstances), extracurricular activities, character, fit, and recommendations. Columbia is definitely a school where it is advantageous to apply early decision as ED admit rates are typically three to four times higher than in the regular round; it was 18 percent for the Class of 2022. The university fills close to 50 percent of its freshman class through the early round. Among the Ivies, only Penn scoops up a higher percentage of its entering class through ED. Even by Ivy League standards, gaining acceptance into Columbia is an intimidating proposition. The aforementioned admitted student bona fides should give you an idea if you have a puncher's chance at success, but no one is a sure thing when only one of every twenty high school superstars is welcomed aboard.

Worth Your Money?

All qualifying students at Columbia receive an aid package that meets 100 percent of their demonstrated need and averages almost $54,000. Columbia does not offer any degree of merit aid, so those without financial need will end up paying the full annual cost of attendance of $80k+ per year. While $320,000 for a bachelor's degree sounds (and probably is) insane, Columbia certainly has a number of degree programs that will lead you into a high-paying job right out of college. It's also hard to undervalue the social capital accrued by spending four years at Columbia, which makes spending a massive amount of money on undergraduate tuition a less onerous proposition.

FINANCIAL
Institutional Type: Private
In-State Tuition: $56,608
Out-of-State Tuition: $56,608
Room & Board: $14,016
Required Fees: $2,822
Books & Supplies: N/A

Avg. Need-Based Aid: $56,829
Avg. % of Need Met: 100%

Avg. Merit-Based Aid: $0
% Receiving Merit-Based Aid: 0%

Avg. Cumulative Debt: $21,406
% of Students Borrowing: N/A

CAREER
Who Recruits
1. eBay
2. Memorial Sloan Kettering
3. Boeing
4. Calgene
5. Arup

Notable Internships
1. Mount Sinai Hospital
2. Google
3. Glassdoor

Top Industries
1. Business
2. Education
3. Research
4. Media
5. Engineering

Top Employers
1. Google
2. Morgan Stanley
3. Citi
4. Goldman Sachs
5. JPMorgan Chase

Where Alumni Work
1. New York City
2. San Francisco
3. Los Angeles
4. Washington, DC
5. Boston

Median Earnings
College Scorecard (Early Career): $83,300
EOP (Early Career): $75,300
PayScale (Mid-Career): $126,800

RANKINGS
Forbes: 14
Money: 81
U.S. News: 3, National Universities
Wall Street Journal/THE: 15
Washington Monthly: 13, National Universities

#CollegesWorthYourMoney

Connecticut College

New London, Connecticut | Admissions Phone: 860-439-2200

ADMISSION
Admission Rate: 38%
Admission Rate - Men: 31%
Admission Rate - Women: 42%
EA Admission Rate: Not Offered
ED Admission Rate: 62%
Admission Rate (5-Year Trend): +1%
ED Admission Rate (5-Year Trend): -3%
% of Admits Attending (Yield): 21%
Transfer Admission Rate: 35%

Offered Wait List: 1,385
Accepted Wait List: 574
Admitted Wait List: 22

SAT Reading/Writing (Middle 50%): 650-710
SAT Math (Middle 50%): 640-720
ACT Composite (Middle 50%): 30-32
Testing Policy: Test Optional
SAT Superscore: Yes
ACT Superscore: Yes

% Graduated in Top 10% of HS Class: 49%
% Graduated in Top 25% of HS Class: 80%
% Graduated in Top 50% of HS Class: 98%

ENROLLMENT
Total Undergraduate Enrollment: 1,844
% Part-Time: 2%
% Male: 39%
% Female: 61%
% Out-of-State: 81%
% Fraternity: Not Offered
% Sorority: Not Offered
% On-Campus (Freshman): 100%
% On-Campus (All Undergraduate): 99%

% African-American: 4%
% Asian: 5%
% Hispanic: 8%
% White: 68%
% Other: 4%
% Race or Ethnicity Unknown: 2%
% International: 7%
% Low-Income: 12%

ACADEMICS
Student-to-Faculty Ratio: 9:1
% of Classes Under 20: 75%
% of Classes Under 40: 97%
% Full-Time Faculty: 74%
% Full-Time Faculty w/ Terminal Degree: 94%

Top Programs
Area Studies
Behavioral Neuroscience
Dance
English
History
International Relations
Psychology
Theatre

Retention Rate: 91%
4-Year Graduation Rate: 78%
6-Year Graduation Rate: 81%

Curricular Flexibility: Somewhat Flexible
Academic Rating: ★★★⭒

Inside the Classroom

Founded as a school for women in the early twentieth century, Connecticut College, known affectionately as Conn College, went co-ed in 1969 and operates today as a unique liberal arts school in the sleepy seaport town of New London. Conn College Camels can pick from an academic menu consisting of forty-one majors, most of which are available as minors as well. There are 1,844 undergraduates on campus, but there is not a single graduate student to be found, which means that, beginning freshman year, the full resources of this school are already at your disposal.

In typical liberal arts fashion, students are required to complete one course in every major discipline: physical and biological sciences, mathematics, social sciences, literature, creative arts, philosophy/religion, and history. There are also requirements in foreign language, writing, and technology. For a laid-back group there is no shortage of academic ambitions as over one-quarter of the Class of 2018 completed a double major. Many also complete a thematic minor that is offered in distinct areas including Modern Greece and Its Background, Non-Violence, or Psychoanalysis: Theories of the Unconscious. Close to 800 courses run each academic year.

The student-faculty ratio is an inviting 9:1, and 75 percent of classes contain fewer than twenty students; 29 percent contain fewer than ten. Conn College's faculty has a reputation for being wholly committed to teaching and forging meaningful relationships with students. Evidence of a personalized experience can be found in the numbers—84 percent of seniors complete a capstone project, 30 percent engage in an individual study with a professor's guidance, and roughly the same number report giving a pubic presentation or performance during their undergraduate career. Slightly more than half of students elect to study abroad. The Class of 2017 completed semesters in thirty-eight countries with Denmark, Italy, and the United Kingdom being the most common destinations.

Consistently named a "top producer" of Fulbright Scholars, Conn College has seen thirty-three students selected in the last five years. Many of those students majored in the school's strong programs in international relations or region-specific programs (e.g., Hispanic Studies, Slavic Studies). Other well-regarded majors include neuroscience, psychology, English, dance, and theatre. In terms of the most frequently conferred degrees, the social sciences at large lead the way (29 percent), followed by biology (17 percent), visual and performing arts (12 percent), psychology (7 percent), and area/ethnic/gender studies (7 percent).

Outside the Classroom

This gorgeous 750-acre campus is wedged between two large bodies of water and features its own hiking trails and arboretum. The gender breakdown still skews strongly in one direction; men make up only 36 percent of the undergraduate population. Three-quarters of the student body participate in competitive sports. For a tiny school it manages to field twenty-eight intercollegiate sports teams (NCAA Division III) as well as a number of intramural squads. Outside of athletic clubs there are roughly seventy student organizations on campus high-lighted by six popular a cappella groups. There are no fraternities or sororities at Conn College, but 98 percent of the student body lives on campus in one of twenty-three residence houses. A close-knit community, Camels come together for some notable campus-wide events like Floralia, Harvestfest, or the massive Seinfeld-inspired Festivus celebration. Public transportation options are plentiful, and the campus and surrounding area are easily bikeable. Even with the relatively close proximity to bigger cities like Boston, New York, and Providence, the school itself estimates that 80 percent of its students stay put on the weekends, making campus a vibrant place seven days a week.

Career Services

The Office of Career Professional Development has eight full-time staff members who specialize in employer relations, general advising, pre-law advising, and connecting students with internships. With a 233:1 stu-dent-to-advisor ratio, Conn College sports a higher level of support than many other schools featured in this guide. Its four-year career program assures that the only interaction with the office isn't a harried and panicked "What do I do now?" conversation right before graduation. Advisors visit the required first-year seminar courses and begin to engage students right away, encouraging them to keep in touch via one-on-one advising sessions as well as by attending sponsored events like Sundays with Alumni, workshops, and joint career fairs such as the Liberal Arts Recruiting Connection in Boston that features on-site interviews with more than thirty compa-nies.

Rising seniors are eligible to spend their summers in a school-funded internship. That's right— all students are guaranteed $3,000 to help fund an internship experience anywhere in the world. Plenty are advertised on CamelLink, but advisers will also work individually with students to unearth additional opportunities. It's a testament to the career services staff that nearly 80 percent of alumni reported that their first job out of school put them on their permanent career path.

E-mail: admission@conncoll.edu | Website: www.conncoll.edu

Professional Outcomes

One year after graduating, 69 percent of the Class of 2018 were engaged in full-time employment, 13 percent were in graduate school, 5 percent were employed part time, and 4 percent were still searching for jobs. Connecticut College produces an interesting blend of career pathways. A solid 24 percent of the Class of 2018 entered the finance industry, but a large swath also veered toward education (17 percent); science, technology, and engineering (15 percent); and health care (14 percent). Those in banking frequently find homes at Bank of America, JPMorgan Chase & Co., and Morgan Stanley. On the public service/health side, three of the largest employers are AmeriCorps, Fulbright, and Sloan Kettering Cancer Center. Other companies employing twenty or more alumni include Pfizer, Massachusetts General Hospital, Deloitte, and UBS. The median salary for midcareer alumni is $56k, slightly less than the median for graduates of UConn, the state's flagship university. Camels end up working predominately in New York (33 percent) and Massachusetts (22 percent), but London/ Norwich, Connecticut; DC, San Francisco, and Hartford claim sizable pockets as well.

Conn College students are known for being grad school ready as a surprising (given the small size of the school) twenty-seven alumni earn their doctoral degrees each year. Examining the graduate school attendees from the classes of 2014-16, it is common for multiple students to land at prestigious schools such as NYU, Columbia, and Yale as well as nearby state schools like UMass and UConn. In recent years graduates have earned spots at just about every top law school in the country including Harvard, Emory, Columbia, Penn, Duke, and Northwestern. Those pursuing medical and dental degrees do so at the likes of Tufts University School of Medicine, NYU School of Medicine, and the University of Texas School of Medicine.

Admission

The school admitted 38 percent of applicants in the 2018 admissions cycle. Over the last five years its acceptance rate has hovered in the 35-40 percent range; its low ebb was 32 percent in 2010. Conn College is test-optional, and unlike most test-optional colleges, the majority of accepted applicants (52 percent) elected not to submit a standardized test score as part of their applications. For those who did, the middle 50 percent range for attending students is 1290-1430 on the SAT and 30-32 on the ACT.

While test scores occupy the "considered" category for the Conn College admissions staff, rigor of coursework, grades, class rank, and character/personal qualities are deemed "most important." Academic performance needs to be strong, but you don't need to be perfect to be considered as 80 percent are in the top 20 percent of their high school class and 49 percent cracked the top 10 percent. Legacy students have an edge and have access to special Admission 101 sessions hosted by the college while they are still in high school. The Class of 2022 has the largest number of legacy students of any class in the school's history. Conn College offers two rounds of early decision, and for those who consider it a top choice, it would be wise to consider partaking. A stunning 62 percent of early applicants were accepted in 2018, accounting for more than 45 percent of the 2018-19 freshman class. In essence, this is not a school with a strict formula for admission. It tends to attract a distinguished applicant pool but does not require Ivy-level qualifications for acceptance. Those who apply early face the best odds.

Worth Your Money?

While 42 percent of undergrads receive merit aid, the average award of $6,494 barely dents the $74k annual cost of attendance. Yet, for a very sizable 58 percent of the student population, 100 percent of financial need is met to the tune of $43,000 per year, making attending Conn College possible for lower- and middle-income students. This is a school that the rich pay close to full price to attend, and the not-rich get generous aid packages. Still, the average debt load carried by alumni is higher than the national average. Therefore, middle-to upper-income students without a solid financial aid offer should carefully consider their future plans before investing in the school.

FINANCIAL
Institutional Type: Private
In-State Tuition: $56,870
Out-of-State Tuition: $56,870
Room & Board: $15,720
Required Fees: N/A
Books & Supplies: $1,000

Avg. Need-Based Aid: $42,713
Avg. % of Need Met: 100%

Avg. Merit-Based Aid: $6,494
% Receiving Merit-Based Aid: 42%

Avg. Cumulative Debt: $33,608
% of Students Borrowing: 45%

CAREER
Who Recruits
1. Amazon
2. JLL
3. Morgan Stanley
4. Deloitte
5. UBS

Notable Internships
1. Sony Music Entertainment
2. Smithsonian
3. J. Crew

Top Industries
1. Business
2. Education
3. Social Services
4. Operations
5. Media

Top Employers
1. Pfizer
2. Google
3. Fidelity Investments
4. JPMorgan Chase
5. Bank of America

Where Alumni Work
1. New York City
2. Boston
3. Norwich, CT
4. Washington, DC
5. San Francisco

Median Earnings
College Scorecard (Early Career): $54,900
EOP (Early Career): $55,500
PayScale (Mid-Career): $100,800

RANKINGS
Forbes: 128
Money: 174
U.S. News: 46, Liberal Arts Colleges
Wall Street Journal/THE: 103
Washington Monthly: 35, Liberal Arts Colleges

#CollegesWorthYourMoney

The Cooper Union for the Advancement of Science & Art

New York, New York | Admissions Phone: 212-353-4120

ADMISSION
Admission Rate: 16%
Admission Rate - Men: 17%
Admission Rate - Women: 15%
EA Admission Rate: Not Offered
ED Admission Rate: 29%
Admission Rate (5-Year Trend): +9%
ED Admission Rate (5-Year Trend): +17%
% of Admits Attending (Yield): 55%
Transfer Admission Rate: 16%

Offered Wait List: 182
Accepted Wait List: 182
Admitted Wait List: 10

SAT Reading/Writing (Middle 50%): 630-720
SAT Math (Middle 50%): 650-790
ACT Composite (Middle 50%): 31-34
Testing Policy: ACT/SAT Required
SAT Superscore: Yes
ACT Superscore: Yes

% Graduated in Top 10% of HS Class: 51%
% Graduated in Top 25% of HS Class: 85%
% Graduated in Top 50% of HS Class: 99%

ENROLLMENT
Total Undergraduate Enrollment: 858
% Part-Time: 0%
% Male: 61%
% Female: 39%
% Out-of-State: 35%
% Fraternity: 4%
% Sorority: 0%
% On-Campus (Freshman): 56%
% On-Campus (All Undergraduate): 13%

% African-American: 3%
% Asian: 21%
% Hispanic: 10%
% White: 31%
% Other: 5%
% Race or Ethnicity Unknown: 8%
% International: 21%
% Low-Income: 20%

ACADEMICS
Student-to-Faculty Ratio: 7:1
% of Classes Under 20: 72%
% of Classes Under 40: 99%
% Full-Time Faculty: 16%
% Full-Time Faculty w/ Terminal Degree: 82%

Top Programs
Architecture
Art
Civil Engineering
Electrical Engineering
Mechanical Engineering

Retention Rate: 91%
4-Year Graduation Rate: 71%
6-Year Graduation Rate: 88%

Curricular Flexibility: Less Flexible
Academic Rating: ★★★⌐

Inside the Classroom

Tuition-free from its founding in 1859 until 2013, The Cooper Union is home to under 900 talented undergraduate students concentrating in art, architecture, and engineering. While tuition has returned (at least until 2029), CU remains an immensely popular destination for its unique programmatic offerings and world-class faculty; hence, it has an Ivy-level acceptance rate of 13 percent.

The Irwin S. Chanin School of Architecture offers a five-year bachelor's program. The School of Art offers a bachelor of fine arts degree with concentrations in painting, sculpture, drawing, film and video, graphic design, photography, and printmaking. The Albert Nerken School of Engineering offers bachelor of engineering degrees in chemical, civil, electrical, and mechanical engineering. All undergraduates must pursue a core curriculum consistent with founder Peter Cooper's insistence on not ignoring the humanities and social sciences in the pursuit of a practical education. As such, a four-semester sequence is required of all students that includes a freshman seminar that focuses on poetry and drama, and three history/sociology courses that follow a chrono-logical sequence from the 1500s to modern day.

No matter your area of study at CU, students report receiving a high degree of attention and mentorship from faculty. With nearly three-quarters of class sections containing fewer than twenty students, learning is an intimate endeavor. Roughly 20 percent elect to study abroad through one of the school's six- to eight-week summer offerings. Engineering students can travel to Spain, Iceland, or Germany while art students have additional options in The Netherlands, France, England, and Sweden. Undergraduate research opportunities are most common in the School of Engineering where all students must complete a senior project.

Accounting for 50 percent of the student body, engineering is the subject in which the largest number of degrees are conferred followed by visual arts and then architecture. All three schools shine in the eyes of employers as well as other institutions of higher education. Graduates of The Cooper Union obtain prestigious fellowships and scholarships at impressive rates. CU has enjoyed thirty-nine Fulbright scholars since 2001, thirteen National Science Foundation Graduate Research Fellowships since 2004, and typically sweeps all four annual Royal Society of Arts-Architecture Student Design Awards.

Outside the Classroom

Most of campus is located in three large buildings: The Foundation Building, 41 Cooper Square, and one fresh-man-only residence hall where 20 percent of undergraduates reside. Yet, being located in the heart of the East Village, your "campus" is really all of New York City. When they aren't up all night working on projects, students can enjoy the array of restaurants, shops, theaters, and museums within easy walking distance of the school or hop one of the nearby subway stops for access to Midtown Manhattan as well as the outer boroughs. CU does have five club sports teams—men's and women's basketball, men's and women's volleyball, and a coed soccer squad. Two fraternities and one sorority have local chapters, but they fall well short of being a dominant force in the social sphere. Over eighty student-run organizations are active on campus including music and drama troupes, a student newspaper, cultural clubs, and professional societies that participate in intercollegiate competitions.

Career Services

The Center for Career Development employs three full-time professional staff members, equating to a 284:1 student-to-advisor ratio that allows for plentiful personalized attention. Undergraduates are always free to book forty-five-minute one-on-one sessions focusing on areas including résumé and cover letter writing, portfolio development, job and internship search strategies, interview preparation, grad school applications, and applica-tions to competitive fellowship and scholarship programs. Current students and alumni can utilize Handshake for a wealth of job postings. Employers attend the fall and spring career fairs and stop by campus for recruiting sessions and on-campus interviews.

The office organizes a multitude of targeted information sessions and networking opportunities for CU students. Recent examples include a roundtable discussion with gallerists and curators, a graduate school information session with Carnegie Mellon, and lunch with alumni. Opportunities for experiential learning are facilitated by career services staff. For instance, art students can partake in the Professional Internship Program for Art that provides undergraduates with a stipend to work at one of a dozen partner NYC-based museums and galleries. Thanks to a full calendar of intimate events catering to art, architecture, and engineering, The Cooper Union's Center for Career Development serves its students admirably.

The Cooper Union for the Advancement of Science and Art

E-mail: admissions@cooper.edu | Website: www.cooper.edu

Professional Outcomes

Due to the exceptionally low numbers of graduates from Cooper Union each year, it is hard to say that large numbers of alumni cluster in any particular company. However, it is fair to state that CU graduates regularly find their way into the most desirable firms within their respective disciplines. Recent graduates of the School of Architecture found homes at many of the world's largest architecture firms such as AECOM, Gensler, Perkins Eastman, and HOK as well as any desirable boutique firm one can name. School of Art alumni can be found at every great museum of art in the county, including the MoMA and the Met, and at prestigious media outlets such as The New Yorker and the New York Times. Engineering grads waltz into an endless list of top companies including Deloitte, ExxonMobil, Google, Goldman Sachs, IBM, and SpaceX. By age thirty-four, alumni of The Cooper Union enjoy median earnings of $64,000.

Forty percent of CU graduates continue their education at top-ranked graduate programs. In the last few years Cooper Union diploma-holders have gone on to advanced study in architecture at Columbia, Harvard, MIT, Princeton, the Rhode Island School of Design, MIT, Penn, and Yale. Art students have been accepted to US-based programs at Cornell, Georgetown, NYU, and Pratt and internationally at The Glasgow School of Art; Oslo Academy of Art; and Goldsmiths, University of London. Engineering students pursuing master's and doctorate degrees have landed spots at Carnegie Mellon, Johns Hopkins, Stanford, Berkeley, and Vanderbilt.

Admission

Among those seeking a spot in the Class of 2022, only 336 of the 2,574 applicants to The Cooper Union gained acceptance, a 13 percent acceptance rate. This is a self-selecting group of students, many of whom have slotted CU as their number one choice, a fact affirmed by the school's robust 61 percent yield rate. The profile of the average accepted student varies greatly by program. Freshmen in the School of Engineering possessed middle-50 percent SAT scores between 1460 and 1540 and ACT composite scores between 33 and 34. Architecture students scored a significantly lower 1190-1410 (26-32 on the ACT). Freshmen studying art held the lowest standardized test scores with middle-50 percent SAT scores between 1080 and 1330 and 24-30 on the ACT. Successful applicants to all three programs generally had A/A- averages. The five categories rated as "most important" to one's admissions prospects at CU are test scores, GPA, rigor of courses, talent/ability, and the level of an applicant's interest.

The admissions office recommends that all applicants "take a well-rounded high school program, preferably in advanced coursework." Program-specific recommendations include that "engineering students should also be well prepared in calculus, chemistry, and physics. Art and architecture applicants should take visual art classes" and that architecture applicants should take pre-calculus in high school. Additional application components are required by the various programs. Engineering applicants are required to submit two SAT subject tests, one in math and one in physics or chemistry as well as a writing supplement. School of Art students must complete a Hometest and submit a portfolio. Those applying to the School of Architecture must complete a studio test. While standardized test scores differ greatly across the three schools, all successful applicants to Cooper Union boast solid academic credentials along with demonstrated gifts in their area of interest. Those seeking to study art or architecture will face a holistic review process; those applying to study engineering will be judged more heavily by their test scores.

Worth Your Money?

After over one hundred years of providing a tuition-free education to undergraduate students, Cooper Union controversially decided, in light of a depleted endowment, to begin charging tuition. While plans exist to progressively reduce tuition over the next decade before returning to a tuition-free policy, those entering the school now encounter an annual cost of attendance of $63,092. However, the school does remain extremely generous with aid, awarding an average annual amount of $24k via merit aid and meeting 100 percent of demonstrated need for most students. Presently, 53 percent of undergraduates receive grants of over $43k per year. While it's not as great as receiving a world-class education gratis, Cooper Union remains worth every dollar and is, undoubtedly, worth your money.

FINANCIAL
Institutional Type: Private
In-State Tuition: $44,550
Out-of-State Tuition: $44,550
Room & Board: $13,017 (room only)
Required Fees: $2,150
Books & Supplies: $1,800

Avg. Need-Based Aid: $43,118
Avg. % of Need Met: 100%

Avg. Merit-Based Aid: $24,241
% Receiving Merit-Based Aid: 86%

Avg. Cumulative Debt: N/A
% of Students Borrowing: N/A

CAREER
Who Recruits
1. AECOM
2. Bloomberg
3. General Motors
4. AT&T
5. Credit Suisse

Notable Internships
1. Con Edison
2. Bloomberg LP
3. PepsiCo

Top Industries
1. Arts & Design
2. Business
3. Engineering
4. Education
5. Operations

Top Employers
1. Con Edison
2. Google
3. Bloomberg LP
4. IBM
5. Amazon

Where Alumni Work
1. New York City
2. San Francisco
3. Los Angeles
4. Boston
5. Philadelphia

Median Earnings
College Scorecard (Early Career): $64,900
EOP (Early Career): $64,300
PayScale (Mid-Career): $126,200

RANKINGS
Forbes: 58
Money: 66
U.S. News: 1, Regional North
Wall Street Journal/THE: N/A
Washington Monthly: N/A

#CollegesWorthYourMoney

Cornell University

Ithaca, New York | Admissions Phone: 607-255-5241

Inside the Classroom

By a wide margin, Cornell boasts the largest undergraduate enrollment of any school in the Ivy League at almost 15,000 students, roughly 5,000 more than the next largest school, the University of Pennsylvania. Located in Ithaca, a certifiable college town in the Finger Lakes region of Upstate New York, Cornell's campus is a seemingly endless 745 acres, and that is not including the adjacent Botanic Gardens owned by the university. A diverse array of academic programs includes ninety majors and 125 minors spread across the university's seven schools/colleges: the College of Agriculture and Life Sciences; College of Architecture, Art and Planning; College of Arts and Sciences; SC Johnson College of Business; College of Engineering; College of Human Ecology; and School of Industrial and Labor Relations.

Most degrees conferred in 2018 were in engineering (17 percent), business (14 percent), agriculture (12 percent), computer science (11 percent), and the social sciences (9 percent). Beginning with the Class of 2023, required courses within the College of Arts & Sciences will include two first-year writing seminars, mastery of a foreign language, and ten distributional requirements. While that sounds like a substantial number of mandated classes, the school does allow certain courses to simultaneously fill more than one distributional requirement.

Classes are a bit larger at Cornell than at many other elite institutions. Still, 57 percent of sections have fewer than twenty students. Introductory courses sometimes take place in larger lecture halls, so 18 percent of courses have an enrollment of more than forty students. Undergraduates do give their professors generally high marks: 93 percent report being satisfied with the instruction they have received, 71 percent report participating in class discussions, 48 percent report completing a thesis/research project, and 62 percent plan on or already have conducted research with a faculty member. Members of Big Red can choose from study abroad opportunities in more than forty countries, and roughly one-third participate.

The SC Johnson College of Business houses two undergraduate schools, both of which have phenomenal reputations. The Cornell School of Hotel Administration is one of the finest such programs in the world, and the Charles H. Dyson School of Applied Economics and Management cracks most lists of the top 10 business programs in the United States. The School of Engineering offers fourteen areas of specialization and is held in high regard by employers and prestigious graduate schools. Highly-desired postgraduate scholarships are procured by Cornell grads at a steady rate. The university has twenty-nine Rhodes Scholars to its credit as well as a regular flow of Fulbright, Schwarzman, Goldwater, and Truman Scholarship award winners.

Outside the Classroom

Ithaca has as much Upstate New York natural splendor as you can handle, from Lake Cayuga to parks to the many breathtaking ravines and gorges. (You've likely seen the "Ithaca is Gorges" T-shirt.) Yet, thanks to frigid weather and the absence of a major metropolis nearby, campus itself and the nearby neighborhoods are where the action is. With a roughly 25 percent participation rate across the fifty-five fraternity and sorority chapters on campus, Greek life dominates much of the social scene. Freshmen are required to live in university housing, although a substantial 48 percent of undergrads live off campus. Student-run organizations can be found for almost anything your mind can fathom. Over 1,000 clubs are active. The Cornell Concert works to bring major acts to campus that suit a variety of tastes from Bob Dylan to Ke$ha. The university also succeeds in luring a fair share of impressive guest speakers to campus each year. The Cornell Daily Sun, founded in 1880, is one of the finest student papers in the country, and the dining hall cuisine and libraries (Hogwarts-esque Uris in particular) receive high marks. Athletics feature eighteen men's and nineteen women's teams competing against NCAA Division I competition as well countless club and intramural opportunities.

Career Services

The Career Services Department has fifty-two full-time staff members, excluding office assistants, who are spread across the various colleges within the university. Those individuals serve as career counselors, internship co-op coordinators, recruiting coordinators, and graduate school advisors in specified disciplines. The 280:1 student-to-advisor ratio is better than average compared to other schools featured in this guide. Among large universities, Cornell's level of support is unparalleled.

Career fairs at Cornell are two-day affairs involving hundreds of Fortune 500, government, and nonprofit employers. In recent years the fall University Career Fair Days have drawn over 6,000 students and 260 employers. Of the Class of 2018, 16 percent found their jobs through on-campus recruiting, 5 percent through career fairs, and 17 percent through an internship or volunteer experience. In an average year, students make over 16,000 advising appointments, and more than 15,000 students attend programs and presentations. Over 500 students take advantage of job-shadowing opportunities offered during winter and spring breaks. Most importantly, 90 percent of students have completed, or plan to complete, an internship/practicum.

Cornell University

E-mail: admissions@cornell.edu | Website: www.cornell.edu

Professional Outcomes

Breaking down the graduates of the College of Arts and Sciences, the largest school at Cornell, 63 percent entered the workforce, 27 percent entered graduate school, 6 percent pursued other endeavors such as travel or volunteer work, and the remaining 4 percent were still seeking employment six months after receiving their diplomas. The top sectors attracting campus-wide graduates in 2018 were financial services (21 percent), consulting (15 percent), technology (14 percent), and health care services (5 percent). Starting salary data varies greatly across schools as well as by major. For example, the average Dyson graduate earns $74,000 while the average College of Agriculture and Life Sciences graduate starts at $60k. College of Engineering students enjoy an average starting salary of $82,000 with a heavy representation at Google, Amazon, Microsoft, and Goldman Sachs. Across all schools the median starting salary was a healthy $66,000.

Of the students from A&S going on to graduate school, 22 percent were pursuing advanced engineering degrees, 9 percent JDs, and 9 percent MDs. Popular destinations included staying at Cornell (especially computer science majors), other Ivies, Stanford, MIT, universities in the UC system, or abroad at Oxford, Cambridge, University of Toronto, or University of St. Andrews. Harvard was the No. 1 destination for biology majors, and Stanford attracted the highest number of chemistry graduates. The ten most frequently attended law schools by Big Red alumni include Columbia, UCLA, Penn, Harvard, and Yale. Those entering medical school typically stay nearby as every one of the ten most popular medical schools was located within the states of New York, New Jersey, or Pennsylvania.

Admission

The deluge of over 51,000 applications for the Class of 2022 was a record setter for Cornell. The acceptance rate of 10.3 percent was an all-time low and has been trending down in recent years. For comparison, Class of 2016 applicants gained acceptance at a 16 percent rate. At Cornell, applicants must apply to one of the eight colleges or schools (counting Dyson and the Hotel School separately), and acceptance rates vary among schools. For example, in the 2017-18 admissions cycle only 3 percent of applicants were accepted into the Dyson School of Applied Economics and Management while the College of Human Ecology admitted 19 percent. Most (83 percent) Cornell freshmen in 2018-19 placed in the top 10 percent of their high school class. The Class of 2022 entered with median SAT/ACT scores of 1480/33; the mid-50 percent ranges were 1390-1540 on the SAT and 32-34 on the ACT. Children of alumni comprised 16.5 percent of the class, and legacy students are believed to have a significant edge, although the school has not been willing to release any statistics in that area. The eight criteria deemed most important by the admissions office are rigor of coursework, grades, test scores, recommendations, essays, extracurriculars, talent/ability, and character/personal qualities. While technically the "easiest" Ivy to get into, that qualifier doesn't mean much these days. Only a fraction away from joining the other seven Ivy League institutions with single-digit acceptance rates, becoming part of Big Red is only a possibility for the crème de la crème of college applicants.

Worth Your Money?

Graduates emerge from their four years of study with an average debt load of just under $30,000, right around the national average. Like many other elite universities, Cornell does not award any merit aid, instead focusing its generosity on students who could not otherwise afford the school. As a result, the $75,000+ list price annual cost of attendance is greatly reduced for students who demonstrate financial need. These students have 100 percent of their need met to the tune of a $43,000 grant. Alumni enjoy starting salaries far superior to those from your average college, making Cornell a phenomenal investment, even if you need to take out sizable loans to attend.

FINANCIAL
Institutional Type: Private
In-State Tuition: $56,550
Out-of-State Tuition: $56,550
Room & Board: $15,201
Required Fees: $672
Books & Supplies: $970

Avg. Need-Based Aid: $42,946
Avg. % of Need Met: 100%

Avg. Merit-Based Aid: $0
% Receiving Merit-Based Aid: 0%

Avg. Cumulative Debt: $29,762
% of Students Borrowing: 41%

CAREER
Who Recruits
1. Four Seasons Hotel and Resorts
2. WeWork
3. Uber
4. Accor
5. Hilton

Notable Internships
1. American Express
2. Lyft
3. PayPal

Top Industries
1. Business
2. Education
3. Operations
4. Research
5. Engineering

Top Employers
1. Google
2. Amazon
3. Microsoft
4. IBM
5. Facebook

Where Alumni Work
1. New York City
2. San Francisco
3. Boston
4. Washington, DC
5. Los Angeles

Median Earnings
College Scorecard (Early Career): $77,200
EOP (Early Career): $79,800
PayScale (Mid-Career): $128,200

RANKINGS
Forbes: 11
Money: 91
U.S. News: 17, National Universities
Wall Street Journal/THE: 9
Washington Monthly: 25, National Universities

#CollegesWorthYourMoney

Dartmouth College

Hanover, New Hampshire | Admissions Phone: 603-646-2875

Inside the Classroom

The smallest school in the Ivy League, Dartmouth plays home to just over 4,400 undergraduate students on its remote, 237-acre New Hampshire campus. Dartmouth has long wrestled with its reputation as one of the most conservative of the Ivy League universities as well as one of the top party schools. Regardless, there are few arguments against the academic superiority of the college that sports sixty majors and a stunning breadth of course selections for an institution of its size.

Dartmouth offers a unique year-round academic calendar with four ten-week terms that allow students maximum flexibility as they pursue internships, paid work, research opportunities, or travel abroad. Undergraduates design their own individual "D-Plan." Needing thirty-five credits for graduation, individuals are free to take anywhere from two to four courses per term. (Most students take three.) Typically, students are expected to spend twelve of the fifteen terms during their natural four-year period on campus, including Sophomore Summer, a mandatory term for rising juniors. All freshmen must take a writing requirement and a first-year seminar course, both designed as intensive workshops to elevate student writing to Dartmouth's high standards.

The learning environment at Dartmouth is extraordinarily intimate. Not only do 62 percent of course sections have under twenty students, but 19 percent has single-digit enrollments. The student-to-faculty ratio is an outstanding 7:1. Undergraduate research opportunities abound with 58 percent of students participating at some point. Further, 88 percent of those participants report having a satisfying experience working with a faculty member in that capacity. The rate of satisfaction is hardly surprising as Dartmouth's faculty consistently rates at the top of rankings/surveys regarding quality of instruction. An extensive study abroad program offers dozens of Dartmouth faculty-led academic experiences around the world, and around half of all students partake.

Top programs offered by Big Green include biology, economics, neuroscience, and government. The social sciences are the most popular, accounting for 34 percent of degrees conferred, followed by mathematics (8 percent), engineering (8 percent), computer science (7 percent), visual and performing arts (5 percent), and history (5 percent). In recent years, an average of fifteen Dartmouth grads have been offered Fulbright Scholarships annually. With sixty-two Rhodes Scholars to its credit, Dartmouth is the sixth highest producer in the history of the award. The Truman Foundation lists Dartmouth as one of its Honor Institutions as many grads have been awarded its $30,000 prize to pursue graduate study in a public service field.

Outside the Classroom

The presence of Greek life at Dartmouth is powerful with over half of the student population belonging to fraternities and sororities. In fact, the school sports one of the highest percentages of Greek-affiliated undergraduates in the entire nation; women join sororities at a 58 percent clip and 48 percent of men sign-up for fraternity life. Over thirty intercollegiate Division I sports are on tap along with two dozen intramural sports and over thirty-five club sports. Roughly three-quarters of Dartmouth men and women participate in some form of athletics. Other highlights include The Dartmouth, America's oldest school newspaper, 170 student-run clubs and organizations, and the Dartmouth Outing Club, the largest collegiate outdoor recreation club in the country. The college owns over 30,000 acres of New Hampshire land that can be enjoyed by students for camping, skiing, hiking, and similar activities. Almost 90 percent of the student body and 100 percent of freshmen live on campus. Dorms earn rave reviews from students, and all are supervised by full-time, live-in community directors. Big Green is living up to its nickname as a green campus with a number of sustainability ventures including transportation, eco-friendly energy options, and its own organic farm/student-operated farmer's market. If you come from an urban environment, the remote feel of Hanover may induce some culture shock, yet Boston is only a two-hour drive away.

Career Services

The Center for Career Development has nine full-time staff members who focus on either career advising or employer relations. The 489:1 student-to-advisor ratio is slightly higher than other schools featured in this guide. However, also available to advise students are the thousands of alumni who volunteer their time as members of the Dartmouth Career Network. Employer Connection Fairs draw over 1,000 students and feature a strong corporate presence. The fall 2019 Engineering Career Fair attracted fifty-one companies including Microsoft, Draftkings, Mastercard, and Wayfair. Students are given a DartBoard account that allows them to access event notifications, on-campus recruiting opportunities, and thousands of internships.

In part because of its unique academic calendar, Dartmouth does an exceptional job facilitating undergraduate internships. Eighty-seven percent of the Class of 2018 participated in at least one internship experience. Many major corporations have elected to become employer partners with the college, a designation that includes, among other things, annual recruiting on campus. Many of those are financial institutions that also grace the list of top employers of Dartmouth grads. (Please see "Professional Outcomes" below.) This alignment of on-campus recruiting and offers of employment at Dartmouth is most impressive.

Professional Outcomes

A great reputation along with a passionate alumni network that is 80,000 strong leads Dartmouth grads to successful transitions into career and graduate school. At the time of receiving their diplomas, 2019 grads had already found employment at a 69 percent clip while 14 percent were headed to graduate school and 14 percent were still weighing their options. Finance is a popular arena for graduates with 26 percent of the Class of 2019 going in that direction. Thus, it is little surprise that included in the top ten employers of Dartmouth grads are a number of investment banks including Goldman Sachs, Morgan Stanley, Bain & Company, Citibank, and Deutsche Bank. Another 21 percent enter the world of consulting. While many start in finance and consulting, a large number of grads plan to enter academia or a career in government down the road. Dartmouth grads will not struggle financially. The median income for Dartmouth grads by age thirty-four is $76,000, thirty-third best of any college in the United States. Upon graduation the majority of the student body migrates to major cities with notably high concentrations in Chicago, DC, New York, Seattle, San Francisco, and Mountain View, California.

Those pursuing graduate and professional degrees often trade one Ivy for another. Harvard, Columbia, and Princeton are three of the most frequent landing spots for Dartmouth grads. Many others continue their studies in one of Dartmouth's own graduate programs or head to other top institutions such as the London School of Economics, Northwestern, or Berkeley. Among the Class of 2019, 20 percent of graduates intended to obtain a medical degree, 10 percent were chasing a law degree, and 14 percent enrolled in PhD programs.

Admission

Like many highly selective schools, Dartmouth's popularity is at an all-time high. The college's yield—the percentage of accepted students who choose to attend—was an all-time high of 61 percent in both 2017-18 and 2018-19. Due to that sky-high yield rate, the number of accepted students fell to only 1,925, the lowest total since the early 1990s. In 2018, Dartmouth shed its double-digit acceptance rate for the first time, falling to 8.7 percent. Five years ago, the admit rate was 12 percent; a decade ago, it was over 18 percent.

The mean SAT is up to 1497, thirty points higher than five years ago, and the mean ACT is 33. Finishing at the top of your class is a must; 95 percent hail from the top 10 percent of their high school graduating class. Legacy students have a fairly strong but not overwhelming presence on campus, comprising 8-9 percent of the student body. Fifteen percent of students are the first in their family to attend college. Alumni interviews are offered but not required. Essays and recommendations are rated as "very important" by the admissions staff. Bottom line: many pine to be part of this Ivy League institution, but earning a spot on the bucolic Hanover campus has never been tougher. Those who wish to experience its renowned teaching faculty and intimate learning environment, rich with hands-on opportunities, will need to bring stellar credentials to the table.

Worth Your Money?

An average annual grant of $53k is delivered to the 2,215 qualifying students, a figure that meets 100 percent of every single student's demonstrated financial need. Most other students will pay the full cost of attendance—$76,718—as there is no merit aid offered at Dartmouth. Those not qualifying for aid are typically in the upper-income brackets with an estimated 20 percent of current undergraduates counting themselves among the 1-percent club, and another 25 percent are from families in the top 5 percent of income levels nationwide. Big Green is unlikely to cost you large amounts of green unless you can comfortably afford it. For that reason, coupled with the stellar postgraduate outcomes you would expect from an Ivy, Dartmouth is, without question, worth the price.

FINANCIAL
Institutional Type: Private
In-State Tuition: $55,605
Out-of-State Tuition: $55,605
Room & Board: $16,374
Required Fees: $2,017
Books & Supplies: $1,100

Avg. Need-Based Aid: $52,542
Avg. % of Need Met: 100%

Avg. Merit-Based Aid: $0
% Receiving Merit-Based Aid: 0%

Avg. Cumulative Debt: $18,903
% of Students Borrowing: 49%

CAREER
Who Recruits
1. Partenon
2. Nomura
3. Oliver Wyman
4. Bridgewater
5. Trinity Partners

Notable Internships
1. PNC
2. Bain & Company
3. ICM

Top Industries
1. Business
2. Education
3. Research
4. Finance
5. Operations

Top Employers
1. Google
2. Goldman Sachs
3. Amazon
4. Morgan Stanley
5. Facebook

Where Alumni Work
1. Boston
2. New York City
3. San Francisco
4. Washington, DC
5. Los Angeles

Median Earnings
College Scorecard (Early Career): $75,500
EOP (Early Career): $76,600
PayScale (Mid-Career): $130,900

RANKINGS
Forbes: 10
Money: 95
U.S. News: 12, National Universities
Wall Street Journal/THE: 12 (T)
Washington Monthly: 34, National Universities

#CollegesWorthYourMoney

Davidson College

Davidson, North Carolina | Admissions Phone: 704-894-2230

ADMISSION
Admission Rate: 19%
Admission Rate - Men: 20%
Admission Rate - Women: 19%
EA Admission Rate: Not Offered
ED Admission Rate: 46%
Admission Rate (5-Year Trend): -7%
ED Admission Rate (5-Year Trend): N/A
% of Admits Attending (Yield): 46%
Transfer Admission Rate: 16%

Offered Wait List: N/A
Accepted Wait List: N/A
Admitted Wait List: N/A

SAT Reading/Writing (Middle 50%): 640-720
SAT Math (Middle 50%): 650-730
ACT Composite (Middle 50%): 29-33
Testing Policy: ACT/SAT Required
SAT Superscore: Yes
ACT Superscore: Yes

% Graduated in Top 10% of HS Class: 73%
% Graduated in Top 25% of HS Class: 97%
% Graduated in Top 50% of HS Class: 100%

ENROLLMENT
Total Undergraduate Enrollment: 1,843
% Part-Time: 0%
% Male: 52%
% Female: 48%
% Out-of-State: 78%
% Fraternity: 30%
% Sorority: 49%
% On-Campus (Freshman): 100%
% On-Campus (All Undergraduate): 95%

% African-American: 7%
% Asian: 5%
% Hispanic: 8%
% White: 67%
% Other: 4%
% Race or Ethnicity Unknown: 1%
% International: 7%
% Low-Income: 12%

ACADEMICS
Student-to-Faculty Ratio: 9:1
% of Classes Under 20: 69%
% of Classes Under 40: 99%
% Full-Time Faculty: 95%
% Full-Time Faculty w/ Terminal Degree: 97%

Top Programs
Biology
Chemistry
Economics
English
History
Physics
Political Science
Psychology

Retention Rate: 95%
4-Year Graduation Rate: 90%
6-Year Graduation Rate: 90%

Curricular Flexibility: Somewhat Flexible
Academic Rating: ★★★★✦

Inside the Classroom

Strolling around Davidson's lush campus, taking in the historic buildings and intellectually engaged student body, it's easy to forget that you are situated about twenty miles north of Charlotte, North Carolina, and not in the heart of New England. The 1,800 students who grace this undergrad-only institution are high achievers who take academics and their school's more-than-just-lip-service Honor Code seriously.

With its small size, the impressive part of the college is the exceptional quality of its offerings, not the breadth of them, as only twenty-nine majors are available. Additional interdisciplinary majors also can be accessed for those seeking another pathway. However, the majority of students stick to traditional areas of concentration with economics, biology, political science, and psychology being the most popular. Required courses include eight classes under the umbrella category of Ways of Knowing that feature, among others, history, rhetoric, quantitative thought, and the visual performing arts. Additional mandated coursework in foreign language, writing, diversity, justice/equality, and physical education must be completed by all students, regardless of major.

The student-to-faculty ratio is 9:1, which allows the college to ensure that 69 percent have fewer than twenty students and 28 percent have enrollments you can count on two hands. Overall, the average number of students per class is only fifteen. Study abroad is encouraged, and more than three-quarters of students elect to study in one of 110 programs around the globe. Undergraduates working side-by-side with their professors is commonplace as over 60 percent of faculty have published with student coauthors at some point.

Top programs at Davidson include political science, chemistry, and English. However, any degree from Davidson is a credential from one of the most respected liberal arts colleges in the country. In fact, it regularly cracks top ten lists of best liberal arts schools and best teaching faculty. Students are no strangers to accolades either; of 467 graduates of the Class of 2018, an almost incomprehensible fifteen students were awarded Fulbright Scholarships. In the same year other members of the graduating class won Boren, Truman, Watson, and Princeton in Africa fellowships/scholarships. In addition, twenty-three alumni have won Rhodes Scholarships.

Outside the Classroom

"Typical" is not a word that applies to any facet of campus life at Davidson. For example, team sports participation is required at the varsity, club, or intramural level. The ten men's and nine women's varsity teams compete in NCAA Division I with the successful men's basketball team atop the popularity charts. Davidson's fourteen Greek houses are all under the purview of one entity, Patterson Court, which ensures that fraternities, sororities, and eating houses all have a social/charitable mission and abide by a common set of rules. Participation is extremely high as 63 percent of male students and 45 percent of females join a Patterson Court house. Students also run over 200 clubs, including Davidson Outdoors, which organizes kayaking, hiking, and climbing trips around the globe as well as in the school's own backyard. The Lake Norman campus, a 110-acre waterfront property only seven miles from the main campus, is reserved for exclusive use by Davidson students. The college's Union Board, the largest student organization, puts on well-attended events including concerts, trivia nights, and movie screenings on a regular basis. The surrounding town of Davidson features many attractions such as an array of student-friendly coffee shops and restaurants as well as a local farmer's market. Those seeking off-campus nightlife and cultural experiences can make that easy twenty-minute drive south to Charlotte.

Career Services

The Center for Career Development (CCD) is staffed by nine full-time staff members, seven of whom have "director" or "assistant director" in their job title. That works out to a student-to-advisor ratio of 205:1, much lower (i.e. better) than the average institution included in this book. Despite the administrative titles, all members of the staff get hands-on with career counseling. In the 2016-17 school year 86 percent of undergrads engaged with the CCD, including 94 percent of all seniors. Over 150 employers recruited on campus including Amazon, Google, Bain, IBM, Deloitte, and Cigna.

One nice aspect of the CCD is its systematic four-year development model that outlines recommended activities for students at all phases of their undergraduate education. As freshmen, Davidson students are encouraged to get comfortable with Handshake and get one-on-one assistance with resume writing. From there, students receive career coaching, help locating an internship, and can participate in the Senior Bootcamp. Close to 150 students per year participate in the school's job-shadowing program, and 98 percent reported that the experience was helpful. The newly launched Insider Series brings professionals in a host of fields (e.g., sports marketing, advertising, and writing careers) to campus to impart career advice. Participation in Career Treks and group visits to corporations and nonprofit agencies has increased significantly in recent years.

Professional Outcomes

Looking at the past five years of available outcomes data, 73-79 percent of graduates landed jobs within six months of graduation, 14-20 percent were enrolled in a graduate program, and 3-4 percent were still seeking employment. Remaining in North Carolina after graduation is a popular choice, but many grads migrate to New York and DC as well. The top three industries favored by graduates are (in order) education, health care, and financial services. Employers of the largest number of Davidson grads include Carolina Healthcare System, Teach for America, the NIH, Wells Fargo, and Bank of America. At age thirty-four, graduates are earning a median salary of slightly over $60k, more than $10k less than Duke and Wake Forest grads but higher salaries than North Carolina rivals UNC or Elon alums.

Of those who attended grad school, the highest number were in health-care-related programs (including MDs), law school, and laboratory sciences. Significant numbers of students pursue advanced degrees at other Southern gems including Vanderbilt, Emory, Duke, Wake Forest, and UNC. In fact, over a five-year period the college sent more law school-bound alumni to UNC Law School (22), Duke (10), and Emory (7) than any other institution. There is also a fair showing of Ivy League acceptances in all graduate disciplines among Wildcat alumni.

Admission

In 2018, Davidson received a modest but all-time high of 5,700 applications, but it accepted an all-time low 19.5 percent into the Class of 2022. For perspective, in 2013, the school accepted 26 percent of applicants, so the school has become a bit more selective in recent years. On standardized tests, enrolled students have a middle 50 percent of 1290-1450 on the SAT and 29-33 on the ACT. The two tests are submitted with equal frequency by Davidson applicants. Davidson students being admitted today do possess slightly higher test scores than students did five years ago. The average GPA of an enrolled student is over 3.93, and 73 percent finished in the top 10 percent of their class; 97 percent finished in the top quartile.

The college has a unique set of admissions criteria atop its list. According to the admissions office, it places the most weight on rigor of coursework, recommendations, volunteer work, and character/personal qualities. Test scores are among the criteria viewed as being next in importance followed by the merely "considered" factors of class rank, GPA, and legacy status. Applying via binding early decision greatly improves your odds. Class of 2022 members who applied ED were accepted at a 46 percent rate compared to only 16 percent in the regular round. Almost two-thirds of the incoming class was filled through the early round, one of the highest figures you will find at any school. One of the most selective liberal arts schools in the South, Davidson's high yield rate (how many accepted students enroll) of 46 percent suggests the applicant pool is self-selecting as well as frequently applying through ED. Those offered admission typically sport excellent grades/test scores, although components of the process are genuinely holistic.

Worth Your Money?

Half of Davidson undergraduates qualify for need-based aid, an area in which the university is notably generous. Almost every student who qualifies for financial aid sees 100 percent of demonstrated need met, and the average annual grant is for over $45,000. Davidson is also more generous with merit aid than your typical highly selective institution, giving 23 percent of current students an average annual award of nearly $20k. At $70,177 in annual cost of attendance, Davidson's list price is a touch lower than many other schools of its ilk and, even better, most of those schools do not pay the full amount. An estimated 50 percent of undergrads have parents who are top 5 percent income-earners, and pretty much everyone else gets a steep discount. With a record of solid graduate outcomes to boot, Davidson is absolutely worth your money.

FINANCIAL
Institutional Type: Private
In-State Tuition: $52,524
Out-of-State Tuition: $52,524
Room & Board: $14,803
Required Fees: $525
Books & Supplies: $1,000

Avg. Need-Based Aid: $45,002
Avg. % of Need Met: 100%

Avg. Merit-Based Aid: $19,973
% Receiving Merit-Based Aid: 23%

Avg. Cumulative Debt: $22,599
% of Students Borrowing: 29%

CAREER
Who Recruits
1. ESPN
2. Barings
3. Deloitte
4. EY
5. BlackArch Partners

Notable Internships
1. Cancer Treatment Centers of America
2. U.S. House of Representatives
3. POLITICO

Top Industries
1. Business
2. Education
3. Social Services
4. Healthcare
5. Operations

Top Employers
1. Wells Fargo
2. Bank of America
3. Wells Fargo
4. US Army
5. Deloitte

Where Alumni Work
1. Charlotte
2. New York City
3. Washington, DC
4. Atlanta
5. Raleigh-Durham, NC

Median Earnings
College Scorecard (Early Career): $58,900
EOP (Early Career): $60,300
PayScale (Mid-Career): $106,900

RANKINGS
Forbes: 48
Money: 87
U.S. News: 17 (T), Liberal Arts Colleges
Wall Street Journal/THE: 54
Washington Monthly: 25, Liberal Arts Colleges

#CollegesWorthYourMoney

Dickinson College

Carlisle, Pennsylvania | Admissions Phone: 717-245-1231

Inside the Classroom

Set in the small town of Carlisle, Pennsylvania, Dickinson College is a liberal arts school with a strong academic reputation that dates back to the earliest days of the United States. In fact, it was founded the same week the United States signed the Treaty of Paris that ended the Revolutionary War. Today, the 2,400 undergraduate students who call Dickinson home are an increasingly diverse group, both in terms of academic/career interests and demographically. In recent years the school has doubled its rate of international students to 13 percent and raised the presence of underrepresented minorities from 15 percent in 2013 to 21 percent in 2017. The school does have a notable gender gap to the tune of a 60/40 split in favor of women.

Freshmen are matched with a professor-advisor and engage in a mandatory first-year seminar intended to hone critical thinking, analysis, and research skills. From there, students must embark on an extensive trek through required coursework in quantitative reasoning, the humanities and arts, the social sciences, laboratory science, foreign language, and four physical education blocks. There are additional boxes to check in the areas of US diversity, global diversity, and a sustainability course.

As students immerse themselves in one of forty-four areas of concentration, Dickinson supports them with a 9:1 student-to-faculty ratio and average class size of fifteen with 75 percent of classes being capped at nineteen students. This type of intimacy allows the school to advertise that "Not only will you have the opportunity to conduct advanced research as an undergraduate that most wouldn't experience until graduate school, you'll also have the chance to work alongside faculty in the process." The majority of students also elect to venture to other continents as part of their undergraduate experience. Offering study abroad opportunities in thirty-nine locations in twenty-four countries across six continents, Dickinson enjoys a 62 percent participation rate.

By discipline, the greatest number of degrees are conferred in the social sciences (27 percent); business (10 percent); biology (9 percent); and area, ethnic, and gender studies (8 percent). The college's foreign language program that features thirteen offerings—including Arabic, Hebrew, and Portuguese—is recognized as one of the top programs in the country. International studies, history, and environmental studies also have particularly strong reputations. Dickinson students are known as a globetrotting and service-oriented bunch. Thus, it is fitting that the college is a leading producer of Fulbright scholars and Peace Corps volunteers.

Outside the Classroom

Dickinson is located in central Pennsylvania about twenty miles from the state capital of Harrisburg. Carlisle may be a small town, yet there are a reasonable number of nearby shopping/dining options, including dozens of restaurants within walking distance. The school's small town location means that a good deal of social life takes place on campus where literally 100 percent of students reside in college-owned housing. Greek life has a strong but not dominant presence with only 4 percent of men joining fraternities but 25 percent of women joining sororities. More than one hundred student clubs exist with the highest concentrations in the performing arts and club sports. For those serious about athletics, the Red Devils compete in NCAA Division III in eleven men's and twelve women's sports. Environmental sustainability is important to the administration and students alike, and with its own organic farm and pledge to be climate neutral by 2020, the college is regularly ranked as one of the top eco-friendly colleges in the country.

Career Services

The Career Center has seven professional employees (not counting the two administrative assistants) who play advising, pre-professional counseling, and employer relations roles. That works out to a 343:1 student-to-advisor ratio, which is about average compared to other schools featured in this guide. One counselor is dedicated to pre-health advising and another guides pre-law students.

Dickinson does not host its own career fairs but does endorse two nearby gatherings, the Capital Region Internship Fair at Penn State Harrisburg and the Not-for-Profit Networking Fair in Philadelphia. However, there are other areas where this office excels. For example, a tremendous 94 percent of students completed an internship, service-learning, or research apprenticeship at some point over their four years of study. In the summer of 2019, more than 400 students completed internships and summer research experiences in thirty states and twenty-one countries. In 2016, the college also launched an externship program in which students can spend between two and ten days over winter break shadowing alums in their workplaces. Unfortunately, only a tiny percentage of alumni report finding their job directly because of the Career Center. Less than 1 percent of 2005-2010 graduates, surveyed in 2015, cited a Dickinson Career Center event as a factor in finding employment. Less than 2 percent (per category) were assisted by an on-campus interview, a job fair, or school-provided online resources. To be fair, there is evidence that the office has made great strides since that time.

Professional Outcomes

One year after graduating, 93 percent of Dickinsonians have found jobs, full-time volunteer work, or have enrolled in graduate school. The most popular industries are, in order, business and industry, education, health and medical services, and nonprofits. Red Devils head to a wide range of organizations/employers with multiple 2018 grads headed to the US Army, the Peace Corps, Teach for America and, on the other end of the spectrum, the Vanguard Group. Many other well-known financial, pharmaceutical, and consulting companies are represented on the list of 2018 graduate destinations as are a host of other nonprofit organizations. Across all graduating years, companies employing more than twenty-five Dickinson alumni include Deloitte, IBM, Morgan Stanley, JPMorgan Chase & Co., Merck, EY, PNC, PwC, Google, and Amazon. The median salary for a Dickinson alum at age thirty-four is $55,000, slightly less than graduates of rival Franklin & Marshall. It's interesting that more alumni can be found in New York City than in Pennsylvania.

Within five years of receiving their diplomas, 55-60 percent of recent grads have entered or finished graduate school. For the Class of 2018, the majority of graduate school-bound new alums found homes in state universities; however, a fair number of prestigious acceptances were sprinkled in including Penn, Tufts, Emory, and Carnegie Mellon (computer science), Johns Hopkins, Columbia, UVA, and NYU. Law school applicants are accepted at a rate of 97 percent with some applicants finding success in Carlisle at Penn State's Dickinson Law School, and two 2018 grads are now attending Notre Dame Law School. Of students recommended for medical school by the college, 75 percent were accepted into at least one institution.

Admission

From 2013-2018 as the highly rated liberal arts admissions world became increasingly more hyper competitive, Dickinson experienced little change. The admit rate in 2018 was 49 percent, slightly friendlier than the 44 percent in 2013. Standardized test scores for admitted students have also remained fairly constant, and the majority do submit them (60 percent submit SATs and 27 percent submit ACTs) even though the school went test-optional a long time ago. The mid-50 percent range on the ACT is 27-31 and 1200-1390 on the SAT. The same goes for class rank, which in 2018-19 saw 41 percent of freshmen hail from the top 10 percent of their high school cohort, and 74 percent finish in the top 25 percent; only 4 percent of this group did not finish in the top half of their class.

Dickinson shows love to students who love them. Sixty-eight percent of early decision applicants were offered admission in 2018, which was a reduction from the previous year. It is unusual for a college to include "demonstrated interest" as one of the most important factors in admissions decisions, but Dickinson does exactly that. With a yield rate of only 21 percent, the vast majority of those accepted into the college elect to attend another institution. A handful of other soft factors also sit atop the list: volunteer work, talent/ability, and character/personal qualities. Despite its status as a highly selective institution, intelligent students with a blemish still have a chance to find a home here. With its test-optional policy, those who excelled in the classroom but struggled on Saturday mornings with a No. 2 pencil in their hand are still in the running as are those with the opposite imperfection—strong SAT-takers who bloomed late as serious-minded students.

Worth Your Money?

An impressively high 61 percent of Dickinson students are awarded some level of need-based aid. While not all see 100 percent of their demonstrated need met, the majority do, and the average annual grant is $42,448. An additional 18 percent of undergraduates receive annual merit aid awards of $12,685, helping to reduce the total cost of attendance that is estimated at over $73k per year. Thanks to that assistance, the amount of debt incurred by the average Dickinson student is less than that of the average college student in the United States. If you were borrowing $100k+ to study the liberal arts, we would caution against selecting this school without first exploring more cost-effective options. However, for those taking on modest amounts of student loans, this is a college worth attending for the intimate class environment and solid graduate outcomes.

FINANCIAL
Institutional Type: Private
In-State Tuition: $55,948
Out-of-State Tuition: $55,948
Room & Board: $14,176
Required Fees: $575
Books & Supplies: $1,250

Avg. Need-Based Aid: $42,448
Avg. % of Need Met: 100%

Avg. Merit-Based Aid: $12,685
% Receiving Merit-Based Aid: 18%

Avg. Cumulative Debt: $26,977
% of Students Borrowing: 56%

CAREER
Who Recruits
1. Gartner
2. Amazon
3. Booz Allen Hamilton
4. PwC
5. PNC

Notable Internships
1. BlackRock
2. IBM
3. Cushman & Wakefield

Top Industries
1. Business
2. Education
3. Operations
4. Social Services
5. Sales

Top Employers
1. US Army
2. Deloitte
3. IBM
4. Morgan Stanley
5. JPMorgan Chase

Where Alumni Work
1. New York City
2. Philadelphia
3. Washington, DC
4. Boston
5. Harrisburg, PA

Median Earnings
College Scorecard (Early Career): $57,400
EOP (Early Career): $55,100
PayScale (Mid-Career): $100,100

RANKINGS
Forbes: 120
Money: 230
U.S. News: 46, Liberal Arts Colleges
Wall Street Journal/THE: 100
Washington Monthly: 49, Liberal Arts Colleges

#CollegesWorthYourMoney

Philadelphia, Pennsylvania | Admissions Phone: 215-895-2400

ADMISSION
Admission Rate: 77%
Admission Rate - Men: 76%
Admission Rate - Women: 78%
EA Admission Rate: 96%
ED Admission Rate: 86%
Admission Rate (5-Year Trend): -5%
ED Admission Rate (5-Year Trend): Previously Not Offered
% of Admits Attending (Yield): 14%
Transfer Admission Rate: 48%

Offered Wait List: 1,215
Accepted Wait List: N/A
Admitted Wait List: 9

SAT Reading/Writing (Middle 50%): 580-670
SAT Math (Middle 50%): 590-710
ACT Composite (Middle 50%): 25-30
Testing Policy: Test Flexible
SAT Superscore: Yes
ACT Superscore: Yes

% Graduated in Top 10% of HS Class: 33%
% Graduated in Top 25% of HS Class: 64%
% Graduated in Top 50% of HS Class: 90%

ENROLLMENT
Total Undergraduate Enrollment: 15,667
% Part-Time: 11%
% Male: 52%
% Female: 48%
% Out-of-State: 49%
% Fraternity: 11%
% Sorority: 10%
% On-Campus (Freshman): 87%
% On-Campus (All Undergraduate): 22%

% African-American: 7%
% Asian: 18%
% Hispanic: 7%
% White: 52%
% Other: 4%
% Race or Ethnicity Unknown: 2%
% International: 11%
% Low-Income: 18%

ACADEMICS
Student-to-Faculty Ratio: 11:1
% of Classes Under 20: 53%
% of Classes Under 40: 85%
% Full-Time Faculty: 54%
% Full-Time Faculty w/ Terminal Degree: 86%

Top Programs
Biomedical Engineering
Civil Engineering
Design
Information Systems
Mechanical Engineering
Nursing
Public Health

Retention Rate: 89%
4-Year Graduation Rate: N/A
6-Year Graduation Rate: 74%

Curricular Flexibility: Less Flexible
Academic Rating: ★★★

Inside the Classroom

Building your campus adjacent to an Ivy League school like the University of Pennsylvania is a solid recipe to end up a higher education afterthought. Yet Drexel, established in 1891, has carved out its own solid reputation as a private research university specializing in engineering, business, and nursing, all bolstered by a ground-breaking and distinctive co-op program that just celebrated its one hundredth anniversary. Drexel Dragons come to the university for its rigorous programs as well as the emphasis placed on experiential learning. They leave, by and large, with well-paying jobs in their area of interest. Practical, career-minded teens find a good partner institution in Drexel University.

There are eighty-plus undergraduate majors to choose from at Drexel, and the academic culture lets you get down to brass tacks quickly. Other than a Composition & Rhetoric course and introductory classes that provide an overview of university life and the co-op experience, most students dive right into their major-specific course-work as freshmen. Business students take courses like Foundations of Economics, Principles of Economics, and Introduction to Analysis. Engineering students are plopped right into Chemistry, Calculus, and Introduction to Engineering Design and Data Analysis. The robust co-op program sees just about every single undergraduate participate. Students can choose between a five-year plan that includes three co-op experiences or a traditional four-year pathway that allows for one co-op placement. The school runs year-round on a quarter calendar to accommodate students on co-ops.

Drexel offers a reasonable 11:1 student-to-faculty ratio with commensurately reasonable class sizes. Fifty-three percent of sections contain nineteen or fewer students, and just a sliver under 10 percent of sections contain fifty or more. Drexel students are encouraged to begin seeking undergraduate research opportunities "as early as the freshman year." An array of research-oriented co-ops exist at local hospitals, museums, and pharmaceutical companies as well. With the emphasis on co-op education, it can be difficult to carve out time to study abroad while at Drexel. Last year, roughly 900 students managed to study internationally at one of sixty locations. Co-ops in foreign countries are another way to access the benefits of this type of experience.

Looking at the number of degrees conferred by discipline, the big three at Drexel are business (25 percent), health professions (21 percent), and engineering (21 percent). Visual and performing arts (9 percent), computer science (4 percent), biology (3 percent), and mathematics (3 percent) round out the list of majors with a sizable representation. The Westphal College of Media Arts & Design has a growing reputation, as do programs in engineering. Also on the rise is Drexel's number of winners of prestigious postgraduate fellowships. In 2019, four undergraduates won Fulbright Scholarships and six former Drexel undergrads took home National Science Foundation Graduate Research Fellowships.

Outside the Classroom

Set on a ninety-six-acre urban campus in University City, the section of Philadelphia that also includes the University of Pennsylvania, Drexel has 87 percent of freshmen residing in university-owned housing, but only 22 percent of the overall student body live on campus. Greek life draws 11 percent of males and 10 percent of female students. There are eighteen NCAA Division I sports teams that compete in the Colonial Athletic Association. Club and intramural sports are huge with over 9,000 participants each year. The Drexel Recreation Center is an 18,000-square-foot facility with all of the fitness amenities one could desire. There are 300 active student organizations on campus and a ton more opportunities for fun in the surrounding area. Drexel students get in free at the Academy of Natural Sciences, the oldest museum of its kind in the country, and can just as easily walk to World Café Live and catch a free concert with a big-name artist every Friday afternoon. Famed art museums, major sporting events, and an excellent food and bar scene are all within a short distance of campus. Student groups like the Campus Activities Board organize group trips to amusement parks, Broadway plays, and host block parties and other special events on campus.

Career Services

The Steinbright Career Development Center is staffed by thirteen full-time staff members who serve as career counselors, pre-law/pre-health advisors, and employer relations specialists. However, there are twenty-four additional professional employees dedicated to the co-op program, bringing the total to thirty-seven staff members who work with undergraduates on career-related matters. That works out to a 419:1 ratio, a respectable figure for a university of Drexel's size and scope. Its three annual career fairs are well attended by employers, but student attendance is lower than one would expect. The Fall Career Fair drew 228 employers and 1,678 students, the Spring Career Fair attracted 109 companies/organizations and 923 students, and the Engineering Career Fair saw 135 employers and 625 students in attendance.

When it comes to career services at Drexel the co-op experiences are, to quote Philadelphia-area native Reggie Jackson, "The straw that stirs the drink." Among surveyed graduates, 84 percent had a co-op experience that was relevant to their current job, and 89 percent landed jobs related to their college majors. More importantly, 48 percent of students received a job offer from one of their co-op employers. Placements are available in thirty-one states and thirty-eight countries, and partner organizations include major players like Goldman Sachs, Lockheed Martin, and Exelon. The strength of this one-of-a-kind co-op program combined with strong employment statistics earns the Steinbright Career Development Center high marks from our staff.

Professional Outcomes

One year after graduating, 96 percent of the class of 2018 had arrived at their next destination; 84 percent were employed, and 12 percent had matriculated into graduate or professional school. The largest employers of Drexel alumni are Comcast, Merck, Vanguard, and Johnson & Johnson. There are also at least one hundred Dragons within GlaxoSmithKline, JP Morgan Chase, SAP (software), Amazon, Microsoft, IBM, Accenture, Deloitte, Google, and EY. Six times as many graduates remain in Philadelphia as go to the second most popular postgraduation destination of New York City. Pockets of Drexel alumni can also be found in DC, San Francisco, Baltimore, Boston, and Los Angeles. The average starting salary for Drexel grads with a full-time job was $59,500.

The predominately career-driven group that attends the university does not immediately move on to graduate schools in large numbers. However, those who do have produced some solid results, particularly those applying to medical and law school. Drexel's medical school acceptance rate was 69 percent, almost thirty points higher than the national average. It offers an accelerated BS/MD program with its own Drexel University College of Medicine. Other commonly attended medical schools include local options Rowan, Temple, Sidney Kimmel Medical College, and the Philadelphia College of Osteopathic Medicine. Eighty-four percent of law school applicants ultimately found a home for their legal education. Recent grads have landed at prestigious law schools at Harvard, the University of Michigan, Vanderbilt, and the University of Pennsylvania as well as a number of local options including Drexel's own law school that opened in 2006.

Admission

Drexel's 30,242 applicants for a place in the freshman class of 2018-19 overwhelmingly received favorable admissions news—77 percent were accepted. That healthy percentage is the norm at Drexel as acceptance rates have been in the 70-80 percent range for some time. Its yield rate, the number of accepted students who actually enroll, is around 14 percent. This is because, for many, Drexel is not their first choice. Still, those who end up attending have a strong academic profile. Freshmen in 2018-19 possessed a mid-50 percent SAT of 1170-1380 and an ACT of 25-30. One-third placed within the top 10 percent of their high school class, and 64 percent were in the top quartile; 49 percent of students sported a GPA of 3.75 or higher and, on the other end, 6 percent had a GPA under 3.0.

Admissions decisions are made in a manner consistent with Drexel's STEM-focus—the hard numbers are of utmost importance. GPA, standardized test scores, class rank, and the rigor of one's high school coursework are deemed "very important" while soft factors like recommendations, essays, and character/personal qualities comprise the second tier. With such a low yield rate, the university looks favorably upon those who will commit to it through binding early decision. The ED acceptance rate in 2018 was 86 percent. In short, Drexel is a rare school with a pre-professional focus that is not terribly difficult to get into. Those with standardized test scores around the 80th percentile and solid but imperfect grades should find a welcome home here.

Worth Your Money?

Drexel graduates earn 18.5 percent above the national average which, even given the focus on business, engineering, and nursing is still an impressive achievement. That salary boost is needed thanks to the $71,600 annual cost of attendance, although students receiving merit aid do receive an average annual grant of $33k. Fortunately, the co-op experience is top notch and frequently leads to gainful employment in one's area of study. Students do not pay tuition during their co-op year and, in fact, are paid a median six-month salary of $18,357. This college is unique and connected enough to be worth the high price tag, particularly for students pursing more pre-professional majors.

FINANCIAL
Institutional Type: Private
In-State Tuition: $52,146
Out-of-State Tuition: $52,146
Room & Board: $14,241
Required Fees: $2,370
Books & Supplies: $1,200

Avg. Need-Based Aid: $33,305
Avg. % of Need Met: 81%

Avg. Merit-Based Aid: $15,641
% Receiving Merit-Based Aid: 35%

Avg. Cumulative Debt: N/A
% of Students Borrowing: N/A

CAREER
Who Recruits
1. Seer Interactive
2. Bentley Systems
3. Johnson & Johnson
4. Spark Therapeutics
5. Lockheed Martin

Notable Internships
1. KPMG
2. Anthropologie
3. Delancy Street Partners

Top Industries
1. Business
2. Engineering
3. Operations
4. Education
5. Healthcare

Top Employers
1. Lockheed Martin
2. Comcast
3. Merck
4. Vanguard
5. Johnson & Johnson

Where Alumni Work
1. Philadelphia
2. New York City
3. Washington, DC
4. San Francisco
5. Baltimore

Median Earnings
College Scorecard (Early Career): $68,800
EOP (Early Career): N/A
PayScale (Mid-Career): $114,800

RANKINGS
Forbes: 226
Money: 382
U.S. News: 97, National Universities
Wall Street Journal/THE: 96 (T)
Washington Monthly: 156, National Universities

#CollegesWorthYourMoney

Duke University

Durham, North Carolina | Admissions Phone: 919-684-3214

Inside the Classroom

Duke is a place where students can be, at once, fanatical, face-painted members of the Cameron Crazies as well as studious, career-minded young people in an Ivy League-caliber academic environment. Close to 6,700 undergrads are joined by more than 9,900 graduate students on this picturesque, 8,800-acre campus in Durham, North Carolina. Nineteen percent go on to earn degrees in the social sciences followed by engineering (15 percent), biology (14 percent), public administration and social services (9 percent), and psychology (7 percent).

The academic offerings at Duke include fifty-three majors, fifty-two minors, and twenty-six interdisciplinary certificates. More than 4,000 undergraduate courses run each semester in the College of Arts & Sciences alone. Rarely do students concentrate solely on one major—83 percent either double major, add a minor, or pursue an additional certificate. Undergraduates encounter a good number of unique academic requirements. All freshmen in the Trinity College of Arts & Sciences must take a first-year seminar and first-year writing course. Before graduation, each individual must take two small group learning experiences that can involve an independent study and/or constructing a thesis. Foreign language and multiple courses under the umbrellas of Areas of Knowledge and Modes of Inquiry also must be tackled.

Class sizes are on the small side—71 percent are nineteen or fewer, and 27 percent are less than ten. A stellar 6:1 student-to-faculty ratio helps keep classes so reasonable even while catering to almost five-figures of graduate students. The Undergraduate Research Support Office does great work connecting students with opportunities to conduct research, either over the summer or during the regular school year. All told, more than half of undergraduates conduct research. More than any other top-ten research institution, Duke students pursue a semester abroad—48 percent elect to venture off to one of the school's 300 partner programs scattered around the world.

Duke has a sterling reputation for academics across the board. The Department of Biology is world class and a leading producer of successful medical school applicants. Programs in economics, English, and public policy consistently earn top ranking as well. Blue Devils win prestigious postgraduate fellowships on a regular basis. Named a top producer of Fulbright Scholars for the last thirteen years, Duke churned out twelve winners in 2018. The university has produced an incredible forty-three Rhodes Scholars in its illustrious history, more than Emory and Vanderbilt combined.

Outside the Classroom

When you enter campus through Duke Gardens, it can feel like you're strolling through a perfectly manicured Disney theme park; everything is pristine and aesthetically pleasing. Thus, no one is anxious to live anywhere other than the university's grounds and 100 percent of freshmen and 85 percent of the entire student body live on campus. With thirty-nine recognized Greek chapters, fraternities and sororities play a major role in social life at Duke. Almost 42 percent of women and 29 percent of men become Greek affiliated. Those who occupy dorms are generally pleased, and the food at Duke is universally praised. Big-time sports is a staple of life on campus as the Blue Devils compete in twenty-three sports in NCAA Division I's vaunted Atlantic Coast Conference. Since the beloved Coach K took over in 1980, the men's basketball squad has made the Final Four a dozen times and has won five national championships. One of the most popular non-sports-related, campus-wide events is the annual Last Day of Classes (LDOC) celebration that draws a large percentage of the student body for activities, beverages, and music. More than 400 student organizations run on campus, including a high-performing mock trial team and The Chronicle, an award-winning student newspaper with a seven-figure budget. The culture of volunteering is strong with an 80 percent participation rate as Blue Devils perform community service in the city of Durham in programs like Engineers Without Borders.

Career Services

The Career Center at Duke is staffed by eight undergraduate career advisors and six employer relations specialists. Not counting other full-time employees who do not work directly with students or the career ambassadors, who are current students, Duke's student-to-advisor ratio calculates to 477:1, which is slightly below average compared to other schools in its weight class. Yet, this is not indicative of anything less than outstanding career services offerings. This assessment can be delivered by one quick fact: An astounding 95 percent of graduating seniors who had lined up their first jobs were hired by companies that work in some capacity with the Duke Career Center.

Undergrads each have their own assigned career counselor, and the school recommends establishing a relationship as a freshman. Two-thirds of graduates reported meeting with a career center staff member at least once over their four years of study. Regular events held include Practice Interview Day, Ignite Your Internship Search, and the Fall Career Fair that includes over one hundred top companies, many of which recruit and offer interviews on campus. Despite having a higher student-to-advisor ratio than the average school profiled in this book, the career center at Duke is among the best in the country at preparing students for high-paying employment and admission into prestigious graduate/professional programs.

Professional Outcomes

At graduation, 71 percent of surveyed seniors in 2018 were set to enter the world of work, 20 percent were continuing into graduate schools, and 2 percent were starting their own businesses. The industries that attract the largest percentage of Blue Devils are finance, IT, health care, business and consulting, and science/research. Companies employing a minimum of three Class of 2018 Duke grads include Google, Capital One, Facebook, Amazon, Microsoft, Oracle, Goldman Sachs, Morgan Stanley, Accenture, and a host of other top-shelf corporations in the areas of technology, finance, and consulting. Thirty-four percent of Duke alumni elect to stay in North Carolina. New York, California, DC, and Massachusetts follow in popularity. The top foreign destinations for employment are the United Kingdom and China. Duke students, on average, do exceptionally well financially, bringing home the eleventh highest salary by age thirty-four of any school in the country, ahead of schools like Georgetown, Stanford, and Caltech.

Of the 20 percent headed into graduate school, a hefty 22 percent are attending medical school, 18 percent are in PhD programs, and 12 percent are entering law school. The med school acceptance rate is 85 percent, more than twice the national average. Eventually, 84 percent of Duke undergraduates will go on to earn an advanced degree. The Class of 2017 saw 146 members apply to law school, scoring an average of 165 on the LSAT, among the highest in the country. Those applicants found their way into just about every top-ranked law school in existence. In the last few years, Blue Devils have pursued a JD at Stanford Law School, University of Chicago Law School, and Harvard Law School, among others.

Admission

Getting into Duke is an Ivy League-level, single-digit proposition. The application pool vying for a place in the Class of 2022 saw only 8.9 percent gain acceptance. That isn't a new trend. Rather, Duke has had an admit rate under 10 percent for the last five years. Among freshmen in 2018-19, 72 percent submitted ACT scores and had a 50th percentile range of 33-35; the SAT range was 1450-1570. An intimidating 95 percent of Blue Devils graduated in the top 10 percent of their high school class, and 98 percent were in the top quartile.

Early decision applicants saw a far more favorable acceptance rate, 21.6 percent versus the regular round rate of 7.3 percent; a sizable 50 percent of the freshman class is cemented during this early round. However, it is worth keeping in mind that athletes and legacy students are typically admitted in the early round, which certainly helps prop up the acceptance rate. Additionally, legacy students comprise 10-13 percent of the student body in any given year, and they typically apply ED. The Duke Admissions Committee considers eight factors as "very important" in admissions decisions: rigor of classes, grades, test scores, essays, recommendations, extracurricular activities, talent/ability, and character/personal qualities. Like the Ivies, Duke routinely rejects valedictorians and teens with perfect standardized test scores. Successful applicants will have exceptional academic credentials, attention-grabbing essays, and special talents that set them apart from a crowded field of aspiring Blue Devils.

Worth Your Money?

Duke's annual cost of attendance is a hair below $77,000, and only 11 percent receive any merit-based aid. The good news for those who are awarded merit aid is that the average award is $57k per year. Further, the 3,103 members of the undergraduate student body who qualify for need-based financial aid receive annual grants of $53k per year, meeting 100 percent of their demonstrated need. The university has the fifteenth largest endowment in the United States ($7 billion), and it puts it to good use, making Duke affordable to those from non-wealthy families. Essentially, the approximately 45 percent of students who come from wealthy families (top 5 percent income) pay the bulk of the sticker price while those from lower-to-middle income homes get significant tuition reductions. Even if you had to take on a lot of debt to attend Duke, this is one school that will almost certainly pay you back many times over; alumni salaries and employment prospects are that strong.

FINANCIAL
Institutional Type: Private
In-State Tuition: $55,880
Out-of-State Tuition: $55,880
Room & Board: $15,588
Required Fees: $2,051
Books & Supplies: $1,434

Avg. Need-Based Aid: $53,214
Avg. % of Need Met: 100%

Avg. Merit-Based Aid: $56,954
% Receiving Merit-Based Aid: 11%

Avg. Cumulative Debt: $21,525
% of Students Borrowing: 32%

CAREER
Who Recruits
1. 4170 Trading LLC
2. Cornerstone Advisors LLC
3. National Security Agency
4. Xerox
5. Qualtrics

Notable Internships
1. Carlyle Group
2. CNBC
3. Instagram

Top Industries
1. Business
2. Education
3. Research
4. Operations
5. Engineering

Top Employers
1. Google
2. Amazon
3. Microsoft
4. Facebook
5. Goldman Sachs

Where Alumni Work
1. Raleigh-Durham, NC
2. New York City
3. Washington, DC
4. San Francisco
5. Boston

Median Earnings
College Scorecard (Early Career): $84,400
EOP (Early Career): $87,500
PayScale (Mid-Career): $132,100

RANKINGS
Forbes: 9
Money: 19
U.S. News: 10, National Universities
Wall Street Journal/THE: 10
Washington Monthly: 5, National Universities

#CollegesWorthYourMoney

Elon University

Elon, North Carolina | Admissions Phone: 336-278-3566

Inside the Classroom

Nestled in the centralized Piedmont region of North Carolina, Elon University is home to 6,100 undergraduates and is—most fittingly for a school whose mascot is the Phoenix—a school on the rise. Not yet an uber-selective school (nearly three-quarters of applicants get in), this modestly sized university is known for its quality undergraduate teaching, experiential learning opportunities, and unparalleled study abroad program. Individualized attention is available at every turn, particularly from a well-staffed and highly effective Career Services Department.

Students choose from sixty majors and can add a number of interesting minors like adventure –based learning, coaching, and multimedia authoring. Regardless of one's area of concentration, all Elon undergrads must work through an extensive core curriculum that is made up of six interrelated parts: two first-year foundations courses focused on developing writing and critical thinking skills; an experiential learning component that requires studying abroad, interning, or conducting independent research; foreign language (can be exempted through AP tests); a total of thirty-two credits in the arts and sciences; eight credit hours of advanced coursework outside one's major; and a capstone seminar as a senior. Ninety-eight percent of students elect to take a one-credit freshman course entitled Elon 101 that, among other things, helps new students map out a graduation plan.

Elon's 12:1 student-to-faculty ratio leads to an average class size of twenty students; 52 percent of sections contain fewer than twenty students. A whopping 78 percent elect to study abroad, the highest participation rate in the country among master's-granting institutions. There are limitless options for overseas study including official Elon Centers Abroad in Shanghai, Dunedin, London, and Florence. Chances for working closely with faculty on research projects are also plentiful; 23 percent of students participate in faculty-mentored research.

Though Elon possesses solid offerings in many disciplines, programs in finance, communication, exercise science, and the performing arts receive the most praise. The areas in which the greatest number of degrees are conferred are business (33 percent), journalism/communication (19 percent), parks and recreation (7 percent), social sciences (7 percent), and social services (7 percent). Elon is recognized as a top producer of Fulbright Scholars seeing eight fellowship winners in 2018; it had forty-five winners between 2013 and 2018. Recent graduates also have received a Truman Scholarship, a Goldwater Scholarship, and grants from the National Science Foundation.

Outside the Classroom

Sixty-four percent of undergrads live on the school's 656-acre grounds. Greek life is a dominant force on the Elon social scene with 39 percent of women joining sororities and 20 percent of men signing up for fraternity life. The 60/40 gender breakdown in favor of women is certainly a factor in social life. It also should be noted that Elon has been rated as one of the LGBTQ-friendlier schools in the country. An athletically inclined student body participates in seventeen NCAA Division I sports as well as twenty-one intercollegiate club teams and eighteen intramural sports. Elon students are known for being involved in their college community as nearly 90 percent contribute some level of volunteer service, and 49 percent hold some type of leadership role in a student organization. There are 250 student-run clubs, including a student-run television station and an award-winning weekly newspaper, The Pendulum. The Elon Speakers Series sees an incredible list of notable figures visit campus each year. In the last few years it has welcomed David Cameron, Anita Hill, and Bob Woodward. The town of Elon is not the world's most exciting place, but those with access to a car are no more than an hour from the larger cities of Durham, Raleigh, and Winston-Salem.

Career Services

The Student Professional Development Center (SPDC) at Elon University has twenty-one professional employees (not counting a number of graduate fellows and apprentices) who play advising, pre-professional counseling, and employer relations roles. That works out to a 295:1 student-to-advisor ratio, which is better-than-average when compared to other schools featured in this guide. This office has sufficient resources to offer individualized services and coordinate large events such as fall and spring job fairs that attract over ninety employers and over 1,000 students. The center also regularly offers smaller events, such as the Accounting Meet and Greet, which attract fifteen firms and 120 undergraduate students. Its Graduate & Professional School Fair brings representatives from fifty institutions to campus each October. In total, 259 employers attended career fairs during the 2017-18 school year.

Thanks to efforts of the Student Professional Development Center, 89 percent of Elon students complete an internship during their four undergraduate years. Members of the class of 2017 interned at a range of employers including The Smithsonian, HBO, Coca-Cola Co., Booz Allen Hamilton, KMPG, and Ralph Lauren. Two-thirds of employed graduates attributed their acquisition of a job directly to networking leads via their internship experience. Companies known to recruit at Elon and/or offer on-campus interviews include Walt Disney Co., ESPN, Oracle, Credit Suisse, EY, PwC, Goldman Sachs, and ABC News. The SPDC facilitates more than 5,600 one-on-one advising appointments per year, an absolutely remarkable number given the modest size of the school.

Professional Outcomes

Results of a survey administered nine months after graduation found that 94 percent of the class of 2018 had found employment, a graduate school, or an internship. That is a significant improvement from five years ago when only 83 percent of graduates had found their next postsecondary or employment home nine months after receiving their diplomas. Of those accepting employment, a magnificent 93 percent reported that their job directly related to their area of study. Top employers of recent Elon graduates include Bloomberg, Deloitte, EY, Google, Goldman Sachs, Red Ventures, and Wells Fargo. Geographically, alumni are dispersed all over the map. A mere quarter of graduates remained in the Tar Heel State while 15 percent migrated to New York and 14 percent to Massachusetts. The average starting salary for an Elon graduate is $43,000. Salaries by the start of midcareer rank seventh among North Carolina colleges and are significantly lower than graduates of Duke, Davidson, or Wake Forest.

Just under one-quarter of 2018 grads gained acceptance into graduate/professional school. Many remain at Elon or continue at other Carolina-based schools such as UNC-Chapel Hill, Duke, Wake Forest, East Carolina University, or North Carolina State. Class of 2018 members gained acceptance into prestigious graduate schools such as Boston University, Columbia, NYU, Penn, and Georgetown. Applicants to medical school typically gain acceptance at the same rate as the national average, around 40 percent. However, in 2017 and 2018, Elon students enjoyed a 52 percent acceptance rate. That group of students earned average MCAT scores that placed them in the 75th percentile. Few graduates in recent years have been accepted into the top medical schools in the country.

Admission

Elon admitted 72 percent of the more than 10,700 applicants for a place in the 2018-19 freshman class. First-year students possessed an average SAT score of 1242 and ACT of 27. Only 25 percent of admitted students finished in the top 10 percent of their high school class, and 57 percent finished in the top quartile. Interestingly, a decade ago, the acceptance rate was a much stingier 42 percent, but the credentials of accepted students were roughly the same. In that time the quality of applicants has remained consistent, but the school's yield rate has declined from 33 percent to 22 percent, leading to more offers of acceptance in order to meet enrollment goals.

The admissions committee rates five factors as of the greatest importance: rigor of secondary curriculum, GPA, standardized test scores, essays, and recommendations. Attributes such as talent/ability as well as work experience, extracurricular activities, and legacy status round out the next tier of considered factors. Applying early decision offers a sizable advantage as 87 percent are accepted in the early round compared to 72 percent in the regular cycle. ED admits account for one-quarter of the freshman class. A school whose reputation is ascending, Elon, for now, remains a welcoming landing spot for teens with solid but unspectacular transcripts. Applying early further increases your odds but may be unnecessary as an admissions strategy unless you are a borderline applicant.

Worth Your Money?

As far as private universities go, a list price of $49,000 (COA) isn't outlandish. A good number of students, 43 percent, receive some type of merit aid, but the awards aren't overly helpful—the average is less than $7,000. Roughly one-third of the undergraduate student body receives need-based aid averaging $16k per recipient. Elon isn't a bargain for most students, but it is a solid deal for a school that provides ample individualized attention and has largely positive student outcomes.

FINANCIAL
Institutional Type: Private
In-State Tuition: $34,850
Out-of-State Tuition: $34,850
Room & Board: $12,230
Required Fees: $469
Books & Supplies: $900

Avg. Need-Based Aid: $15,516
Avg. % of Need Met: 59%

Avg. Merit-Based Aid: $6,895
% Receiving Merit-Based Aid: 43%

Avg. Cumulative Debt: $30,625
% of Students Borrowing: 35%

CAREER
Who Recruits
1. Walt Disney Company
2. SAS
3. Oracle
4. Net Suite
5. Vanguard

Notable Internships
1. ABC's The View
2. Aflac
3. Merrill Lynch

Top Industries
1. Business
2. Education
3. Sales
4. Operations
5. Media

Top Employers
1. Wells Fargo
2. Bank of America
3. EY
4. PwC
5. IBM

Where Alumni Work
1. Winston-Salem, NC
2. New York City
3. Raleigh-Durham, NC
4. Washington, DC
5. Charlotte

Median Earnings
College Scorecard (Early Career): $51,900
EOP (Early Career): $47,300
PayScale (Mid-Career): $93,700

RANKINGS
Forbes: 133
Money: 319
U.S. News: 84, National Universities
Wall Street Journal/THE: 143 (T)
Washington Monthly: 282, National Universities

#CollegesWorthYourMoney

Emory University

Atlanta, Georgia | Admissions Phone: 404-727-6036

ADMISSION
Admission Rate: 19%
Admission Rate - Men: 20%
Admission Rate - Women: 18%
EA Admission Rate: Not Offered
ED Admission Rate: 26%
Admission Rate (5-Year Trend): -7%
ED Admission Rate (5-Year Trend): N/A
% of Admits Attending (Yield): 28%
Transfer Admission Rate: 25%

Offered Wait List: 4,983
Accepted Wait List: 2,660
Admitted Wait List: 0

SAT Reading/Writing (Middle 50%): 660-730
SAT Math (Middle 50%): 690-790
ACT Composite (Middle 50%): 31-34
Testing Policy: ACT/SAT Required
SAT Superscore: Yes
ACT Superscore: No

% Graduated in Top 10% of HS Class: 84%
% Graduated in Top 25% of HS Class: 98%
% Graduated in Top 50% of HS Class: 100%

ENROLLMENT
Total Undergraduate Enrollment: 7,086
% Part-Time: 1%
% Male: 40%
% Female: 60%
% Out-of-State: 79%
% Fraternity: 28%
% Sorority: 25%
% On-Campus (Freshman): 99%
% On-Campus (All Undergraduate): 63%

% African-American: 8%
% Asian: 21%
% Hispanic: 10%
% White: 39%
% Other: 4%
% Race or Ethnicity Unknown: 1%
% International: 17%
% Low-Income: 19%

ACADEMICS
Student-to-Faculty Ratio: 9:1
% of Classes Under 20: 60%
% of Classes Under 40: 82%
% Full-Time Faculty: 88%
% Full-Time Faculty w/ Terminal Degree: 96%

Top Programs
Biology
Business Administration
Chemistry
English
Film and Media
International Studies
Neuroscience and Behavioral Biology
Philosophy

Retention Rate: 95%
4-Year Graduation Rate: 83%
6-Year Graduation Rate: 90%

Curricular Flexibility: Somewhat Flexible
Academic Rating: ★★★★✓

Inside the Classroom

Widely viewed as a "Southern Ivy," Emory University hosts almost 8,000 elite undergraduates on its Atlanta-based campus. To be more geographically precise, the prestigious school, which boasts the sixteenth largest endowment of any university in the United States, is located in the Druid Hills section of Atlanta, home to the Centers for Disease Control as well as one of the wealthiest neighborhoods in the entire state of Georgia. This midsize university offers a diverse array of majors (70+) and minors (50+), and more than half of Emory students pursue more than one area of study.

All freshmen must complete a first-year seminar in which they are tasked with stretching their critical thinking and research skills as they explore one of a series of fascinating topics in an intimate setting with a faculty member. The immersion and support don't stop there; all freshmen also must take a one-credit advising program called PACE (Pre-Major Advising Connections at Emory) in which they work with a faculty advisor and peer mentor to explore academic pathways. Ultimately, the greatest number of students go on to earn degrees in the social sciences (17 percent), business (16 percent), biology (14 percent), mathematics (7 percent), and psychology (5 percent).

One unique feature of Emory is that one of its undergraduate divisions, Oxford College, about forty-five minutes away, functions as a small liberal arts college for freshmen and sophomores. Oxford students knock out many of their lower-level courses before declaring a major and attending upper-level courses at Emory. No matter which school you attend, hands-on learning opportunities abound. A healthy 56 percent of Emory's student body works directly with a faculty member on academic research. Also noteworthy is the fact that 60 percent of courses have class sizes of under twenty students, a number comparable to many smaller liberal arts colleges.

Emory is notable for its renowned Woodruff School of Nursing and Goizueta School of Business. It also routinely rates well in biology, neuroscience, creative writing, and political science. Undergrads at Emory have a strong history of winning national awards; the school boasted fourteen Fulbright Scholars in 2018-19 alone and has produced twenty Rhodes Scholars in its history. Further, Emory churns out more Teach for America candidates than any other midsize school in the United States, and it is also a leading producer of students who join the Peace Corps upon graduation.

Outside the Classroom

Ninety-nine percent of freshmen and 63 percent of all undergraduates reside in university-owned housing. Many also live in Greek houses as 28 percent of men pledge fraternities and 25 percent of women join sororities. Emory claims over 550 student-run clubs and sports teams, and Oxford College adds another eighty to that diverse list. Volunteer Emory organizes twenty to thirty service trips per week, and over 80 percent of students participate in one or more of the opportunities for community service each year. If you are looking for top-of-the-line collegiate athletics, Emory may not be a great fit. Despite the absence of nationally televised football games, roughly 400 non-scholarship athletes compete in a variety of Division III athletic competitions. Another 600+ students compete in one or more of Emory's club sports, which include everything from flag football to golf to swimming. Impressive amenities, such as two Olympic-size swimming pools and a rock climbing arena, also are available for recreational use. Notable campus-wide events include Wonderful Wednesdays, a weekly open-invite celebration that can include anything from a petting zoo to a volunteer fair and an annual town hall with former President Jimmy Carter. Off campus there is something for everyone with Atlanta's nightlife and natural beauty (a nature trail begins on Oxford's campus) right in your backyard.

Career Services

The Career Center at Emory is staffed by thirteen full-time professional employees as well as four additional full-time staff members who exclusively serve business majors at Goizueta. That equates to a student-to-advisor ratio of 417:1, slightly below average compared to the other institutions included in this book. Spring and fall job fairs are well attended (over 1,000 students each), and approximately 200 companies recruit on campus each year. Each year, more than 12,000 jobs and internships are posted on Handshake, 350+ events are held, and 1,500 one-on-one counseling sessions take place.

Typical career-prep services are available to undergraduate students. Resumes, cover letters, and personal statements can be submitted online for editing by a staff member with fairly quick turnaround times. High Five networking events are held at least once a year for ten career categories including legal, data science, green, STEM, and government and public policy. A full slate of guests, many of whom are Emory alums, discuss their careers with undergraduate attendees. At any time, students can access alumni as well as internship opportunities through their Handshake account. Emory Connects: Career Discovery Days provides students with job-shadowing opportunities in the Atlanta area.

Professional Outcomes

Within three months of graduation 43 percent of Emory grads are already employed, and 92 percent have arrived at their next destination. The top ten employers of Emory's Class of 2018 include Ernst & Young, PricewaterhouseCoopers, Google, Goldman Sachs, BlackRock, and Accenture. Past graduating classes have had a significant numbers of Eagles (the schools lesser-known mascot) land at Deloitte, PwC, the Home Depot, Facebook, and the Coca-Cola Company. Teach for America is the largest employer of the previous three graduating classes. While a healthy number of Emory grads found employment in Georgia, the top destinations for the Class of 2018 included non-Southern locales New York City, DC, LA, Chicago, and Philadelphia. Graduates of the Goizueta Business School found strong starting salaries with the majority going into either finance (median salary: $80k) or consulting (median salary: $69k). Eighty-eight percent of graduates from the Woodruff School of Nursing found employment within three months at an average salary of $53k. The median salary across all schools in 2018 was $60k.

A healthy number of Emory grads pursue further education upon graduation. Last year, more than ten Emory grads/alums received acceptance letters from the following top law schools: Columbia, Berkeley, Michigan, Northwestern, and Georgetown. Every one of the forty-three seniors who applied directly to law school received at least one acceptance. Med school acceptances included Duke, Johns Hopkins, Vanderbilt, and USC. Overall, the most commonly attended graduate schools included Emory itself, Columbia, Duke, University of Chicago, NYU, Penn, Harvard, and Stanford.

Admission

Emory received a record number of applications in 2018—27,559; only 5,104 were accepted, an overall acceptance rate of 18.5 percent, down from a 25 percent acceptance rate only two years ago and a 22 percent clip in 2017. Admitted students out of the 2018 applicant pool had a median SAT score of 1500 or above. That means half of those accepted into Emory's Class of 2022 scored in the 99th percentile nationally on standardized tests. Among those who went on to enroll, the mid-50 percent ranges were 1350-1420 on the SAT and 31-34 on the ACT. The average GPA on a 4.0 scale was 3.78, and few students possessed a GPA under a 3.5.

While high test scores and near-perfect grades (83 percent were in the top 10 percent of their high school classes) are close to prerequisites, Emory does employ a holistic review process that carefully considers letters of recommendations, essays, and how you spent your time outside the classroom. It is a fairly common strategy for students to submit applications to both Emory and Oxford. The latter is slightly less selective with a 19.8 acceptance rate (vs. a 15.6 acceptance rates at Emory College). It is also important to note that 49 percent of first-year students at Emory were admitted through early decision, and the ED acceptance rate was eight points higher than the regular round rate. Thus, if Emory is your first choice, applying early may be a good idea. In sum, Emory is a highly selective, elite school where competition for a spot-on campus is growing more difficult every year. Nothing short of straight A's in a rigorous selection of courses, along with a 1500+ SAT score, puts you in good standing to earn a place in one of the South's most prestigious universities.

Worth Your Money?

Almost all Emory students who qualify for financial aid see 100 percent of their demonstrated need met by the university. That translates to 48 percent of the undergraduate student body receiving an average grant of $44,463 per year. In addition, 22 percent of students are given a merit award of almost $30k, which means few students pay the full $71,588 annual cost of attendance. Emory does a tremendous job of opening its doors to students from every socioeconomic background as the median family income for current students (estimated by tax return data) is much lower than many other private institutions of its ilk. Given that grads enjoy top-shelf employment prospects and generous financial aid, Emory is likely to be worth every dollar it will cost you.

FINANCIAL
Institutional Type: Private
In-State Tuition: $53,070
Out-of-State Tuition: $53,070
Room & Board: $14,972
Required Fees: $734
Books & Supplies: $1,224

Avg. Need-Based Aid: $44,463
Avg. % of Need Met: 100%

Avg. Merit-Based Aid: $29,911
% Receiving Merit-Based Aid: 22%

Avg. Cumulative Debt: $29,658
% of Students Borrowing: 34%

CAREER
Who Recruits
1. American Express
2. SunTrust
3. Turner Construction
4. Macy's
5. BNP Paribas

Notable Internships
1. ExxonMobil
2. Booz Allen Hamilton
3. BlackRock

Top Industries
1. Business
2. Healthcare
3. Education
4. Research
5. Social Services

Top Employers
1. Centers for Disease Control
2. Deloitte
3. EY
4. PwC
5. Google

Where Alumni Work
1. Atlanta
2. New York City
3. Washington, DC
4. San Francisco
5. Boston

Median Earnings
College Scorecard (Early Career): $66,000
EOP (Early Career): $67,800
PayScale (Mid-Career): $110,800

RANKINGS
Forbes: 55
Money: 127
U.S. News: 21, National Universities
Wall Street Journal/THE: 22
Washington Monthly: 83, National Universities

#CollegesWorthYourMoney

Fairfield University

Fairfield, Connecticut | Admissions Phone: 203-254-4100

ADMISSION

Admission Rate: 60%
Admission Rate - Men: 61%
Admission Rate - Women: 60%
EA Admission Rate: 61%
ED Admission Rate: 88%
Admission Rate (5-Year Trend): -10%
ED Admission Rate (5-Year Trend): +26%
% of Admits Attending (Yield): 16%
Transfer Admission Rate: 34%

Offered Wait List: 3,287
Accepted Wait List: 1,005
Admitted Wait List: 11

SAT Reading/Writing (Middle 50%): 600-660
SAT Math (Middle 50%): 590-680
ACT Composite (Middle 50%): 26-30
Testing Policy: Test Optional
SAT Superscore: Yes
ACT Superscore: Yes

% Graduated in Top 10% of HS Class: 37%
% Graduated in Top 25% of HS Class: 77%
% Graduated in Top 50% of HS Class: 96%

ENROLLMENT

Total Undergraduate Enrollment: 4,177
% Part-Time: 5%
% Male: 40%
% Female: 60%
% Out-of-State: 72%
% Fraternity: Not Offered
% Sorority: Not Offered
% On-Campus (Freshman): 95%
% On-Campus (All Undergraduate): 73%

% African-American: 2%
% Asian: 3%
% Hispanic: 7%
% White: 76%
% Other: 2%
% Race or Ethnicity Unknown: 5%
% International: 4%
% Low-Income: 17%

ACADEMICS

Student-to-Faculty Ratio: 12:1
% of Classes Under 20: 41%
% of Classes Under 40: 98%
% Full-Time Faculty: 45%
% Full-Time Faculty w/ Terminal Degree: 93%

Top Programs
Accounting
Communication
English
Finance
Marketing
Nursing
Politics

Retention Rate: 90%
4-Year Graduation Rate: 78%
6-Year Graduation Rate: 81%

Curricular Flexibility: Less Flexible
Academic Rating: ★★★

Inside the Classroom

If you're seeking a high-caliber Catholic/Jesuit institution and don't have the grades and test scores for Georgetown, Holy Cross, Boston College, or Fordham, say hello to a new friend named Fairfield University. This school may not have the national name recognition of its Jesuit brethren but, rest assured, this Connecticut university of 4,100+ undergraduates has its share of stellar students and no shortage of connections to the nearby corporate world of New York City, including many of Wall Street's premier firms.

No matter which of the forty-seven majors you happen to be pursuing, a significant amount of time will be spent fulfilling the required Magis Core Curriculum, beginning with the Class of 2023. Totaling forty-five credits (15 courses), students must complete Introduction to Rhetoric and Composition and Introduction to Philosophy as well as coursework in math, history, religious studies, modern or classical language, and additional forays into the behavioral and social sciences, literature, natural sciences, and visual and performing arts. Business majors, of which there are many (stats to follow), take a whole extra set of mandated coursework including Calculus, Introduction to Microeconomics, and Introduction to Macroeconomics.

A 12:1 student-to-faculty ratio is fully felt in the classroom as courses average only twenty students per section. While 41 percent come in under that marker and only a smattering of sections contain forty+ students, the greatest number of courses have enrollments in the twenty to twenty-nine range. Each year 300+ faculty-directed undergraduate research projects are completed and shown-off at the university's Annual Research and Creative Accomplishments Symposium. Study abroad programs have a 30 percent participation rate, and opportunities are available to travel to sixty sites across forty countries on five continents.

Fairfield is primarily known for its business program, which serves as a pipeline to many of the top financial/accounting/consulting firms in the country. A whopping 43 percent of degrees conferred are from the highly respected Dolan School of Business. Next in popularity are majors within the health professions (12 percent) and communication (9 percent)—both areas also receive high marks at Fairfield. Fulbright winners have trailed off in recent years, but the school has had as many as nine in a single year in the not-too-distant past. However, landing fellowships is rarely the postgraduate goal of this business-minded group.

Outside the Classroom

Housing is guaranteed for all four years, but just below three-quarters of students elect to live on the school's 200-acres campus. Demographically, two things at Fairfield stand out. One, the lack of ethnic diversity is real—77 percent of the class of 2022 identifies as white, and secondly, women make up 60 percent of the undergraduate population. As at many Jesuit institutions, Greek life doesn't exist here, but there are plenty of social opportunities around; for many years Fairfield made appearances on top party school lists, but today it cracks prominent lists measuring schools with the happiest students and best quality of life. With twenty NCAA Division I teams boasting a combined forty-two NCAA tournament appearances in school history, Fairfield certainly has plenty of sports to offer. While the Stags' fan base is quiet compared to a place like fellow Jesuit school Boston College, it is still significant that 10 percent of the student body are Division I athletes. There are over one hundred clubs and activities to enjoy, including twenty intramural sports and twenty-five club teams. Being just sixty miles from NYC is an advantage not only for networking but for weekend trips. Campus itself cannot unreasonably be assigned adjectives like "idyllic" and "stunning." It's location on the Connecticut coast turns the nearby beach into an extension of campus; in fact, 400 seniors each year live in beachfront homes and apartments.

Career Services

The Career, Leadership, and Professional Development (CLPD) staff at Fairfield is comprised of seven full-time employees who work in employer development, recruitment, and experiential learning and internship coordination. The 570:1 student-to-advisor ratio is only average compared to the schools featured in this guidebook, but that does not appear to prevent the CLPD staff from directly touching the lives of almost every student. The office hosts four career fairs per year, including general expos in the fall and spring and smaller affairs specific to nursing and law school. The most recent Fall Career Fair was attended by 123 employers and 745 students. Companies in attendance included EY, KPMG, Morgan Stanley, and Epsilon.

Events including mock interviews, job shadowing, industry nights, resume-writing workshops, and employer presentations occur on a regular basis. The Stags4Hire platform connects students with job opportunities and can help book on-campus interviews. An impressive 47 percent of Class of 2018 members reported that they found their first job through on-campus recruiting/interviewing opportunities during their senior year. Among that same cohort, 602 participated in internships, and 20 percent of 2018 grads cited that experience as directly leading to their first full-time employment opportunity. Taking full advantage of their proximity to NYC, Fairfield's CLPD provides all of the internship and employment opportunities one could hope for.

Professional Outcomes

Fairfield's Class of 2018 found its next destination within six months of graduating at a hard-to-beat 98 percent clip. Financial services was the most commonly entered industry (21.8 percent), followed by healthcare/nursing (18.2 percent), communications/marketing (17.3 percent), and science/biotech/technology (7.8 percent). Many major investment banks, accounting firms, and consulting companies employ large numbers of Fairfield alumni. For example, PwC, Deloitte, Morgan Stanley, JP Morgan & Chase Co., EY, UBS, and Merrill Lynch all employ one hundred or more Stags, and Fairfield grads also have strong representation at IBM, Goldman Sachs, Citi, and Prudential. Thus, it's no wonder that the average starting salary is a healthy $56,000, not including bonuses. Connecticut is not the primary destination for graduates. Rather, New York City attracts the greatest number of alumni with Boston second and Hartford a distant third.

A shade under 30 percent of 2018 grads enrolled directly in graduate or professional school. The breakdown of programs was as follows: business (42.5 percent), education (14.5 percent), arts and sciences (14.5 percent), engineering (10.7 percent), health care (7.5 percent), and law (7 percent). The university has produced roughly thirty graduates per year that go on to earn their degrees in medicine and dentistry. Medical schools where recent grads have been admitted include Johns Hopkins, Georgetown, and the Albert Einstein College of Medicine. Those headed to law school do so at a range of institutions that includes elite schools Fordham, Boston College, and Cornell. Graduate schools pursued and attended by Stag alumni run the gamut of selectivity, but those with high GPAs are in the running for a place in elite graduate institutions.

Admission

Applications to the Class of 2023 set a record for the school as over 12,300 lined up for the chance to become a Stag. The 11,361 applications Fairfield received for a place in the class of 2022 saw 60 percent admitted, still an unintimidating acceptance rate despite the school's rising reputation. Fairfield is a test-optional school, but the vast majority of the 2018-19 freshman class did submit test scores with the SAT being the people's choice. The mid-50 percent SAT range was 1190-1340 and the ACT range was 26-30. Thirty-seven percent finished in the top 10 percent of their high school class, 77 percent were in the top quartile, but almost 5 percent did not land in the top half, giving hope to late bloomers with some blemishes on their transcripts. The average GPA was 3.65, but plenty of students with lower GPAs received acceptance letters; in fact, 16 percent of accepted students had lower than a 3.25.

The four factors the committee lists as being of supreme importance are rigor of curriculum, GPA, recommendations, and the essay. On the next tier of still "important" factors are an interview, extracurricular activities, first-generation status, character/personal qualities, talent/ability, work experience, volunteer work, and demonstrated interest. It's definitely a good idea to visit campus and interview in order to let the university know you are serious about attending. Fairfield only has a 16 percent yield rate, meaning that 84 percent of those accepted into the school do not ultimately enroll. Applying early decision is a good way to punch your ticket to campus as those going the ED route enjoyed an 88 percent acceptance rate.

Worth Your Money?

On the surface, Fairfield, being a not terribly selective, high-priced private school is an unlikely candidate for this guide. Yet, Fairfield succeeds where many others in its class fail. For one, thanks to generous merit and need-based aid, even parents in high-income brackets can expect to pay an average annual COA of $40k, which is $25k less than the sticker price. Parents in lower-income brackets receive commensurate discounts (90 percent of students receive some type of aid) and, with strong graduate outcomes and connections to major corporations, this university could make financial sense for students of all income levels, especially if they have business-related aspirations. However, it is worth noting that the average cumulative debt for Fairfield grads is higher than the national average.

FINANCIAL
Institutional Type: Private
In-State Tuition: $47,650
Out-of-State Tuition: $47,650
Room & Board: $14,710
Required Fees: $700
Books & Supplies: $1,150

Avg. Need-Based Aid: $16,564
Avg. % of Need Met: 84%

Avg. Merit-Based Aid: $17,099
% Receiving Merit-Based Aid: 92%

Avg. Cumulative Debt: $38,596
% of Students Borrowing: 64%

CAREER
Who Recruits
1. FBI
2. Deloitte
3. Ipsos
4. McIntyre Group
5. TEKsystems

Notable Internships
1. Major League Baseball
2. PwC
3. Deutsche Bank

Top Industries
1. Business
2. Education
3. Finance
4. Sales
5. Operations

Top Employers
1. PwC
2. Deloitte
3. Morgan Stanley
4. UBS
5. EY

Where Alumni Work
1. New York City
2. Boston
3. Hartford, CT
4. Philadelphia
5. Washington, DC

Median Earnings
College Scorecard (Early Career): $72,100
EOP (Early Career): $69,900
PayScale (Mid-Career): $116,900

RANKINGS
Forbes: 135
Money: 139
U.S. News: 3, Regional North
Wall Street Journal/THE: 199 (T)
Washington Monthly: N/A

#CollegesWorthYourMoney

Florida State University

Tallahassee, Florida | Admissions Phone: 850-644-6200

ADMISSION
Admission Rate: 37%
Admission Rate - Men: 37%
Admission Rate - Women: 37%
EA Admission Rate: N/A
ED Admission Rate: Not Offered
Admission Rate (5-Year Trend): -20%
ED Admission Rate (5-Year Trend): Not Offered
% of Admits Attending (Yield): 34%
Transfer Admission Rate: 28%

Offered Wait List: Not Offered
Accepted Wait List: Not Offered
Admitted Wait List: Not Offered

SAT Reading/Writing (Middle 50%): 610-680
SAT Math (Middle 50%): 590-670
ACT Composite (Middle 50%): 26-30
Testing Policy: ACT/SAT Required
SAT Superscore: Yes
ACT Superscore: Yes

% Graduated in Top 10% of HS Class: 39%
% Graduated in Top 25% of HS Class: 84%
% Graduated in Top 50% of HS Class: 98%

ENROLLMENT
Total Undergraduate Enrollment: 32,472
% Part-Time: 11%
% Male: 43%
% Female: 57%
% Out-of-State: 11%
% Fraternity: 14%
% Sorority: 23%
% On-Campus (Freshman): 82%
% On-Campus (All Undergraduate): 21%

% African-American: 9%
% Asian: 3%
% Hispanic: 21%
% White: 60%
% Other: 4%
% Race or Ethnicity Unknown: 1%
% International: 2%
% Low-Income: 27%

ACADEMICS
Student-to-Faculty Ratio: 21:1
% of Classes Under 20: 57%
% of Classes Under 40: 82%
% Full-Time Faculty: 82%
% Full-Time Faculty w/ Terminal Degree: 93%

Top Programs
Criminology
Education
Information Technology
Motion Picture Arts
Political Science
Psychology
Real Estate
Risk Management

Retention Rate: 93%
4-Year Graduation Rate: 66%
6-Year Graduation Rate: 83%

Curricular Flexibility: Somewhat Flexible
Academic Rating: ★★★✓

Inside the Classroom

Founded in 1851, FSU is one of the state's oldest institutions of higher education as well as one of the nation's finest public research universities. A wide range of baccalaureate degrees—107 to be precise—are available to more than 33,000 undergraduate students, a group possessing increasingly impressive academic credentials with every passing year. Bound by excellent academics and athletics, FSU's student body and alumni are, with good reason, proud to call themselves Seminoles.

The greater university is comprised of sixteen distinct colleges, and all except the College of Law and College of Medicine offer undergraduate degree programs. All students must meet a number of state and university requirements as they progress through their four years of study. Regardless of academic concentration, thirty-six semester hours of coursework are mandated in the areas of quantitative and logical thinking, English composition, natural sciences, social sciences/history, humanities, and cultural practices/ethics, and two semesters of foreign language.

The student-to-faculty is a rather high 22:1, which translates into larger class sizes. Over 16 percent of sections contain more than fifty students, and 7 percent have more than one hundred. However, that is balanced by the 40 percent of sections that contain fewer than twenty students. Out-of-class undergraduate research is taken advantage of by one-quarter of students, and the school plans to greatly expand such offerings. An abundance of study abroad choices include special summer programs in Panama, Florence, London, and Valencia, Spain. FSU has sixty academic programs available in twenty locations throughout the world; one in five students elects to participate.

FSU boasts a number of standout academic programs including those in the College of Motion Picture Arts, the premier film school in the region. The College of Business is extremely well regarded in the corporate world as the real estate, marketing, accounting, management, and insurance programs are all highly ranked. Twenty-two percent of degrees conferred fall under the business umbrella. The social sciences (17 percent), biology (9 percent), psychology (7 percent), and homeland security (6 percent) are next in popularity. More Seminoles have landed prestigious postgraduate fellowships in recent years than ever. Eight graduates took home Fulbright Scholarships in 2018; Gilman Scholarships have gone to twenty-one recent undergrads, and three have become Rhodes scholars in the past twelve years.

Outside the Classroom

Florida State could easily be called Extrovert U—95 percent of undergrads participate in at least one on-campus activity. Just about everyone cheers on the Seminole football team as well as seventeen other NCAA Division I teams competing in the esteemed Atlantic Coast Conference (ACC). Forty sports clubs and a thriving intramural program draw widespread participation. The Bobby E. Leach center offers students recreational amenities including a sixteen-lane pool and indoor track, and all of the exercise equipment one could ever desire. While campus is a sizable 477 acres, only 20 percent of undergrads live on site, almost exclusively freshmen. Greek life is a driving force on campus despite a temporary ban in 2017 after a tragic hazing death. The school has a 22 percent participation rate across its twenty-eight fraternities and twenty-six sororities. Those seeking non-Greek, non-sports activities can pick from one of more than 650 recognized student organizations. Approximately 2,000 students become engaged in community service projects each year. Club Downunder, a student-run venue in town, brings notable comedy and musical acts to Tallahassee on a regular basis. The Student Life Cinema plays free movies for students six night a week. Tallahassee offers plenty of nightlife and cultural opportunities and can be easily accessed via public transit.

Career Services

The Career Center at Florida State University employs forty-one full-time staff members (not including office assistants) who work in career advising, employer relations, and experiential learning. This student-to-advisor ratio of 805:1 is below average compared to the other institutions included in this book. Of course, the size and scope of the operation is massive, and FSU's Career Center does a solid job of reaching a healthy number of the 30,000 undergraduate students through a variety of means.

The university puts on twenty job fairs per year that attract close to 1,450 employers and 11,500 students. Annually, the office puts on 1,200+ programs/workshops drawing a total audience of greater than 40,000. Florida State's internship participation rate was 66 percent for the Class of 2018. An impressive 7,700+ students obtain internship/co-op positions, and close to 8,600 students find other opportunities for experiential learning. Over 40 percent of graduates who found employment credited the Career Center with providing them the lead. Many big-time corporations recruit on campus including PepsiCo, KPMG, and PricewaterhouseCoopers. Close to 5,000 on-campus interviews are conducted each year. Despite a high student-to-counselor ratio, Florida State's Career Center deploys its resources efficiently, reaching an extremely high percentage of the student body.

Florida State University

E-mail: admissions@admin.fsu.edu | Website: www.fsu.edu

Professional Outcomes

Two-thirds of 2018 FSU grads already had a job offer in hand when they threw their caps toward the sky in celebration. Within six months of graduation, 87 percent had achieved positive outcomes; 69 percent were employed full time. The top five sectors employing Seminoles are (in order) education, technology, retail, financial, and health. Employers hiring the greatest number of FSU alumni include Apple, Northrup Grumman, EY, General Motors, and Deloitte. The average starting salary for graduates is a shade over $50k. Among ACC schools, FSU ranks toward the bottom in terms of median salary by midcareer, coming in at thirteenth of fourteen, behind Pitt and slightly ahead of the University of Louisville with alumni, by some measures, making roughly half as much as Duke graduates. Geographically, the greatest number of alumni remain in Florida but large numbers also relocate to Massachusetts, Georgia, Texas, Washington State, and California.

Roughly one-quarter of Florida State grads elect to immediately pursue admission into an advanced degree program; 75 percent of those who apply receive at least one acceptance. A typical graduating class sees over one hundred students accepted into medical schools and over 200 accepted into law schools. Students enjoy graduate school acceptances at a wide range of state and private universities with some recent alumni landing at prestigious institutions including Emory, Johns Hopkins, MIT, Northwestern, Georgetown, Vanderbilt, and the University of Chicago.

Admission

The acceptance rate into Florida State's Class of 2022 dipped below 40 percent for the first time, hitting 37 percent as the university received a record 50,314 applications. Only five years ago, the university received fewer than 30,000 applications and accepted more than half. Enrolled freshmen possessed middle-50 percent SAT scores of 1200-1350 and ACT scores of 26-30. For perspective, a decade ago, the ranges were 1090-1270 and 23-28, indicating a notable increase in the academic caliber of the average first-year student. A solid 39 percent of FSU freshmen finished in the top 10 percent of their high school class; 84 percent were in the top quarter. A GPA of 3.75 or higher was possessed by 85 percent of first-year students in 2018-19.

The admissions committee ranks the rigor of an applicant's secondary school record above all other factors but also strongly weights GPA, standardized test scores (the ACT is the more commonly submitted test), talent/ability, and state residency (out-of-state applicants face tougher prospects and were admitted at a rate of 19.5 percent). Class rank, extracurricular activities, and essays are merely "considered." Due to the immense volume of applicants, the university does not offer admissions interviews. While FSU does not offer a binding early decision option, it does have two deadlines—one in November and one in February. The November deadline is preferable as this early round typically sees acceptance rates close to 60 percent. Over 80 percent of attendees are residents of the Sunshine State, and admissions standards are more lax for residents than outsiders. With draws like elite sports, beautiful weather, and an excellent academic reputation, the number of applicants to FSU is likely to continue to rise. Candidates should be mindful of the increasingly selective admissions process and the need to post strong ACT/SAT scores and grades, above all else.

Worth Your Money?

An in-state cost of attendance of just over $22,000 puts places like FSU in the "absurd bargain" category. Unusual for a state school, over half of students also receive some level of merit aid that averages a not inconsequential $6k per year. While the school rarely meets full demonstrated need, it does give financial grants to 48 percent of the undergraduate student body with an average award of $14,597. Even for the 20 percent of students who do not have residency status, the out-of-state COA is a reasonable $37k. Attending Florida State and paying $37k per year is especially appealing if you are entering a field in which grads enjoy high average starting salaries like computer science ($66k), engineering ($68k), or math and sciences ($64k).

FINANCIAL
Institutional Type: Public
In-State Tuition: $4,640
Out-of-State Tuition: $19,806
Room & Board: $10,780
Required Fees: $1,877
Books & Supplies: $1,000

Avg. Need-Based Aid: $14,597
Avg. % of Need Met: 81%

Avg. Merit-Based Aid: $6,078
% Receiving Merit-Based Aid: 52%

Avg. Cumulative Debt: $22,840
% of Students Borrowing: 49%

CAREER
Who Recruits
1. Grant Thorton LLC
2. Enterprise
3. Aldi
4. Northrop Grumman
5. KPMG

Notable Internships
1. Equifax
2. Walt Disney Company
3. Royal Carribean Cruises

Top Industries
1. Business
2. Education
3. Operations
4. Sales
5. Social Services

Top Employers
1. IBM
2. Raymond James
3. JPMorgan Chase
4. Amazon
5. Microsoft

Where Alumni Work
1. Tallahassee, FL
2. Miami
3. Tampa, FL
4. Orlando, FL
5. Atlanta

Median Earnings
College Scorecard (Early Career): $46,400
EOP (Early Career): $46,400
PayScale (Mid-Career): $92,700

RANKINGS
Forbes: 151
Money: 102
U.S. News: 57, National Universities
Wall Street Journal/THE: 208 (T)
Washington Monthly: 81, National Universities

#CollegesWorthYourMoney

Fordham University

Bronx, New York | Admissions Phone: 718-817-4000

ADMISSION
Admission Rate: 46%
Admission Rate - Men: 45%
Admission Rate - Women: 47%
EA Admission Rate: 54%
ED Admission Rate: 53%
Admission Rate (5-Year Trend): -1%
ED Admission Rate (5-Year Trend): Previously
Not Offered
% of Admits Attending (Yield): 11%
Transfer Admission Rate: 44%

Offered Wait List: 9,215
Accepted Wait List: 2,423
Admitted Wait List: 68

SAT Reading/Writing (Middle 50%): 620-700
SAT Math (Middle 50%): 630-730
ACT Composite (Middle 50%): 28-32
Testing Policy: ACT/SAT Required
SAT Superscore: Yes
ACT Superscore: Yes

% Graduated in Top 10% of HS Class: 44%
% Graduated in Top 25% of HS Class: 76%
% Graduated in Top 50% of HS Class: 97%

ENROLLMENT
Total Undergraduate Enrollment: 9,645
% Part-Time: 5%
% Male: 43%
% Female: 57%
% Out-of-State: 58%
% Fraternity: Not Offered
% Sorority: Not Offered
% On-Campus (Freshman): 76%
% On-Campus (All Undergraduate): 50%

% African-American: 4%
% Asian: 11%
% Hispanic: 15%
% White: 56%
% Other: 4%
% Race or Ethnicity Unknown: 2%
% International: 9%
% Low-Income: 20%

ACADEMICS
Student-to-Faculty Ratio: 15:1
% of Classes Under 20: 50%
% of Classes Under 40: 98%
% Full-Time Faculty: 41%
% Full-Time Faculty w/ Terminal Degree: 92%

Top Programs
Communication and Culture
English
Finance
Global Business
International Studies
Performing Arts
Psychology

Retention Rate: 90%
4-Year Graduation Rate: 79%
6-Year Graduation Rate: 83%

Curricular Flexibility: Somewhat Flexible
Academic Rating: ★★★✦

Inside the Classroom
With campuses in both Manhattan and the Bronx, Fordham University, a private Jesuit school with 175 years of tradition, has hit new heights of popularity and prestige in recent years; it shows no signs of slowing down. As one of the top twenty-five most expensive schools in the United States, paying for Fordham may be even more challenging than getting accepted. Yet, for those who can afford it, this is a wonderful place to live and learn for four years. Of course, paying back loans becomes easier when you enter a high-paying field like business, which accounts for 29 percent of all degrees conferred. Next in popularity are social sciences (19 percent), communication and journalism (13 percent), psychology (7 percent), and the visual and performing arts (6 percent).

The university offers more than seventy majors, minors, and pre-professional programs. Regardless of concentration area, on their way to earning 124 credits all Rams (minus many pursuing a bachelor of science) are required to tackle from one to four semesters of foreign language. Freshmen must complete an advanced composition course, Computational Reasoning, Philosophy of Human Nature, Faith and Critical Reason, and one seminar course designated as *Eloqeuntia Perfecta* that focuses on enhancing students' written and oral communication ability. As students progress to sophomore, junior, and senior year they are required to tackle additional courses in philosophy, literature, life science, theology, the performing arts, natural science, and ethics.

Fordham's 15:1 student-to-faculty ratio leads to average class sizes of twenty-two. Some classes will be on the smaller side as 52 percent of sections contain nineteen or fewer students. Rarely will an undergrad end up in a classroom of more than forty students. A substantial 45 percent of the student body spend a semester abroad at one of the school's 110 programs in fifty-two countries. The undergraduate research program has awarded 1.5 million dollars to students over the last decade and saw thirty-eight undergrads obtain coauthor status on professor-published work in 2017 alone.

The university's theater and dance programs are world-renowned for sending countless alumni to Broadway and Hollywood. Gabelli is a top-rated business program with standout programs in international business and finance and serves as a pipeline to many large firms. Another point of pride is the phenomenal number of graduates who earn competitive national scholarships/fellowships. Fordham has produced 132 Fulbright scholarships since 2003. Grads also regularly win Beinecke, Gates-Cambridge Harriman, and Truman Scholarships/Fellowships.

Outside the Classroom
The undergraduate experience will differ depending on whether you attend the Rose Hill Campus in the Bronx or the Lincoln Center campus in Manhattan. At Lincoln Center there are two large high-rises that offer every convenience imaginable. Of course, Manhattan has all of the culture, shopping, dining, and entertainment you could ever dream of. The Bronx campus offers fourteen residential buildings and is near the New York Botanical Garden, the Bronx Zoo, Yankee Stadium, and Little Italy. Between the two sites, roughly half of the student body lives on campus. Greek Life at Fordham is a complete non-factor—the university does not have any fraternities or sororities. Instead, 160 student-run organizations provide opportunities for social bonding. Athletics are popular as the Rams field twenty-three teams in NCCA Division I and also run twenty-four club and intramural sports. Over 4,000 students participate in community service each year, contributing over one million collective hours. The school's newspaper, *The Observer*, enjoys a loyal readership and has garnered widespread praise. Yet, no feature of campus life will play a bigger role in the Fordham experience than its Big Apple location, which opens the doors to limitless possibilities on a daily basis.

Career Services
The Career Services office at Fordham is staffed by thirteen professional employees who specialize in areas that include undergraduate counseling and employer relations. That 723:1 student-to-advisor ratio is significantly higher than many of the other schools featured in this guide. In order to reach the masses, the office puts on four career fairs in the fall and two in the spring. Some are specific to areas like finance, STEM, or government while others are more general. The school attempts to engage with students beginning in their freshman year, encouraging first-years to meet one-on-one with an advisor, attend a resume/cover letter workshop, and take personality assessments. Subsequent activities are designed for sophomore, junior, and senior year as students master the office's three goals: awareness, preparedness, and presentation.

Fordham University

E-mail: enroll@fordham.edu | Website: www.fordham.edu

A phenomenal 81 percent of 2018 graduates completed at least one internship during their undergraduate years. An examination of how recent graduates found their jobs reveals the following breakdown: internships (12 percent), on-campus recruiting (2 percent), career fairs (2 percent), and CareerLink (6 percent). The vast majority found employment primarily through non-school resources. Yet plenty of opportunities exist to expand one's contacts by taking advantage of a Ram alumni network of over 175,000 individuals embedded in top companies across the globe. Despite a less-than-ideal student-to-counselor ratio and a low percentage of students attributing their job acquisition to the direct efforts of career services, Fordham grads do enjoy better-than-average employment and graduate school outcomes.

Professional Outcomes

Class of 2018 graduates found employment, graduate school, or other meaningful activities at a 90 percent clip within six months of receiving their degrees. Almost three-fifths of this group landed employment and enjoyed an average salary of $55,280, higher than the national average. Financial services was, by a large margin, the most common industry followed by advertising/PR, media and communications, health care, and accounting. Significant numbers of 2018 grads found homes at major companies including Ernst & Young (27), JP Morgan Chase & Co. (24), PwC (17), KMPG (15), NBC Universal (14), and Deloitte (12). A sizable number of graduates also moved into working for nonprofit organizations such as the Jesuit Volunteer Corps, AmeriCorps, or the Peace Corps.

Those aiming for graduate school found homes at a variety of excellent institutions. The greatest number of 2018 graduates landed at Fordham (139), NYU (22), and Columbia (17). Some also gained acceptance into Penn, Georgetown, Boston University, and George Washington. Law school applicants were successful 95 percent of the time, a rate 17 percent higher than the national average. In recent years, Fordham alumni have gone on to Harvard Law School, University of Pennsylvania Law School, Cornell Law School, and Northwestern University School of Law. Those applying to professional health programs, including medical school, gained acceptance at a 76 percent rate compared to the national average of 45 percent.

Admission

Fordham offered admission to 46 percent of the over 46,000 applicants vying for a place in the class of 2022. Those who ultimately enrolled possessed a mean test score of 1354 and a mean high school GPA of 3.64 on a 4.0 scale. In 2014, a 1350 would have placed in the 75th percentile of all Fordham freshmen. The mid-50 percent standardized test score ranges were 1250-1430 Forty-four percent of freshmen finished in the top 10 percent of their high school cohort, and 76 percent placed in the top quarter; three percent did not place in the top half. While 45 percent of entering freshmen in 2018-19 possessed better than a 3.75 GPA, 12 percent did earn a 3.25 or under in high school.

The admissions committee prioritizes the usual factors of rigor of coursework, GPA, and standardized test scores. Softer factors including recommendations, essays, talent/ability, volunteer work, and extracurricular activities are given secondary consideration.

In part because it serves as a safety school for many elite students aiming for Ivies or Ivy equivalents, Fordham has an exceptionally low yield rate—around 10 percent of admitted students actually enroll. Therefore, demonstrating your genuine interest in attending and applying early decision are strategic moves that serious applicants should consider. ED applications to the university are surprisingly low, but acceptance rates are higher than during the regular cycle (53 percent versus 40 percent). Like many schools in Manhattan, Fordham's rising popularity can be best summed up by the real estate cliché of location, location, location. Always a school that required students to have reasonably strong credentials, Fordham is entering a new strata and is now a viable option for very accomplished students.

Worth Your Money?

An annual total cost of attendance exceeding $75,000 sounds prohibitive, but a good number of students do obtain aid, either need based or merit. Sixty-three percent of current undergraduates receive an annual merit aid award of $20,744, and 59 percent of students qualify for grants that average over $32k. Unfortunately, only a small number see 100 percent of their need covered by the university. The average graduate owes more than $37k in loans, but starting salaries tend to be solid, making it worth incurring a moderate amount of debt, particularly for students pursuing study within Fordham's strongest programs, most notably business.

FINANCIAL
Institutional Type: Private
In-State Tuition: $52,980
Out-of-State Tuition: $52,980
Room & Board: $18,510
Required Fees: $1,413
Books & Supplies: $1,039

Avg. Need-Based Aid: $32,045
Avg. % of Need Met: 80%

Avg. Merit-Based Aid: $20,744
% Receiving Merit-Based Aid: 63%

Avg. Cumulative Debt: $37,429
% of Students Borrowing: 62%

CAREER
Who Recruits
1. EY
2. Teach for America
3. Standard Motor Products
4. Enterprise
5. Northwestern Mutual

Notable Internships
1. The Philadelphia Zoo
2. NBCUniversal
3. Spotify

Top Industries
1. Business
2. Education
3. Social Services
4. Operations
5. Finance

Top Employers
1. NYC Department of Education
2. Teach for America
3. NBCUniversal
4. JPMorgan Chase
5. US Army

Where Alumni Work
1. New York City
2. Washington, DC
3. Boston
4. Los Angeles
5. Philadelphia

Median Earnings
College Scorecard (Early Career): $59,200
EOP (Early Career): $63,300
PayScale (Mid-Career): $112,500

RANKINGS
Forbes: 141
Money: 376
U.S. News: 74, National Universities
Wall Street Journal/THE: 176 (T)
Washington Monthly: 301, National Universities

#CollegesWorthYourMoney

Lancaster, Pennsylvania | Admissions Phone: 717-358-3953

ADMISSION
Admission Rate: 35%
Admission Rate - Men: 31%
Admission Rate - Women: 39%
EA Admission Rate: Not Offered
ED Admission Rate: 58%
Admission Rate (5-Year Trend): -1%
ED Admission Rate (5-Year Trend): -11%
% of Admits Attending (Yield): 26%
Transfer Admission Rate: 38%

Offered Wait List: 2,106
Accepted Wait List: N/A
Admitted Wait List: N/A

SAT Reading/Writing (Middle 50%): 620-690
SAT Math (Middle 50%): 640-750
ACT Composite (Middle 50%): 28-32
Testing Policy: Test Optional
SAT Superscore: Yes
ACT Superscore: Yes

% Graduated in Top 10% of HS Class: 59%
% Graduated in Top 25% of HS Class: 84%
% Graduated in Top 50% of HS Class: 97%

ENROLLMENT
Total Undergraduate Enrollment: 2,309
% Part-Time: 1%
% Male: 45%
% Female: 55%
% Out-of-State: 72%
% Fraternity: 20%
% Sorority: 27%
% On-Campus (Freshman): 100%
% On-Campus (All Undergraduate): 99%

% African-American: 6%
% Asian: 5%
% Hispanic: 10%
% White: 55%
% Other: 2%
% Race or Ethnicity Unknown: 3%
% International: 18%
% Low-Income: 17%

ACADEMICS
Student-to-Faculty Ratio: 9:1
% of Classes Under 20: 68%
% of Classes Under 40: 99%
% Full-Time Faculty: 89%
% Full-Time Faculty w/ Terminal Degree: 95%

Top Programs
Biology
Business, Organizations & Society
Economics
Environmental Studies
Political Science
Public Health
Sociology

Retention Rate: 92%
4-Year Graduation Rate: 78%
6-Year Graduation Rate: 83%

Curricular Flexibility: Somewhat Flexible
Academic Rating: ★★★★

Inside the Classroom
Situated on the pastoral hills of Lancaster County, Pennsylvania, most famous for its large Amish community, Franklin & Marshall has carved out its own stellar reputation ever since its two namesake colleges merged in 1853. An undergraduate population of almost 2,300 gets to choose from a generous liberal arts menu that features fifty-nine academic programs. Never content to rest on its laurels, F&M is in the middle of a $200 million fundraising campaign entitled "Now to Next" that is designed to take this already excellent school to even greater heights.

The educational experience at F&M is guided by its "Connections" curriculum, a series of requirements divided into three phases: Introduction, Exploration, and Concentration. Freshmen must take two small, intensive seminar classes that immerse them in the world of intellectual discourse, academic writing, and the art of oral presentation. Next, students tackle courses in the arts, humanities, social and natural sciences, foreign language, and non-Western cultures. As a culminating experience, students complete a capstone project that may involve research alongside a professor.

Franklin & Marshall's student-faculty ratio is 9:1, and 67 percent of classes have fewer than twenty students enrolled; 29 percent are in the twenty to twenty-nine range. The average classroom contains eighteen students. Juniors are encouraged to spend a semester abroad, and 55 percent oblige, jetting off to locations from Argentina to Vietnam. Grants through the Hackman Scholars program allow approximately seventy-five students to conduct research with faculty each summer. Many more Diplomats research with faculty through other means during the academic year and, by graduation, 35 percent of students have engaged in a research experience.

The greatest number of degrees conferred at the college are in the social sciences (23 percent), interdisciplinary studies (14 percent), biology (12 percent), business (10 percent), physical sciences (7 percent), and psychology (5 percent). Programs in public health and environmental science receive high marks. In addition, students in the official pre-med program and related majors have experienced a high degree of success in earning acceptances into medical school. F&M students are no strangers to prestigious fellowships, having produced six Fulbright Scholars in 2018 and seven in 2017. The Class of 2018 also saw graduates awarded fellowships from Public Policy and International Affairs, Princeton in Asia, and Princeton in Africa.

Outside the Classroom
Lancaster, Pennsylvania, may be notable primarily for its Amish population, but there is a surprisingly large downtown area replete with a full array of shopping, eating, and entertainment options. Those seeking the excitement of a bigger city will have a bit of a car ride ahead of them—Philly is eighty miles away. Being in a relatively remote locale, the center of social life at F&M is on campus where 99 percent of the student population resides. Greek life is a big part of the Franklin and Marshall tradition, dating back to the school's founding, and it enjoys a robust participation rate of 20 percent for men and 27 percent for women. Participation in athletics is also central to campus life. Being a small school and fielding twenty-seven sports teams, mostly in NCAA Division III, translates to over 30 percent of the student body being comprised of varsity athletes. Outside of sports and frats/sororities, there are roughly one hundred active, student-run organizations that cover everything from a cappella to seven student-run publications. The vast majority of incoming freshmen performed community service in high school, and that practice continues while at F&M through numerous volunteer groups as well as through Greek organizations.

Career Services
The Office of Student and Post Graduate Development (OSPGD), a mouthful to say, is staffed by eleven full-time professionals. That works out to a 210:1 student-to-advisor ratio, which is better than average compared to other schools featured in this guide. Noteworthy for a small liberal arts school, F&M employs expert advisors who specialize in health care professions and law school advising so that undergrads on those tracks can receive specialized guidance. In the 2018-19 academic year an impressive 2,540 (more than one per student) one-on-one advising sessions were conducted.

Students seeking a personal touch in advising will appreciate the OPSGD's availability to meet one-on-one to discuss internship opportunities, professional pathways, or graduate school planning. A commendable 80 percent of the student body engages with the office each year. The sixth annual Job and Internship Fair, held in 2018, drew roughly eighty employers, and 106 employers recruited at some point on campus during the same year. The office puts on about 150 events each year with a total attendance of over 3,200. Other career-oriented offerings include Life After F&M, a handy feature that allows current Diplomats to view the types of jobs held by graduates of every major offered at the college. With each student's Handshake account, they also can access a database of 800+ alumni and parent mentors more than happy to dispense career advice. With a high level of engagement and positive graduate outcomes, the OSPGD receives a positive rating from our staff.

Professional Outcomes

Shortly after graduation, 97 percent of 2018 F&M grads are either employed or continuing their educational journey. The most frequently pursued industries are education (20 percent), finance and insurance (16 percent), research and development (7 percent), public administration (7 percent), and social/community service (7 percent). Students find work at a cornucopia of interesting companies and organizations from HBO to the Selective Mutism Research Institute to Sotheby's. Across all graduating years the companies with the greatest number of Diplomats on staff are Morgan Stanley, Deloitte, Vanguard, EY, Merrill Lynch, IBM, Wells Fargo, and Citi. Sixty-five percent of graduates stay in the Northeast, and 19 percent head down South. There are more alumni living in New York City than in Philadelphia. Salary data for alumni at age thirty-four reveals a median income of $58k, slightly higher than grads of more prestigious Pennsylvania-based liberal arts schools Swarthmore and Haverford.

F&M boasts excellent results for premed students. Over a three-year period, 89 percent of students with at least a 3.3 GPA and an MCAT score in the 67th percentile or better were accepted into medical school. That includes admissions into schools of medicine at Harvard, Yale, Johns Hopkins, Penn, and Georgetown. Those seeking a legal education head to universities such as Villanova, Harvard, William & Mary, NYU, Yale, Tulane, and UC Berkeley. Of the 18 percent of graduates furthering their education, there is a genuine mix of prestigious and less prestigious graduate programs, but it is fair to say that excelling at F&M at least puts you in the running for a spot at a top graduate school.

Admission

Applications to F&M surged to record levels as 9,502 poured in for a place in the Class of 2023, and 30 percent were accepted. The implementation of a full-blown test-optional strategy could be behind the massive spike. In 2018, Franklin & Marshall admitted 35 percent of more than 6,500 applicants. The Class of 2022 possessed mid-50 percent standardized test scores of 1260-1440 on the SAT and 28 to 32 on the ACT. Those scores were almost identical to the profile of the average member of the graduating Class of 2018 that had a similar admit rate of 36 percent. In other words, not much has changed in recent years. F&M continues to place the highest value on rigor of coursework, GPA, class rank, and character/personal qualities. On that last factor, it particularly values athletic participation/leadership; an insanely high percentage of incoming students played a varsity sport in high school. Fifty-nine percent of freshmen in the 2018-19 academic year finished in the top 10 percent of their high school cohort; 84 percent were in the top 25 percent.

F&M faces stiff competition for students as it must compete with a high number of other excellent liberal arts schools in PA and the surrounding states. Its yield rate (the percentage of accepted students who enroll) is only 26 percent, which means the admissions staff is particularly interested in qualified applicants for whom F&M is a top choice. Thus, it is no surprise that the early decision acceptance rate is 58 percent, far more favorable than that of the regular round; 57 percent of the 2018-19 freshman cohort came through the ED round. Not a school with a formulaic admissions algorithm, F&M students do typically share two common traits—excellent high school grades and strong interest in attending the college.

Worth Your Money?

Attending Franklin & Marshall will cost you $73k per year unless you are among the 54 percent of undergraduates who demonstrate financial need, in which case you see 100 percent of your financial need met. The average grant is for almost $47,000. Merit-based aid is not offered. Overall, F&M does an admirable job of making the school affordable for those from a wide range of socioeconomic backgrounds. However, middle-to-upper income students who cannot comfortably afford F&M's price and who fail to qualify for significant need-based aid should consider their desired path after college before committing. For everyone else, investing in an F&M degree is likely worth the money.

FINANCIAL
Institutional Type: Private
In-State Tuition: $56,450
Out-of-State Tuition: $56,450
Room & Board: $14,050
Required Fees: $300
Books & Supplies: $1,200

Avg. Need-Based Aid: $46,628
Avg. % of Need Met: 100%

Avg. Merit-Based Aid: $5,000
% Receiving Merit-Based Aid: 13%

Avg. Cumulative Debt: $27,149
% of Students Borrowing: 54%

CAREER
Who Recruits
1. W.B. Mason
2. The JDK Group
3. Travelers
4. ScribeAmerica
5. S&T Bank

Notable Internships
1. New Jersey Office of the Governor
2. Acacia Finance
3. Audible

Top Industries
1. Business
2. Education
3. Operations
4. Finance
5. Sales

Top Employers
1. Morgan Stanley
2. Deloitte
3. UBS
4. Vanguard
5. EY

Where Alumni Work
1. New York City
2. Philadelphia
3. Lancaster, PA
4. Washington, DC
5. Boston

Median Earnings
College Scorecard (Early Career): $58,900
EOP (Early Career): $57,800
PayScale (Mid-Career): $109,700

RANKINGS
Forbes: 114
Money: 166
U.S. News: 38, Liberal Arts Colleges
Wall Street Journal/THE: 91 (T)
Washington Monthly: 21, Liberal Arts Colleges

#CollegesWorthYourMoney

Franklin W. Olin College of Engineering

Needham, Massachusetts | Admissions Phone: 781-292-2222

Inside the Classroom

Perhaps the most highly-regarded school of its size in the entire United States, The Franklin W. Olin College of Engineering was founded in the early 2000s as an experimental, cutting-edge training ground for budding engineers. Today, this Boston-area institution has an undergraduate enrollment of 390 students who are every bit as brilliant as the talent at Caltech or MIT. Academically, there is only one item on the menu here but, boy, is it delicious. Every single degree conferred at Olin has "engineering" in its name: electrical and computer engineering, mechanical engineering, or general engineering with a concentration area such as bioengineering, computing, or design and robotics.

No matter one's major, all students most take a collection of core courses that the college deems essential to its mission, giving its students the engineering toolkit needed to "have a positive impact in the real world." Those required classes are tied to three interconnected themes: Design and Entrepreneurship, Modeling and Analysis, and Systems and Control. Students also work through a concentration in either the arts and humanities or entrepreneurship that can be completed at partner colleges Brandeis, Wellesley, or Babson. Unlike most engineering schools where students knock out a laundry list of math and science requirements before taking a deep dive into their engineering-specific coursework, Olin students take three such courses in their first semester.

Many classes are taught in a studio environment to encourage collaboration, and a number of courses are co-taught by professors from different disciplines. Classes are generally reasonably small; 54 percent of class sections contain fewer than twenty students. The school's 8:1 student- to-faculty ratio translates into an enormous amount of individualized attention and invitations to participate in research. Students can easily track down current research projects and contact information on the school's website and can obtain funding for their efforts via the Undergraduate Research Fund. Additionally, students can elect to take advantage of study abroad programs in thirty-five foreign locations. Half of students ultimately do spend a semester in a foreign country, a notably high percentage for an engineering school.

As chronicled in more detail in our "Professional Outcomes" section, the Franklin W. Olin College of Engineering may not be a household name for the average American, but employers and elite graduate schools adore its graduates every bit as much as those from Stanford or Carnegie Mellon. For such an incredibly small school, Olin graduates annually take home a number of prestigious awards. Two students/alumni won Fulbright Scholarships in 2018, and one took home a National Science Foundation Graduate Research Fellowship. Eight recent grads were named Grand Challenge Scholars by the National Academy of Engineers.

Outside the Classroom

Not far from Wellesley and Babson, Olin College of Engineering's Needham locale places it only eighteen miles outside of Boston. It features a seventy-acre campus lined with buildings as new as the college itself. Nearly all students reside on campus in one of two residence halls. No frats or sororities operate at this institution. There are no NCCA sports because it would be interesting to field teams from a pool of 345 engineering geniuses. However, thanks to agreements forged with nearby schools, Olin students can participate in intramural leagues at Babson or Wellesley. Additionally, Olin does field its own intercollegiate soccer and ultimate Frisbee teams. Fans of the outdoors can connect with hiking trails on campus and all around Needham and the town of Wellesley. There are plenty of student-run clubs with an engineering/innovation emphasis, including the Olin robotic sailing team that competes in global competitions, Olin Baja—a vehicle design competition, and AERO—a drone and plane designing team. Historic Needham is a safe suburb with plenty of restaurants, shops, museums, and cultural events.

Career Services

The Office of Postgraduate Planning consists of three professional employees, equating to a superior student-to-advisor ratio of 130:1, among the best of any school in the country. The office's mission is aligned to that of the school's—to assist future engineers in finding meaningful opportunities for hands-on training. This mission is accomplished to the tune of 98 percent of those graduating in 2018 having had a technical internship or research experience; 89 percent had more than one such experience. The Fall Career Fair is attended by more than fifty top companies. Given that this works out to about one company for every two seniors, this attendance is extraordinary and speaks to how desirable Olin students are in the eyes of employers.

With only thirteen years' worth of graduates, the total alumni base has yet to reach 1,000—it will cross that mark in 2020—but the industry connections made via the school's Corporate Partners Program open countless doors. In the past year undergrads landed internships at organizations including Tesla, Bose, GE, Microsoft, and Google. Thanks to a focus on experiential learning, ample industry connections, and exceptional starting salaries for grads, Olin's career services is held in high esteem by our staff.

Franklin W. Olin College of Engineering

E-mail: info@olin.edu | Website: www.olin.edu

Professional Outcomes

For a school exclusively graduating engineers, it isn't a surprise that alumni tend to find good-paying jobs. The average starting salary for recent graduates is in excess of $80,000. Electrical and computer engineers have averaged over $90K while mechanical engineers are at the low end with $67k in compensation. Over the past decade, the companies employing the greatest number of alumni are Google (39), Microsoft (26), athenahealth (22), Apple (14), and Amazon (11). In 2018, Shift, Bose, Cognex, MITRE, Nutonomy, and Raytheon all hired more than one Olin graduate. While a majority of graduates find work in Massachusetts, a large number also migrate to California where Silicon Valley welcomes them with open arms.

Olin College of Engineering undergrads have gone on to prestigious graduate engineering programs in impressive numbers. Since 2006 more than twenty graduates have gone to Stanford, MIT, and Harvard. The school also has sent double-digit numbers of alumni to Carnegie Mellon, Cornell, and Berkeley. Perusing the lists of graduate school acceptances, it is rare that anyone attends anything less than one of the world's most prestigious institutions. The majority of those hopping right into advanced studies are pursuing PhDs.

Admission

The 85 freshmen in the Class of 2022 are an impressive group, no matter the metric. With an average unweighted GPA of 3.9 and middle 50 percent standardized test scores of 1470-1540 on the SAT and 34-35 on the ACT, Olin students are nothing shy of Ivy caliber. In 2018, the school's acceptance rate was 16 percent, but it has dipped as low as 13 percent in recent years.

Applicants can rest assured that they will be viewed in three dimensions as a number of factors beyond grades and test scores are considered "very important" to the admissions committee. Those include essays, recommendations, interview, extracurricular activities, talent/ability, character/personal qualities, and level of demonstrated interest in the college. In fact, those considerations all rate ahead of standardized test results. Yet, consideration of those traditional factors is only half of the acceptance process. Each year, roughly 225-250 applicants are selected by Olin College of Engineering to visit during a Candidates' Weekend—a process closer to how most schools hire faculty than select their undergraduates. The prospective students are put through a design challenge, an individual interview, and group exercise to help evaluate which students would bring the most to and benefit the most from the Olin College of Engineering. Getting into Olin is a marathon; it is not a school you even apply to unless you are 100 percent committed to attending. Elite academic prowess is only one of many prerequisites for consideration to join this small but potent engineering juggernaut.

Worth Your Money?

The total annual cost of attendance at Franklin W. Olin is a hair below $76,000. Thankfully, 39 percent of the undergraduate population receives need-based aid averaging $50k per year, and merit awards with an average yearly value of $25k are distributed generously. Even if you didn't receive any aid, you're always safe investing in a college where the average starting salary exceeds the annual cost of attending. Olin is such a school, and with engineering being the only pathway, you are just about guaranteed a solid return on your educational investment.

FINANCIAL
Institutional Type: Private
In-State Tuition: $52,164
Out-of-State Tuition: $52,164
Room & Board: $16,872
Required Fees: $3,336
Books & Supplies: $200

Avg. Need-Based Aid: $50,188
Avg. % of Need Met: 100%

Avg. Merit-Based Aid: $25,295
% Receiving Merit-Based Aid: 100%

Avg. Cumulative Debt: $20,480
% of Students Borrowing: 40%

CAREER
Who Recruits
1. Cognex Corporation
2. Ford Motor Company
3. General Electric
4. Watts
5. Tableau

Notable Internships
1. Ford Motor Company
2. Raytheon
3. Tableau Software

Top Industries
1. Engineering
2. Education
3. Research
4. Information Technology
5. Business

Top Employers
1. Google
2. Microsoft
3. Apple
4. athenahealth
5. Skydio

Where Alumni Work
1. Boston
2. San Francisco
3. Seattle
4. New York City
5. Los Angeles

Median Earnings
College Scorecard (Early Career): N/A
EOP (Early Career): N/A
PayScale (Mid-Career): N/A

RANKINGS
Forbes: N/A
Money: N/A
U.S. News: N/A
Wall Street Journal/THE: N/A
Washington Monthly: N/A

#CollegesWorthYourMoney

George Mason University

Fairfax, Virginia | Admissions Phone: 703-993-2400

ADMISSION
Admission Rate: 81%
Admission Rate - Men: 77%
Admission Rate - Women: 84%
EA Admission Rate: 85%
ED Admission Rate: Not Offered
Admission Rate (5-Year Trend): +19%
ED Admission Rate (5-Year Trend): Not Offered
% of Admits Attending (Yield): 23%
Transfer Admission Rate: 83%

Offered Wait List: 1,889
Accepted Wait List: 1,770
Admitted Wait List: 187

SAT Reading/Writing (Middle 50%): 570-660
SAT Math (Middle 50%): 550-660
ACT Composite (Middle 50%): 24-30
Testing Policy: ACT/SAT Required
SAT Superscore: Yes
ACT Superscore: No

% Graduated in Top 10% of HS Class: 18%
% Graduated in Top 25% of HS Class: 50%
% Graduated in Top 50% of HS Class: 87%

ENROLLMENT
Total Undergraduate Enrollment: 26,192
% Part-Time: 19%
% Male: 50%
% Female: 50%
% Out-of-State: 10%
% Fraternity: 5%
% Sorority: 8%
% On-Campus (Freshman): 64%
% On-Campus (All Undergraduate): 23%

% African-American: 11%
% Asian: 20%
% Hispanic: 15%
% White: 39%
% Other: 5%
% Race or Ethnicity Unknown: 3%
% International: 6%
% Low-Income: 24%

ACADEMICS
Student-to-Faculty Ratio: 17:1
% of Classes Under 20: 30%
% of Classes Under 40: 73%
% Full-Time Faculty: 48%
% Full-Time Faculty w/ Terminal Degree: 90%

Top Programs
Accounting
Criminology, Law and Society
Computer Science
Economics
Government and International Politics
History
Information Technology

Retention Rate: 86%
4-Year Graduation Rate: 47%
6-Year Graduation Rate: 70%

Curricular Flexibility: Less Flexible
Academic Rating: ★★★

Inside the Classroom
If you had to describe George Mason University in five adjectives or less, large, public, affordable, career-focused, and politically conservative (the Koch brothers are/were major donors) would be apt selections. Outsiders sometimes find the number of GMU students surprising; there are 37,000+ of them, more than 25,000 of whom are undergraduates. The high numbers of commuters can hide the actual scope of the university that features ten undergraduate schools and colleges and approximately seventy distinct academic programs. You can get a sense of the pre-professional feel of the student body simply by examining the areas where the greatest number of degrees are conferred. Business (20 percent) is followed by the social sciences (11 percent), health professions (10 percent), computer and information sciences (9 percent), and engineering (6 percent).

Mason aims to make every one of its graduates an "engaged citizen and well-rounded scholar who is prepared to act." Toward that goal it requires a journey through the "Mason Core," a forty-three credit collection of foundation, exploration, and integration requirements. Among the mandatory topics one must tackle are written communication, oral communication, quantitative reasoning and information technology, literature, arts, natural sciences, and other liberal arts staples. That trek will take you the equivalent of three full semesters. The Honors College requires twelve additional credits.

As a result of a 17:1 student-to-faculty ratio and over 11,000 graduate students, class sizes at GMU are rarely small, but it tends to be a mixed bag, and many sections do feature relatively modest numbers. Thirty percent of sections enroll nineteen or fewer students, 27 percent have forty or more students, and the remaining sections lie in between. More intimate educational experiences can be sought in the form of undergraduate research, which roughly half of all students ultimately engage in. There are plenty of summer research opportunities, but you can also take courses designated as Discovery of Scholarship, Scholarly Inquiry, or Research & Scholarship Intensive that offer built-in supervised research. Presently, only ten percent of GMU students study abroad, but the school does sponsor 140+ programs, including travel to the school's own international campus in South Korea.

The Volgenau College of Engineering, which houses a top-tier Information Technology Department, and the School of Business are both extremely reputable in the eyes of prospective employers, and the school's Northern Virginia location allows many to connections with industry to be forged via internships and face-to-face recruiting opportunities. Recent grads have also captured a growing number of prestigious fellowships and scholarships. In 2018, five students won Boren Awards, and in 2019, the school produced a Truman Scholarship winner and has boasted a handful of Fulbright Scholars in recent years.

Outside the Classroom
Only 63 percent of freshmen and 22 percent of the overall undergraduate population reside in on-campus housing. There are many students who commute and/or live in (sometimes) cheaper off-campus housing in Arlington, Falls Church, Annandale, or Manassas. Because 85 percent of GMU students are Virginia residents, they are usually in fairly close proximity to their families. Greek life exists but doesn't dominate; 5 percent of men join frats, and 8 percent of women join sororities. While DC isn't exactly in your backyard at Mason, it is like having a beautiful park right down the street. The heart of the city is only fifteen miles from campus. Meanwhile, the 677 wooded acres that comprise the school's grounds are home to 500+ student-run clubs. There are hundreds of events to attend for free at the Center for the Arts, organic gardens that can be fully utilized by students, two pools, and loads of intramural and club sports. On the more serious athletic front, the Patriots' 462 student-athletes compete in twenty-two NCAA Division I sports with a men's basketball team good enough to have made a Final Four run this millennium. The Hub Student Center is another place where a student body with a large contingent of commuters can coalesce and mingle, but surveys indicate that, at present, the social scene at Mason has room for improvement. Seniors offer much lower ratings of indicators like "sense of belonging" and "involvement in campus activities" than the quality of academic instruction they received.

Career Services
George Mason University Career Services employs twenty-four professionals (not including office assistants, the webmaster, or peer advisors). Roles include employer outreach, industry advisor, career counselor, and career fair manager. That works out to a 1,041:1 student-to-advisor ratio, poorer than the average ratio when compared to other institutions included in this guidebook but not altogether unusual for a school of Mason's size. The career services staff still manages to help more than 20,000 unique students each year, approximately 81 percent of all undergraduate students, which is impressive.

George Mason University

E-mail: admissions@gmu.edu | Website: www2.gmu.edu

This level of outreach helps to explain why, among employed class of 2018 members, 82 percent were in jobs that aligned with their career goals. Some connections are made through fall and spring career fairs that draw 150 employers and 1,500+ students each semester. The internship outlook is aided by the prime location of the university as well as cultivated relationships with many companies. There are fifteen Fortune 500 Companies and, of course, every government agency within a stone's throw. Within the Civil Engineering Department over 90 percent of undergrads complete at least one internship. Over 100,000 Mason alumni, who are mainly concentrated in the Beltway area, also greatly aid the job and internship hunt.

Professional Outcomes

Six months after receiving their degrees 82 percent of the class of 2018 had accepted a job offer or started work in a graduate program. The most commonly entered industries were education (21 percent), government (15 percent), technology (11 percent), health (9 percent), consulting (6 percent), and finance (6 percent). GMU grads flow into major consulting firms like Booz Allen Hamilton, Deloitte, and Accenture, financial institutions like Capital One and Freddie Mac, and engineering/tech firms like General Dynamics, IBM, and Microsoft. Class of 2018 graduates also secured employment at Lockheed Martin, the Smithsonian, the Department of Homeland Security, the Kennedy Center, and CBS News. The vast majority of recent grads stay in the area as 92 percent work in DC, Virginia, or Maryland. New York City and San Francisco also have sizable numbers of Mason alumni. Including bonuses, the median first year salary for a GMU grad is $61,000.

George Mason is presently conducting a feasibility study for creating its own medical college. In the meantime, it offers two guaranteed admissions, joint-degree programs with Virginia Commonwealth University and George Washington University. George Mason does have its own institution for legal education—the Antonin Scalia Law School—and it offers a 3+3 bachelor's/JD program. Across all disciplines Mason graduates tend to pursue advanced degrees either at Mason itself or at other area schools including George Washington, American University, or the University of Maryland.

Admission

At 81 percent George Mason has one the highest acceptance rates of any school featured in this guide, making it an excellent choice for someone with less-than-stellar credentials but a desire to attend a school with tremendous resources. The school is test-optional for those with a strong GPA (It cites a mid-50 percent mark as 3.3-3.9, a record of honors and AP courses, and an impressive list of extracurricular activities that demonstrate leadership). Most applicants end up submitting standardized test scores—71 percent of the Class of 2022 submitted SAT scores, and 9 percent produced ACT results. The mid-50 percent ranges were 1120-1320 on the SAT and 24-30 on the ACT. Only 18 percent of 2018-19 freshman placed in the top 10 percent of their high school class, half were in the top quartile, and 87 percent were in the top 50 percent. The average GPA was 3.7, but 27 percent were below 3.5, giving hope to those who may have hit some bumps along their academic road.

GMU values the rigor of one's high school courses and the GPA earned above all else. Class rank, standardized test scores, and intangibles like talent/ability and character/personal qualities come next. There are no interviews offered as part of the process, nor is there an option for binding early decision. An early action deadline of November 1 will get students a decision by December 15. Entry to Mason is competitive, but compared to many other schools of its class, the bar is easier to clear.

Worth Your Money?

As a state resident George Mason is an unequivocal steal at under $12,500 in tuition. Out-of-staters will pay almost three times as much, making it a question of (a) will Mason provide me with significantly better academics/job prospects than public universities in my own state, and (b) will my potential area of study warrant the extra cost? For example, an applicant from Pennsylvania intent on majoring in education would be unlikely to get a solid return on investment depending, of course, on the degree of merit and need-based aid.

FINANCIAL
Institutional Type: Public
In-State Tuition: $9,060
Out-of-State Tuition: $32,520
Room & Board: $11,460
Required Fees: $3,402
Books & Supplies: $1,200

Avg. Need-Based Aid: $7,840
Avg. % of Need Met: 63%

Avg. Merit-Based Aid: $6,312
% Receiving Merit-Based Aid: 36%

Avg. Cumulative Debt: $30,790
% of Students Borrowing: 60%

CAREER
Who Recruits
1. CoStar
2. BAE Systems
3. Andersen Tax
4. Boeing
5. Black Horse

Notable Internships
1. Verizon
2. Cisco
3. BAE Systems

Top Industries
1. Business
2. Education
3. Infromation Technology
4. Operations
5. Engineering

Top Employers
1. Booz Allen Hamilton
2. Deloitte
3. Northrop Grumman
4. Capital One
5. Freddie Mac

Where Alumni Work
1. Washington, DC
2. New York City
3. Richmond, VA
4. San Francisco
5. Baltimore

Median Earnings
College Scorecard (Early Career): $59,900
EOP (Early Career): $56,500
PayScale (Mid-Career): $105,700

RANKINGS
Forbes: 177
Money: 64
U.S. News: 153, National Universities
Wall Street Journal/THE: 184
Washington Monthly: 51, National Universities

#CollegesWorthYourMoney

Colleges Worth Your Money **George Mason University** 111

Washington, District of Columbia | Admissions Phone: 202-994-6040

ADMISSION

Admission Rate: 42%
Admission Rate - Men: 42%
Admission Rate - Women: 42%
EA Admission Rate: Not Offered
ED Admission Rate: 70%
Admission Rate (5-Year Trend): +9%
ED Admission Rate (5-Year Trend): N/A
% of Admits Attending (Yield): 26%
Transfer Admission Rate: 40%

Offered Wait List: 4,963
Accepted Wait List: 2,081
Admitted Wait List: 14

SAT Reading/Writing (Middle 50%): 640-720
SAT Math (Middle 50%): 640-740
ACT Composite (Middle 50%): 29-32
Testing Policy: Test Optional
SAT Superscore: Yes
ACT Superscore: Yes

% Graduated in Top 10% of HS Class: 56%
% Graduated in Top 25% of HS Class: 88%
% Graduated in Top 50% of HS Class: 98%

ENROLLMENT

Total Undergraduate Enrollment: 12,546
% Part-Time: 10%
% Male: 39%
% Female: 61%
% Out-of-State: 96%
% Fraternity: 14%
% Sorority: 17%
% On-Campus (Freshman): 98%
% On-Campus (All Undergraduate): 60%

% African-American: 7%
% Asian: 11%
% Hispanic: 10%
% White: 50%
% Other: 4%
% Race or Ethnicity Unknown: 6%
% International: 11%
% Low-Income: 12%

ACADEMICS

Student-to-Faculty Ratio: 13:1
% of Classes Under 20: 53%
% of Classes Under 40: 80%
% Full-Time Faculty: 43%
% Full-Time Faculty w/ Terminal Degree: 95%

Top Programs
Communication
Finance
History
International Affairs
International Business
Political Science
Public Health
Public Policy

Retention Rate: 93%
4-Year Graduation Rate: 74%
6-Year Graduation Rate: 82%

Curricular Flexibility: Somewhat Flexible
Academic Rating: ★★★✦

Inside the Classroom

Appropriately located only four blocks from the White House, the university named after our nation's first president educates over 12,500 undergraduate students and an additional 15,500 graduate students. One of the pricier schools in the United States, George Washington University, nevertheless, has rarely been in higher demand since its founding in 1821. Thanks to the popularity of DC as a college setting and a number of highly regarded academic programs, GW has become increasingly selective, catering to a more talented group of students today than it did at the turn of the millennium.

GW undergraduates choose from seventy majors spread across nine colleges: the Columbian College of Arts & Sciences, Corcoran School of the Arts & Design, School of Business, School of Engineering & Applied Science, Elliot School of International Affairs, School of Media & Public Affairs, School of Medicine & Health Sciences, School of Nursing, and the Milken Institute School of Public Health. All GW students must complete one course in mathematics or statistics, one course in natural and/or physical laboratory sciences, two courses in social sciences, one course in humanities, and two writing-intensive courses. From there, another set of college/major-specific requirements follow, but general education requirements tend not to be overly restrictive.

The school's 13:1 student-to-faculty ratio translates to a mix of small, medium, and large undergraduate sections. Eleven percent of courses have single-digit enrollments, 10 percent have over fifty students, and the majority fall in the ten to thirty range. In recent years the university has invested in increasing the number of undergraduate research experiences available to its students through the GW Center for Undergraduate Research and Fellowships. The efforts are paying off as a record 160 undergrads presented at the 2017 GW Research Days, a two-day event held in April. Close to half of Colonials study abroad for one semester in Europe (65 percent), Asia (10 percent), Latin America (8 percent), Africa (7 percent), or Australia (6 percent).

Standout programs at GW include political science, international affairs, communications, and public health. Any degree earned from the university will serve students well when they vie for positions at top companies and elite graduate schools. The social sciences (34 percent) are the area in which the greatest number of degrees are awarded followed by business (17 percent), health professions (12 percent), engineering (5 percent), and communications/journalism (5 percent). A service-oriented institution, GW is proudly the number one producer of Peace Corps volunteers among midsize universities, and it also churns out Teach for America members at one of the highest rates in the country. Twelve of the forty-nine GW students who applied were named Fulbright Scholars in 2017. That success rate of 24 percent is higher than the rate at Harvard, Princeton, or Columbia.

Outside the Classroom

Freshmen, sophomores, and (as of 2018) juniors are all required to live in one of twenty-six residence halls situated on the university's two campuses. Three-quarters of freshmen reside at the main Foggy Bottom Campus, and the other 25 percent of first-years live at the Mount Vernon Campus that is three miles away in Northwest DC. Over 2,500 students, 14 percent of men and 17 percent of women, are Greek affiliated, making fraternities and sororities powerful social forces at GW. The school's robust sports program includes twenty-seven NCAA Division I teams. An additional 1,000 students participate in club sports, and the intramural programs scoop up the rest of the athletically inclined undergrads. The 475 registered student organizations collectively offer 1,200 leadership positions, and 87 percent of undergraduates are involved with at least one group. Noteworthy guest speakers appear with regularity through the GW Speaker Series. Of course, what's on campus is only the first layer of recreational opportunities at George Washington. The Foggy Bottom campus is only a few miles from the National Mall and many of the best museums in the country. As a bridge between the school and outside city, GW's flexible meal plans allow you to visit ninety partner restaurants, cafes, and grocery stores around DC. At GW, your life outside the classroom can involve every corner of the District of Columbia.

Career Services

The Center for Career Services is staffed by twenty-four full-time employees, including eight individuals with the title of career coach as well as other professionals focusing on employer relations and graduate school advising. That calculates to a student-advisor ratio of 420:1, within the average range of institutions profiled in this guide. Personalized career coaching is readily available. The office received high marks from students who exited in 2017 as 95 percent agreed that career programs had helped enhance their career development. Large-scale events, such as the Fall Career Fair, attracted more than one hundred employers in 2018. Fall and spring career fairs generally attract in the neighborhood of 1,400 GW undergrads and alumni.

George Washington University

E-mail: gwadm@gwu.edu | Website: www.gwu.edu

Internships are completed by 68 percent of undergraduates and 54 percent are either paid or awarded a stipend for their work. Thanks to the university's far-reaching connections and prime location, internships are procured at thousands of different companies/organizations each year, from the US Congress to the Smithsonian to the NFL Players Association. More than 800 employers engaged with GW students through a combination of on- and off-campus events. The school also enjoys an alumni base of over 250,000 that leads to ample opportunities for networking. In sum, the Center for Career Services does a solid job facilitating internships and utilizing its DC locale and huge, well-connected alumni base to produce decent outcomes for its graduates.

Professional Outcomes

Within six months of leaving GW 87 percent of the Class of 2018 had found their way to gainful employment or graduate school while 13 percent were still job hunting. Of the 61 percent of grads already in the workplace, two-thirds were in a for-profit industry, 25 percent had entered a nonprofit position, and 8 percent were working in government. Among the most popular sectors for GW grads were health care (9 percent), legal and law enforcement (6 percent), management/consulting (6 percent), accounting (5 percent), public relations (5 percent), and defense (5 percent). Close to one-third enjoyed starting salaries above $60,000 while 49 percent earned less than $50,000. The median salary earned by newly minted grads from 2014-2017 was $46k. Close to four-fifths of recent grads remained in the Mid-Atlantic region with the West and Mountain regions a distant second.

A healthy 23 percent of those earning their diplomas in 2018 immediately turned their attention to earning an advanced degree. Among that group were 66 percent seeking master's degrees, 14 percent entering law school, 6 percent entering a doctoral program, and 7 percent pursuing a medical degree. Looking at the last four graduating classes as a whole, 488 students have continued their studies at George Washington. The next most commonly attended institutions were Columbia University (48), Georgetown (42), Johns Hopkins (37), and NYU (31).

Admission

Of 26,590 Class of 2022 hopefuls, GW admitted 11,100 for an acceptance rate of 42 percent. That number has shown volatility over current attendees' lifetimes, hitting as low as 32 percent in 2010 and as high as 80 percent in 1998 when today's seniors were in diapers. Freshmen during the 2018-19 school year earned excellent grades in high school as 56 percent finished in the top 10 percent of their class, and 88 percent landed in the top 25 percent. Of those submitting standardized test results the middle 50 percent of SAT scores were 1280-1460 and 29-32 on the ACT.

The admissions committee rates two factors—rigor of secondary school record and GPA—as carrying the greatest weight in the process. The next tier of factors includes the essay, volunteer work, recommendations, talent/ability, and extracurricular activities. GW has been test-optional since 2015, and a fair number of applicants do forgo submitting standardized test scores. Of the 2,800 freshmen in the Class of 2022, 1,419 submitted SAT scores and 955 submitted ACT scores. Given that a fair number of students likely submitted results from both tests, more than a quarter of those enrolled are likely to have been accepted sans test scores. Over the past two decades GW has grown into a highly selective and sought-after university in one of the country's hottest cities. Still, this institution is in a dogfight for top students and rewards those who apply early, typically accepting 70 percent through ED versus 40 percent in the regular cycle.

Worth Your Money?

Attending a private college in the fifth most expensive US city isn't going to come cheap. GW will set you back $74k per year for total cost of attendance. Three-fifths of students do receive a merit aid award averaging almost $23k, which makes the university slightly more affordable. For the 47 percent of undergrads who qualify for need-based financial aid, an average annual award of $35,000 puts a dent in the total costs, but the school does not meet 100 percent of the demonstrated need for the majority of eligible students. George Washington grads emerge with higher-than-average debt loads, thus prospective students need to carefully determine whether this school is a good financial fit for them, given their individual circumstances. Students pursuing study in the areas of business, communication, politics and policy enjoy better prospects for a strong ROI.

FINANCIAL
Institutional Type: Private
In-State Tuition: $54,459
Out-of-State Tuition: $54,459
Room & Board: $14,300
Required Fees: $90
Books & Supplies: $1,400

Avg. Need-Based Aid: $35,061
Avg. % of Need Met: 88%

Avg. Merit-Based Aid: $22,777
% Receiving Merit-Based Aid: 60%

Avg. Cumulative Debt: $35,454
% of Students Borrowing: 47%

CAREER
Who Recruits
1. Becton, Dickinson and Co.
2. Consumer Financial Protection Bureau
3. Westat
4. Turner Construction
5. Gunnison Consulting

Notable Internships
1. United States Senate
2. NBC News
3. Macy's

Top Industries
1. Business
2. Education
3. Operations
4. Social Services
5. information Technology

Top Employers
1. Booz Allen Hamilton
2. Deloitte
3. IBM
4. U.S. House of Representatives
5. Capital One

Where Alumni Work
1. Washington, DC
2. New Yor City
3. San Francisco
4. Boston
5. Philadelphia

Median Earnings
College Scorecard (Early Career): $69,600
EOP (Early Career): $63,900
PayScale (Mid-Career): $115,300

RANKINGS
Forbes: 78
Money: 235
U.S. News: 70, National Universities
Wall Street Journal/THE: 72
Washington Monthly: 54, National Universities

#CollegesWorthYourMoney

Georgetown University

Washington, District of Columbia | Admissions Phone: 202-687-3600

ADMISSION
Admission Rate: 15%
Admission Rate - Men: 16%
Admission Rate - Women: 14%
EA Admission Rate: N/A
ED Admission Rate: Not Offered
Admission Rate (5-Year Trend): -3%
ED Admission Rate (5-Year Trend): Not Offered
% of Admits Attending (Yield): 49%
Transfer Admission Rate: 7%

Offered Wait List: 2,593
Accepted Wait List: 1,754
Admitted Wait List: 16

SAT Reading/Writing (Middle 50%): 680-750
SAT Math (Middle 50%): 690-780
ACT Composite (Middle 50%): 31-34
Testing Policy: ACT/SAT Required
SAT Superscore: Yes
ACT Superscore: No

% Graduated in Top 10% of HS Class: 89%
% Graduated in Top 25% of HS Class: 97%
% Graduated in Top 50% of HS Class: 99%

ENROLLMENT
Total Undergraduate Enrollment: 7,459
% Part-Time: 6%
% Male: 44%
% Female: 56%
% Out-of-State: 98%
% Fraternity: Not Offered
% Sorority: Not Offered
% On-Campus (Freshman): 100%
% On-Campus (All Undergraduate): 77%

% African-American: 6%
% Asian: 9%
% Hispanic: 10%
% White: 50%
% Other: 5%
% Race or Ethnicity Unknown: 5%
% International: 15%
% Low-Income: 13%

ACADEMICS
Student-to-Faculty Ratio: 11:1
% of Classes Under 20: 60%
% of Classes Under 40: 87%
% Full-Time Faculty: 49%
% Full-Time Faculty w/ Terminal Degree: 80%

Top Programs
Economics
Finance
Global Health
Government
History
International Business
International Politics
Psychology

Retention Rate: 96%
4-Year Graduation Rate: 89%
6-Year Graduation Rate: 94%

Curricular Flexibility: Somewhat Flexible
Academic Rating: ★★★★

Inside the Classroom

The nation's oldest Catholic and Jesuit university also happens to be one of the best institutions in the country and one of the premier training grounds for future political bigwigs. Spired campus buildings, cobblestone walkways, and tree-lined streets give Georgetown an elegant aesthetic and an air of sophistication that perfectly matches the rigorous educational experience and conservative/traditional campus vibe.

The university's 7,400 undergraduates and 11,700 graduate students are divided among nine schools/colleges, but only four are open to undergrads. Applicants to Georgetown must select one of these four schools: Georgetown College, McDonough School of Business, the Walsh School of Foreign Service, or the School of Nursing & Health Studies. Core requirements vary by school but are fairly extensive. For example, Georgetown College requires one course in the humanities and writing and two courses per discipline in theology, philosophy, math/science, social science, foreign language, and diversity for a total of fourteen required courses. There are forty-four majors within Georgetown College, seven business-oriented majors within McDonough, four tracks in the nursing school, and eight majors within the Walsh School of Foreign Service.

For a large university with a heavy presence of graduate students, Georgetown maintains a personalized and intimate learning environment. The student-faculty ratio is 11:1, and 60 percent of classes enroll fewer than twenty students. While some classes are a bit larger, only 6 percent cross the fifty-student threshold. There are many ways that students can seek funding for independent research projects or become an assistant to faculty members via the Georgetown Undergraduate Research Opportunities Program. Summer research can lead to the completion of a senior thesis that can be presented at the College Academic Council Research Colloquium every spring. A phenomenal 57 percent of Hoya undergrads participate in one of the schools 200 study abroad programs that are spread across fifty countries.

Those desiring to join the world of politics or diplomacy are in the right place. The Government and International Affairs programs are among the best in the country. For those with their eyes on a finance career, McDonough is one of the most esteemed business schools one can find. The greatest number of degrees are conferred in the social sciences (35 percent) followed by business (26 percent), interdisciplinary studies (6 percent), and foreign language (5 percent). Georgetown is regularly a top producer of distinguished fellowship winners. In 2018, it produced thirty Fulbright Scholars, placing it in the top five in the nation. It typically also sees multiple Truman, Boren, Gilman International, and Marshall Scholars from each graduating class.

Outside the Classroom

The scenic and safe Georgetown area of DC is littered with high-end restaurants and shops. Only a short Metro ride away, the opportunities for museums, live music, fine cuisine, sporting events, and a pulsating nightlife are endless. A touch over three-quarters of undergrads live on campus.

The twenty-three NCAA Division I sports teams are part of the fabric of Hoya life, particularly the men's basketball team. More than 2,500 students participate in intramural sports, utilizing the school's superb facilities that include Yates Field House. Due to the clash of values between the Jesuits and Greek life, fraternities and sororities are not recognized by the school, but they have enjoyed a recent rise in popularity despite their unofficial status. Religion is a guiding force at the university as more than half of the student body identify as Catholic. The campus ministry is popular, and many students are part of faith-based or secular volunteer organizations. In total, there are 250 active student organizations that offer an array of clubs focused on spirituality, culture, academics, and the arts. The Georgetown University Lecture Fund brings an incredible lineup of luminaries from the realms of politics, entertainment, business, media, and social activism to speak on campus.

Career Services

The Cawley Career Education Center is manned by fourteen professionals (not counting office managers and administrative assistants). That gives it a student-to-advisor ratio of 531:1, below average compared to the pool of institutions included in this book. Yet, that does not translate to a poor delivery of services. In fact, the staff boasts over 13,000 interactions with undergraduate students each year, almost twice the population of the student body; by graduation, over 90 percent have engaged with the career center. In a given year, counselors spend approximately 800 collective hours meeting one-on-one with students to discuss professional pathways and dole out career/graduate school advice.

In a single school year Georgetown arranged for 2,460 interviews on campus and attracted more than 1,800 attendees at both its fall and spring career expos. Over 200 corporations, government, and nonprofit employers met with students at those events. Additionally, sixty-five companies visited campus to host information sessions with undergraduates. With a strong and active alumni base, the Hoya Career Connection sees roughly 15,000 internship/employment opportunities posted per year. Despite not having an elite student-advisor ratio, Cawley's extensive counseling offerings/events, proficiency with facilitating on-campus recruiting by top-level employers, and tremendous student outcomes earned it top grades from our staff.

Georgetown University

E-mail: guadmiss@georgetown.edu | Website: www.georgetown.edu

Professional Outcomes

Within six months of graduating 75 percent of members of the Class of 2018 entered the workforce, 16 percent went directly into a graduate or professional program of study, and 5 percent were still seeking employment. In past years the number of fresh alums entering grad school has been significantly greater—as high as 24 percent. The Class of 2018 sent massive numbers of graduates to a number of major corporations including Deloitte (26), Citi (24), JPMorgan Chase (22), PricewaterhouseCoopers (21), EY (18), Morgan Stanley (17), McKinsey & Company (11) and Goldman Sachs (10), and a number of other multinational financial institutions. As one might ascertain from this list of companies, the most popular industries were consulting (15 percent), investment banking (14 percent), and internet and software (8 percent). By far, New York and remaining in DC are the two most popular postgraduate destinations, although a fair number also migrate to Virginia, California, Massachusetts, and Maryland. The financial picture for Georgetown graduates is rosy. They enjoy an average starting salary of $61,000, well above the national average.

Over the past six years, medicine and law have been the top two graduate fields chosen by Hoya alumni. Each year roughly forty to fifty-five grads entered law school, and another forty to fifty-five entered med school. An incredibly high percentage elect to remain at Georgetown—forty-seven members of the Class of 2018 entered graduate school at their alma mater. The number two choice was Columbia with eighteen students. In fact, since 2007 Georgetown and Columbia have been the two most frequently attended graduate schools. The other schools on that list are almost exclusively elite institutions including Harvard, Yale, Duke, Northwestern, USC, NYU, Tufts, and the University of Chicago.

Admission

Like many other prestigious universities, Georgetown registered its all-time high in applications received and all-time low acceptance rate for the class of 2022. Of the almost 23,000 applications, slightly more than 3,330 were admitted for an acceptance rate of 14.5 percent. The average SAT score of those accepted was the highest ever at 1467. For enrolled freshmen in 2018-19, the mid-50 percent range was 1370-1530 on the SAT and 31-34 on the ACT. Grades must be equally exceptional for serious consideration; 89 percent of enrolled students finished in the top 10 percent of their high school class. The profile of students admitted today has much in common with those admitted five years ago.

Georgetown does not have an early decision option but does offer nonbinding early action. However, applying early yields little advantage as the university's early round acceptance rates tend to be lower than in the regular round. Also noteworthy, the university does not allow Score Choice, the option that permits applicants to select which standardized scores are reported to prospective schools and which are not. The admissions office rates nine factors as being "very important," most notably first-generation status, a consideration weighted this heavily by few other schools. In the 2018-19 academic year 11 percent of admitted students were the first in their family to attend college. The most selective school in the DC Metro area, Georgetown attracts growing lines of extremely well-qualified candidates each year. There are few admissions surprises here. Test scores around the 97th percentile and near-perfect grades in an AP-heavy course load are required.

Worth Your Money?

A year at Georgetown will cost you close to $78,000 if you do not receive any financial aid. Like many similarly elite institutions, it is more focused on providing sizable grants to those with true financial need. For the 38 percent of current students who qualify for financial aid, Georgetown meets 100 percent of their demonstrated need, which works out to an average annual amount of $45,572. Unless you plan to enter a low-paying field and need to take on an excessive amount of debt, this school is well worth paying for as the Georgetown name will open doors for you well into adulthood.

FINANCIAL
Institutional Type: Private
In-State Tuition: $55,440
Out-of-State Tuition: $55,440
Room & Board: $17,638
Required Fees: $618
Books & Supplies: N/A

Avg. Need-Based Aid: $45,572
Avg. % of Need Met: 100%

Avg. Merit-Based Aid: $0
% Receiving Merit-Based Aid: 0%

Avg. Cumulative Debt: $25,726
% of Students Borrowing: 37%

CAREER
Who Recruits
1. BMO Capital Markets
2. AlphaSights
3. RBC Capital Markets
4. Capital One
5. Charles River Associates

Notable Internships
1. U.S. Securities and Exchange Commission
2. Vanguard
3. Goldman Sachs

Top Industries
1. Business
2. Education
3. Social Services
4. Operations
5. Media

Top Employers
1. Deloitte
2. Google
3. PwC
4. Citi
5. Goldman Sachs

Where Alumni Work
1. Washington, DC
2. New York City
3. San Francisco
4. Boston
5. Los Angeles

Median Earnings
College Scorecard (Early Career): $93,500
EOP (Early Career): $84,400
PayScale (Mid-Career): $122,200

RANKINGS
Forbes: 15
Money: 61
U.S. News: 24, National Universities
Wall Street Journal/THE: 29
Washington Monthly: 9, National Universities

#CollegesWorthYourMoney

Georgia Institute of Technology

Atlanta, Georgia | Admissions Phone: 404-894-4154

ADMISSION
Admission Rate: 23%
Admission Rate - Men: 19%
Admission Rate - Women: 29%
EA Admission Rate: 26%
ED Admission Rate: Not Offered
Admission Rate (5-Year Trend): -19%
ED Admission Rate (5-Year Trend): Not Offered
% of Admits Attending (Yield): 39%
Transfer Admission Rate: 29%

Offered Wait List: 3,511
Accepted Wait List: 2,265
Admitted Wait List: 72

SAT Reading/Writing (Middle 50%): 680-750
SAT Math (Middle 50%): 710-790
ACT Composite (Middle 50%): 31-34
Testing Policy: ACT/SAT Required
SAT Superscore: Yes
ACT Superscore: Yes

% Graduated in Top 10% of HS Class: 89%
% Graduated in Top 25% of HS Class: 97%
% Graduated in Top 50% of HS Class: 99%

ENROLLMENT
Total Undergraduate Enrollment: 16,049
% Part-Time: 11%
% Male: 62%
% Female: 38%
% Out-of-State: 34%
% Fraternity: 28%
% Sorority: 33%
% On-Campus (Freshman): 97%
% On-Campus (All Undergraduate): 43%

% African-American: 7%
% Asian: 22%
% Hispanic: 7%
% White: 47%
% Other: 4%
% Race or Ethnicity Unknown: 3%
% International: 10%
% Low-Income: 15%

ACADEMICS
Student-to-Faculty Ratio: 23:1
% of Classes Under 20: 45%
% of Classes Under 40: 78%
% Full-Time Faculty: 88%
% Full-Time Faculty w/ Terminal Degree: 99%

Top Programs
Architecture
Business
Chemistry
Computer Science
Engineering
Industrial Design
Mathematics
Physics

Retention Rate: 97%
4-Year Graduation Rate: 40%
6-Year Graduation Rate: 87%

Curricular Flexibility: Less Flexible
Academic Rating: ★★★★

Inside the Classroom

Downtown Atlanta is home to one of the world's undisputed best public technological institutes. The Georgia Institute of Technology, more commonly referred to as Georgia Tech, educates more than 16,000 undergraduates as well as another 16,000-plus graduate students who are on track to be the next generation of leaders in the engineering, computer science, and related fields. While still catering to locals (68 percent are Georgia residents), Tech has managed to grow its national reputation in recent years and has blossomed from a top public tech university to simply a top tech university.

Georgia Tech is divided into six colleges: the College of Design, the College of Computing, the College of Engineering, the College of Sciences, Ivan Allen College of Liberal Arts, and Scheller College of Business. Altogether, more than 115 majors and minors are available to undergraduates; all students are held to a stringent list of core requirements that is partially governed by the state. Must-take courses include Constitution & History, Communication Outcomes, Quantitative Outcomes, and Introduction to Computing as well as requirements in humanities/fine arts/ethics, social sciences, and wellness (physical education).

Being a large research university, the student-to-faculty ratio is a less-than-ideal 23:1, leading to some larger undergraduate class sections. In fact, 35 percent of courses had enrollments of more than thirty students in 2018-19. On the other end of the spectrum, 29 percent of sections had single-digit enrollments. While not all of your professors will know you by name, there are plenty of ways that motivated students can strike up meaningful faculty-student relationships. For example, 30 percent of aerospace engineering majors collaborate on research with their professors. In the School of Chemical and Biomolecular Engineering that figure rises to 60 percent. Over half of Tech students have gone abroad by the time they graduate, with a growing number electing to complete internships in a foreign land rather than academic coursework. Last year, 135 undergraduate students participated in a global internship.

Georgia Tech's engineering and computer science programs are at the top of any "best programs" list. The Scheller College of Business boasts top programs in management information systems, production/operation management, quantitative analysis, and supply chain management/logistics. The architecture school also receives national recognition. In terms of total number of degrees conferred, the most popular areas of study are engineering (60 percent), computer science (17 percent), and business (10 percent). Those pursuing prestigious fellowships/scholarships have done well in recent years. In 2016, five students won Fulbright Scholarships. Others have succeeded at taking home Astronaut, Udall, Truman, and Marshall Scholarships. Two undergrads from one major—electrical engineering—won National Science Fellowships in 2018.

Outside the Classroom

Georgia Tech's 400-acre, wooded campus contains the vast majority of freshmen (98 percent), but only 45 percent of the overall student body lives in the school's forty residence halls. The rest find apartments or housing in surrounding neighborhoods like Buckhead, Home Park, Westside, or Atlantic Station. The Yellow Jackets field seventeen varsity intercollegiate athletic teams. The school's nine men's and eight women's teams participate in the Atlantic Coast Conference (ACC). Add twenty intramural sports, forty-three sports clubs, and one of the largest outdoor recreation programs around, and the result is an extremely athletically-inclined student body. Those who aren't involved with sports typically find another place to connect, whether it's in one of the more than 400 student organizations or fifty Greek organizations. Tech is a Greek-heavy school with 28 percent of men and 33 percent of women belonging to a fraternity or sorority. Campus provides plenty of chances for social engagement, but those seeking more can enjoy all that Atlanta has to offer.

Career Services

The Georgia Tech Center for Career Discovery and Development, cleverly nicknamed C2D2, employs twenty full-time staff members (not counting IT professionals and office assistants). That collection of career advisors, employee relations specialists, and graduate school counselors works out to a student-to-counselor ratio of 679:1, below average compared to the pool of institutions included in this book. Despite this unremarkable number, C2D2 is able to put on impressive, large-scale events that enhance student outcomes. The Fall Career Fair is the school's largest, featuring over 400 employers including Accenture, Capital One, GM, and Intel, and 5,000 students attend each year. The school also forges formal corporate partnerships with big-time companies including Google, Airbnb, Qualcomm, Northrup Grumman, and ConocoPhillips. Corporations routinely host information sessions on campus.

Internships and co-op programs receive some of the highest marks in the country. Thirty-five percent of undergrads choose to enter the school's three-semester co-op program, which leads to a five-year degree, while many others complete a one- or two-semester internship. In 2017, C2D2 placed 1,068 students in internships and another 1,307 in co-op programs. Individualized appointments are encouraged as early as freshman year to begin planning potential career and graduate school pathways. Overall, Georgia Tech's career services does a fantastic job of funneling undergraduates into the world's premier employers at high starting salaries.

Georgia Institute of Technology

E-mail: admission@gatech.edu | Website: www.gatech.edu

Professional Outcomes

Graduates in the Class of 2018 procured employment at a rate of 78 percent by the time they were handed their diplomas. The median salary reported by that group was $70,500. The highest median salary of $99k went to graduates of the School of Computer Science. By midcareer, Georgia Tech alumni enjoy the second highest salary of the most selective public universities in the country. You will find alumni at every major technology in the world. Just examining those who have LinkedIn profiles, 969 Yellow Jackets work at Google, 853 at Microsoft, 789 at Amazon, 759 at IBM, 586 at Apple, 327 at Facebook, and 170 at Uber. The bulk of graduates remain in the Atlanta metro area. The next three most popular destinations are San Francisco, New York City, and Washington, DC.

At the time of their exit surveys, 21 percent of 2018 grads planned on pursuing an advanced degree within the next year. Many remain on campus to earn advanced engineering degrees through Georgia Tech, but the school's reputation is such that gaining admission into other top programs including MIT, Carnegie Mellon, Berkeley, Stanford, and Caltech is an achievable feat. Those same schools are institutions where Tech alumni have gone on to work as professors and researchers.

Admission

Only 22 percent of applicants to the Class of 2022 were admitted, a slight decrease from the 23 percent who were admitted the prior year. Freshmen during the 2018-19 school year possessed middle-50 percent scores of 1390-1540 on the SAT and 31-34 on the ACT, and 94 percent had a GPA of over 3.75. A staggering 89 percent of first-year students hailed from the top 10 percent of their high school classes; 97 percent were in the top 25 percent. Only a decade ago, the university admitted 63 percent of applicants, and the 75th percentile of test-takers placed close to the Class of 2022's 25th percentile. Clearly, this school is infinitely more difficult to get into than it was only a short time ago.

Three factors can give you an advantage in your quest to gain acceptance at Tech: (1) if you are from Georgia, (2) if you are female, and (3) if you apply early action. In 2017-18, the acceptance rate for Peach State residents was 44 percent, more than double the out-of-state figure. The following cycle the acceptance rate for female applicants was 29 percent versus only 19 percent for male applicants. The early action acceptance rate was 26 percent versus 17 percent for the general pool. For all applicants, the admissions committee places the most emphasis on the rigor of one's high school coursework, GPA, and extracurricular activities. Test scores, essays, talent/ability, character, and personal qualities, volunteer work, and work experience are among the factors in the next tier. Getting into Georgia Tech has become a harrowing enterprise and is a wholly different experience than for previous generations. Applying early will help, but nonresident men, in particular, will still face extremely unfavorable odds.

Worth Your Money?

Georgia residents are looking at an annual cost of attendance of $31k which, when you consider that the median starting salary is well over two times that amount, makes Georgia Tech an exceptional bargain. Even better, merit aid is generously distributed with 63 percent of undergrads landing, on average, a $12,777 award each year. That includes the Stamps President's Scholars Program that gives a free ride to forty highly qualified applicants each year. Need-based aid is granted to 40 percent of students with the average amount in the range of $12,500. Only a small percentage of aid recipients see 100 percent of their demonstrated need met. Even if you received limited aid and/or were paying out-of-state tuition, which brings the COA to $52k, Tech would still prove a worthwhile investment of your time and money.

FINANCIAL
Institutional Type: Public
In-State Tuition: $10,008
Out-of-State Tuition: $30,604
Room & Board: $11,884
Required Fees: $2,416
Books & Supplies: $800

Avg. Need-Based Aid: $14,630
Avg. % of Need Met: 66%

Avg. Merit-Based Aid: $12,777
% Receiving Merit-Based Aid: 63%

Avg. Cumulative Debt: $32,760
% of Students Borrowing: 36%

CAREER
Who Recruits
1. SunTrust Bank
2. Caterpillar
3. The Clorox Company
4. Equifax
5. Rockwell Automation

Notable Internships
1. NASA
2. Procter & Gamble
3. Uber

Top Industries
1. Engineering
2. Business
3. Operations
4. Information Technology
5. Research

Top Employers
1. Google
2. Microsoft
3. Amazon
4. Home Depot
5. Apple

Where Alumni Work
1. Atlanta
2. San Francisco
3. New York City
4. Washington, DC
5. Seattle

Median Earnings
College Scorecard (Early Career): $79,100
EOP (Early Career): $78,900
PayScale (Mid-Career): $133,400

RANKINGS
Forbes: 65
Money: 27
U.S. News: 29, National Universities
Wall Street Journal/THE: 68 (T)
Washington Monthly: 48, National Universities

#CollegesWorthYourMoney

Grinnell College

Grinnell, Iowa | Admissions Phone: 641-269-3600

ADMISSION
Admission Rate: 24%
Admission Rate - Men: 23%
Admission Rate - Women: 26%
EA Admission Rate: Not Offered
ED Admission Rate: 58%
Admission Rate (5-Year Trend): -11%
ED Admission Rate (5-Year Trend): +9%
% of Admits Attending (Yield): 26%
Transfer Admission Rate: 4%

Offered Wait List: 1,447
Accepted Wait List: 274
Admitted Wait List: 33

SAT Reading/Writing (Middle 50%): 670-750
SAT Math (Middle 50%): 700-790
ACT Composite (Middle 50%): 30-34
Testing Policy: ACT/SAT Required
SAT Superscore: Yes
ACT Superscore: Yes

% Graduated in Top 10% of HS Class: 68%
% Graduated in Top 25% of HS Class: 90%
% Graduated in Top 50% of HS Class: 99%

ENROLLMENT
Total Undergraduate Enrollment: 1,716
% Part-Time: 2%
% Male: 46%
% Female: 54%
% Out-of-State: 92%
% Fraternity: Not Offered
% Sorority: Not Offered
% On-Campus (Freshman): 100%
% On-Campus (All Undergraduate): 88%

% African-American: 5%
% Asian: 8%
% Hispanic: 7%
% White: 50%
% Other: 5%
% Race or Ethnicity Unknown: 6%
% International: 19%
% Low-Income: 22%

ACADEMICS
Student-to-Faculty Ratio: 9:1
% of Classes Under 20: 65%
% of Classes Under 40: 100%
% Full-Time Faculty: 82%
% Full-Time Faculty w/ Terminal Degree: 99%

Top Programs
Biology
Biological Chemistry
Chemistry
Economics
History
Physics
Political Science
Sociology

Retention Rate: 92%
4-Year Graduation Rate: 78%
6-Year Graduation Rate: 84%

Curricular Flexibility: Very Flexible
Academic Rating: ★★★★✔

Inside the Classroom

Long a bastion of progressive, free-thinking liberal arts education, Grinnell College, set in remote Iowa, has never been a more popular destination in its more than 170-year history than it is today. Rising numbers of applications and shrinking acceptance rates have raised the caliber of the nearly 1,700 young people who currently occupy campus.

Grinnell offers twenty-seven distinct bachelor's degrees and over 500 courses each semester, and students have an immense deal of autonomy with course selection. In fact, nothing better epitomizes the school's philosophy than its list of graduation requirements that are more a list of the maximum number of courses a student can take in any one area rather than a list of minimal expectations. The only required course is the First-Year Tutorial, a ten- to fourteen-student, writing-intensive seminar with topics ranging from the artist Kendrick Lamar to the comic strip Calvin & Hobbes. Outside of that one course, your education is personally crafted through the college's Individually-Advised Curriculum that sees students working closely with a faculty advisor to make the most of their educational journey.

Thanks to a 9:1 student/faculty ratio and no competition from graduate students, two-thirds of classes have fewer than twenty students, and 24 percent of sections have single-digit student enrollments. Participating in research is a normal part of an undergraduate education at Grinnell. Overall, 43 percent of Grinnell undergrads participate in one on- or off-campus research experience that was not simply built into their coursework. Mentor Advanced Projects, which see faculty closely work with students on scholarly or creative works, were participated in by 71 percent of the subset who had some type of research experience. Thirty percent of that group conducted research at another location such as Duke University, Georgetown University, or Carnegie Mellon University. International study is also a fairly common part of a Grinnell education with 50 percent of students studying abroad. The Grinnell-in-London program is a popular option, offering a semester's worth of courses on English politics, history, and theater.

A top producer of PhDs in both the sciences and the social sciences, Grinnell has strong offerings across the board, with programs in biology, chemistry, economics, and history receiving particularly high praise. The largest number of degrees are conferred in English, foreign languages, biology, and computer science. A fast riser, the computer science program now graduates seventy students per year versus only fifteen four years ago. Grinnell students fare extraordinarily well at obtaining competitive scholarships. Graduates in the Class of 2017 captured Watson, Fulbright, and NIH scholarships/fellowships. Grinnell is one of the top Fulbright-producing institutions in the country with seven recipients in 2018 and ten in 2016.

Outside the Classroom

Over 85 percent of students live on campus in small residence halls that house between fifty and sixty students. Grinnell has a long tradition of being fraternity and sorority free, instead favoring an "inclusive and open-minded" social scene. One-third of students engage in varsity athletics; the school fields twenty NCAA Division III teams that compete in the Midwest Conference. Intramurals draw heavy participation with soccer, volleyball, flag football, and basketball being among the most popular. Two-thirds of students participate in community service projects, and opportunities include teaching at a local prison, a buddies program for nearby children, and Alternative Breaks at impoverished areas around the United States. There are more than one hundred student organizations as silly and relaxed as the Zombie Movie Club or as serious as the local chapter of the Roosevelt Institute Campus Network. With its remote location amidst the cornfields of Iowa, there's not much to explore in the surrounding area. Fortunately, campus itself is a nurturing and lively place.

Career Services

For a school of just over 1,700, the Center for Careers, Life, and Service (CLS) employs an astounding twenty-two full-time staff members that includes those specializing in career advising (14), employer relations, internships, and fellowships and awards. That equates to a student-to-advisor ratio of 77:1, better than every school except Wellesley that is featured in this guide. The personalized attention that staffing level affords enables the CLS to adhere to its core belief that "one's impact, satisfaction, and sense of purpose are maximized when one is able to align their values, strengths, and curiosities." To that aim, students are assigned a CLS exploratory advisor before they even set foot on campus. In the 2018-19 academic year the office had 4,469 one-one-one advising contacts with students, which works out to more than two per student!

While its somewhat remote location and small student body makes it tough to host a large-scale career fair, the school compensates by hosting/facilitating over 180 smaller events each year including career treks, workshops, alumni panels, and networking receptions. Seventy-seven companies recruited on campus in the last academic year. Grinnell does a solid job facilitating internship experiences with a 44 percent participation rate among 2017 graduates. Of that group, 31 percent completed two internships, and 19 percent completed four.

Internships were procured around the globe including stops at BMW China, Amazon Japan, the White House, the United Nations, Facebook, IBM, and Twitter. Thirty-five percent of the employed members of the class of 2017 stated that their first job was exactly what they wanted to be doing, and 46 percent viewed their position as a "good stepping stone." Grinnell's CLS offers unparalleled support and has an excellent track record of helping students secure valuable internships, meaningful first jobs, and graduate school acceptances.

Professional Outcomes

Upon graduation 59 percent of the Class of 2017 headed into the workforce, 22 percent to graduate school, 7 percent to postgraduate service, and 5 percent earned fellowships. Of the 59 percent entering employment, 88 percent had already procured full-time jobs. Multiple members of this cohort accepted positions with Amazon and Google while others were hired by desirable organizations that included the Federal Reserve Board, Deloitte, the Brookings Institute, Goldman Sachs, and the Centers for Disease Control. The most commonly entered fields were IT/computing (15 percent), education (14 percent), business (13 percent), and research/science (11 percent). The mean salary of those employed was roughly $45,500, and the median was a slightly lower $42,500. Illinois attracted the highest number of graduates, slightly more than Iowa itself. California, New York, and Minnesota were the next most popular locations for Grinnell grads.

Forty percent of those entering graduate school in 2018 were pursuing PhDs in the hard sciences, 10 percent were headed to law school, and an equal percentage were bound for medical school. Law school acceptances included top-tier institutions Harvard and the University of Chicago, and one student was granted admission to the Johns Hopkins University School of Medicine. Other members were admitted to various advanced degree programs at Cambridge, Yale, Carnegie Mellon, and Cornell (NY). Overall, 86 percent of law school applicants received at least one acceptance, and 57 percent of medical school applicants were successful, which was twelve points higher than the national average.

Admission

The acceptance rate has jumped around in the last few years between 20 and 29 percent. That is far more selective than Grinnell was only a short time ago. For example, in the 2010-11 cycle Grinnell accepted 43 percent of applicants. That year it received only 2,969 applications, but it received 7,345 for a place in the Class of 2022. Standardized test scores of attending freshmen are higher as well—the mid-50 percent SAT score is 1320-1530 and 30-33 on the ACT. Approximately 80 percent of Grinnell students hail from the top 10 percent of their high school classes.

Admissions factors rated by the committee as being "very important" are rigor of secondary curriculum, GPA, class rank, and recommendations. The four categories that fall under "important" are standardized test scores, extracurricular activities, and talent/ability. Most members of the Class of 2022 were deeply involved during high school with 81 percent participating in community service, 71 percent in the fine arts, 65 percent in athletics, and 43 percent held jobs. Applying through early decision yields a major advantage as 58 percent of applicants receive positive news, more than double the regular rate. Early decision applicants comprise 44 percent of the incoming class, meaning that a large number of spots are already filled by the time the regular cycle rolls around. Even with Grinnell's transformation into a highly sought-after liberal arts college, the process remains holistic. Grades and test scores certainly matter, but unique talents and high school involvement play a major role as well. We can't stress enough how advantageous applying early is for students dead-set on studying at this now-elite Iowa school.

Worth Your Money?

The cost of attendance at Grinnell College is $67,646. One-quarter of undergrads receive a merit aid award averaging $19k. More encouragingly, two-thirds of attendees receive need-based grants with an annual value of roughly $45,000. Further, Grinnell manages to meet the full-demonstrated need of 100 percent of aid-eligible students. Starting salaries are generally on the lower side coming out of this college, which is perhaps attributed to the many Grinnellians in the academic and non-profit sectors; however, that isn't a big deal for most, thanks to the generosity of the aid packages being distributed. The average graduate comes out of Grinnell with less than $19,000 in debt, a very manageable sum.

FINANCIAL
Institutional Type: Private
In-State Tuition: $53,872
Out-of-State Tuition: $5,387
Room & Board: $13,292
Required Fees: $482
Books & Supplies: N/A

Avg. Need-Based Aid: $45,007
Avg. % of Need Met: 100%

Avg. Merit-Based Aid: $18,811
% Receiving Merit-Based Aid: 25%

Avg. Cumulative Debt: $18,694
% of Students Borrowing: 60%

CAREER
Who Recruits
1. Epic Systems
2. Morningstar
3. Nationwide
4. Teach for America
5. Google

Notable Internships
1. U.S. Forest Service
2. MasterCard
3. Resorative Justice Project

Top Industries
1. Education
2. Business
3. Research
4. Social Services
5. Media

Top Employers
1. Google
2. Amazon
3. Epic
4. U.S. State Department
5. Wells Fargo

Where Alumni Work
1. Des Mones, IA
2. Chicago
3. New York City
4. Washington, DC
5. Minneapolis

Median Earnings
College Scorecard (Early Career): $49,100
EOP (Early Career): $47,300
PayScale (Mid-Career): $96,500

RANKINGS
Forbes: 80
Money: 205
U.S. News: 14 (T), Liberal Arts Colleges
Wall Street Journal/THE: 57
Washington Monthly: 21, Liberal Arts Colleges

#CollegesWorthYourMoney

Hamilton College

Clinton, New York | Admissions Phone: 315-859-4421

Inside the Classroom

Recent years have been kind to Alexander Hamilton. His legacy has sparked a mega-hit Broadway musical, a Pulitzer Prize-winning biography, and the liberal arts college in Clinton, New York, that bears his name—Hamilton College—has achieved new heights of prestige, claiming a place among the best liberal arts schools in the United States.

Close to 1,900 undergraduate students can choose from forty-three areas of concentration, but education at Hamilton is about so much more than merely choosing a major. The unique open curriculum is immensely flexible and caters to student passions and curiosity over a rigid list of required courses. While there are no distributional requirements, certain skill areas must be addressed as you work your way through the thirty-two courses needed for graduation. That includes three writing-intensive courses, one quantitative/symbolic reasoning course, one physical education course, and an area of concentration that includes a senior project.

The student-to-faculty ratio is 9:1, and without any pesky graduate students to get in the way, face time with professors is a regular occurrence. In fact, 37 percent of all classes have nine or fewer students; 76 percent have nineteen or fewer. Each summer more than 140 students engage in high-level undergraduate research with a faculty member. Two-thirds of Hamilton students study off campus for a semester, although those locations are not always foreign countries. Many participate in domestic study programs in NYC, DC, or Boston while others take advantage of international opportunities like the school's own renowned Chinese language program in Beijing or one of one hundred other approved programs around the globe.

Economics, government, and biology are among the strongest and most popular majors; Other standout programs include public policy, mathematics, and environmental studies. Hamilton students fare extremely well in competition for prestigious national fellowships, capturing a shocking number when considering the small size of each graduating class. The Class of 2019 won seven Fulbright Scholarships, a Critical Language Scholarship, a National Science Foundation Graduate Research Fellowship, and a Watson Fellowship; six juniors also won Gilman Scholarships last year.

Outside the Classroom

Just about everyone lives in university housing—roughly 98 percent to be precise—leading to a cohesive atmosphere on the college's 1,350-acre campus. Greek life is strange in that it is nonresidential following a series of reforms over the past decade. While roughly one-quarter of Hamilton students belong to a fraternity or sorority, those organizations do not play nearly as prominent a role on campus as they once did. The school's twenty-nine teams (15 women's, 14 men's) compete as the Colonials in the New England Small College Athletic Conference (NESCAC) with other elite liberal arts schools Amherst, Bates, Bowdoin, Middlebury, Tufts, Wesleyan, and Williams. There are 550 student-athletes donning the buff-and-blue colors, accounting for 30 percent of the total student body. Add that total to the seventeen club and twelve intramural teams and it can feel like just about everyone is, technically, an athlete. Yet, with almost 200 active student organizations, there are plenty of ways to get involved outside of competitive team sports. The Hamilton Association for Volunteering, Outreach, and Charity (HAVOC) attracts hundreds of civic-minded students each year. The Hamilton Outing Club is the largest club on campus and organizes weekend camping/hiking/skiing trips to the Adirondacks as well as more exotic locations around the world. Amazing speakers come to town as part of the Sacerdote Great Names Series. In recent years Hamilton has hosted David Cameron, Bill and Hillary Clinton, Desmond Tutu, Jon Stewart, Colin Powell, and Jimmy Carter.

Career Services

The Maurice Horowitch Career Center is staffed by twelve professionals with expertise in career development, employer development, and health professions advising. That works out to a 155:1 student-to-advisor ratio, which is significantly stronger than most schools featured in this guide. Each student is assigned a career advisor who works with that student throughout the four-year journey. On the job-finding front, the center assists "students in developing skills in self-assessment, career exploration, resume preparation, interviewing, and uncovering job leads that will empower them to proactively manage their own careers." Yet, that is all steeped in the belief that career planning is a developmental process that unfolds over a lifetime.

The college does not host any large-scale career expos, but numerous employers do visit campus each year to host informational sessions or to recruit/interview candidates. Hamilton's Career Center does a superb job assisting students with finding opportunities for experiential learning. Nine in ten members of the class of 2019 had at least one internship over the course of the four years, and an incredible 70 percent had two. Alumni are highly supportive of current students and are willing to present on campus or offer job-shadowing experiences; 75 percent of alumni in a recent survey stated they would be happy to supply current students with career advice. Hamilton's 22,500 alumni rank in the top 1 percent when measured by the percentage that donate to their alma mater. Students can join Handshake to find internship and career possibilities and My Hamilton to network with alumni. Despite not hosting a notable career fair, the individualized attention and care that Hamilton shows its undergrads results in tremendously overall positive postgraduate and career outcomes.

Professional Outcomes

Examining the 477 graduates in Hamilton's class of 2018, an enviable 95 percent wasted no time landing jobs, graduate school acceptances, or fellowships. The most commonly entered industries were business (18 percent), education (13 percent), finance (12 percent), and science and technology (9 percent), health care (9 percent), and marketing/sales (7 percent). Among the employers welcoming multiple graduates aboard were Wayfair, Goldman Sachs, Teach for America, Dana Farber Cancer Institute, Kantar Consulting, and Deutsch Bank. New York City, Boston, and DC were the most popular destinations. Median compensation by midcareer (age thirty-four) is roughly $60,000, comparable to other elite Northeastern liberal arts colleges such as Middlebury, Tufts, and Colby.

Only 11 percent of 2018 graduates went directly into an advanced degree program. Of that group, 35 percent were studying a STEM field, 23 percent health care, and 6 percent went to law school. Law school acceptances over the past three years have included Georgetown, the University of Virginia, NYU, Penn, Yeshiva University, Washington University, Boston College, and Boston University. Medical school/veterinary school acceptances in that same period have included Columbia University, Penn, Temple, Tufts, SUNY, the University of Rochester, and Boston University. Other Hamilton graduates have been accepted into master's programs at Stanford, Cornell, USC, the University of Chicago, Vanderbilt, and others. Clearly, a degree from Hamilton opens doors to some of the world's top graduate/professional programs.

Admission

Hamilton saw 6,240 applicants for a coveted spot in the Class of 2022, but only 21 percent of that group made the cut, and only 36 percent of those admitted ultimately enrolled in the college. Most applicants provide SAT or ACT scores, but this institution is test-flexible and allows three AP/IB/SAT subject tests to be submitted in lieu of the SAT/ACT. The mid-50 percent range on the SAT was 1350-1510 and 31-34 on the ACT. The vast majority of students finished near the top of their high school class; 81 percent were in the top decile and 98 percent placed in the top quartile. Hamilton's admissions statistics have remained highly consistent over the past decade, so the level of selectivity should not come as a surprise to anyone.

The admissions committee's top priorities are an applicant's GPA, class rank, and the rigor of their coursework. Standardized test scores, essays, recommendations, character/personal qualities, and an interview comprise the second tier of key factors. Because Hamilton is competing for applicants with a host of other elite liberal arts schools, it favors those willing to commit via binding early decision; the acceptance rate for early applicants is more than double that (42 percent) of those in the regular pool (19 percent). Further, early acceptances make up 51 percent of the freshman class, leaving only a limited number of seats in the spring. To be a competitive applicant you should be in the top 10 percent of your graduating class and have standardized test scores in the 95th percentile or higher. If you're on the cusp and Hamilton is your top choice, definitely apply ED.

Worth Your Money?

If you have a genuine need for financial aid to make your education possible, Hamilton will usually answer the bell. In the 2018-19 academic year the college awarded over half of its undergraduates an average grant of $45,000, taking some of the sting out of the $70,000 sticker price for full cost of attendance. In 2008 Hamilton ceased offering merit aid to admitted applicants, a rare and admirable practice in the world of higher education. With 100 percent of its focus on making college affordable to lower- and middle-class students, higher-earning families can expect to pay full freight. Still, this school, with its minuscule class sizes, truly exceptional academics, and powerful network is, in the end, worth the money for most teens.

FINANCIAL
Institutional Type: Private
In-State Tuition: $54,080
Out-of-State Tuition: $54,080
Room & Board: $13,870
Required Fees: $540
Books & Supplies: $1,000

Avg. Need-Based Aid: $45,196
Avg. % of Need Met: 100%

Avg. Merit-Based Aid: $0
% Receiving Merit-Based Aid: 0%

Avg. Cumulative Debt: $20,582
% of Students Borrowing: 44%

CAREER
Who Recruits
1. Merrill Lynch
2. NERA Economic Consulting
3. Isaacson Miller, Inc.
4. Teach for America
5. Kantar Consulting

Notable Internships
1. Credit Suisse
2. CNBC
3. UBS

Top Industries
1. Business
2. Education
3. Operations
4. Media
5. Finance

Top Employers
1. Morgan Stanley
2. Goldman Sachs
3. Google
4. Wayfair
5. Citi

Where Alumni Work
1. New York City
2. Boston
3. Washington, DC
4. San Francisco
5. United Kingdom

Median Earnings
College Scorecard (Early Career): $60,200
EOP (Early Career): $60,300
PayScale (Mid-Career): $108,100

RANKINGS
Forbes: 59
Money: 177
U.S. News: 14 (T), Liberal Arts Colleges
Wall Street Journal/THE: 59 (T)
Washington Monthly: 19, Liberal Arts Colleges

#CollegesWorthYourMoney

Cambridge, Massachusetts | Admissions Phone: 617-495-1551

ADMISSION
Admission Rate: 5%
Admission Rate - Men: 5%
Admission Rate - Women: 5%
EA Admission Rate: 15%
ED Admission Rate: Not Offered
Admission Rate (5-Year Trend): -1%
ED Admission Rate (5-Year Trend): Not Offered
% of Admits Attending (Yield): 82%
Transfer Admission Rate: 1%

Offered Wait List: N/A
Accepted Wait List: N/A
Admitted Wait List: N/A

SAT Reading/Writing (Middle 50%): 720-780
SAT Math (Middle 50%): 740-800
ACT Composite (Middle 50%): 33-35
Testing Policy: ACT/SAT Required
SAT Superscore: Yes
ACT Superscore: No

% Graduated in Top 10% of HS Class: 94%
% Graduated in Top 25% of HS Class: 99%
% Graduated in Top 50% of HS Class: 100%

ENROLLMENT
Total Undergraduate Enrollment: 6,788
% Part-Time: 0%
% Male: 51%
% Female: 49%
% Out-of-State: 84%
% Fraternity: Not Offered
% Sorority: Not Offered
% On-Campus (Freshman): 99%
% On-Campus (All Undergraduate): 97%

% African-American: 8%
% Asian: 20%
% Hispanic: 11%
% White: 38%
% Other: 7%
% Race or Ethnicity Unknown: 2%
% International: 13%
% Low-Income: 15%

ACADEMICS
Student-to-Faculty Ratio: 7:1
% of Classes Under 20: 72%
% of Classes Under 40: 87%
% Full-Time Faculty: 85%
% Full-Time Faculty w/ Terminal Degree: 94%

Top Programs
Biology
Chemistry
Economics
Mathematics
Political Science
Physics
Psychology
Statistics

Retention Rate: 98%
4-Year Graduation Rate: 87%
6-Year Graduation Rate: 98%

Curricular Flexibility: Somewhat Flexible
Academic Rating: ★★★★★

Inside the Classroom

The oldest university in the United States, founded 140 years before the United States itself was even a concept, it is also the most iconic and, in many ways, revered institution of higher learning. Worldwide, Harvard is the envy of other universities and the dream destination for countless teenage geniuses and overachievers. For 6,800 young people, the Ivy League university in Cambridge, Massachusetts, is their reality, and learning from Nobel Laureates, Pulitzer Prize winners, and global leaders in every field is an everyday occurrence.

There are fifty undergraduate fields of study referred to as concentrations; many are interdisciplinary. Nearly 3,900 courses are on the menu, so learning options are extensive. Core requirements are minimal outside of expository writing, which all freshmen must conquer, proficiency in a foreign language (which must be achieved by the end of sophomore year), and a trek through the program in general education. The latter requirement ensures that undergrads are exposed to four main areas: aesthetics and culture, ethics and civics; histories, societies, and individuals; and science and technology in society. Roughly half of students complete some type of senior thesis, but there are no requirements in that area.

Even with a graduate population of almost 14,000 to cater to, undergraduate class sizes still tend to be on the smaller side with 42 percent of sections having single-digit enrollments and 72 percent being capped at nineteen. Graduates report an 82 percent satisfaction rate with the experience within their academic concentration. Summer research experiences are taken advantage of by 38 percent of the student body. Approximately 60 percent of students study abroad at a number of locations in South America, Africa, Europe, or Asia.

Economics, government, and computer science are the three most popular areas of concentration at Harvard. Those programs, along with ones in biology, chemistry, physics, math, statistics, sociology, history, English, and psychology all sit atop most departmental ranking lists. The university also occupies the top position in the all-time Rhodes Scholar rankings with 347 to its credit, more than the combined total from Stanford, Penn, Dartmouth, Brown, MIT, Cornell, and Columbia. Other prestigious postgraduate fellowships are awarded to Harvard students with regularity including the Fulbright, which was captured by sixteen members of the Class of 2018. The list of all-time alumni accolades could go on forever and includes ninety-six Nobel Laureates and eight US presidents.

Outside the Classroom

Possessing a bottomless endowment, the school never needs to cut corners on any programs, campus infrastructure, or amenities—and it shows. Freshmen live together at a centralized campus location adjacent to the famed Harvard Yard and then, as sophomores, move into one of twelve stately, upper-class houses, each with its own set of traditions and sense of community. Greek life, once thriving, has taken a dip in recent years after university officials enacted new regulations to deter membership in single-sex clubs. Students who participate forfeit eligibility for leadership positions in athletics or student government and will not be recommended for prestigious scholarships. Fortunately, a bevy of other social clubs exist in the form of 450 student-run organizations including the history-rich Hasty Pudding Club and the Phillips Brooks House Association that runs eighty-six volunteer organizations. Of course, studying is also a popular "hobby," and the Harvard Library is the largest academic library in the world and boasts a staff of nearly 800. *The Harvard Crimson* is a premier college newspaper with a long and storied history—Franklin Roosevelt and John F. Kennedy are among its alums—and *The Harvard Lampoon* is one of the world's oldest humor magazines, one that has helped launch talents ranging from John Updike to Conan O'Brien. Athletics also play a prominent role in Harvard's culture, both past and present, as the school fields forty NCAA Division I sports teams, evenly split between men's and women's squads. Cambridge itself is a bustling hub of culture, nightlife, and entertainment. Downtown Boston is only a twelve-minute ride away on the city's easily accessible public transit system.

Career Services

The Center for Career Development (CCD) has nineteen professional staff members (excluding students, assistants, and IT staff) who are dedicated to tasks including employer relations, career counseling, and summer funding opportunities. The 352:1 student-to-advisor ratio is about average compared to other schools featured in this guide. Yet, the closer you look into Harvard's career services, locating another "average" feature is a nearly impossible task.

The CCD hosts more than 300 events annually that are attended by 9,600 students. It also organizes twenty independent career fairs, each targeting a particular sector that attracts just under 6,000 net attendees. The OCS logs 6,700 advising appointments per year and manages to engage with 70 percent of the total undergraduate student body. Crimson Careers, the office's online database, posts 8,000+ jobs/internships from thousands of unique employers. On-campus recruiting occurred on a regular basis with 180 employers, including just about any big-name company you can think of, conducting over 5,100 interviews on site in Cambridge. More than three-quarters of students participate in a summer internship during their four years of study. In short, career services are what you would expect from America's preeminent university—exceptional.

Harvard University

E-mail: college@fas.harvard.edu | Website: www.college.harvard.edu

Professional Outcomes

The Crimson class of 2018 saw 15 percent of students head directly into graduate/professional school. Of the 65 percent of graduates entering the world of work, 18 percent were entering the financial services field, another 18 percent were entering the world of consulting, and technology/engineering attracted 14 percent. Over 1,000 Harvard alumni presently work for Google and over 500 for Microsoft, McKinsey & Company, and Goldman Sachs. More than 250 are employed at Amazon, Facebook, and Bain & Company. Postgraduation, Harvard students tend to cluster in three main states—New York, California, and Massachusetts. Those three states collectively reel in 57 percent of newly minted alumni. Remuneration is excellent with 53 percent of graduates reporting starting salaries over $70k and 11 percent taking home $110k+ in base pay. By midcareer, grads have the third highest median salaries in the Ivy League.

Turning our attention to those moving on to graduate school, Harvard grads with at least a 3.5 GPA typically enjoy acceptance rates into medical school of 90 percent or greater, demolishing the national average. Harvard grads tend to trade one high prestige school for another when pursuing an advanced degree. Many also stay close to home—Harvard Medical School (HMS), Harvard Law School, and the Graduate School of Arts & Sciences all accept more Harvard College graduates than those from any other single institution. It is estimated that approximately one-fifth of the HMS student body already spent four years in Cambridge as an undergraduate.

Admission

Harvard's admission rate for the Class of 2022 was 4.6 percent, an all-time low. Applicants fare better in the early action round that sports a 14.5 percent acceptance rate; the regular round rate is an almost comically low 2.9 percent. This was the first year in school history that the overall percentage of admitted students dipped below 5 percent. For historical context, at the turn of the millennium, 12 percent of applicants were welcomed aboard. The mid-50 percent SAT range for enrolled freshmen in 2018-19 was 1460-1590; over 85 percent of students scored above a 700 on each portion of the exam. It's not shocking that 94 percent of students admitted earned a place in their high school class's top decile. An insanely high number—84 percent—of admitted students elect to enroll. In other words, Harvard is second choice for few students.

The admissions staff does not rank any factor as being "very important" or even "important." All of the usual factors—grades, SATs, essays, and so on—are "considered." Demonstrated interest is not considered, which is unsurprising in light of the aforementioned yield rate. Legacy students comprise roughly one-third of the student body and enjoy an acceptance rate five times that of non-legacy applicants. For information about the role of race in admissions at Harvard, simply consult any newspaper. Getting into Harvard is the subject of plenty of (mostly awful) movies for a reason—it is a mammoth task set against harrowing odds. Even valedictorians with perfect test scores are not immune from rejection. However, impeccable credentials of that nature will at least allow you the opportunity to roll the dice with a realistic chance of success.

Worth Your Money?

Asking if Harvard is worth the money is a bit like John C. Reilly's character in Stepbrothers, Dale Doback, asking if bonito fish are big. Yes, Dale, bonito fish are big, and Harvard is worth the $78,300 annual cost of attendance. Merit aid barely exists at the university but, thanks to a $38 billion endowment, the 54 percent of the undergraduate population that is eligible for financial aid sees 100 percent of its need met; the total annual value is an extremely generous $57,000. Harvard is one of the rare schools where the average graduate's salary exceeds the annual cost of attendance, so even if you did have to take out loans to attend, it would be more than worth the expense.

FINANCIAL
Institutional Type: Private
In-State Tuition: $47,730
Out-of-State Tuition: $47,730
Room & Board: $17,682
Required Fees: $4,195
Books & Supplies: $1,000

Avg. Need-Based Aid: $56,771
Avg. % of Need Met: 100%

Avg. Merit-Based Aid: $0
% Receiving Merit-Based Aid: 0%

Avg. Cumulative Debt: $13,372
% of Students Borrowing: 17%

CAREER
Who Recruits
1. Putnam Investments
2. Akuna Capital
3. Atlantic Media
4. Vertica
5. Environmental Defense Fund

Notable Internships
1. McKinsey & Company
2. NASA Jet Propulsion Laboratory
3. Jane Street Capital

Top Industries
1. Business
2. Education
3. Research
4. Operations
5. Media

Top Employers
1. Google
2. Microsoft
3. Goldman Sachs
4. McKinsey & Company
5. IBM

Where Alumni Work
1. Boston
2. New York City
3. San Francisco
4. Washington, DC
5. Los Angeles

Median Earnings
College Scorecard (Early Career): $89,700
EOP (Early Career): $81,500
PayScale (Mid-Career): $146,800

RANKINGS
Forbes: 1
Money: 14
U.S. News: 2, National Universities
Wall Street Journal/THE: 1
Washington Monthly: 2, National Universities

#CollegesWorthYourMoney

Claremont, California | Admissions Phone: 909-621-8011

ADMISSION
Admission Rate: 14%
Admission Rate - Men: 10%
Admission Rate - Women: 24%
EA Admission Rate: Not Offered
ED Admission Rate: 19%
Admission Rate (5-Year Trend): -5%
ED Admission Rate (5-Year Trend): -3%
% of Admits Attending (Yield): 39%
Transfer Admission Rate: 7%

Offered Wait List: 509
Accepted Wait List: 327
Admitted Wait List: 0

SAT Reading/Writing (Middle 50%): 720-760
SAT Math (Middle 50%): 770-800
ACT Composite (Middle 50%): 34-34
Testing Policy: ACT/SAT Required
SAT Superscore: Yes
ACT Superscore: Yes

% Graduated in Top 10% of HS Class: 87%
% Graduated in Top 25% of HS Class: 98%
% Graduated in Top 50% of HS Class: 100%

ENROLLMENT
Total Undergraduate Enrollment: 889
% Part-Time: 0%
% Male: 51%
% Female: 49%
% Out-of-State: 56%
% Fraternity: Not Offered
% Sorority: Not Offered
% On-Campus (Freshman): 100%
% On-Campus (All Undergraduate): 98%

% African-American: 3%
% Asian: 19%
% Hispanic: 20%
% White: 31%
% Other: 11%
% Race or Ethnicity Unknown: 6%
% International: 10%
% Low-Income: 16%

ACADEMICS
Student-to-Faculty Ratio: 8:1
% of Classes Under 20: 57%
% of Classes Under 40: 93%
% Full-Time Faculty: 88%
% Full-Time Faculty w/ Terminal Degree: 99%

Top Programs
Biology
Chemistry
Computer Science
Engineering
Mathematical and Computational Biology
Mathematics and Statistics
Physics

Retention Rate: 97%
4-Year Graduation Rate: 85%
6-Year Graduation Rate: 92%

Curricular Flexibility: Somewhat Flexible
Academic Rating: ★★★★★

Inside the Classroom

To the average college-bound teen, Harvey Mudd may not have the name recognition that other schools of its caliber enjoy. While it may sound a bit like a Depression-era comic strip, the smallest of the colleges within the illustrious Claremont Consortium (Pomona, Claremont McKenna, Scripps, and Pitzer are the others) is routinely rated one of the best liberal arts colleges in the entire country and one of the top STEM institutions in the world.

A little under 900 undergraduate students occupy this tiny 33-acre campus; however, it is surrounded by the aforementioned affiliated colleges, giving the experience a less claustrophobic feel. Only six majors are offered: biology, chemistry, computer science, engineering, mathematics, and physics. All are incredibly strong. Students also have the option to combine certain disciplines into what amounts to a double major. In preparing a small army of future engineers and scientists, Harvey Mudd has been at the forefront of preaching a balanced education. The school requires a significant amount of coursework in the humanities, backing up its stated belief that "technology divorced from humanity is worse than no technology at all."

Class sizes are not always as small as the school itself. While 57 percent of courses have an enrollment under twenty, another 37 percent enroll between twenty and thirty-nine students. Regardless, Mudd prides itself on offering graduate-level research opportunities and experiential learning to all undergrads. The college backs up its philosophical stance with cold, hard cash, allocating three million dollars annually to facilitate student-faculty research. Students can participate during the school year or during the Summer Undergraduate Research Program that entails ten weeks of full-time laboratory work. The Clinic Program groups juniors and seniors and lets them work on a real-world problem for corporate or agency sponsors for 1,200 to 1,500 hours over the course of one year. It is not uncommon for participants to end up with their name on a patent.

The college routinely produces winners of scholarships from the National Science Foundation, the Astronaut Scholarship Foundation, the Department of Energy, the Department of Defense, the Watson Fellowship, and the Mindlin Prize for Innovative Ideas in Science. The faculty also regularly receive accolades for their teaching. The National Science Foundation recognized the Chemistry Department as the top per capita producer of chemistry PhDs in the country.

Outside the Classroom

Campus life at Mudd is, in part, defined by the fact that you are not confined to one campus. After all, Pomona, Pitzer, Scripps, and CMC all share the same 560 acres of land, not to mention a whole lot else. For athletics, Harvey Mudd, Claremont, and Scripps combine forces to compete in twenty-one NCAA Division III men's and women's sports. Club and intramural sports from ultimate Frisbee, equestrian, and roller hockey to water polo are available as well. Both cross-consortium and Mudd-only clubs and activities are plentiful and diverse, ranging from a poker club to a lettuce-eating competition (seriously). With Los Angeles just a half-hour drive away, Claremont is located in close proximity to all of the restaurants, museums, theaters, and even Disneyland, if you so desire. Mudd's dorms are known for having district personalities, but one common thread is that the college is known, in general, to be a friendly and accepting place.

Career Services

HMC's Career Services Office has four full-time professional staff members working on grad school/career advising and employer recruitment. That equates to a 222:1 student-to-advisor ratio, which is among the best of any college featured in this guide. Career Services is highly accessible to students, and it even offers walk-in hours from 1 to 4 p.m. each week day. Staff members are more than happy to offer one-on-one attention, and students take advantage as the office held 891 sessions, just over one per student, in the 2017-18 school year.

Harvey Mudd hosts a Fall Software Fair, a Fall General STEM Fair, and a Spring Fair that can be attended by all members of the consortium, which can draw as many as 160+ employers per year. The three fairs draw almost 2,000 student participants per year. Companies that recruit on campus comprise a who's who of tech royalty: Google, Microsoft, Facebook, Space X, and Uber. In fact, many of those companies, along with other major corporations, conducted interviews on HMC's campus. Undergrads routinely land summer internships at an equally impressive array of technology companies. In examining the breakdown of where Mudd grads end up receiving job offers, there is a clear correlation with the employer relations efforts of the Career Services Office. Overall, HMC's career services earns top grades from the College Transitions staff.

Professional Outcomes

The highest number of recent Harvey Mudd graduates is scooped up by the following companies (in order of representation): Google, Facebook, Microsoft, and Northrup Grumman. Across all graduating years, significant numbers of alumni also can be found at Apple, Raytheon, Intel, Boeing, and the NASA Jet Propulsion Laboratory. Software and technology is, by far, the career field of choice with aerospace a distant second. HMC grads end up in high-paying jobs that are directly related to their major as the 95 percent of seniors who report landing a job related to their college major confirms. The most common job titles held immediately out of college are software engineer, industrial engineer, and electrical engineer. Graduates average an impressive $87,500 starting salary, a phenomenal number even when accounting for the preponderance of STEM majors. By some measures, that is the highest graduate starting salary of any institution in the United States.

Many Harvey Mudd grads—close to one-quarter—go directly into graduate school programs. The highest number of 2018 grads pursued advanced degrees at the following institutions: Stanford (6), Cornell (5), USC (4), UC-Santa Barbara (2), Columbia (2), and the University of Washington (2). One student from the same class attended each of Harvard, Carnegie Mellon, Caltech, and Johns Hopkins. The most pursued graduate field of study at those elite schools are computer science, mathematics, physics, and engineering. A healthy 72 percent of those attending grad school are presently working toward a PhD.

Admission

A decade ago, over 30 percent of applicants to Harvey Mudd were accepted; five years ago, that number fell to 20 percent. In recent years HMC's admit rate has hovered in the 13 to 15 percent range; it was 15 percent for applicants aspiring to join the Class of 2022. However, it is important to note that the profile of the average accepted student has not changed significantly and, unlike many other elite colleges across the United States, the number of applicants has not skyrocketed in the past few years. Early decision applicants made up 39 percent of the acceptance pool, which means applying early may be a good idea if Mudd is your top choice. The ED rate was 19 percent, which was a touch better than the 14 percent encountered during the regular application round.

An overwhelming 87 percent of accepted applicants finished in the top 10 percent of their high school class, and just about everyone placed at least in the top 25 percent. Valedictorians and salutatorians make up an impressive 23 percent of the student body. Standardized test scores need to be high to garner serious consideration. The mid-50 percent range on standardized tests for freshmen in 2018-19 was 1490-1560 on the SAT and 34-35 on the ACT. HMC is one of those rare schools that requires two SAT subject tests in addition to the SAT/ACT. One of those two tests must be the Math Level 2 exam on which accepted students typically score a 750 or better. The school lists essays and recommendations as being "very important" factors in admissions decisions. In sum, Harvey Mudd is not a school that you add to your college list on a whim. It is an institution for those with a proven track record within the realm of science and engineering. Excellent grades in AP/IB course work, along with standardized test scores well above the 95th percentile, are just about prerequisites for serious consideration.

Worth Your Money?

At almost $77,000 per year, a degree from Harvey Mudd won't come cheap, but the majority of undergraduates do not pay the full cost. On the merit aid front, the college awards an average of $15k to 44 percent of the student body. Even better, 49 percent of attendees see 100 percent of their financial need met, which averages out to $45k in aid each year, knocking the total cost down closer to state school levels. As a result, HMC helps many students from lower- and middle-income families attend the school. While that does result in a higher-than-average postgraduate debt load, alumni enjoy such strong job prospects that paying back loans will not be overly worrisome. No matter your circumstances, if you have a chance to go to Mudd, start packing your bags.

FINANCIAL
Institutional Type: Private
In-State Tuition: $56,331
Out-of-State Tuition: $56,331
Room & Board: $18,127
Required Fees: $545
Books & Supplies: $800

Avg. Need-Based Aid: $45,244
Avg. % of Need Met: 100%

Avg. Merit-Based Aid: $14,678
% Receiving Merit-Based Aid: 44%

Avg. Cumulative Debt: $31,594
% of Students Borrowing: 46%

CAREER
Who Recruits
1. Palantir
2. The Aerospace Corporation
3. Oracle
4. Boeing
5. Farmers Insurance

Notable Internships
1. Google
2. Salesforce
3. PayPal

Top Industries
1. Engineering
2. Research
3. Business
4. Education
5. information Technology

Top Employers
1. Google
2. Microsoft
3. Apple
4. Northrop Grumman
5. Facebook

Where Alumni Work
1. Los Angeles
2. San Francisco
3. Seattle
4. San Diego
5. New York City

Median Earnings
College Scorecard (Early Career): $88,800
EOP (Early Career): $82,400
PayScale (Mid-Career): $158,200

RANKINGS
Forbes: 23
Money: 136
U.S. News: 23, Liberal Arts Colleges
Wall Street Journal/THE: N/A
Washington Monthly: 48, National Universities

#CollegesWorthYourMoney

Haverford College

Haverford, Pennsylvania | Admissions Phone: 610-896-1350

ADMISSION
Admission Rate: 19%
Admission Rate - Men: 19%
Admission Rate - Women: 18%
EA Admission Rate: Not Offered
ED Admission Rate: 44%
Admission Rate (5-Year Trend): -5%
ED Admission Rate (5-Year Trend): -1%
% of Admits Attending (Yield): 41%
Transfer Admission Rate: 19%

Offered Wait List: 1,349
Accepted Wait List: 613
Admitted Wait List: 11

SAT Reading/Writing (Middle 50%): 680-750
SAT Math (Middle 50%): 690-780
ACT Composite (Middle 50%): 32-34
Testing Policy: ACT/SAT Required
SAT Superscore: Yes
ACT Superscore: Yes

% Graduated in Top 10% of HS Class: 95%
% Graduated in Top 25% of HS Class: 97%
% Graduated in Top 50% of HS Class: 100%

ENROLLMENT
Total Undergraduate Enrollment: 1,310
% Part-Time: 0%
% Male: 49%
% Female: 51%
% Out-of-State: 86%
% Fraternity: Not Offered
% Sorority: Not Offered
% On-Campus (Freshman): 100%
% On-Campus (All Undergraduate): 98%

% African-American: 7%
% Asian: 13%
% Hispanic: 10%
% White: 53%
% Other: 3%
% Race or Ethnicity Unknown: 3%
% International: 11%
% Low-Income: 16%

ACADEMICS
Student-to-Faculty Ratio: 9:1
% of Classes Under 20: 78%
% of Classes Under 40: 96%
% Full-Time Faculty: 85%
% Full-Time Faculty w/ Terminal Degree: 99%

Top Programs
Biology
Chemistry
English
History
Mathematics
Philosophy
Physics
Political Science

Retention Rate: 97%
4-Year Graduation Rate: 88%
6-Year Graduation Rate: 92%

Curricular Flexibility: Very Flexible
Academic Rating: ★★★★★

Inside the Classroom

Serving 1,353 remarkably accomplished undergraduate students, Haverford College, situated on Philly's ritzy Main Line, has 186 years of history and a reputation as one of the best liberal arts colleges in the country. Affectionately known as "The Ford," the college is part of the Tri-College Consortium with nearby Bryn Mawr and Swarthmore, which also happen to be among the crème de la crème of liberal arts schools. Students can take courses at those two schools as well through Penn's Wharton School of Business via an additional alliance known as the Quaker Consortium.

Haverford offers twenty-nine majors, thirty-one minors, thirteen concentrations, and eleven consortium programs— areas of study that can be pursued at partner campuses. All students must fulfill a first-year writing requirement, a two-course language requirement, and a quantitative or symbolic reasoning requirement, and students need to take an uncredited physical education course prior to their junior year. Every student produces a senior thesis, a work of original research/scholarship under the close supervision of a faculty member. Teens seeking a relatively open curriculum that encourages exploration and the pursuit of one's unique passions will adore Haverford.

The school's 9:1 student-to-faculty ratio and exclusive emphasis on undergraduate education leads to exceptionally intimate classes, 39 percent of which have fewer than ten students, and 76 percent have fewer than twenty. Plenty of summer research opportunities exist in which students can work alongside faculty, and some STEM students conduct and present original research through the Undergraduate Science Research Symposium. The study abroad program has a 49 percent participation rate, and students can choose from seventy-six programs in thirty-four countries.

The most popular areas of study at Haverford include the social sciences (26 percent), physical sciences (13 percent), psychology (10 percent), biology (9 percent), mathematics (8 percent), foreign language (7 percent), and computer science (5 percent). All majors are highly respected in the eyes of graduate institutions and potential employers, but programs in English, physics, and political science receive especially high marks. Science majors and those on a premed track gain acceptance to prestigious PhD programs and medical schools at an eye-popping rate. Graduates are also no strangers to competitive national awards/fellowships. In the school's history it claims twenty Rhodes Scholars, 104 Fulbright Scholars, sixty-three Watson Fellows, forty-eight National Science Foundation Fellows, and two Goldwater Scholars.

Outside the Classroom

Ninety-eight percent of students live on this stunningly beautiful 216-acre campus; first-years are assigned to one of four residence halls. There are no fraternities or sororities at Haverford. Even with such a tiny student body, Haverford fields twenty-three varsity sports teams that compete in NCAA Division III. Combined with the seven club sports teams, 53 percent of undergrads participate in athletics. The college's 145 student-run organizations include an array of pre-professional and service-oriented groups as well as plenty of recreational/ performance options such as the Martial Arts Alliance, contemporary dance, and a number of a cappella groups. HAVOC is an outdoor adventure group that has a strong membership. The mock trial team placed second in the nation in 2017. Fellow Tri-Co member schools Bryn Mawr and Swarthmore offer plenty of additional chances for social connection, both formal and informal. All that the city of Philadelphia has to offer is only eight miles away. The Main Line area itself offers plenty of dining, cultural, and entertainment choices. The college's Honor Code and governing Honor Council are central to the life at Haverford. Tenets of the code include un-proctored exams, no RAs in dorms, and tolerance of people of all backgrounds and orientations.

Career Services

The Center for Career & Professional Advising (CCPA) employs four individuals who specialize in career counseling, pre-law advising, and health professions advising; another four staff members are part time. With a 338:1 student-to-advisor ratio, Haverford compares favorably against most of the other colleges featured in this guide. The resources are deployed efficiently as in a given year the CCPA engages in 800+ advising sessions, reaches over 80 percent of the student body in some capacity, and makes a great effort to reach first-year students. In fact, 94 percent of freshmen report engaging with the office. The level of personalized advising is also evident by the annual number of resume critiques, 600+.

In hosting 150 information sessions and workshops per year, there are almost daily opportunities for students to sharpen their pre-professional skills and connect with potential employers. Large- scale career fairs are typically a joint effort of the Tri-College Consortium, along with Bryn Mawr and Swarthmore. Haverford alone draws more than one hundred employers to campus for its career fairs. The CCPA funds more than 140 internships per year and helps facilitate 190 on-campus interviews. Additionally, the college has more than 1,000 alumni association volunteers who provide hundreds of job-shadowing and externship experiences to current students. The CCPA delivers ample personalized attention to undergraduates and does an unsurpassed job assisting students with acceptance into top graduate schools.

Haverford College

E-mail: admission@haverford.edu | Website: www.haverford.edu

Professional Outcomes

Six months after leaving Haverford 63 percent of the Class of 2018 had found employment, 18 percent had enrolled in graduate school, and 9 percent were still job hunting. Among the employed, education was the most common industry (22 percent) followed by business (12 percent), the sciences (10 percent), community services (9 percent), and health care (9 percent). Employers hiring multiple recent Haverford grads include Google, The Vanguard Group, IBM, Booz Allen Hamilton, Amazon, the National Institutes of Health, and the Children's Hospital of Philadelphia. Midcareer salaries are comparable to other elite liberal arts schools such as Wesleyan, Colby, Swarthmore, and Bates; the median income at age thirty-four is $57,200. Staying in the Philly metro area is the number one choice of alumni. New York City, various international destinations, Boston, and DC are next in popularity.

Almost a quarter of Haverford grads continue to advanced degree programs right out of undergrad. In 2018, the most commonly entered fields of study were STEM (41 percent), medicine (18 percent), law (16 percent), and arts and humanities (12 percent). Graduate schools accepting the highest number of recent alumni include Yale, Columbia, the University of Chicago, Penn, Harvard, Johns Hopkins, and the University of North Carolina at Chapel Hill. Those applying to medical school have extraordinary success as the college's 90 percent rate of acceptance from 2015-18 more than doubles the national average of 42 percent. Haverford undergrads average MCAT scores in the 85th percentile of all test takers. In the last three years 100 percent of those applying to law school received at least one letter of acceptance. Of that cohort, 32 percent were accepted into a top fifteen law school, and 94 percent had found homes at a top one hundred law school.

Admission

Admissions for a place in the Class of 2022 was the most selective round in the school's history; a record 4,682 applications were received, and only 18.7 percent were accepted. A staggering 95 percent of enrolled freshmen earned a place in the top 10 percent of their high school class and sported a mid-50 percent test score of 1370-1530 on the SAT and 32-34 on the ACT. Five years ago, the acceptance rate was a slightly higher 22 percent, but the academic profile of the average admitted applicant was similar to that of a 2018 enrollee.

According to the admissions committee the most important factors in the decision-making process are rigor of coursework, GPA, essays, recommendations, extracurricular activities, and character/personal qualities. Class rank, standardized test scores, talent/ability, work experience, and volunteer work make up the second rung of considered data points. Items like the interview, first-generation status, or legacy status are given a lesser degree of consideration. Applying early decision can be a significant advantage. In the most recent cycle ED applicants were accepted at a far more generous 44 percent clip and comprised 55 percent of that year's incoming freshmen. Even with a self-selecting applicant pool that results in modest application numbers, Haverford is an exceptionally difficult school to gain acceptance into. A near 19 percent acceptance rate is almost misleadingly encouraging, and applicants sizing up their chances will be better informed by the high level of academic achievement displayed by successful applicants. Applying ED should be given serious consideration if Haverford is among your top choices.

Worth Your Money?

Haverford's annual cost of attendance is among the highest in the country at $76,414 but, on the positive end, it meets 100 percent of demonstrated need for those who qualify. The total average annual grant is over $52,000, helping make the school affordable for those not in the highest income brackets. However, an estimated 40 percent of attending students come from families in the top 5 percent of annual income nationwide and, typically, those individuals will pay full price. If you can afford the upfront costs, or if you receive a sufficiently sized financial aid award, becoming part of this elite institution will likely prove worth the investment in the long run.

FINANCIAL
Institutional Type: Private
In-State Tuition: $56,200
Out-of-State Tuition: $56,200
Room & Board: $16,770
Required Fees: $752
Books & Supplies: $1,194

Avg. Need-Based Aid: $51,777
Avg. % of Need Met: 100%

Avg. Merit-Based Aid: $0
% Receiving Merit-Based Aid: 0%

Avg. Cumulative Debt: $11,000
% of Students Borrowing: 37%

CAREER
Who Recruits
1. Chatham Financial
2. FDIC
3. Janney Montgomery Scott
4. Boston Consulting Group
5. Analysis Group

Notable Internships
1. Boston Consulting Group
2. Spotify
3. U.S. House of Representatives

Top Industries
1. Education
2. Business
3. Research
4. Healthcare
5. Media

Top Employers
1. Google
2. Children's Hospital of Philadelphia
3. Facebook
4. US State Department
5. Deloitte

Where Alumni Work
1. New York City
2. Philadelphia
3. Washington, DC
4. Boston
5. San Francisco

Median Earnings
College Scorecard (Early Career): $60,700
EOP (Early Career): $57,200
PayScale (Mid-Career): $112,300

RANKINGS
Forbes: 49
Money: 126
U.S. News: 11, Liberal Arts Colleges
Wall Street Journal/THE: 39
Washington Monthly: 11, Liberal Arts Colleges

#CollegesWorthYourMoney

Hempstead, New York | Admissions Phone: 516-463-6700

ADMISSION
Admission Rate: 63%
Admission Rate - Men: 58%
Admission Rate - Women: 67%
EA Admission Rate: 70%
ED Admission Rate: Not Offered
Admission Rate (5-Year Trend): +4%
ED Admission Rate (5-Year Trend): Not Offered
% of Admits Attending (Yield): 9%
Transfer Admission Rate: 63%

\# Offered Wait List: 143
\# Accepted Wait List: 45
\# Admitted Wait List: 24

SAT Reading/Writing (Middle 50%): 580-660
SAT Math (Middle 50%): 570-670
ACT Composite (Middle 50%): 24-30
Testing Policy: Test Optional
SAT Superscore: Yes
ACT Superscore: Yes

% Graduated in Top 10% of HS Class: 28%
% Graduated in Top 25% of HS Class: 49%
% Graduated in Top 50% of HS Class: 59%

ENROLLMENT
Total Undergraduate Enrollment: 6,701
% Part-Time: 6%
% Male: 45%
% Female: 55%
% Out-of-State: 38%
% Fraternity: 8%
% Sorority: 10%
% On-Campus (Freshman): 65%
% On-Campus (All Undergraduate): 43%

% African-American: 9%
% Asian: 11%
% Hispanic: 12%
% White: 55%
% Other: 3%
% Race or Ethnicity Unknown: 3%
% International: 6%
% Low-Income: 23%

ACADEMICS
Student-to-Faculty Ratio: 13:1
% of Classes Under 20: 48%
% of Classes Under 40: 95%
% Full-Time Faculty: 39%
% Full-Time Faculty w/ Terminal Degree: 93%

Top Programs
Accounting
Criminology
Finance
Journalism
Performing Arts
Public Relations
Radio, Television & Film

Retention Rate: 82%
4-Year Graduation Rate: 52%
6-Year Graduation Rate: 63%

Curricular Flexibility: Somewhat Flexible
Academic Rating: ★★★

Inside the Classroom

Looking at Hofstra University today, one sees a private university of 6,700 undergraduate students spread across a gorgeous and imposing Long Island campus. Its roots as a commuter school for Long Island residents have long since faded from view as the student body is now comprised of almost 50 percent out-of-state and international students. While still a common safety school choice for high-achieving Northeasterners aiming for schools like Fordham and Boston University, Hofstra's national reputation is undoubtedly on the rise. It remains an excellent academic institution with tremendous resources to help students find their way to a successful career. Even better, it also is accessible to students with imperfect academic profiles—at least for now.

There are 160 programs for undergraduates spread across the various colleges housing liberal arts, engineering, business, communications, and nursing/health professions. While the core curriculum varies from school to school, most Hofstra students are required to complete coursework in the humanities, natural sciences, history, philosophy, foreign language, quantitative reasoning, two introductory writing courses, and two advanced writing courses. In total there are thirty-three credits worth of distributional requirements for students in the College of Liberal Arts and Sciences. First-year seminars are courses reserved for freshmen that enroll nineteen or fewer students, focus on a specific topic of interest, and help new students acclimate to college-level work.

The average undergraduate class size is twenty, and the student-faculty ratio is a favorable 13-to-1. The great bulk of courses enroll between eleven and twenty-nine students; 11 percent are single-digit enrollment courses, and only 2 percent of sections contain more than fifty students. Opportunities to participate in undergraduate research are managed by each department separately. Students in the Honors College have an easier time procuring opportunities as supervised independent research is built into the program. Full-length study abroad opportunities are offered in locations that include Amsterdam, China, Florence, Rome, and Ireland. Many students prefer short-term international sessions offered in January (three weeks) or summer (five weeks).

The Zarb School of Business draws almost a quarter of the student body for good reason; it is a well-regarded business school with strong connections to many major banks and consulting firms. It also boasts one of the nation's best simulated trading rooms. The Lawrence Herbert School of Communication is widely known in the media industry, and Hofstra students enter in large numbers—15 percent of the total degrees conferred are in communication/journalism. Health professions, social sciences, and psychology are third, fourth, and fifth in popularity, respectively. Winning national postgraduate fellowships is not a major focus of Hofstra seniors. They have won an occasional Fulbright Scholarship, a Critical Language Scholarship in 2018, and Gilman Scholarship in 2019.

Outside the Classroom

Only 65 percent of freshmen and roughly 45 percent of the overall undergraduate student body live on campus in one of thirty-five residence halls. There are traditional dorms as well as high-rise options that, collectively, offer single, double, triple, quad, and suite-style living options. Within the limits of the 240-acre campus are eighteen eateries, six theaters, an arboretum, bird sanctuary, and an art museum that houses 5,000 works and artifacts. Hofstra's gorgeous, tree-lined grounds are deservedly included on many "most beautiful campus" lists. The twenty-nine fraternities and sororities attract 8 percent of men and 10 percent of women, creating an atmosphere with a noticeable Greek presence, but not a suffocating one. The sports teams, for many years known as the Flying Dutchmen, now compete as the Pride at the NCAA Division I level in the Colonial Athletic Association. There are twenty-one varsity sports—ten men's and eleven women's teams. There are 200+ student-run clubs at Hofstra, including plenty of performance, cultural, or pre-professional options and a big-time collegiate radio station, WRHU, which also serves as the radio home of the National Hockey League's New York Islanders. Hempstead is not the safest area or most desirable part of town, but this is made up for by having an amenity-filled campus and being only a twenty-five-minute drive from famed Jones Beach in Long Island and, of course, being only a forty- to fifty-minute trip from all that New York City has to offer.

Career Services

Hofstra's Career Center is manned by eight professionals with expertise in career coaching, corporate outreach, and diversity and inclusion initiatives. That works out to an 838:1 student-to-advisor ratio, which is higher than the average school in this guide but not awful when compared to other midsize universities. The Fall Career and Internship Fair was attended by 130+ employers, and the center routinely offers in-person and online workshops, field trips to companies, networking events, and on-campus interview days with employers.

Drawing employers to campus and placing current students with big-name organizations is aided by the school's location and the tight connections that the Career Center has forged with New York City employers.

Hofstra's internship numbers for undergraduates are particularly strong. With the help of career services staff members, 73 percent of Hofstra students participate in at least one internship, and the average student completes 2.31 such experiences. Class of 2017 grads interned at hundreds of organizations including Berkshire Hathaway, Last Week Tonight with John Oliver, ABC News, and the Securities and Exchange Commission. Current students can also benefit from connecting with the 140,000 living alumni, 1,000 of whom are active volunteers for the school and more than willing to assist with career exploration and the job search.

Professional Outcomes

Within six months of exiting with their diplomas, 92 percent of Class of 2017 grads had found employment or a graduate school destination; within a year that figure rose to 99 percent, with 91 percent employed and 33 percent pursuing an advanced degree, which includes some overlap as many individuals were doing both. Northwell Health, the largest health care provider in New York State, is also the largest employer of Hofstra alumni. Other companies employing more than one hundred Flying Dutchmen/Pride alums include JPMorgan Chase, Citi, PwC, Morgan Stanley, EY, Deloitte, Estee Lauder, and NBC Universal. Among the Class of 2017, grads went on to a number of interesting careers with professional sports teams, major media outlets, and political groups. The median starting salary was $50,000 with 20 percent of the class bringing home less than $40k and 30 percent making over $60k. Just about everyone stays in the Greater New York City area with Boston, Philly, and DC picking up the crumbs.

Grad school is a common next step for those receiving their Hofstra degree as 33 percent enrolled within a year, and 44 percent planned to pursue further study within five years. Class of 2017 members matriculated into a wide array of graduate and professional schools including every SUNY and CUNY institution as well as many elite universities like Harvard, Yale, Carnegie Mellon, Northwestern, Rice, MIT, and Stanford. The school offers its undergraduates a 4+4 BS/MD option in conjunction with its own Zucker School of Medicine. Other medical schools attended by recent grads include the Albert Einstein College of Medicine, Icahn School of Medicine, and SUNY Downstate. There were eleven different law schools attended by Class of 2017 members with William & Mary highlighting an otherwise middling list.

Admission

Sixty-three percent of the 27,620 applicants for a spot in the Class of 2022 were accepted, but a minuscule 9 percent of those accepted actually enrolled in the university. Of those that became 2018-19 freshmen, 90 percent had over a 3.0 GPA, 28 percent were in top 10 percent of their high school class, and 59 percent were in top 25 percent. The average SAT score was 1238, and the average ACT score was 27. The mid-50 percent ranges were 1150 to 1330 on the SAT and 24 to 30 on the ACT. The university's degree of selectivity has remained constant in recent years. Acceptance rates and grades from the early 2010s are comparable to those today. Standardized test scores have risen, but much of that can be attributed to going test-optional (more on that in a moment).

The five factors viewed as the most important by the admissions committee are GPA, class rank, rigor of secondary school record, recommendations, and the essay. Hofstra went test-optional in 2014 but, presently, three-quarters of applicants still submit standardized test scores. Interviews are listed as "important" but are not a required part of the process. Extracurricular activities, talent/ability, and character/personal qualities also play a major factor in the process. For a school that has such a low yield rate (the percent of accepted students that enroll), it is surprising that it does not offer a binding early decision option, but it does offer early action. Hofstra remains a realistic option for B students who take some advanced coursework in high school.

Worth Your Money?

Hofstra is an expensive school, registering a $63,000 annual cost of attendance, but it is generous with both need-based and merit aid as the average grants in both areas are approximately $20k-23k. The Long Island location can make this school worth the money for those with a clear plan of how to take advantage of the school's New York City connections. Students without a preprofessional focus and for whom costs are a concern should also consider more affordable options.

FINANCIAL
Institutional Type: Private
In-State Tuition: $44,640
Out-of-State Tuition: $44,640
Room & Board: $15,708
Required Fees: $1,060
Books & Supplies: $1,000

Avg. Need-Based Aid: $23,169
Avg. % of Need Met: 70%

Avg. Merit-Based Aid: $20,251
% Receiving Merit-Based Aid: 36%

Avg. Cumulative Debt: N/A
% of Students Borrowing: 63%

CAREER
Who Recruits
1. Cox Media Group
2. Stanley Black & Decker
3. Raytheon
4. Partners Healtcare
5. Boston Children's Hospital

Notable Internships
1. The Tonight Show
2. The Carlyle Group
3. CNN NY News Bureau

Top Industries
1. Business
2. Education
3. Operations
4. Sales
5. Finance

Top Employers
1. Northwell Health
2. JPMorgan Chase
3. Citi
4. Morgan Stanley
5. PwC

Where Alumni Work
1. New York City
2. Boston
3. Philadelphia
4. Washington, DC
5. Los Angeles

Median Earnings
College Scorecard (Early Career): $53,100
EOP (Early Career): $55,700
PayScale (Mid-Career): $110,400

RANKINGS
Forbes: 292
Money: 609
U.S. News: 162, National Universities
Wall Street Journal/THE: 228
Washington Monthly: 379, National Universities

#CollegesWorthYourMoney

Illinois Institute of Technology

Chicago, Illinois | Admissions Phone: 312-567-3025

ADMISSION
Admission Rate: 58%
Admission Rate - Men: 57%
Admission Rate - Women: 61%
EA Admission Rate: Not Offered
ED Admission Rate: Not Offered
Admission Rate (5-Year Trend): +1%
ED Admission Rate (5-Year Trend): Not Offered
% of Admits Attending (Yield): 21%
Transfer Admission Rate: 58%

Offered Wait List: Not Offered
Accepted Wait List: Not Offered
Admitted Wait List: Not Offered

SAT Reading/Writing (Middle 50%): 600-680
SAT Math (Middle 50%): 620-720
ACT Composite (Middle 50%): 26-31
Testing Policy: ACT/SAT Required
SAT Superscore: Yes
ACT Superscore: Yes

% Graduated in Top 10% of HS Class: 50%
% Graduated in Top 25% of HS Class: 78%
% Graduated in Top 50% of HS Class: 95%

ENROLLMENT
Total Undergraduate Enrollment: 3,026
% Part-Time: 8%
% Male: 69%
% Female: 31%
% Out-of-State: 25%
% Fraternity: 7%
% Sorority: 6%
% On-Campus (Freshman): 73%
% On-Campus (All Undergraduate): 43%

% African-American: 5%
% Asian: 15%
% Hispanic: 16%
% White: 35%
% Other: 4%
% Race or Ethnicity Unknown: 3%
% International: 17%
% Low-Income: 34%

ACADEMICS
Student-to-Faculty Ratio: 12:1
% of Classes Under 20: 46%
% of Classes Under 40: 84%
% Full-Time Faculty: 56%
% Full-Time Faculty w/ Terminal Degree: 82%

Top Programs
Aerospace Engineering
Architecture
Computer Science
Finance
Mechanical Engineering
Information Technology and Management

Retention Rate: 90%
4-Year Graduation Rate: 37%
6-Year Graduation Rate: 72%

Curricular Flexibility: Somewhat Flexible
Academic Rating: ★★★

Inside the Classroom

A rare school that educates more advanced degree-seekers than undergraduate students, the Illinois Institute of Technology—traditionally referred to as IIT but rebranded in 2001 as Illinois Tech—is a private research university with roughly 3,000 undergrads and 40+ undergraduate majors, mostly in the realms of engineering, business, computer science, and architecture.

Located on Chicago's South Side, this school has a large international presence with forty-eight countries represented as well as a phenomenally high number of Pell Grant recipients as 30 percent of undergraduates present with serious financial need. This is significant because Illinois Tech has a reputation not just for producing grads who earn excellent salaries but for facilitating social and economic mobility as well.

Undergraduates study in one of six undergraduate divisions: the Armour College of Engineering, the College of Architecture, the College of Science, the Lewis College of Human Sciences, the School of Applied Technology, or the Stuart School of Business. The university has four learning goals associated with its core curriculum: (1) commitment to positive change in their communities, nations, and the world; (2) the ability to think critically and viewing problems as opportunities for innovation; (3) the ability to collaborate professionally and ethically; and (4) communicate effectively. Toward those aims, one must take three courses in the humanities, three in the social or behavioral sciences, three in science or engineering, one computer science course, and complete thirty-six hours of coursework with a substantial focus on oral or written communication. A 600 SAT reading score will get you out of introductory writing.

The student-to-faculty ratio is 12:1, but with so many graduate students to serve, undergraduate course sections are not small across the board; rather, they vary from 20 percent of sections that boast a single-digit enrollment to the 16 percent of courses that enroll more than forty students. Yet, an Illinois Tech education provides many opportunities for students to have close contact with faculty. For example, the Interprofessional Projects (IPRO) Program features "teams of students from a variety of majors that develop solutions to real-world problems using design-centered methodology and innovative thinking." Completing two IPROs is a graduation requirement. The Elevate program connects students with undergraduate research and other experiential learning opportunities as early as freshman year. There are 42 study abroad programs in which IIT students can participate, although as with most technical institutions, the bulk of undergrads remain on campus for all four years.

The most popular major is computer science followed by architecture and mechanical engineering. Overall, 51 percent of the degrees conferred are in engineering, 17 percent in computer science, and 14 percent in architecture. The School of Applied Technology offers one of the most respected information technology programs in the country and serves as a pipeline to many top tech companies. The College of Architecture has a similarly sterling national reputation. Programs in engineering and computer science are also strong.

Outside the Classroom

Illinois Tech's 120-acre urban campus is home to only 43 percent of the undergraduate population; the majority of students live in university-owned housing and are graduate students. Freshmen and sophomores are required to live on campus, but commuters who live with their parents and transfers are often granted exemptions. There are two traditional dormitories and two "villages" that are collections of smaller residence halls. S.R. Crown Hall and the McCormick Tribune Campus Center are architecturally unique, and the campus as a whole sometimes cracks "most beautiful" lists. Many students self-identify as "nerds," and the rigorous academics and male-heavy population (only 37 percent of students are female) can limit social life. Greek life has a moderate presence on campus drawing 8 percent of men and 7 percent of women. There are seventeen varsity intercollegiate sports teams—nine men's and eight women's—many of which compete in NCAA Division III. More than 150 student-run organizations are available, and the BOG serves as a popular hub thanks to its free, eight-lane bowling alley and abundance of arcade games. Campus is only three miles south of downtown Chicago and about one mile from Guaranteed Rate Field where the Chicago White Sox play baseball. Plenty of bars, jazz clubs, museums, zoos, and an aquarium are a short distance from campus.

Career Services

The main Career Services Office at IIT consists of five professional employees, but the Stuart School of Business has its own separate office with three full-time employees bringing the school's total to eight career services professionals. That works out to a student-advisor ratio of 378:1, within the average range of schools profiled in the book. Freshmen are encouraged to begin working with a career counselor during their first semester. In addition to the professional staff members, eight peer counselors also are available to those looking to get the jump on vocational exploration.

Staff members are always willing to assist with "résumé and cover letter writing, networking advice, company research assistance, mock interviews, (and) dinner/business etiquette workshops." Two-day career fairs are held on campus each semester, and more than 150 employers attended the September 2018 fair alone, including industry giants Amazon, Goldman Sachs, NBCUniversal, and Grainger. The school claims 78,500 living alumni, many of whom are concentrated in tech companies in Chicago, making networking conditions favorable. That can come in handy when pursuing for-credit internships or co-ops during the school year or during the summer term. However, the school does not release information about what percentage of students complete one or more internships or what percentage of the undergraduate student body is serviced by the office in any capacity in a given year.

Professional Outcomes

Illinois Tech grads can be found in sizable numbers within major corporations including Motorola, Amazon, Microsoft, Google, Apple, Accenture, JPMorgan Chase, IBM, EY, and Cisco. The Greater Chicago area plays home to more than half of IIT alumni with San Francisco, New York City, Seattle, and Los Angeles and international destinations including India, Brazil, and Spain all attracting fairly large numbers of Scarlet Hawks. Starting salaries as well as midcareer compensation figures are the strongest in the state of Illinois and among the highest anywhere when compared to other highly selective private universities. The school also ranks high for social mobility, lifting more students whose families fall in the bottom 20 percent income bracket into the top 20 percent than any other school in the state.

Those continuing to graduate school often stay at Illinois Tech, which offers degrees in engineering, science, architecture, business, design, human sciences, applied technology, and law. For premed students, the medical school acceptance rate is "often above the national average." A dual degree program is offered in partnership with Midwestern University's Chicago College of Osteopathic Medicine. Recent students have earned it a place among top medical schools like the Northwestern University Feinberg School of Medicine, New York University School of Medicine, and the University of Michigan Medical School.

Admission

With an acceptance rate of 58 percent, the Illinois Institute of Technology is not looking to shut the door on those with imperfect credentials, yet some of that hefty number is attribute to self-selection. The mid-50 percent SAT range of 2018-19 freshmen is 1220-1400 and the ACT range is 26-31. Surprisingly, and perhaps encouragingly—depending on your circumstances—16 percent of attending students scored less than a 600 on the math section of the SAT, 24 percent scored under a 600 on the verbal section. Half of freshmen earned a place in the top 10 percent of their respective high school class, 78 percent were in the top quartile, and 95 percent were in the top 50 percent. All of those numbers, including the overall acceptance rate, are similar to those from five years ago, despite a spike in the total number of applications.

Like most engineering-focused schools, the hard numbers are paramount when it comes to making admissions decisions. Standardized test scores, GPA, and the level of rigor of one's coursework are of the utmost importance while factors such as class rank and recommendations are also given weight by the committee. Female applicants enjoy slightly better admissions prospects with an acceptance rate of 61 percent compared to men at just under 57 percent. There is no early decision process at Illinois Tech, rather, applications are accepted on a rolling basis beginning on October 1 with a priority deadline of December 1. Applying on the early side is your best bet regardless of whether IIT is your number one choice or one of many irons in the fire.

Worth Your Money?

On paper, the cost of attendance at IIT is greater than $65,000 per year. However, 97 percent of students receive some type of aid, and even families with an income above $135,000 receive an average scholarship and grant combo adding up to $32,000 annually. As a result, the school is a worthy investment for most as solid-paying tech, finance, and architecture jobs in the Chicago area await your arrival postgraduation

FINANCIAL
Institutional Type: Private
In-State Tuition: $47,480
Out-of-State Tuition: $47,480
Room & Board: $13,582
Required Fees: $1,800
Books & Supplies: $1,250

Avg. Need-Based Aid: $36,584
Avg. % of Need Met: 86%

Avg. Merit-Based Aid: $26,980
% Receiving Merit-Based Aid: 39%

Avg. Cumulative Debt: $32,671
% of Students Borrowing: 54%

CAREER
Who Recruits
1. Webber, LLC
2. Wise Equation Solutions
3. W.W. Grainger
4. AVG Automation
5. CCC Information Services

Notable Internships
1. BMW
2. Salesforce
3. Motorola

Top Industries
1. Engineering
2. Business
3. Infromation Technology
4. Operations
5. Education

Top Employers
1. Amazon
2. Motorola
3. Google
4. Microsoft
5. Apple

Where Alumni Work
1. Chicago
2. San Francisco
3. India
4. New York City
5. Seattle

Median Earnings
College Scorecard (Early Career): $69,100
EOP (Early Career): $72,300
PayScale (Mid-Career): $118,500

RANKINGS
Forbes: 208
Money: 213
U.S. News: 2, National Universities
Wall Street Journal/THE: 137 (T)
Washington Monthly: 60, National Universities

#CollegesWorthYourMoney

Indiana University Bloomington

Bloomington, Indiana | Admissions Phone: 812-855-0661

ADMISSION
Admission Rate: 77%
Admission Rate - Men: 78%
Admission Rate - Women: 76%
EA Admission Rate: N/A
ED Admission Rate: Not Offered
Admission Rate (5-Year Trend): +5%
ED Admission Rate (5-Year Trend): Not Offered
% of Admits Attending (Yield): 24%
Transfer Admission Rate: 65%

\# Offered Wait List: 2,835
\# Accepted Wait List: 467
\# Admitted Wait List: 427

SAT Reading/Writing (Middle 50%): 580-670
SAT Math (Middle 50%): 570-690
ACT Composite (Middle 50%): 24-31
Testing Policy: ACT/SAT Required
SAT Superscore: Yes
ACT Superscore: Yes

% Graduated in Top 10% of HS Class: 35%
% Graduated in Top 25% of HS Class: 69%
% Graduated in Top 50% of HS Class: 95%

ENROLLMENT
Total Undergraduate Enrollment: 33,301
% Part-Time: 4%
% Male: 50%
% Female: 50%
% Out-of-State: 35%
% Fraternity: 23%
% Sorority: 20%
% On-Campus (Freshman): 89%
% On-Campus (All Undergraduate): 37%

% African-American: 5%
% Asian: 6%
% Hispanic: 6%
% White: 69%
% Other: 4%
% Race or Ethnicity Unknown: 0%
% International: 9%
% Low-Income: 19%

ACADEMICS
Student-to-Faculty Ratio: 16:1
% of Classes Under 20: 37%
% of Classes Under 40: 75%
% Full-Time Faculty: 86%
% Full-Time Faculty w/ Terminal Degree: 88%

Top Programs
Accounting
English
Entrepreneurship
History
Finance
Music
Psychology
Public Management

Retention Rate: 91%
4-Year Graduation Rate: 64%
6-Year Graduation Rate: 78%

Curricular Flexibility: Somewhat Flexible
Academic Rating: ★★★

Inside the Classroom

From coast to coast, flagship public universities have seen their admissions standards skyrocket in recent years. Students for whom the University of Maryland, the University of Wisconsin, or any school within the University of California system would have been a safety school a decade ago now find themselves sweating out admissions decisions each spring. Fortunately, this is not so at Indiana's famed Bloomington campus where more than three-quarters of applicants who apply still receive a friendly Midwestern welcome, and both the quality and price of the education that await are exceptionally solid. That combination of accessibility, quality, and variety— IU offers 200+ majors—draws more out-of-state and international students than you might expect. Only 57 percent of IU undergraduates are from in state, and 7 percent of the student body are international students hailing from 120+ countries.

Unlike many large universities made up of numerous schools and colleges, Indiana is not overeager to assign and confine you to a particular program. Upon entering IU, freshmen are housed within the University Division, and they remain there for one or two years in order to figure out their academic direction. This gives all freshmen time to begin wrestling with the Common Ground Curriculum that involves completing courses in six areas: English composition, mathematical modeling, arts and humanities, social and historical studies, natural and mathematical sciences, and world languages and cultures. Of note for any foreign language averse students, there are ways to fill the latter requirement without learning another language. Students who are members of the Hutton Honors College also typically need to complete a senior thesis within their academic departments.

The university's 16:1 student-to-faculty ratio is not bad for a school of Indiana's size, and it does make an effort to keep undergraduate classes on the small side. While there are a number of introductory courses that transpire in giant lecture halls, 63 percent of all sections contain no more than twenty-nine students. Experiential learning opportunities are available to those who seize them; 27 percent of arts and sciences students completed research with a faculty member. On the study abroad front, 26 percent of 2018 A&S graduates spent a semester in a foreign country. In total, the school offers 360 programs in sixty-five countries and twenty languages.

Business/marketing is the most popular major accounting for 25 percent of the total degrees conferred. Kelley is an acclaimed business school that draws immense national respect, ranking up there in prestige with Goizueta (Emory), McDonough (Georgetown), and its neighbor to the north, Mendoza (Notre Dame). Indiana, notably, did not offer an engineering program until recently, making Purdue a much better local public option for anyone entering that field of study. However, the computer and information science degree program has tight ties to top tech companies, and it is the school's second most frequently conferred degree at 9 percent. The other degrees most commonly awarded are in social services (8 percent), parks and recreation (8 percent), journalism (7 percent), and biology (7 percent). Plenty of students from all academic backgrounds capture competitive postgraduate scholarships. In 2019, the school's haul included eleven Critical Language Scholarships, ten Fulbrights, and a Churchill Scholarship. The previous year undergraduates won a hard-to-fathom twenty-one Fulbright Scholarships.

Outside the Classroom

The university houses 89 percent of freshmen but only 37 percent of the overall undergraduate student body on its sprawling 1,936-acre campus. Living options include thirteen residence halls, eleven apartment complexes, and more than twenty residential thematic communities. For everyone else, there are plenty of affordable off-campus apartments within close proximity. Fraternities and sororities play an enormous role in social life as 23 percent of men and 20 percent of women join Greek organizations; there are seventy to choose from. There are twenty-four varsity sports, and many boast Big Ten championships, yet one shines above the rest as Hoosier hoops is nothing short of a religion in Bloomington, and you'll never find one of the 17,222 seats within Assembly Hall unfilled during men's basketball games. For those looking for lower-key athletics, there are more than seventy club and intramural sports at your disposal. Overall, Indiana University is home to more than 750 student organizations featuring clubs ranging from calligraphy to bass fishing. Bloomington gets high marks as a safe and enjoyable college town, and there are always events going on whether it's a free show at the spectacular Musical Arts Center or a community service opportunity—students donated a total of 225,000 hours last year. Indianapolis is a fifty-mile highway drive away, making it an option for a quick weekend getaway.

Career Services

The university has a main Career Development Center for those who enter undecided as well as discipline-specific career services offices housed within each undergraduate college. There are eighty-six full-time staff members dedicated to career advising, experiential education, and employer relations. The university's overall 389:1 student-to-counselor ratio is one of the best for a public institution of Indiana's immense size. This staff's output is astounding whether measured by its 23,428 one-on-one counseling sessions per year or its large-scale efforts that include booking 1,761 companies to attend the school's many career fairs.

Last year alone, 9,778 internships were completed by IU students in both for-credit and noncredit placements. Over 2,000 employers recruited at Bloomington, and hiring organizations conducted a collective 11,020 on-campus interviews. Among the major corporations actively recruiting and interviewing on campus are EY, PwC, Deloitte, Oracle, JPMorgan Chase & Co., Microsoft Corporation, Anheuser-Busch, Epic Systems, Procter & Gamble, and Grainger, Inc. Just a quick glance at the university calendar reveals a frenetic pace of career fairs taking place in the fall of 2019, including targeted events for those interested in business, media, social services, finance, public health, internships, the creative arts, and the hard sciences. Any way you measure it, the IU career services staff's output is prodigious and helps set undergraduates up for successful postgraduation transition.

Professional Outcomes

Indiana University tracks the postgraduate outcomes from each undergraduate school. Looking at the College of Arts & Sciences, by far the largest group of students, Class of 2018 grads reached their next employment or graduate school destination at a 93 percent rate within six months of receiving their degrees. Fifty-three percent had procured their first jobs, and one-quarter of students were in grad school; only 7 percent of those looking for jobs were unable to land one in that time. The most frequently entered industries (from A&S) were arts & entertainment, education, retail, and advertising. The median starting salary for A&S grads was $37,500. In the Kelley School of Business, 96 percent were placed successfully within six months, and the median starting salary was $62,000. School of Informatics, Computing & Engineering grads had comparable starting salaries and an identical 96 percent success rate. Among the largest employers of Hoosier alumni are local pharmaceutical giant Eli Lilly, EY, Amazon, PwC, Salesforce, Deloitte, IBM, Oracle, Microsoft, Accenture, and Google. Indianapolis, Chicago, Bloomington, and New York City are the locales where you can find the greatest concentration of Indiana graduates.

Among the most frequently attended graduate schools by members of the Class of 2018 were Indiana Bloomington (including its own law and medical schools), Purdue, Loyola Chicago, Northwestern, and Columbia. Indiana is a premed factory with 275 applicants to med school in 2018-19 alone; that is the thirteenth highest in the nation. Impressively, the well-regarded Indiana University School of Medicine was the second most frequently attended graduate school overall. That was aided by the fact that the in-state acceptance rate at this medical school is 48 percent, six times higher than the out-of-state rate. The university also operates two separate law schools, one in Indianapolis and one in Bloomington, and both draw large numbers of IU undergraduates. A combined BA/JD program can be completed in six years.

Admission

Of all the flagship universities profiled in this book, Indiana has the most relaxed admissions standards as 77 percent of those who applied for a place in the Class of 2022 were welcomed aboard. The mid-50 percent SAT scores for attending freshman were 1150-1360 and the ACT mid-50th was a wide-ranging 24-31. The school became test-optional in 2020. The majority— 58 percent—sported GPAs of 3.75 or better, and 35 percent finished in the top 10 percent of their high school class. More encouragingly for less-than-perfect applicants is the fact that 31 percent of undergrads did not place in the top quartile of their graduating cohort, and 24 percent possessed cumulative GPAs under 3.5.

With roughly 44,000 applications to wade through, the admissions committee must first rely on the easy-to-assess credentials of class rank, GPA, standardized test scores, and level of academic rigor. The application essay is "important," but factors like extracurricular activities, recommendations, and volunteer work are merely "considered." While there is no binding early decision option available, IU does offer an early action round with a deadline of November 1, also the deadline for the most complete scholarship consideration. The acceptance rate at this university has actually gone up in the last five years—it had been in the high 60s. Thanks to declining enrollment numbers the last three years, the admissions standards show no sign of stiffening any time soon.

Worth Your Money?

Indiana residents enjoy not only a reasonable tuition cost that is a touch under $11,000 but a modest room-and-board price as well when compared to other schools of roughly the same quality. For comparison, room and board alone at Notre Dame would cost an extra $20,000 over four years. Nonresidents should consider their aid package and program of study (business-related fields are your best bet) before packing off to Bloomington, as out-of-state rates are approaching that of many private colleges. Hoosiers cannot go wrong heading to Bloomington for their bachelor's degree, no matter what field of interest they plan to study.

FINANCIAL
Institutional Type: Public
In-State Tuition: $9,342
Out-of-State Tuition: $34,117
Room & Board: $10,466
Required Fees: $1,339
Books & Supplies: $930

Avg. Need-Based Aid: $12,806
Avg. % of Need Met: 71%

Avg. Merit-Based Aid: $7,592
% Receiving Merit-Based Aid: 36%

Avg. Cumulative Debt: $28,352
% of Students Borrowing: 44%

CAREER
Who Recruits
1. Macy's
2. Anheuser-Busch
3. Grant Thornton LLC
4. Oracle
5. Insight Global

Notable Internships
1. The Economist
2. Grant Thornton LLP
3. Bain & Company

Top Industries
1. Business
2. Education
3. Operations
4. Sales
5. Social Services

Top Employers
1. Eli Lily and Company
2. EY
3. Amazon
4. PwC
5. Salesforce

Where Alumni Work
1. Indianapolis
2. Chicago
3. Bloomington, IN
4. New York City
5. Washington, DC

Median Earnings
College Scorecard (Early Career): $47,700
EOP (Early Career): $40,100
PayScale (Mid-Career): $97,100

RANKINGS
Forbes: 131
Money: 97
U.S. News: 79 (T), National Universities
Wall Street Journal/THE: 123 (T)
Washington Monthly: 47, National Universities

#CollegesWorthYourMoney

Johns Hopkins University

Baltimore, Maryland | Admissions Phone: 410-516-8171

Inside the Classroom

High schoolers who dream of entering the medical profession look to North Baltimore as their Mecca—more specifically, to Johns Hopkins University, Charm City's prestigious, midsized research institution. Yet, four years at Johns Hopkins is so much more than merely a prelude to seven years of medical school. With fifty-two majors as well as forty-seven minors, JHU excels in everything from its bread-and-butter medical-related majors to international relations and dance. Of the five undergraduate schools within the university, the vast majority of students reside in either the Krieger School of Arts and Sciences or the Whiting School of Engineering. However, the Carey School of Business, School of Education, and Peabody Institute also award bachelor's degrees.

All Hopkins bachelor's-seekers must meet distributional requirements covering the basics: humanities, natural sciences, social and behavioral sciences, quantitative and mathematical sciences, and engineering. Writing-intensive courses also are mandated regardless of one's major. Students are encouraged to broaden their horizons by double majoring or selecting a minor, and 70 percent do so. First-year experience courses help to transition students to the school and second-year experience courses assist with community-building and career planning.

Boasting an enviable 8:1 student-to-faculty ratio and 75 percent of course sections with an enrollment under twenty, face time with professors is a reality. That presents a phenomenal opportunity to learn directly from a group that includes four Nobel Laureates, four Medal of Science winners, and two recipients of the Presidential Medal of Freedom. Fittingly for America's first research university, 80 percent of JHU undergraduates complete a research experience while working closely with a faculty member. Each year, hundreds of students receive significant funding for independent projects through the Hopkins Office for Undergraduate Research.

Universally respected by employers and graduate schools alike, many departments carry a high level of clout, including biology, chemistry, English, and international studies. Biomedical engineering, public health, and nursing, which happen to be the three most popular majors, can also be found at the top of the national rankings. In 2019, there were twenty-two Fulbright Scholars named from the university. Johns Hopkins grads also are competitive in landing Luce, Truman, Marshall, Goldwater, and National Science Foundation Graduate Research Fellowships.

Outside the Classroom

The 140-acre Homewood campus located in North Baltimore is the site of the School of Engineering and the School of Arts & Sciences. The dorms located at Homewood house most underclassmen and feature dining halls that garner generally high praise. Despite the excellent chow, upperclassmen tend to outgrow university-owned housing; a slight majority of students, 52 percent, live off campus. The twenty-two Greek organizations each have their own charitable focus and attract 27 percent of the undergraduate student body. Nicknamed the Blue Jays, athletes compete in twelve men's and ten women's sports in NCCA Division III. Over 400 student organizations are active at JHU. Groups centered on community service tend to be the most popular. The Center for Social Concern connects students with over seventy-five local organizations. For those interested in a medical career, you'll have the chance to volunteer in one of fifteen local hospitals, including Johns Hopkins' own facilities. Popular traditions include the three-day Spring Fair, the nation's largest student-run fair. Famous guest speakers from all walks of life regularly visit campus and draw engaged audiences. Homewood is a only a few miles from the bustle of Baltimore's Inner Harbor so, even though the area immediately surrounding campus isn't the most inviting, culture and nightlife can easily be found.

Career Services

The Homewood Career Center is staffed by seventeen full-time professional employees that work with and on behalf of undergraduates in the areas of career development, employer engagement, internship coordination, and event planning. This figure does not include administrative assistants, IT, graduate advisors, or marketing professionals. Possessing a student-to-advisor ratio of 311:1, JHU is superior to many of the institutions included in this book.

In 2018-19, the Career Center engaged 1,999 undergraduates in one-to-one career coach appointments. More than ninety employers, including many Fortune 1000 companies, conducted 716 interviews on campus. Over 15,000 jobs and internship opportunities were available on Handshake. Homewood hosts three major career fairs each year: the flagship Fall Career Fair with more than 150 employers, the STEM & Innovation Career Fair with forty targeted companies attending, and the spring Nonprofit Career Fair that also focuses on internship procurement. All told, 170 companies attended career fairs at JHU, and 247 companies recruited on campus. The university also provides a number of internships that are built-in to each academic department. Those include credit-bearing options in orthopedic surgery, film and media studies, business, and computational biology. An exceptional 85 percent of undergraduates complete one internship over their four years of study; it is not unusual to complete two.

Professional Outcomes

The Class of 2018 saw 97 percent of graduates successfully land at their next destination within six months of exiting the university; 54 percent of graduates entered the world of employment and a robust 35 percent went directly to graduate/professional school. Of those entering the workforce, the most popular industries were research, engineering and IT, consulting, finance, and health care. Johns Hopkins University and its affiliated medical institutions were the largest employer of recent graduates, scooping up sixty-four Class of 2017 members. Other prominent companies landing more than a handful of fresh JHU alums were Deloitte, Accenture, Booz Allen Hamilton, Morgan Stanley, and ScribeAmerica. Across all graduating years you'll find hundreds of Hopkins grads working for IBM, Google, Microsoft, Facebook, and Apple. The average starting salary across all majors was $60,768.

Johns Hopkins' sterling reputation also helps land its undergrads at premier graduate schools. Engineering is the most popular graduate field with 27 percent of 2017 graduates going in that direction. Medical school was the second most common endeavor at 17 percent. The overall admit rate to medical schools was a healthy 79 percent. Law school grads also found homes at an above-average 90 percent clip. Johns Hopkins itself is the most frequently attended graduate school, and it's not even close, with 147 Class of 2017 grads continuing their educations in Baltimore. The next five most frequently attended institutions were Harvard, Penn, Columbia, Duke, and Stanford.

Admission

If Johns Hopkins' aim in 2018 was to become one of a dozen or so elite universities with a single-digit admissions rate, it only missed that goal by a matter of percentage points; 10.6 percent of undergraduates were admitted into the Class of 2022. That follows a pattern of declining acceptance rates over the past few years. For historical context, the school admitted one-quarter of applicants only a decade ago. The SAT middle 50 percent range in 2008 was 1320-1480; today it is 1470-1560. Given that the former 75th percentile SAT score is now the 25th percentile score, it's pretty clear that Johns Hopkins has grown increasingly competitive in recent years. For those taking the ACT, the mid-50 percent is a tight range of 33-34.

Current students landed in the top 10 percent of their high school classes at a 96 percent clip, so impeccable grades in the most competitive curriculum available is pretty much a prerequisite for consideration. The average unweighted GPA for 2018-19 freshman was 3.93, meaning that more than one or two imperfections on a transcript can be a disqualifier. Leadership qualities and community service are also highly valued. In the university's own words, it is "looking for students who can think beyond their limits, who don't see 'impossible' as a roadblock, and who will not only elevate themselves but also those around them." Early decision applicants will see improved odds as their acceptance rate is more than three times that of the regular round (30 percent vs. 9 percent). Further, 46 percent of the Class of 2022 was accepted via ED. Always a highly selective school, Johns Hopkins is now in the upper-upper tier of selectivity along with the Ivies, Stanford, and a small cadre of elite liberal arts colleges. Only those with first-rate test scores and transcripts need apply.

Worth Your Money?

If your family is a lower-to-mid tier income bracket, Johns Hopkins will provide you with every dollar of financial aid you need to attend the university. Presently, 47 percent of the undergraduate population benefits from that generosity with an average need-based grant of $47,492. The annual cost of attendance is approaching $75,000, and of those families making incomes in the top 5 percent nationally (an estimated 40 percent of current students' families do), you can expect to pay close to full price. Even for those taking out loans to attend, JHU is the type of school that it is almost always OK to pay up for. With fantastic job and professional school prospects down the road, the $300,000 investment will be well worth it in the long run.

FINANCIAL
Institutional Type: Private
In-State Tuition: $53,740
Out-of-State Tuition: $53,740
Room & Board: $15,836
Required Fees: N/A
Books & Supplies: $1,240

Avg. Need-Based Aid: $47,492
Avg. % of Need Met: 100%

Avg. Merit-Based Aid: $10,602
% Receiving Merit-Based Aid: 1%

Avg. Cumulative Debt: $25,697
% of Students Borrowing: 46%

CAREER
Who Recruits
1. Dean & Company
2. Bloomberg
3. Lockheed Martin
4. Bain & Company
5. McKinsey & Co.

Notable Internships
1. Twitter
2. NASA Jet Propulsion Laboratory
3. National Institutes of Health

Top Industries
1. Business
2. Education
3. Research
4. Engineering
5. Healthcare

Top Employers
1. Booz Allen Hamilton
2. Google
3. Deloitte
4. IBM
5. Microsoft

Where Alumni Work
1. Baltimore
2. Washington, DC
3. New York City
4. San Francisco
5. Boston

Median Earnings
College Scorecard (Early Career): $73,200
EOP (Early Career): $75,000
PayScale (Mid-Career): $117,100

RANKINGS
Forbes: 22
Money: 125
U.S. News: 10, National Universities
Wall Street Journal/THE: 12 (T)
Washington Monthly: 56, National Universities

#CollegesWorthYourMoney

Kenyon College

Gambier, Ohio | Admissions Phone: 740-427-5776

ADMISSION
Admission Rate: 36%
Admission Rate - Men: 33%
Admission Rate - Women: 38%
EA Admission Rate: Not Offered
ED Admission Rate: 70%
Admission Rate (5-Year Trend): -3%
ED Admission Rate (5-Year Trend): +12%
% of Admits Attending (Yield): 24%
Transfer Admission Rate: 30%

Offered Wait List: 1,857
Accepted Wait List: 907
Admitted Wait List: 4

SAT Reading/Writing (Middle 50%): 640-730
SAT Math (Middle 50%): 640-740
ACT Composite (Middle 50%): 29-33
Testing Policy: ACT/SAT Required
SAT Superscore: Yes
ACT Superscore: Yes

% Graduated in Top 10% of HS Class: 55%
% Graduated in Top 25% of HS Class: 79%
% Graduated in Top 50% of HS Class: 96%

ENROLLMENT
Total Undergraduate Enrollment: 1,719
% Part-Time: 0%
% Male: 45%
% Female: 55%
% Out-of-State: 87%
% Fraternity: 27%
% Sorority: 32%
% On-Campus (Freshman): 100%
% On-Campus (All Undergraduate): 99%

% African-American: 4%
% Asian: 4%
% Hispanic: 8%
% White: 70%
% Other: 5%
% Race or Ethnicity Unknown: 3%
% International: 7%
% Low-Income: 10%

ACADEMICS
Student-to-Faculty Ratio: 10:1
% of Classes Under 20: 80%
% of Classes Under 40: 99%
% Full-Time Faculty: 80%
% Full-Time Faculty w/ Terminal Degree: 88%

Top Programs
English
History
International Studies
Neuroscience
Performing Arts
Political Science
Sociology

Retention Rate: 91%
4-Year Graduation Rate: 85%
6-Year Graduation Rate: 89%

Curricular Flexibility: Very Flexible
Academic Rating: ★★★★

Inside the Classroom

When your list of notable alumni includes Paul Newman, National Humanities Medal recipient E.L. Doctorow, and largely forgotten US President Rutherford B. Hayes, it's clear that your college is a unique and special place. Kenyon College in rural Gambier, Ohio, has a history of excellence in drama, English, and across the broader liberal arts that produces passionate and talented alumni who are ready, willing, and able to carve out their legacies within their chosen disciplines.

Kenyon offers thirty-three majors and an additional thirteen concentrations that allow students to complete their education with few nondepartmental core requirements. All undergrads must demonstrate proficiency in a foreign language (AP opt-out is available) and take a quantitative reasoning course, but other than that, a Kenyon education is open and flexible. A senior capstone awaits all would-be graduates and can take many forms, but the project must demonstrate a student's skills in writing, speaking, collaborating and "distinguish the essential from the trivial." This latter requirement epitomizes Kenyon's emphasis on critical thought throughout one's four years of study.

The student-faculty ratio is 10-to-1, and the most common class size is fifteen. Thirty-two percent of classes are even more intimate, offering single-digit enrollments. Close relationships develop with faculty and often lead to opportunities to engage in undergraduate research. Summer research programs available to students include the Kenyon Summer Scholars Program, a joint program with Ohio State, and the Summer Science Program that sees more than thirty student-professor pairs collaborate on research for an eight- to ten-week period. Roughly half of each junior class packs up its bags and heads off to a distant land for a semester abroad. Students choose from more than 190 programs in fifty countries across Africa, Asia, Australia, Europe, and the Americas; the school also sponsors programs in England and in Rome.

English, economics, psychology, and political science are easily the school's four most popular majors. As alluded to earlier, the drama program is one of the country's finest and has a lengthy alumni list of recognizable actors and performers. It's rare to identify an institution's English program as having an elevated reputation in the minds of employers and graduate schools, but Kenyon's would be one of the exceptions. For a relatively small school, Kenyon graduates procure nationally competitive scholarships and fellowships at an exceptional clip. In 2018, the college had a dozen Fulbright winners and two Goldwater recipients. It has been a top Fulbright producer for the last decade.

Outside the Classroom

Kenyon's 1,000-acre campus is located forty-five miles from bustling Columbus and includes a 500-acre nature preserve. All students live on campus, and freshmen are clustered in special residence halls near the Gund Commons. Facilities receive rave reviews from students including the Kenyon Athletic Center that includes tennis courts, a pool, and an indoor track. Approximately 30 percent of Kenyon undergraduates are involved in Greek life but, uniquely, fraternities and sororities are situated within residence halls, leading to a more integrated experience. Close to one-third of students are on the roster of one of the school's twenty NCAA Division III athletic teams (ten men's and ten women's). Plenty of club and intramural sports are available for those seeking a less formal sports pursuit. Intramurals include offbeat games like cornhole and capture the flag. Beyond Greek organizations and sports teams, there are 120 student organizations to consider including five a cappella groups, numerous community service opportunities, and the Kenyon College Dance & Dramatics Club that puts on high-quality student productions. Nature lovers can hike the six miles of trails in the school's own preserve along the Kokosing River or join the Outdoors Club that takes backpacking and whitewater rafting trips to more adventurous locations such as the Monongahela National Forest of West Virginia.

Career Services

The Career Development Office (CDO) employs six professional staff members who work in career development or graduate school advising. With a 280:1 student-to-advisor ratio, Kenyon provides a higher-than-average level of support when compared against the other institutions in this guidebook. While it doesn't host a large-scale career fair, it does offer employer/graduate school information sessions at a rate of fifteen to twenty per month. The CDO's strengths lie in its willingness to give individualized attention to students and its involved alumni network.

The online Kenyon Career Network helps link current students to alumni working in their field of interest; there are 8,000 alumni willing to offer their advice and assistance. Job-shadowing opportunities are plentiful, and experiences have included trips to the New York Times, Random House, and the Federal Reserve Bank of Chicago. The office is adept at helping students find internships, and recent grads have had stints with organizations such as the Museum of Modern Art, the San Diego Padres, and the Library of Congress. In recent years 65-70 percent of employed graduates reported that their jobs were related to their desired career path. Only 66 percent of graduates reported that Kenyon was effective at preparing them for the work of employment. Those indicators suggest that not all graduates are fully satisfied with the career services delivered at this school.

Professional Outcomes

Popular fields for Kenyon grads include education, health care, marketing, nonprofit management, research, and writing and editing. Due to Kenyon's small size and the diversity of its academic programs, it lacks dense concentrations of alumni at particular companies. Economics majors often land as financial analysts or advisors at firms including BlackRock, Wells Fargo, JP Morgan, or Goldman Sachs. English and journalism majors end up at a diverse array of publishing houses, talent agencies, news organizations, and consulting companies. New York City, DC, Columbus, Chicago, and Boston are the five cities drawing the greatest numbers of Kenyon alumni. Median salary for Kenyon grads by the start of midcareer is a modest $48,000, but that can partially be explained by the fact that many alumni pursue lengthy graduate/professional programs that typically pay financial dividends later in life. Other comparable schools including Vassar, Carleton, and Occidental rank similarly.

The 18 percent of graduates who directly enter an advanced degree program enjoy extraordinary success. Within five years of completing their undergraduate education at Kenyon, 50 percent have already finished an advanced degree program and 70 percent are enrolled in one. Law and business school applicants find success at a 99 percent clip and, among medical school candidates with a minimum GPA of 3.25, the acceptance rate is a phenomenal 90 percent. Recent grads have been welcomed into the top law schools at Yale, NYU, Berkeley, Stanford, UVA, Michigan, and the University of Chicago. Future doctors are currently training at prestigious medical schools including Johns Hopkins, Duke, Harvard, Tufts, Vanderbilt, and Northwestern. A successful undergraduate career at Kenyon will make possible admission into the finest graduate and professional schools in the world. Across all disciplines, 98 percent of those applying to an advanced degree program are accepted by one of their top three choices.

Admission

A rarity among elite liberal arts schools, Kenyon's acceptance rate has risen in recent years. The class of 2019 acceptance rate hit an all-time low of 24 percent, but the Class of 2022 rate was a significantly friendlier 36 percent. The latest incoming freshman class possessed an average GPA of 3.97 and middle-50 percent standardized test scores of 1280-1470 on the SAT and 29-33 on the ACT. Three years ago, when the acceptance rate was a dozen points lower, the SAT range was 1240-1420; the average GPA was the same. Therefore, one can conclude that the profile of the average Kenyon student has not changed much in recent years.

The admissions committee values four factors above all others: rigor of courses, GPA, recommendations, and essays. Test scores, class rank, the interview, talent/ability, extracurricular activities, character/personal qualities, and the level of an applicant's interest make up the next rung of important considerations. Facing stiff competition from other elite liberal arts schools, Kenyon very much wants to know if you truly want to go there. Applying early decision is the ultimate sign of devotion, and that act is rewarded. Almost 70 percent of ED applicants were accepted, and they comprise a good portion of each incoming class; 43 percent of the Class of 2022 was admitted via ED. Kenyon is looking for academically curious and talented students who are actively involved in their schools/communities. Excellent grades are a must, and demonstrating interest is more valuable here than at your average college. If your heart is set on Kenyon, strongly consider demonstrating your loyalty by applying early.

Worth Your Money?

The 43 percent of current Kenyon students who qualify for financial aid receive grants averaging $41,000 per year; the college meets 100 percent of student need. To help lower the $71k cost of attendance, it also offers annual awards of $13k in merit aid to 42 percent of the undergraduate population. This school is definitely worth your money but, as when considering any institution, we would caution against taking on an excessive amount of debt if you are pursuing a major that is unlikely to lead to fiscal stability upon graduation.

FINANCIAL
Institutional Type: Private
In-State Tuition: $56,430
Out-of-State Tuition: $56,430
Room & Board: $12,580
Required Fees: $2,140
Books & Supplies: N/A

Avg. Need-Based Aid: $41,461
Avg. % of Need Met: 100%

Avg. Merit-Based Aid: $13,317
% Receiving Merit-Based Aid: 42%

Avg. Cumulative Debt: $26,271
% of Students Borrowing: 46%

CAREER
Who Recruits
1. GBQ Partners
2. DHL Supply Chain
3. Skylight Financial Group
4. TEKsystems
5. Verizon

Notable Internships
1. Penguin Random House
2. Guggenheim Museum
3. Morgan Stanley

Top Industries
1. Business
2. Education
3. Media
4. Operations
5. Social Services

Top Employers
1. JPMorgan Chase
2. Cleveland Clinic
3. Google
4. Amazon
5. US State Department

Where Alumni Work
1. New York City
2. Washington, DC
3. Columbus, OH
4. Chicago
5. Boston

Median Earnings
College Scorecard (Early Career): $48,700
EOP (Early Career): $48,000
PayScale (Mid-Career): $103,800

RANKINGS
Forbes: 71
Money: 248
U.S. News: 27 (T), Liberal Arts Colleges
Wall Street Journal/THE: 91 (T)
Washington Monthly: 47, Liberal Arts Colleges

#CollegesWorthYourMoney

Lafayette College

Easton, Pennsylvania | Admissions Phone: 610-330-5100

ADMISSION
Admission Rate: 29%
Admission Rate - Men: 26%
Admission Rate - Women: 33%
EA Admission Rate: Not Offered
ED Admission Rate: 52%
Admission Rate (5-Year Trend): -5%
ED Admission Rate (5-Year Trend): -1%
% of Admits Attending (Yield): 27%
Transfer Admission Rate: 14%

\# Offered Wait List: 2,332
\# Accepted Wait List: 948
\# Admitted Wait List: 2

SAT Reading/Writing (Middle 50%): 620-700
SAT Math (Middle 50%): 630-740
ACT Composite (Middle 50%): 27-32
Testing Policy: ACT/SAT Required
SAT Superscore: Yes
ACT Superscore: Yes

% Graduated in Top 10% of HS Class: 52%
% Graduated in Top 25% of HS Class: 78%
% Graduated in Top 50% of HS Class: 96%

ENROLLMENT
Total Undergraduate Enrollment: 2,642
% Part-Time: 1%
% Male: 48%
% Female: 52%
% Out-of-State: 81%
% Fraternity: 24%
% Sorority: 34%
% On-Campus (Freshman): 100%
% On-Campus (All Undergraduate): 92%

% African-American: 5%
% Asian: 4%
% Hispanic: 7%
% White: 65%
% Other: 3%
% Race or Ethnicity Unknown: 6%
% International: 9%
% Low-Income: 9%

ACADEMICS
Student-to-Faculty Ratio: 10:1
% of Classes Under 20: 62%
% of Classes Under 40: 98%
% Full-Time Faculty: 80%
% Full-Time Faculty w/ Terminal Degree: 98%

Top Programs
Economics
Engineering
English
Film and Media Studies
Government and Law
International Affairs
Psychology

Retention Rate: 93%
4-Year Graduation Rate: 83%
6-Year Graduation Rate: 87%

Curricular Flexibility: Somewhat Flexible
Academic Rating: ★★★★

Inside the Classroom

Nearing its 200th birthday, this elite liberal arts school named after the Revolutionary War hero the Marquis de Lafayette, offers a rare blend of an intimate academic experience mixed with big- time sports and prominent Greek life. Roughly 2,500 students comprise the student body at this undergraduate-only liberal arts school in quiet Easton, Pennsylvania. Undergrads are a high-caliber lot, possessing academic credentials only a touch below archrival Lehigh University.

Lafayette offers fifty-one areas over four academic divisions: engineering, humanities, natural sciences, and the social sciences. It also allows for self-designed majors such as behavioral economics, environmental issues and policy, or nanoscience. All undergrads delve into a first- year seminar during fall of their freshman year, a course designed to strengthen writing, thinking, and speaking abilities. Other required components of the school's common course of study include a year of foreign language, a quantitative reasoning course, two classes under the umbrella of global and multiculturalism, and at least a singular foray into each of the college's academic divisions.

One-on-one attention from professors is a reality at Lafayette, thanks to a 10:1 student-to-faculty ratio and no graduate students to compete with. A solid 62 percent of sections contain fewer than twenty students; 16 percent enroll nine or fewer. By the time senior year is nearing its completion, 52 percent of students have completed a research experience with a faculty member. The school invests almost half a million dollars annually in funding undergraduate research. A majority of students also have studied for a semester in a foreign country as 60 percent of graduates elect to study abroad in one of fifty locations. In addition to semester-long options, Lafayette offers truncated study abroad opportunities during semester breaks.

Of the 609 degrees conferred in 2018, engineering was the discipline in which the largest number of degrees were earned, accounting for a whopping 22 percent. The engineering program is one of the best in the country among non-doctoral granting institutions. Economics was the next most commonly conferred degree and is also one of Lafayette's strongest. Other popular and well-regarded programs include psychology, international affairs, and film studies. On the whole, Lafayette students well with employers and top graduate schools but also experience success when applying for prestigious fellowships. Named a top Fulbright producer, Lafayette had four winners in 2017-18. In recent years, it has had graduates land Gilman, Goldwater, and Udall Scholarships.

Outside the Classroom

In sleepy Easton, 96 percent of undergrads lay their heads at night inside college-owned housing. Greek life, which was under a microscope after a 2012 hazing death, has survived and thrived, still drawing 39 percent of the student body into fraternities and sororities. Athletics are also a central part of the Lafayette experience as the Leopards compete in twenty-three NCAA Division I sports as well as in more than fifty club and intramural programs. Games against rival Lehigh garner a high level of interest. Over 200 student-run organizations are active. For those interested in the performing arts, twenty-four such clubs are on the menu. There are forty-three cultural and/or service organizations that help contribute a collective 20,000 annual hours of charitable engagement. Nature lovers aren't far from the Pocono Mountains that offer all of the hiking, snowboarding, skiing, tubing, and fishing you can handle. Almost equidistant (in terms of travel time) between New York City and Philadelphia, big-city fun is only a car ride away. Easton is a small town with plenty of history and some nice eateries, but campus is the hub of the social experience.

Career Services

The recently renamed Gateway Career Center is staffed by eleven professional employees (not counting office assistants or database managers) who work in career counseling, employer relations, internship coordination, or graduate school advising. That 236:1 student-to-advisor ratio is better-than-average when compared to other schools featured in this guide. Thanks to such generous staffing, counselors can offer distinct services to students at every phase of their college education, beginning with career exploration activities during freshman year. Mock interviews, resume development, internship/externship discovery, or individualized career/grad school counseling is available at any time.

Large-scale events, such as the Fall Career Fair, attract more than sixty employers including Goldman Sachs, ExxonMobil, and Fidelity Investments. The Gateway Career Center does an excellent job guiding students into internships and other meaningful opportunities for hands-on learning. By senior year 78 percent of Lafayette undergrads have completed an internship, externship, or other field experience. A robust 40 percent of recent grads found their jobs directly through campus recruiting and/or the alumni network. On-campus interviews take place October-November and again from February-April. With a high level of personalized offerings and excellent career and graduate school outcomes, the Gateway Career Center accomplishes its mission on behalf of its undergraduates.

Professional Outcomes

Within six months of graduation, a stellar 97 percent of the Class of 2018 had already landed full-time jobs or were enrolled in graduate/professional school. The most commonly procured jobs are in business development, education, operations, engineering, sales, finance, and research. Companies employing large numbers of Lafayette alumni include Merck, IBM, Morgan Stanley, Citi, Merrill Lynch, JP Morgan Chase Co., Deloitte, and EY. The average early career salary for a Lafayette graduate is over $62,000; by midcareer the average income reaches $121,000. Despite being a Pennsylvania institution, Philadelphia is the second most popular landing spot for alumni; New York City attracts nearly three times as many Leopards. Large pockets of alumni also can be found in DC, Boston, and San Francisco.

Those attending graduate school frequently land at some of the top programs in the country within their respective disciplines. Recent economics majors have entered business/econ programs at Stanford, the University of Chicago, and Yale. Government majors have gone on to study at Penn, Harvard, and GW. Chemistry majors go on to pursue PhDs at institutions such as Tulane, Princeton, and Emory. Medical school applicants with a 3.6 GPA or above enjoy a 75 percent acceptance rate, and dental school candidates find homes at a 94 percent clip. Recent graduates have matriculated into medical schools at Georgetown, UVA, Brown, Dartmouth, and Boston University. Law school applicants found homes at a perfect 100 percent rate, and those acceptances included many top law schools.

Admission

The 9,236 students jostling for a spot in the Lafayette Class of 2022 were granted acceptance at a 29 percent rate. The Class of 2021 was admitted at a slightly more generous 31 percent. The Class of 2022 possessed an average SAT score of 1345, ACT of 30, and average GPA of 3.51. Twenty-three incoming freshmen were the valedictorian or salutatorian of their high school classes; 52 percent hailed from the top 10 percent, and 78 percent from the top quarter. A decade ago, Lafayette was a touch easier to get into. The acceptance rate in 2008-09 was 37 percent, and the 75th percentile SAT score was 1370, a figure closer to the average SAT score held by today's freshmen. However, students' class rank from that year shows that 65 percent placed in the top 10 percent of their high school classes, and 93 percent were in the top quarter. Taken together, those figures paint a muddled picture of whether Lafayette is more or less difficult to gain acceptance into than it was a decade ago.

In the eyes of the admissions committee at Lafayette, two factors receive the highest level of consideration—rigor of coursework and GPA. The next tier of factors includes test scores, class rank, essays, recommendations, extracurricular activities, the interview, character/personal qualities, and talent/ability. Those applying early decision were accepted at a 52 percent clip and accounted for more than half of entering freshmen in the 2018-19 academic year. Lafayette is a competitive institution but not out of reach for students with SAT scores in the 1300s and/or a less-than-pristine transcript. Applying early yields a strong advantage in the admissions process as the acceptance rate is higher, and a large chunk of the spots in the freshman class are already occupied by the time applicants enter the regular round.

Worth Your Money?

The annual bill to attend Lafayette exceeds $73,000. Eleven percent of undergrads do receive merit aid averaging $29k. Only one-third of undergraduates currently attending Lafayette receive any aid at all. The good news is that those who are awarded a grant see 100 percent of their need met, and the average total is over $45,000. The school's excellent offerings in engineering and strong networks in Philly and NYC lead to generally high starting salaries, making it possible for most to pay their student loans without too much economic pain.

FINANCIAL
Institutional Type: Private
In-State Tuition: $54,512
Out-of-State Tuition: $54,512
Room & Board: $16,264
Required Fees: $1,240
Books & Supplies: $1,000

Avg. Need-Based Aid: $44,741
Avg. % of Need Met: 100%

Avg. Merit-Based Aid: $29,253
% Receiving Merit-Based Aid: 11%

Avg. Cumulative Debt: $26,341
% of Students Borrowing: 39%

CAREER
Who Recruits
1. Gilbane Building
2. Crayola
3. SMC Partners
4. MarketAxess
5. Whiting-Turner Contracting

Notable Internships
1. Disney Streaming Services
2. RCA Records
3. Cisco

Top Industries
1. Business
2. Education
3. Operations
4. Engineering
5. Sales

Top Employers
1. Merck
2. IBM
3. Morgan Stanley
4. Citi
5. Deloitte

Where Alumni Work
1. New York City
2. Philadelphia
3. Allentown, PA
4. Boston
5. Washington, DC

Median Earnings
College Scorecard (Early Career): $68,600
EOP (Early Career): $75,300
PayScale (Mid-Career): $122,500

RANKINGS
Forbes: 57
Money: 67
U.S. News: 39, Liberal Arts Colleges
Wall Street Journal/THE: 87 (T)
Washington Monthly: 26, Liberal Arts Colleges

#CollegesWorthYourMoney

Lawrence University

Appleton, Wisconsin | Admissions Phone: 920-832-6500

Inside the Classroom

The history of Lawrence University, a tiny liberal arts school in Appleton, Wisconsin, is as unique as its present-day educational offerings. One of the earliest (ninth, to be precise) coeducational colleges in the United States and one of the top music conservatories anywhere, the nearly 1,500 undergraduates on campus today enjoy an intimate academic environment in which the largest number of degrees conferred are in the performing arts. It is the only school in the nation whose college of arts and sciences and music conservatory are both 100 percent populated by undergraduates. There are thirty-five distinct majors as well as the option to complete a five-year double major from both the conservatory and A&S; like we said, LU is unique.

Operating on a trimester calendar, the academic year is comprised of ten-week fall, winter, and spring sessions. For more than seventy years, part of the LU core curriculum has been a yearlong Freshman Studies program that in a small, seminar-style classroom explores questions like "What is the best sort of life for human beings? Are there limits to human knowledge? How should we respond to injustice and suffering?" From there, Lawrence undergrads encounter a dose of humanities, natural science, social science, and fine arts offerings and must show competency in a foreign language, quantitative reasoning, and a writing/speaking-intensive course. Every graduate completes a Senior Experience that can take the form of a paper, performance, portfolio, or exhibition.

An 8:1 student/faculty ratio allows for extremely small class sizes—the majority of sections contain only ten to nineteen students, and many independent study/1:1 music instruction courses also are available. With Lawrence being a "university" in name only, undergraduate research opportunities are wide open. Professors are expected to allow undergraduates access to their research studies; for example, every member of the Chemistry Department has to run an active research group. The Lawrence University Research Fellows (LURF) program offers a stipend during ten-week, research-focused terms. All told, close to two-thirds of LU students gain hands-on research experience at some point during their four years of study. The college strongly encourages students to study abroad, and roughly 40 percent take the plunge. Sponsored opportunities include the London Lawrence Center or the Francophile Seminar in Dakar, Senegal.

Biology (14), social sciences (19 percent), and performing arts (22 percent) comprise the most popular areas of study at LU. The latter includes Lawrence's world-renowned Conservatory of Music, which enrolls approximately 350 undergraduates. Extremely strong natural science programs allow the university to be a top producer of future STEM PhDs. It is also a top producer of Fulbright Scholars, with five to its credit in the 2018-19 year. Other prestigious fellowships won by Class of 2018 members include a Watson Fellowship and a Goldwater Scholarship.

Outside the Classroom

Lawrence's 88-acre campus houses 100 percent of freshmen and 94 percent of the undergraduate student body in five residence halls. The Greek presence is minimal with 8 percent of men affiliated with frats and 10 percent of women members of sororities. One-quarter of the population are NCAA Division III varsity athletes competing on one of the ten men's or nine women's squads known as the Vikings. Non-sports events that draw many participants include Fall Festival, Winter Carnival, and the Great Midwest Trivia Contest, a fifty-hour marathon that has drawn national media attention. There are over one hundred clubs and activities, and virtually every student on campus is involved in at least one. Volunteer organizations are popular, and students give a collective 10,000 hours per year. Three or four times per year campus will close for an hour while everyone flocks to Memorial Chapel for convocation where a famous speaker like Maya Angelou or David Sedaris will address the student body. If the Appleton campus that overlooks the Fox River doesn't provide enough natural beauty for you, the college also owns 425+ acres on the shores of Lake Michigan that can be utilized for hiking, ice skating, and camping. Appleton is a safe and enjoyable small town with a population around 70,000 that contains ample bars, restaurants, and shops. The town is only about a thirty-minute drive from Green Bay and about ninety minutes from Milwaukee.

Career Services

The Center for Career, Life and Community Engagement employs eight full-time staff members in employer and alumni relations, Career advisor, and pre-professional advising and major fellowships. That student-to-advisor ratio of 184:1 is strong when compared to other colleges featured in this guide, and it allows the career services staff to carve out time even for freshmen. All first-years are encouraged to come in for at least a fifteen- or twenty-minute counseling session. The center's stated mission is "preparing students for lives of achievement, responsible and meaningful citizenship, lifelong learning, and personal fulfillment," and it offers ample one-on-one counseling toward those aims.

Lawrence University

Students can locate internship opportunities through Lawrence Link or through face-to-face counseling sessions. Many students pursue internships with nonprofit institutions, charitable organizations, and museums, although several recent undergrads have landed positions at Apple, Google, and JPMorgan Chase. In part due to the school's small size and location, recruiting or on-campus interviewing visits from major employers are not frequent occurrences, and the school does not host a major job fair. Unfortunately, LU does not publicize data such as the percentage of students who land an internship, the number of in-person counseling sessions per year, or information about employers visiting campus. In the absence of such information and given the low starting salaries of recent graduates, it appears that some improvement may be needed in those areas.

Professional Outcomes

Of the 329 graduates in the Class of 2017, an impressive 98 percent had already reached their next employment or postsecondary destination. Among the 57 percent of that group who had landed their first jobs, fifty-eight grads were working in business/finance, forty-one in social services/nonprofit, eighteen in the arts, thirteen in health care/pharmaceutical, and twelve in media/communications. Companies presently employing more than a dozen Lawrence alumni include Deloitte, Epic Systems, Wells Fargo, Northwestern Mutual, US Bank, and UnitedHealth Group. Most students continue to reside in the Midwest after graduating. Greater Chicago; Oshkosh, Wisconsin; Greater Minneapolis-St. Paul; and Greater Milwaukee boast the greatest number of alums. Starting salaries for recent graduating classes average around $42,000, lower than many in its peer group that includes St. Olaf, Grinnell, and Carleton (whose graduates pull in over $10k more).

Over the last few years graduates have gone on to master's and doctoral programs at a wide range of universities on the prestige spectrum. Highlighting that list are elite schools Carnegie Mellon, Duke, Dartmouth, Emory, Georgetown, University of Pennsylvania, and Washington University in St. Louis. Medical school acceptance rates fluctuate between 67 and 75 percent, significantly higher than the national average, even in down years. Recent graduates have matriculated into medical schools at Johns Hopkins, the University of Chicago, Northwestern, Boston University, and the University of Wisconsin. According to the National Science Foundation, Lawrence produces the fourteenth most future science and engineering PhDs among liberal arts colleges.

Admission

It's hard to find a school of better quality that has a greater acceptance rate than Lawrence's 62 percent. The university is trending in a more selective direction as the admit rate was an even more generous 73 percent five years ago, but chances remain strong, even for less-than-perfect high schoolers. While 35 percent did place in the top 10 percent of their graduating class and 31 percent possessed a GPA of greater than 3.75, many others brought more middling credentials to the table. The average GPA for admitted students is 3.46, and 31 percent did not land in the top 25 percent of their high school cohort. This school does not require SATs or ACTs but, among those who elected to submit scores anyway, the mid-50 percent range was 1210-1450 on the SAT and 27-31 on the ACT.

Lawrence was early to the test-optional party, jettisoning mandatory standardized test submission in 2006. As a result, GPA, rigor of coursework, class rank, talent/ability, and character/personal qualities are perched atop the list of most important factors. The admissions essay, recommendations, extracurricular activities, and an interview, which is recommended but not required, make up the second rung of "important factors." Test scores are merely "considered"; 41 percent of enrolled freshmen did submit SAT scores to go along with 31 percent who submitted results from the ACT. Few apply early decision; only twenty-four did so in 2018, and twenty were accepted. A safety school for many applying to even more prestigious Midwestern liberal arts institutions, only about 20 percent of those admitted actually enroll. Thus, it is advantageous to communicate your genuine interest in attending throughout the application process.

Worth Your Money?

The sticker price (including room and board and all fees) at Lawrence is $61,716, but few receive an annual bill for that amount. Over two-thirds of undergraduates receive need-based aid for an average of $39,000, and 43 percent of those awarded aid see 100 percent of their demonstrated need met. A substantial number of students, approximately one-third, receive an average merit aid award of more than $26k. Because the most commonly studied fields at LU are not among the highest paying, students need to adjust the value of loans they are willing to take out accordingly. That said, this school provides an amazing educational experience, particularly for those interested in performance and academia, and it typically provides enough financial aid to make a Lawrence degree affordable.

FINANCIAL
Institutional Type: Private
In-State Tuition: $48,822
Out-of-State Tuition: $48,822
Room & Board: $10,719
Required Fees: $300
Books & Supplies: $900

Avg. Need-Based Aid: $39,106
Avg. % of Need Met: 95%

Avg. Merit-Based Aid: $26,419
% Receiving Merit-Based Aid: 33%

Avg. Cumulative Debt: $31,136
% of Students Borrowing: 67%

CAREER
Who Recruits
1. M3 Insurance
2. Enterprise Holdings
3. Hauser Advertising
4. McAdam Financial
5. Air Wisconsin Airlines, LLC

Notable Internships
1. American Museum of Natural History
2. Uber
3. EY

Top Industries
1. Education
2. Business
3. Operations
4. Arts & Design
5. Social Services

Top Employers
1. US Bank
2. Epic
3. Northwestern Mutual
4. Target
5. Wells Fargo

Where Alumni Work
1. Chicago
2. Oshkosh, WI
3. Minneapolis
4. Milwaukee
5. New York City

Median Earnings
College Scorecard (Early Career): $44,100
EOP (Early Career): $44,500
PayScale (Mid-Career): $98,800

RANKINGS
Forbes: 193
Money: 183
U.S. News: 58, Liberal Arts Colleges
Wall Street Journal/THE: 189 (T)
Washington Monthly: 107, Liberal Arts Colleges

#CollegesWorthYourMoney

Lehigh University

Bethlehem, Pennsylvania | Admissions Phone: 610-758-3100

ADMISSION
Admission Rate: 22%
Admission Rate - Men: 20%
Admission Rate - Women: 25%
EA Admission Rate: Not Offered
ED Admission Rate: 60%
Admission Rate (5-Year Trend): -9%
ED Admission Rate (5-Year Trend): 0%
% of Admits Attending (Yield): 37%
Transfer Admission Rate: 24%

\# Offered Wait List: 7,737
\# Accepted Wait List: 3,358
\# Admitted Wait List: 69

SAT Reading/Writing (Middle 50%): 620-690
SAT Math (Middle 50%): 650-760
ACT Composite (Middle 50%): 29-33
Testing Policy: ACT/SAT Required
SAT Superscore: Yes
ACT Superscore: Yes

% Graduated in Top 10% of HS Class: 58%
% Graduated in Top 25% of HS Class: 88%
% Graduated in Top 50% of HS Class: 99%

ENROLLMENT
Total Undergraduate Enrollment: 5,047
% Part-Time: 1%
% Male: 54%
% Female: 46%
% Out-of-State: 73%
% Fraternity: 30%
% Sorority: 39%
% On-Campus (Freshman): 99%
% On-Campus (All Undergraduate): 63%

% African-American: 3%
% Asian: 8%
% Hispanic: 10%
% White: 63%
% Other: 3%
% Race or Ethnicity Unknown: 4%
% International: 9%
% Low-Income: 17%

ACADEMICS
Student-to-Faculty Ratio: 9:1
% of Classes Under 20: 50%
% of Classes Under 40: 82%
% Full-Time Faculty: 76%
% Full-Time Faculty w/ Terminal Degree: 95%

Top Programs
Accounting
Computer Science
Earth and Environmental Sciences
Engineering
Finance
International Relations
Psychology

Retention Rate: 94%
4-Year Graduation Rate: 72%
6-Year Graduation Rate: 87%

Curricular Flexibility: Somewhat Flexible
Academic Rating: ★★★★

Inside the Classroom

Emblematic of the American economy as a whole, the once great industrial town of Bethlehem, Pennsylvania, is now highlighted by a research university known for preparing the next generation of problem-solving engineers. Lehigh University is a research powerhouse that caters to only 5,075 undergraduate students, allowing for lots of individualized attention from expert faculty in world-class facilities. There are three colleges within the larger university: the College of Arts & Sciences, the College of Business & Economics, and the prestigious Rossin College of Engineering and Applied Sciences.

Despite its modest size, Lehigh offers more than one hundred undergraduate degree programs and runs 2,300+ courses each school year. Academic requirements vary by school but, notably, none possess a foreign language mandate. In the College of Arts & Sciences students must complete two semesters of Composition & Literature, First-Year Seminar, one math course, and eight credits in each of the humanities, natural sciences, and social sciences. The core curricula in the College of Business & Economics includes foundational courses in decision-making and business principles as well as introductory coursework in accounting, economics, marketing, management, and finance (no matter which of those concentrations you choose). Lastly, all business students must complete a senior capstone project. Within the Rossin College of Engineering and Applied Science undergrads must knock out ten credits of English and economics and thirteen credits in the humanities. There are also two innovative programs that require a foray into other disciplines—the Integrated Business & Engineering Honors Program (IBE) and the Integrated Degree Engineering, Arts & Sciences Honors Programs (IDEAS).

Lehigh has a 9:1 student-to-faculty ratio, but classes aren't as tiny as one might expect with such favorable staffing numbers. The average class size is twenty-nine but, on the plus side, 45 percent of courses have enrollments of nineteen or fewer. Undergraduate research is commonplace, particularly within the engineering school. Each year, 40 percent of engineering students gain faculty-led research experience. Additionally, 43 percent of graduates engage in some type of international experience, whether it's a semester of academic study abroad or a foreign-based internship. Roughly half of those students took courses in one of 250 study abroad programs approved by the university.

With a highly ranked engineering school, it's easy to view Lehigh as primarily a techie haven. Surprisingly, the majority of students pursue other programs, with Lehigh's well-regarded business school drawing the most majors (34%). Competitive fellowship and scholarship programs look favorably upon the university. Ten undergrads were awarded Gilman Scholarships in 2018, and three students won National Science Foundation Fellowships the year prior.

Outside the Classroom

Lehigh's three contiguous campuses account for 1,600 picturesque acres. Only 65 percent of students live on campus, and most of those are underclassmen who are required to reside in college-owned housing. The school plans to add 1,000 undergraduate students by 2026 and is presently building additional on-campus housing to accommodate the increased student population. Even with 35 percent of students living off campus, this is an incredibly involved student body with 99 percent involved in some type of extracurricular activity. Greek life is a powerful force with 43 percent of women joining sororities and one-third of men pledging a fraternity. On the athletics front, the Mountain Hawks compete in twenty-five intercollegiate sports, mostly in the NCAA Division I Patriot League. An additional forty-three intramural and club teams claim another 2,900 participants annually. On the non-sports front there are 200+ student organizations at Lehigh and over 250 art events on campus annually. Service-oriented clubs are popular and account for 65,000 collective hours of community service per year. Bethlehem is known more for its industrial history as a hub of steel production than for a thrilling nightlife, but students with a car can get to Philly in an hour and a half or New York City in a little over two hours.

Career Services

The Center for Career and Professional Development (CCPD) is staffed by ten professional employees (not counting business managers or interns) who work in career counseling, employer engagement, or graduate school advising. That 507:1 student-to-advisor ratio is within the average range of universities profiled in this guide. Yet, by almost any metric, the level of support offered to the school's undergraduates is of superior quality.

In 2017-18, the CCPD enticed more than 6,900 attendees to its events (more than the entire undergraduate population). The fall and spring career expos draw large student crowds and are attended by as many as 140 employers, including many major corporations. Counselors held an outstanding 2,468 one-on-one advising sessions and achieved 12,000+ total engagements through in-person and online interaction. Perhaps most impressive is the number of on-campus interviews conducted in 2017-18—2,754—more than double the number of graduating seniors that year. Lehigh's career services staff also does a superb job facilitating internships and other valuable immersive experiences. An exceptional 89 percent of Class of 2018 members completed at least one internship or externship. Lehigh's Center for Career and Professional Development provides a top-notch level of service to its undergraduate clientele, and those efforts translate into stellar employment and graduate school outcomes.

Professional Outcomes

The Class of 2018 quickly found its way toward the next productive step in their lives with 95 percent landing jobs or grad school placements within six months of leaving Lehigh. Among graduates of the School of Business and Economics, the top industries entered by graduates were financial services (28 percent), accounting (19 percent), consulting (9 percent), and marketing (6 percent). Top employers of recent business degree earners include Amazon, CitiGroup, Deloitte, EY, KPMG, Morgan Stanley, and PwC. Rossin College of Engineering and Applied Science graduates flocked to companies such as ExxonMobil, GE, Google, IBM, Lockheed Martin, Merck, and Microsoft. Arts & Sciences graduates secured employment at places like CBS, People Magazine, and the National Institutes of Health. Across all three schools, the average starting salary was $65,000 with computer science majors on the high end at $87k and math and natural sciences majors on the low end at $48k.

Of those heading straight to graduate/professional school, 31 percent were studying engineering, 24 percent were pursuing business degrees, 10 percent were training for health professions, and 4 percent had entered law school. In 2018, a phenomenal 91 percent of medical school applicants found at least one acceptance. That cohort possessed an average GPA of 3.7 and MCAT scores in the 85th percentile. Recent med school acceptances included Boston University School of Medicine, Harvard School of Dental Medicine, and Johns Hopkins School of Medicine. Over the past three years law school applicants were successful 93 percent of the time and were welcomed by institutions such as the University of Pennsylvania, Tulane, Temple, and Villanova. Those pursuing a master's or a PhD from the Class of 2018 did so at Columbia, Duke, Stanford, Berkeley, Brown, Johns Hopkins, and a number of other first-class universities.

Admission

Lehigh experienced a 13 percent spike in applications between 2018 and 2017 that led to an all-time low 22 percent acceptance rate for those jockeying for a spot in the Class of 2022. Freshmen entering Lehigh for the 2018-19 school year possessed middle-50 percent scores of 1270-1450 on the SAT and 29-33 on the ACT. A similar number of students submit scores from each exam. Fifty-eight percent of entering freshmen in 2018-19 placed in the top decile of their high school class, and 88 percent were in the top quartile.

Five factors sit perched atop the list of criteria considered by the Lehigh admissions committee: rigor of courses, GPA, recommendations, extracurricular activities, and character/personal qualities. The next rung of factors deemed "important" include standardized test scores, essays, talent/ability, volunteer work, and demonstrated interest. On the subject of demonstrated interest, Lehigh places high value on an applicant's level of commitment to attending the university. To quantify that importance, early decision applicants are admitted at a rate of 60 percent, almost three times the acceptance rate during the regular cycle. Early decision applicants comprised 56 percent of the incoming class. Women face slightly better odds, generally sporting acceptance rates 5-7 percent better than male applicants. Clearly, applying early is a major edge at Lehigh, but you'll need to be toward the top of your class and have taken a healthy dose of AP and honors courses, particularly in STEM areas.

Worth Your Money?

Those who don't qualify for financial aid will not receive much help from Lehigh—fewer than 10 percent of attendees receive merit aid. Fortunately, the $71,465 annual cost of attendance is knocked down significantly for the 43 percent of undergraduates who qualify for need-based aid; many see 100 percent of their demonstrated need met by the university, and the average annual grant is for $45k. With extremely high starting salaries, this school is likely to pay you back, particularly if you major in the business/engineering realm.

FINANCIAL
Institutional Type: Private
In-State Tuition: $54,790
Out-of-State Tuition: $54,790
Room & Board: $14,160
Required Fees: $450
Books & Supplies: $1,000

Avg. Need-Based Aid: $44,745
Avg. % of Need Met: 97%

Avg. Merit-Based Aid: $11,097
% Receiving Merit-Based Aid: 9%

Avg. Cumulative Debt: $35,109
% of Students Borrowing: 50%

CAREER
Who Recruits
1. Knowles Corporation
2. Mineral Technologies Inc.
3. SIG
4. Tge LiRo Group
5. Crayola

Notable Internships
1. Prudenial Financial
2. Barclays
3. Visa

Top Industries
1. Business
2. Engineering
3. Education
4. Operations
5. Research

Top Employers
1. Merck
2. EY
3. PwC
4. IBM
5. Deloitte

Where Alumni Work
1. New York City
2. Allentown, PA
3. Philadelphia
4. Boston
5. Washington, DC

Median Earnings
College Scorecard (Early Career): $81,900
EOP (Early Career): $81,200
PayScale (Mid-Career): $134,100

RANKINGS
Forbes: 67
Money: 111
U.S. News: 50 (T), National Universities
Wall Street Journal/THE: 55
Washington Monthly: 71, National Universities

#CollegesWorthYourMoney

Loyola University Maryland

Baltimore, Maryland | Admissions Phone: 410-617-5012

Inside the Classroom

College consumers can sometimes find the Loyola brand hard to grasp. After all, there is Loyola University Chicago, Loyola University New Orleans, Loyola Marymount University in Los Angeles, and the school we are profiling here—Loyola University Maryland—and *none* of the schools is affiliated in any way with the others. While all honor St. Ignatius, the Jesuit founder, Loyola University Maryland is its own distinct entity and is a rare school where the acceptance rate and four-year graduation rate both hover around 80 percent. Offering thirty-five undergraduate programs through its three schools, Loyola College (arts and sciences), the Sellinger School of Business and Management, and the School of Education, Loyola services an undergraduate population of 3,879, only 20 percent of whom are Maryland residents

Consistent with the Jesuit ideology of *cura personalis*, Loyola has created a liberal arts curriculum designed to help develop the whole person and produce well-rounded citizens. This extensive seventeen-course set of requirements includes writing, history, literature, foreign language, social sciences, fine arts, mathematics, theology, philosophy, ethics, and diversity. Students in the small-but-excellent Honors Program follow an identical path but complete their core curriculum within honors-only sections.

A 12:1 student-to-faculty ratio leads to average class sizes of only twenty students. The vast majority of courses enroll between ten and twenty-nine students, 12 percent have a single-digit enrollment, and of 906 total sections only fourteen contained forty or more undergraduates. Students are encouraged to apply for undergraduate research opportunities such as the Hauber Summer Research Fellowship Program which, in 2019, gave fourteen students in the natural and applied sciences fields a chance to conduct ten weeks of independent research. Biology majors can enroll in two courses that facilitate experiential research opportunities. Those with wanderlust will find plenty of kindred spirits and no shortage of options; there are twenty countries that students can choose from as study abroad options, and the participation rate exceeds 60 percent, one of the highest figures of any master's-granting school in the nation.

Almost two-fifths of the degrees conferred are in the area of business/marketing, making it, by far, the school's most popular area of concentration. Next are communication/journalism (10 percent), the social sciences (8 percent), psychology (7 percent), and biology (6 percent). The Sellinger School of Business and Management has a solid reputation beyond the immediate region, and the Department of Communication has an excellent record of placing students within media organizations. The school's push for international study translated to a record number of Fulbright Scholars in 2019 with eight winners. Additionally, three current students captured Gilman Scholarships.

Outside the Classroom

If you are looking for a school where just about everyone lives in a tightknit community on campus, then the Loyola Maryland experience is for you. Freshmen occupy university-owned dorms at a 97 percent clip, and 82 percent of the total student body resides on this 81-acre wooded campus that isn't what you'd expect to find in the middle of Baltimore. Loyola's seventeen residence halls are some of the best-rated college accommodations in the entire country. As is the case at many Jesuit institutions, there are no sororities or fraternities at this school, but there are 200+ clubs, including seventeen community service organizations, fourteen dance groups, and twelve honors societies. Service is popular as 80 percent of the student body engages in some type of charitable endeavor. Religion plays a major role as students are predominately Catholic—27 percent attended Catholic high schools. The gender split on campus is approaching 60/40 in favor of women. Loyola has a strong athletics program that features eighteen NCAA Division I teams that play in the Patriot League. Johns Hopkins is its biggest rival, and the annual lacrosse showdown is a big deal. There are also twenty-six club teams, and 20 percent of students participate in intramural leagues. Recreational amenities include a ten-lane pool, rock climbing wall, and indoor track. Not known as a big party school, there are plenty of safe commercial pockets in the city of Baltimore worth exploring, and DC is only an hour away for weekend trips.

Career Services

The Career Center at Loyola Maryland is manned by seven professionals with expertise in career counseling and employer outreach. That works out to a 554:1 student-to-advisor ratio, which is within the average range of colleges featured in this guide. This office keeps careful track of its own statistics that paint a picture of a supportive and highly available career services staff offering ample opportunity to connect with relevant employers.

In the 2017-18 school year the office posted 12,805 jobs and 4,661 internships on Handshake, held 2,218 counseling appointments, and attracted 2,307 students to networking events, workshops, career fairs, and information sessions. For a small university, it's highly impressive that 111 companies and organizations interviewed seniors on campus. In total, 194 unique employers visited campus. A helpful alumni base 60,000 strong is also willing to lend a hand to those about to launch their careers. If you're looking to land a position far from Baltimore, Loyola Marymount's Career Center has reciprocity with twenty-eight other Jesuit institution's career centers around the country. The school also has forged many strong internship partners. For example, within the Department of Writing, partners include nine publications and ten nonprofits that regularly take Loyola interns. Career fairs drew eighty-nine employers, and official sponsors of the fairs included Bank of America, Dixon Hughes Goodman (the largest accounting firm in the South), and CareFirst BlueCross BlueShield. In sum, the Loyola Career Center directly connects with more than half of the undergraduate student body each year and facilitates a solid number of industry connections, making it a highly useful resource for all current students.

Professional Outcomes

Members of the Class of 2017 found their way to their next employment, volunteer, or grad school home within six months of receiving their diplomas at a stellar 97 percent clip. Major companies and organizations employing members of this cohort include Accenture, Booz Allen Hamilton, Bloomberg, Goldman Sachs, NASA, the National Institutes of Health, the New York Giants (NFL), Sony/ATV Music Publishing, and Walt Disney Company. Employers of the overall greatest number of alumni include T. Rowe Price, Northrup Grumman, Morgan Stanley, JPMorgan Chase, PwC, EY, Black & Decker, and Deloitte. The average starting salary for a Loyola graduate is $51,000 with social sciences majors bringing home a mean salary of $41k and degree-earners in the natural and applied sciences averaging $58k. Baltimore, New York City, DC, Philly, and Boston woo the most Greyhound alumni.

Twenty-three percent of the members of the Class of 2017 immediately enrolled in graduate or professional school after completing their undergraduate work at Loyola Maryland. Many stayed in the area, either at Loyola itself, the University of Maryland, or in the DC or Philadelphia areas at schools like George Washington, Temple University, or Villanova. Some members earned a spot at elite graduate institutions like Brown, Columbia, Duke, Northwestern, and the University of Pennsylvania. Over the last decade the percentage of successful law school applicants has vacillated between 77 percent and 93 percent, and Loyola grads are currently pursuing their legal education at Villanova, George Washington, UC Berkeley, and the University of Maryland. From 2015-2019 medical school applicants who obtained a committee letter supporting their candidacy enjoyed a 72 percent acceptance rate. Recent acceptances include some of the top medical schools in the country such as Boston University, Tufts, Harvard, and Georgetown.

Admission

Getting into Loyola is not a harrowing process, even if you hit a few bumps along your academic road. The acceptance rate for a place in the Class of 2022 was an unintimidating 79 percent, and that doesn't show any signs of falling as the school has only a 13 percent yield rate; in other terms, 87 percent of those who are accepted ultimately enroll at another institution. Loyola is test-optional, but most 2018-19 freshman submitted scores—63 percent included SATs and 25 percent included ACTs as part of their applications. The mid-50 percent scores were 25-30 on the ACT and 1140-1320 on the SAT. The average high school GPA earned by entering members of this class was 3.5, and while 28 percent ranked in the top decile of their graduating class and 61 percent were in the top quartile, 10 percent did not even rank in the top 50 percent.

This committee means what it says when it declares that it does "not use a formula or have strict cutoffs. Instead, the admission office's goal is to conduct a balanced and individual review, taking a number of factors into account." At the top of that list are GPA, rigor of secondary school record, recommendations, the essay, and character/personal qualities. Extracurricular activities, volunteer work, and talent/ability also receive strong consideration. Loyola is a school where bright but perhaps late-blooming teens can find a welcoming institution that will offer a top-notch Jesuit education.

Worth Your Money?

Living on campus brings the total annual sticker price to a whopping $67,380, a steep price to pay for any school. At that cost, it is hard to justify attending Loyola University Maryland if you are in a situation where you will need to take out large loans; the average Greyhound's debt is over $32,000. However, it is worth applying to see what kind of aid package you receive. Freshmen in 2018-19 who qualified for some type of aid averaged a package just shy of $19,000. If the total cost of attendance is comparable to other institutions to which you are accepted, a degree from this university can certainly make it worth your money.

FINANCIAL
Institutional Type: Private
In-State Tuition: $48,700
Out-of-State Tuition: $48,700
Room & Board: $14,710
Required Fees: $1,565
Books & Supplies: $1,250

Avg. Need-Based Aid: $18,861
Avg. % of Need Met: 88%

Avg. Merit-Based Aid: $18,390
% Receiving Merit-Based Aid: 75%

Avg. Cumulative Debt: N/A
% of Students Borrowing: N/A

CAREER
Who Recruits
1. Legg Mason
2. Baltimore Orioles
3. T. Rowe Price
4. Cisco
5. Stanley Black & Decker

Notable Internships
1. LGT Capital Partners
2. National Bank of Canada
3. Fidelity Investments

Top Industries
1. Business
2. Education
3. Operations
4. Finance
5. Sales

Top Employers
1. T. Rowe Price
2. Northrop Grumman
3. Morgan Stanley
4. JPMorgan Chase
5. PwC

Where Alumni Work
1. Baltimore
2. New York City
3. Washington, DC
4. Philadelphia
5. Boston

Median Earnings
College Scorecard (Early Career): $68,100
EOP (Early Career): $69,800
PayScale (Mid-Career): $111,200

RANKINGS
Forbes: 124
Money: 303
U.S. News: 4, Regional North
Wall Street Journal/THE: 208 (T)
Washington Monthly: N/A

#CollegesWorthYourMoney

Macalester College

St. Paul, Minnesota | Admissions Phone: 651-696-6357

ADMISSION
Admission Rate: 41%
Admission Rate - Men: 40%
Admission Rate - Women: 42%
EA Admission Rate: Not Offered
ED Admission Rate: 52%
Admission Rate (5-Year Trend): +7%
ED Admission Rate (5-Year Trend): -1%
% of Admits Attending (Yield): 25%
Transfer Admission Rate: 13%

Offered Wait List: 426
Accepted Wait List: 238
Admitted Wait List: 0

SAT Reading/Writing (Middle 50%): 650-730
SAT Math (Middle 50%): 660-770
ACT Composite (Middle 50%): 29-33
Testing Policy: ACT/SAT Required
SAT Superscore: Yes
ACT Superscore: Yes

% Graduated in Top 10% of HS Class: 63%
% Graduated in Top 25% of HS Class: 91%
% Graduated in Top 50% of HS Class: 99%

ENROLLMENT
Total Undergraduate Enrollment: 2,174
% Part-Time: 2%
% Male: 40%
% Female: 60%
% Out-of-State: 82%
% Fraternity: Not Offered
% Sorority: Not Offered
% On-Campus (Freshman): 100%
% On-Campus (All Undergraduate): 60%

% African-American: 3%
% Asian: 8%
% Hispanic: 8%
% White: 58%
% Other: 6%
% Race or Ethnicity Unknown: 0%
% International: 16%
% Low-Income: 17%

ACADEMICS
Student-to-Faculty Ratio: 10:1
% of Classes Under 20: 73%
% of Classes Under 40: 98%
% Full-Time Faculty: 71%
% Full-Time Faculty w/ Terminal Degree: 94%

Top Programs
Anthropology
Chemistry
Economics
Environmental Studies
Geography
International Studies
Mathematics
Political Science

Retention Rate: 96%
4-Year Graduation Rate: 85%
6-Year Graduation Rate: 90%

Curricular Flexibility: Somewhat Flexible
Academic Rating: ★★★★⏸

Inside the Classroom
One might expect a small liberal arts school in Minnesota to be set in a remote tundra, its own little universe surrounded by a stark landscape and frigid air. In the case of Macalester College, the frigid air would be accurate, but this collection of 2,133 undergraduate students is a rarity in the liberal arts world—it is situated in the metropolis of St. Paul on the border of Minneapolis. While typically lagging slightly behind rival Carleton College in most rankings, Macalester is every bit in the same league, boasting a strong reputation for rigorous academics that draw 85 percent of the school's student body from outside Minnesota and a stunning 24 percent from ninety-seven foreign countries.

International students aren't flocking to Mac for the weather or Great Plains scenery; they are here for the academic reputation. Students can choose from thirty-nine majors and over 800 courses that are offered each academic year. Requirements for all students are fairly straightforward and include a first-year course that is a small, writing-intensive seminar, courses in each of the schools four divisions—Fine Arts, Humanities, Social Studies, and Natural Science and Mathematics, and courses in multiculturalism and internationalism. Perhaps the most notable mandate is in foreign language where proficiency equivalent to four semesters of study must be demonstrated.

Being an undergraduate-only institution, Macalester students enjoy the full benefits of the school's 10:1 student-to-faculty ratio. The average class size is only seventeen students, and 17 percent of class sections have single-digit enrollments. Fewer than 2 percent of the overall courses contain more than forty students, so the chances are high that you will never be in a course where the professor does not know your name. That level of intimacy leads to plentiful chances for being part of faculty-led research, including through the Collaborative Summer Research Program that provides stipends for student-faculty research ventures. In total, 54 percent of students participate in some form of undergraduate research. Study abroad opportunities, typically twelve weeks in length, are taken advantage of by 60 percent of Macalester undergrads.

As an elite liberal arts institution with no attached graduate schools, Macalester possesses strong offerings across many different disciplines. Programs in economics, international studies, and mathematics are among the best anywhere. In addition, science majors of all varieties benefit from the school's strong reputation for premed and preparing future PhD scientists. Prestigious postgraduate fellowships are routinely awarded to Mac seniors. In the last decade, grads have walked away with fifty-seven Fulbright Scholarships, including eight such awards in 2018 alone. In that same time, students and alumni have procured a Rhodes Scholarship, thirty-nine National Science Foundation Fellowships, nine Watson Fellowships, four Goldwater Scholarships, and three Truman Scholarships.

Outside the Classroom
Due to limited availability of college-owned housing, only 60 percent of Macalester students live on campus. However, 100 percent of freshmen live in one of four residence halls for first-years; sophomores, who are also required to live on campus, have their own dorms as well. There is no Greek life here, so undergrads find other ways to forge deep bonds. With twenty-one sports teams and roughly 400 student-athletes, one-quarter of the student population dons a Scots jersey as they compete in NCAA Division III. Intramurals and club teams also draw heavy participation, leading to a majority of Mac students being involved in some type of formalized athletics. There are also ninety-nine student-run organizations, including eleven musical ensembles, student theater groups with 125 participants, three student publications, including the popular Mac Weekly, and a campus radio station, WMCN. The LGBTQ+ population on campus is notably large—25 percent identify in that category. This cozy 53-acre campus provides ample activity, but access to the city nightlife is quite easy by car. The Mall of America is less than a fifteen-minute drive from the college, and students also enjoy Minnesota's pro sports scene, museums, restaurants, and nightlife.

Career Services
The Career Development Center is staffed by seven professionals (not counting graduate/undergraduate fellows or office assistants), equating to a student-to-advisor ratio of 305:1, better than the average college included in this book. That level of support allows the CDC to implement its four-phase process of "explore/design/connect/launch" that ultimately results in favorable outcomes for graduates. Events such as the fall and spring career fairs are small in scale—the fall 2018 Career Fair was attended by thirty-five employers. In the 2018-19 school year, it held 1,918 one-on-one advising appointments and enticed 103 employers to recruit on campus.

Internships and/or mentored research experiences are enjoyed by 72 percent of Macalester undergraduates. Internships, specifically, are obtained and completed by 60 percent of students. In 2017-18, almost 400 students engaged in credit-bearing internships at organizations as varied as the US Department of State, EY, Minnesota Public Radio, the New York University School of Medicine, and Lockheed Martin. This strong internship program sets up students for a successful transition into a meaningful first job. Among 2018 grads who found employment within six months of leaving, 91 percent said their first job was congruent with their interests. While Macalester grads do not go on to earn high starting salaries, they do find fulfilling jobs aligned with their interests and have success entering and completing top graduate/professional degree programs.

Professional Outcomes

Six months after graduating 94 percent of the Macalester Class of 2018 had found employment, graduate school, or a fellowship; 6 percent were still actively seeking their next destination. Fifty-five percent of those finding employment landed with for-profit corporations, 20 percent with nonprofit organizations, 15 percent with educational institutions, and 9 percent with federal, state, or local government. Employers of recent grads include ABC News, Google, Goldman Sachs, Dow Chemical Company, McKinsey & Company, the ACLU, the National Cancer Institute, and National Geographic. Across all sectors, the average starting salary was $47,000. Geographically, 52 percent of grads elected to stay in the North Star State while many others migrated to the West Coast (13 percent), East Coast (11 percent) or overseas (8 percent).

Graduates from 2012-2017 most frequently attended graduate schools such as the University of Washington – Seattle (28), University of Wisconsin – Madison (25), Harvard (21), Georgetown (19), NYU (17), and Johns Hopkins (16). Those from the classes of 2017 and 2018 who enrolled in graduate school entered science and mathematics programs at a 42 percent rate. In those same years, 100 percent of Macalester grads who applied to graduate school received at least one acceptance. From 2007-2016 the college ranked fourteenth among liberal arts schools with the most grads who went on to earn PhDs. Among students with at least a 3.5 GPA and decent MCAT scores, 90 percent were admitted to at least one medical school. Recent medical school acceptances include Tufts University, Northwestern, Brown, and Washington University in St. Louis. The most popular medical school attended by alumni is the University of Minnesota – Twin Cities.

Admission

Macalester received just under 6,000 applications for admission into the Class of 2022, and it admitted 41 percent; of that group, 25 percent went on to enroll in the school. Admitted students averaged a 1430 on the SAT and a 32 on the ACT. An impressive 70 percent hailed from the top decile of their high school's graduating class. The profile of the average freshman who enrolls is a bit more down to earth with 63 percent in the top 10 percent of their high school class and a 33 ACT representing the 75th percentile. Comparing this incoming freshman class to the freshman cohort of a decade earlier, there are few differences to be found. With a comparable acceptance rate and almost identical standardized test scores, this is one liberal arts school that has not changed much in recent years.

The admissions committee ranks the rigor of one's secondary programming and GPA earned as the two most critical factors in the process. The second rung of still "important" factors is comprised of SAT/ACT scores, recommendations, essays, extracurricular activities, and character/personal qualities. Macalester insists that it does not consider demonstrated interest in the admissions process, an unusual move for a school with a relatively low yield rate (the percent of accepted students who go on to enroll). That being said, applying via early decision is a wise choice for those committed to attending the college as the ED acceptance rate is 52 percent. Attracting students from all fifty states and eighty-eight countries, this school's Minnesota locale draws talented applicants from around the world. Lots of AP courses and excellent grades should set up candidates for success.

Worth Your Money?

Sixty-eight percent of the Macalester student population receives need-based aid for an average grant of $42,916 per year. Of those that qualify, 63 percent see 100 percent of their demonstrated need met by Mac, with many others receiving packages that cover nearly all of their college costs. Unfortunately, if you don't qualify for need-based aid, do not expect much in the way of merit aid—most likely you'll be paying close to the full annual cost of attendance of $73,500. With so many graduates pursuing advanced degrees, average early career earnings aren't spectacular, but Mac is still a school with phenomenal long-term career outcomes, and a very wise investment for students who can afford the price without racking up higher-than-average debt.

FINANCIAL
Institutional Type: Private
In-State Tuition: $56,062
Out-of-State Tuition: $56,062
Room & Board: $12,592
Required Fees: $230
Books & Supplies: $1,191

Avg. Need-Based Aid: $42,916
Avg. % of Need Met: 100%

Avg. Merit-Based Aid: $15,361
% Receiving Merit-Based Aid: 20%

Avg. Cumulative Debt: $24,880
% of Students Borrowing: 66%

CAREER
Who Recruits
1. ScribeAmerica
2. ESRI
3. BMO Capital Markets
4. Twin Cities Public Television
5. Airbnb

Notable Internships
1. Minnesota Wild
2. U.S. Bank
3. U.S. House of Representatives

Top Industries
1. Business
2. Education
3. Social Services
4. Research
5. Operations

Top Employers
1. Wells Fargo
2. UnitedHealth Group
3. Target
4. Epic
5. 3M

Where Alumni Work
1. Minneapolis
2. New York City
3. San Francisco
4. Washington, DC
5. Chicago

Median Earnings
College Scorecard (Early Career): $47,600
EOP (Early Career): $47,000
PayScale (Mid-Career): $100,400

RANKINGS
Forbes: 86
Money: 371
U.S. News: 25, Liberal Arts Colleges
Wall Street Journal/THE: 83
Washington Monthly: 36, Liberal Arts Colleges

#CollegesWorthYourMoney

Marist College

Poughkeepsie, New York | Admissions Phone: 845-575-3226

ADMISSION
Admission Rate: 46%
Admission Rate - Men: 51%
Admission Rate - Women: 43%
EA Admission Rate: 52%
ED Admission Rate: 89%
Admission Rate (5-Year Trend): +9%
ED Admission Rate (5-Year Trend): -1%
% of Admits Attending (Yield): 25%
Transfer Admission Rate: 70%

Offered Wait List: 4,592
Accepted Wait List: 983
Admitted Wait List: 106

SAT Reading/Writing (Middle 50%): 580-660
SAT Math (Middle 50%): 570-660
ACT Composite (Middle 50%): 24-29
Testing Policy: Test Optional
SAT Superscore: Yes
ACT Superscore: Yes

% Graduated in Top 10% of HS Class: 22%
% Graduated in Top 25% of HS Class: 51%
% Graduated in Top 50% of HS Class: 85%

ENROLLMENT
Total Undergraduate Enrollment: 5,670
% Part-Time: 9%
% Male: 42%
% Female: 58%
% Out-of-State: 53%
% Fraternity: 3%
% Sorority: 3%
% On-Campus (Freshman): 95%
% On-Campus (All Undergraduate): 61%

% African-American: 4%
% Asian: 3%
% Hispanic: 10%
% White: 73%
% Other: 3%
% Race or Ethnicity Unknown: 5%
% International: 2%
% Low-Income: 14%

ACADEMICS
Student-to-Faculty Ratio: 16:1
% of Classes Under 20: 45%
% of Classes Under 40: 100%
% Full-Time Faculty: 41%
% Full-Time Faculty w/ Terminal Degree: 78%

Top Programs
Business Administration
Communication
Criminal Justice
Fashion Design
Information Technology and Systems
Political Science

Retention Rate: 87%
4-Year Graduation Rate: 76%
6-Year Graduation Rate: 83%

Curricular Flexibility: Somewhat Flexible
Academic Rating: ★★★

Inside the Classroom

Competing for attention in the world of New York State institutions of higher education must feel like raising your hand to volunteer while surrounded by equally eager-to-contribute NBA centers. As a school serving 5,700 undergraduates, Marist College is overshadowed by smaller and more selective options that include Hamilton, Colgate, Vassar, and Skidmore as well as the more famous larger universities Cornell, Rochester, and Syracuse—and that's not even considering schools in New York City. Yet, there are many reasons you should get to know Marist, an accessible school for solid-but-imperfect high schoolers that succeeds in providing a world-class education to undergraduates who go on to land enviable internships with regularity, study abroad at exceptional rates and, as a whole, experience tremendous postgraduate success.

Marist offers forty-seven distinct bachelor's programs but is ultimately a true liberal arts institution that requires its undergrads to complete a core curriculum. As freshmen, students engage in a first-year seminar and a course called Writing for College, both of which incorporate themes related to "Cultural Diversity, Nature & the Environment, Civic Engagement, and/or Quantitative Reasoning." There are thirty-six credits worth of distributional courses of study including ethics and justice, fine arts, history, literature, mathematics, natural science, philosophy, and social science. Additionally, although this can overlap with distributional requirements, students must also tackle a four-course "Pathway," choosing from twenty-three courses including African Diaspora Studies, Gender Studies, and Public Health Studies.

Marist has average class sizes in the eighteen to twenty-six range and a 16:1 student-to-faculty ratio—few sections are single-digit seminars or large lectures. On the less-than-ideal side, the majority of Marist's professors are adjuncts, 348 versus 232 full timers. On the plus side, undergrads enjoy the real-world knowledge brought by those nontenure-track professors, and few complain about availability outside the classroom. Marist is supportive of undergraduate research, particularly in the hard sciences where completion of a research project is often a graduation requirement. Marist sees 50 percent of its students study abroad as part of the college's robust international program that is rated among the best in the country.

The School of Management and the School of Communication are quite popular as business and communication are, by far, Marist's two most commonly conferred degrees. They are also among Marist's strongest. It is also noteworthy that the School of Mathematics and Computer Science has had a joint study program with IBM for more than three decades. This intensive collaboration frequently leads to employment at IBM after graduation. With many grads entering corporate America, applications to prestigious national fellowship programs are sparse, but twenty-six grads have won Fulbright Scholarships in the past fifteen years.

Outside the Classroom

Two-thirds of the undergraduate population at Marist live on campus in a combination of corridor, suite, apartment, and townhouse-style residences. The 150+ acre campus is spectacularly set on the shores of the Hudson River. On the border of what arguably qualifies as "Upstate" New York, Poughkeepsie is about an hour and half drive from the heart of New York City. On campus, there are three fraternities and four sororities with around 300 members, giving Greek life a modest presence of roughly 5 percent of the undergraduate population. Playing in NCAA Division I, the Red Foxes field twenty-three varsity sports teams. For less serious athletes there are eleven club teams as well as an extensive intramural program that draws an incredible 65 percent of students. Overall, there are more than eighty student-run clubs and organizations. The Hudson Valley offers plenty worth exploring, from the ample natural beauty ripe for hiking and canoeing to the commerce of the popular Poughkeepsie Galleria Mall. While the school's Catholic origins are no longer officially linked to the school, the largest student group at Marist is the Campus Ministry that has a membership of 1,300 students. At 58 percent female, there is a noticeable gender gap at this school.

Career Services

The Center for Career Services (CCS) at Marist is staffed by five professionals with expertise in career coaching, employer relations, and graduate school advising. That works out to a 1,140:1 student-to-advisor ratio that is much higher than the average school in this guide. We do, however, take it as a positive sign that the Student Services Department (which includes the CCS) received a thumbs-up from 95 percent of grads. As the CCS states, "It's never too early to begin the process of learning how your interests and passions turn into long-term career aspirations." To back up that ideal, the CCS offers daily walk-in hours, scheduled one-on-one career counseling appointments, and weekly workshops on topics like resumes, cover letters, interviewing, and building a personal brand online.

Large events take place regularly, including the two annual Career and Internship Fairs. The fall 2018 fair attracted sixty employers and 700 students. An annual Graduate School Forum brings forty graduate and professional schools to campus to meet with prospective students. The CCS also maintains an active Alumni Career Network of former students in a variety of fields who are willing to volunteer their time to mentor. Efforts such as those lead to an extremely healthy 83 percent internship participation rate for Marist undergrads. In 2017, over 1,100 internships were completed at organizations including the Brooklyn Nets (NBA), CBS, Goldman Sachs, HBO, Morgan Stanley, Seventeen Magazine, and Madison Square Garden. Success in helping its students secure experiential and networking opportunities ends up leading to positive career and graduate school outcomes for the vast majority of students.

Professional Outcomes

Red Foxes strutting across the graduation stage in 2017 went on to find employment or a graduate school home at a terrific 98 percent rate by the time they filled out their first-destination survey. Major employers of Marist alums include IBM, which presently employees over 700 individuals, as well as JP Morgan Chase, EY, Macy's Citi, Morgan Stanley, Deloitte, and NBC Universal Media. Members of the Class of 2017 headed to a number of media powerhouses including iHeartRadio, Fox News, Random House, and the MLB Network as well as other major companies Adidas, Coach, Lockheed Martin, Northrup Grumman, and Moody's. The Greater New York City area draws approximately two-thirds of grads; Boston, Atlanta, Albany, and Hartford attract their own slivers of each graduating class. Midcareer median salaries are in the same range as other excellent schools in this guide such as UC Santa Barbara, Texas A&M, Colby, and American University.

The percent of Class of 2017 members pursuing graduate/professional degrees varied greatly across disciplines. Thirty-six percent of those in the School of Social & Behavioral Sciences enrolled in graduate school followed by the School of Science (28 percent), the School of Computer Science & Mathematics (16 percent), and the School of Liberal Arts (14 percent). In terms of selectivity, a wide range of institutions were attended including elite universities Cornell, Penn, Harvard, Columbia, and Oxford. Over the last decade, 70 percent of medical school applicants were accepted to at least one institution, a figure that is more than twenty-five points higher than the national average. Acceptances have included Georgetown Medical School, Albany Medical College, New York Medical College, SUNY Upstate Medical Center at Syracuse, Medical College of Virginia, and the Albert Einstein School of Medicine. Recent law school acceptances have included William & Mary, the University of Texas, and Northeastern University.

Admission

In 2018, Marist received over 11,000 applications, accepted 46 percent, and saw one-quarter of those accepted ultimately go on to enroll. The Class of 2022 possessed mid-50 percent SAT scores 1210-1340 and 26-30 on the ACT. In the classroom, this cohort earned an average high school GPA of 3.3, and only 22 percent of its members placed in the top decile of their high school class. Not only can students gain acceptance into Marist without a pristine transcript, but the college also became test-optional back in 2011. Thirty-seven percent of the Class of 2022 elected not to submit standardized test scores, and in the years since it went test-optional, the average scores have predictably gone up a bit because those with lower scores simply do not submit.
The other qualifications, such as GPA and class rank, have remained fairly constant over the last decade.

According to the admissions office Marist applicants "should rank in the top half of their graduating class and hold a recalculated average of 3.3 or better." The school also likes to see some honors and/or Advanced Placement courses on an applicant's transcript. Evidence of leadership and extracurricular participation are valued by the committee as well. With lots of liberal arts competition both Upstate and around New York City, Marist finds itself fighting for quality freshmen each year. Thus, committing to the school via early decision gives you a massive edge in the admissions game; in 2018, the college accepted an overwhelming 86 percent of ED applicants. It filled 22 percent of the Class of 2022 via binding early-round applicants.

Worth Your Money?

Tuition fees plus room and board bring the total sticker price to over $58,000, making a four-year degree a $200,000+ venture. Fortunately, through a combination of merit and need-based aid, the net price ends up under $40k per year, even for families in the top income brackets. While not cheap by any means, Marist has the type of NYC corporate connections that can eventually open doors to lucrative and interesting careers that will likely return your investment.

FINANCIAL
Institutional Type: Private
In-State Tuition: $41,800
Out-of-State Tuition: $41,800
Room & Board: $15,920
Required Fees: $700
Books & Supplies: $1,125

Avg. Need-Based Aid: $20,548
Avg. % of Need Met: 73%

Avg. Merit-Based Aid: $11,813
% Receiving Merit-Based Aid: 41%

Avg. Cumulative Debt: $39,035
% of Students Borrowing: 64%

CAREER
Who Recruits
1. IBM
2. EY
3. KPMG
4. UBS
5. The Met

Notable Internships
1. ESPN
2. Sony Music Entertainment
3. American Red Cross

Top Industries
1. Business
2. Sales
3. Operations
4. Education
5. information Technology

Top Employers
1. IBM
2. JPMorgan Chase
3. EY
4. Macy's
5. Citi

Where Alumni Work
1. New York City
2. Boston
3. Atlanta
4. New York City
5. Hartford, CT

Median Earnings
College Scorecard (Early Career): $56,900
EOP (Early Career): $59,500
PayScale (Mid-Career): $101,000

RANKINGS
Forbes: 189
Money: 189
U.S. News: 10, Regional North
Wall Street Journal/THE: 398 (T)
Washington Monthly: N/A

#CollegesWorthYourMoney

Massachusetts Institute of Technology

Cambridge, Massachusetts | Admissions Phone: 617-253-3400

Inside the Classroom

A beacon of egalitarianism and meritocracy, the Massachusetts Institute of Technology is less about legacy and more about the future. MIT doesn't care who your grandfather was or how far you can throw a football; it is seeking the world's sharpest and most innovative minds in engineering, the sciences, mathematics, and related fields who, one day, will create the world the rest of us will merely inhabit. Graduate students account for the majority of students enrolled at MIT, but the nearly 4,500 undergraduates pursue one of fifty-three majors and fifty-eight minors in this world-class research institution that continues to be one of the world's most magnetic destinations for science geniuses.

There are five separate schools within MIT: the School of Architecture and Planning; the School of Engineering; the School of Humanities, Arts, and the Social Sciences; the Sloan School of Management; and the School of Science. There are a number of broad academic requirements across all five schools including an eight-subject humanities, arts, and social sciences requirement and a six-subject science requirement that includes two terms of calculus, two terms of physics, one term of chemistry, and one term of biology. Additionally, students must complete two courses under the designation of "restricted electives" in science and technology, a laboratory requirement, and a physical education course.

The student-to-faculty ratio is an astonishing 3-to-1, and even with a substantial focus on graduate programs, the class sizes are intimate. An exceptional 43 percent of class sections have single-digit enrollments, and 70 percent of courses contain fewer than twenty students. MIT is known for having one of the best formalized undergraduate research programs in the country. The Undergraduate Research Opportunities Program (UROP) operates year-round and helps connect 91 percent of undergrads to a research experience with an MIT faculty member. Studying abroad is strongly encouraged, and the school offers some fantastic opportunities through programs such as MIT Madrid, Imperial College Exchanges (London), and departmental exchange programs in South Africa, France, and Japan.

The highest numbers of degrees conferred in 2018 were in the following majors: computer science and engineering (251), electrical engineering and computer science (161), mathematics (76), and physics (55). Just about every program at MIT sits at or near the top of any rankings. The most sought after employers and grad schools aggressively recruit alumni. Graduates win nationally competitive fellowships and scholarships on a routine basis. In 2019, five students were awarded Marshall Scholarships; in 2018, eight of the forty finalists for Hertz Fellowships were MIT grads, and fourteen students in the Department of Chemistry alone were awarded National Science Foundation Graduate Research Fellowships.

Outside the Classroom

The campus' 166 acres include twenty-six acres of playing fields, twenty acres of green spaces and gardens, and eighteen student residences that house the 90 percent of students who live on campus, a requirement for freshmen. It may be a bit of a surprise that the school's thirty-seven fraternities, sororities, and living groups attract 43 percent of male students and 28 percent of females. Around half live in frat/sorority/living group housing, and the other half reside in dorms. Falling victim to stereotypes, one might not immediately assume that MIT would have an athletically-inclined student body. However, the school fields thirty-three varsity sports teams (16 women's, 15 men's, 2 co-ed), most of which compete in NCAA Division III against other New England colleges. The intramural program is bursting at the seams with over 4,000 participants annually. Another 800 students are members of thirty-three club teams. Plenty of culture/creativity can be found on campus in one of MIT's twelve museums and galleries (The MIT Museum draws 150,000 visitors each year). There are also more than sixty arts, dance, music, and writing organizations for students. The school is devoted to environmental sustainability, and the campus and surrounding area are designed for a car-free lifestyle that remains highly convenient. With forty-four bike-sharing stations, six subway stations, and twenty-nine bus routes in the surrounding area, students can navigate Cambridge with ease. Harvard's campus is less than one mile away, and downtown Boston is easy to reach. For reference, Fenway Park is less than two miles from campus.

Career Services

MIT Global Education & Career Development (GECD) has sixteen professional staff members who are directly involved in employer relations, career counseling, and graduate school advising. That 278:1 student-to-advisor ratio is better than average compared to other schools featured in this guide. The office provides top-notch individualized counseling and also puts on phenomenal large-scale events. The MIT Fall Career Fair is an unmatched event that sees around 450 companies and 5,000 students attend. If you can think of a desirable tech/finance company, chances are it has a booth at the event. Even the less-epic Spring Career Fair attracts seventy employers including Northrup Grumman, Wayfair, Bank of America, the Walt Disney Company, Cisco, and Twitter.

With assistance from the GECD, 87 percent of MIT undergraduates complete at least one internship. Almost one-quarter of those participating in internships received a full-time job offer from that same organization. The GECD played a direct role in helping many others land jobs through various means as 20 percent found employment through on-campus recruiting, 19 percent through faculty/GECD connections, and 18 percent through career fairs. In a single year the GECD hosted 130 different employers, which led to a collective 2,609 interviews held on campus. An additional 1,072 employers posted 2,595 unique jobs online in an effort to lure MIT seniors. MIT students sell themselves, so career services staff have a role akin to managing the '27 Yankees. Still, the office does a world-class job of setting up its highly desired undergrads with premium opportunities.

Professional Outcomes

The Class of 2018 saw 54 percent of its members enter the world of employment and 39 percent continue on their educational paths. By industry, the highest percentage of graduates found jobs in engineering (24 percent), computer technologies (23 percent), consulting (14 percent), and finance/banking (14 percent). The top employers included Accenture, Oracle, Facebook, Amazon, Microsoft, Northrop Grumman, Goldman Sachs, Google, General Motors, the US Navy, Apple, Bain & Company, Boeing, and McKinsey. The mean starting salary for an MIT bachelor's degree holder was $88,381, and the median was $85,000.

The most frequently attended graduate schools are a who's who of elite institutions including MIT itself, which accounted for 177 members of the Class of 2017 with Stanford a distant second, attracting twenty-two graduates. Also making the list were Princeton, California Institute of Technology, Columbia, Northwestern, University of Chicago, University of California at Berkeley, and University of Michigan. The most common degree being pursued was a PhD (43 percent), and the second most common was a master's of engineering (41 percent). Only 6 percent were entering medical/dental/veterinary school, and 1.6 percent were headed to law school. Medical school acceptance rates typically land in the 80-95 percent range for grads/alumni, more than double the national average.

Admission

Applicants for a place in the Class of 2022 encountered a murderous 6.7 percent acceptance rate. Freshmen entering MIT in the fall of 2018 possessed SATs with a middle-50 percent range of 1500-1570 and ACTs with middle-50 percent scores of 34-36. Students were almost unanimously from the top 10 percent of their high school classes—97 percent boasted that achievement. MIT offers a nonbinding early action option with a November 1 deadline, but it yields little in the way of an admissions edge. The acceptance rate for the early round is usually almost identical to that of the regular round.

The MIT admissions committee rates character/personal qualities as "very important," and just about everything else—rigor of courses, GPA, test scores, essays, recommendations, interview, extracurricular activities—in the next tier of importance. While a nice nod to the importance of character, every one of the aforementioned factors ranked as merely "important" have to be close to perfect for it to even enter the equation. Legacy status is not considered at MIT, a rarity among elite universities, meaning that the alumni connection of your mother, grandfather, or brother plays zero role in helping you gain admission. Despite a large intercollegiate sports program, athletic prowess plays a minimal role in admissions decisions as well. MIT is as close to a true meritocracy as you can find in the world of higher education. The most brilliant and innovative minds from around the globe are admitted regardless of family name or lacrosse skills. Rather, a sparkling academic record, near-perfect test scores, and impressive STEM-focused experiences/accomplishments outside the classroom will rule the day.

Worth Your Money?

Yes…Need more? Going to MIT is punching your ticket to any number of lucrative careers. If you need financial assistance, this school will meet 100 percent of your demonstrated need; the average grant is for roughly $49,000. The full cost of attendance is $73,160.

FINANCIAL
Institutional Type: Private
In-State Tuition: $53,450
Out-of-State Tuition: $53,450
Room & Board: $16,390
Required Fees: $340
Books & Supplies: $820

Avg. Need-Based Aid: $49,010
Avg. % of Need Met: 100%

Avg. Merit-Based Aid: $0
% Receiving Merit-Based Aid: 0%

Avg. Cumulative Debt: $22,696
% of Students Borrowing: 29%

CAREER
Who Recruits
1. Hudson River Trading
2. Nvidia
3. Five Rings Technology
4. Stripe
5. AB InBev

Notable Internships
1. Jane Street Capital
2. Airbnb
3. Shell

Top Industries
1. Business
2. Engineering
3. Education
4. Research
5. Operations

Top Employers
1. Google
2. Apple
3. Microsoft
4. Amazon
5. IBM

Where Alumni Work
1. Boston
2. San Francisco
3. New York City
4. India
5. Washington, DC

Median Earnings
College Scorecard (Early Career): $104,700
EOP (Early Career): $98,500
PayScale (Mid-Career): $155,200

RANKINGS
Forbes: 4
Money: 7
U.S. News: 3 (T), National Universities
Wall Street Journal/THE: 2
Washington Monthly: 3, National Universities

#CollegesWorthYourMoney

Middlebury College

Middlebury, Vermont | Admissions Phone: 802-443-3000

ADMISSION
Admission Rate: 17%
Admission Rate - Men: 18%
Admission Rate - Women: 16%
EA Admission Rate: Not Offered
ED Admission Rate: 47%
Admission Rate (5-Year Trend): -1%
ED Admission Rate (5-Year Trend): +12%
% of Admits Attending (Yield): 41%
Transfer Admission Rate: 9%

\# Offered Wait List: 1,215
\# Accepted Wait List: 914
\# Admitted Wait List: 24

SAT Reading/Writing (Middle 50%): 660-730
SAT Math (Middle 50%): 670-770
ACT Composite (Middle 50%): 31-34
Testing Policy: Test Flexible
SAT Superscore: Yes
ACT Superscore: Yes

% Graduated in Top 10% of HS Class: 80%
% Graduated in Top 25% of HS Class: 95%
% Graduated in Top 50% of HS Class: 99%

ENROLLMENT
Total Undergraduate Enrollment: 2,579
% Part-Time: 1%
% Male: 47%
% Female: 53%
% Out-of-State: 94%
% Fraternity: Not Offered
% Sorority: Not Offered
% On-Campus (Freshman): 100%
% On-Campus (All Undergraduate): 95%

% African-American: 4%
% Asian: 7%
% Hispanic: 10%
% White: 62%
% Other: 5%
% Race or Ethnicity Unknown: 2%
% International: 11%
% Low-Income: 12%

ACADEMICS
Student-to-Faculty Ratio: 8:1
% of Classes Under 20: 66%
% of Classes Under 40: 95%
% Full-Time Faculty: 84%
% Full-Time Faculty w/ Terminal Degree: 96%

Top Programs
Economics
English
Environmental Studies
History
International & Global Studies
Neuroscience
Performing Arts
Political Science

Retention Rate: 96%
4-Year Graduation Rate: 83%
6-Year Graduation Rate: 91%

Curricular Flexibility: Somewhat Flexible
Academic Rating: ★★★★✦

Inside the Classroom
Located between the Green Mountains and the Adirondacks, Middlebury College is heading toward the summit of Northeastern liberal arts colleges. In the same conversation as (although always ranked just behind) Williams and Amherst, Middlebury's 2,500 undergraduate students are an exceptionally accomplished crew. Even the frigid Vermont winters do little to take away from the beauty of the college's historic 350-acre campus or the natural grandeur of the surrounding area. A quintessential New England liberal arts college aesthetically, "Midd" also plays that role when it comes to the classroom experience.

Offering forty-seven departments and programs in which to major and minor, the college requires all students to complete one course in seven of the following eight categories: literature, the arts, philosophical and religious studies, historical studies, physical and life sciences, deductive reasoning and analytical processes, social analysis, and foreign language. Undergrads also must complete four additional courses that meet the cultures and civilization requirement. Mandatory writing-intensive seminars must be tackled—one as a freshman and the second by the end of the sophomore year.

The school's 8:1 student-faculty ratio allows 100 percent of courses to be taught by professors, not graduate assistants. Most classes are small; the mean class size is nineteen, and 19 percent of sections contain fewer than ten students. The Summer Research at Middlebury program funds 130 students annually to work alongside faculty in a variety of disciplines. Each year, more than 50 percent of juniors take a semester abroad in one of ninety programs in forty countries. The college's robust international program includes Middlebury Schools Abroad in Argentina, Brazil, Cameroon, Chile, China, France, Germany, India, Israel, Italy, Japan, Jordan, Morocco, Russia, Spain, the United Kingdom, and Uruguay.

Middlebury is renowned for its Language Department as well as international studies. Graduate schools know the value of a Middlebury education (see med school acceptance rates below). The college also produces a large number of national fellowship/scholarship winners. In the 2017-18 school year graduates/alumni took home three Watson Fellowships, Four National Science Foundation Graduate Research Fellowships, thirteen Fulbright Scholarships, and five Critical Language Scholarships.

Outside the Classroom
Implementing the Oxford/Cambridge system of residential housing, all Middlebury undergraduates are required to live in one of more than sixty on-campus buildings. First-year students are assigned to one of five larger Commons where they will reside until the end of their sophomore year. More than thirty faculty/staff members regularly eat in the Commons allowing for classroom discussions to continue over a meal. That leaves no room for Greek life, which vanished two decades ago (limited "social houses" do remain). With thirty-one varsity sports teams competing in the NCAA New England Small College Athletic Conference, the Middlebury Panthers put a sizable portion of its undergraduate population in uniform. Less committed athletes can enjoy a full array of club and intramural sports as well as the school's eighteen-hole golf course, 3.5-mile jogging trail, 2,200-seat ice hockey rink, or six-lane indoor track. Midd offers more than 170 student-run organizations with options in all the usual realms—performing arts, spiritual, social, student government, and more. Outdoor activity clubs that engage in climbing, hiking, kayaking, skiing, and camping are among the most popular groups. Student theater productions are also well attended. The town of Middlebury is tiny and quiet, so some students make the just-under-an-hour drive to Burlington. Montreal, Canada, is the closest cosmopolitan destination with Boston and New York more than three hours away.

Career Services
The Center for Careers and Internships is staffed by sixteen full-time staff members who specialize in areas such as employer relations, career advising, heath professions and STEM advising, and internships and early engagement. Its 156:1 student-to-advisor ratio places it among the most supportive career services offices of any college profiled in this guide. Middlebury's career counselors are rarely found not actively engaging undergraduates in career/grad school planning. In 2017, the office coordinated 240 events and workshops, and advisors held 2,700 individual student sessions.

For a school of modest size, Middlebury brought an impressive ninety employers to campus to host information sessions and facilitated 500 on-campus interviews in 2017. Every year it helps 800 undergrads find internships and contribute $800,000 to help fund unpaid summer work experiences. More than 5,500 opportunities for jobs and internships are posted online. Further, a generous alumni base is more than willing to assist current Panthers—more than 7,500 alums in a range of professions wait to connect on MiddNet. While the Center for Careers and Internships three- to six-months out employment rate is not as high as that of some other comparably staffed elite schools, Middlebury grads regularly find their way to careers they find meaningful and fulfilling, including many at some of the country's best companies.

Middlebury College

E-mail: admissions@middlebury.edu | Website: www.middlebury.edu

Professional Outcomes

Three months after graduating, 70 percent of the Class of 2018 had landed jobs, 12 percent were in graduate school, and 13 percent were still searching for employment. That was an improvement over the classes of 2016 and 2017 that saw 21-22 percent of alumni still hunting for jobs in the same time frame. The most commonly held jobs fell under the category of "social impact-related careers" (21 percent), followed by financial services (15 percent), consulting (12 percent), technology (11 percent), and health care and science (10 percent). Interestingly, the number of Middlebury grads entering tech-related fields has grown by 55 percent in the last three years. Google is now one of the leading employers of alumni alongside Morgan Stanley, Goldman Sachs, Deloitte, Amazon, and JP Morgan. With a median mid-career salary in the range of $62,000, Middlebury grads are in a similar income bracket with those from Williams, Brandeis, and Bowdoin.

Middlebury students with solid grades will be viewed favorably by graduate and professional schools should they wish to continue their education. Graduate schools attended by members of the Class of 2017 included Columbia, Georgia Tech, Harvard Law School, Oxford, Stanford, and Yale. Members of the Class of 2018 who applied to medical school sported an average GPA of 3.7, a median MCAT score in the 90th percentile, and were accepted at an 89 percent clip (the 2017 figure was 83 percent). Over the last eight years, the most frequently attended medical schools include Tufts, Boston University, Geisel (Dartmouth), and NYU.

Admission

Middlebury College admitted 17 percent of the 9,227 applicants for a place in the Class of 2022. Of those receiving an acceptance letter, 41 percent went on to enroll at the college. The middle-50 percent standardized tests scores of those who enrolled were 1330-1500 on the SAT and 31-34 on the ACT. There is a relatively even split between those submitting scores from each exam. One of the rare test-flexible institutions, Middlebury requires students to submit (a) SAT results (b) ACT results or (c) three SAT subject scores. For those choosing the latter option, the three tests must be from three distinct disciplines (i.e., Math I and Math II will not count as two tests).

Six factors sit atop the pecking order of most important as applicants are being evaluated by the admissions committee: rigor of secondary coursework, GPA, class rank, extracurricular activities, talent/ability, and character/personal qualities. Test scores, recommendations, essays, and racial/ethnic status comprise the second tier of "important" factors. Those who commit to the college through binding early decision are rewarded with a 47 percent acceptance rate, more than three times that of the regular cycle. Middlebury has remained similarly selective throughout the twenty-first century. One decade ago, the acceptance rate was a touch lower at 16 percent; the average test scores were a touch lower too, but the average enrollee looked similar to a 2018-19 freshman. The college continues to use a genuinely holistic approach in the admissions process, and the test-flexible policy can be useful for a certain type of applicant. Even when considering the "special" students being accepted via the early round, ED still provides borderline applicants with an increased chance at getting in.

Worth Your Money?

Middlebury's list price is about the going rate for elite liberal arts institutions with a total annual cost of attendance of $74k. However, if you qualify for need-based aid, the college will meet your full level of need; the average award is $49k. As with most schools that meet a student's full demonstrated need, there isn't much, if any, merit aid money to go around. A school of superior quality, Middlebury rates as a rare liberal arts school that will pay you back multiple times over the course of your life, even if the upfront costs are steep.

FINANCIAL
Institutional Type: Private
In-State Tuition: $55,790
Out-of-State Tuition: $55,790
Room & Board: $16,040
Required Fees: $426
Books & Supplies: $1,000

Avg. Need-Based Aid: $48,993
Avg. % of Need Met: 100%

Avg. Merit-Based Aid: $0
% Receiving Merit-Based Aid: 0%

Avg. Cumulative Debt: $18,955
% of Students Borrowing: 50%

CAREER
Who Recruits
1. Analysis Group
2. Goldman Sachs
3. Oak Hill Advisors
4. ScribeAmerica
5. CIA

Notable Internships
1. Tesla
2. Bain & Company
3. Merrill Lynch

Top Industries
1. Business
2. Education
3. Media
4. Social Services
5. Operations

Top Employers
1. Google
2. Goldman Sachs
3. Morgan Stanley
4. Amazon
5. Deloitte

Where Alumni Work
1. New York City
2. Boston
3. Washington, DC
4. San Francisco
5. Glen Falls, NY

Median Earnings
College Scorecard (Early Career): $58,200
EOP (Early Career): $61,800
PayScale (Mid-Career): $109,800

RANKINGS
Forbes: 36
Money: 186
U.S. News: 7, Liberal Arts Colleges
Wall Street Journal/THE: 35
Washington Monthly: 6, Liberal Arts Colleges

#CollegesWorthYourMoney

Mount Holyoke College

South Hadley, Massachusetts | Admissions Phone: 413-538-2023

ADMISSION
Admission Rate: 51%
Admission Rate - Men: Not Offered
Admission Rate - Women: 51%
EA Admission Rate: Not Offered
ED Admission Rate: 58%
Admission Rate (5-Year Trend): +4%
ED Admission Rate (5-Year Trend): +8%
% of Admits Attending (Yield): 33%
Transfer Admission Rate: 40%

Offered Wait List: 598
Accepted Wait List: 313
Admitted Wait List: 0

SAT Reading/Writing (Middle 50%): 640-720
SAT Math (Middle 50%): 650-780
ACT Composite (Middle 50%): 29-32
Testing Policy: Test Optional
SAT Superscore: Yes
ACT Superscore: Yes

% Graduated in Top 10% of HS Class: 47%
% Graduated in Top 25% of HS Class: 83%
% Graduated in Top 50% of HS Class: 98%

ENROLLMENT
Total Undergraduate Enrollment: 2,208
% Part-Time: 1%
% Male: 0%
% Female: 100%
% Out-of-State: 73%
% Fraternity: Not Offered
% Sorority: Not Offered
% On-Campus (Freshman): 99%
% On-Campus (All Undergraduate): 96%

% African-American: 4%
% Asian: 10%
% Hispanic: 7%
% White: 45%
% Other: 4%
% Race or Ethnicity Unknown: 2%
% International: 27%
% Low-Income: 13%

ACADEMICS
Student-to-Faculty Ratio: 9:1
% of Classes Under 20: 77%
% of Classes Under 40: 96%
% Full-Time Faculty: 78%
% Full-Time Faculty w/ Terminal Degree: 97%

Top Programs
Area Studies
Biology
Computer Science
English
Environmental Studies
International Relations
Psychology

Retention Rate: 92%
4-Year Graduation Rate: 77%
6-Year Graduation Rate: 83%

Curricular Flexibility: Somewhat Flexible
Academic Rating: ★★★★

Inside the Classroom

Stately, majestic, and Hogwarts-esque are three of the most common adjectives used to describe the grounds of Mount Holyoke College, an exclusively female liberal arts school located in South Hadley, Massachusetts. Situated ninety miles west of Boston, MHC is home to over 2,200 undergraduates and is part of the Five College Consortium with nearby Amherst, Smith, Hampshire, and UMass-Amherst. With fifty departmental and interdepartmental majors as well as the option to design your own major, MHC students, nicknamed "Lyons" after the college's founder, are free to follow their academic passions, an attribute that helps explain the incredible percentage of alumni that go on to earn PhDs.

By liberal arts college standards Mount Holyoke requires a minimal amount of core coursework. While working toward the completion of the 128 credits needed for graduation, students must complete one class in each of the humanities, sciences, social sciences, and mathematics. A freshman seminar focused on sharpening writing skills is mandatory as is one semester of foreign language study, one course focused on multicultural perspectives, and physical education. Thanks to membership in the Five College Consortium, undergrads can take a good number of courses at one of the other institutions but must complete two of their final three years of study on the MHC campus.

Professors are known for their accessibility and commitment to undergraduate education. Thanks to a 9-to-1 student-to-faculty ratio, roughly three-quarters of sections contain fewer than twenty students; 14 percent are single-digit seminar classes. Opportunities to research and publish alongside faculty are definitely available, and many 200- and 300-level courses have independent research baked-in as a requirement. Across all disciplines, more ambitious students can arrange summer research internships with professors. More than one hundred study abroad options are on the table, but preferred MHC-affiliated programs are definitely worth considering. Those targeted college-run programs include Globalization, Development, and Environment in Costa Rica; Economic Transformation and Business in Shanghai; and the Associated Kyoto Program that allows students to attend a full academic year of classes in Japan.

MHC isn't a school where one or two programs are more popular and/or more respected than the rest. Rather, strong programs are found across a variety of fields—for example, in biology, English, and international relations. Among undergrads, there is a fairly even distribution between the humanities (28 percent), social sciences (35 percent), and science and mathematics (36 percent). Fellowships award season is usually kind to Mount Holyoke grads. In 2018, MHC students took home seven Fulbright Scholarships, two Davis Project for Peace awards, and two Critical Language Scholarships awarded by the US State Department.

Outside the Classroom

Roughly 95 percent of undergraduates live on campus in one of eighteen residential halls. The last time sororities existed on campus was 1910 when they were dissolved for being "undemocratic." The college's thirteen sports teams compete in NCAA Division III, including a stellar equestrian program. Of the over one hundred student organizations, a cappella and glee are among the most popular along with volunteerism in many forms. Each year over half of MHC students volunteer at local schools, hospitals, YMCAs, and other community organizations. Speakers, including many authors, appear frequently on campus to give well-attended talks. Thanks again to membership in the Five College Consortium, social opportunities are expanded to include those offered at Smith, UMass, Amherst, and Hampshire. Campus, which is almost always cited as one the nation's prettiest, is a spacious 800 acres that features notable man-made highlights such as the MHC Art Museum, a fitness center that is less than a decade old, and an eighteen-hole golf course in addition to natural highlights such as two lakes and several hiking trails. South Hadley is a small town exploding with quaint New England charm. Those seeking more adventure can make the two-hour trip to Boston.

Career Services

The Career Development Center (CDC) is staffed by ten professionals (not counting communications staff or admin assistants) who work directly with, or on behalf of, students in the following capacities: career counseling, internships, experiential learning, and external relations. That 221:1 student-to-advisor ratio is superior to the majority of schools featured in this guidebook. Ample individualized attention is at the fingertips of undergraduates—thirty-minute advising sessions are available as often as once per week for current students or three times per year for recent graduates. The CDC does not host many large events itself; rather, it takes advantage of the school's geographic location and takes part in events such as the Smith College Life Sciences & Technology Fair, the UMASS Amherst Computer Science & Engineering Fair, and the MIT Asian Career Fair.

Through an approach dubbed the "Lynk," Mt. Holyoke strives to systematically assist students in connecting their curriculum to their future career. That goal is accomplished through the offering of experiential learning opportunities, internship connections (funding is guaranteed), industry site visits, and networking with past students who have entered fields of interest. In fact, a thriving career directory maintained by the college connects undergrads with 20,000 willing-to-help alumni, and almost 1,400 students connect with a member of that directory each year. Overall, the CDC excels in helping young women find their next destination as evidenced by a low percentage of students still seeking employment six months out and the strength of its graduate school preparation (more in a moment). Even with salaries on the lower end and a dearth of on-campus recruiting, the Mount Holyoke Career Development Center works hard to connect its students to fulfilling and relevant career paths.

Professional Outcomes

Six months after commencement 63 percent of 2018 grads had found employment, 20 percent had entered graduate/professional school, 7 percent had landed fellowships/internships, and only 5 percent were still searching for jobs. Education was the most frequently entered field (26 percent). It was followed by technology, science, and engineering (11 percent); social services, public administration, or advocacy (10 percent); and health care (8 percent). The top Lyon employers of 2018 included Google, Goldman Sachs, Barclay's, and Boston Children's Hospital. Microsoft, IBM, Harvard University, and Amazon also employ a healthy number of Lyons. Given the number of grads entering the public sector or pursuing graduate degrees, it isn't shocking that average salary statistics for alumni tend to be on the low side. The midcareer median salary is $49k, more than $7,000 less than the median salary for a Wellesley graduate. Over one-third of students remain in Massachusetts after obtaining their diplomas. Plenty of alumni also can be found in New York, California, or international locales.

Ten years after graduation close to 80 percent of alumni have enrolled in graduate or professional school. The college produces an exceptional number of future STEM PhDs. Between 2004-2013 it saw 171 of its graduates go on to earn doctorates in hard sciences. In recent years the law school acceptance rate has fluctuated between 75 percent and 100 percent. Recent acceptances include Harvard Law School, Boston College, University of Michigan, and Stanford. Medical school acceptance rates tend to be above average, and recent graduates have attended Johns Hopkins, Tufts, Emory, Columbia, UVA, and Washington University. Across all disciplines the graduate schools accepting the most recent alumni included Yale, Cornell, NYU, and Duke. Massachusetts-based Simmons, UMASS-Amherst, and Mt. Holyoke itself also cracked the list.

Admission

The 3,699 applicants for membership in the Class of 2022 saw a generous—particularly by the standards of this book—51 percent succeed, and one-third of those who were accepted ultimately enrolled in the college. The profile of the typical Mt. Holyoke student is quite different than your average college that has an acceptance rate of more than 50 percent. The middle-50 percent range for SATs was 1290-1500, and 47 percent of those attending placed in the top decile of their high school class; 83 percent were in the top quartile. Just under 60 percent earned GPAs of 3.75 or higher.

Four factors reign supreme in the eyes of the admissions committee: rigor of coursework, GPA, recommendations, and essays. Factors such as class rank, the interview, extracurricular activities, talent/ability, character/ personal qualities, volunteer work, and work experience also are deemed "important" in the evaluation process. Missing from this list are standardized test scores because Mount Holyoke is a test-optional school. Among freshmen in the 2018-19 school year, 57 percent submitted SATs and 23 percent submitted ACTs as part of their applications. Given that some applicants likely submitted both SAT and ACT scores, it is fair to infer that more than one-quarter of current students were admitted via test-optional applications. A self-selecting applicant pool leads to a deceptively high acceptance rate. Yet, the women who are offered admission at Mount Holyoke tend to be high achieving with impressive high school transcripts to their names. Those sure that this is the Seven Sisters school for them can gain a slight advantage by applying early—58 percent of 2018 ED applicants were admitted.

Worth Your Money?

Mt. Holyoke has an annual cost of attendance approaching the $70,000 mark, yet thanks to the generosity of its aid offers, many pay far less. In fact, 63 percent of the undergraduates at the college qualify for need-based aid, and the average grant in $37k, a figure that covers 100 percent of demonstrated need for every single recipient. Further, the school is not stingy with merit aid either, dishing out an average package of $20,000 per year to 26 percent of the student population. While many graduates don't immediately land high-paying jobs, the swarms of alumni earning advanced degrees do just fine financially in the long run.

FINANCIAL
Institutional Type: Private
In-State Tuition: $52,040
Out-of-State Tuition: $52,040
Room & Board: $15,320
Required Fees: $218
Books & Supplies: $950

Avg. Need-Based Aid: $36,597
Avg. % of Need Met: 100%

Avg. Merit-Based Aid: $20,388
% Receiving Merit-Based Aid: 26%

Avg. Cumulative Debt: $25,538
% of Students Borrowing: 66%

CAREER
Who Recruits
1. ESPN
2. Life Technologies
3. Forester Capital, LLC
4. NERA Economic Consulting
5. Analysis Group

Notable Internships
1. United States Senate
2. Nike
3. The Coca-Cola Company

Top Industries
1. Education
2. Business
3. Social Services
4. Media
5. Research

Top Employers
1. Google
2. MassMutual
3. Microsoft
4. Amazon
5. Goldman Sachs

Where Alumni Work
1. New York City
2. Boston
3. Springfield, MA
4. Washington, DC
5. San Francisco

Median Earnings
College Scorecard (Early Career): $48,600
EOP (Early Career): $48,900
PayScale (Mid-Career): $92,100

RANKINGS
Forbes: 137
Money: 234
U.S. News: 32, Liberal Arts Colleges
Wall Street Journal/THE: 61 (T)
Washington Monthly: 38, Liberal Arts Colleges

#CollegesWorthYourMoney

New York, New York | Admissions Phone: 212-998-4500

ADMISSION
Admission Rate: 20%
Admission Rate - Men: 20%
Admission Rate - Women: 20%
EA Admission Rate: Not Offered
ED Admission Rate: 35%
Admission Rate (5-Year Trend): -12%
ED Admission Rate (5-Year Trend): +3%
% of Admits Attending (Yield): 43%
Transfer Admission Rate: 25%

Offered Wait List: N/A
Accepted Wait List: N/A
Admitted Wait List: N/A

SAT Reading/Writing (Middle 50%): 650-720
SAT Math (Middle 50%): 660-790
ACT Composite (Middle 50%): 29-34
Testing Policy: Test Flexible
SAT Superscore: Yes
ACT Superscore: Yes

% Graduated in Top 10% of HS Class: 71%
% Graduated in Top 25% of HS Class: 100%
% Graduated in Top 50% of HS Class: 100%

ENROLLMENT
Total Undergraduate Enrollment: 26,733
% Part-Time: 4%
% Male: 42%
% Female: 58%
% Out-of-State: 67%
% Fraternity: 4%
% Sorority: 7%
% On-Campus (Freshman): 84%
% On-Campus (All Undergraduate): 42%

% African-American: 7%
% Asian: 19%
% Hispanic: 15%
% White: 28%
% Other: 4%
% Race or Ethnicity Unknown: 6%
% International: 21%
% Low-Income: 22%

ACADEMICS
Student-to-Faculty Ratio: 9:1
% of Classes Under 20: 61%
% of Classes Under 40: 87%
% Full-Time Faculty: 45%
% Full-Time Faculty w/ Terminal Degree: 94%

Top Programs
Business and Political Economy
Computer Science
Film and Television
Finance
Global Public Health
Journalism
Mathematics
Performing Arts

Retention Rate: 94%
4-Year Graduation Rate: 77%
6-Year Graduation Rate: 85%

Curricular Flexibility: Somewhat Flexible
Academic Rating: ★★★★

Inside the Classroom

A genuine melting pot, even by the standards of the city in which it is located, New York University's campus is graced by talented young people of every ethnicity, from every socio-economic status, and from every corner of the globe. All told, there are more than 50,000 students presently enrolled at NYU, just less than half of whom are undergraduates. With more than 230 areas of undergraduate study, the talents and passions of this student body are as diverse as its demographic makeup.

NYU is divided into a number of smaller (but still quite large) colleges organized by discipline. Schools with undergraduate programs include the College of Arts & Sciences; Tisch School of the Arts; Tandon School of Engineering, Steinhardt School of Culture, Education, and Human Development; Silver School of Social Work; Rory Meyers College of Nursing; Stern School of Business; College of Global Public Health; and the Gallatin School of Individualized Study where students can create their own liberal arts course of study. There are five parts to NYU's core curriculum that must be tackled by all arts and sciences students. Within other colleges, alterations are made in some areas. The core is comprised of (1) a research- and writing-focused first-year seminar capped at eighteen students, (2) a course in expository writing, (3) two years of language study, (4) Foundations of Contemporary Culture, and (5) Foundations of Scientific Inquiry.

With over 30,000 graduate students and a similar number of undergrads, you might expect undergraduate courses to be held in large lecture halls, even with a 9:1 student-to-faculty ratio. However, NYU manages to run a commendable 59 percent of its classes with an enrollment under twenty students; only 10 percent of courses contain more than fifty students. The school puts a great deal of money into undergraduate research, and it has been running an Undergraduate Research Conference for over forty years. Summer research opportunities are plentiful, including through the School of Engineering's ten-week summer research program for rising juniors and seniors. With more than 4,400 students studying in foreign countries each year, NYU sends more undergrads abroad than any other US university.

While all schools within NYU have solid reputations that will open doors to top corporations and grad schools alike, Stern holds the distinction as one of the top undergraduate business programs in the country. For those entering film, dance, drama, or other performing arts, Tisch is as prestigious a place as you can find to study, and the alumni list is full of Hollywood legends. In recent years NYU has seen an increase in the number of students winning highly competitive postgraduate scholarships. In 2019, Fulbright Scholarships were awarded to fourteen exiting seniors. The school has seen more than one Rhodes Scholar named each of the last three years with the Abu Dhabi campus producing more Rhodes winners than any other school in the country.

Outside the Classroom

Campus life at NYU is best described in one word: diverse. The make-up of the student body is 28 percent international, the highest percentage of any US school, as its students hail from 115 countries. With sizable Asian, Latino, and African American populations, only about one-fifth of the students are classified as white. Life outside the classroom is every bit as diverse as the demographics as NYU truly has something for everyone. The school's twenty-two dorms provide housing for 12,000 students (including some graduate students); overall, 43 percent of undergrads live on campus. With eleven men's and ten women's varsity teams competing in NCAA Division III sports as well as an extensive club and intramural program, NYU has enough opportunity to satisfy the athletically-inclined but is far from a "sports school." Greek life is also available but tempered with single-digit participation rates in sororities and fraternities. There are 300 student organizations open to all students as well as hundreds more school-specific clubs (e.g., Stern-only, Tandon-only). Performance-based groups abound and often sport incredible alumni lists such as those from the Hammerkatz sketch comedy, Tisch New Theater, and WNYU radio. Plenty of quirky, niche options also are available such as the uber-popular Milk and Cookies Club. The university's Greenwich Village location means all that New York City has to offer is at your fingertips. International cuisine, Broadway shows, world-renowned museums, top musical and comedy acts, and shopping can all be part of your daily existence.

Career Services

The Wasserman Center for Career Development has fifty professional staff members who work in areas such as career counseling, recruitment, and student employment. That 580:1 student-to-advisor ratio is a bit higher than the average school featured in this guide. Catering to the career services needs of more than 25,000 full-time undergrads is a massive task. Fortunately, NYU's staff is up to it, hosting large-scale events such as the Fall Job & Internship Fair as well as other industry-specific events throughout the year including real estate, nursing, government, and hospitality and tourism.

Of the employed members of the Class of 2018, 56 percent landed their jobs through an NYU resource. Among the resources rated "most helpful" by job/internship seekers were NYU CareerNet, NYU Connections, and the NYU On-Campus Recruiting Program. Those landing summer jobs and internships along the way also attributed their procurement of positions directly to Wasserman at a similar 54 percent clip. The top summer internship destinations include PwC, EY, Credit Suisse, Accenture, Barclay's, Bank of America, and Wells Fargo. Thirteen percent of employed graduates were the recipients of promotions stemming from summer internships. A solid 42 percent of employed grads received job offers prior to commencement. More than half a million alumni are situated in companies and organizations around the world, leaving no shortage of networking opportunities.

Professional Outcomes
Within six months of graduating, 97 percent of NYU Class of 2018 graduates had successfully landed at their next destination. Of that group, 85 percent were employed and 15 percent were in graduate school. Over half of grads received more than one job offer. The top industries for employment were entertainment/media (20 percent), financial services/banking (17 percent), health care (13 percent), computer science/technology (11 percent), and consulting (10 percent). Large numbers of alumni can be found at major corporations such as Google, Deloitte, Morgan Stanley, Goldman Sachs, IBM, JP Morgan Chase, Citi, and Amazon. The mean starting salary is $65,000 with a mean signing bonus of almost $12k. In 2018, New York was (by more than ten times) the most popular destination over number two choice California. New Jersey, DC, and Massachusetts were next in attracting the highest numbers of recent alumni.

Of the 15 percent of the Class of 2018 attending graduate school, 18 percent were seeking degrees in arts/humanities/social sciences, 13 percent were in medical school, and 10 percent were in law school. Elite graduate and professional schools are well within the grasp of an NYU alum, including the university's own top-ranked Stern School of Business, School of Law at New York University, and the School of Medicine at New York University (Langone). Even though the number of students directly matriculating into graduate school is relatively small, 48 percent stated that they planned to continue their education within the next five years.

Admission
Acceptance rates at NYU have experienced a rapid decline in recent years. In 2013, a solid 35 percent of applicants were accepted; in 2017, that figure dipped to 28 percent before plummeting to 20 percent in 2018. In total, the university received over 71,000 applications for a place in the Class of 2022. This cohort boasted a mid-50 percent SAT score of 1310-1510, an all-time high for an incoming class at NYU; the ACT mid-50 percent range was 29-34. The average GPA was 3.62, and 40 percent of freshmen possessed a 3.75 or higher. Close to three-quarters of entering freshmen placed in the top decile of their high school class, and every single individual was at least in the top quartile.

The overwhelming volume of applicants makes an in-depth, personalized admissions process unfeasible. Rather, the committee relies primarily on hard numbers like GPA, class rank, and standardized test scores. Participation in a highly rigorous course load is also a must, and special talents/abilities are given serious consideration. Essays, recommendations, extracurricular activities, and character/personal qualities also are deemed important in the process. NYU does offer an early decision round that yields more favorable acceptance rates than those in the regular round. ED applicants to the Class of 2022 were successful 35 percent of the time versus 18 percent in the regular cycle. *Warning:* This is a school where high school guidance counselors, thinking of NYU-bound students they worked with a few years ago, may not be aware of the increased selectivity demonstrated by the university in the last few years. Applicants with a genuine shot will be near the top of their graduating class and will have standardized test scores in the 95th percentile.

Worth Your Money?
NYU is not nearly as generous with financial aid as many other elite schools that strive to meet 100 percent of demonstrated student need. In fact, the university is downright stingy--only 12 percent of those who qualify for aid see all of their need met; instead, the average annual grant for those found eligible is $31,839. The overall cost of attendance is $75,502, and merit aid awards are extremely uncommon and typically for very low amounts. The university is an exceptional place to learn, but for $300,000 in total costs you'll need to weigh your expected future salary (based on the field you intend to enter) versus the amount of debt you are willing to take on. Of course, if you are aiming to study at any New York City school, the living costs will be on the high side, but the benefits may be great.

FINANCIAL
Institutional Type: Private
In-State Tuition: $50,684
Out-of-State Tuition: $50,684
Room & Board: $18,684
Required Fees: $2,624
Books & Supplies: $752

Avg. Need-Based Aid: $31,839
Avg. % of Need Met: 65%

Avg. Merit-Based Aid: $5,040
% Receiving Merit-Based Aid: 5%

Avg. Cumulative Debt: $29,923
% of Students Borrowing: 43%

CAREER
Who Recruits
1. Infosys
2. BNP
3. Netflix
4. PayPal
5. Eileen Fisher

Notable Internships
1. United Nations
2. Credit Suisse
3. NYU Langone Health

Top Industries
1. Business
2. Education
3. Media
4. Arts & Design
5. Operations

Top Employers
1. Google
2. JPMorgan Chase
3. Citi
4. Morgan Stanley
5. Amazon

Where Alumni Work
1. New York City
2. Los Angeles
3. San Francisco
4. Washington, DC
5. Boston

Median Earnings
College Scorecard (Early Career): $61,900
EOP (Early Career): $58,100
PayScale (Mid-Career): $117,700

RANKINGS
Forbes: 35
Money: 206
U.S. News: 29, National Universities
Wall Street Journal/THE: 31
Washington Monthly: 107, National Universities

#CollegesWorthYourMoney

North Carolina State University

Raleigh, North Carolina | Admissions Phone: 919-515-2434

ADMISSION
Admission Rate: 47%
Admission Rate - Men: 44%
Admission Rate - Women: 49%
EA Admission Rate: 61%
ED Admission Rate: Not Offered
Admission Rate (5-Year Trend): 0%
ED Admission Rate (5-Year Trend): Not Offered
% of Admits Attending (Yield): 34%
Transfer Admission Rate: 42%

Offered Wait List: 4,133
Accepted Wait List: 4,127
Admitted Wait List: 20

SAT Reading/Writing (Middle 50%): 620-680
SAT Math (Middle 50%): 630-710
ACT Composite (Middle 50%): 27-31
Testing Policy: ACT/SAT Required
SAT Superscore: Yes
ACT Superscore: Yes

% Graduated in Top 10% of HS Class: 48%
% Graduated in Top 25% of HS Class: 85%
% Graduated in Top 50% of HS Class: 99%

ENROLLMENT
Total Undergraduate Enrollment: 25,199
% Part-Time: 11%
% Male: 53%
% Female: 47%
% Out-of-State: 9%
% Fraternity: 13%
% Sorority: 17%
% On-Campus (Freshman): 97%
% On-Campus (All Undergraduate): 38%

% African-American: 6%
% Asian: 7%
% Hispanic: 6%
% White: 67%
% Other: 4%
% Race or Ethnicity Unknown: 7%
% International: 4%
% Low-Income: 21%

ACADEMICS
Student-to-Faculty Ratio: 14:1
% of Classes Under 20: 35%
% of Classes Under 40: 76%
% Full-Time Faculty: 86%
% Full-Time Faculty w/ Terminal Degree: 92%

Top Programs
Architecture
Agricultural Science
Animal Science
Design
Engineering
Sport Management
Textile Design and Management

Retention Rate: 94%
4-Year Graduation Rate: 54%
6-Year Graduation Rate: 81%

Curricular Flexibility: Less Flexible
Academic Rating: ★★★⭐

Inside the Classroom

Of the University of North Carolina System's seventeen campuses, UNC-Chapel Hill, the flagship, understandably has the highest national profile by a wide margin. Yet, those in the know are aware that North Carolina State University (NC State) has emerged as a highly competitive and elite academic institution in its own right. Located in the state capital of Raleigh, NC State is at the heart of the Research Triangle—in fact, the school is one its vertices with the aforementioned UNC-Chapel Hill and Duke University accounting for the others. Some would be surprised to learn that among entering freshmen in 2018-19, the average SAT score was 1320 and that the group included 230 valedictorians and salutatorians. The quality of the 25,200 undergraduates is matched by the school's superb academic offerings in engineering, architecture, agriculture, design, business, and so much more.

The general education program requires all students to conquer thirty-nine credits of mandated coursework in the following areas: mathematical science, natural sciences, humanities, social sciences, health and exercise studies, US diversity, interdisciplinary studies, global studies, and technology fluency. Everyone also engages with an Introduction to Writing class and the demonstration of foreign language proficiency, but it's extremely easy to opt out of a foreign language if you choose, as long as you took two years of courses in the same language in high school.

Thanks to a reasonable 14:1 student-to-faculty ratio, you won't exclusively have classes in enormous lecture halls. Rather, NC State offers its undergraduates a mix of experiences with 64 percent of sections enrolling twenty-nine or fewer students and 16 percent enrolling fifty or more. The Office of Undergraduate Research works diligently to connect star students to faculty research projects, which leads to over 600 student presentations at spring/summer poster sessions. The "Speed-Data-ing" program brings together 250 underclassmen to learn about current research being conducted by NC State professors. The university has put a good deal of emphasis on raising its study abroad participation rate in recent years, and those efforts have been fruitful; 22 percent of undergraduates now study abroad, and there has been a 75 percent increase in participation by underrepresented students over the past seven years.

Engineering is the most popular area of concentration as 27 percent of Class of 2019 graduates earned a degree in that field. Business/marketing comes in second at 15 percent followed by biology (8 percent) and agriculture (7 percent). NC State has an exceptional regional reputation and an expanding national one with the College of Engineering now found near the top of many rankings. Programs in design, architecture, and animal science are also very strong. Wolfpack members also are gaining the attention of the most prestigious postgraduate fellowship organizations. In 2019, National Science Foundation Graduate Research Fellowships went to fourteen NC State students. Another four students won Goldwater Scholarships, four captured Fulbright Scholarships, and thirteen were awarded Gilman Scholarships.

Outside the Classroom

Freshmen overwhelmingly reside on campus as they are required to do; 97 percent of all first-year students live in university-run housing. Among all undergraduates, 38 percent live on campus in one of twenty residence halls that are a mix of suite, hotel, and traditional buildings. Greek houses draw their fair share of the population with 17 percent of women joining sororities and 13 percent of men pledging fraternities. More than 550 athletes participate as part of the twenty-three varsity athletic teams that have combined to capture four national championships, including the legendary 1983 NCAA champion men's basketball team. Wolfpack fans are a rabid bunch, and they rank in the top ten for hoops attendance in the United States. The Talley Student Union, built in 2015, is the central hub for 700+ student organizations including a daily newspaper, a popular college radio station, and plenty of cultural, performance-based, political, and pre-professional organizations. The school's 2,110-acre campus is within a few miles of many of Raleigh's finest attractions including North Carolina's state art, natural history, and history museums; multiple parks and arboretums; and the beautiful Lake Johnson Park.

Career Services

The NCSU Career Development Center employs eighteen professionals who function as career identity coaches, career counselors, employer relations specialists, and pre-professional advisors. There are numerous other departments within individual colleges that employ another five career services staff members to bring the total of full-time, professional employees to twenty-three, which works out to a 1008:1 student-to-advisor ratio, higher than the average school featured in this guidebook.

Still, 50 percent of Class of 2019 members had received counseling in the Career Development Center, and the vast majority found the experience to be a positive one. A solid two-thirds of employed Class of 2019 members stated that their job was "directly related" to their major, a sign that career counseling staff are pointing students in the right direction. The greatest number of students reported that their internship/externship had been most helpful in their job search (43 percent) followed by a career fair at NC State (29 percent). In the Poole College of

Management, the co-op/internship completion rate was 85 percent. Co-op participation is encouraged, and students can complete up to three alternating semesters of paid work experience. NC State offers 1,000 different work rotations, making it one of the largest university co-op programs in the country. Major employers are regular visitors to campus, and career expos such as the Engineering Career Fair, Poole College of Management Career & Internship Fair, and the Ag & Sciences Career Expo collectively draw hundreds of top hiring organizations to Raleigh. Being situated in the Triangle means that many big-time companies are nearby and loaded with Wolfpack alumni.

Professional Outcomes

Approximately 75 percent of students graduating in May 2019 reported that they planned to pursue employment after receiving their diplomas, and half had already secured a job offer. Members of that class obtaining a full-time job reported an average starting salary of $54,734 (with a slightly higher median). Of that cohort, 71 percent were remaining in the state of North Carolina for work with a large percentage situated in the Research Triangle area of Raleigh, Durham, and Chapel Hill. San Francisco, DC, New York City, and Atlanta also attracted a fair number of graduates. Including all graduating years, the companies employing the largest number of Wolfpack alumni are Cisco, Red Hat and SAS (major NC-based software companies), IBM, Lenovo, Amazon, Microsoft, Intel, Google, Deloitte, Facebook, and Salesforce. Many recent graduates also work for the university itself and for the Wake County Public School System.

Upon graduation, one-fourth of Class of 2019 members indicated that their plan was to attend graduate/professional school. Forty-six percent of that group planned to continue their educational journey at NC State, and 70 percent planned to attend a school in North Carolina. An encouraging 88 percent stated that they were attending their first-choice institution. The most commonly pursued degree was a master's (67 percent) followed by a professional degree (18 percent) and a doctoral degree (15 percent). Each year roughly 300 NC State students apply to medical school and another 150 to dental school. Recent med school acceptances include prestigious programs at Duke, UNC-Chapel Hill, UVA, Wake Forest, and Emory. Between 75 and 80 percent of those recommended by the Health Professions Advising Center are accepted into at least one medical school. Law candidates find similar positive results, and schools like Yale, Duke, UNC-Chapel Hill, and Washington & Lee regularly visit NC State to recruit.

Admission

The present iteration of NC State is highly selective, which may come as a shock even to an older relative who attended the university. In fact, the 25th percentile SAT score of attending freshmen in 2018-19 is close to the 75th percentile figure from a decade prior. The acceptance rate is now 47 percent, and the applicant pool is more competitive than ever. Those attending possess impressive mid-50 percent standardized test ranges of 27-31 on the ACT and 1250-1390 on the SAT with an even number of students submitting results from both exams. They also earned the grades to match those test scores with an average unweighted GPA of 3.76 (the average weighted GPA is 4.59). A solid 58 percent hailed from the top 10 percent of their high school class, and 85 percent placed in the top quartile.

With more than 30,000 applicants annually, NC State admissions officers rely heavily on factors like SAT scores, GPA, class rank, and the rigor of one's course load. All other factors are mere considerations, unlikely to exert significant influence on the decision. There are no early action or early decision options at NC State, but we recommend that every serious applicant submit by the Nov. 1 priority deadline rather than waiting until mid-January. Thirty-four percent of those accepted ultimately enroll in the school compared with over 50 percent in 2000 when the school drew one-third as many applicants. Despite the lower yield rate, it is fair to say that NC State is a more desirable landing spot than ever for high-achieving North Carolina residents.

Worth Your Money?

When an annual tuition bill is in the four-figures it instantly qualifies as an absurd bargain. NC State's tuition is actually around one-sixth the cost of North Carolina private schools like Duke, Davidson, or Wake Forest. For the 15 percent of Wolfpack members not from in state, thanks to low housing costs, the total cost of attendance is not obscene, coming in at under $45k. Therefore, the value of this degree for a nonresident would be context dependent—engineering, computer science, and design students are more than likely to see favorable returns. For a resident, it's a no-brainer investment.

FINANCIAL
Institutional Type: Public
In-State Tuition: $6,535
Out-of-State Tuition: $25,878
Room & Board: $11,078
Required Fees: $2,566
Books & Supplies: $1,082

Avg. Need-Based Aid: $10,104
Avg. % of Need Met: 73%

Avg. Merit-Based Aid: $5,811
% Receiving Merit-Based Aid: 11%

Avg. Cumulative Debt: $24,002
% of Students Borrowing: 51%

CAREER
Who Recruits
1. John Deere
2. Smithfield
3. GSK
4. Allstate
5. SAS

Notable Internships
1. Barclays
2. Red Hat
3. Cisco

Top Industries
1. Business
2. Engineering
3. Operations
4. Education
5. Research

Top Employers
1. Cisco
2. SAS
3. IBM
4. Lenovo
5. Red Hat

Where Alumni Work
1. Raleigh-Durham, NC
2. Charlotte
3. Winston-Salem, NC
4. Washington, DC
5. San Francisco

Median Earnings
College Scorecard (Early Career): $52,500
EOP (Early Career): $52,300
PayScale (Mid-Career): $106,500

RANKINGS
Forbes: 139
Money: 40
U.S. News: 84, National Universities
Wall Street Journal/THE: 104
Washington Monthly: 74, National Universities

#CollegesWorthYourMoney

Northeastern University

Boston, Massachusetts | Admissions Phone: 617-373-2200

Inside the Classroom

If Northeastern University was a middle-aged person headed to a twentieth high school reunion, it would easily earn the distinction as the least recognized individual in the room. Few institutions have undergone such a substantial metamorphosis in such a short time. Beginning in the 1990s NU decided to reverse-engineer the *US News* rankings and make a grab for increased prestige. At the time, the school was ranked the 162nd best university in the nation. As of 2019 it is close to cracking the top forty. Today, the average undergraduate student possesses a 4.2 GPA and a 1459 on the SAT, literally 400+ higher than two decades ago. You read that correctly—400 points!

On the menu for this suddenly top-flight breed of undergrads are all the trappings of a major research university, including ninety-two majors and 142 combined majors available at Northeastern's seven undergraduate schools. All students are required to walk the NUpath, the school's core curriculum that is "built around essential, broad-based knowledge and skills—such as understanding societies and analyzing data—integrated with specific content areas and disciplines." There are eleven components to the NUpath that involve forays into the natural and designed world, creative expression and innovation, culture, formal and quantitative reasoning, societies and institutions, analyzing data, differences and diversity, ethical reasoning, writing across audiences, integrating knowledge and skills through experience, and a capstone course as you near completion of your chosen major(s).

More than two-thirds of Husky classrooms contain nineteen or fewer students, and 11 percent have single-digit enrollments. Large lecture hall courses crammed with undergrads are rare at this school—only 6 percent of sections sport a student enrollment of fifty or more. A 14:1 student-to-faculty ratio makes these cozy class sizes possible, an impressive feat considering the school has almost 8,700 graduate students to serve as well. Since 2006 Northeastern has added an incredible 650 tenured and tenure-track faculty members. Undergraduate research opportunities exist in all departments, and experiential learning of some type is had by virtually all graduates, thanks to the school's illustrious and robust co-op program. NU students have not only become more accomplished but also more worldly. Last academic year, 3,820 students had a global experience in one of eighty-eight countries, and 538 students participated in a co-op program overseas.

The D'Amore-McKim School of Business is a top-ranked school and offers one of the best international business programs anywhere, and the both the College of Engineering and College of Computer Science are highly respected as well. Criminal justice, architecture, and nursing are three other majors that rate near the top nationally. Business/marketing (25 percent) and engineering (17 percent) account for the largest percentages of degrees conferred. The social sciences (12 percent), health-related professions (10 percent), and biology (8 percent) round out the list of most popular majors. In 2019, Northeastern grads fared better than ever in procuring nationally competitive scholarships. Nine took home Fulbright Scholarships, five were awarded Gilman Scholarships, and two won Truman Scholarships.

Outside the Classroom

Northeastern is split down the middle in terms of those who live in on-campus housing and those who do not. All freshmen and sophomores are required to live in the dorms, and most have at least one or two roommates. Campus offers six large quad areas and twenty eateries. Greek life is fairly strong with 10 percent of men and 17 percent of women joining frats and sororities. The 73-acre urban campus is situated in the true heart of downtown Boston and within one mile of Fenway Park, Newbury Street, and the Museum of Fine Arts. With such a premier location, the beloved city of Boston is truly an extension of your campus, but there are also plenty of university-sponsored activities to keep you busy. Over 400 student clubs and organizations and the Northeastern University Hus-skiers and Outing Club (NUHOC), student government, and forty club sports teams are among the most popular. In total, 3,000 students participate in club and intramural sports. Spectator sports are not a focal point of NU life—the football program was dissolved in 2009— but of the sixteen existing NCAA Division I squads, the Huskies hockey team reigns supreme. The spirit of volunteerism is huge at NU as students have contributed a collective 1.4 million hours since 2006.

Career Services

Thirty-six counselors, employer relations specialists, and experiential learning coordinators comprise the NU Employer Engagement and Career Design Office (EECD), which doesn't count admin assistants or IT professionals. Working out to a student-to-advisor ratio of 512:1, NU offers a high level of support for an institution with more than 18,000 undergraduates. Northeastern University has long held a reputation as one of the premier career services providers in the nation, and it's not hard to see why.

Career counselors received incredibly high reviews from students as 96 percent report progress on their career goals after only one session; 100 percent felt it was worth their time to return for a follow-up. The EECD has forged relationships with over 3,000 employers and, through its employer-in-residence program, representatives from those organizations spend up to one day per week for an entire year interacting with students, making personal connections, and offering career tips. The fall 2018 Career Fair was attended by 260 employers and the spring Engineering and Technology Career Fair usually draws 4,000+ students and 140 companies. Perhaps the most impactful role of this office is to facilitate co-op placements. Ninety-six percent of NU graduates spend at least one semester in a co-op placement, and 50 percent of students receive a job offer from their co-op partner; 2,900+ employers participate each year. By almost any metric, the Employer Engagement and Career Design services stand out from the pack, easily earning its staff near universal praise.

Professional Outcomes

Nine months after leaving Northeastern 92 percent of students have landed at their next employment or graduate school destination. Huskies entering the job market are quickly rounded up by the likes of State Street, Fidelity Investments, IBM, and Amazon, all of whom employ 500+ Northeastern alums. Between 200 and 500 employees at Wayfair, Google, Amazon, Oracle, IBM, and Apple have an NU lineage. Whether or not they originally hailed from New England, the vast majority of graduates remain in the Greater Boston area. Next in popularity are New York City, San Francisco, DC, Los Angeles, Philadelphia, and Seattle. Starting salaries are above average, in part due to the stellar co-op program, and compensation is in the same range as other highly selective schools including Fordham and Boston University.

Strange for a school with such excellent career services, Northeastern does not publicize its law school or med school acceptance rates or release a list of the most frequently attended graduate schools by NU alumni. The highly ranked Northeastern University School of Law does take a large number of its own undergraduates. More than one alum is currently enrolled at such law schools as Suffolk, Harvard, Fordham, and Boston College. While Northeastern does not have its own medical college, many graduates go on to attend top institutions. Multiple recent grads are currently attending such medical schools as UMass, Harvard, UConn, and Tufts. In short, while NU is strangely mysterious about its graduate/professional school outcomes data, it has no reason to be; Huskies routinely continue their educations at some of the best universities in the United States.

Admission

Only 18 percent of the 62,000 applicants for a place in the 2019-20 freshman class received a letter of acceptance. The middle-50 percent stats for admitted (not committed) students included a 4.1-4.5 GPA, a 1450-1540 SAT range, and 33-35 on the ACT. Over three-quarters placed in the top 10 percent of their high school graduating class. A decade ago, the school received only 34,000 applications, and a far less menacing 41 percent were let through the door. Freshmen in 2009-10 possessed middle 50 percent SAT scores of 1200-1370. Any way you measure it, the level of selectivity is far greater than even in the most recent past.

An applicant's GPA, rigor of courses, standardized test scores, essay, and recommendation letters are all categorized as "very important" admissions factors by this committee. Admissions officers at Northeastern place soft factors such as extracurricular activities, talent/ability, character, personal qualities, volunteer work, and work experience on the next rung of "important" categories. Class rank, first-generation status, ethnic status, geographical residence, and the level of demonstrated interest comprise the "considered" factors in the admissions process. As to why geographical residence is a considered factor, the university received only 49 percent of its applications from outside New England in 2006; in 2019, it received 65 percent from outside the region. That is all part of the university's aforementioned quest to enhance its national reputation. Northeastern's desirability and prestige have risen at a lightning pace, making it exactly the type of school that even a well-intentioned school counselor or parent can easily misjudge in terms of the current odds of gaining admission. This is a school that generally only accepts students with standardized test scores in the top 3 percent and who have virtually flawless transcripts. Applying via binding early decision is definitely a serious consideration. Of the 1,107 who did so last year, 41 percent were successful.

Worth Your Money?

Northeastern has a list price cost of attendance in excess of $72,000 per year, and the need-based aid situation is less than ideal. Only two-thirds of those applying for financial aid received an award. Compare that to nearby Boston College and Boston University, each of which awarded need-based grants to 88 percent and 82 percent, respectively, of those who applied. The better news is that over half of Northeastern students receive a merit aid award averaging $19,500, at least bringing the total four-year costs closer to $200,000. In short, this school is worth your money if you are aiming to enter a high-paying field and/or have parents who can afford the hefty tuition payments. Then the connections the school provides are worth a substantial amount. However, middle-class students set on entering public service would likely not see their investment returned and could accumulate a good deal of debt along the way.

FINANCIAL
Institutional Type: Private
In-State Tuition: $52,420
Out-of-State Tuition: $52,420
Room & Board: $16,930
Required Fees: $1,086
Books & Supplies: $1,000

Avg. Need-Based Aid: $35,299
Avg. % of Need Met: 100%

Avg. Merit-Based Aid: $19,488
% Receiving Merit-Based Aid: 51%

Avg. Cumulative Debt: N/A
% of Students Borrowing: N/A

CAREER
Who Recruits
1. IBM
2. Siemens
3. Staples
4. Coleman
5. Northwestern Mutual

Notable Internships
1. Wayfair
2. Vogue
3. Tesla

Top Industries
1. Business
2. Engineering
3. Operations
4. Education
5. information Technology

Top Employers
1. State Street
2. Fidelity Investments
3. Amazon
4. IBM
5. Wayfair

Where Alumni Work
1. Boston
2. New York City
3. San Francisco
4. Washington, DC
5. Los Angeles

Median Earnings
College Scorecard (Early Career): $67,400
EOP (Early Career): $61,800
PayScale (Mid-Career): $109,700

RANKINGS
Forbes: 182
Money: 135
U.S. News: 40, 74, National Universities
Wall Street Journal/THE: 93 (T)
Washington Monthly: 141, National Universities

#CollegesWorthYourMoney

Northwestern University

Evanston, Illinois | Admissions Phone: 847-491-7271

ADMISSION
Admission Rate: 8%
Admission Rate - Men: 8%
Admission Rate - Women: 8%
EA Admission Rate: Not Offered
ED Admission Rate: 27%
Admission Rate (5-Year Trend): -6%
ED Admission Rate (5-Year Trend): -8%
% of Admits Attending (Yield): 56%
Transfer Admission Rate: 15%

Offered Wait List: 2,861
Accepted Wait List: 1,859
Admitted Wait List: 24

SAT Reading/Writing (Middle 50%): 700-760
SAT Math (Middle 50%): 730-790
ACT Composite (Middle 50%): 33-35
Testing Policy: ACT/SAT Required
SAT Superscore: Yes
ACT Superscore: No

% Graduated in Top 10% of HS Class: 92%
% Graduated in Top 25% of HS Class: 100%
% Graduated in Top 50% of HS Class: 100%

ENROLLMENT
Total Undergraduate Enrollment: 8,231
% Part-Time: 2%
% Male: 49%
% Female: 51%
% Out-of-State: 68%
% Fraternity: 34%
% Sorority: 39%
% On-Campus (Freshman): 100%
% On-Campus (All Undergraduate): 60%

% African-American: 6%
% Asian: 18%
% Hispanic: 13%
% White: 45%
% Other: 6%
% Race or Ethnicity Unknown: 4%
% International: 9%
% Low-Income: 14%

ACADEMICS
Student-to-Faculty Ratio: 6:1
% of Classes Under 20: 78%
% of Classes Under 40: 93%
% Full-Time Faculty: 86%
% Full-Time Faculty w/ Terminal Degree: 100%

Top Programs
Biology
Communication Studies
Economics
Engineering
Journalism
Performing Arts
Political Science
Social Policy

Retention Rate: 97%
4-Year Graduation Rate: 84%
6-Year Graduation Rate: 95%

Curricular Flexibility: Somewhat Flexible
Academic Rating: ★★★★★

Inside the Classroom

Like the neighboring University of Chicago, Northwestern University is a highly selective academic institution that operates on a quarter system and is located in Illinois, but the similarities end there. Where the UChicago has a reputation as a breeding ground for future academics/researchers, Northwestern's vibe is more pre-profession-al, athletic, and Greek-inclined, but the 8,200 undergraduates who attend must bring equally flawless academic credentials to the table—otherwise, they will find themselves among the 92 percent of applicants left outside the gates.

Northwestern is home to six undergraduate schools: Weinberg College of Arts and Sciences; McCormick School of Engineering and Applied Science; School of Education and Social Policy; School of Communication; Medill School of Journalism, Media, Integrated Marketing Communications; and Bienen School of Music. Academic requirements vary by school. Weinberg, which enrolls half of all Wildcats, requires two first-year seminars, the demonstration of proficiency in a foreign language and in writing as well as two courses each in six intellectual divisions. Overall, coursework requirements are extensive but not particularly narrow.

The quarter system allows students to take four courses at a time rather than the typical five. Even so, the aca-demic demands are intense, and Northwestern students work hard for their grades. Fortunately, the academic experience is far from an anonymous endeavor. The university has a phenomenal 6:1 student-faculty ratio, and a spectacular 42 percent of class sections have nine or fewer students enrolled; 78 percent have fewer than twenty enrollees. Faculty receive generally favorable reviews from undergraduate students with 93 percent either "very satisfied" or "generally satisfied" with the quality of instruction; 92 percent awarded one of those two pos-itive ratings when asked about the availability of their professors. A solid 58 percent of Northwestern students have the chance to conduct research with a faculty member at some point during their undergraduate years.

The social sciences account for the greatest numbers of degrees conferred (22 percent), followed by communi-cations/journalism (14 percent), engineering (13 percent), biology (8 percent), visual and performing arts (7 percent), and psychology (7 percent). Medill is widely regarded as one of the country's best journalism schools. The McCormick School of Engineering also achieves top rankings, along with programs in economics, social policy, and theatre. Students from all majors bring home prestigious postgraduate fellowships at an enviable rate. In 2018 alone, the school produced twenty-six Gilman Scholars awarded through the US State Depart-ment, twenty-four Fulbright Scholarships, and twenty National Science Foundation Research Fellowships. In total, the Class of 2018 took home a ridiculous 268 competitive national/global scholarships.

Outside the Classroom

Northwestern, like its elite peers Duke, Stanford, and USC, offers top-level academics without sacrificing any of the major college frills like football and frat parties. With forty-six Greek organizations drawing 30 percent of men and 39 percent of women, fraternities and sororities exert a significant degree of influence over the social scene. Athletics are also a strong part of the university's culture with eight men's and eleven women's teams competing in NCAA Division I. The Wildcats are the lone private school competing in the Big Ten Conference, which is otherwise made up of athletic powerhouses like Penn State, Ohio State, and Michigan. NU undergrads report that 91 percent are "deeply involved" with a student organization or athletic team. Nearly half the student population reported that same level of involvement with a community service project. Of the school's 350 student-run clubs, pre-professional organizations, service-oriented groups, and the *Daily Northwestern*—named the nation's top student paper by the Society of Professional Journalists—are among the most popular. Evanston is roughly thirty to forty-five minutes from downtown Chicago (depending on traffic). One of the famous North Shore suburbs of Chicago, Evanston is an affluent city with plenty of high-end restaurants and coffee shops. Natural beauty is easy to find as the school owns a lakefront beach that is on campus. Approximately 60 percent of students (and 99.9 percent of freshmen) elect to live in on-campus housing that is highlighted by thirteen residence halls, each accommodating anywhere from 25-500 students.

Career Services

Northwestern Career Advancement (NCA) employs nineteen full-time professionals who work directly with or on behalf of undergraduate students. That includes career counselors, career advisors, and employer relations staff but does not include graduate advisors, interns, or IT specialists. The student-to-advisor ratio of 443:1 puts NU in the average range compared to other institutions included in this book. Career counselors keep extensive walk-in hours and arrange a number of career-related events, large and small, from the two-day Fall Internship and Job Fair with over 150 employers to more intimate workshops and employer information sessions that are held throughout the year.

Northwestern University

E-mail: ug-admission@northwestern.edu | Website: www.northwestern.edu

A phenomenal 90 percent of graduates reported they engaged in at least one experiential learning opportunity, and 64 percent reported engaging in between two and four such activities. When looking specifically at internships, 76 percent reported landing at least one summer of paid or unpaid experience. The Northwestern Network Mentorship Program now has 5,000 alumni across ninety industries and sixty-six countries ready and willing to help current students with their career planning. The NCA has corporate partnerships with a host of top-notch companies including Accenture, Deloitte, PwC, Capital One, and JP Morgan. The NCA does not publish statistics related to outreach (percentage of students engaging with the office), but thanks to a stellar record of arranging experiential learning opportunities/internships and strong corporate connections, Northwestern's career services still gets a thumbs up from our staff.

Professional Outcomes

Six months after graduating, 72 percent of the Class of 2018 had found employment, 23 percent were in graduate school, and only 3 percent were still looking for work. The four professional fields attracting more than 10 percent of Wildcat alumni were business/finance (20 percent), consulting (15 percent), communications/marketing/media (13 percent), and engineering (12 percent). Employers included an impressive group of media outlets including the BBC, NBC News, the *Washington Post*, and NPR. Across all other industries Wildcats had strong representation at all of the usual corporate giants including Boeing, Google, IBM, Deloitte, PepsiCo, Northrup Grumman, and Goldman Sachs. More than 50 percent of graduates remained in the Midwest, roughly a quarter moved to the East Coast, and 12 percent migrated to California. Across all majors the average starting salary was $59k while engineering and applied sciences students averaged $78k with the lowest income belonging to communications students who earned $43k.

Of the recent alum's headed straight to graduate school, 18 percent were pursuing medical degrees, 13 percent were beginning PhD programs, and 6 percent were entering law school. Engineering, medicine, and business were the three most popular graduate areas of concentration. Members of the Class of 2017 pursued advanced degrees at seven of the eight Ivy League Schools—Stanford, MIT, Carnegie Mellon, UChicago, and Oxford—among a host of other elite institutions. Northwestern is a prolific producer of future MDs; 232 applied in the 2018-19 school year alone.

Admission

The trend toward increasing selectivity continued at Northwestern in 2018 as, for the ninth straight year, the admission rate fell. After hitting single digits for the first time in 2017, only 8.5 percent were admitted into the Class of 2022. The profile of the average freshman in the 2018-19 school year was a mid-50 percent SAT of 1430-1550 and an ACT (by far the more commonly submitted test) was 33-35. A decade ago, when 26 percent of applicants were accepted, the ACT range was a significantly lower 30-32. The percent of freshmen in the top 10 percent of their high school class also has increased during that time, jumping from 85 percent to 92 percent.

According to the admissions office, rigor of courses, GPA, class rank, and standardized test scores are the only four factors that are "very important" in the admissions process. Last year, early decision applicants comprised 56 percent of the incoming classes and enjoyed increased chances of getting in. The regular decision acceptance rate in 2018 was only 6.4 percent compared to 27 percent in the ED round. Northwestern has always been a highly selective school, but the bar has been raised even higher in recent years. Those who wish to find a home on this picturesque North Shore campus next fall must bring excellent credentials to the table and should strongly consider applying early decision.

Worth Your Money?

The average Northwestern graduate who took out loans owes $32,000+, which is a tad more than the national average. This is to be expected at a school that costs over $77,500 per year and does not award much merit aid. Yet, for the 46 percent of undergrads who qualify for need-based aid, the school could not be more generous. It met 100 percent of every student's demonstrated financial need with the average grant approaching $52,000 per year. Those in the toughest spot are children of the middle-class who do not qualify for aid. Still, with very few exceptions, this is a school worth paying for. Even in programs such as journalism that do not generally lead to high-paying first jobs, the networks you will gain at Northwestern are likely to end up paying career dividends many decades down the road.

FINANCIAL
Institutional Type: Private
In-State Tuition: $56,232
Out-of-State Tuition: $56,232
Room & Board: $17,019
Required Fees: $459
Books & Supplies: $1,638

Avg. Need-Based Aid: $51,686
Avg. % of Need Met: 100%

Avg. Merit-Based Aid: $4,964
% Receiving Merit-Based Aid: 4%

Avg. Cumulative Debt: $32,395
% of Students Borrowing: 35%

CAREER
Who Recruits
1. Nielsen
2. Aldi
3. AQR
4. Roland Berger
5. Flow Traders

Notable Internships
1. Brookings Institute
2. HSBC
3. BlackRock

Top Industries
1. Business
2. Education
3. Media
4. Operations
5. Research

Top Employers
1. Google
2. Accenture
3. Amazon
4. Microsoft
5. Deloitte

Where Alumni Work
1. Chicago
2. New York City
3. San Francisco
4. Los Angeles
5. Washington, DC

Median Earnings
College Scorecard (Early Career): $69,000
EOP (Early Career): $72,600
PayScale (Mid-Career): $115,400

RANKINGS
Forbes: 17
Money: 62
U.S. News: 9, National Universities
Wall Street Journal/THE: 11
Washington Monthly: 32, National Universities

#CollegesWorthYourMoney

Oberlin College

Oberlin, Ohio | Admissions Phone: 440-775-8411

Inside the Classroom

A Midwestern version of Oregon's Reed College in terms of the originality and progressive leanings of the student body, Oberlin College in Ohio is an extremely strong provider of a liberal arts education. Known primarily for its top-ranked Conservatory of Music and as a factory for future PhDs, particularly in the hard sciences, Oberlin enrolls more than 2,800 undergraduates. Boasting fifty majors and an additional forty-three minors and concentrations, the college provides an educational setting where professors in just about all of your classes will not only know your name but, amazingly, perhaps even your goals and interests.

As part of the curriculum exploration requirement, two courses each are required in each of the college's three divisions: Arts & Humanities, Mathematics & Natural Sciences, and the Social Sciences. Two of the thirty-two total courses taken must be classified as writing and another two as meeting the Quantitative & Formal Reasoning requirement. Three additional courses must have a Cultural Diversity designation. Students are encouraged—but not required—to become proficient in a foreign language. Overall, Oberlin's mandated coursework is not cumbersome, especially compared to many liberal arts schools of its ilk.

Thanks to its almost entirely undergraduate student population, the effects of Oberlin's 9:1 student-to-faculty ratio are fully felt. Of all the courses at the college, 78 percent had nineteen or fewer students enrolled, and 37 percent contained fewer than ten students. Professors are generous with their time in an academic environment conducive to the formation of mentorships. Undergraduate research opportunities are not hard to locate. In fact, according to the school, "Many students coauthor articles with faculty, which are published in scholarly journals and presented at national meetings." The Office of Study Away helps arrange for roughly 40 percent of graduates to study in a foreign land. School-run opportunities such as Oberlin-in-London are on the table as are ninety affiliated programs.

In terms of sheer volume, the greatest number of degrees conferred in 2019 were in history (55), politics (51), biology (48), English (46), and economics (45). The Conservatory of Music has a worldwide reputation as one or more of its representative alumni are in every major ensemble in the United States. Programs in the natural sciences have sterling reputations, leading to remarkable medical school acceptance rates and the aforementioned number of future PhD scientists and researchers. Highly competitive postgraduate fellowship-granting organizations adore Oberlin grads. In 2017, an astonishing fourteen grads and alumni were named Fulbright Scholars, and the school routinely produces Gilman, Critical Language, Goldwater, and Marshall winners as well.

Outside the Classroom

If you understand Oberlin's vibe it will not surprise you that there are no frats or sororities on campus. Instead, Oberlin requires students to live in either college-owned housing or student-run co-ops all the way through graduation. Some co-ops offer "theme living" centered on commonalities such as an obsession with sci-fi, disability status, sustainability/environmental concerns, or a love of ancient Mediterranean culture. With more than 175 clubs and organizations, twenty-one varsity teams, and thirty-one intramural and club sports, just about every one of Oberlin's undergraduate students is involved in something. The Yeoman and Yeowomen compete within NCAA Division III with 350 athletes competing at that level. If you happen to like live classical music you're in luck—the school's conservatory puts on hundreds of concerts each year. Guest speakers, often intellectuals and authors, regularly attract large crowds at Oberlin. There are a wealth of organizations catering to political/social causes and musical/theatrical performance as well as seven student-run publications. To generalize, most Oberlin students are politically liberal and enjoy challenging social norms. Most students stick around campus, and the small town of Oberlin's quaintness is best exemplified by its claim of having one of the last single-screen movie theaters in the country. For those with access to a car, Cleveland is only a forty-minute drive away.

Career Services

The Career Development Center employs five professional staff members who work in career development or graduate school advising (not counting technical support or administrative assistants). With a 565:1 student-to-advisor ratio, Oberlin provides a lower-than-average level of career services support than many comparable liberal arts schools featured in this guide. While the office does encourage one-on-one appointments and walk-ins, large-scale events like career fairs are lacking, and on-campus recruiting by major employers is not a routine occurrence.

Beginning in 2019, Oberlin began hosting Career Communities covering nine sectors (e.g., entrepreneurship and innovation, professions in music, and science and technology). Up to thirty juniors and seniors can join each community, which includes a guaranteed summer internship and a set of industry-specific mentors. Each community meets as a group six times per semester. Oberlin helps to arrange summer and winter term internships for all interested students, primarily through the use of its online resources. The Oberlin Alumni Database is a platform from which current students can seek job advice from alumni. The office also recommends connecting with 7,000 alumni via LinkedIn. New programs such as the Career Communities show Oberlin's commitment to expanding its career services offerings.

Professional Outcomes

In the years 2015-2017, graduates entering business found homes at companies such as United Shore, Edward Jones, and Liberty Mutual Insurance. Publishing, media, and entertainment companies that scooped up recent grads include MSNBC, *New York Magazine*, and NBCUniversal, Inc. In part because so many students go on to enter careers in research and academia, even age thirty-four median salaries are quite low—one study ranked Oberlin sixty-third of sixty-four selective liberal arts schools in this department. However, it is important to note that many Oberlin graduates do go on to remunerative careers. New York is home to the highest number of alumni followed by San Francisco, Cleveland, DC, and Boston.

Over the last few years multiple students have gone on to pursue advanced degrees at Harvard, Stanford, MIT, Brown, Columbia, Princeton, and the University of Michigan. Graduates fare well in gaining acceptance into med school, sporting an 80 percent success rate, nearly double the national average. Recent grads have enrolled in medical school at the University of Pennsylvania, Baylor College of Medicine, and SUNY Upstate Medical University. Law school applicants have enjoyed an 83 percent acceptance rate and have found homes at the likes of Yale, Indiana, and Wake Forest. Oberlin also has a reputation for churning out future PhDs and, in fact, is among the top ten schools across all disciplines in producing graduates who go on to earn their doctoral degrees.

Admission

An unintimidating 39 percent of the 6,269 applicants for a place in the Class of 2022 were successful, but that number hardly tells the story of how competitive the Oberlin admissions process really is. Admitted students possessed middle-50 percent test scores of 30-34 on the ACT and 1320-1520 on the SAT. The average weighted GPA was 4.0, and the average unweighted GPA was 3.7. An overwhelming 91 percent of students ranked in the top quarter of their high school classes, 65 percent placed in the top 10 percent, and 21 percent were in the top 1 percent. Twenty-nine percent of those accepted went on to enroll in the college. Of those who joined the college, the mid-50 percent SAT range was 1280-1480, and 54 percent placed in the top decile of their graduating class.

Standardized test scores, GPA, class rank, and the rigor of one's secondary school record are the four factors weighted most heavily in the process. Secondary factors include essays, recommendations, talent/ability, character/personal qualities, and the seemingly polar opposite categories of legacy and first-generation applicants. Those who apply via early decision enjoy a 49 percent acceptance rate and account for roughly one-third of each incoming class. Oberlin is definitely a college where the self-selecting applicant pool results in a deceptively high acceptance rate. Make no mistake—you need to bring extremely strong grades to the table (only 14 percent of enrolled high school freshmen possessed GPAs under 3.25) and strong standardized test scores (only 7 percent had SAT reading scores under 600). Applying early is a worthwhile maneuver for those clamoring to spend the next four years in rural Ohio at this liberal arts gem. The ED acceptance rate is 49 percent compared with 35 percent in the regular round.

Worth Your Money?

Oberlin is one of the exclusive club of colleges that meets 100 percent of all undergraduates' demonstrated need. Half of all students receive an average annual aid package that exceeds $41,000. Equally encouraging is the fact that 81 percent of students net merit aid; the average award is approximately $19,000. With an annual cost of attendance of $72,628, those "discounts" are most appreciated, especially because many graduates pursue careers that are not among the most lucrative and/or require many additional years of education beyond the bachelor's degree. Admitted students should consider their future plans before committing. However, Oberlin's top-notch academics and generous aid make it a worthy investment for most.

FINANCIAL
Institutional Type: Private
In-State Tuition: $54,346
Out-of-State Tuition: $54,346
Room & Board: $16,338
Required Fees: $706
Books & Supplies: $930

Avg. Need-Based Aid: $41,979
Avg. % of Need Met: 100%

Avg. Merit-Based Aid: $18,961
% Receiving Merit-Based Aid: 81%

Avg. Cumulative Debt: $27,523
% of Students Borrowing: 41%

CAREER
Who Recruits
1. Cleveland Clinic
2. Sony Pictures
3. City Year
4. Epic
5. Microsoft

Notable Internships
1. Gotham Group
2. Colgate-Palmolive
3. Fidelity Investments

Top Industries
1. Education
2. Business
3. Media
4. Arts & Design
5. Social Services

Top Employers
1. Google
2. Apple
3. Amazon
4. Microsoft
5. IBM

Where Alumni Work
1. New York City
2. San Francisco
3. Cleveland
4. Boston
5. Washington, DC

Median Earnings
College Scorecard (Early Career): $40,800
EOP (Early Career): $38,900
PayScale (Mid-Career): $96,800

RANKINGS
Forbes: 85
Money: 539
U.S. News: 33, Liberal Arts Colleges
Wall Street Journal/THE: 96 (T)
Washington Monthly: 101, Liberal Arts Colleges

#CollegesWorthYourMoney

Occidental College

Los Angeles, California | Admissions Phone: 323-259-2700

Inside the Classroom

A rare liberal arts dynamo in an urban setting, Occidental College, one of the oldest schools on the West Coast, is home to 2,055 undergraduate students. Situated only eight miles from downtown Los Angeles, Occidental attracts a diverse set of talented and community-oriented young people. Non higher-education aficionados may have first heard of the college when Barack Obama burst onto the political scene; he attended the school through sophomore year before transferring to Columbia University. Along with the Claremont colleges, the school known affectionately as Oxy is among the best liberal arts institutions west of the Mississippi.

Thirty-four majors are on tap, but all students must plow through the Oxy Core Program that is designed to "encourage critical thinking, problem-solving, effective communication and productive engagement with issues of difference, diversity and community." Before students even arrive on campus they must complete a summer reading assignment centered on an annual theme. Once class commences, students engage in the Cultural Studies Program, two small seminar courses intended to introduce students to collegiate-level writing and discourse.

Oxy offers an enviable 9:1 student-to-faculty ratio and an average class size of eighteen students. Not a single class contains over fifty students, and 90 percent enroll fewer than thirty. The Undergraduate Research Center facilitates a plethora of hands-on experiences including a ten-week mentored summer program and limitless chances to pursue independent and course-based academic research during the regular school year. At the end of the summer, 120+ students present their research findings. Over two-thirds of undergraduates become global citizens during their time at Occidental through international internships and fellowships or through participation in the study abroad program. Faculty-led programs are available at a variety of destinations around the globe including Italy, Costa Rica, China, the Czech Republic, and Austria. Its partnership with the United Nations provides a one-of-a-kind opportunity for a cohort of students to live in New York, intern at the UN, and take courses with Occidental professors at the same time.

The most popular degree programs at Oxy, all of which carry strong reputations with employers and top-tier graduate schools, are economics, biology, sociology, psychology, diplomacy and world affairs, mathematics, and urban and environmental policy. Prestigious postgraduate scholarship programs look kindly on those with a degree from Oxy. Ten Rhodes Scholars graduated from the school that has been a top ten producer of Fulbright Fellowships for the last decade; nine seniors took home Fulbrights in 2019 alone.

Outside the Classroom

Hardly your typical urban campus, Occidental's 120 acres are among the most notably beautiful higher education homes in the entire country. Countless Hollywood productions (e.g., *Clueless*, *90210*) have selected Occidental as a filming location. The amenities are more in line with a private resort than a typical college. It features a 25,000-square-foot facility only for tennis, a thirty-four-meter deep pool only for water polo, and dining services that serve restaurant-quality cuisine. Just over four-fifths of the student population reside in one the school's thirteen residence halls, and there are seven Greek organizations that attract a modest membership. Roughly 25 percent of undergrads compete on one of twenty-one NCAA Division III sports teams. Tigers also have the option of joining eight club sports teams or any number of intramural athletic leagues. A full array of student organizations exist as well—115 in total—with everything from Oxy TV to a microfinance club. Wandering off campus and into the Eagle Rock and Highland Park sections of Northeast Los Angeles provides easily accessible entertainment, and downtown LA is only a short drive away, which is relevant because 60 percent of Oxy students bring a car to school. In addition, destinations including Venice Beach and Disneyland are less than an hour away.

Career Services

The Hameetman Career Center (HCC) has six full-time professional staff members working in career advising, pre-health advising, and national/international fellowship application guidance. The CDO's 343:1 student-to-advisor ratio is better than average when compared to other colleges featured in our guidebook. Additionally, the center trains four career peer advisors to assist their fellow undergrads. The six core services provided by the office are "(1) career education and career advice; (2) access to internships; (3) pre-law advice; (4) employer, alumni, and parent engagement; (5) job search; and (6) employer recruiting events." It conducted 1,650 one-on-one advising appointments last year alone.

The most recent Oxy Career Fair was attended by sixty-three employers and 380 students. Hosting more than 200 events each year, the HCC also brings 120 employers to campus each year for recruiting purposes. Including all events and individual counseling appointments, it interacts with 2,500 students annually. Internships hosting Oxy students in recent years include Mercedes Benz Shanghai, the Office of the Mayor of Los Angeles, the *Los Angeles Times*, and the NASA Jet Propulsion Laboratory. This office aims to reach students in their freshman year and first presents their services to incoming students at orientation with an eye toward preparing them for a productive first summer experience. Impressive employment and graduate enrollment statistics indicate that its approach works, earning Occidental's Hameetman Career Center praise from current and former students alike.

Professional Outcomes

One year after graduation, 94 percent of Occidental alumni are employed, pursuing graduate studies, or engaged in both simultaneously. By sector, the largest numbers of grads enter community service/education (25 percent), STEM (23 percent), and management/business/finance (20 percent). Among the largest employers of Oxy alumni are the Los Angeles Unified School District, Kaiser Permanente, Microsoft, NASA Jet Propulsion Laboratory, Google, Morgan Stanley, and Amazon. Also on the list are a number of universities that employ Occidental grads after they earn advanced degrees. Most Tigers remain on the prowl in California—mainly LA or San Fran, although there are large alumni clusters on the East Coast, especially in New York City and DC. Midcareer average salaries are in the six figures and among the highest of any institution in the country. According to PayScale, recent graduates earn an average of $51,000 and, by midcareer, bring home $108,000.

Close to three-quarters of Oxy alumni eventually earn one or more advanced degrees. Recent graduates have gone on to continue their educations at Harvard, Stanford, NYU, University of Chicago, UCLA, USC, and UC Berkeley. Those pursuing law degrees have done so at Stanford, USC, UCLA, University of Pennsylvania, Yale, Columbia, Vanderbilt, and Emory. Each year Occidental sees roughly twenty graduates and alumni accepted into medical school, including many of the finest universities in the country. On a per capita basis, the college is also one of the most prolific producers of future PhDs in the country. According to the National Science Foundation, Oxy ranks nineteenth among liberal arts colleges in this category. In short, graduate and professional schools respect the college's reputation and know that those who post an impressive undergraduate GPA have fully earned it.

Admission

Of the 7,281 applicants vying for a place in Occidental College's 2018-19 freshman class, 37 percent were admitted, and 565 ultimately enrolled. Members of the Class of 2022 held a median unweighted GPA of 3.7, SAT score of 1350, and an ACT score of 30. Students were generally active outside the classroom as 52 percent of freshmen played a sport in high school, 75 percent volunteered in their community, and 28 percent played a musical instrument. Over three-fifths placed within the top decile of their high school graduating class; 86 percent landed in the top quarter.

An admissions review from the Occidental staff is a genuinely holistic process. As the committee states, "Creative, soulful, funny, introspective—all words to describe some of our most memorable applicants, but the common thread is always authenticity." That philosophy is supported by GPA, rigor of secondary school record, and the application essay as the triumvirate of admissions factors designated as "most important." Class rank, standardized test scores, recommendations, extracurricular activities, character/personal qualities, volunteer work, and work experience make up the next rung of "important" factors. Men may receive a slight edge in the admissions process as they make up 43 percent of the student body, but the admit rate for men and women is generally comparable. Those applying early decision received a "yes" 48 percent of the time. Occidental is a rare elite college that is not test-optional, but it does not make supremely high test scores a firm prerequisite for serious consideration. In fact, 45 percent of freshmen who took the ACT possessed a composite score between 24 and 29. The college has an extremely low yield rate of 12 percent, which means that it is always on the lookout for students who demonstrate interest and view the school as their number one choice.

Worth Your Money?

An education at Occidental is a phenomenal and highly personalized experience. Of course, providing such an intimate and supportive learning environment costs money. As a result, the annual cost of attendance is $73,102, and while 46 percent of students are awarded merit aid, the average amount is $12k, which puts only a small dent in the overall price. Fortunately, those with significant financial need will see 100 percent of their need met by the school. That translates to 57 percent of current undergraduates receiving grants of almost $42k, helping to make the Occidental experience far more affordable and a worth investment. Middle-income students without a significant financial aid offer should consider their career plans before agreeing to attend.

FINANCIAL
Institutional Type: Private
In-State Tuition: $54,090
Out-of-State Tuition: $54,090
Room & Board: $15,496
Required Fees: $596
Books & Supplies: $1,220

Avg. Need-Based Aid: $41,521
Avg. % of Need Met: 100%

Avg. Merit-Based Aid: $12,332
% Receiving Merit-Based Aid: 46%

Avg. Cumulative Debt: $32,055
% of Students Borrowing: 55%

CAREER
Who Recruits
1. NASA Jet Propulsion Laboratory
2. Northwestern Mutual
3. Aflac
4. Bank of America
5. Teach for America

Notable Internships
1. Calvin Klein
2. Paramount Pictures
3. Pfizer

Top Industries
1. Business
2. Education
3. Operations
4. Media
5. Social Services

Top Employers
1. Kaiser Permanente
2. Google
3. NASA Jet Propulsion Laboratory
4. Microsoft
5. Amazon

Where Alumni Work
1. Los Angeles
2. San Francisco
3. New York City
4. Seattle
5. Orange County, CA

Median Earnings
College Scorecard (Early Career): $50,600
EOP (Early Career): $49,000
PayScale (Mid-Career): $105,700

RANKINGS
Forbes: 102
Money: 251
U.S. News: 39, Liberal Arts Colleges
Wall Street Journal/THE: 99
Washington Monthly: 62, Liberal Arts Colleges

#CollegesWorthYourMoney

The Ohio State University – Columbus

Columbus, Ohio | Admissions Phone: 614-292-3980

Inside the Classroom

Anyone who has ever seen a college football game, even a flicker of one while flipping channels on a Saturday afternoon, will immediately associate the name Ohio State with gray football helmets covered in buckeye leaves. Yet, football is hardly the only draw at the great state of Ohio's flagship university, one of the top public research institutions anywhere. Over 46,000 undergraduate students now grace the Columbus campus, 66 percent of whom are Ohio natives, 21 percent of whom are from out of state, and 13 percent of whom are international students. As you will see in the "Admissions" section below, if you want to gain access to the 2021 version of OSU, you'd better be one of the best students in your high school graduating class.

With 200+ undergraduate majors and eighteen schools and colleges housed within OSU, there are a number of curricular requirements that vary among the many academic programs. However, all Buckeyes must take a liberal arts core that includes writing, quantitative skills, natural science, literature, visual and performing arts, history, social science, and a foreign language. From there it's all about completing your major, but students can find electives in just about anything you can imagine because the university offers 12,000 courses.

A 19-to-1 student-to-faculty ratio leads to fairly large classes as only 27 percent of sections enroll fewer than twenty students, so expect a fair number of courses in a large lecture hall setting. In fact, 36 percent of courses contain forty or more undergraduate students. Still, aggressive students can find opportunities to work closely with faculty. The Office of Undergraduate Research & Inquiry helps 800 students participate in annual Denman Undergraduate Research Forum and fifty+ students receive funding from OSU for summer research. All told, approximately 20 percent of students gain research experience. The same percentage of undergraduates elect to study abroad in one of 200 programs spread across seventy countries, the highest figure of any Big Ten university.

Business saw the greatest percentage of degrees conferred at 18 percent followed by engineering (14 percent), biology (9 percent), health professions (9 percent), and the social sciences (9 percent). It makes sense that so many flock to the business and engineering schools as they are among the highest rated undergraduate programs in their respective disciplines. Top companies adore new Buckeye grads, and hundreds of alums can be found at some of the top tech companies, banks, and accounting firms in the United States. In recent years the university has produced between five and eleven Fulbright Scholars annually and as many as six Boren Scholars, thirteen Gilman Scholars, four Goldwater Scholars, and eleven National Science Foundation Graduate Research Fellowship honorable mentions.

Outside the Classroom

There's a little something for everyone on this anything-but-little 1,665-acre campus that ranks third largest in the United States in sheer size. If you are seeking Greek life, you can find it—12 percent of women join sororities and 8 percent of men enter fraternities. The sports scene is epic in scope whether you are a casual athlete wanting to join one of the sixty+ club teams and numerous intramural leagues or one of the 1,000+ big-time athletes on the Buckeyes' thirty-six varsity teams. Football Saturdays are kind of a big deal as more than 102,000 fans of the Scarlet and Gray pack Ohio Stadium. In total, 1,300 student organizations are awaiting your participation on the Columbus campus alone. Only 32 percent of students live in university-owned housing so, for many, sports and club activities are a way to stay connected. Many aspects of OSU campus life receive rave reviews in surveys—from the food to general happiness to LGBTQ friendliness, the university gets a giant thumbs up from its own students. Ohio's capital city is almost equidistant from Cincinnati and Cleveland, about a two-hour car ride. Skiing, camping, and hiking opportunities can be found much closer to satisfy those with a craving for nature.

Career Services

Buckeye Careers is a university-wide office staffed by four professionals, yet the bulk of the counseling takes place within discipline-specific career services offices housed within individual colleges. Including career coaches and other professional staff from the College of Arts & Sciences (14), College of Engineering (9), Fisher School of Business (6), and smaller undergraduate schools, there are forty-two professional members on the OSU career services team. The university's overall 1,115:1 student-to-counselor ratio is poor compared to many other schools in this guide, but there are myriad facts and figures that suggest the university is preparing students for successful postgraduation outcomes.

The fall 2018 Career and Internship Fair was attended by 218 employers and more than 4,000 students, 93 percent of whom rated the event as helpful. The Fisher School of Business has its own career fair that brings 185 companies to campus in the fall and another 130 in the spring. In a typical year, an eye-popping thirty-six career fairs are held. A solid 71 percent of Ohio State graduates completed at least one internship, and those students have been 2.8 times more likely to receive a job offer prior to graduation than their peers who did not complete an internship. Within the Fisher School of Business, 95 percent of graduates participated in an internship or other intensive work experience; Fisher also conducts over 1,100 mock interviews per year. Three-quarters of grads believe the university prepared them well for the job market. Within the School of Education and Human Ecology alone there are just shy of 600 one-on-one counseling sessions taking place every academic year. Despite less-than-desirable staffing levels, Ohio State University's career services is well-run and manages to have a positive impact on students' lives.

Professional Outcomes

Class of 2019 graduates were primarily entering the world of employment (71 percent) while 26 percent were already accepted into graduate or professional school. Hordes of Buckeyes can be found in the offices of many of the nation's leading companies. More than 2,000 alumni work for JPMorgan Chase, more than 1,000 are employed by Cardinal Health and Nationwide, and at least 300 OSU grads inhabit the halls of Amazon, Oracle, IBM, Microsoft, Google, and Apple. Roughly half of graduates settle in for the long haul in the Columbus area, and many others remain in the state, residing in Cleveland or Cincinnati. New York, Chicago, DC, and San Francisco also attract a fair number of alumni. Overall, the average starting salary for a recent graduate is $54,000, a figure buoyed by the high number of business and engineering grads the school produces.

Of the more than one-quarter of recent grads directly matriculating into graduate or professional school, many continue in one of OSU's own ninety-four doctoral programs, ninety-seven master's programs, or excellent law and medical schools. In the last few years law school-bound graduates have earned admission at universities including UVA, Penn, Fordham, Harvard, George Washington, Georgetown, Case Western, and Cornell. Over 500 graduates apply to medical school each year, and some have gone on to prestigious medical institutions like Harvard Medical School, Duke University School of Medicine, and Johns Hopkins School of Medicine. In sum, Ohio State grads attend a wide variety of graduate schools, and they can absolutely earn their way into some of the best institutions in the world.

Admission

Fifty-two percent of the 48,077 applicants for a place in the Class of 2022 gained acceptance, but that figure hardly tells the whole story of just how selective the flagship Columbus campus has become. The ACT is, by far, the more commonly submitted test, and members of the 2018-19 freshman class possessed a mid-50 percent ACT composite score of 27-32; the SAT range was 1240-1370. Even more shocking is the fact that 63 percent of enrolled students finished in the top 10 percent of their high school classes; 94 percent were in the top quartile. Ohio State has become significantly more competitive in recent years. A decade ago, it received fewer than half as many applications as it does today, admitted 62 percent of the pool, and the ACT range was far lower than today at 25-30; the average ACT score today is 29.3.

The OSU admissions staff promises a holistic review of each application but does rank the concrete factors of class rank, standardized test scores, GPA, a rigor of curriculum as "very important" in the process. Essays, extracurricular activities, talent/ability, first-generation status (few schools give this factor so much weight), volunteer work, and work experience get second billing. In a broad sense, OSU seeks individuals who are "not only smart but willing to lead; who see strength in diversity of people and ideas; who seek collaboration when solving problems; and who make use of all opportunities to figure out what kind of impact they want to have in the world." In 2008 in-staters represented 82 percent of the student body; today, that figure is only 66 percent. The influx of out-of-staters and international students has caused the school to make huge jumps in selectivity. As a result, Buckeye state residents need to be A/A- students with standardized test scores in at least the 90th percentile to be on solid footing.

Worth Your Money?

Ohio residents have a cost of attendance of $27,000 per year, making the cost of a four-year degree from a well-respected university very reasonable. The out-of-state cost of attendance is a shade over $48,000 per year. Approximately 30 percent of undergrads receive a small merit aid award, but as is typical at public institutions, the need-based aid tends to be a bit more substantial. Close to half of current students receive some level of grant with an average award of $11,692. In state, OSU is an easy choice and a spectacular value; out of state it may be worth paying for certain top programs, particularly those that lead to careers with above-average starting salaries.

FINANCIAL
Institutional Type: Public
In-State Tuition: $11,084
Out-of-State Tuition: $32,061
Room & Board: $12,708
Required Fees: N/A
Books & Supplies: $1,168

Avg. Need-Based Aid: $11,692
Avg. % of Need Met: 72%

Avg. Merit-Based Aid: $6,800
% Receiving Merit-Based Aid: 31%

Avg. Cumulative Debt: $27,453
% of Students Borrowing: 52%

CAREER
Who Recruits
1. Abercrombie & Fitch
2. Cargill
3. Nestle
4. Sherwin-Williams
5. Marriott International

Notable Internships
1. Sun National Bank
2. Walt Disney World
3. U.S. Department of State

Top Industries
1. Business
2. Education
3. Operations
4. Healthcare
5. Sales

Top Employers
1. JPMorgan Chase
2. Nationwide
3. Cardinal Health
4. Amazon
5. IBM

Where Alumni Work
1. Columbus, OH
2. Cleveland
3. Cincinnati
4. New York City
5. Chicago

Median Earnings
College Scorecard (Early Career): $46,100
EOP (Early Career): N/A
PayScale (Mid-Career): $98,600

RANKINGS
Forbes: 121
Money: 152
U.S. News: 54 (T), National Universities
Wall Street Journal/THE: 86
Washington Monthly: 95, National Universities

#CollegesWorthYourMoney

University Park, Pennsylvania | Admissions Phone: 814-865-5471

ADMISSION
Admission Rate: 56%
Admission Rate - Men: 52%
Admission Rate - Women: 60%
EA Admission Rate: N/A
ED Admission Rate: Not Offered
Admission Rate (5-Year Trend): +1%
ED Admission Rate (5-Year Trend): Not Offered
% of Admits Attending (Yield): 27%
Transfer Admission Rate: 46%

Offered Wait List: 105
Accepted Wait List: 76
Admitted Wait List: 41

SAT Reading/Writing (Middle 50%): 580-660
SAT Math (Middle 50%): 580-700
ACT Composite (Middle 50%): 25-30
Testing Policy: ACT/SAT Required
SAT Superscore: No
ACT Superscore: No

% Graduated in Top 10% of HS Class: 43%
% Graduated in Top 25% of HS Class: 76%
% Graduated in Top 50% of HS Class: 96%

ENROLLMENT
Total Undergraduate Enrollment: 40,363
% Part-Time: 3%
% Male: 53%
% Female: 47%
% Out-of-State: 34%
% Fraternity: 17%
% Sorority: 20%
% On-Campus (Freshman): 99%
% On-Campus (All Undergraduate): 35%

% African-American: 4%
% Asian: 6%
% Hispanic: 7%
% White: 65%
% Other: 3%
% Race or Ethnicity Unknown: 2%
% International: 12%
% Low-Income: 14%

ACADEMICS
Student-to-Faculty Ratio: 14:1
% of Classes Under 20: 31%
% of Classes Under 40: 71%
% Full-Time Faculty: 86%
% Full-Time Faculty w/ Terminal Degree: 83%

Top Programs
Architecture
Business
Criminal Justice
Earth Sciences
Economics
Engineering
Information Sciences and Technology
Kinesiology

Retention Rate: 93%
4-Year Graduation Rate: 66%
6-Year Graduation Rate: 85%

Curricular Flexibility: Less Flexible
Academic Rating: ★★★

Inside the Classroom
"We are Penn State," the signature slogan of Pennsylvania State University, is one of the more recognizable chants echoing across any college campus in the United States. More than 40,000 undergraduates reside in State College, nicknamed Happy Valley, a moniker that has weathered scandal and continues to be a destination point for Pennsylvanians as well as many out-of-staters and international students who make up 42 percent of today's student population. Not only does PSU have one the world's largest and most passionate alumni bases, it also possesses as diverse an academic menu as you will find anywhere with its 275 majors and a number of top-ranked programs in a host of disciplines.

There are forty-five credits worth of general education requirements that you'll need to fulfill whether you are studying turfgrass science, toxicology, or telecommunications—all actual majors at PSU. Fifteen of those credits will come through introductory courses in writing, speaking, and quantification, and thirty will come via explorations of the humanities, natural sciences, social and behavioral sciences, the arts, and health and wellness. First-year engagement courses help students hone study and research skills and introduce freshmen to resources around campus. Students also must take courses that satisfy the categories of writing across the curriculum, United States cultures, and international cultures, but those can overlap with the aforementioned forty-five credits worth of distributional mandates.

Unlike some public research universities that can have student-to-faculty ratios greater than 20:1, PSU boasts a stellar 14:1 ratio. That level of support allows 61 percent of classes to have an enrollment below thirty students. Still, you will take some intro courses in massive lecture halls, and 17 percent of sections enroll more than fifty undergraduates. Even at such a large institution, it is possible to get involved in undergraduate research. Eberly College of Science professors are running upwards of 3,000 research projects per year, and the school has a well-maintained and up-to-date database of undergraduate research positions. All told, 20 percent of graduates report having engaged in undergraduate research. Twenty-three percent of Penn Staters avail themselves of study abroad opportunities in one of 300 programs in fifty countries.

Penn State University's College of Engineering is rated exceptionally well on a national scale, cracking the top twenty-five on just about everyone's list, and even hits the top ten in some sub- disciplines such as industrial and biological engineering. It's no wonder that engineering is the most popular field of study at the university, accounting for 18 percent of the degrees conferred. The Smeal College of Business is equally well regarded, also earning high rankings in everything from supply chain management to accounting to marketing. This school not only ranks among top undergraduate public business colleges in the United States but among all colleges, and it attracts 16 percent of total degree-seekers. In addition to gaining positive attention from the engineering and business communities, PSU is viewed favorably by prestigious national fellowship organizations. In 2019, ten graduates captured Fulbright Scholarships as well as one or more Boren, Critical Language, Astronaut, Marshall, and Goldwater Scholarships in the last two years.

Outside the Classroom
Only 35 percent of Nittany Lions technically live in university-owned housing, but that doesn't quite capture the cohesive spirit of the PSU community. Greek life is a major social force at the school as 17 percent of men join frats and 20 percent of women become members of sororities. A tragic hazing death a few years back led to a shutdown of one fraternity and increased administrative scrutiny of the practices of others. Unfortunately, the school is no stranger to national controversy. Yet, even after the infamous Sandusky scandal, Penn State football is a tradition like no other as 106,000 pack into Beaver Stadium to watch the Lions battle with Big Ten rivals like Ohio State, Michigan, and Nebraska. Thon, an annual charity dance marathon, is one of the grandest and most impressive events on campus, raising over $10 million to fight childhood cancer in 2019. With over 1,000 clubs and activities to choose from, it's hard not to find your niche at Penn State. Campus itself covers almost 8,000 acres and contains its own arboretum, the Palmer Art Museum, and the famous (and delicious) Penn State Creamery. State College may be in the middle of nowhere, but it truly is the ultimate college town, walkable and brimming with terrific restaurants, bars, and shops.

Career Services
Not counting graduate assistants and office managers, there are thirty full-time employees occupying the Bank of America Career Services Center at University Park. However, there are additional offices that serve specialty groups such as the Career Resources & Employer Relations department housed within the College of Engineering that is staffed by seven professionals, the Smeal College of Business that has nine career services employees, and eleven other staff members are spread across campus in other departments. Based on this grand total of fifty-seven career counselors, internship coordinators, employer relations specialists, and related positions, the student-to-counselor ratio is 708:1, higher than most of the schools featured in this guide, but not at all bad for a school of PSU's size.

Pennsylvania State University – University Park

E-mail: admissions@psu.edu | Website: www.psu.edu

Career fairs, such as the major one held each fall, are massive undertakings, some featuring 300+ companies. The Fall Career Fair is four days in length, and that time is divided to cover technical jobs, nontechnical jobs, internships, and interviews. It also offers many smaller (but still large) targeted fairs in areas such as nursing, education, graduate school, small business and startups, and impact (nonprofits). The majority of graduates, 63 percent, report participating in at least one internship while at University Park. More than one 2018 graduate held an internship position at companies like Amazon, Pfizer, and Xerox. Within the first week of students returning to school for the 2019-20 school year, Microsoft and Lockheed Martin were already actively recruiting on campus. PSU does not publish statistics on how many students take advantage of career services offerings, but it is clear that this staff facilitates powerful, door-opening opportunities for those proactive enough to seek them out.

Professional Outcomes

By the day of graduation, 72 percent of Nittany Lions have found their next employment or graduate school home; within some of the universities many colleges, that rate is even higher. Upon receiving their diplomas, 82 percent of Smeal College of Business Class of 2018 grads already had their next step lined up. They flock in large numbers to some of the nation's best finance, accounting, consulting, and technology firms. More than 500 PSU alumni are currently working at each of IBM, Deloitte, PwC, Amazon, EY, JPMorgan Chase, Microsoft, Google, and Oracle. Hundreds more work at Citi, Salesforce, and Facebook. Philadelphia, New York City, Pittsburgh, DC, San Francisco, Boston, and Los Angeles all have a strong PSU alumni presence. The median salary for Penn State grads ten years after arriving at the school averages $50,000. Of course, salaries vary greatly by academic discipline; business graduates' salaries start at $60,000 while engineering students start at over $70,000.

Medical school acceptance rates for PSU graduates hover around 60 percent, well above the national average, an impressive figure when considering that over 300 students applied in 2019. Seventy percent of those accepted into medical school enroll at Pennsylvania-based institutions including the Penn State College of Medicine. Overall, presently PSU alumni are enrolled in sixty medical schools throughout the country. Likewise, many prelaw students go on to pursue legal educations at one of the university's two law schools (Penn State Law and Dickinson Law), other strong local options like Temple or Villanova, or prestigious national universities like the University of North Carolina, Stanford, Cornell, or Wake Forest.

Admission

The nearly 53,000 Nittany Lion hopefuls seeking a place in the Class of 2022 were accepted at a 56 percent rate, a figure that somewhat undersells how competitive gaining admission right out of high school truly is (transferring later is easier). For some, Penn State is a clear number one choice and often a family tradition, for other Pennsylvania students it occupies mere safety status. Overall, the yield rate—the percentage of accepted students who go on to enroll—is 27 percent. Freshmen who entered the university in 2018-19 possessed mid-50 percent standardized test scores of 1160-1330 on the SAT and a composite score of 25-30 on the ACT. One-quarter of applicants scored over a 700 on the math portion of the SAT; only 12 percent achieved the same on the verbal section. With 43 percent of freshmen having earned a place in the top ten percent of their high school class and 76 percent in the top quartile, most Penn State admits sport strong grades, generally a mix of A's and B's in at least some AP and honors courses.

The only two "very important" factors in the admissions process are GPA and standardized test scores. The rigor of one's high school coursework sits alone in the next tier of still "important" factors. Soft factors like essays, extracurricular activities, work experience, talent/ability, character/personal qualities as well as state residency status and ethnicity are "considered" in candidate evaluation. An early option allows students to submit an application by November 1. After that admission is rolling, but you should absolutely meet the priority date of November 30.

Worth Your Money?

PSU's in-state tuition cost of roughly $18,500 and total cost of attendance of $32,000+ isn't as cheap as, for example, schools in New York's SUNY system that have a COA approximately $10k cheaper. A non-Keystone State resident would pay a COA of over $50,000, which would not make sense in most circumstances. Denizens of Pennsylvania will generally reap the benefits of this flagship institution's strong reputation and incomprehensibly vast alumni network.

FINANCIAL
Institutional Type: Public
In-State Tuition: $17,416
Out-of-State Tuition: $34,480
Room & Board: $11,884
Required Fees: $1,034
Books & Supplies: $1,840

Avg. Need-Based Aid: $6,578
Avg. % of Need Met: 64%

Avg. Merit-Based Aid: $5,444
% Receiving Merit-Based Aid: 33%

Avg. Cumulative Debt: $38,695
% of Students Borrowing: 53%

CAREER
Who Recruits
1. Google
2. Grant Thorton LLP
3. Oracle
4. PNC
5. Accenture

Notable Internships
1. Anheuser-Busch
2. Morgan Stanley
3. Aramark

Top Industries
1. Business
2. Operations
3. Education
4. Engineering
5. Sales

Top Employers
1. IBM
2. PwC
3. Amazon
4. Johnson & Johnson
5. EY

Where Alumni Work
1. Philadelphia
2. New York City
3. Pittsburgh
4. State College, PA
5. Washington, DC

Median Earnings
College Scorecard (Early Career): $50,100
EOP (Early Career): $50,900
PayScale (Mid-Career): $105,500

RANKINGS
Forbes: 117
Money: 291
U.S. News: 57 (T), National Universities
Wall Street Journal/THE: 105 (T)
Washington Monthly: 120, National Universities

#CollegesWorthYourMoney

Pepperdine University

Malibu, California | Admissions Phone: 310-506-4392

Inside the Classroom

The incongruity of a resort-like university located in Malibu that only lifted its ban on dancing in the late 1980s is hard to reconcile. Maybe the most beautiful campus in the world, Pepperdine is also a bastion of evangelical Christianity and largely conservative politically. On the academic menu for the 3,300 undergrads at Seaver College (the school's undergraduate wing) are forty-five majors and forty minors with the most commonly conferred degrees being in business/marketing (26 percent), communication/journalism (19 percent), general social sciences (11 percent), psychology (10 percent), and parks and recreation (8 percent). Only 2 percent pursue degrees in religion, but its influence is interwoven into the fabric of both the academic experience and the social scene.

Among the nineteen courses that constitute Pepperdine's general education requirements for all undergraduates are three classes under the umbrella of Christianity and Culture. Other mandated areas of study include the American experience, Western cultures, human institutions and behavior, world civilizations, fine arts, mathematics, laboratory science, and speech and rhetoric. First-year seminars are intended to sharpen skills in the areas of communication, critical thinking and learning how to "apply the university's Christian mission." Those seminars tackle big-picture topics that include science and religion, the nature of conscience, and the pain of betrayal. Students must continually update a writing portfolio that is formally evaluated as the junior writing portfolio when students reach their third year of study.

A 13:1 student-to-faculty ratio is solid, and faculty are fully deployed with the aim of creating an intimate liberal arts classroom setting. The average class contains nineteen students, and one-quarter of courses will contain fewer than ten students. There are three formal programs for undergraduate research: the Summer Undergraduate Research Program, the Cross-disciplinary/Interdisciplinary Undergraduate Research Program, and Academic Year Undergraduate Research Initiative. Close to two-thirds of Seaver students study abroad and build global experience in locations such as Buenos Aires, Florence, London, and Shanghai.

The Graziadio Business School has a strong reputation that penetrates far beyond the school's home state. The Communication Division also registers on many national ranking lists. Thanks in part to the school's focus on international experience, five 2018 graduates won Fulbright Scholarships, and six took home the award in 2017. Recent grads also have, on occasion, been awarded Gilman, Boren, and National Science Foundation fellowships.

Outside the Classroom

The university's 835-acre grounds can be found in the number one or two position in just about any nationwide ranking of "most beautiful campuses." Given its size and luxurious feel, it's a bit strange that under 60 percent of the undergraduate population lives on campus, however 98 percent of freshmen do reside in university-owned housing. Dorms and on-campus apartments are single-sex, and overnight visitors of the opposite sex are prohibited. The alcohol policies are also enforced more than at your average college. Gender-wise, Seaver has a 60/40 split in favor of women, 32 percent of whom join sororities while 23 percent of men join fraternities. A relatively athletic undergraduate student body participates on seventeen NCAA Division I sports teams (the Waves) that have produced an impressive fifty-two Olympians in the school's history. There are plenty of intramural and club teams as well as four fitness centers and an Olympic-size swimming pool. One hundred and ten student organizations are active, and more than 1,000 on-campus events are hosted each semester. A focus on service leads three-fifths of students to engage in volunteer work with over 80,000 hours contributed each year. Pepperdine is nestled in the Santa Monica Mountains only minutes from some of the world's premier surfing beaches. As another bonus, campus is only thirty miles west of Los Angeles, so Hollywood is only a short car ride away.

Career Services

Pepperdine Career Services employs eight full-time professional staff members (not counting office managers) working as counselors, industry specialists, events managers, and employer relations coordinators. That works out to a 402:1 student-to-counselor ratio, within the average range of institutions profiled in this book. This department offers a solid blend of one-on-one counseling and large-scale events such as industry-specific career fairs in business, health and sciences, nonprofit and government, and arts/entertainment/media. There is also a more generalized Spring Career Expo attended by fifty+ employers and graduate schools.

A phenomenal 96 percent of Class of 2017 grads had at least one internship, work experience, or formal undergraduate research experience. Four-fifths had a minimum of one internship in their four years of undergraduate education. Over 1,000 unique internship sites hosted members of this cohort. Each year, 150+ employers recruit on site at Pepperdine, conducting information sessions as well as on-campus interviews. The alumni network is always happy to be involved in assisting current students. Over 500 alumni volunteer to work with undergraduates directly, and 110,000 living alumni can be found around the globe. A formalized Career Coaching Program has set up 350 students with alumni mentors who have guided them through each stage of the career exploration and development process since its inception in 2001. An above-average level of next-step support and reasonably successful student outcomes makes Pepperdine Career Services a strong performing outfit.

Professional Outcomes

Members of the Seaver Class of 2018 landed at their next destination within six months of graduating at an 89 percent clip with 68 percent employed full time, 18 percent admitted to graduate school, 3 percent volunteering, and 11 percent seeking their first job or a graduate school home. Of those entering the world of work, three-quarters were in the for-profit sector, 18 percent with nonprofit/government entities, and 8 percent pursuing entrepreneurial ventures. Deloitte, Disney, EY, Facebook, PwC, Sony Pictures, and the US Senate and House of Representatives all hired 2017 graduates. Other companies employing fifty or more alumni include Kaiser Permanente, Apple, Google, Wells Fargo, and Amazon. Many graduates remain in California as Los Angeles and Orange County are the two most common landing spots. Other West Coast locales including San Diego, San Francisco, and Seattle also sport sizable numbers of alums. When compared to other elite California-based schools, mid-career median salaries rank lower than Pomona but higher than Occidental.

Class of 2018 graduates were admitted to graduate/professional school at an 83 percent rate. Training in a medical field was the choice of 22 percent of that group, and 12 percent matriculated into law school. In a typical year, twenty to thirty grads apply to medical school, and 70-80 percent are successful. Recent students have gained acceptance to medical schools at Georgetown; Emory; USC; University of California, San Diego; and Washington University in St. Louis. Those going the law school route study at many fine institutions including Pepperdine's own law school. In the last few years, others have been admitted to Harvard Law School, UCLA School of Law, and NYU School of Law. No matter your postgraduate pursuit, a solid transcript and a Pepperdine degree will leave you with many strong graduate/professional school options.

Admission

In the 2018 admission cycle, the university admitted 35 percent of 12,134 applicants. Those who were offered a place in the Class of 2022 had a mid-50 percent range of 28-32 on the ACT, 1270-1420 on the SAT, and 3.62-3.95 as their cumulative GPA. Applicants who accepted positions at the university and comprised the freshman class had a 25-30 ACT range, a 1200-1390 SAT range, and an average GPA of 3.64. "Only" 49 percent of that cohort placed in the top 10 percent of their high school class, a low figure compared to many other elite universities. Further, 20 percent did not place in the top quartile, so there is some leeway here for students with imperfect academic transcripts.

There are seven factors rated as "very important" by the admissions committee, most notably religious affiliation because Pepperdine, as noted earlier, is a Christian school. The other more common critical factors are: rigor of coursework, GPA, application essay, extracurricular activities, talent/ability, and character/personal qualities. Standardized tests, recommendations, and volunteer work make-up the second rung of still "important" factors. The yield rate (percent of those accepted who actually enroll) is only 18 percent, which means that Pepperdine is definitely interested to know if you are a student who truly places the university at the top of your college list. Since it offers only early action and does not have a binding early decision program, demonstrating interest is a good idea if you are serious about this school. Admissions standards at Pepperdine today are almost identical to those of five years ago. It remains a niche institution for devout Christians with strong academic credentials.

Worth Your Money?

Pepperdine's annual cost of attendance exceeds $74,000, making it one of the most expensive colleges in the country. Just about everyone entering the school applies for need-based aid, but only 53 percent of those seeking a grant actually receive one; the average amount is over $37,000, slicing the COA in half. Roughly one-quarter of current students receive an average merit aid grant of $15k. There aren't exactly dozens of academically competitive, conservative Christian universities with a beachfront view; so, if that's the description of your ideal school, Pepperdine will likely be worth your money, especially if you have plans to enter the fields of business or communication.

FINANCIAL
Institutional Type: Private
In-State Tuition: $55,640
Out-of-State Tuition: $55,640
Room & Board: $15,670
Required Fees: $252
Books & Supplies: $1,250

Avg. Need-Based Aid: $37,652
Avg. % of Need Met: 77%

Avg. Merit-Based Aid: $15,207
% Receiving Merit-Based Aid: 25%

Avg. Cumulative Debt: $34,335
% of Students Borrowing: 51%

CAREER
Who Recruits
1. PennyMac
2. Disney
3. Universalizer
4. Sony Pictures Entertainment
5. REX-Real Estate Exchange Inc.

Notable Internships
1. United Nations
2. U.S. Securities and Exchange Commission
3. Farmers Insurance

Top Industries
1. Business
2. Education
3. Operations
4. Sales
5. Healthcare

Top Employers
1. Boeing
2. Kaiser Permanente
3. Wells Fargo
4. Walt Disney
5. Amazon

Where Alumni Work
1. Los Angeles
2. Orange County, CA
3. San Francisco
4. San Diego
5. New York City

Median Earnings
College Scorecard (Early Career): $65,500
EOP (Early Career): $55,800
PayScale (Mid-Career): $103,900

RANKINGS
Forbes: 129
Money: 244
U.S. News: 50 (T), National Universities
Wall Street Journal/THE: 137 (T)
Washington Monthly: 203, National Universities

#CollegesWorthYourMoney

Pitzer College

Claremont, California | Admissions Phone: 909-621-8129

ADMISSION
Admission Rate: 13%
Admission Rate - Men: 17%
Admission Rate - Women: 12%
EA Admission Rate: Not Offered
ED Admission Rate: 30%
Admission Rate (5-Year Trend): -1%
ED Admission Rate (5-Year Trend): N/A
% of Admits Attending (Yield): 47%
Transfer Admission Rate: 10%

Offered Wait List: 707
Accepted Wait List: 234
Admitted Wait List: 4

SAT Reading/Writing (Middle 50%): 670-730
SAT Math (Middle 50%): 670-760
ACT Composite (Middle 50%): 30-33
Testing Policy: Test Optional
SAT Superscore: Yes
ACT Superscore: Yes

% Graduated in Top 10% of HS Class: 62%
% Graduated in Top 25% of HS Class: 83%
% Graduated in Top 50% of HS Class: 98%

ENROLLMENT
Total Undergraduate Enrollment: 1,106
% Part-Time: 2%
% Male: 44%
% Female: 56%
% Out-of-State: 56%
% Fraternity: Not Offered
% Sorority: Not Offered
% On-Campus (Freshman): 100%
% On-Campus (All Undergraduate): 73%

% African-American: 6%
% Asian: 10%
% Hispanic: 14%
% White: 45%
% Other: 7%
% Race or Ethnicity Unknown: 6%
% International: 12%
% Low-Income: 14%

ACADEMICS
Student-to-Faculty Ratio: 10:1
% of Classes Under 20: 69%
% of Classes Under 40: 99%
% Full-Time Faculty: 80%
% Full-Time Faculty w/ Terminal Degree: 97%

Top Programs
Environmental Analysis
Human Biology
Media Studies
Organizational Studies
Political Studies
Psychology
Sociology

Retention Rate: 91%
4-Year Graduation Rate: 77%
6-Year Graduation Rate: 84%

Curricular Flexibility: Somewhat Flexible
Academic Rating: ★★★★

Inside the Classroom

Every member school within the Claremont Consortium has its own distinct personality—Harvey Mudd is for engineering geniuses, Scripps is a highly selective women's college, Pomona and CMC are premier liberal arts colleges that battle East Coast schools Swarthmore, Amherst, and Williams for the top spot in the national rankings. Then there is Pitzer College, a liberal arts powerhouse in its own right with an emphasis on service learning and global engagement that has experienced logarithmic leaps in selectivity itself since the dawn of the new millennium. Cozy in size, hosting a mere 1,100 students, Pitzer still manages to offer forty+ majors and twenty minors and, as a bonus, students are free to take more than 2,000 courses across the consortium.

Graduating from Pitzer involves the completion of thirty-two courses including a minimum of eleven required courses that are part of meeting the college's education objectives. That involves two courses in the humanities and fine arts, two in the behavioral and social sciences, and one each in written expression, quantitative reasoning, and the natural sciences. Sequences covering social justice/social responsibility and intercultural understanding global/local also must be completed. The class on social justice requires active community engagement. First-year experience courses are taught on a variety of topics, are capped at fifteen students, and involve "close textual analysis, broadly conceived, and effective writing strategies for diverse audiences and purposes."

A 10:1 student-to-faculty ratio and no graduate student presence leads to an average class size of fifteen students, and 69 percent of sections enroll nineteen or fewer students. In 2018-19, only one course section was larger than forty students. Finding mentorship is doable in this atmosphere and can lead to undergraduate research opportunities such as those at the Keck Science Department, which also services CMC and Scripps students. Those opportunities can occur in the summer or during senior year while completing a required thesis. With one of the highest study abroad percentages of any school at 75 percent, Pitzer runs eight foreign programs and offers access to thirty-two international exchange programs.

The most popular majors at Pitzer are (1) psychology, (2) environmental analysis, (3) economics, (4) sociology, (5) media studies, and (6) self-designed degrees. Nearly all programs have the full admiration of graduate/professional schools as well as prestigious scholarship programs, but majors within the social and behavioral sciences (e.g. psychology and sociology) typically draw the most praise. In fact, Pitzer has produced the most Fulbright Scholars from an undergraduate-only institution for six straight years. In 2019, ten seniors and recent alumni captured Fulbrights, three were named Napier Fellows, and two students won Gilman Scholarships. Students also captured one Goldwater Scholarship, a National Science Foundation Graduate Research Fellowship, a Princeton in Asia Fellowship, and a Davis Project for Peace Award. Not bad for a school with fewer than 250 graduates per year.

Outside the Classroom

Every single Pitzer freshman and 73 percent of all students live in six dorms on the school's thirty-one-acre campus. Dorms receive glowing reviews as environmentally responsible housing and their farm-to-table program that is ranked as one of the best in the country. From those two facts you're likely picking up on the school's ethos and can guess that it does not have fraternities or sororities. Pitzer does have a joint athletics department with Pomona College that features twenty-one NCAA Division III varsity sports teams known as the Sagehens. There are 250+ clubs students can join, many of which are of the cross-college variety. Every single member of the Pitzer community gives back through service. In total, students, faculty, and staff commit approximately 100,000 hours to community-based projects each year. Activism carries over to student govern-ment, which is consistently passionate and vocal whether the issue is undergraduate housing costs or a recent ban on study abroad in Israel. Pitzer Outdoor Adventure (POA) is also immensely popular and regularly leads its large membership on hiking, cycling, climbing, camping, and surfing trips. Those seeking big-city fun will relish in the fact the City of Angels can be reached in less than an hour.

Career Services

Career Services at Pitzer has only three full-time professional staff members, yet being such a small college, that number still works out to a solid 360:1 student-to-advisor ratio, slightly better than the average college featured in our guidebook. Those individuals work directly with students and hold the titles of director, assistant director, and career counselor; they also have a highly-qualified office assistant. For such a tiny operation, the level of outreach is spectacular as 75 percent of freshmen engage with career services. Overall, approximately two-thirds of the student body utilize career services, and 33 percent take advantage of walk-in counseling appointments each year. It hosts roughly ninety events per year that attract almost 800 student participants.

Being part of the Claremont Consortium has as many advantages with regard to career development as it is does with regard to academics. Over 350 companies recruit annually at the 5Cs, and Pitzer students enjoy full access to networking and on-campus interviews. The office also does an excellent job financially supporting students' job-exploration endeavors. Roughly fifty students per year receive financial assistance from the Pitzer Internship Fund, which enables students to complete unpaid or low-paid experiential learning opportunities. Roughly forty students engage in a job-shadowing experience with an alum over winter break. Overall, this is an accessible office that greatly benefits from its affiliation with its neighbor schools.

Professional Outcomes

Upon receiving their degrees, 50 percent of 2018 Pitzer graduates had already found full-time employers, 18 percent were headed to graduate school, and 12 percent were entering fellowship, internship, or service programs. Among those employed, the most popular industries were finance/business (29 percent), tech/engineering (17 percent), health/medicine/research (17 percent), entertainment/arts (13 percent), education (6 percent), and nonprofit (6 percent). Employers presently issuing paychecks to more than ten Pitzer alumni include Google, Kaiser Permanente, the Los Angeles Unified School District, and Accenture. Graduates tend to be a globetrotting bunch, and the 11,000 living alumni can be found all over the map, although roughly half settle in Los Angeles or San Francisco. Median salaries, even ten years after graduation, are on the lower end of selective colleges. While plenty of Pitzer grads go on to pursue high-paying finance and tech jobs, many others choose PhD programs, medical school, or fellowship programs abroad that can delay financial returns.

Members of the Class of 2018 headed to prestigious graduate schools including Vanderbilt, Oxford, USC, Northwestern, Columbia, and Johns Hopkins. In 2017, it also sent graduates to UC Berkeley, the University of Pennsylvania, and Stanford. For premed students, the college offers a Joint Medical Program with the Western University of Health Sciences admitting up to six students each year. The W.M. Keck Science Department services Scripps, Claremont McKenna, and Pitzer, so all students have access to an excellent premed curriculum and facility. Those heading to law school in recent years have matriculated into a wide range of institutions that includes Notre Dame, UC Berkeley, Georgetown, Santa Clara, and Loyola Marymount University.

Admission

Applicants to the Class of 2022 were admitted at only a 13 percent clip, a rate similar to five years ago but far below that of 2005 when the admit rate was 39 percent. Even that 39 percent figure represented a sharp decline from a more forgiving admissions era in the 1990s. An early adopter of test-optional policies, Pitzer stopped requiring SAT or ACT scores in 2003, and more applicants take advantage of that option here than at most other test-optional institutions. Among 2018-19 freshmen, only 30 percent of students submitted an SAT score, and an identical 30 percent submitted an ACT result. Unsurprisingly, the test scores of freshmen who divulged them tended to be strong; the mid-50 percent range was a 1320-1490 on the SAT and a 30-33 on the ACT. It's within the realm of high school performance that successful Pitzer applicants set themselves apart. Sixty-two percent placed within the top 10 percent of their graduating class, and 83 percent were in the top quartile. The average GPA for an entering member of the Class of 2022 was 3.94.

The admissions process at Pitzer is highly personalized, and each application receives a lengthy review. A rigorous high school course load, a high GPA, a strong essay, and the demonstration of solid and unique character/personal qualities are at the forefront of the decision-making process. Recommendations, volunteer work, talent/ability, and extracurricular activities are also important factors. If you are a borderline applicant who is serious about getting in, applying early decision may be the way to go; 30 percent of applicants were accepted—135 students—almost half the freshman class.

Worth Your Money?

Pitzer has notably generous financial aid as roughly 40 percent of undergraduates received an average annual package of $41,042. That assistance helps greatly lessen the blow of a $56k list tuition price and $73k+ cost of attendance. While median salaries are on the low side, being part of the world-renowned Claremont Consortium allows access to premier facilities and professors and opens doors to the most competitive grad schools, fellowships and, should you choose, major corporations. You wouldn't want to pay $300,000 for a humanities degree without a clear plan for how to pay back those loans. Again, thanks to merit aid and need-based awards from the school, you are unlikely to be asked to pay anything approaching the full sticker price.

FINANCIAL
Institutional Type: Private
In-State Tuition: $55,734
Out-of-State Tuition: $55,734
Room & Board: $17,432
Required Fees: $284
Books & Supplies: $1,100

Avg. Need-Based Aid: $41,042
Avg. % of Need Met: 100%

Avg. Merit-Based Aid: $5,749
% Receiving Merit-Based Aid: 4%

Avg. Cumulative Debt: $17,848
% of Students Borrowing: 40%

CAREER
Who Recruits
1. City Year
2. Apple
3. Amazon
4. JumpStart
5. Accenture

Notable Internships
1. FX Networks
2. Collins Aerospace
3. Apple

Top Industries
1. Business
2. Education
3. Operations
4. Social Services
5. Media

Top Employers
1. Kaiser Permanente
2. Los Angeles Unified School District
3. Google
4. Wells Fargo
5. Accenture

Where Alumni Work
1. Los Angeles
2. San Francisco
3. New York City
4. Seattle
5. Portland, OR

Median Earnings
College Scorecard (Early Career): $48,700
EOP (Early Career): $43,500
PayScale (Mid-Career): $96,600

RANKINGS
Forbes: 54
Money: 522
U.S. News: 35, Liberal Arts Colleges
Wall Street Journal/THE: 77
Washington Monthly: 109, Liberal Arts Colleges

#CollegesWorthYourMoney

Pomona College

Claremont, California | Admissions Phone: 909-621-8134

ADMISSION
Admission Rate: 8%
Admission Rate - Men: 9%
Admission Rate - Women: 7%
EA Admission Rate:
ED Admission Rate: 17%
Admission Rate (5-Year Trend): -6%
ED Admission Rate (5-Year Trend): -3%
% of Admits Attending (Yield): 53%
Transfer Admission Rate: 8%

Offered Wait List: 826
Accepted Wait List: 527
Admitted Wait List: 67

SAT Reading/Writing (Middle 50%): 700-760
SAT Math (Middle 50%): 700-780
ACT Composite (Middle 50%): 31-34
Testing Policy: ACT/SAT Required
SAT Superscore: Yes
ACT Superscore: Yes

% Graduated in Top 10% of HS Class: 91%
% Graduated in Top 25% of HS Class: 100%
% Graduated in Top 50% of HS Class: 100%

ENROLLMENT
Total Undergraduate Enrollment: 1,679
% Part-Time: 1%
% Male: 48%
% Female: 52%
% Out-of-State: 74%
% Fraternity: 5%
% Sorority: Not Offered
% On-Campus (Freshman): 99%
% On-Campus (All Undergraduate): 98%

% African-American: 10%
% Asian: 15%
% Hispanic: 17%
% White: 34%
% Other: 7%
% Race or Ethnicity Unknown: 5%
% International: 12%
% Low-Income: 19%

ACADEMICS
Student-to-Faculty Ratio: 8:1
% of Classes Under 20: 70%
% of Classes Under 40: 99%
% Full-Time Faculty: 79%
% Full-Time Faculty w/ Terminal Degree: 98%

Top Programs
Chemistry
Economics
Environmental Analysis
International Relations
Mathematics
Media Studies
Psychology
Public Policy Analysis

Retention Rate: 97%
4-Year Graduation Rate: 89%
6-Year Graduation Rate: 94%

Curricular Flexibility: Somewhat Flexible
Academic Rating: ★★★★★

Inside the Classroom

Considered the preeminent institution among the Claremont Consortium, Pomona College in Claremont, California, is much like the elite liberal arts schools of the Northeast—Williams and Amherst—only with perfect weather, gorgeous beaches, and Disneyland in relatively close proximity. Pomona also boasts one of the lowest acceptance rates in the country, one that is on par, from a selectivity standpoint, with Yale, Columbia, Brown, and MIT. That said, if you are one of the rare individuals capable of gaining entrance, you won't find a better or more rigorous liberal arts education anywhere.

There are forty-eight majors and minors to select from with the most popular being social sciences (20 percent), math/statistics (12 percent), computer science (10 percent), and physical sciences (9 percent). More than 600 courses are on the menu at Pomona alone, but students can access any of the Claremont Consortium's 2,700 courses. Everyone begins with a critical inquiry seminar as a freshman and must complete coursework designated as writing intensive, speaking intensive, and analyzing difference. Breadth of study requirements demand that undergrads complete one course in the following six categories: criticism, analysis, and contextual study of works of the human imagination; social institutions and human behavior; history, values, ethics, and cultural studies; physical and biological sciences; mathematical and formal reasoning; and creation and performance of works of art and literature. There are literally eight ways to meet the college's foreign language requirement including AP scores, SAT IIs, and passing three semesters of language, but all eight demand the demonstration of proficiency.

The school's 186 professors are dedicated to the task of undergraduate education. Pomona's 8:1 student-to-teacher ratio leads to an average class size of only fifteen students. There are only six of 412 courses that ran in 2018-19 that contained more than forty students. Small classes also lead to the forging of student-professor bonds that help 53 percent of the undergraduate population conduct research alongside a faculty member. Each summer 200 students remain on campus for such an endeavor. Close to 50 percent of Pomona students travel abroad to one of fifty-nine programs in thirty-four countries.

All of the college's academic offerings are highly respected by employers, graduate/professional schools, and national fellowship/scholarship competitions. Majors in economics, international relations, chemistry, and mathematics receive especially high marks. One-quarter of Pomona students apply for at least one competitive fellowship. Of the students in the Class of 2019 who applied for Fulbright Scholarships, nine were successful; thirteen won the previous year. Three captured Watson Scholarships in 2019, and a remarkable ten grads and alumni were awarded National Science Foundation Graduate Research Fellowships.

Outside the Classroom

Pomona's bustling campus is spread across 140 acres and contains fifteen residence halls and three dining halls; 98 percent of students live in campus housing. There are two co-ed fraternities on campus that student members themselves describe as "just a bunch of dorks that hang out sometimes." Unlike Claremont, Mudd, and Scripps that combine for athletics, Pomona fields its own squads. The twenty-one varsity teams play as the Sagehens in NCAA Division III; 20 percent of the student body are members of a varsity team, and many others participate in club and intramural athletics. Student life at Pomona is, in part, defined by the multitude of opportunities to enjoy the resources of the other Claremont Colleges—Pitzer, Scripps, Harvey Mudd, and CMC. More than 250 clubs can be accessed by students of any of the five schools. On the Loose is a popular outdoors club that organizes 150 excursions into natural settings each year. Students can tend to their own plot at an on-campus organic farm, perform for the Claremont Colleges Ballroom Dance Company, write for the *Student Life* newspaper, or connect with volunteer opportunities through the Draper Center for Community Partnerships. While campus itself receives rave reviews, few complain about the school's enviable location either. Less than an hour from campus, students can access all of the fun Los Angeles has to offer as well as some of the most beautiful beaches in the country.

Career Services

The Career Development Office (CDO) has seven full-time professional staff members working on grad school/career advising, employer relations, and experiential learning coordination. The CDO's 243:1 student-to-advisor ratio is better than the average college featured in our guidebook. Pomona's staff puts its resources to good use, engaging 80 percent of freshmen through lunches where the CDO's offerings are introduced. Each year, the office engages in over 1,800 one-on-one counseling appointments, more than one per enrolled undergraduate student. Two-thirds of seniors directly engage with counselors.

On a more global scale, Pomona students can connect with more than 8,500 employers through the school's membership in three consortia groups: the Claremont Consortium, the Career and Internship Connection, and the Liberal Arts Career Network. More than 500 employers engage in on-campus recruiting at Pomona each year, including many that attend winter break recruiting programs. Unique internship opportunities are available such as the Pomona College Internship Program (PCIP) that funds students to intern domestically in places like DC or New York or abroad in cities like Bangkok or Tokyo. Roughly 130 students were awarded PCIP positions during the 2017-18 school year along with an additional eighty students in the summer. By senior year 89 percent of students have participated in at least one internship, and 70 percent have completed two or more. Thanks to loads of individualized attention and ways to connect directly with top employers and graduate schools, Pomona's career services is highly regarded by our staff.

Professional Outcomes

Whether entering the corporate world or a nonprofit position, employers adore Pomona grads. Overall, the largest number of Pomona alumni can be found in the offices of Google, Kaiser-Permanente, Microsoft, Amazon, and Facebook. Looking at grads from 2014-2018, many computer science majors ended up at the aforementioned tech giants. In that same time, more than one economics major landed a job at Goldman Sachs, Wells Fargo, Morgan Stanley, or Accenture. Majors in the hard sciences frequently landed at top research laboratories and hospitals. The three most popular geographical landing spots were Los Angeles, San Francisco, and New York City. Midcareer salaries are middle-of-the-pack among elite schools and are commensurate with other highly selective liberal arts schools like Williams, Middlebury, and Colby.

Of the 16 percent of Class of 2018 members who were accepted directly into graduate school, the three most frequently attended institutions were a not-too-shabby list of the University of Cambridge, the University of Oxford, Stanford, Harvard, and Cornell. When Pomona students go to law school they attend only the best. Thirty percent of alumni were admitted into top-five law schools; nearly three-quarters were admitted into top-fourteen schools. Med school applicants were admitted at a 70 percent clip, and in recent years more than one Pomona graduate has enrolled in medical school at USC, UCLA, University of Washington, and Emory University. In short, attending Pomona as an undergraduate will put you in a direct pipeline into the world's best graduate/professional schools.

Admission

Pomona now sits among the most ultra-selective schools in the world after admitting only 6.9 percent of the 10,245 students fighting for a spot in the Class of 2022. It accepted only 8.2 percent and 9.1 percent, respectively, in the previous two cycles. Of those offered spots in the 2018-19 freshman class, 95 percent were in the top decile of their high school class, and 91 percent of those actually attending earned that distinction. The median SAT score was 1495, and the median ACT score was 34. The mid-50 percent ranges for those who actually enrolled were 1400-1540 and 31-34. Students submitted SAT and ACT scores at a fairly even rate. International admits hailed from forty-four countries, and 57 percent of admitted domestic applicants were students of color. A high yield rate of 53 percent indicates that teens who apply to Pomona are likely to attend the college if accepted.

Getting in is a genuinely holistic process that strongly weights wide-ranging factors including rigor of curriculum, GPA, class rank, standardized test scores, essays, recommendations, extracurricular activities, talent/ability, and character/personal qualities. The committee does not factor in demonstrated interest, and interviews are merely "considered." Two hundred seven members of the Class of 2022 were admitted via early decision at a rate of 16.5 percent, which suggests that ED does provide an admissions edge. Of note, Pomona did accept twenty-eight transfer applicants in 2018, a higher number than many other elite institutions. In 1914, the school's president declared, "Let only the eager, thoughtful, and reverent enter here." Over a century later those criteria hold true with the addendum of near-perfect test scores and placement atop your high school graduating class. Like other schools with single-digit acceptance rates, there is an element of randomness that can leave valedictorians and possessors of 1600 SAT scores wondering why they were rejected.

Worth Your Money?

Pomona may have a sky-high sticker price, but it does everything in its power to make attending the school a possibility for students who otherwise could not afford it. In meeting 100 percent of the need of every eligible student, it awards an average of $54,000 per year to 57 percent of its undergraduate population. For everyone who can afford the $74k+ annual cost of attendance, that will be the actual cost because Pomona does not award merit aid. If you are offered a rare chance to attend Pomona, you should take advantage. With a superior reputation in academic and corporate circles alike, this college is definitely worth your money.

FINANCIAL
Institutional Type: Private
In-State Tuition: $54,380
Out-of-State Tuition: $54,380
Room & Board: $17,218
Required Fees: $382
Books & Supplies: $1,000

Avg. Need-Based Aid: $54,404
Avg. % of Need Met: 100%

Avg. Merit-Based Aid: $0
% Receiving Merit-Based Aid: 0%

Avg. Cumulative Debt: $17,303
% of Students Borrowing: 30%

CAREER
Who Recruits
1. Kaiser Permanente
2. Saatchi & Saatchi
3. UPS
4. JPMorgan Chase
5. AlphaSights

Notable Internships
1. :Los Angeles Review of Books
2. U.S. Senate
3. Spotify

Top Industries
1. Business
2. Education
3. Research
4. Media
5. Operations

Top Employers
1. Google
2. Microsoft
3. Kaiser Permanente
4. Amazon
5. Facebook

Where Alumni Work
1. Los Angeles
2. San Francisco
3. New York City
4. Seattle
5. Washington, DC

Median Earnings
College Scorecard (Early Career): $58,100
EOP (Early Career): $62,000
PayScale (Mid-Career): $117,200

RANKINGS
Forbes: 12
Money: 60
U.S. News: 5, Liberal Arts Colleges
Wall Street Journal/THE: 23
Washington Monthly: 8, Liberal Arts Colleges

#CollegesWorthYourMoney

Princeton University

Princeton, New Jersey | Admissions Phone: 609-258-3060

ADMISSION
Admission Rate: 5%
Admission Rate - Men: 5%
Admission Rate - Women: 6%
EA Admission Rate: 15%
ED Admission Rate: Not Offered
Admission Rate (5-Year Trend): -2%
ED Admission Rate (5-Year Trend): Not Offered
% of Admits Attending (Yield): 69%
Transfer Admission Rate: 1%

Offered Wait List: 1,125
Accepted Wait List: 844
Admitted Wait List: 0

SAT Reading/Writing (Middle 50%): 710-770
SAT Math (Middle 50%): 730-800
ACT Composite (Middle 50%): 32-35
Testing Policy: ACT/SAT Required
SAT Superscore: Yes
ACT Superscore: No

% Graduated in Top 10% of HS Class: 94%
% Graduated in Top 25% of HS Class: 99%
% Graduated in Top 50% of HS Class: 100%

ENROLLMENT
Total Undergraduate Enrollment: 5,428
% Part-Time: 2%
% Male: 51%
% Female: 49%
% Out-of-State: 82%
% Fraternity: Not Offered
% Sorority: Not Offered
% On-Campus (Freshman): 100%
% On-Campus (All Undergraduate): 94%

% African-American: 8%
% Asian: 21%
% Hispanic: 10%
% White: 41%
% Other: 5%
% Race or Ethnicity Unknown: 1%
% International: 12%
% Low-Income: 19%

ACADEMICS
Student-to-Faculty Ratio: 5:1
% of Classes Under 20: 74%
% of Classes Under 40: 87%
% Full-Time Faculty: 84%
% Full-Time Faculty w/ Terminal Degree: 94%

Top Programs
Economics
Engineering
History
Mathematics
Philosophy
Physics
Politics
Public Policy

Retention Rate: 98%
4-Year Graduation Rate: 87%
6-Year Graduation Rate: 96%

Curricular Flexibility: Somewhat Flexible
Academic Rating: ★★★★★

Inside the Classroom

The fourth oldest college in the United States is also an institution whose very name rings of wealth, privilege, and power—Princeton University. A charter member of the so-called Big Three alongside Harvard and Yale, Princeton has the smallest undergraduate population of that elite trio, but that doesn't stop it from churning out a disproportionate number of leaders and luminaries. Alumni include three current members of the US Supreme Court, eighteen Nobel Prize winners, business giants like Jeff Bezos and Steve Forbes, and countless other influential politicians, actors, writers, and scientific geniuses. We're hardly breaking new ground here—suffice to say that Princeton is Princeton.

Once noted for its policy of grade deflation, Princeton ended that practice five years ago, and GPAs have been on the rise since, providing a source of relief to current and future undergraduates. The majority of students are required to take a freshman writing seminar, one course in each of epistemology and cognition, ethical thought and moral values, historical analysis, and quantitative reasoning as well as two courses in each of literature and the arts, social analysis, and science and technology. All students must demonstrate proficiency in a foreign language. Central to a Princeton education is the culminating senior thesis project that is developed through one-on-one mentorship with a faculty member.

An absurdly low 5:1 student to faculty ratio does, as you might expect, translate to tiny class sizes for undergraduates. Just a touch over three-quarters of class sections have an enrollment of nineteen or fewer students, and 35 percent have fewer than ten students. Princeton is known for its commitment to undergraduate teaching, and students consistently rate professors as accessible and helpful. The Office of Undergraduate Research, formed in 2014, assists Tigers in locating faculty members with whom they can jointly conduct research in the summer or during a regular term. The university offers more than one hundred study abroad programs in forty-three countries; over half of its students take advantage.

As evidenced by the partial list of Princeton alumni, graduates of the university find themselves well received by the worlds of employment and top graduate schools. That goes for recipients of any degree, but the Engineering Department is widely recognized as one of the country's best as is the Woodrow Wilson School of Public and International Affairs. Prestigious scholarship programs love to go Tiger hunting. Thirty-three students and alumni made off with Fulbright Scholarships in 2018, three were named Rhodes Scholars, four became Schwarzman Scholars, and so many National Science Foundation Graduate Research Fellowships were procured that seven students won them from the Electrical Engineering program alone.

Outside the Classroom

An attractive and historic 500-acre campus plays home to 96 percent of Princeton undergraduates who are guaranteed housing for all four years. Freshmen and sophomores are required to live in one of six Residential College houses, each staffed by a live-in faculty member and full administrative team intent on creating a "strong sense of community, collaboration, and mutual respect, and to support individual initiative and personal growth."

Sports are serious at Princeton as the Tigers field thirty-seven varsity men's and women's squads that compete in NCAA Division I, and the school is the all-time leader in Ivy League titles. A sizable 18 percent of the undergraduate students compete at that level, and many others join one of the thirty-seven club sports teams. There are no officially recognized Greek organizations on campus, but that doesn't mean fraternities and sororities do not exist. In fact, 15-20 percent of the undergraduate population joins a Greek organization, and many more go through the "Bicker" process in an attempt to gain entry into one of the university's storied and exclusive "Eating Clubs" that are located in mansions on what is known as "The Street." The 135-member Ivy Club, immortalized by F. Scott Fitzgerald in *This Side of Paradise*, is Princeton's version of a Skull and Bones secret society. For everyone else, there are 300 student organizations that include popular dance troupes, singing groups, fifteen chaplaincies, the *Daily Princetonian* (one the oldest collegiate papers), and the 500-member American Whig-Cliosophic Society. The oldest debate team in the country, it was actually founded by James Madison. Princeton's location fifty-five miles from both Philadelphia and New York City means that big-city fun is always only a reasonable car or train ride away.

Career Services

Career Services at Princeton University has twenty professional staff members (excluding peer career advisors, assistants, and IT staff) who are dedicated to tasks such as pre-law advising, employer engagement, career advising, and alumni engagement. That 263:1 student-to-advisor ratio is superior to the average college featured in this guide. In addition to loads of individualized attention, Princeton also offers large-scale events such as the Fall HireTigers Career Fair that features one hundred top employers, and the school's online Handshake system sees over 42,000 applications for 6,500 jobs and internships each year.

An endless stream of impressive data supports the excellent work of the Career Services office. In 2016-17, counselors engaged students in 5,651 one-on-one advising sessions and attracted 11,541 attendees at 396 unique career services events. Close to 3,800 students participated in student-alumni engagement programs, and 46 percent of undergraduate participants reported that those sessions helped influence their postgraduate plans. More than 3,100 on-campus employer interviews took place each year. Overall, Princeton has recruiting relationships with an astronomical 13,669 employers. Highly personalized career and graduate school advising, along with ample resources and a supportive alumni base, assure graduating Tigers that a multitude of wonderful pathways await them post-commencement.

Professional Outcomes

Ninety-four percent of the Class of 2017 (the most recent class for which data is available) achieved their postgraduation plans within six months. Full-time employment was the first destination for 72.5 percent of those surveyed with professional, scientific, and technical services being the top industry, attracting 18 percent of graduates. The next most commonly entered industries were finance and insurance (13 percent), information (6 percent), and educational services (5 percent). Companies presently employing hundreds of Tiger alumni include Google, Goldman Sachs, Microsoft, McKinsey & Company, Morgan Stanley, IBM, and Facebook. The average salary reported by the 293 graduates entering the business and financial operations field was $73k while the school's 107 grads holding computer/mathematical positions averaged $107k. Those finding jobs in education, health care, or social services generally made less than $40k. The majority of grads remain in the Northeast and Mid-Atlantic regions, but 8 percent head to international destinations such as China, the United Kingdom, and South Korea.

The Class of 2017 saw 17.5 percent of its members head directly to graduate/professional school. Princeton alumni typically choose equally prestigious graduate schools to attend. Members of the Class of 2017 flocked in the largest numbers to Stanford (21), Penn (11), Princeton (11), Harvard (11), Cambridge (11), Columbia (10), and Oxford (10). The most frequently pursued degree was a master's (40 percent) followed by a PhD (34 percent), medical school (11 percent), and law school (5 percent). In recent years, Princeton undergrads have received acceptances into medical school 82-90 percent of the time, more than double the national average.

Admission

On the surface, Princeton's 5.5 percent acceptance rate for the Class of 2022 is extremely intimidating, as are the middle-50 percent of enrolled freshman test scores of 1430-1560 for the SAT and 32-35 for the ACT. Taking a granular look only makes things worse. Applicants with an unweighted GPA of 4.0 were only successful 8.1 percent of the time, and those with SATs north of 1500 had an 8 percent acceptance rate. Candidates with a 3.75 GPA or a 1350 SAT score were accepted less than 3 percent of the time.

The committee ranks nine factors as being most important in making admissions decisions: rigorous curriculum, GPA, class rank, essays, recommendations, standardized test scores (Princeton recommends two SAT subject tests), extracurricular activities, talent/ability, and character/personal qualities. Sorry, Risky Business fans, but alumni interviews are merely "considered." In 2018, single-choice early action (SCEA) applicants experienced a 14.7 percent acceptance rate, the lowest early-round acceptance rate in the school's history. There are a fair number of legacy admits, particularly in the early round. Overall, 14 percent of incoming freshmen in 2018-19 had Tiger lineage. One hundred seventy freshmen were international students representing sixty-three countries. Any way you slice it, getting into Princeton is a harrowing undertaking that will, more often than not, result in failure, even for some of the most accomplished applicants. Those who are successful typically have near-perfect to perfect test scores and GPAs and a "hook" to seal the deal.

Worth Your Money?

If you qualify for financial aid, your family won't pay a dime more than it can afford. That is the case for the 61 percent of current undergrads who qualify for need-based aid; they receive an annual award of $54,270. The university does not award merit aid. The average student graduates from Princeton with less than $10k in debt, less than one-third the national average. Of course, graduates also regularly walk into financially rewarding positions, so taking on any amount of debt to attend this school would absolutely be worth the sacrifice.

FINANCIAL
Institutional Type: Private
In-State Tuition: $49,450
Out-of-State Tuition: $49,450
Room & Board: $16,360
Required Fees: $890
Books & Supplies: $1,050

Avg. Need-Based Aid: $54,270
Avg. % of Need Met: 100%

Avg. Merit-Based Aid: $0
% Receiving Merit-Based Aid: 0%

Avg. Cumulative Debt: $9,059
% of Students Borrowing: 18%

CAREER
Who Recruits
1. Bain & Company
2. Schlumberger
3. MIT Lincoln Laboratory
4. Blackstone Group
5. Uber

Notable Internships
1. US Department of State
2. Jane Street
3. Bain & Company

Top Industries
1. Business
2. Education
3. Research
4. Engineering
5. Finance

Top Employers
1. Google
2. Goldman Sachs
3. Microsoft
4. McKinsey & Company
5. Facebook

Where Alumni Work
1. New York City
2. San Francisco
3. Washington, DC
4. Boston
5. Philadelphia

Median Earnings
College Scorecard (Early Career): $74,700
EOP (Early Career): $90,700
PayScale (Mid-Career): $139,400

RANKINGS
Forbes: 5
Money: 3
U.S. News: 1, National Universities
Wall Street Journal/THE: 5 (T)
Washington Monthly: 8, National Universities

#CollegesWorthYourMoney

Purdue University – West Lafayette

West Lafayette, Indiana | Admissions Phone: 765-494-1776

ADMISSION
Admission Rate: 58%
Admission Rate - Men: 52%
Admission Rate - Women: 67%
EA Admission Rate: N/A
ED Admission Rate: Not Offered
Admission Rate (5-Year Trend): -2%
ED Admission Rate (5-Year Trend): Not Offered
% of Admits Attending (Yield): 27%
Transfer Admission Rate: 41%

Offered Wait List: 5,276
Accepted Wait List: 4,409
Admitted Wait List: 565

SAT Reading/Writing (Middle 50%): 590-680
SAT Math (Middle 50%): 590-730
ACT Composite (Middle 50%): 25-32
Testing Policy: ACT/SAT Required
SAT Superscore: Yes
ACT Superscore: Yes

% Graduated in Top 10% of HS Class: 32%
% Graduated in Top 25% of HS Class: 69%
% Graduated in Top 50% of HS Class: 96%

ENROLLMENT
Total Undergraduate Enrollment: 32,672
% Part-Time: 4%
% Male: 57%
% Female: 43%
% Out-of-State: 39%
% Fraternity: 18%
% Sorority: 20%
% On-Campus (Freshman): 94%
% On-Campus (All Undergraduate): 41%

% African-American: 3%
% Asian: 9%
% Hispanic: 5%
% White: 63%
% Other: 4%
% Race or Ethnicity Unknown: 2%
% International: 14%
% Low-Income: 19%

ACADEMICS
Student-to-Faculty Ratio: 13:1
% of Classes Under 20: 38%
% of Classes Under 40: 73%
% Full-Time Faculty: 87%
% Full-Time Faculty w/ Terminal Degree: 98%

Top Programs
Agriculture
Business
Chemistry
Computer and Information Technology
Computer Science
Engineering
Nursing
Pharmacy

Retention Rate: 92%
4-Year Graduation Rate: 56%
6-Year Graduation Rate: 81%

Curricular Flexibility: Somewhat Flexible
Academic Rating: ★★★✦

Inside the Classroom
After dominating Wabash College in an 1892 football contest, a newspaper reporter labeled the brutes from Purdue University as "burly boiler makers." It was intended to be derogatory—a dig at an engineering and agricultural education—but it was almost immediately embraced by not only the football team but the entire university. As the twenty-first century has progressed, Purdue University, the public STEM university in Indiana, has grown to where it now educates roughly 33,000 undergraduates and another 10,000 graduate students and draws bright techie teens from well beyond the Hoosier State's ninety-two counties. Indiana residents comprise only 52 percent of the total undergraduate population at Purdue while 34 percent hail from out of state, and 14 percent are international students.

Waves of new students crash onto Purdue's West Lafayette campus each year filling up ten discipline-specific colleges in the pursuit of 200+ undergraduate majors. Yet, whether you are a member of the College of Engineering or the College of Education, you'll have to complete the same core curriculum, a thirty-credit concoction that lists among its ingredients written communication, information literacy, oral communication, science, quantitative reasoning, human behavior, and human cultures. The school's renowned Honors College welcomes 700 freshmen each fall and offers small class sizes, honors housing, and special leadership opportunities.

But class sizes are reasonable for all students, not only those in the Honors College. For a school of immense size, Purdue offers a strong 13:1 student-to-faculty ratio that leads to 38 percent of course sections having an enrollment of nineteen or fewer. You can also expect a balance of larger lectures as well as 20 percent of cours-es enroll more than fifty students. Undergraduate research opportunities are afforded to around 2,000 students per year. Undergrads can connect with professors on research projects during the academic year or apply to participate in a Summer Research Fellowship. A similar number, 2,400 students per year, elect to study abroad at one of 400 programs in sixty countries.

Engineering and engineering technologies majors earn 33 percent of the degrees conferred by the university. It makes sense that so many take advantage. After all, Purdue's College of Engineering cracks the top ten on almost every list of best engineering schools. The Krannert School of Management is also well regarded by employers around the country; 16 percent of degrees conferred are in business. Other popular majors include computer science (8 percent), agriculture (6 percent)—both are incredibly strong. Nationally Competitive Schol-arships have been captured by recent grads of all academic backgrounds, including as many as six Fulbright Scholarships per year and a multitude of National Science Foundation Graduate Research Fellowships.

Outside the Classroom
Male-heavy to the tune of 57 percent (a typical STEM disproportionality), two-fifths of the Purdue undergraduate student body lives on campus. Freshman housing is only guaranteed to those who sign a housing contract by early May; 94 percent of first-year students follow through. There are over ninety fraternity and sorority houses, and 18 percent of men and 20 percent of women partake in Greek life. Nearly 1,000 clubs and activities are available, and among those who participate, 66 percent cited their involvement as one of the major reasons they remain at the university. A hard-to-fathom 18,000 students participate in one of forty intramural sports—there are 300 flag football teams alone. There is also no shortage of big-time sports to consume as a fan. A top-ranked marching band helps cheer on the eighteen NCAA Division I squads that compete in the Big Ten Conference. Purdue has sent thirty players to the NBA, and the football team has appeared in eighteen post-season bowl games. Campus food receives favorable reviews as does the sprawling 2,000-acre campus and its proximity to traditional college town fare and basic entertainment. In addition, Indianapolis can be reached within about an hour by car, and Chicago is a nice weekend destination that is only a two-hour drive away.

Career Services
There are twenty-one professional staff members (not counting administrative assistants) occupying the offices of Purdue University's Center for Career Opportunities & Pre-Professional Advising (CCO). The majority have the title of career services consultant while others specialize in pre-professional advising. The university's overall 1,556:1 student-to-counselor ratio is high compared to most other schools profiled in this guidebook. Fortunately, the center is adept at organizing large-scale events, connecting with industry leaders, and facilitating experiential learning and networking opportunities for its undergraduate students.

The Industry Roundtable, held every September, is the largest student-run career fair in the United States, drawing 400 companies and 12,000+ students. A business-specific career fair attracts another 2,000 students, the Agricultural Career Fair brings one hundred companies to campus, and Purdue also offers fairs for aviation, civil engineering, hospitality/tourism, aerospace, and construction management. This robust operation brings a total of 1,400 employers to campus each year for recruiting and/or on-campus interviews. Internship numbers are equally impressive—81 percent engage in at least one internship experience during their four years of study, 28 percent complete two experiences, and 24 percent engage in three or more. Catering to the career services needs of nearly 33,000 undergraduates with limited staff may be a logistical battle, but it is one that Purdue's CCO is managing to win. What it lacks in the ability to hand-hold, it makes up for in the scope of offerings and the positive career results for graduates.

Professional Outcomes

Shortly after receiving their diplomas, 70 percent of members of the Class of 2018 were headed to the world of employment, 21 percent were continuing their educational journey in graduate/professional school, and a mere 3.5 percent were still seeking employment. The top industries entered by Purdue grads in 2018 were (1) health care, pharmaceuticals, and medical devices; (2) finance, insurance, and consulting; (3) higher education; and (4) airline, aviation, and aerospace. Companies employing the greatest number of 2018 graduates included General Motors (31), Amazon (24), PepsiCo (22), Lockheed Martin (19), and Boeing (19). The average starting salary was an exceptional $59,500 across all degree programs. Liberal arts and education majors earned an average salary in the neighborhood of $40k while engineering students brought home $68k. The majority of alumni remain in Indiana with Chicago, San Francisco, New York, and DC rounding out the five next most common destinations.

Purdue enjoys professional school acceptance rates that are "slightly above" the national averages. In 2018-19, the school saw 163 of its seniors apply to medical school, and many went on to attend the Indiana University School of Medicine and other Midwestern institutions including the University of Minnesota and the University of Illinois. Given the academic concentrations of many undergrads, law school is not an immensely popular choice. Interestingly, Purdue purchased an unaccredited online law school in 2017, and it is still working toward recognition from the American Bar Association. Looking at all grad school applicants, 346 graduates in the Class of 2018 who continued their educations did so in state. Illinois, New York, and California all attracted fifty+ graduate/professional students including top institutions like NYU, UC Berkeley, and the University of Chicago.

Admission

Purdue – West Lafayette received 53,439 applications for a spot in the Class of 2022 and admitted a friendly 58 percent of wanna-be Boilermakers. Of those who were admitted and ultimately enrolled, the mid-50 percent standardized test scores were 1190-1390 on the SAT and 25-32 on the ACT. Math scores are generally stronger than reading scores—38 percent of freshmen scored above a 700 on the SAT while only 19 percent hit that same target on the reading section. Roughly one-third placed in the top 10 percent of their high school class, but only 69 percent were in the top quartile, giving more than a glimmer of hope to applicants with a few blemishes on their transcripts and who aren't looking to pursue either engineering or computer science. Earning entry into these majors can prove considerably more difficult.

The university's admissions staff looks foremost at the hard numbers of GPA and standardized test scores as well as the rigor of your high school curriculum. First-generation status is among the categories occupying the next rung of "important" factors. It is joined by essays, extracurricular activities, recommendations, and character/personal qualities. Women enjoyed a 67 percent acceptance rate compared to 52 percent for male applicants. There is no binding early decision option, but there is an early action round with a November 1 deadline. Acceptance rates at Purdue are definitely on the decline. In 2007 the school received approximately 20,000 applications and accepted 79 percent of the pool. Despite the rise in selectivity, Purdue remains one of the top STEM-focused universities that accepts solid-but-imperfect applicants.

Worth Your Money?

Tuition for Hoosier State residents remains a tremendous bargain at a hair under $10K. Nonresidents and international students will pay upward of $29k in tuition which, given the graduates' employment and salary data, is still not a bad price. Like most STEM-oriented schools, Purdue is highly likely to return your investment many times over. The only person for which this school would not make complete sense is an out-of-state applicant taking loans to pursue a non-STEM/business degree.

FINANCIAL
Institutional Type: Public
In-State Tuition: $9,208
Out-of-State Tuition: $28,010
Room & Board: $10,030
Required Fees: $784
Books & Supplies: $1,160

Avg. Need-Based Aid: $12,787
Avg. % of Need Met: 77%

Avg. Merit-Based Aid: $5,333
% Receiving Merit-Based Aid: 28%

Avg. Cumulative Debt: $28,440
% of Students Borrowing: 38%

CAREER
Who Recruits
1. Cognex Corporation
2. Endress + Hauser
3. Lockheed Martin
4. General Motors
5. General Electric

Notable Internships
1. Caterpillar
2. Qualcomm
3. PepsiCo

Top Industries
1. Business
2. Engineering
3. Operations
4. Education
5. Sales

Top Employers
1. Amazon
2. Microsoft
3. IBM
4. Google
5. Apple

Where Alumni Work
1. Indianapolis
2. Lafayette, IN
3. Chicago
4. San Francisco
5. New York City

Median Earnings
College Scorecard (Early Career): $55,100
EOP (Early Career): $48,800
PayScale (Mid-Career): $110,000

RANKINGS
Forbes: 118
Money: 55
U.S. News: 57, National Universities
Wall Street Journal/THE: 46
Washington Monthly: 41, National Universities

#CollegesWorthYourMoney

Reed College

Portland, Oregon | Admissions Phone: 503-777-7511

Inside the Classroom

"A band of fierce intellectuals and the distinctive institution that nurtures them. All in for rigorous scholarship and the joy of intellectual pursuit." Thus reads the twitter profile of an elite liberal arts school of fewer than 1,500 undergraduates located in Portland, Oregon—the one-and-only Reed College. It would be difficult to create a statement that more aptly sums up this unique institution that, for many, serves primarily as a prelude to a PhD program.

Twenty-three academic departments collectively offer forty majors, fourteen of which are interdisciplinary (e.g., history-literature or mathematics-economics). One of the most storied features of a Reed education is the mandatory, year-long freshman Humanities 110 course that comprehensively explores Greco-Roman culture and its many influences. However, in spring 2018, after a series of student-led protests over the course's "Eurocentrism," the school agreed to alter the course to include the study of other cultures. As with the aforementioned twitter statement, that anecdote also helps paint a picture of the Reed experience.

Grades at the college are, paradoxically, both (a) difficult to earn and (b) completely unknown to the students themselves. To ensure that the emphasis on the classroom remains on learning for learning's sake, grades are issued but not shared with students until graduation. The average GPA earned is 3.1, and only eleven students have graduated with a perfect 4.0 in the last three decades. The educational experience is highly personalized, and students work directly with their professors. Class sizes average seventeen students, and the student-to-faculty ratio is 9:1. Study abroad opportunities exist at fifty-two partner university programs in twenty-three countries. The college funds a number of undergraduate research opportunities for students to work alongside faculty, and all students are required to complete their own senior thesis, which is essentially a mini-dissertation under the guidance of a faculty advisor.

The areas in which the highest number of degrees are conferred are the social sciences (17 percent), biology (13 percent), interdisciplinary studies (11 percent), foreign languages (10 percent), psychology (9 percent), and English (7 percent). All majors are viewed favorably by elite graduate programs that are fully aware of the exceptional level of rigor baked into every academic program at the college. English, math, and physics receive particularly strong praise. Competitive fellowship and scholarship programs are also acutely aware of Reed's excellence and pluck up graduates at exceptionally high rates. In 2018, of a graduating class of just over 300 students, six won Fulbright awards and one took home a Truman Scholarship. In its history, Reed grads have won thirty-two Rhodes Scholarships, sixty-seven Watson Fellowships, and 174 National Science Foundation Fellowships.

Outside the Classroom

Downtown Portland is only ten minutes away, making Reed's location in the southeastern corner of the city ideal for finding culture, the arts, and entertainment. Public transportation is easy to navigate, so just about anything the uber-progressive City of Roses has to offer is accessible. While 98 percent of freshmen live on campus, only 67 percent of the total student body resides in university-owned housing. Others live in affordable off-campus housing that is easy to locate in the immediate area. There are no fraternities or sororities at Reed, nor is there any semblance of highly completive athletics. There are, however, five intercollegiate club teams in which athletically-inclined students may wish to participate. While most Reedies would say their primary outside-the-classroom activity is "studying," there are ninety student-run organizations from which to choose, including KRRC, the campus radio station; *Quest*, the student body's independent newspaper; and typically "Reedish" groups like the Sky Appreciation Society. Renn Fayre, an annual campus-wide, weekend-long party for graduating seniors is an out-of-control event that is truly beloved by students. Notable amenities include a recently renovated ski cabin on Mt. Hood that students are free to use, and the Watzik Sports Center that boasts a pool, sauna, and climbing wall.

Career Services

The Center for Life Beyond Reed (CLBR) employs five full-time staff members giving it a 297:1 student-to-advisor ratio that is about average for a college included in this guidebook. The guiding mission of the office since a 2012 rebranding is to help students "try to connect the intellectual passions they cultivate during their time here to successful careers."

On the practical side, the CLBR offers six full-day senior boot camps where students can receive help with resumes, online professional profiles, interview techniques, and helpful contacts in students' areas of interest. In recent years, it has increased engagement with freshmen and sophomores, encouraging earlier 1:1 advising sessions. The Fall Job Fayre features a limited number of employers and drew only eighty students in 2017. Handshake and the Reed Career Network are the places online to find a job, internships, or connect with alumni. Winter Shadow internships allow current students to join alumni in their places of business. With an intense focus on preparing the next generation of academics and researchers, the campus is not swarming with corporate recruiters, yet Reed does maintain some productive relationships with employers—Microsoft, for example, contributed $500,000 toward the development of the college's computer science program. Acknowledging its immense level of success in placing students at elite graduate and professional schools, the CLBR serves its unique student population well in spite of below-average starting salaries (more on that in a moment).

Professional Outcomes

An examination of Reed's alumni database reveals that the three most common occupational pathways are business (28 percent), education (25 percent), and self-employment (19 percent). Included among the most frequent current employers are Microsoft Corporation, Kaiser Permanente, Portland Public Schools, Intel Corporation, the US Department of State, National Institutes of Health, and Apple. Because of the incredible number of students who flock to academia (more on this later), many institutions of higher education are also employers of large numbers of Reed alumni. Salary figures for graduates are low. In fact, at age thirty-four the median Reed graduate makes only $37k, lowest among any of the nation's elite liberal arts colleges. However, it is important to put that number in proper context because that is the age when many Reed alumni may be completing an advanced degree.

Reed is rarely the final stop on a student's academic journey. In College Transitions' analysis of National Science Foundation data, Reed was the No. 1 producer of future PhD holders across all academic disciplines as determined by percentage of graduates attaining that degree. By discipline, Reed was in either first or second place for English, history, biology, and physics. The list of the universities where the highest concentration of grads pursue their doctorates is phenomenal. Included on that list are MIT, Harvard, Stanford, Yale, Berkeley, and Princeton. MBAs were earned at institutions that include Penn, Georgetown, Columbia, and UChicago. Reedies who went the legal route obtained their JDs primarily from top-tier law schools. Recent med school applicants have enjoyed a 70 percent acceptance rate, and many have attended similarly impressive universities as those in other fields already mentioned.

Admission

Reed College's 35 percent acceptance rate does not do its level of selectivity justice, not that the college cares. Admirably, this institution has long been anti-rankings and has no interest in PR efforts to drum up more applicants for the purpose of enhancing its status. It receives fewer than 6,000 applications per year. Its students are a self-selecting crew who choose to apply to this unique liberal arts school in Portland, Oregon. The middle-50 percent range for enrolled students is 1310-1520 on the SATs and 30-33 on the ACTs. Grades/class rank numbers are impressive but do not automatically exclude those with an imperfect transcript; 55 percent finished in the top 10 percent of their high school class, 78 percent were in the top 25 percent, and 70 percent of students typically sport a GPA of 3.75 or above.

The Reed Admissions Office only designates three factors as being "very important" in its evaluation process: rigor of secondary school record, grades, and essays. Factors deemed "important" are standardized test scores, class rank, interview, demonstrated interest, and recommendations. This is a college that, like Wesleyan on the opposite coast, is looking for intellectual risk-takers whose passion comes through in their writing and in conversation. Applying early definitely helps as 52 percent of ED applicants are accepted (a figure that is unaffected by athletes). Teens who are destined to be Reedies are the ones who fall in love with the school in the first place. Brilliant young people with an open mind who eschew convention will be thrilled to find a home here. Of course, strong credentials will help to make that goal a reality.

Worth Your Money?

At a cost of $75,000 and little available in the way of merit aid, many pay a steep price for attending this institution. Over 50 percent of Reed students do qualify for need-based aid and receive average annual grants of $40k. Undoubtedly, the academic experience here is uniquely wonderful and a perfect fit for a certain type of budding intellectual. Yet, if you don't qualify for need-based aid and don't come from a wealthy family, you would have to make sure that the $300,000+ bill for tuition would make sense as part of your life plan. Interestingly, the average student loan debt among Reed graduates is lower than the national average.

FINANCIAL
Institutional Type: Private
In-State Tuition: $58,130
Out-of-State Tuition: $58,130
Room & Board: $14,620
Required Fees: $310
Books & Supplies: $1,050

Avg. Need-Based Aid: $40,278
Avg. % of Need Met: 100%

Avg. Merit-Based Aid: $0
% Receiving Merit-Based Aid: 0%

Avg. Cumulative Debt: $21,697
% of Students Borrowing: 48%

CAREER
Who Recruits
1. TerraCotta Group LLC
2. First Book
3. Cranial Technologies
4. Teach for America
5. Wayfair

Notable Internships
1. Melville House Publishing
2. RTI International
3. Whitney Museum of American Art

Top Industries
1. Business
2. Education
3. Research
4. Media
5. Operations

Top Employers
1. Google
2. Microsoft
3. Apple
4. Intel
5. Amazon

Where Alumni Work
1. Portland, OR
2. San Francisco
3. New York City
4. Seattle
5. Los Angeles

Median Earnings
College Scorecard (Early Career): $42,200
EOP (Early Career): $36,900
PayScale (Mid-Career): $104,900

RANKINGS
Forbes: 105
Money: 665
U.S. News: 68, Liberal Arts Colleges
Wall Street Journal/THE: 75 (T)
Washington Monthly: 40, Liberal Arts Colleges

#CollegesWorthYourMoney

Rensselaer Polytechnic Institute

Troy, New York | Admissions Phone: 518-276-6216

ADMISSION
Admission Rate: 43%
Admission Rate - Men: 41%
Admission Rate - Women: 47%
EA Admission Rate: Not Offered
ED Admission Rate: 47%
Admission Rate (5-Year Trend): +2%
ED Admission Rate (5-Year Trend): -6%
% of Admits Attending (Yield): 20%
Transfer Admission Rate: 57%

\# Offered Wait List: 5,769
\# Accepted Wait List: 3,845
\# Admitted Wait List: 3

SAT Reading/Writing (Middle 50%): 640-720
SAT Math (Middle 50%): 690-780
ACT Composite (Middle 50%): 29-33
Testing Policy: ACT/SAT Required
SAT Superscore: Yes
ACT Superscore: No

% Graduated in Top 10% of HS Class: 64%
% Graduated in Top 25% of HS Class: 92%
% Graduated in Top 50% of HS Class: 98%

ENROLLMENT
Total Undergraduate Enrollment: 6,628
% Part-Time: 0%
% Male: 68%
% Female: 32%
% Out-of-State: 66%
% Fraternity: 30%
% Sorority: 16%
% On-Campus (Freshman): 100%
% On-Campus (All Undergraduate): 57%

% African-American: 4%
% Asian: 14%
% Hispanic: 9%
% White: 50%
% Other: 6%
% Race or Ethnicity Unknown: 1%
% International: 15%
% Low-Income: 15%

ACADEMICS
Student-to-Faculty Ratio: 13:1
% of Classes Under 20: 52%
% of Classes Under 40: 83%
% Full-Time Faculty: 90%
% Full-Time Faculty w/ Terminal Degree: 94%

Top Programs
Architecture
Business
Engineering
Computer Science
Game Design
Information Technology and Web Science
Physics

Retention Rate: 92%
4-Year Graduation Rate: 62%
6-Year Graduation Rate: 86%

Curricular Flexibility: Somewhat Flexible
Academic Rating: ★★★★

Inside the Classroom

Founded almost 200 years ago, Rensselaer Polytechnic Institute is America's first technological research university and still one of its best. Fittingly situated on the eastern bank of the Hudson River in the Industrial Revolution hotspot of Troy, New York, RPI is the proud home of 6,628 of the brightest and most innovative technical undergraduate minds anywhere. This is merely perpetuating a long history of producing high achievers in the tech world. Including both faculty and alumni, Rensselaer claims eighty-five members of the National Academy of Engineering, five members of the National Inventors Hall of Fame, and a Nobel Prize winner in physics.

There are five undergraduate schools within the larger university: The School of Architecture; the Lally School of Management; the School of Science; the School of Engineering; and the School of Humanities, Arts, and Social Sciences. All students take what is known as the HASS Core, a six course, twenty-four-credit foray into the humanities and social sciences. Beyond that, the academic programs are tailored to different schools and degree programs. There is no foreign language requirement, although the school does offer coursework in Mandarin Chinese for interested students.

The student-to-faculty ratio at RPI is 13:1, and with only about 1,300 graduate students to serve, there is plenty of time and attention left for undergraduates. Students will encounter various class sizes over the course of their four years of study. A solid 51 percent of sections contain fewer than twenty students; 13 percent will have fifty or more students. Being a research institution, RPI attracts $103 million in research funding each year, meaning that the school's 500 faculty members are constantly in the middle of projects that require student assistance. Students can participate during the academic year for credit or during the summer when select individuals receive $4,000 to work full time in a lab. International study is also encouraged at one of the school's affiliate universities in thirteen countries including Australia, Finland, and Singapore.

Engineering is the most commonly conferred degree area, accounting for 54 percent of 2018 graduates. Computer and information sciences was second (17 percent), followed by business/marketing (6 percent), engineering technology (5 percent), and biology (4 percent). The School of Engineering has a brilliant reputation with employers worldwide and is always near the top of the rankings for its programs in mechanical, aerospace, computer, electrical, and biomedical engineering. Physics, architecture, and computer science are also strong. Graduates do not apply to prestigious fellowship programs in droves, but the school does capture an occasional Fulbright or Truman Scholarship. RPI does, however, typically produce more than one annual National Science Foundation Graduate Research Fellowship winner.

Outside the Classroom

The school's 296-acre suburban campus only houses 57 percent of the student body as many upperclassmen seek off-campus apartments or join fraternities or sororities. Slightly over one-quarter of men and women elect to join Greek organizations. Those numbers are down after several chapters were suspended or dissolved in recent years. For a technical school, RPI boasts a highly athletic student body. Sixty-three percent of incoming freshmen participated in varsity athletics in high school, and forty-two individuals were the captains of their squads. There are twenty-three varsity men's and women's sports teams, twenty-two of which compete in NCAA Division III. The exception is men's hockey, which is one of the oldest and best teams in the entire country, having produced a long list of NHL stars over the years. Including the university's thriving intramural and club programs, 80 percent of RPI students are involved in athletics. With over 200 student organizations, students have their pick of non-sports/Greek sources of camaraderie. For example, the RPI Players has put on 300 theatrical shows over its ninety-year history, and there are nineteen service-oriented groups that serve the local community. In addition, fitness classes run by professional instructors are available just about every day at the Mueller Center. Troy itself may lack excitement, but the state capital of Albany is only ten miles away, and scenic retreats like the Berkshires or Catskills are under two hours away.

Career Services

The Center for Career and Professional Development consists of eight professional employees, which calculates to a student-to-advisor ratio of 796:1, a bit higher than the average school featured in this guide. However, that less-than-deal statistic is not at all representative of the exceptional work done by RPI's career services staff. Other numbers tell a different story, such as the ninety-five annual events hosted by the school that draw almost 1,900 undergrads, and the 1,912 one-on-one counseling appointments that take place. And that doesn't even include the employer recruiting numbers that are even more eye-popping.

Rensselaer Polytechnic Institute

E-mail: admissions@rpi.edu | Website: www.rpi.edu

In the 2017-18 school year career fairs drew 403 employers to campus, and 102 employers conducted 1,923 on-campus interviews. Companies also hosted 132 information sessions for RPI students that same year. Companies that recruit on campus include Cisco, the Blackstone Group, Deloitte, Johnson & Johnson, and Credit Suisse. Rensselaer Alumni Connect is a platform with over 2,500 active users, 79 percent of whom are willing to introduce others to connections while 83 percent are willing to answer industry-specific questions. Internship and co-op opportunities abound, and large numbers of students land co-op positions at Hasbro (27), NASA Jet Propulsion Laboratory (10), and Walt Disney World (7). Thanks to an endless parade of recruiters flowing into campus, high starting salaries, and plenty of individualized attention, the CCPD has earned a reputation for stellar work.

Professional Outcomes

As they receive their diplomas, 55 percent of RPI grads have already landed a job, 24 percent have committed to a graduate school, and 16 percent are still seeking their next destination. The largest numbers of 2017 grads were hired by companies that included UnitedHealth (17), United Technologies (16), General Dynamics (16), Boeing (14), and IBM (12). Massive numbers of alumni hold leadership positions in corporations like Google, Pratt & Whitney, General Motors, GE, and Microsoft. Geographically, 68 percent of graduates remain in the Northeast, 10 percent head to the West—primarily to Silicon Valley—and 8 percent land in the Southeast. The Class of 2017 enjoyed an average starting salary of $69,220. By midcareer RPI alumni have achieved one of the highest median salaries of any elite college, slightly ahead of other tech powerhouses including Caltech, Carnegie Mellon, and Lehigh University.

Of the nearly one-quarter of 2017 grads who were entering an advanced degree program, many were headed to some of the nation's best schools. Recent grads have been accepted by the likes of Carnegie Mellon University, Duke University, Massachusetts Institute of Technology, Northwestern University, Texas A&M, and the University of Chicago. Those intent on medical school have the option to apply to RPIs seven-year BS/MD program with affiliate Albany Medical College. Recent medically-minded grads have enjoyed acceptances at the likes of Harvard Medical School and Cornell University College of Veterinary Medicine. Those intent on law school also have the option of a combined degree, in this case a BS/JD at either Albany or Columbia University.

Admission

RPI was deluged by applications from Class of 2022 hopefuls, receiving an all-time high of 20,403. While the acceptance rate of 43 percent will do little to scare off prospective students, the composition of the 2018-19 freshman class was an impressive one. The average SAT score was 1409, and 161 netted a perfect score on either the critical reading or math section. A solid 64 percent placed in the top 10 percent of their high school class, 92 percent were in the top quarter, and ninety-five students earned either valedictorian or salutatorian status. The average GPA of an entering freshman was 3.91, and 69 percent of this cohort had a cumulative GPA of over 3.75. Comparing this incoming crop of freshmen to those from five years ago reveals that not much has changed admissions-wise in the recent past.

There is nothing opaque about the way in which applicants are evaluated by the Rensselaer Admissions Committee. The most strongly weighted factors are GPA, test scores (72 percent submit SATs), class rank, and the rigor of one's high school coursework. Of secondary importance are application essays, recommendations, extracurricular activities, and character/personal qualities. Unusual for a tech school, males and females have fairly similar acceptance rates. In 2018, men were accepted at a 41 percent clip, and women were welcomed 46.5 percent of the time. The yield rate at RPI is around 20 percent, which means only one of five admitted students goes on to enroll. However, applying early decision provides only a modest advantage; 47 percent of ED applicants were admitted into the Class of 2022. Also of note, transfer students fare well at this institution as 57 percent of the 496 applicants were accepted in 2018. Rensselaer Polytechnic Institute is looking for students with GPAs above a 3.75 in most or all honors and AP courses and who scored in the 95th percentile on standardized tests. The criteria is fairly simple.

Worth Your Money?

Rensselaer's annual cost of attendance is a pretty high $73,816; the good news is that starting salaries for graduates just about matches that sum. Over one-third of entering students do get an offer of merit aid that averages almost $22k, and more than half of attendees qualify for a need-based grant with an average value of $39k. Attending a STEM-heavy school like RPI is almost always a good bet for getting an excellent return on your educational investment, even if the up-front cost is quite high.

FINANCIAL
Institutional Type: Private
In-State Tuition: $54,000
Out-of-State Tuition: $54,000
Room & Board: $15,580
Required Fees: $1,378
Books & Supplies: $2,858

Avg. Need-Based Aid: $38,861
Avg. % of Need Met: 82%

Avg. Merit-Based Aid: $21,836
% Receiving Merit-Based Aid: 36%

Avg. Cumulative Debt: $34,595
% of Students Borrowing: 63%

CAREER
Who Recruits
1. U.S. Nuclear Regulatory Commission
2. Etsy
3. GlobalFoundries
4. Apprenda
5. American Airlines

Notable Internships
1. Regeneron Pharmaceuticals
2. NASA
3. Pfizer

Top Industries
1. Engineering
2. Business
3. Operations
4. Information Technology
5. Education

Top Employers
1. IBM
2. Pratt & Whitney
3. Google
4. Boeing
5. GE

Where Alumni Work
1. New York City
2. Albany, NY
3. Boston
4. San Francisco
5. Washington, DC

Median Earnings
College Scorecard (Early Career): $82,000
EOP (Early Career): $84,100
PayScale (Mid-Career): $134,100

RANKINGS
Forbes: 113
Money: 217
U.S. News: 50 (T), National Universities
Wall Street Journal/THE: 122
Washington Monthly: 78, National Universities

#CollegesWorthYourMoney

Rhodes College

Memphis, Tennessee | Admissions Phone: 901-843-3700

Inside the Classroom

Rhodes College's Memphis location places it among the rare liberal arts schools located in an urban setting. (Occidental in Los Angeles is another such school featured in this guide.) Just four miles from the world famous Beale Street, Rhodes, founded in 1848, is one of the top colleges in the region. A progressive, service-oriented student body of just over 2,000 students flocks to Rhodes for its small classes, awesome location, and nurturing environment that leads many on the path to top graduate and professional programs.

The school offers fifty majors and minors and a great deal of academic autonomy along the way. The foundations requirements can be meet by roughly 400 varied courses that cover target areas such as written communication, becoming an active and engaged citizen, gaining proficiency in a second language, and understanding scientific approaches to the natural world. As part of this experience students choose between two signature courses: The Search for Values in the Light of Western Religion and History and Life: Then and Now, both of which were developed after World War II. Freshmen also must engage in the first-year experience requirement, an integrative, year-long program focused on becoming an active student-citizen as well as a first year writing seminar.

A 10:1 student-to-faculty ratio leads to an amazingly intimate average class size of only fourteen students. Only 3.7 percent of course sections contain more than twenty-nine students. Ninety-eight percent of the 224 faculty members hold the highest degree available in their fields, so you will not be taught by TAs or adjuncts. A great deal of resources are committed to undergraduate education. For example, Rhodes puts an astounding sum of money into its physical science programs, having committed $34 million to a new science center in 2017. As a result, the school produces an incredible number of PhDs (more on this under "Professional Outcomes"). Three-quarters of students at this institution engage in some form of undergraduate research. Opportunities are plentiful in every academic discipline to collaborate with faculty on research projects, and the annual Undergraduate Research and Creativity Symposium is a chance to show off student projects. An affiliation with St. Jude's Children's Research Hospital leads to intensive summer research opportunities for those in the hard sciences. A solid 65 percent of students elect to study abroad, and the school offers many Rhodes faculty-led locations around the world.

While the sciences may be the area for which Rhodes receives the greatest recognition (biology is the most popular major), business, psychology, and international studies are also strong and attract large numbers of undergrads. Since the turn of the millennium, Rhodes graduates have earned thirty-one Fulbright Scholarships, fourteen Goldwater Scholarships, eleven Watson Fellowships, five Truman Scholarships, five National Science Foundation Graduate Fellowships, two Luce Scholarships, and one Rhodes Scholarship.

Outside the Classroom

This 123-acre wooded oasis in midtown Memphis is home to 70 percent of all undergraduates. Students are required to live in residence halls for their first two years. Most residence halls are intimate places of under one hundred students where everyone knows everyone. A 56/44 percent breakdown in favor of women certainly has an impact on student life. Greek life is a defining characteristic of social life at Rhodes with 40 percent of women joining a sorority and 34 percent of men pledging a fraternity. Participation in sports is also common with twenty-one men's and women's varsity teams competing in NCAA Division III athletics. The Bryan Campus Life Center offers ample facilities for recreational sports and fitness. For non-jocks, there are more than one hundred student-run organizations, and over 80 percent of students engage in community service activities. The mock trial team is exceptionally strong in national competitions. With the Lynx Lair serving as a hub for food, social events, and frequent concerts, lectures, and films there is rarely a dull moment around Rhodes. Of course, with Memphis as your backyard there are always exciting excursions for entertainment, culture, or dining. The Memphis Zoo, the Memphis Brooks Museum of Art, and the National Civil Rights Museum are only a few miles away. Campus is walker-friendly, but bikes are popular as well. The city of Memphis has over 200 miles of bike infrastructure to help ensure safety.

Career Services

The Career Services Office at Rhodes has three full-time staff members—the director, a first- and second-year counselor, and a third- and fourth-year counselor. Its 663:1 student-to-advisor ratio does not compare favorably to other liberal arts schools featured in this guide, but the push for personalized service is evident everywhere you look. The school encourages meeting one-on-one with advisors two or three times in the freshman year as well during sophomore year. Few schools promote that level of contact so early in a student's undergraduate career.

Every fall, representatives from over one hundred graduate and professional schools travel to Rhodes' campus to attend the Graduate School Exposition. The 2019 Career Fair was attended by over fifty employers, including many national corporations such as AutoZone, Raymond James, and St. Jude's Research Hospital. Over 80 percent of undergraduates complete at least one internship. Those numbers are bolstered by career services partnerships with over one hundred local, national, and global employers. Many of the 13,000 alums are willing to lend a hand to a current student or recent grad seeking to network.

Professional Outcomes

Within one year of receiving their diplomas, 98 percent of Rhodes grads have found their way into the world of employment or are pursuing an advanced degree program. Among the companies employing the largest number of alumni are St. Jude's Children's Hospital, Deloitte, EY, FedEx, Raymond James, and PwC. Midcareer salaries are the second highest among any Tennessee institution, behind only Vanderbilt. Yet, it is worth noting that Vandy grads earn over $20k more by age thirty-four. Greater Memphis is where most graduates remain. Many others situate themselves in Greater Nashville, Atlanta, DC, New York, or Dallas.

A superb 86 percent of those applying to graduate school get into their top-choice institution. Medical and law school applicants are accepted at higher rates than the national average. Those with a 3.4 GPA and above the 57th percentile on the MCAT are accepted into medical school at an identical 86 percent clip and, overall, applicants enjoy a 65 percent acceptance rate. In 2018, an impressive forty-two graduates were accepted into med school. Rhodes is in the top 10 percent of science PhD-producing undergraduate schools in the country, and it is ranked fifteenth overall in the number of physics majors who go on to receive a doctorate in physics or astronomy. Recent graduates have been accepted into programs at elite universities including Brown, Columbia, Georgetown, Harvard Law School, New York University School of Law, and Yale Divinity School. Medical schools attended by recent grads include Tufts, Dartmouth, Boston University, Wake Forest, and UVA.

Admission

With a 45 percent acceptance rate for a place in the Class of 2022, Rhodes College is a rare school that provides an elite education without putting applicants through a harrowing admissions process with dreadfully unfavorable odds. The 5,092 hopefuls who submitted applications were a strong bunch, but those who were successful didn't have to sport a perfect transcript. The SAT mid-50 percent range was 1240-1410, although the ACT was submitted more than twice as often; 28-31 was the mid-50 percent ACT score, and half of ACT takers had a composite score above 30. Three-quarters of admitted freshmen held a weighted GPA of 3.75 or higher, 54 percent finished in the top decile of their high school class, and 85 percent were in the top quartile. The average GPA of incoming 2018-19 freshman was 3.92.

Rigor of secondary school record, GPA, and class rank sit atop the list of most important factors in the eyes of the admissions office. Factors considered as "important" include standardized test scores, essays, recommendations, character/personal qualities, legacy status, and racial/ethnic status. Only 24 percent of those accepted actually enrolled, thus the college values those who demonstrate interest, particularly in the form of committing through early decision. As a result, 63 percent of ED applicants were accepted in 2018. In their own words, Rhodes uses a "holistic approach to evaluate every facet of your application to get a better sense of the whole you." Obviously, the school is looking for students with strong grades in a demanding curriculum, but students do not need to have perfect test scores and grades for consideration at this fine liberal arts institution.

Worth Your Money?

Rhodes sticker-price cost of attendance of almost $62,000 isn't particularly tough to swallow, at least when considered against the cost of many comparable institutions. Yet, Rhodes delivers merit aid packages to two-thirds of its undergrads, lowering the cost by an average of $26k per year. Further, almost half of all students receive need-based aid at an average annual total of $33k. Given the cost that most people actually pay, Rhodes College is a fairly priced option that will afford you a one-of-a-kind educational experience.

FINANCIAL
Institutional Type: Private
In-State Tuition: $47,580
Out-of-State Tuition: $47,580
Room & Board: $11,403
Required Fees: $310
Books & Supplies: $1,125

Avg. Need-Based Aid: $32,532
Avg. % of Need Met: 93%

Avg. Merit-Based Aid: $26,103
% Receiving Merit-Based Aid: 66%

Avg. Cumulative Debt: $24,187
% of Students Borrowing: 48%

CAREER
Who Recruits
1. St. Jude's Children's Research Hospital
2. Raymond James
3. Methodist Healthcare
4. PeaceCorps
5. Teach for America

Notable Internships
1. Graystar Real Estate
2. Christie's
3. FedEx

Top Industries
1. Business
2. Education
3. Operations
4. Social Services
5. Healthcare

Top Employers
1. St. Jude Children's Research Hospital
2. Deloitte
3. EY
4. Raymond James
5. FedEx

Where Alumni Work
1. Memphis
2. Nashville
3. Atlanta
4. Washington, DC
5. New York City

Median Earnings
College Scorecard (Early Career): $53,600
EOP (Early Career): $52,000
PayScale (Mid-Career): $97,800

RANKINGS
Forbes: 150
Money: 282
U.S. News: 53 (T), Liberal Arts Colleges
Wall Street Journal/THE: 134 (T)
Washington Monthly: 171, Liberal Arts Colleges

#CollegesWorthYourMoney

Rice University

Houston, Texas | Admissions Phone: 713-348-7423

ADMISSION
Admission Rate: 11%
Admission Rate - Men: 11%
Admission Rate - Women: 11%
EA Admission Rate: Not Offered
ED Admission Rate: 22%
Admission Rate (5-Year Trend): -6%
ED Admission Rate (5-Year Trend): -3%
% of Admits Attending (Yield): 41%
Transfer Admission Rate: 11%

Offered Wait List: 3,296
Accepted Wait List: 2,137
Admitted Wait List: 31

SAT Reading/Writing (Middle 50%): 700-760
SAT Math (Middle 50%): 750-800
ACT Composite (Middle 50%): 33-35
Testing Policy: ACT/SAT Required
SAT Superscore: Yes
ACT Superscore: Yes

% Graduated in Top 10% of HS Class: 87%
% Graduated in Top 25% of HS Class: 96%
% Graduated in Top 50% of HS Class: 99%

ENROLLMENT
Total Undergraduate Enrollment: 3,992
% Part-Time: 2%
% Male: 52%
% Female: 48%
% Out-of-State: 53%
% Fraternity: Not Offered
% Sorority: Not Offered
% On-Campus (Freshman): 99%
% On-Campus (All Undergraduate): 71%

% African-American: 7%
% Asian: 26%
% Hispanic: 15%
% White: 33%
% Other: 4%
% Race or Ethnicity Unknown: 2%
% International: 12%
% Low-Income: 19%

ACADEMICS
Student-to-Faculty Ratio: 6:1
% of Classes Under 20: 72%
% of Classes Under 40: 87%
% Full-Time Faculty: 78%
% Full-Time Faculty w/ Terminal Degree: 97%

Top Programs
Architecture
Biochemistry
Biology
Cognitive Science
History
Engineering
Kinesiology
Music

Retention Rate: 97%
4-Year Graduation Rate: 86%
6-Year Graduation Rate: 95%

Curricular Flexibility: Somewhat Flexible
Academic Rating: ★★★★★

Inside the Classroom

With just shy of 4,000 undergraduates, Rice is at once a powerhouse research institution *and* a place where world-class instruction is the norm. The university's illustrious faculty includes multiple Nobel Prize and National Medal of Science winners as well as countless recipients of any prestigious fellowship or award that one can name. And the best news is that undergraduates have the chance to learn from that distinguished lot.

Rice offers more than fifty majors across six broad disciplines: engineering, architecture, music, social science, humanities, and natural science. Double majoring is more common at Rice than your average university; roughly 20 percent of students graduate with a double major. Speaking of majors, there is a greater diversity of majors than one might assume at a STEM-famous school. The most commonly conferred degrees are in engineering (19 percent), the social sciences (15 percent), parks and recreation (9 percent), computer science (7 percent), biology (7 percent), and mathematics (5 percent).

Boasting a student-to-faculty ratio of 5.6:1, Rice offers a spectacularly intimate learning experience. Class sizes are ideally small with 72 percent containing fewer than twenty students and a median class size of only fourteen. Undergraduate research opportunities abound with 62 percent of graduates participating in academic research during their four years. Those experiences are open to freshmen through the Century Scholars Program and to all underclassmen through the Rice Undergraduate Scholars Program. Study abroad options are available in seventy countries, including collaborative programs with some of the top schools in the world including The London School of Economics, Oxford, and Cambridge; approximately 30 percent of Rice students elect to spend a semester in another country.

Programs in biology, biochemistry, cognitive science, and music are incredibly strong, while the School of Architecture and the George R. Brown School of Engineering are among the highest ranking schools in their disciplines. It is also notable that Rice is doing its part to close the STEM gender gap; the school is among the national leaders in producing female engineers, and it also boasts a 32 percent clip of female computer science majors, almost twice the national average. When it comes to procuring scholarships and fellowships upon graduation, Owls fare well, regularly producing Fulbright Scholars, Marshall Scholars, Watson Fellows, Hertz Fellows, and an occasional Rhodes Scholar (a dozen in its history).

Outside the Classroom

Central to student life at Rice is the Oxford/Cambridge-style (or more familiarly, Yale-style) residential college system. Upon matriculation, students are assigned to one of eleven residential colleges that contain their own dorms, dining halls, common areas, and faculty sponsors. Each college has its own student-run government, unique traditions, and social events. Those seeking a strong Greek life will have to look elsewhere as Rice has always operated free of fraternities and sororities. Rice does not have a particularly fervent sports culture either despite seven men's and seven women's varsity teams competing in NCAA Division I competition. The most notable squad is the baseball team that is always competing for national titles. Opportunities for intramural and club team participation are vast and include sports like aikido, badminton, and water polo. Student-run clubs are plentiful as well with over 250 to select from. The *Rice Thresher*, the student newspaper, is widely read and regularly wins national awards. While campus life is abuzz with activity, many venture into the city of Houston to enjoy the nightlife and cultural events in such close proximity.

Career Services

The Rice Center for Career Development (CCD) is staffed by eleven full-time professional employees, which equals a student-to-advisor ratio of 363:1, better-than-average when compared with the other institutions included in this book. Additional peer career advisors, embedded in each residential college, offer services such as resume reviews or assistance with locating internship opportunities. Internships opportunities can also be discovered at the Career and Internship Expo, which is attended by more than one hundred employers, and through RICElink, which posts internships open exclusively to current Owls. The CCD also facilitates Owl Edge Externships, job-shadowing experiences that last from one day to a full week.

The university does a phenomenal job of facilitating on-campus interviews with roughly 150 employers conducting over 1,600 interviews each year. It also hosts one hundred+ events that connect students to potential employers from formal career fairs to casual events like the Chili Cook-Off. The CCD does a superb job with outreach as it attracts more than 3,500 non-grad student visits per year, close to one visit per undergraduate. It's little surprise that 55 percent of graduates found their first job directly through the CCD office. In short, it is hard to imagine a career services office accomplishing more for its undergraduates than the CCD does for its students at Rice.

Rice University

E-mail: admi@rice.edu | Website: www.rice.edu

Professional Outcomes

Six months after graduation only 6 percent of Rice grads are still seeking employment. The overwhelming majority have found careers or a graduate school home. Companies that are known to pluck more than their fair share of employees each year from Rice's senior class include Deloitte, Capital One, JP Morgan Chase, Google, and Microsoft. Over one hundred alumni are also current employees of companies such as Shell, ExxonMobil, Chevron, Amazon, Accenture, and Facebook. Median starting salaries for Rice grads far exceed national averages. Across all majors the average starting salary is $69k. That encompasses engineering majors at the high end ($79k) and humanities majors at the low end ($52k). Texas is among the most common destinations for recent grads, but many also flock to California, New York, Wisconsin, and Washington State.

Over one-third of graduates move directly into graduate or professional school. That group fares well in gaining admission to elite graduate institutions; Harvard, Yale, Stanford, MIT, Columbia, and Berkeley are among the schools that absorb the highest number of Rice applicants. Rice is also known for producing a strong number of successful medical school applicants each year. A robust 38 percent of graduate school attendees are enrolled in medical school. Baylor College of Medicine and the med schools in the UT system are popular destinations for future doctors. Other recent grads are presently attending Harvard Medical School, Duke University School of Medicine, and Stanford Medical School.

Admission

Rice's acceptance rate for the Class of 2022 plummeted to an all-time low of 11 percent. That flirtation with the single-digit club was a steep fall from the 15-17 percent acceptance rates of the last few years. The number of applications received by the university topped 20,000 for the first time, and that figure has more than doubled in the last decade. The ACT mid-50 percent range is 33-35. The 75th percentile score on the math section was a perfect 800, and the reading range was 700-760. More than 88 percent of students earned above a 700 in math, and 77 percent earned the same in reading. In 2014, "only" 64 percent of Rice's freshman class scored above a 700 on the verbal section, and 75 percent reached that mark on the math portion. This is a clear indicator that Rice's diminishing acceptance rate is, in fact, indicative of an increasingly selective student profile.

Early decision applicants, as would be expected, enjoy a better acceptance rate of 22 percent, but an applicant's bona fides still need to meet the university's sky-high standards. Rice lists more factors as being "very important" than most elite schools, granting this designation to rigor of courses, GPA, class rank, test scores, essays, recommendations, talent/ability, and character/personal qualities. An intimidating 89 percent of Rice students placed in the top 10 percent of their high school class, and 96 percent were in the top quartile. In 2018, Rice instituted an expedited system of reviewing applications; it now takes two admissions officers fewer than ten minutes to review each candidate and assign a numerical rating, a 5 being the highest. With that in mind, to have a realistic chance of getting in, the admissions staff shouldn't have to dig very deep to find reasons to say "Yes." A quality essay and glowing recommendations will help, but you'll need a sparkling academic profile and in-range test scores to make it through the first wave.

Worth Your Money?

For the 39 percent of students who qualify for need-based financial aid, Rice delivers by meeting 100 percent of every individual's demonstrated need. That equates to over $44k per year, which certainly helps make the $67,000 annual cost (already a reasonable list price relative to the marketplace) of attendance more affordable. Further, 11 percent of students qualify for merit-based aid that averages $21,740. Graduates not only encounter incredibly high starting salaries, they also have less debt, on average, than the average college graduate in the United States. Needless to say, Rice is worth the cost of admissions no matter who you are or how much you have to pay.

FINANCIAL
Institutional Type: Private
In-State Tuition: $48,330
Out-of-State Tuition: $48,330
Room & Board: $14,140
Required Fees: $782
Books & Supplies: $1,200

Avg. Need-Based Aid: $44,044
Avg. % of Need Met: 100%

Avg. Merit-Based Aid: $21,740
% Receiving Merit-Based Aid: 11%

Avg. Cumulative Debt: $24,635
% of Students Borrowing: 24%

CAREER
Who Recruits
1. DMC, Inc.
2. INT Software
3. Quantlab
4. Oxy
5. Chevron

Notable Internships
1. The Blackstone Group
2. Jane Street
3. Houston Rockets

Top Industries
1. Business
2. Education
3. Engineering
4. Research
5. Operations

Top Employers
1. Google
2. Shell
3. ExxonMobil
4. Chevron
5. Microsoft

Where Alumni Work
1. Houston
2. San Francisco
3. Dallas
4. Austin
5. New York City

Median Earnings
College Scorecard (Early Career): $65,400
EOP (Early Career): $76,700
PayScale (Mid-Career): $129,500

RANKINGS
Forbes: 21
Money: 24
U.S. News: 17, National Universities
Wall Street Journal/THE: 16
Washington Monthly: 101, National Universities

#CollegesWorthYourMoney

Rochester Institute of Technology

Rochester, New York | Admissions Phone: 585-475-6631

ADMISSION
Admission Rate: 70%
Admission Rate - Men: 75%
Admission Rate - Women: 68%
EA Admission Rate: Not Offered
ED Admission Rate: 84%
Admission Rate (5-Year Trend): +10%
ED Admission Rate (5-Year Trend): -1%
% of Admits Attending (Yield): 19%
Transfer Admission Rate: 56%

Offered Wait List: 914
Accepted Wait List: 346
Admitted Wait List: 40

SAT Reading/Writing (Middle 50%): 600-690
SAT Math (Middle 50%): 620-720
ACT Composite (Middle 50%): 27-32
Testing Policy: ACT/SAT Required
SAT Superscore: Yes
ACT Superscore: Yes

% Graduated in Top 10% of HS Class: 39%
% Graduated in Top 25% of HS Class: 73%
% Graduated in Top 50% of HS Class: 94%

ENROLLMENT
Total Undergraduate Enrollment: 13,513
% Part-Time: 8%
% Male: 62%
% Female: 38%
% Out-of-State: 47%
% Fraternity: 4%
% Sorority: 2%
% On-Campus (Freshman): 96%
% On-Campus (All Undergraduate): 51%

% African-American: 4%
% Asian: 9%
% Hispanic: 7%
% White: 63%
% Other: 4%
% Race or Ethnicity Unknown: 6%
% International: 6%
% Low-Income: 30%

ACADEMICS
Student-to-Faculty Ratio: 13:1
% of Classes Under 20: 49%
% of Classes Under 40: 88%
% Full-Time Faculty: 73%
% Full-Time Faculty w/ Terminal Degree: 54%

Top Programs
Computer Science
Engineering
Film and Animation
Game Design and Development
Imaging Science
Management Information Systems
Photographic Arts

Retention Rate: 89%
4-Year Graduation Rate: 28%
6-Year Graduation Rate: 70%

Curricular Flexibility: Less Flexible
Academic Rating: ★★★

Inside the Classroom

Since 1829 the Rochester Institute of Technology has been more than simply a technical school that churns out large quantities of engineers each year. With additional strengths in art and animation and design, this institution genuinely desires to "shape the future and improve the world through creativity and innovation." Even by STEM-focused school standards, the training at RIT is highly focused on career readiness and launches students into hands-on learning opportunities from the start of their freshman year. Large compared to other schools of its ilk like RPI and WPI, Rochester Institute of Technology educates approximately 16,000 under-graduates and another 3,100 graduate students. Half are from New York State, but students from all over the United States as well as one hundred countries brave the frigid Upstate New York weather in order to attend this accessible school that offers many standout programs and some of the best connections to industry of any school in the country.

The co-op program is the fourth oldest in the country, and just about all students complete a one- or two-semester paid learning experience after finishing their first two years of academic study. There are nine under-graduate colleges at RIT, and while all have distinct course requirements the school's signature general education curriculum touches every single student. Students earning a bachelor's of science degree in engineering, for example, need to take sixty credit hours of general education courses—including first-year writing—and a number of perspectives courses that cover categories such as social, ethical, global, artistic, mathematics, scientific principles, and natural science inquiry. One immersion sequence that involves a three-course, deep dive into a particular topic also must be built into every undergrad's program.

RIT's 13:1 student-to-faculty ratio and a genuine commitment to undergraduate teaching leads to a respectable 49 percent of sections enrolling fewer than twenty students, and only 11 percent of courses contain more than forty students. Additionally, RIT provides an array of undergraduate research opportunities including the Biological Sciences Research Scholars Program, the Chemistry Research Scholars Program, Economics Undergraduate Research, and the Undergraduate Research Symposium that saw 212 students give presentations in the 2018-19 academic year. Ample opportunities exist to study abroad, but few undergraduates elect to take advantage.

The most popular majors at this school are engineering, information sciences, visual and performing arts, and business. The Gleason College of Engineering and the Golisano College of Computing and Information Sciences are top-of-the-line. The latter houses RIT's game design program, which is the best on the entire East Coast. Strong film, art, and design programs also churn out successful graduates. Few pursue postgraduate fellow-ships, but the school does produce roughly one Fulbright Scholar and two Goldwater Scholars each cycle.

Outside the Classroom

RIT guarantees housing to freshmen and can accommodate about half the total undergraduate population in a mix of residence halls, apartments, the RIT Inn and Conference Center, Greek housing, and the global village. Like too many institutes of technology, the male-to-female ratio is heavily skewed at 2-to-1, which certainly has an impact on aspects of campus life. There are thirty fraternities and sororities on campus, but in the scope of such a large school, Greek life only draws single-digit participation. While RIT doesn't award athletic scholar-ships, it does field twenty-four NCAA varsity sports teams including Division I men's and women's ice hockey as well as many highly-competitive Division III teams. RIT is so competitive, in fact, rumors have swirled about a step-up to Division I. There are 300 clubs and organizations, including an extensive intramural sports program that signs up roughly half of the student body and plenty of opportunities for competitive or friendly gaming; video games are a way of life here. One of the greenest campuses around with a focus on sustainability, the 1,159 acres owned by the school offer federally designated wetlands, ample native plantings and wildlife, and a 200-acre area where most buildings are concentrated. There's enough to do on campus and in the classroom to mitigate the impact of an otherwise unexciting locale.

Career Services

The Office of Career Services and Cooperative Education (OCSCE) is staffed by twenty-seven professional staff members (not counting office assistants) who play roles such as career advisor, employer engagement and partnerships coordinator, and alumni relations coordinator. Rochester Institute of Technology's 593:1 student-to-advisor ratio is slightly higher than the average school featured in this guide, but it unquestionably has sufficient personnel to get the job done. Large- scale, university-wide career fairs are put on twice per year, drawing 726 companies and 3,500 students. Numerous boutique fairs cater to groups such as future accoun-tants, civil engineers, and teachers. On a more personal level, the office also arranges "tailored orientations, workshops, and one-on-one advisement. It also plans and promotes events such as career fairs, workshops, and speakers from industry," and that's only the tip of the iceberg.

The co-op program, more than a century old, sees 2,300+ participants per year in co-op with employers from all fifty states and forty countries. The list of co-op and internship partners is incredible—Boeing, the CIA, EY, Fisher Price, Walt Disney World, SpaceX, NASA, Google, and literally dozens of other equally impressive organizations. RIT has 2,200 employer partners. The off-the-charts employer relations accomplishments do not stop there; the career services staff posts 10,000 jobs per year and facilitates 5,400 on-campus interviews, far more than the number of seniors at RIT, meaning many are interviewing with multiple companies. More than 850 companies recruit on campus every single year. In sum, the Rochester Institute of Technology offers an exceptional level of support to its undergraduates through its robust co-op program as well as all of the one-on-one attention you could desire.

Professional Outcomes

Within six months of graduation 95.4 percent of the 2,495 members of the Class of 2017 had found employment or a full-time graduate program. Major companies presently employing more 500 RIT alums include Xerox and Paychex, both with offices in Rochester. Between 200 and 450 employees of IBM, Microsoft, Apple, Intel, Amazon, Google, and Cisco were educated at RIT. Many graduates remain in the Upstate New York area while large numbers of other RIT alumni flock to New York City, Boston, DC, and San Francisco. Median income levels by midcareer are in the same neighborhood as fellow New York institutions including the University of Rochester, Fordham, and Syracuse. Starting salary figures vary greatly by major with College of Business grads landing median starting salaries between $43,000 (marketing majors) and $53,000 (finance majors), and just about all engineering grads being compensated at more than $60k. Computer science majors had a median compensation package of $83k right out of school.

The Class of 2017 saw an exceptionally low 8.8 percent of graduates electing to pursue an advanced degree; the prior year saw 12.5 percent continuing their educations postgraduation. While only a small number of RIT grads head directly to grad school, those who do typically head to some of the world's best such as Carnegie Mellon, Duke, Harvard, Johns Hopkins, MIT, Rhode Island School of Design, Penn, UVA, and the University of Michigan. The number of seniors applying to medical school has risen in recent years and is now between forty and forty-five applicants annually. Historically, the school has an 80-85 percent acceptance rate, but that number includes non-MD graduate programs in the health professions. Recent graduates have landed at top medical schools including Columbia University Vagelos College of Physicians and Surgeons, Emory University School of Medicine, Geisel School of Medicine at Dartmouth, and Georgetown University School of Medicine.

Admission

Applicants to the Rochester Institute of Technology benefit from a fairly generous acceptance rate that is typically in the mid-to-high 50-percent range. Students apply to individual colleges within the larger university, and standards vary from program to program. For example, 2018-19 freshmen in the Saunders College of Business had mid-50 percent standardized test scores of 1170-1340 on the SAT and 26-31 on the ACT. Successful College of Engineering applicants had similar ranges of 1190-1350 on the SAT and 25-31 on the ACT. The highest achieving group were freshmen in the Golisano College of Computing and Information Sciences who scored 1380-1450 on the SAT and 29-34 on the ACT. Across all schools and majors the average entering GPA was 3.7; two-fifths placed in the top decile of their high school class, nearly three-quarters were in the top quartile, and all but 5 percent ranked in the top half.

This admissions committee looks, first and foremost, for applicants who engaged in a rigorous high school course load and achieved a solid mix of A's and B's. The four factors that make-up the second tier of admissions considerations are standardized test scores, class rank, recommendations, and the essay. It is important to note that the school is now test-optional, but only for applicants to the College of Liberal Arts. Roughly 1,300 apply via early decision, and RIT rewards their pledge of loyalty with a 66 percent ED acceptance rate. For the level of excellence at this institution, the Rochester Institute of Technology continues to have rather unintimidating admissions standards. While average test scores have risen in recent years, some of that can be attributed to SAT score inflation. The acceptance rate and general academic expectations for entry have remained steady over the past decade.

Worth Your Money?

Yes. That's the short answer for anyone coming to RIT to study engineering or computer science. The school keeps the sticker price reasonable, by market standards, at a bit over $45k for tuition and under $60k total cost of attendance. Over three-quarters of attending students receive some level of need-based aid and, even for families in the upper income brackets, the total COA annually comes out in the mid-$30k range. Those coming for liberal arts, business, or an art and design degree would have to weigh RIT's offer against their other options to find the most sensible deal.

FINANCIAL
Institutional Type: Private
In-State Tuition: $45,244
Out-of-State Tuition: $45,244
Room & Board: $13,540
Required Fees: $646
Books & Supplies: $2,082

Avg. Need-Based Aid: $29,475
Avg. % of Need Met: 87%

Avg. Merit-Based Aid: $11,700
% Receiving Merit-Based Aid: 14%

Avg. Cumulative Debt: $41,202
% of Students Borrowing: 75%

CAREER
Who Recruits
1. General Electric
2. Google
3. Microsoft
4. Intel
5. IBM

Notable Internships
1. GE Aviation
2. Electronic Arts
3. L.L. Bean

Top Industries
1. Engineering
2. Business
3. Operations
4. Information Technology
5. Arts & Design

Top Employers
1. Xerox
2. Paychex
3. IBM
4. Microsoft
5. Apple

Where Alumni Work
1. Rochester, NY
2. New York City
3. Boston
4. Washington, DC
5. San Francisco

Median Earnings
College Scorecard (Early Career): $62,400
EOP (Early Career): $62,400
PayScale (Mid-Career): $106,600

RANKINGS
Forbes: 337
Money: 369
U.S. News: 104 (T), National Universities
Wall Street Journal/THE: 153 (T)
Washington Monthly: 219, National Universities

#CollegesWorthYourMoney

Rose-Hulman Institute of Technology

Terre Haute, Indiana | Admissions Phone: 812-877-8213

ADMISSION
Admission Rate: 68%
Admission Rate - Men: 66%
Admission Rate - Women: 76%
EA Admission Rate: 84%
ED Admission Rate: Not Offered
Admission Rate (5-Year Trend): +12%
ED Admission Rate (5-Year Trend): Not Offered
% of Admits Attending (Yield): 16%
Transfer Admission Rate: 54%

\# Offered Wait List: 357
\# Accepted Wait List: 137
\# Admitted Wait List: 50

SAT Reading/Writing (Middle 50%): 610-700
SAT Math (Middle 50%): 660-780
ACT Composite (Middle 50%): 28-33
Testing Policy: ACT/SAT Required
SAT Superscore: Yes
ACT Superscore: Yes

% Graduated in Top 10% of HS Class: 64%
% Graduated in Top 25% of HS Class: 93%
% Graduated in Top 50% of HS Class: 100%

ENROLLMENT
Total Undergraduate Enrollment: 2,085
% Part-Time: 1%
% Male: 75%
% Female: 25%
% Out-of-State: 65%
% Fraternity: 37%
% Sorority: 26%
% On-Campus (Freshman): 98%
% On-Campus (All Undergraduate): 55%

% African-American: 3%
% Asian: 6%
% Hispanic: 5%
% White: 65%
% Other: 5%
% Race or Ethnicity Unknown: 1%
% International: 15%
% Low-Income: 17%

ACADEMICS
Student-to-Faculty Ratio: 11:1
% of Classes Under 20: 54%
% of Classes Under 40: 100%
% Full-Time Faculty: 96%
% Full-Time Faculty w/ Terminal Degree: 98%

Top Programs
Biomedical Engineering
Chemical Engineering
Civil Engineering
Computer Science
Electrical Engineering
Mechanical Engineering

Retention Rate: 92%
4-Year Graduation Rate: 67%
6-Year Graduation Rate: 81%

Curricular Flexibility: Less Flexible
Academic Rating: ★★★★

Inside the Classroom

When searching for the top engineering schools you naturally encounter a number of prestigious, doctoral-granting research universities like Stanford, MIT, UC Berkeley, and Carnegie Mellon. When looking for small engineering schools, Caltech and Harvey Mudd are typically the easiest ones to locate. Likely off your radar is a small private college in Terra Haute, Indiana, that, year after year, tops the charts among engineering schools whose highest degree is a master's. The Rose-Hulman Institute of Technology offers only nineteen undergraduate degree programs to 2,200 students, mostly from the Midwest, but they go on to phenomenal postgraduate successes.

Operating on the quarter system, courses are swift and rigorous, and pretty much everything you learn will be related to your major. Engineering students (the bulk of the student body) dive right in as first-semester freshmen by taking a heavy dose of math, science, and introductory engineering courses. The whole first year of study has room for only two electives in the realm of rhetoric/composition, the humanities, or social sciences. Foreign language is not among the requirements at this institution.

A student-to-faculty ratio of 11:1 and a minimal presence of graduate students bodes well for both class sizes and having introductory classes that are taught by full-time faculty members. The average class size is twenty, and 54 percent of sections are smaller than that. Giant lecture halls simply don't exist at Rose-Hulman as only two sections of 457 contained greater than forty students. Undergraduate research is commonplace at this school and can be arranged through the Independent Project/Research Opportunities Program that connects you to faculty mentors and sets you on the path toward presenting your work at the End-of-Quarter Symposium. Ten-week summer research apprenticeships also are available. International opportunities can be procured through the Global E3, a consortium of sixty engineering schools of which Rose-Hulman is a member, or through participation in Engineers without Borders. This is a rare institute of technology that pushes its students to pursue an international experience; it even hosts an annual Study Abroad Fair as part of those efforts.

The engineering major accounts for 79 percent of all degrees conferred, and there's a good reason for its popularity; this program is viewed among the best by prospective employers and graduate schools, and not just in the Midwest. Rose-Hulman's reputation for excellence in engineering stretches from Silicon Valley to the East Coast. Unique undergraduate engineering programs include optical engineering and international computer science; CS, in general, is the second-most popular degree program (13 percent).

Outside the Classroom

Even more than your average STEM-focused school, the gender disparity is significant to the tune of a 75/25 split favoring males. (The school didn't become coed until 1995.) Greek life at Rose-Hulman is booming with 37 percent of men joining fraternities and 26 percent of women involved with the school's sororities. All but a handful of freshmen live on campus (it is a requirement). And 55 percent of the total undergraduate student body lives in one of ten dormitories or apartment complexes. Despite its small size, the school still fields twenty NCAA Division III sports teams, the Fightin' Engineers, who compete in the Heartland Collegiate Athletic Conference. That translates to a full quarter of the student body participating in varsity athletics. There are also ninety clubs, including a popular student newspaper, radio station, and film club plus plenty of intramural sports such as archery, ballroom dancing, scuba, and yoga. The general social hub on campus is the Mussallem Unio, with well-reviewed cuisine, a giant Connect Four board, and a lakefront view—what more can you ask for? Rose-Hulman is set on a 1,300-acre property, but the majority of campus is confined to a 200-acre tract. Terra Haute isn't exactly Midtown Manhattan, but it's not that far from a number of major Midwestern destinations with trips to Indianapolis, Chicago, Louisville, Cincinnati, or St. Louis doable on a weekend.

Career Services

The Career Services and Employer Relations Office at Rose-Hulman consists of five professional employees, which computes to a student-to-advisor ratio of 440:1, in the average range compared to other schools featured in this guide. However, it is notable that this career services office puts "employer relations" right in its own title, and the statistics in that area prove that this inclusion is more than warranted.

A stunning 894 companies participated in events hosted by career services or had contact with students that was facilitated by career services staff in the last academic year. As a school of 2,200+ undergraduates, that figure is absurdly good. In total, 1,392 interviews were conducted by companies on campus, also a ridiculously strong number when you consider there were fewer than 500 seniors. Historically, 94 percent of seniors have had at least one opportunity for experiential learning via undergraduate research, co-op placement (50+ companies participate in the school's co-op program), or an internship. Three career fairs held annually in the fall, winter, and spring are extremely well attended by students as well as major hiring organizations. The fall 2018 fair drew a school record 251 companies, some of which conducted on-the-spot interviews with students. In short, thanks to the vast network of employers connected to this career services office, Rose-Hulman job-seekers are not the hunters but the hunted.

Rose-Hulman Institute of Technology

E-mail: admissions@rose-hulman.edu | Website: www.rose-hulman.edu

Professional Outcomes

Of the 487 graduates who strutted the stage in 2018, an enviable 98 percent had landed at their next desti-nation, whether employment or graduate school, within six months of exiting. Further, students in ten of the school's programs enjoyed a 100 percent success rate. Top employers of Class of 2018 graduates includ-ed Boston Scientific, Cook Group, Texas Instruments, Caterpillar, Honeywell, Raytheon, and Rolls Royce. Raytheon, Microsoft, and Indianapolis-based pharmaceutical giant Eli Lilly also have a strong representation of Rose-Hulman-affiliated employees. The average first-year salary for a Rose-Hulman grad is just shy of $70,000, and some members of the Class of 2018 took home a not-too-shabby $120,000 in first-year wages. The ma-jority of alumni remain in Indiana with Indianapolis and Terra Haute being the two favorite destinations. Smaller pockets of graduates can be found in Chicago, Cincinnati, San Francisco, and Seattle.

Fifteen percent of the Class of 2018 (74 students) enrolled in graduate school directly out of undergrad. They entered thirty-five universities, including many of the world's most distinguished such as Johns Hopkins, Carnegie Mellon, Duke, Northwestern, Washington University in St. Louis, Georgia Tech, Cornell, Notre Dame, and Rice University. Two 2018 graduates matriculated into medical school, and one 2017 graduate was on the path to becoming a medical doctor. No one from the previous two classes decided to attend law school. Clearly, and not surprisingly, the records demonstrate that students come to Rose-Hulman to enter technology/engineering fields.

Admission

Rose-Hulman's acceptance rate for membership in the Class of 2022 was an unimposing 68 percent. Compare that to other premier institutes of technology with phenomenal job placement rates and starting salaries and you might breathe a sigh of relief. Of course, the applicant pool is a self-selecting group with an affinity for STEM learning, and that leads to an impressive freshman class academic profile. The Class of 2022 had a mid-50 percent SAT range of 1270-1480 and ACT range of 28-33. Sixty-four percent of 2018-19 freshmen earned a place in the top 10 percent of their high school class while 93 percent were in the top quartile. Nearly four-fifths of students had a GPA over 3.75, and only 6 percent had under a 3.5. Suddenly, that sigh of relief feels like a distant memory. Interestingly, the school does accept a lower percentage of applicants in some cycles. Only a few years ago, the acceptance rate was under 60 percent as rates can fluctuate quite a bit at a school with a small applicant pool of under 4,500 students.

Rigor of secondary coursework and grades are the two most important factors for admission followed by standardized test scores, class rank, recommendations, and extracurricular activities. The acceptance rate for female applicants is 76 percent compared to the rate for males of 66 percent. This schools offers multiple early action application deadlines but no binding early decision option. In the admissions office's own words, successful applicants are "typically at the top of their high school graduating classes with scores in the 95th percentile on the SAT or ACT – plus they have taken a lot of high school science, math and English."

Worth Your Money?

This is a rare case where an annual cost of attendance of $70,000 does little to derail the financial futures of the student population. Freshmen receiving need-based aid net an average annual award of more than $30,000; average merit aid packages for those eligible neared $12,000. Even without financial aid, Rose-Hulman is definitely worth the private school cost thanks to phenomenal placement rates at top companies and extremely high starting salaries, even by STEM standards.

FINANCIAL
Institutional Type: Private
In-State Tuition: $46,641
Out-of-State Tuition: $46,641
Room & Board: $14,766
Required Fees: $930
Books & Supplies: $1,500

Avg. Need-Based Aid: $30,676
Avg. % of Need Met: 65%

Avg. Merit-Based Aid: $11,737
% Receiving Merit-Based Aid: 81%

Avg. Cumulative Debt: $43,459
% of Students Borrowing: 58%

CAREER
Who Recruits
1. Archer Daniels Midland
2. Whirlpool
3. Allegant Air
4. Kinze Manufacturing
5. Ingredion Incorporated

Notable Internships
1. Rolls-Royce
2. Halliburton
3. Tesla

Top Industries
1. Engineering
2. Operations
3. Business
4. Information Technology
5. Education

Top Employers
1. Eli Lily and Company
2. Cummins Inc.
3. Rolls-Royce
4. Caterpillar Inc.
5. Google

Where Alumni Work
1. Indianapolis
2. Terra Haute, IN
3. Chicago
4. Cincinnati
5. San Francisco

Median Earnings
College Scorecard (Early Career): $80,900
EOP (Early Career): $83,600
PayScale (Mid-Career): $135,800

RANKINGS
Forbes: 110
Money: 336
U.S. News: N/A
Wall Street Journal/THE: 103
Washington Monthly: N/A

#CollegesWorthYourMoney

Rutgers University – New Brunswick

Piscataway, New Jersey | Admissions Phone: 732-445-4636

ADMISSION
Admission Rate: 60%
Admission Rate - Men: 60%
Admission Rate - Women: 60%
EA Admission Rate: N/A
ED Admission Rate: Not Offered
Admission Rate (5-Year Trend): +1%
ED Admission Rate (5-Year Trend): Not Offered
% of Admits Attending (Yield): 28%
Transfer Admission Rate: 55%

Offered Wait List: N/A
Accepted Wait List: N/A
Admitted Wait List: N/A

SAT Reading/Writing (Middle 50%): 590-680
SAT Math (Middle 50%): 600-730
ACT Composite (Middle 50%): 25-31
Testing Policy: ACT/SAT Required
SAT Superscore: Yes
ACT Superscore: Yes

% Graduated in Top 10% of HS Class: 38%
% Graduated in Top 25% of HS Class: 72%
% Graduated in Top 50% of HS Class: 95%

ENROLLMENT
Total Undergraduate Enrollment: 36,039
% Part-Time: 6%
% Male: 50%
% Female: 50%
% Out-of-State: 6%
% Fraternity: N/A
% Sorority: N/A
% On-Campus (Freshman): 84%
% On-Campus (All Undergraduate): 43%

% African-American: 7%
% Asian: 27%
% Hispanic: 13%
% White: 38%
% Other: 4%
% Race or Ethnicity Unknown: 2%
% International: 9%
% Low-Income: 30%

ACADEMICS
Student-to-Faculty Ratio: 16:1
% of Classes Under 20: 42%
% of Classes Under 40: 73%
% Full-Time Faculty: 50%
% Full-Time Faculty w/ Terminal Degree: 99%

Top Programs
Accounting
Computer Science
Criminal Justice
English
History
Pubilc Health
Supply Chain Management

Retention Rate: 93%
4-Year Graduation Rate: 61%
6-Year Graduation Rate: 80%

Curricular Flexibility: Somewhat Flexible
Academic Rating: ★★★

Inside the Classroom

Rutgers-New Brunswick, the flagship campus of the school's three locations (Camden and Newark being the others), is one of the oldest universities in the country. Founded in 1766 as one of nine colleges in Colonial America, the New Brunswick campus today is a top state research university that is home to more than 36,000 undergraduates. Garden State residents comprise 83 percent of the student body, but there has been a push in recent years to attract more out-of-staters, partially for monetary reasons. Presently, there are representatives of all fifty states and 115 countries on campus as the number of nonresidents increases each year. No matter where you're from, you'll enjoy the benefits of Rutgers massive operation that is divided into seventeen schools and colleges, collectively offering one hundred+ undergraduate majors.

Core requirements are variable across different programs, but members of the School of Arts & Sciences, by far the university's largest college, have a ten- to fourteen-course core. Mandates include fulfilling coursework in areas such as diversities and inequalities, our common future, natural sciences, social and historical analysis, arts and humanities, writing and communication, and quantitative and formal reasoning. In the School of Engineering, first-year coursework will look quite different as students must conquer courses that include General Chemistry for Engineers, Calculus, Analytical Physics, and Introduction to Computers for Engineers; non-STEM coursework is minimal for engineering students. A host of first-year initiatives, including Byrne Seminars and First Year Interest Group Seminars, leads to a freshman retention rate of 93 percent, a tremendous achievement for a public university.

Impressive for a school its size and scope, Rutgers boasts a 13:1 student-to-faculty ratio. As a result, it can offer a reasonable number of smaller, seminar-style courses to undergraduates. Thirty-nine percent of class sections have an enrollment of nineteen or fewer students compared to only 21 percent of sections that contain more than fifty undergrads. Rutgers offers 180 study abroad programs in fifty countries, but few take advantage; the participation rate is a paltry 2 percent. Undergraduate research, on the other hand, attracts more takers. The Aresty Research Center serves as a clearinghouse that matches undergraduates with faculty members conducting research in an area of interest; there are presently 1,500 faculty partners. An annual Undergraduate Research Symposium has showcased thousands of student projects in its fifteen+ years of existence.

The areas of study in which the greatest number of degrees are conferred are business (17 percent), engineering (11 percent), health professions (10 percent), biology (9 percent), social sciences (8 percent), and computer science (8 percent). Rutgers Business School sends many majors to top Wall Street investment banks, and programs in computer science, public health, and criminal justice have a terrific national reputation. Competitive scholarship and fellowship organizations also show lots of love to Scarlet Knights. Students and alumni received twenty-three Fulbright Scholarships in 2019 to go with three Goldwater Scholarships, two Schwarzman Scholarships, a Gates-Cambridge Scholarship, and a Truman Scholarship.

Outside the Classroom

Rutgers-New Brunswick's sprawling 2,685-acre campus is divided into five distinct, interconnected campuses. Despite one of the largest undergraduate housing operations of any school in the United States, only 43 percent of students (roughly 16,000) live on campus in one of 136 residence hall buildings or university-owned apartment complexes. The Greek scene is on the rise at Rutgers as the school now has over 3,800 members of eighty+ fraternities and sororities, all of which are located off campus. The Scarlet Knights compete in NCAA Division I athletics in ten men's and fourteen women's sports. Highpoint.com Stadium is the only Division I football stadium in the NY/NJ region, but it rarely fills its 52,000-seat capacity. Rutgers students would rather play sports than watch them as a member of one of fifty-seven club teams or fifty intramural leagues. The school's five fitness and recreation centers attract more than 5,000 visitors per day; ten outdoor fields and parks also are available for student use. There are also 500+ student-run organizations, including a top-ranked Model UN team and the Rutgers University Dance Marathon that raised over one million dollars for pediatric illnesses in 2019 alone. The Zimmerli Art Museum houses one of the top collegiate collections around, and there are plenty of live musical and theatrical acts that visit campus. Rutgers' excellent location makes weekend trips to Philly, New York, or the Jersey Shore a painless one-hour car ride.

Career Services

Thirty-seven professional employees staff the Rutgers University Career Services (UCS) Office in areas such as career exploration, career development, and employer relations. The university's overall student-to-counselor ratio of 973:1 is higher than the average school featured in this guidebook, but not alarmingly so when compared to other large public universities. Despite the monumental task of connecting with more than 36,000 students, the UCS has made some inroads as it currently interacts, in some form, with 56 percent of the student population each year. In 2017, the office saw a 90 percent increase in first-year student contact as it aims to connect with more freshmen. In 2018-19, the UCS conducted 4,817 one-on-one advising appointments.

E-mail: admissions@ugadm.rutgers.edu | Website: www.newbrunswick.rutgers.edu

There are plenty of large-scale offerings designed to benefit the student population. Career fair attendance is solid with 3,400 students connecting with 300 companies in the fall and 4,700 engaging with 265 employers in the spring. Another 641 unique employers visited career fairs in 2018-19. There were more than 3,400 on-campus interviews conducted with Rutgers seniors that same year. The CareerKnight online database of job and internship opportunities receives hundreds of thousands of annual hits. The Road to Wall Street mentoring program led to over 90 percent of participants landing competitive summer internships; the overall internship completion rate for graduates is an estimated 28 percent. Job search boot camps draw solid reviews as 100 percent of attendees said they have a better awareness of the next steps in the process as a result of attending. With 352,000 living alumni, there is always a Scarlet Knight networking opportunity in your field of interest. Roughly two-fifths of graduates say that the Rutgers UCS contributed to their career success.

Professional Outcomes

Upon graduation, 80 percent of Rutgers students have their next stop, whether it's a first job or graduate school, squared away. Three-fifths of the Class of 2018 were headed directly to the world of employment where the companies hiring the largest number of grads included Amazon, Johnson & Johnson, L'Oréal, and JP Morgan Chase. Investment banks like Goldman Sachs and Citi also employ hundreds of alumni. More than 300 current employees of Verizon, Bristol-Meyers Squibb, Novartis, Amazon, Pfizer, and Google also have Scarlet Knight lineage. The median starting salary across all majors was $52,500. The median starting salary for engineering majors was $65,000 while arts and sciences grads brought home $47,500. The bulk of graduates, approximately 75 percent, end up settling in New Jersey/the Greater New York area. Philadelphia, DC, and San Francisco are next in popularity.

One-fifth of the 2018 graduating class matriculated into full-time graduate or professional school. The most frequently attended universities were Rutgers, NYU, Columbia, and fellow Jersey institution Rowan University. Of the 483 graduates of the Class of 2018 who applied to medical school, 52 percent gained acceptance, a bit above the national average. Those sporting a 3.7 GPA or higher were even more successful, gaining acceptance at a 75 percent clip. Ninety-one of those accepted matriculated into one of Rutgers' two medical colleges. Rowan University's Cooper Medical School and School of Osteopathic Medicine were by far the most commonly attended institutions. Prestigious acceptances included Duke, Georgetown, Cornell, UVA, and Stanford. Future lawyers also end up in droves at Rutgers own highly reputable law school as well as at Villanova, Penn, Fordham, and Notre Dame.

Admission

Unlike at so many other premier flagship universities around the nation, the acceptance rate at Rutgers-New Brunswick has not plummeted in recent years. Those seeking entry into the Class of 2022 were given the thumbs up 59 percent of the time. Still, the quality of the applicant pool has risen dramatically over the 2000s. Freshmen entering Rutgers' School of Arts & Sciences in the 2018-19 school year had mid-50 percent standardized test scores of 1270-1430 on the SAT, 26-33 on the ACT, and a weighted GPA of 3.6-4.1. Right around two-fifths of current students placed in the top 10 percent of their high school class, and three-quarters landed in the top 25 percent. Five years ago, the acceptance rate at the university was a comparable 61 percent, but the SAT range was a far lower 1040-1290.

The factors deemed most important by the admissions committee are GPA, standardized test scores, and rigor of secondary curriculum. Extracurricular involvement is the lone category dubbed "important," and factors like state residency, essays, class rank, first-generation status, and volunteer work are "considered." Rutgers does offer an early action deadline of November 1, but no binding early decision plan is available. An average in the B+/A- range and standardized test scores in the 85th percentile put you firmly in play for an invitation to attend the New Brunswick campus right out of high school. Otherwise, a start at the Camden or Newark campus may be the only option. Out-of-state applicants may find slightly more relaxed admission standards, given the university's push to recruit applicants from outside New Jersey.

Worth Your Money?

Rutgers doesn't have the endowment to meet anything close to your full level of financial need, but it does award grants averaging $13,025 to 54 percent of current undergraduates. The school, however, is more generous with merit aid than your average public university, giving one-fifth of students an annual award close to $12k. The in-state cost of attendance is $32,443, which is not a bad deal for a flagship public school in the Northeastern United States. Out-of-state students would pay close to $49k per year COA, which would be a curious move for students not receiving aid, given the likelihood that better deals would be available.

FINANCIAL
Institutional Type: Public
In-State Tuition: $12,230
Out-of-State Tuition: $29,012
Room & Board: $13,075
Required Fees: $3,177
Books & Supplies: $1,350

Avg. Need-Based Aid: $13,025
Avg. % of Need Met: 55%

Avg. Merit-Based Aid: $11,734
% Receiving Merit-Based Aid: 20%

Avg. Cumulative Debt: $34,113
% of Students Borrowing: 60%

CAREER
Who Recruits
1. Aerotek
2. Automatic Data
3. Enterprise Holdings
4. Insight Global
5. Robert Half

Notable Internships
1. Colgate-Palmolive
2. NBCUniversal
3. New York Giants

Top Industries
1. Business
2. Education
3. Operations
4. Healthcare
5. Sales

Top Employers
1. Johnson & Johnson
2. Verizon
3. Bristol-Myers Squibb
4. JPMorgan Chase
5. Novartis

Where Alumni Work
1. New York City
2. Philadelphia
3. Washington, DC
4. San Francisco
5. Boston

Median Earnings
College Scorecard (Early Career): $57,900
EOP (Early Career): $58,400
PayScale (Mid-Career): $111,000

RANKINGS
Forbes: 123
Money: 50
U.S. News: 62, National Universities
Wall Street Journal/THE: 130
Washington Monthly: 39, National Universities

#CollegesWorthYourMoney

San Diego State University

San Diego, California | Admissions Phone: 619-594-6336

ADMISSION
Admission Rate: 34%
Admission Rate - Men: 33%
Admission Rate - Women: 35%
EA Admission Rate: Not Offered
ED Admission Rate: Not Offered
Admission Rate (5-Year Trend): -3%
ED Admission Rate (5-Year Trend): Not Offered
% of Admits Attending (Yield): 24%
Transfer Admission Rate: 20%

Offered Wait List: 2,853
Accepted Wait List: 1,276
Admitted Wait List: 46

SAT Reading/Writing (Middle 50%): 560-650
SAT Math (Middle 50%): 550-660
ACT Composite (Middle 50%): 22-28
Testing Policy: ACT/SAT Required
SAT Superscore: Yes
ACT Superscore: Yes

% Graduated in Top 10% of HS Class: 29%
% Graduated in Top 25% of HS Class: 68%
% Graduated in Top 50% of HS Class: 93%

ENROLLMENT
Total Undergraduate Enrollment: 30,393
% Part-Time: 10%
% Male: 45%
% Female: 55%
% Out-of-State: 11%
% Fraternity: 11%
% Sorority: 13%
% On-Campus (Freshman): 72%
% On-Campus (All Undergraduate): 19%

% African-American: 4%
% Asian: 13%
% Hispanic: 31%
% White: 33%
% Other: 7%
% Race or Ethnicity Unknown: 4%
% International: 7%
% Low-Income: 35%

ACADEMICS
Student-to-Faculty Ratio: 25:1
% of Classes Under 20: 28%
% of Classes Under 40: 70%
% Full-Time Faculty: 49%
% Full-Time Faculty w/ Terminal Degree: 88%

Top Programs
Art
Communication
Criminal Justice
International Business
Kinesiology
Psychology

Retention Rate: 89%
4-Year Graduation Rate: 37%
6-Year Graduation Rate: 75%

Curricular Flexibility: Less Flexible
Academic Rating: ★★★

Inside the Classroom
They say that a rising tide lifts all boats. As the University of California system has become ultra-competitive over the past decade, the California State University system has seen many of its schools become beneficiaries of an overflow of uber-qualified applicants. San Diego State University, offering a highly affordable education in a gorgeous and temperate setting, is one such institution. A diverse school of over 30,000 undergraduates, one-third of its students are Hispanic, and roughly the same percentage are first-generation students. Most hail from the Golden State, but 7 percent of the population are international students representing one of 114 countries. Don't be scared off by the low acceptance rate (34 percent); you don't need straight A's in high school to gain access to this excellent research university that boasts nearly 160 undergraduate majors, minors, and pre-professional programs.

The general education requirements at SDSU are the breadth portion of one's education experience and will comprise approximately one-third of an undergraduate's time at the university. Forty-nine units are required, including nine units of communications and critical thinking courses; thirty-one units of foundational study in the humanities; social and behavioral sciences; and natural sciences and quantitative reasoning; and nine units in "explorations" that are upper-division courses you cannot begin until junior year. After completing sixty credits, all students must take and pass a writing placement assessment. Some majors require you to learn a language other than English while some, like engineering, do not. Lastly, there is a mandated course called American Institutions in which you must demonstrate your knowledge of California government, the US Constitution, and American history.

Like many other schools in the California State University system, cheap tuition and heavy enrollment leads to a high student-to-faculty ratio. San Diego State sports a 25:1 ratio and, consequently, classes tend to be on the large side. Thirty percent of course sections enroll more than forty students, and only 28 percent of sections contain fewer than twenty students. To help connect students to faculty mentors and undergraduate research opportunities, the school maintains a useful database of current professors seeking assistance. Summer research programs and an annual Undergraduate Research Symposium provide additional experiences in that realm. In 2018, a solid 33 percent of grads reported studying abroad. In total, 3,000 SDSU students take a semester outside of the United States each year.

Business/marketing accounts for 22 percent of the degrees conferred, making it the school's most popular area of study. Next in line are the social sciences (10 percent), engineering (8 percent), health professions (8 percent), psychology (7 percent), and parks and recreation (7 percent). You won't find the engineering or computer science programs at the top of any rankings lists, but that doesn't have much of an impact on employment, thanks to the booming local tech and startup scene. Because of its emphasis on international study, many graduates go on to win fellowships that take them all around the globe. SDSU has had as many as nine Fulbright award winners in recent years, and it often has multiple recipients of Boren, Critical Language, and Gilman Scholarships. SDSU also has had several undergraduates receive National Science Foundation Graduate Research Fellowships over the last few years.

Outside the Classroom
On-campus housing is limited, and preference is given to freshmen who take advantage at a 72 percent clip. Overall, only 19 percent of undergraduates reside in university-owned housing. However, there is plenty to bond the student body and create cohesion on campus. Eleven percent of men and 13 percent of women belong to the university's fifty+ fraternities and sororities. In addition to Greek life, annual campus-wide events like AzFest and Homecoming Weekend unify the 30,000+ undergrads, as do basketball and football games. The Aztecs field nineteen NCAA Division I sports teams, and famous alumni athletes include Marshall Faulk (NFL), Tony Gwynn (MLB), and 2019 NBA Finals MVP Kawhi Leonard. There are 350+ student organizations including KCR College Radio that has a long history and large listenership, intramural sports that draw thousands of participants, and the Aztec Unity Project that is committed to local community service projects. Viejas Arena, where the Aztecs play basketball, doubles as a major concert venue drawing acts like the Chainsmokers, the Foo Fighters, and Drake—basically a major act every week. San Diego weather, sunsets, and seventeen miles of coastline are all free benefits of attending SDSU. Additionally, there are multiple beaches less than ten miles from campus. The Aquaplex is, essentially, a free resort on campus for student use. It features two outdoor pools and a twenty-person spa; such is life at San Diego State.

Career Services
The main San Diego State Career Services Office employs nineteen full-time professional staff members (not counting administrative assistants) working as internship coordinators, career counselors, employer outreach specialists, and experiential learning specialists. There are an additional four staff members working out of the Fowler College of Business, bringing the campus-wide total to twenty-three, which works out to a 1,304:1 student-to-counselor ratio, poorer than the average school profiled in this book.

San Diego State University

E-mail: admissions@sdsu.edu | Website: www.sdsu.edu

SDSU offers four large-scale career fairs in the fall semester and another four fairs in the spring semester. One hundred ten employers attend the Fall 2018 Career and Internship Fair, and the Nonprofit and Education Career Fair in the spring draws thirty employers. In addition, the Graduate & Professional School Fair draws representative from ninety+ institutions. A solid 49 percent of Class of 2018 graduates reported completing at least one internship. Workshops are offered on a regular basis on useful topics such as Applying for Federal Jobs, Personal Branding Using Social Media, and Planning for Graduate School. Career counselors specialize in a variety of fields and encourage fifty-minute one-on-one career exploration sessions or fifteen-minute walk-in appointments. The Aztec Mentor Program connects juniors and seniors to alumni in their fields of interest for a minimum of eight hours of mentorship. In sum, programmatic offerings by SDSU's Career Services Office are impressive, but they do not publicize statistics on how many counseling sessions take place or how many on-campus interviews with employers occur each year.

Professional Outcomes

At the time of receiving their degrees, 72 percent of newly-minted 2018 SDSU graduates already had their next phase of life planned. Thirty-four percent of that group had secured full-time employment, 21 percent were engaged in military service/volunteer work/part-time employment, and 17 percent were entering graduate or professional school. The mean reported salary for those offered full-time employment was $53,000. Qualcomm and Apple are the two largest employers of Aztec alumni, and they are followed by LPL Financial, Amazon, Intuit, Google, ServiceNow (cloud computing), Microsoft, Facebook, Salesforce, and Robert Half. All of the most common geographic landing spots for alumni are within California borders; San Diego keeps a large chunk of grads while Los Angeles, San Francisco, and Orange County also have fairly strong representation.

In 2019, there were sixty-four SDSU graduates applying to medical school and, while the university lacks its own affiliated hospital/medical schools, many future physicians do remain in the state of California at universities like UC-San Diego, UC-Davis, UC-Riverside, UCLA, and Western University of Health Sciences; others move out of state to the University of Michigan, Tufts, and the University of South Carolina. Likewise, many law students remain in state at schools such as the University of San Diego School of Law, the Thomas Jefferson School of Law, Loyola Law School, Santa Clara School of Law, and UC-Davis. SDSU offers a pre-law society, mock trial team, and targeted pre-law advising to those considering a legal education.

Admission

Only 34 percent of the 69,043 applicants for a place in the Class of 2022 were accepted into the university; 24 percent of that group went on to enroll at SDSU. Despite the intimidating acceptance rate, there is plenty of room at this school for solid but less-than-perfect applicants as evidenced by the wide range of test scores and GPAs that are accepted. The mid-50 percent standardized test scores for 2018-19 freshmen were 1110-1310 on the SAT and 22-28 on the ACT. Twenty-nine percent of that cohort placed within the top 10 percent of their high school class, 68 percent were in the top quartile, and 93 percent landed in top half. While 54 percent of Class of 2022 members possessed a high school GPA of 3.75 or above, 21 percent earned under a 3.5. A decade ago, almost 30,000 fewer students applied, but the acceptance rate was similar. Yet, SAT scores were substantially lower, and less than half as many students held 3.75+ GPAs. The school's freshman class today is 1,500+ students larger than the freshman group of ten years ago.

The admissions committee needs to work quickly to sift through the deluge of applications it receives each year. As a result, it reviews standardized test scores, GPA, rigor of courses, state residency, and literally nothing else. Soft factors like essays, recommendations, and extracurricular activities play no role in the admissions process at San Diego State. There is no early action or early decision option at SDSU, but the admissions deadline is extremely early—everything must be completed by November 30. In spite of the low acceptance rate, students should be able to accurately gauge their odds given the relatively formulaic evaluation process. Those solidly in the middle of the wide ranges of standardized test scores can feel good about their chances.

Worth Your Money?

The process to qualify for out-of-state students to earn residency status has tightened in recent years, making it almost certain that international and non-California residents will pay roughly $42,000 per year total cost of attendance. In-state COA is estimated at $30,500, with only $7,500 of that figure covering basic tuition. Thus, those living at home or commuting can attend the university at an absurdly low cost. Like the other twenty-two schools in the California State University System, SDSU is affordable and, with its excellent ties to industry, job prospects for most graduates are bright.

FINANCIAL
Institutional Type: Public
In-State Tuition: $5,742
Out-of-State Tuition: $17,622
Room & Board: $17,752
Required Fees: $1,768
Books & Supplies: $1,969

Avg. Need-Based Aid: $10,300
Avg. % of Need Met: 68%

Avg. Merit-Based Aid: $3,500
% Receiving Merit-Based Aid: 25%

Avg. Cumulative Debt: $21,327
% of Students Borrowing: 45%

CAREER
Who Recruits
1. Bainbridge
2. Cox Communications
3. GoSite
4. ASML
5. Marriott International

Notable Internships
1. BAE Systems
2. Cushman & Wakefield
3. U.S. Senate

Top Industries
1. Business
2. Operations
3. Education
4. Sales
5. Engineering

Top Employers
1. Qualcomm
2. Apple
3. EY
4. Amazon
5. Intuit

Where Alumni Work
1. San Diego
2. Los Angeles
3. San Francisco
4. Orange County, CA
5. Germany

Median Earnings
College Scorecard (Early Career): $51,000
EOP (Early Career): $51,000
PayScale (Mid-Career): $102,800

RANKINGS
Forbes: 181
Money: 74
U.S. News: 147 (T), National Universities
Wall Street Journal/THE: 270 (T)
Washington Monthly: 144, National Universities

#CollegesWorthYourMoney

Santa Clara University

Santa Clara, California | Admissions Phone: 408-554-4700

ADMISSION

Admission Rate: 50%
Admission Rate - Men: 47%
Admission Rate - Women: 52%
EA Admission Rate: 63%
ED Admission Rate: 73%
Admission Rate (5-Year Trend): 0%
ED Admission Rate (5-Year Trend): +18%
% of Admits Attending (Yield): 17%
Transfer Admission Rate: 46%

Offered Wait List: 2,620
Accepted Wait List: 1,776
Admitted Wait List: 149

SAT Reading/Writing (Middle 50%): 630-700
SAT Math (Middle 50%): 640-740
ACT Composite (Middle 50%): 28-32
Testing Policy: ACT/SAT Required
SAT Superscore: Yes
ACT Superscore: Yes

% Graduated in Top 10% of HS Class: 49%
% Graduated in Top 25% of HS Class: 82%
% Graduated in Top 50% of HS Class: 97%

ENROLLMENT

Total Undergraduate Enrollment: 5,520
% Part-Time: 1%
% Male: 51%
% Female: 49%
% Out-of-State: 28%
% Fraternity: Not Offered
% Sorority: Not Offered
% On-Campus (Freshman): 96%
% On-Campus (All Undergraduate): 56%

% African-American: 3%
% Asian: 16%
% Hispanic: 18%
% White: 48%
% Other: 7%
% Race or Ethnicity Unknown: 2%
% International: 4%
% Low-Income: 12%

ACADEMICS

Student-to-Faculty Ratio: 10:1
% of Classes Under 20: 46%
% of Classes Under 40: 98%
% Full-Time Faculty: 62%
% Full-Time Faculty w/ Terminal Degree: 94%

Top Programs
Accounting
Bioengineering
Communication
Computer Science and Engineering
Finance
Public Health
Psychology

Retention Rate: 95%
4-Year Graduation Rate: 84%
6-Year Graduation Rate: 91%

Curricular Flexibility: Less Flexible
Academic Rating: ★★★★✦

Inside the Classroom

If you were asked to name a premier university in the heart of California's Silicon Valley, chances are your immediate answer would be Stanford. Yet, those who aren't likely to be among the 4.3 percent of accepted applicants at Stanford might want to turn their attention to the Valley's second most prestigious school, one that has over ten times the acceptance rate. Santa Clara University is a Jesuit school with a growing national reputation; right now, 73 percent of undergraduates still hail from California, and major tech firms love to recruit at this excellent institution located in their own backyard.

Students can pursue fifty degrees offered by three undergraduate colleges: the College of Arts & Sciences, the School of Engineering, and the Leavey School of Business. Santa Clara's core curriculum is designed to provide "a humanistic education that leads toward an informed, ethical engagement with the world." To accomplish that students must take (1) foundations courses in critical thinking and critical writing, cultures and ideas, a second language, mathematics, and religion, theology, and culture; (2) explorations courses in ethics, civic engagement, diversity, additional religion/theology courses, and all of the traditional prerequisites in the natural sciences, social sciences, and the arts; and (3) integrations courses in advanced writing, experiential learning for social justice, and a pathways class that requires students to make connections across disciplines. It's a tall order, involves a certain amount of religious study, and doesn't leave a ton of room for electives.

Santa Clara caters to 5,500 undergraduate students as well as another 3,100 graduate students but, thanks to a 10:1 student-to-faculty ratio, it keeps classes reasonably sized. While you won't find many single-digit enrollment seminars, 46 percent of course sections do contain fewer than twenty students. Undergraduate research opportunities are built into many academic programs, particularly in the sciences, and students can partner with willing professors for credited research study. In addition, study abroad opportunities are available on all six continents fit for human habitation, and more than 500 students take advantage each year.

The most commonly conferred degrees are in business (25 percent), engineering (17 percent) and the social sciences (14 percent). The Leavey School of Business offers highly ranked management information systems, accounting, and entrepreneurship degree programs. The engineering program is respected by employers, and computer science students fare extraordinarily well in the Silicon Valley job market, which happens to be one of the most competitive in the world. Graduates of SCU do not seek prestigious fellowships in droves, but many of those who do are successful. In 2018, seven grads/alumni procured Fulbright Scholarships, and one took home a Udall Scholarship; an alum even won a Rhodes Scholarship in 2017.

Outside the Classroom

The 106-acre campus houses only 56 percent of the undergraduate student body; however, 96 percent of first-years do reside in university-owned dorms. There are ten fraternities and six sororities at Santa Clara, and although none of them are affiliated with the university (they were dropped in 2001), Greek life still plays a significant social role. For a school of its size, athletics are surprisingly serious at SCU as the Broncos compete at the NCAA Division I level and field nineteen intercollegiate teams. Intramural sports draw an astonishing 3,800 participants every year on 500 teams in sports ranging from soccer to ping-pong. Almost every student is involved in at least one (if not two or three) of the 125 organizations presently operating. The Ruff Riders, a booster organization, is one of the largest groups of its kind with over 1,000 members. Into the Wild is another popular club that plans outdoor excursions to locations such as Big Sur, the beaches of Santa Cruz, and Lake Tahoe. World-class recreational facilities exist on campus for fitness enthusiasts such as the 45,000-square-foot Malley Fitness Center and the Sullivan Aquatic Center. The University's Silicon Valley location means that plenty of high-end cultural, dining, and entertainment options are at your fingertips, and San Francisco is only an hour away by car.

Career Services

Santa Clara's Career Center has seven full-time professional staff members working as career development specialists, employer relations specialists, and coordinators of experiential learning. The 786:1 student-to-advisor ratio is below average when compared with the other institutions featured in this guide. However, the center has many strengths, particularly its deep connections to major Silicon Valley companies. Each year, the Fall Career Fair draws many top employers (including tech companies) as well as over 1,000 undergraduates. Another STEM-specific fair in October brings in another 650 students in search of jobs. Across the school's six annual career fairs, 470 employers manned booths and spoke with SCU students.

Santa Clara University

E-mail: admission@scu.edu | Website: www.scu.edu

More than 6,000 employers recruit Santa Clara undergraduates through a mix of Career Center programs and the online job board available through the Handshake platform, and 65 percent of students utilize their account. Over 900 on-campus interviews take place each academic year. Recruiting companies include Disney, Tesla, Apple, Oracle, Cisco, Kaiser Permanente, and NBC Universal. Almost four-fifths of those completing an SCU degree completed at least one internship position during their time at the university. This school boasts an alumni network 100,000 strong, and many are willing to assist current students with finding their first job. Thanks to the strength of its employer recruiting efforts and internship program, SCU's Career Center gets high marks from our staff.

Professional Outcomes

Within six months of receiving their degrees, 83 percent of Santa Clara graduates have landed jobs, started graduate school, or committed to a full-time service program. Of those employed, the five most commonly entered industries are business development, engineering, education, entrepreneurship, and sales. The companies presently employing the greatest number of Bronco alumni are all tech giants including Cisco, Apple, Google, Oracle, Facebook, and Adobe. The median starting salary for all grads is $53,000 with engineering ($70k) and business majors ($60k) enjoying the highest compensation, and math/natural sciences grads on the low end ($38k). Roughly two-thirds of alumni remain in the Bay Area. Other West Coast destinations such as Los Angeles, Seattle, Portland, Sacramento, and San Diego also attract a fairly large number of grads.

Many graduates who continue their education at the master's or doctoral level do so at one of Santa Clara's own excellent grad programs; the same goes for law school. Over the last fifteen years, 90 percent of SCU medical school applicants with a minimum of MCAT score of 505 and a GPA of 3.5 or higher have been accepted by at least one institution. However, many fail to meet those criteria as only 40 percent of overall applicants in that period have been accepted, slightly lower than the national average. The three most frequently attended medical schools are fellow Jesuit institutions Creighton, Georgetown, and Loyola (Chicago). A look at where Class of 2017 and 2018 grads were pursuing additional education includes a wide range of schools that includes UCLA, Berkeley, USC, the University of Washington, and Duke University.

Admission

Growing in popularity, Santa Clara crossed the 16,000 application mark with the Class of 2022; that represented a 47 percent increase since 2009. A seemingly soft 49 percent of applicants were granted admission, but a glance at the profile of the average accepted applicant is more informative as to the school's level of selectivity. Successful applicants averaged an unweighted GPA of 3.8 and scores of 1407 on the SAT and 31 on the ACT. Notably, only 17 percent of admitted students went on to enroll in the freshman Class of 2018-19. Of those who actually enrolled in the university, the middle-50 percent SAT range was still a solid 1270-1440. Just a shade under 50 percent placed in the top decile of their high school class, and 82 percent finished in the top quartile.

The admissions committee ranks three categories as most important: rigor of secondary school record, GPA, and essays. The list of factors ranked as "important" is far longer and includes class rank, recommendations, standardized test scores, volunteer work, racial/ethnic status, first generation status, legacy status, and extracurricular activities. While the process can be viewed as holistic, the university does not offer an evaluative interview. Due to the aforementioned low yield rate of only 17 percent, Santa Clara is always happy to have strong applicants who are willing to commit to the school. As a result, a whopping 73 percent of early decision applicants gain admission. Santa Clara University is a school that is attracting more applicants every year as its national reputation climbs to new heights. A deceptively high acceptance rate does not do full justice to the caliber of undergraduate it currently attracts. Borderline candidates who have a strong desire to attend should definitely consider applying early decision.

Worth Your Money?

At almost $74,000 in total annual cost of attendance, Santa Clara is an expensive proposition any way you slice it. The university does dangle an average merit aid award of almost $16k to two-fifths of students to bring the price down a bit, but only 37 percent of all undergrads qualify for need-based grants that average close to $33,000. A Santa Clara degree won't come cheap, but that's okay for business and engineering students who will be heading to high-paying careers in Silicon Valley. Those intending to pursue majors in less immediately lucrative disciplines need to calculate whether the finances make sense for them to attend this school.

FINANCIAL
Institutional Type: Private
In-State Tuition: $52,998
Out-of-State Tuition: $52,998
Room & Board: $15,507
Required Fees: $636
Books & Supplies: $1,971

Avg. Need-Based Aid: $33,180
Avg. % of Need Met: 79%

Avg. Merit-Based Aid: $15,875
% Receiving Merit-Based Aid: 41%

Avg. Cumulative Debt: $25,640
% of Students Borrowing: 36%

CAREER
Who Recruits
1. Stryker Corporation
2. Gap Inc.
3. Tesla
4. Teach for America
5. Kiva

Notable Internships
1. McAfee
2. Yelp
3. Vera Wang

Top Industries
1. Business
2. Engineering
3. Education
4. Operations
5. Sales

Top Employers
1. Cisco
2. Apple
3. Google
4. Oracle
5. Facebook

Where Alumni Work
1. San Francisco
2. Los Angeles
3. Seattle
4. Sacramento
5. Portland, OR

Median Earnings
College Scorecard (Early Career): $72,600
EOP (Early Career): $72,500
PayScale (Mid-Career): $134,700

RANKINGS
Forbes: 51
Money: 144
U.S. News: 54 (T), National Universities
Wall Street Journal/THE: 87 (T)
Washington Monthly: 137, National Universities

#CollegesWorthYourMoney

Scripps College

Claremont, California | Admissions Phone: 909-621-8149

ADMISSION
Admission Rate: 24%
Admission Rate - Men: Not Offered
Admission Rate - Women: 24%
EA Admission Rate: Not Offered
ED Admission Rate: 32%
Admission Rate (5-Year Trend): -11%
ED Admission Rate (5-Year Trend): -20%
% of Admits Attending (Yield): 33%
Transfer Admission Rate: 16%

Offered Wait List: 780
Accepted Wait List: 388
Admitted Wait List: 4

SAT Reading/Writing (Middle 50%): 660-740
SAT Math (Middle 50%): 640-740
ACT Composite (Middle 50%): 30-33
Testing Policy: ACT/SAT Required
SAT Superscore: Yes
ACT Superscore: Yes

% Graduated in Top 10% of HS Class: 69%
% Graduated in Top 25% of HS Class: 98%
% Graduated in Top 50% of HS Class: 100%

ENROLLMENT
Total Undergraduate Enrollment: 1,048
% Part-Time: 1%
% Male: 0%
% Female: 100%
% Out-of-State: 55%
% Fraternity: Not Offered
% Sorority: Not Offered
% On-Campus (Freshman): 100%
% On-Campus (All Undergraduate): 94%

% African-American: 4%
% Asian: 17%
% Hispanic: 14%
% White: 53%
% Other: 5%
% Race or Ethnicity Unknown: 3%
% International: 5%
% Low-Income: 12%

ACADEMICS
Student-to-Faculty Ratio: 10:1
% of Classes Under 20: 77%
% of Classes Under 40: 100%
% Full-Time Faculty: 77%
% Full-Time Faculty w/ Terminal Degree: 99%

Top Programs
Area Studies
Art
Biology
English
Media Studies
Politics
Psychology

Retention Rate: 92%
4-Year Graduation Rate: 81%
6-Year Graduation Rate: 88%

Curricular Flexibility: Somewhat Flexible
Academic Rating: ★★★★↙

Inside the Classroom

While the East Coast is swarming with high-end women's colleges such as Wellesley, Smith, Bryn Mawr, Barnard, and Mt. Holyoke, there is only one such jewel resting closer to the Pacific Ocean. Scripps College, a member of the five-school Claremont Consortium, is the West Coast's lone elite all-female institution, making it a highly desirable destination for young women seeking a classic liberal arts education in a nurturing and supportive academic environment without the lonely, harsh winters of the Northeast.

There are sixty-five majors available to Scripps undergrads, including some that are accessible through membership in the Consortium. Curricular requirements at Scripps are extensive, requiring a three-semester dive into interdisciplinary humanities coursework that tackles the essential question of "What makes a community?" through a combination of lecture, seminar-style discussions, and a self-designed project. All undergraduates must demonstrate competency in mathematics, foreign language, and writing. Along the way, one course must be taken in each of the four divisions: fine arts, natural sciences, letters, and social sciences. Within one's major, a minimum of eight courses must be tackled, culminating in the completion of a senior thesis, which 100 percent of graduates must complete.

A 10:1 student to faculty ratio at a school with zero grad students breeds an intimate learning atmosphere where professors are genuinely dedicated to undergraduate learning. A lack of competitiveness should not be mistaken for a lack of rigor. Scripps is loaded with driven students, 28 percent of whom elect to double major. As part of the required senior thesis, many undergraduates also have the chance to assist professors with academic/scientific research. Due to the absence of graduate students who would gobble up such positions, research opportunities are readily available for credit during the academic year as well on a full-time basis during the summer; the Scripps Undergraduate Research Fellowship is one such program. Study abroad programs in forty countries are taken advantage of by nearly two-thirds of the student body, giving Scripps one of the highest participation rates of any college in the United States.

The top five majors are (in order) biology/life sciences; social sciences; psychology; area, ethnic, and gender studies; and visual/performing arts. Each possesses a very strong reputation. Regardless of your major, however, graduate/professional schools know that earning a degree from Scripps is no small achievement. Prestigious scholarship committees also look kindly upon the school as Scripps is regularly a top twenty-five producer of Fulbright winners, taking home an incredible (considering the size of the graduating class) nine awards in 2018. Two additional 2018 grads took home Watson Fellowships, and one was awarded a Davis Projects for Peace Fellowship.

Outside the Classroom

At Scripps, 96 percent of students live on the school's modestly sized 30-acre campus in one of eleven immaculately maintained dorms or in thematic housing options catering to those with goals and interests in common such as The Stem, Pre-Health Living Learning Community, and the Substance Free Community. There are no sororities at Scripps. Sports exist but are a combined effort with Harvey Mudd, and Claremont McKenna that, collectively, field eleven NCAA Division III teams. Fitness and recreational facilities are shared with Pitzer, Pomona, Harvey Mudd, and CMC. That means students have access to four swimming pools, four fitness centers, and a dozen playing fields. There are roughly thirty Scripps-only student-run organizations, but there are also more than 250 clubs that can be accessed by students of any of the five schools. One of the more notable social hubs is the Motley Coffeehouse, founded in 1974 and run entirely by Scripps students. In fact, the feminist, environmental, and social justice vibe makes its coffeehouse a perfect embodiment of the college's values and ethos. The college also boasts its own art museum, the Williamson Gallery, which contains works by many notable American artists. Of course, cultural options are hardly confined to the campus limits with Los Angeles only a forty-five minute car ride away.

Career Services

The Career Planning & Resources Office (CP&R) has four full-time professional staff members working as career counselors. Scripps' 267:1 student-to-advisor ratio is better than the average college featured in our guidebook. It may be a small office, but you won't find a more proactive group of counselors at any college in the country as the CP&R meets with 90 percent of freshmen within the students' first three weeks on campus. Larger events are typically joint affairs with the other esteemed members of the Claremont Consortium.

E-mail: admission@scrippscollege.edu | Website: www.scrippscollege.edu

Scripps takes pride in its facilitation of student internships and has the stats to prove it; 86 percent of graduates held at least one internship, and close to one-quarter completed three or more. Internship locations of note include 20th Century Fox, the California Department of Justice, and the Smithsonian. Career Treks whisk Scripps students off to metropolitan areas around the country to meet with alumni who are working in the same field of interest. Former students are always willing to lend a hand to current ones and can connect with soon-to-be grads through the Alumni Book, a compilation of student resumes. A week-long Emerging Professionals Program featuring alumni, recruiters, and CP&R counselors can be accessed for free. The office also offers a Financial Literacy Program to teach undergraduates about everything from budgeting to investing to filing taxes.

Professional Outcomes

Women land jobs at some of the world's leading companies after receiving their diplomas. The top employers of Scripps alumni include Google, Kaiser Permanente, and Amazon. Many go on to work for universities, particularly after earning additional degrees (more on this in a moment). Schools employing significant numbers of Scripps alumni include Pomona, Scripps, Stanford, UCLA, and UC-San Diego. Recent graduates also have landed positions at BlackRock, CBS, Goldman Sachs, Facebook, and Pfizer. Median salaries by midcareer are quite a bit lower than fellow Consortium member schools Pomona and Claremont McKenna, but they are comparable to other elite women's colleges such as Bryn Mawr. Most Scripps alumni remain on the West Coast with the largest percentage in Los Angeles followed by San Francisco, Seattle, Portland, San Diego, and Orange County. The most popular East Coast destinations are New York City, DC, and Boston.

An advanced degree is in the cards for most Scripps grads, and it isn't usually too far in the future—two-thirds complete a graduate/professional program within five years of receiving their bachelor's degrees. Recent grads have pursued further study at institutions such as Caltech, Harvard, MIT, Vanderbilt, Oxford, Brown, Northwestern, and Tufts. Scripps knows what it's doing when it comes to premeds, thanks to its Post-Baccalaureate Premedical Program that boasts a 98 percent+ acceptance rate; traditional undergrads also fare well above the national average. Those eyeing law school also find favorable results; recent grads have been accepted at top-tier law schools such as Emory, Georgetown, the University of Chicago, Berkeley, and the University of Michigan.

Admission

Thirty-one percent of the 3,160 women who applied for a place in the Class of 2022 were accepted. One-third of the overall applicant pool went on to enroll. Freshmen in 2018-19 possessed a middle-50 percent score of 1300-1480 on the SAT and 30-33 on the ACT. An impressive 69 percent came from the top decile of their high school class; 98 percent placed in the top quarter. Over 80 percent sported a GPA of 3.75 or greater; 92 percent earned above a 3.5.

The admissions committee seeks "to build a community of curious and engaged students who are eager to contribute their diverse interests, backgrounds, and experiences to our academic and residential community." As such, they weight nine factors as being "very important" to admissions decisions: rigor of coursework, GPA, test scores, class rank recommendations, essays, extracurricular activities, talent/ability, and character/personal qualities. Applying early decision at Scripps does yield an edge; 32 percent of ED applicants were accepted into the Class of 2022 versus 24 percent of regular round applicants. Those accepted in the early round comprised 36 percent of the incoming freshman class. Scripps has become more competitive as the 2000s have marched on. A decade ago, the acceptance rate was a healthier 43 percent, and average SAT/ACT scores were a bit lower. The West Coast's highest-ranked women's college is looking for students with not only strong academic credentials but a solid extracurricular resume.

Worth Your Money?

At almost $74,000 the sticker price cost of attendance for Scripps College is undoubtedly on the high side. However, the 38 percent of undergraduates who are determined eligible for need-based aid all see 100 percent of their need met; the average grant is for $40k. Additionally, 15 percent of students do receive a merit aid package that averages $22k. Of course, you would never want to go into six figures worth of debt in order to obtain an undergraduate degree, but if attending Scripps is financially feasible for your family, the quality of the educational experience and networks/resources offered by the Consortium make this school worth some level of sacrifice.

FINANCIAL
Institutional Type: Private
In-State Tuition: $54,806
Out-of-State Tuition: $54,806
Room & Board: $16,932
Required Fees: $218
Books & Supplies: $800

Avg. Need-Based Aid: $39,735
Avg. % of Need Met: 100%

Avg. Merit-Based Aid: $22,131
% Receiving Merit-Based Aid: 15%

Avg. Cumulative Debt: $17,756
% of Students Borrowing: 34%

CAREER
Who Recruits
1. DaVita
2. Nielsen
3. Pfizer
4. Nordstrom
5. Brancart & Brancart

Notable Internships
1. ALCU
2. Louis Vuitton
3. KPMG

Top Industries
1. Education
2. Business
3. Social Services
4. Media
5. Research

Top Employers
1. Google
2. Kaiser Permanente
3. Amazon
4. Microsoft
5. Seattle Children's

Where Alumni Work
1. Los Angeles
2. San Francisco
3. Seattle
4. New York City
5. Portland, OR

Median Earnings
College Scorecard (Early Career): $54,100
EOP (Early Career): $46,400
PayScale (Mid-Career): $98,600

RANKINGS
Forbes: 60
Money: 308
U.S. News: 33, Liberal Arts Colleges
Wall Street Journal/THE: 65
Washington Monthly: 97, Liberal Arts Colleges

#CollegesWorthYourMoney

Sewanee – The University of the South

Sewanee, Tennessee | Admissions Phone: 931-598-1238

ADMISSION
Admission Rate: 65%
Admission Rate - Men: 65%
Admission Rate - Women: 66%
EA Admission Rate: 83%
ED Admission Rate: 86%
Admission Rate (5-Year Trend): +5%
ED Admission Rate (5-Year Trend): +12%
% of Admits Attending (Yield): 21%
Transfer Admission Rate: 70%

Offered Wait List: 513
Accepted Wait List: 101
Admitted Wait List: 9

SAT Reading/Writing (Middle 50%): 610-700
SAT Math (Middle 50%): 590-690
ACT Composite (Middle 50%): 25-31
Testing Policy: Test Optional
SAT Superscore: Yes
ACT Superscore: Yes

% Graduated in Top 10% of HS Class: 30%
% Graduated in Top 25% of HS Class: 61%
% Graduated in Top 50% of HS Class: 92%

ENROLLMENT
Total Undergraduate Enrollment: 1,698
% Part-Time: 1%
% Male: 49%
% Female: 51%
% Out-of-State: 78%
% Fraternity: 56%
% Sorority: 64%
% On-Campus (Freshman): 100%
% On-Campus (All Undergraduate): 99%

% African-American: 5%
% Asian: 2%
% Hispanic: 5%
% White: 81%
% Other: 3%
% Race or Ethnicity Unknown: 0%
% International: 4%
% Low-Income: 20%

ACADEMICS
Student-to-Faculty Ratio: 10:1
% of Classes Under 20: 60%
% of Classes Under 40: 99%
% Full-Time Faculty: 71%
% Full-Time Faculty w/ Terminal Degree: 95%

Top Programs
Biology
Economics
English
Environment & Sustainability
History
International & Global Studies
Politics

Retention Rate: 89%
4-Year Graduation Rate: 78%
6-Year Graduation Rate: 84%

Curricular Flexibility: Somewhat Flexible
Academic Rating: ★★★✦

Inside the Classroom

People flying over the historic campus of the University of the South, sometimes referred to as "Sewanee" might, in a moment of panic, fret that they had accidentally hopped aboard an international flight and were passing directly over Oxford or Cambridge. This breathtaking campus that includes 13,000 acres of natural beauty known affectionately as "The Domain" is situated on Tennessee's Cumberland Plateau. The pretty packaging is not misleading; the University of the South delivers a powerful academic punch, and it isn't quite as picky as many other top schools as to who gets to step into the ring. While designated a "university," Sewanee is really more of a liberal arts college of approximately 1,700 undergrads and fewer than one hundred graduate students.

Offering thirty-six majors and forty-three minors, undergrads are exposed to a wide scope of liberal arts study, no matter their area of concentration. All students must complete a designated writing-intensive course by the end of their sophomore year as well as coursework fulfilling six "learning objectives." Literary analysis, understanding the arts, and seeking meaning require one course each while multiple classes are required in exploring past and present, the scientific and quantitative view, and language and global studies. Two physical education and wellness classes also must be tackled prior to graduation.

A 10:1 student-to-faculty ratio and a limited number of grad students means that undergraduate teaching remains the primary focus at Sewanee. The average class size is seventeen students, and 99+ percent of course sections have an enrollment under thirty. Opportunities to conduct research with faculty members are not only plentiful, they are often funded by the university. Recent students have collaborated on fascinating research projects on topics such as Adolescent Substance use Perception in Southern Appalachia; Synthesis of New, More Effective Anti-Cancer Metallopharmaceuticals; and Corporate Political Contributions and Stock Returns. Study abroad options that are a summer, a semester, or a full year in length are embarked upon by roughly half of all Sewanee students. European Studies and British Studies are two of the most popular global programs offered by the college.

The degrees most commonly conferred are in biology, economics, English, history, international and global studies, and environment studies. All are strong, but Sewanee's English Department has a leading national reputation. Thanks to the Tennessee Williams Writers-in-Residence program, accomplished authors from around the globe come to teach at Sewanee, and English majors routinely continue their studies at the likes of Princeton, Yale, Duke, and the University of Chicago. The school has also historically had success in helping its students procure the most distinguished graduate fellowships. Sewanee was named a top producer of Fulbright Scholars with four winners in 2018 alone, and forty-seven students have claimed Watson Scholarships since they were first made available in 1968. Incredibly, the school claims twenty-six Rhodes Scholars in its history, more than Amherst, the University of Pennsylvania, or Georgetown.

Outside the Classroom

Just about the entire student body, 98.5 percent to be precise, live in the dorms or in other on-campus housing. Greek life is extremely popular at Sewanee as the eleven fraternities and ten sororities attract an overwhelming 80 percent of undergraduates in rushing. When it's all said and done, 64 percent of women and 56 percent of men end up Greek affiliated. Involvement in some type of sport is also common. Eleven men's and thirteen women's Division III athletic teams are joined by 30 percent of the student population. Another eight club teams and plenty of intramural sessions draw many more. More than ninety student-run organizations are active with the most popular being the Student Government Association, the Order of Gown (focusing on campus spirit and traditions), and the Student Activity Board. If climbing, caving, hiking, biking, or canoeing is more your style, then the Sewanee Outing Program (SOP) is a must-join organization. In addition to taking outdoorsy road trips, the SOP also takes full advantage of the pristine beauty of the aforementioned Domain. With Chattanooga only an hour away and Nashville an hour-and-a-half car ride from campus, Sewanee students can access big-city fun on the weekends.

Career Services

The Career and Leadership Development Office (CLD) employs five full-time staff members, four of whom are titled director or assistant director, yet all work directly in counseling undergraduates. That equates to a student-to-staff ratio of 351:1, in the average range compared to the other institutions included in this book. The CLD does manage to reach 97 percent of students by the time they graduate, and a hard-to-beat 99 percent report being satisfied by the guidance they receive. Events such as the annual Graduate and Professional School Fair draws reps from more than thirty-five programs including Tulane, Vanderbilt, and UGA's law schools, Wake Forest's MBA program, and Emory's School of Theology. An annual Beyond the Gates event sees close to fifty alumni from all walks of professional life spend a weekend mentoring current juniors and seniors as they ready themselves for the job search.

Via the Sewanee Pledge, the university guarantees funding for one unpaid internship or research experience for every single student. Each year, more than 200 such stipends are granted for unpaid internships alone. Over 150 Sewanee-exclusive internship opportunities are posted each year, creating a favorable environment for students to gain the inside track on desirable opportunities. Recent students have interned at *Style Magazine*, Accenture, the World Wildlife Fund, and US Forest Service. The CLD at the University of the South, thanks to a high level of connection and personalized counseling, succeeds in assisting the bulk of graduates reach their next destination.

Professional Outcomes

Within six months of their commencement ceremony, 98 percent of Sewanee grads have found some form of employment or have begun their graduate studies. Three-quarters have obtained full-time employment with the most popular sectors being business/finance/consulting (37 percent), arts/entertainment/sports/media/publishing (10 percent), government/politics/policy/law (10 percent), health care/medicine/research (10 percent), education (9 percent), and environment/sustainability/natural resources (7 percent). Organizations employing recent graduates include Booz Allen Hamilton, Sony Pictures, Warby Parker, BlackRock, and Massachusetts General Hospital. The largest number of total alumni can be found at Wells Fargo, Deloitte, Regions Bank, and Vanderbilt University Medical Center. Median income by midcareer is an unspectacular $47k, comparable to the figures at Colorado College, Smith, or Grinnell. Many alumni remain in the South after graduation as Nashville, Atlanta, and Chattanooga are the most frequent destinations. However, DC and New York City also contain large pockets of grads.

The majority of those in the Class of 2018 who pursued advanced degrees entered master's programs (36) followed by law school (10), medical school (8), and PhD programs (6). Elite graduate school acceptances included Johns Hopkins, Georgetown, Vanderbilt, Washington University in St. Louis, and the University of Michigan. Law schools attended included the University of North Carolina, University of Arkansas, NYU, and Samford University. Medical school acceptances in the last several years included East Carolina University and the University of Texas.

Admission

Sewanee is a rare top school that, even in 2020, still lacks a menacing acceptance rate—its 53.9 percent is about as friendly as you will find among top colleges. The entering Class of 2022 held strong academic credentials, sporting middle-50 percent standardized test scores of 1250-1390 on the SAT and 27-32 on the ACT, which is submitted by the majority of applicants, and an average high school GPA of 3.74. You don't need to be at the top of your high school class to gain admittance as only 30 percent placed in the top decile and 61 percent in the top quartile. The school's selectivity level is similar to that of a full decade ago.

A test-optional school, the University of the South places a strong emphasis on the rigor of one's secondary school record, GPA, and recommendations. Second billing is granted to the application essay, extracurricular activities, character/personal qualities, volunteer work, and work experience. A relatively low yield rate of 21 percent means that almost four-fifths of those accepted enroll elsewhere. While the university does not rank demonstrated interest as an important factor in admissions decisions, the committee certainly appreciates those who apply via binding early decision. In fact, 86 percent of those applying ED are accepted. A fine and distinctive education can be yours at this exceptionally beautiful Tennessee campus without the typical crucible of admissions-related stress found at many of the schools featured in this book. Students with strong but not outstanding resumes are welcomed through this holistic-minded and test-optional admissions process.

Worth Your Money?

The overall cost of attendance of $62,290 is high, but it is not an exorbitant sticker price in the world of small liberal arts schools. This is particularly true since three-fifths of undergrads qualify for an average merit aid award of almost $20k. Forty-seven percent of undergrads qualify for an average need-based award of $29,262, but only 32 percent of those who qualify for aid see 100 percent of their need met. If your family has limited funds (like most), you'll want to see how much merit and need-based aid you are awarded before making a decision on whether Sewanee is the right choice for your wallet.

FINANCIAL
Institutional Type: Private
In-State Tuition: $46,200
Out-of-State Tuition: $46,200
Room & Board: $13,268
Required Fees: $272
Books & Supplies: $1,200

Avg. Need-Based Aid: $29,262
Avg. % of Need Met: 83%

Avg. Merit-Based Aid: $19,708
% Receiving Merit-Based Aid: 60%

Avg. Cumulative Debt: $28,976
% of Students Borrowing: 43%

CAREER
Who Recruits
1. Springbot
2. JumpCrew
3. Showtime Networks
4. Accenture
5. Harris Williams & Co.

Notable Internships
1. UBS
2. Wells Fargo
3. U.S. Senate

Top Industries
1. Business
2. Education
3. Social Services
4. Operations
5. Sales

Top Employers
1. Wells Fargo
2. Regions Bank
3. CBRE
4. Deloitte
5. Capital One

Where Alumni Work
1. Nashville
2. Atlanta
3. Chattanooga, TN
4. Washington, DC
5. New York City

Median Earnings
College Scorecard (Early Career): $45,500
EOP (Early Career): $46,600
PayScale (Mid-Career): $97,800

RANKINGS
Forbes: 154
Money: 388
U.S. News: 43, Liberal Arts Colleges
Wall Street Journal/THE: 141 (T)
Washington Monthly: 99, Liberal Arts Colleges

#CollegesWorthYourMoney

Skidmore College

Saratoga Springs, New York | Admissions Phone: 518-580-5570

Inside the Classroom

Founded as a women's college at the turn of the twentieth century, Skidmore still serves more women than men today, but going co-ed isn't the most notable shift that has occurred at this private liberal arts college in Upstate New York. The school's 2,500 undergrads, affectionately known as "Skiddies," have become an increasingly higher-achieving lot as the school has transformed from selective to highly selective over the past decade. What has remained is its reputation as a free-spirited student body and extremely accessible and student-friendly faculty that have long defined Skidmore.

An undergraduate-only institution, there are forty-three majors to choose from with the most popular being business, English, psychology, political science, economics, studio art, theater, biology, and environmental studies. All students begin by completing a first-year experience that is highlighted by participation in the Scribner Seminars where students begin to grasp the level of rigor that will be expected as they launch their collegiate studies. Foundations courses include Applied Quantitative Reasoning, Global Cultural Perspectives, Language Study, and Writing. Inquiry courses include Artistic Inquiry through Practice, Humanistic Inquiry and Practice, and Scientific Inquiry through Practice. It's hard to earn a diploma without completing some type of a culminating project; 75 percent complete a senior capstone, 53 percent engage in independent study, and 32 percent produce a senior thesis or advanced research project.

With no graduate students around to suck up professorial attention, undergrads reap the full benefits of the school's student-faculty ratio of 8-to-1. Skidmore's average class size is only sixteen students, and 94 percent of sections have fewer than thirty students. Over one-quarter of sections enroll only single digits. Each year roughly 500 students, 20 percent of the student body, engage in research with a faculty mentor, including eighty students who participate in the Summer Student-Faculty Research Program. Internships and service-learning courses are a normal part of the Skidmore experience. Three-fifths of students study abroad at one of 120 programs in forty-five countries, a rate of participation that places it at the very top in the nation.

Known for its superior undergraduate teaching, a Skidmore degree will carry enough prestige to open doors to top employers and graduate schools, particularly in the aforementioned areas that are among the most popular majors. The school produces a surprisingly modest number of competitive postgraduate scholars and fellows. Many years it produces a finalist for a National Science Foundation, Goldwater, or Mitchell Scholarship, but it does not consistently take home the big prizes.

Outside the Classroom

Approximately 90 percent of students reside in one of Skidmore's eight residence halls, which are split evenly on a North and a South campus spread over 1,000 enchanting acres. The only Greek life at Skidmore can be found in courses in the classics; there are no frats or sororities in the "Skidmore bubble." An almost 60/40 split along gender lines in favor of women certainly has an impact on social life. There are 120 active student-run clubs and nineteen Division III varsity sports teams (10 women's and 9 men's) nicknamed the Thoroughbreds. There are plenty of club sports and intramural leagues for less serious competitors. Amenities are first-class, from the apartment-style dorms to the award-winning dining services to the 150-acre North Woods oasis that can be used for anything from meditation to skiing. Saratoga Springs is a small city of 30,000, but its funky downtown is only a ten-minute walk from campus. Skidmore is located thirty minutes from Albany and three full hours from popular road trip destinations like New York City, Boston, and Montreal. Those seeking more nature-oriented recreation can easily travel to the Berkshires, Adirondacks, or Green Mountains.

Career Services

The Career Development Center (CDC) at Skidmore College is staffed by eight professionals with counseling expertise in a variety of fields. That works out to a 333:1 student-to-advisor ratio that is solidly in the average range compared to other institutions in this guidebook. The CDC hosts an annual networking event called Career Jam that was attended by 219 students and seventy-four alumni, parents, and employers in 2017. The annual Graduate and Professional School Expo attracts representatives from roughly forty-five universities to Skidmore. Students also can travel off campus to corporate destinations along the East Coast as part of the Road Trips to the Real World program.

In the 2017-18 academic year the CDC conducted 2,081 one-on-one counseling sessions, brought seventy-four employers to Saratoga Springs for recruiting purposes, and facilitated 323 on-campus interviews. An impressive 274 employers attend the college's job fairs. Nearly 85 percent of students participate in an internship during their time at Skidmore, and many are funded by the school. Students nab intriguing internships at places such as Tesla, *The Daily Show with Trevor Noah*, the NBA, *Esquire Magazine*, and Memorial Sloan Kettering Cancer Center. The career services staff encourages individual meetings as early as freshman year in its effort to support "all students and alumni through the creative process of integrating their liberal arts education and experiences into a satisfying career." Skidmore's CDC boasts strong internship numbers; however, with 10 percent of grads still seeking employment six months after graduation, there is room for improvement.

Skidmore College

E-mail: admissions@skidmore.edu | Website: www.skidmore.edu

Professional Outcomes

Three-quarters of 2018 Skidmore grads were employed within six months of completing their degrees, 14 percent were enrolled in graduate school, and 10 percent were still seeking employment. The most frequently entered industries were arts, audio/visual technology, and communications (15 percent); education and training (14 percent); STEM (13 percent); business (11 percent); and marketing, sales, and service (10 percent). The median starting salary range for Class of 2018 grads was $40,000-$49,999. Intriguing employers included the Metropolitan Opera, Penguin Random House, NBC Universal, Estee Lauder, and Vineyard Vines. Fairly large numbers of Skiddies can be found at major corporations including Google, Morgan Stanley, EY, Amazon, JPMorgan Chase, Fidelity Investments, and IBM. The greatest concentration of alumni can be found in Greater New York City with Boston, Albany, San Francisco, and Washington, DC, the next most popular landing spots.

Graduate acceptances procured by the Class of 2018 included Ivies like Harvard, Cornell, Dartmouth, and Columbia as well as other elite institutions like Johns Hopkins, Tufts, and NYU. Skidmore students are accepted to medical school at a rate "far above the national average." Many recent med school-bound grads have attended NY-based schools like SUNY Upstate, SUNY Stony Brook, or the University of Buffalo. Class of 2017 and 2018 members matriculated into law schools at Duke, Penn State, and the University of Miami.

Admission

For 2018-19 freshman hopefuls, only 27 percent were accepted (24.5 percent were accepted the previous year), and the average SAT was 1250-1380; a dozen years ago, 39 percent of applicants got in. It is important to note that Skidmore adopted a test-optional policy in 2016 that has led to a spike in applications. Among enrolled freshman, 48 percent submitted SAT scores, and another 27 percent submitted ACT scores, so the majority of accepted applicants are not going the test-optional route. Many students, but far from all, rank near the top of their graduating high school classes; 38 percent of members of the Class of 2022 placed in the top decile, and 78 percent earned a spot in the top quartile.

In the eyes of the admissions office the rigor of secondary coursework is the only factor that rises to "most important" status. From there, class rank, GPA, essays, recommendations, extracurricular activities, talent/ability, character/personal qualities, work experience, volunteer work, and demonstrated interest are on equal footing as "important" factors. As a test-optional school, SATs and ACTs are relegated to "considered" status. In the most recent admissions cycle the acceptance rate for early decision applicants was 51 percent compared to 25 percent in the regular cycle, and ED students made up 53 percent of the freshman class. A more competitive school than in the recent past, those set on Skidmore definitely should consider applying ED and should at least go out of their way to demonstrate serious interest in the college. While test-optional, strong standardized test scores can still help you win over the admissions committee.

Worth Your Money?

Need-based grants averaging $46,400 are awarded to 42 percent of undergraduates at Skidmore. That helps defray the $71,480 in total costs each year for those with genuine financial need. Unfortunately, merit aid is only made available to 2.8 percent of the undergraduate population; thus, you are unlikely to get a significant tuition discount unless you qualify for a grant. If your parents can afford Skidmore, it is a wonderful place to spend four years learning and growing. On the other hand, we would not recommend taking on large amounts of debt in order to study theater, English, studio art, or any other popular but typically low-paying major without a clear postgraduate career and financial plan.

FINANCIAL
Institutional Type: Private
In-State Tuition: $53,258
Out-of-State Tuition: $53,258
Room & Board: $14,494
Required Fees: $1,162
Books & Supplies: $1,300

Avg. Need-Based Aid: $46,400
Avg. % of Need Met: 100%

Avg. Merit-Based Aid: $15,000
% Receiving Merit-Based Aid: 3%

Avg. Cumulative Debt: $24,987
% of Students Borrowing: 42%

CAREER
Who Recruits
1. New England Center for Children
2. M&T Bank
3. EY
4. NYS Department of Health
5. Carney Sandoe & Associates

Notable Internships
1. Scholastic
2. WHYY
3. Airbnb

Top Industries
1. Business
2. Education
3. Arts and Design
4. Operations
5. Media

Top Employers
1. Morgan Stanley
2. EY
3. JPMorgan Chase
4. Google
5. Fidelity Investments

Where Alumni Work
1. New York City
2. Boston
3. Albany, NY
4. San Francisco
5. Washington, DC

Median Earnings
College Scorecard (Early Career): $49,700
EOP (Early Career): $47,500
PayScale (Mid-Career): $99,700

RANKINGS
Forbes: 101
Money: 167
U.S. News: 39, Liberal Arts Colleges
Wall Street Journal/THE: 93 (T)
Washington Monthly: 83, Liberal Arts Colleges

#CollegesWorthYourMoney

Smith College

Northampton, Massachusetts | Admissions Phone: 413-585-2500

ADMISSION
Admission Rate: 31%
Admission Rate - Men: Not Offered
Admission Rate - Women: 31%
EA Admission Rate: Not Offered
ED Admission Rate: 49%
Admission Rate (5-Year Trend): -12%
ED Admission Rate (5-Year Trend): +2%
% of Admits Attending (Yield): 34%
Transfer Admission Rate: 33%

Offered Wait List: 923
Accepted Wait List: 458
Admitted Wait List: 68

SAT Reading/Writing (Middle 50%): 670-750
SAT Math (Middle 50%): 670-770
ACT Composite (Middle 50%): 31-34
Testing Policy: Test Optional
SAT Superscore: Yes
ACT Superscore: Yes

% Graduated in Top 10% of HS Class: 72%
% Graduated in Top 25% of HS Class: 96%
% Graduated in Top 50% of HS Class: 100%

ENROLLMENT
Total Undergraduate Enrollment: 2,502
% Part-Time: 0%
% Male: 0%
% Female: 100%
% Out-of-State: 81%
% Fraternity: Not Offered
% Sorority: Not Offered
% On-Campus (Freshman): 100%
% On-Campus (All Undergraduate): 95%

% African-American: 7%
% Asian: 9%
% Hispanic: 12%
% White: 48%
% Other: 5%
% Race or Ethnicity Unknown: 6%
% International: 14%
% Low-Income: 21%

ACADEMICS
Student-to-Faculty Ratio: 8:1
% of Classes Under 20: 70%
% of Classes Under 40: 94%
% Full-Time Faculty: 94%
% Full-Time Faculty w/ Terminal Degree: 98%

Top Programs
Area Studies
Biology
Education & Child Study
Economics
Engineering
Government
Psychology
Sociology

Retention Rate: 93%
4-Year Graduation Rate: 83%
6-Year Graduation Rate: 89%

Curricular Flexibility: Very Flexible
Academic Rating: ★★★★✦

Inside the Classroom

You will not find a more wide-open curriculum or liberal/progressive ethos at any women's school in the country than that of Smith College; only a few coeducational institutions—perhaps Vassar or Wesleyan—can go toe-to-toe with Smith on both fronts. Its list of alumnae supports that claim with Gloria Steinem, Julia Child, and Sylvia Plath all being Smith grads (Nancy Reagan was the ideological oddball). From a Seven Sisters admissions standpoint, Smith is more selective than Mt. Holyoke but less selective than Wellesley, Bryn Mawr, or Barnard. A member of the Five College Consortium, students can cross-enroll at Mt. Holyoke, UMass, Amherst, and Hampshire. In addition to the forty-five academic departments and programs and 1,000 courses offered each academic year at Smith, an additional 4,000 courses can be accessed at partner universities.

Smith's seven major fields of knowledge are literature, historical studies, social science, natural science, mathematics and analytical philosophy, the arts, and foreign language. Forays into each are "recommended," but the only nonnegotiable requirement is one writing-intensive course in the first or second semester of the freshman year. Otherwise, graduation requirements dictate that sixty-four credits must be taken outside of one's major. What that distribution looks like is entirely up to you. Young women seeking the ultimate level of undergraduate academic freedom will adore the Smith experience.

There are 290 professors at Smith, translating to a student-faculty ratio of 9:1. With only a small number of graduate students to worry about, 22 percent of undergraduate sections have single-digit enrollments, and 70 percent of total class sections enroll fewer than twenty students. Each summer, eighty Smithies spend their time working side-by-side with a professor on a research project. Around 40 percent of undergrads spend a semester abroad in one of a hundred programs on six continents, including some programs taught in the native tongue for those proficient in a foreign language.

The social sciences are most popular at Smith, accounting for 22 percent of the degrees conferred, with programs in economics and government carrying very strong reputations. Next in line is biology (11 percent), psychology (8 percent), foreign language (7 percent), and engineering (6 percent). Thanks to a strong decade-long push toward increasing the number of women studying such fields as engineering, mathematics, and the hard sciences, greater than two-fifths of current students are majoring in a STEM field. Smith is also the Fulbright Scholarship capital of the world producing an awe-inspiring 188 winners in the past dozen years. Recent students also have captured Goldwater and Udall Scholarships as well as National Science Foundation Graduate Research Fellowships.

Outside the Classroom

Every freshman, and 95 percent of the total undergraduate population, lives in college-owned housing. There are thirty-seven self-governing houses, each with its own dining hall, that accommodate between ten and one hundred students; most have a mix of freshmen through seniors. No sororities operate at this school. Smith offers eleven varsity sports that compete in NCAA Division III as well as extensive intramural and club sports programs that include oddities like Quidditch and Futsal. The Outing Club is a popular way to enjoy the area's natural beauty through hikes, canoeing trips, and rock-climbing adventures. Approximately 120 student-run organizations are available with a wide selection of cultural groups, political and student government groups, and community service clubs. Each year 200+ volunteers dedicate 10,000+ hours of community service through the Jandon Center for Community Engagement. Smith's membership in the Five College Consortium leads to additional social and extracurricular opportunities on the campuses of Mt. Holyoke, UMass, Amherst, and Hampshire. Culture and relaxation can be found on campus at the Smith College Museum of Art or the school's own botanical garden. The town of Northampton is two hours west of Boston and features plenty of restaurants and an artsy vibe that meshes well with this particular college community.

Career Services

The Lazarus Center for Career Development at Smith is staffed by ten professionals, including six career advisors and internship and employer relations specialists. The 245:1 student-to-advisor ratio is better than the average school featured in this guidebook. For a small school, it puts on a fairly large Fall Career Fair that draws eighty+ companies and graduate schools. It also organizes the Spring Life Sciences, Technology & Engineering Fair that attracts thirty+ employers. In addition, Smith partners with MIT and UMass Amherst to offer access to additional off-site career fairs. Membership in the Selective Liberal Arts Consortium affords the women of Smith chances to participate in interview days with major corporations in Washington, DC, and New York City.

Last year, 176 companies recruited on campus, an exceptional figure for a small liberal arts school. More than 6,600 job and internship opportunities are posted each year on Handshake. Praxis grants of up to $3,500 are awarded to roughly 400 undergraduates per year to pursue unpaid internships. Current students also benefit from the network of 48,000 alumnae spread across 120 countries who are known for being generous with their time and offers of mentorship. While the school's starting salary numbers leave something to be desired, the Lazarus Center for Career Development excels in employer relations, procurement of prestigious scholarships, and offers ample individualized attention for those who seek it.

Professional Outcomes

Two years after graduating 91 percent of Smith alumnae have found employment, and 42 percent have begun their graduate studies. More than twenty-five alumnae can be found at the US Department of State, Google, IBM, Johnson & Johnson, Accenture, Fidelity Investments, Deloitte, Microsoft, JPMorgan Chase, and Amazon. Many Smith women rise to high ranks within their respective organizations and corporations. Twenty years after graduation, 10 percent of alumnae report holding a chief executive position, and an additional 8 percent are stationed in other executive-level positions. Median career incomes are on the lower side compared to other elite schools and are comparable to those of Mt. Holyoke. Surprising given its locale, Boston is only the second-most popular destination for grads. New York City is number one with Springfield (Massachusetts), San Francisco, and DC also toward the top of the list.

Within ten years of receiving their bachelor's degrees more than three-quarters of Smith grads have earned or are working toward an advanced degree. The five most frequently attended graduate schools are Columbia, NYU, Harvard, Smith itself, and Boston University. Medical and law school acceptance rates are strong. Smith undergrads with a 3.3 GPA and a minimum of 507 on the MCAT were accepted into medical school at an 87 percent clip. The law school acceptance rate is consistently over 80 percent.

Admission

In seeking a place in the Class of 2022, almost 5,800 hopefuls applied to Smith; 31 percent were accepted, and 34 percent of that group ultimately enrolled. The college went test-optional a full decade ago, but 43 percent of the 2018-19 freshman class submitted SAT scores, and an additional 30 percent included ACT results as part of their applications. The mid-50 percent ranges on those exams were a 1340-1510 on the SAT and 31-34 on the ACT. Seventy-two percent of freshmen earned a spot in the top 10 percent of their high school class, and 96 percent placed in the top 25 percent; the average GPA was 3.98. Five years ago, 43 percent of women who applied were accepted at Smith, and the standardized test score range was a much lower 1220-1450 on the SAT and 28-31 on the ACT.

As stated by the committee, "Most applications are read by two members of the admission staff, and every part of your folder reveals another facet of your life." That holistic review places the greatest emphasis on five factors: rigor of coursework, GPA, recommendations, essays, and character/personal qualities. The second rung of important factors are class rank, an interview, extracurriculars, and talent/ability. Those applying through the early decision round received a boost to their admissions prospects to the tune of a 49 percent acceptance rate. Further, ED applicants accounted for 47 percent of the incoming freshman class. While not at the selectivity level of Wellesley or Barnard, Smith College has become increasingly more difficult to gain acceptance into in recent years. A sparkling high school transcript is nonnegotiable, and showing commitment through submitting an early decision application is recommended for borderline applicants who have Smith as their clear first choice.

Worth Your Money?

With a cost of attendance of $74,618, a Smith degree won't come cheap for those who do not qualify for institutional aid. The good news is that 61 percent of undergraduates do, indeed, qualify for need-based grants that average almost $50,000 annually. Merit aid awards are harder to come by and, when given, are only for a fraction of the need-based grants. Smith students have superb graduate/professional school and employment outcomes, making this school a solid choice for anyone who can afford it.

FINANCIAL
Institutional Type: Private
In-State Tuition: $53,940
Out-of-State Tuition: $53,940
Room & Board: $18,130
Required Fees: $284
Books & Supplies: $800

Avg. Need-Based Aid: $50,491
Avg. % of Need Met: 100%

Avg. Merit-Based Aid: $14,564
% Receiving Merit-Based Aid: 8%

Avg. Cumulative Debt: $22,083
% of Students Borrowing: 58%

CAREER
Who Recruits
1. Amazon Robotics
2. The Beacon Group
3. Woodard & Curran
4. Audible
5. Collins Aerospace

Notable Internships
1. National Institutes of Health
2. Goldman Sachs
3. Roosevelt Park Zoo

Top Industries
1. Business
2. Education
3. Healthcare
4. Social Services
5. Media

Top Employers
1. Google
2. IBM
3. Johnson & Johnson
4. Accenture
5. JPMorgan Chase

Where Alumni Work
1. New York City
2. Boston
3. Springfield, MA
4. San Francisco
5. Washington, DC

Median Earnings
College Scorecard (Early Career): $46,200
EOP (Early Career): $46,200
PayScale (Mid-Career): $98,200

RANKINGS
Forbes: 81
Money: 206
U.S. News: 11, Liberal Arts Colleges
Wall Street Journal/THE: 41
Washington Monthly: 28, Liberal Arts Colleges

#CollegesWorthYourMoney

Southern Methodist University

Dallas, Texas | Admissions Phone: 214-768-2058

Inside the Classroom

Wealthy and moderately conservative—such is the reputation of Southern Methodist University in Dallas, Texas, a midsized private institution with a loyal alumni base and plenty of financial backing. Historically, a large percentage of the school's 6,500 undergraduates come from families earning incomes in the top 5 percent of all families in the United States. While "Methodist" is in its name, only 14 percent of students identify as affiliating with that denomination; twice as many are Catholic. Academically, the Cox School of Business has one of the most respected faculties in the world, but that is by no means the only high-profile academic department; the public policy, sports management, performing arts, music, and film programs shine almost as brightly. In total, SMU offers one hundred+ majors and eighty-five minors.

The university's curriculum was revised in 2016 and now involves fulfilling foundation, depth, and breadth requirements. While that may sound extensive, the school offers great flexibility within those categories, and many courses within one's major will naturally fulfill some of the various mandates. Seven "proficiencies and experiences" can be met through a combination of coursework and noncredit activities that address each of human diversity, information literacy, oral communication, writing, community engagement, global engagement, and quantitative reasoning.

Thanks in part to an 11:1 student-to-faculty ratio, 59 percent of classes enroll fewer than twenty students, and fewer than 9 percent of classes enroll fifty+ undergraduates. Opportunities for personal connection and guidance extend beyond the classroom as 1,000 current SMU students have participated in undergraduate research or apprenticeships. Grants for independent research through an Engaged Learning Fellowship or a Summer Research Assistantship that pays students to work alongside faculty members for twenty-nine hours per week also are available. An annual symposium and an undergraduate-only research journal provide outlets through which you can share those valuable experiences. The 150 study abroad programs in fifty countries attract more than one-quarter of Mustangs at some point during their four years of study.

This career-minded student body gravitates toward preprofessional degrees, particularly in business (26 percent) and engineering (9 percent). SMU's Cox School of Business is top-ranked and has especially strong ties to Wall Street. Programs in engineering, sports management, and the performing arts are also very well regarded. Most fresh SMU grads are targeting high-paying jobs or entering the graduate/professional school of their choosing, but a small number each year aim for (and win) prestigious fellowships. Mustangs are awarded between two and five Fulbright Scholarships per year, two to four Gilman Scholarships, and an occasional Goldwater or Truman Scholarship.

Outside the Classroom

Almost every freshman resides in one of the university's eleven Residential Commons (which also houses sophomores), and 54 percent of all undergraduates call the dorms home; upperclassmen occupy six separate communities. Greek life is a huge part of the social fabric at SMU with 24 percent of men joining fraternities and 37 percent of women affiliating with a sorority. Sports are also a major force as the Mustangs field seventeen teams that compete in the American Athletic Conference against Division I competition. Impressively, SMU has won eighteen conference championships in the last five years. The football tradition at SMU is strong despite a series of recruiting scandals in the '80s that led to the team being banned for the 1987 season. Now, money flows into the program legally, including the $27 million that funded a new indoor practice facility that opened in 2019. New buildings are popping up everywhere you look across campus, whether it's the 50,000-square-foot Gerald J. Ford Hall for Research and Innovation or the Crain Family Centennial Promenade running through the heart of campus. The school routinely places near the top of "most beautiful campus" lists. Those not thrilled by Greeks and sports can still choose from over 200 campus organizations or venture into Dallas as the city's downtown area is only a few miles from the school.

Career Services

The Hegi Family Development Center has eight full-time employees as well as two graduate assistants. Professionals fill roles such as career counselor and employer relations specialist, and the overall student-to-counselor ratio is 807:1, poorer than most midsized universities profiled in this guide. Events that take place on campus, including career fairs, draw as many as one hundred employers and 575 students. The All Majors Career Fair held in the fall of 2019 attracted fifty+ employers including heavy hitters like American Airlines, Southwest, Hershey's, Mary Kay, and Home Depot.

Southern Methodist University

E-mail: ugadmission@smu.edu | Website: www.smu.edu

SMU's connected alumni base helps sustain strong school-to-employer bonds that lead to ample internship opportunities, particularly in the Dallas area. Business majors land internships at major investment firms and banks like Goldman Sachs, Citi, and JPMorgan Chase. A tremendous 90 percent of Lyle School of Engineering undergraduates complete at least one internship. Services offered by the Hegi Family Development Center include one-day externships, one-on-one career counseling that staff recommends "early and often," and the facilitation of on-campus interviews with recruiters from 160 companies, including some in the Fortune 500. Becoming a Mustang enables undergraduates of all socioeconomic backgrounds to connect to industry through networking, experiential learning opportunities, and impactful corporate relationships.

Professional Outcomes

At the moment they receive their diplomas, over two-thirds of graduates already have their first jobs or graduate school destinations in hand. Six months after graduation, that figure rises to 93 percent. The major corporations employing the greatest number of Mustangs are Lockheed Martin, AT&T, EY, IBM, JPMorgan Chase, Microsoft, Deloitte, American Airlines, Accenture, Oracle, Amazon, and Goldman Sachs. While close to half of SMU alums stay close to their alma mater in the Dallas-Fort Worth area, many relocate to New York City, Los Angeles, San Francisco, or DC for work. Average salaries for graduates of the Cox School of Business ranged between $50k for management majors to $70k for finance majors. Across all colleges and majors the average starting salary was $55,000.

In a typical year, one-quarter of seniors elect to continue their education in pursuit of a graduate or professional degree. SMU itself is a popular choice, but graduates have no shortage of options, including at the nation's top universities. Of the eighty-three SMU grads applying to begin medical school in 2018, a solid 58 percent gained acceptance, better than the national average that year of 43 percent. Acceptances included the Baylor College of Medicine, Perelman School of Medicine at the University of Pennsylvania, University of Texas at Austin Dell Medical School, and Vanderbilt University School of Medicine. The roughly one hundred pre-law students enjoy an annual acceptance rate hovering between 70 and 85 percent. Each year, forty students enter the Pre-Law Scholars Program, which puts them on track to attend SMU's Dedman School of Law upon graduation. Other grads in recent years have entered prestigious law schools such as those at Columbia, Cornell, Duke, Penn, Stanford, and Yale.

Admission

The 12,603 applicants to the Class of 2022 was a slight dip from the previous two admissions cycles but a still a big jump from the roughly 8,000 applications received in 2009. Fifty-one percent of Class of 2022 applicants were accepted, and 24 percent of those admitted chose to attend SMU. Standardized test scores have demonstrated a strong and consistent upward trend over the past decade; in 2008 the average SAT score was 1228, and the average ACT score was 27. Today, the average SAT score is 1363, and the average ACT score is a 30. Almost half finished in the top decile of their high school class, and 80 percent were at least in the top quartile. The average GPA for incoming freshmen is 3.63, and 45 percent of that group possessed a 3.75 or higher.

There are five "very important" factors given top priority by the SMU Admissions Committee: GPA, standardized test scores, rigor of coursework, recommendations, and application essays. That holistic and deep review also grants "important" status to class rank, extracurricular activities, talent/ability, and character/personal qualities. Demonstrated interest is a minor factor in the process as are first-generation or legacy status. Southern Methodist University offers an early decision option with a November 15 deadline that yields a small admissions edge; ED applicants get in at a 61percent clip. SMU also offers a second ED option with a January 15 deadline.

Worth Your Money?

Along with schools like Columbia, USC, and the University of Chicago, Southern Methodist University is near the top of the list of schools with the highest sticker prices in the country. The estimated total cost of attendance for an SMU student in 2019-20 was $76,786. So is a non-Ivy worth an Ivy price tag? Perhaps, especially after accounting for financial aid. The university is generous with merit scholarships, awarding 73 percent of students an average of $28,000 per year. Need-based aid is also disbursed freely to the point that the average cost of attendance, even for families in the highest income bracket, is $43,000; families making $75k-$110k pay $32,500 per year, less than half the list price. Many majors within the Cox School of Business and Lyle School of Engineering start their careers with salaries that will easily cover a reasonable student loan payment.

FINANCIAL
Institutional Type: Private
In-State Tuition: $50,200
Out-of-State Tuition: $50,200
Room & Board: $16,750
Required Fees: $6,360
Books & Supplies: $800

Avg. Need-Based Aid: $18,691
Avg. % of Need Met: 86%

Avg. Merit-Based Aid: $27,685
% Receiving Merit-Based Aid: 73%

Avg. Cumulative Debt: $38,086
% of Students Borrowing: 28%

CAREER
Who Recruits
1. Vira Insight
2. Epsilon
3. Dell
4. Frost Bank
5. Bank of America

Notable Internships
1. Dallas Mavericks
2. Cushman & Wakefield
3. Dell

Top Industries
1. Business
2. Education
3. Operations
4. Engineering
5. Sales

Top Employers
1. Lockheed Martin
2. AT&T
3. EY
4. IBM
5. Accenture

Where Alumni Work
1. Dallas
2. India
3. Houston
4. New York City
5. Austin

Median Earnings
College Scorecard (Early Career): $60,700
EOP (Early Career): $55,400
PayScale (Mid-Career): $110,400

RANKINGS
Forbes: 91
Money: 357
U.S. News: 64 (T), National Universities
Wall Street Journal/THE: 84 (T)
Washington Monthly: 308, National Universities

#CollegesWorthYourMoney

St. Olaf College

Northfield, Minnesota | Admissions Phone: 507-786-3025

ADMISSION
Admission Rate: 50%
Admission Rate - Men: 49%
Admission Rate - Women: 50%
EA Admission Rate: Not Offered
ED Admission Rate: 76%
Admission Rate (5-Year Trend): -9%
ED Admission Rate (5-Year Trend): +13%
% of Admits Attending (Yield): 29%
Transfer Admission Rate: 37%

Offered Wait List: 911
Accepted Wait List: 448
Admitted Wait List: 51

SAT Reading/Writing (Middle 50%): 600-700
SAT Math (Middle 50%): 590-710
ACT Composite (Middle 50%): 25-32
Testing Policy: ACT/SAT Required
SAT Superscore: Yes
ACT Superscore: Yes

% Graduated in Top 10% of HS Class: 41%
% Graduated in Top 25% of HS Class: 72%
% Graduated in Top 50% of HS Class: 96%

ENROLLMENT
Total Undergraduate Enrollment: 3,048
% Part-Time: 1%
% Male: 43%
% Female: 57%
% Out-of-State: 53%
% Fraternity: Not Offered
% Sorority: Not Offered
% On-Campus (Freshman): 100%
% On-Campus (All Undergraduate): 94%

% African-American: 3%
% Asian: 7%
% Hispanic: 7%
% White: 69%
% Other: 4%
% Race or Ethnicity Unknown: 1%
% International: 10%
% Low-Income: 15%

ACADEMICS
Student-to-Faculty Ratio: 12:1
% of Classes Under 20: 50%
% of Classes Under 40: 95%
% Full-Time Faculty: 64%
% Full-Time Faculty w/ Terminal Degree: 97%

Top Programs
Area Studies
Biology
Chemistry
Economics
Exercise Science
Mathematics
Religion

Retention Rate: 91%
4-Year Graduation Rate: 82%
6-Year Graduation Rate: 86%

Curricular Flexibility: Less Flexible
Academic Rating: ★★★✦

Inside the Classroom

Easier to gain acceptance into than neighbor/rival Carleton, St. Olaf College is a strong liberal arts school in Northfield, Minnesota, that is home to roughly 3,000 undergraduates. Just as in 1889 when the college first opened its frost-covered doors, St. Olaf retains a strong affiliation with the Lutheran Church. Running on a 4-1-4 schedule, students take four courses during fourteen-week semesters and one course during the one month in between. Students are nicknamed Oles (pronounced OH-Leez), and they enjoy a robust academic program of eighty-five+ majors, concentrations, and pre-professional options.

General education requirements are extensive, even by the standards of a traditional liberal arts school. This intensive regiment of coursework includes Foundation Studies, which is comprised of a first-year writing seminar, mastery of a foreign language, courses in oral communication and writing in context as well as abstract and quantitative reasoning and studies in physical movement. Freshman courses in biblical studies and theology are also mandates as well as a litany of courses across the humanities, natural sciences, and social sciences.

With a 12:1 student-to-faculty ratio and no graduate students there is ample room for mentor-mentee relationships to flourish. Exactly half of all course sections contain fewer than twenty students, and another 36 percent contain twenty to twenty-nine students. Graduation surveys reveal students who are immensely satisfied with the St. Olaf academic experience. Ninety-four percent agreed that faculty made them better critical thinkers, 88 percent touted the quality of outside-the-classroom interactions with professors, and 87 percent said coursework improved their written expression. There are multiple avenues in which students can pursue research experiences on or off campus. On-campus options include applying for ten-week summer stints through the Collaborative Undergraduate Research & Inquiry program, a Steen Fellowship to encourage independent research, or an independent study conducted for credit. Studying abroad is a staple of life for Oles; three-quarters spend a semester studying off campus, the vast majority at an international locale.

The most commonly conferred degrees are in economics, biology, psychology, mathematics, and the visual and performing arts. Many departments at St. Olaf have exceptional national reputations including religion and theology, mathematics/statistics, and physical sciences. The most coveted fellowship and scholarship organizations definitely pay special attention to graduates of this institution. In fact, the college has produced an astounding five Rhodes Scholars since 1995. In that same time, 119 graduates have taken home Fulbright Scholarships, including thirteen members of the Class of 2019.

Outside the Classroom

With 95 percent of students living on campus or in college-owned housing nearby, the student body functions as a fairly cohesive unit. Students remain on campus for a variety of sound reasons. For one, dining hall cuisine is regularly rated among the country's best, and for another no Greek life exists at St. Olaf. So-called "Honor Houses" are the closest thing to frats or sororities, but they are residences based on common academic areas of study or special interests. There are twenty-one such houses at the college, including ones focused on common bonds such as Norwegian languages, Muslim identity, or the environment. The Oles field twenty-five athletic teams (13 men's, 12 women's) that compete in NCAA Division III. A hefty portion of the student body—500 undergraduates—are members of a varsity sports squad. There are more than 200 clubs active at the school. Those who enjoy the outdoor life will adore the 325 adjoining acres of woodlands, wetlands, and prairie that students can freely roam. Environmentally conscious policies include running 100 percent on carbon-free electrical power and a connection to fifteen local food producers to promote sustainability. The school's location near Carleton College opens additional chances for socialization as does the fact that Minneapolis and St. Paul are both less than fifty miles away.

Career Services

The Piper Center for Vocation and Career is staffed by eleven professional employers serving roles such as counselor, alumni engagement, and employer relations. Additionally, the college trains twenty-eight peer advisors to add an extra layer of student support. Counting only professional employees, St. Olaf sports a student-to-advisor ratio of 276:1, lower than the average school included in this book. Thanks to those favorable numbers, 79 percent of undergraduates meet with either a career coach or peer advisor each academic year. Among graduates, just shy of 90 percent reported they were adequately prepared for life beyond college.

On-campus events include an annual Recruiting Showcase featuring some of the top corporate employers of Oles and a Government and Nonprofit Career Fair open to all Minnesota college students. The college also participates in the statewide Private College and Career Fair that features 260+ employers. Opportunities for experiential learning are wide ranging and taken advantage of by most students as 86 percent of undergrads complete at least one internship, job-shadowing, or field experience over the course of their four years on campus. A tightknit and helpful alumni base regularly avail themselves to assist current undergrads. Alumni events like Ole Biz, which brings over a hundred graduates to Minneapolis, invites current students to learn about ten industries while networking their hearts out. The Piper Center excels in setting students up with meaningful experiences and important alumni connections, and it has a direct line to many of the region's largest corporate employers.

Professional Outcomes

Examining the outcomes for the graduating classes of 2017 and 2018, between 73 and 79 percent immediately enter the workforce and between 17 and 23 percent matriculate into graduate/professional school. In 2017, four percent of grads were still seeking their next step six months after graduation; in 2018 not a single student reported failing to find their next destination. The great majority of alumni remain in the Greater Minneapolis-St. Paul area (more than ten times as many as relocate to second-choice destination Chicago), which impacts what companies hire the most Oles. To name names, alumni have the largest representation at Target, UnitedHealth Group, the Mayo Clinic, Wells Fargo, Medtronic, 3M, and US Bank. Midcareer median salaries fall in the same range as other Minnesota academic powerhouses Carleton and Macalester.

While many pursuing higher education choose to stay in the Midwest, every year the college sends at least one graduate to the likes of Columbia, Yale, or Cornell to pursue an advanced degree. St. Olaf students in a premed area of concentration and who have a GPA of 3.59 or better gain acceptance to medical school at a solid 75 percent clip. The most commonly attended medical school is the University of Minnesota-Twin Cities, but recent grads have gone on to study at the University of Michigan Medical School, Washington University in St. Louis School of Medicine, and Wake Forest Medical School. Law school applicants have gone on to elite universities including Harvard, Emory, Georgetown, and UCLA. The school is also a top producer of future PhDs, placing eleventh among baccalaureate colleges in the number of graduates who go on to earn doctoral degrees in their respective fields.

Admission

Exactly half of those who applied for a position in St. Olaf's Class of 2022 were granted acceptance. One decade ago, the acceptance rate was 59 percent of an applicant pool that was only one-third the size of the 2022 class. Attending freshmen in the 2018-19 school year possessed a middle-50 percent SAT range of 1190-1410 and a wide-ranging ACT composite of 25-32. The ACT was, by far, the test of choice; it was submitted by 73 percent of applicants. Just over 50 percent of freshmen boasted GPAs of over 3.75, but one-quarter of attendees had below a 3.5. Forty-one percent fell within the top decile of their graduating class, and 72 percent placed in the top quarter.

Rigorous coursework, GPA, and the application essay are of paramount importance to the admissions committee followed by a second tier of factors including standardized test scores, class rank, recommendations, an interview, extracurricular activities, talent/ability, and character/personal qualities. Showing a commitment to the college is rewarded on the admissions end; early decision applicants were accepted at a friendly rate of 76 percent. Overall, St. Olaf has a yield rate of 29 percent, which means that just under one-in-three accepted students actually go on to enroll. Earning admission into St. Olaf is more than a simple numbers game; a holistic approach by the committee rewards "smart, ambitious, creative people who want to be challenged." Even if you lack perfect grades or ACT scores, a candidate can still make a compelling case for acceptance into this fine Midwestern liberal arts institution.

Worth Your Money?

Total cost of attendance at St. Olaf will run you just short of $63,000 per year, yet few pay that amount. Two-thirds of Oles receive some form of financial aid, and the overall value of each need-based award is $37k, ultimately making this school affordable for those with financial need. Considering the high rate of internship participation, close contact with major companies, and accessible faculty, St. Olaf is likely worth your money.

FINANCIAL
Institutional Type: Private
In-State Tuition: $49,710
Out-of-State Tuition: $49,710
Room & Board: $11,270
Required Fees: $0
Books & Supplies: $1,000

Avg. Need-Based Aid: $36,531
Avg. % of Need Met: 100%

Avg. Merit-Based Aid: $17,556
% Receiving Merit-Based Aid: 46%

Avg. Cumulative Debt: $29,907
% of Students Borrowing: 64%

CAREER
Who Recruits
1. Lewin Group
2. Cerner Corporation
3. Thomson Reuters
4. North Sky Capital
5. MatrixCare

Notable Internships
1. Game Informer Magazine
2. MITRE
3. 9/11 Tribute Museum

Top Industries
1. Education
2. Business
3. Operations
4. Social Services
5. Healthcare

Top Employers
1. UnitedHealth Group
2. Target
3. Mayo Clinic
4. Wells Fargo
5. U.S. Bank

Where Alumni Work
1. Minneapolis
2. Chicago
3. New York City
4. San Francisco
5. Denver

Median Earnings
College Scorecard (Early Career): $50,400
EOP (Early Career): $48,600
PayScale (Mid-Career): $101,900

RANKINGS
Forbes: 116
Money: 133
U.S. News: 62, Liberal Arts Colleges
Wall Street Journal/THE: 156 (T)
Washington Monthly: 60, Liberal Arts Colleges

#CollegesWorthYourMoney

Stanford University

Stanford, California | Admissions Phone: 650-723-2091

ADMISSION
Admission Rate: 4%
Admission Rate - Men: 4%
Admission Rate - Women: 4%
EA Admission Rate: N/A
ED Admission Rate: Not Offered
Admission Rate (5-Year Trend): -1%
ED Admission Rate (5-Year Trend): Not Offered
% of Admits Attending (Yield): 82%
Transfer Admission Rate: 1%

Offered Wait List: 870
Accepted Wait List: 681
Admitted Wait List: 30

SAT Reading/Writing (Middle 50%): 700-770
SAT Math (Middle 50%): 720-800
ACT Composite (Middle 50%): 32-35
Testing Policy: ACT/SAT Required
SAT Superscore: Yes
ACT Superscore: Yes

% Graduated in Top 10% of HS Class: 96%
% Graduated in Top 25% of HS Class: 100%
% Graduated in Top 50% of HS Class: 100%

ENROLLMENT
Total Undergraduate Enrollment: 7,087
% Part-Time: 0%
% Male: 50%
% Female: 50%
% Out-of-State: 59%
% Fraternity: 18%
% Sorority: 24%
% On-Campus (Freshman): 100%
% On-Campus (All Undergraduate): 93%

% African-American: 7%
% Asian: 22%
% Hispanic: 16%
% White: 34%
% Other: 9%
% Race or Ethnicity Unknown: 1%
% International: 10%
% Low-Income: 15%

ACADEMICS
Student-to-Faculty Ratio: 5:1
% of Classes Under 20: 69%
% of Classes Under 40: 85%
% Full-Time Faculty: 67%
% Full-Time Faculty w/ Terminal Degree: 76%

Top Programs
Computer Science
Economics
Engineering
Human Biology
International Relations
Mathematics
Physics
Psychology

Retention Rate: 99%
4-Year Graduation Rate: 75%
6-Year Graduation Rate: 94%

Curricular Flexibility: Somewhat Flexible
Academic Rating: ★★★★★

Inside the Classroom

Fittingly situated in the heart of Silicon Valley sits one of the tech industry's top feeder schools and one of the premier research universities in the world. Among Stanford's many quantifiable boasts and brags are the lowest acceptance rate in the country, the nation's second-largest college endowment, the best all-around athletic department in the country, the second-highest total of affiliate-won Nobel Prizes, and the highest graduate starting salaries for any non-STEM-exclusive institution. At Stanford, the list of accomplishments could go longer than a vintage John Elway (an alum) deep ball.

Over 7,000 undergrads and another 8,000 graduate students occupy this expansive campus that is the sixth largest in the nation. For perspective on its size, 19,000 bicycle parking spots can be found on university grounds. There are three undergraduate schools at Stanford: The School of Humanities & Sciences that houses 61 percent of the student body, the School of Engineering, and the School of Earth, Energy, and Environmental Sciences. All undergraduates must complete three courses in writing and rhetoric, one year of a foreign language, and a freshman course entitled Thinking Matters in which students choose from a full menu of courses covering a host of intellectual topics from Race in American Memory to How Does Your Brain Work? The Ways of Thinking, Ways of Doing requirement comprises eleven additional courses in ethical reasoning, applied quantitative reasoning, and aesthetic and interpretive inquiry. Further requirements are major specific. Some programs require a senior capstone, research component, practicum or, for foreign language, an oral proficiency review.

A virtually unmatched 4:1 student-to-faculty ratio sets the Cardinal students up for a personalized classroom experience and an incredible amount of face time with some of the leaders in their respective fields. Two-thirds of classes have fewer than twenty students, and 35 percent have a single-digit enrollment. Stanford puts unmatched resources behind undergraduate research; more than $5.6 million in grant funding is allocated each year to support roughly 1,000 student research projects. Close to 900 students study abroad annually through the Bing Overseas Studies Program in eleven international cities.

The School of Engineering is one of the best in the world; all of its sub disciplines sit atop any list of best engineering programs. Programs in computer science, physics, mathematics, international relations and economics are arguably the best anywhere. In terms of sheer volume, the greatest number of degrees are conferred each year in engineering (18 percent), computer science (18 percent), interdisciplinary studies (15 percent), and the social sciences (12 percent). With ninety-six Rhodes Scholars to its credit, Stanford ranks fourth on the all-time list. In 2018, the school produced twenty Fulbright winners, five Schwartzman Scholars, a Truman Scholar, and in recent years has produced a multitude of winners of just about any prestigious post-grad scholarship one can name.

Outside the Classroom

Stanford is where you can receive a world-class education and experience the excitement of a typical college experience. The Cardinal have a rich sports tradition with its sixteen men's and twenty women's NCAA Division I teams. The excellence the university expects in the classroom in matched on the field; the Athletic Department has won the Directors' Cup, given to the most successful college athletic program, for twenty-four consecutive years, and at least one team has won an NCAA national championship in each of the last forty-two years. With an additional forty club teams, over 900 undergraduates compete in intercollegiate athletics. Fraternities and sororities are thriving on campus with a 25 percent participation rate across twenty-nine Greek organizations. Over 600 student organizations are active including sixty student-led community service organizations, the widely circulated Stanford Daily, and a vast array of ethnic/cultural groups. Ninety-two percent of undergrads live on Stanford's sprawling 8,180-acre campus in the heart of the San Francisco Peninsula. The surrounding area of Palo Alto, America's wealthiest town, is full of natural and manmade beauty and any cultural, culinary, or entertainment delight one could seek. The university itself puts its bottomless endowment to use with immaculately manicured grounds, well-maintained dorms, state-of-the-art recreational facilities, and restaurant-quality campus dining options. Simply put, the campus aesthetics at Stanford are every bit as breathtaking as the quality of its academics.

Career Services

BEAM (Bridging Education, Ambition, & Meaningful Work) is Stanford's career services office. It employs twenty-five professional staff members who work in the Career Catalysts, Career Communities, and Career Ventures divisions. The 282:1 student-to-advisor ratio is lower than the average school featured in this guide. The three aforementioned divisions speak to the unique and comprehensive career services approach at Stanford. There is a sincere effort to get students to align their career interests with their identities and passions, cultivate a personalized network of mentors/guides, and connect directly with employers. BEAM does a fantastic job with all three phases of that process.

E-mail: admission@stanford.edu | Website: www.stanford.edu

In 2017-18, the career services staff facilitated 19,344 "meaningful connections" between current students and alumni/industry professionals and initiated 37,818 "meaningful opportunities" for undergraduates to carve out a pathway toward their employment or graduate school destination. BEAM sponsors fourteen to sixteen career fairs per year, posts over 10,000 job and internship opportunities on Handshake, and runs the superb Stanford Alumni Mentoring program. Major companies recruit on campus on a constant basis because (a) of the incredible talent pool and (b) the school is located in Silicon Valley, home to most of the world's largest tech companies. Stanford facilitates internships at over 700 unique sites, and close to half of all students complete two internships as part of their undergraduate education; two-thirds complete at least one. With a robust career services department and spectacular graduate outcomes (see below), BEAM earns every ounce of its stellar reputation.

Professional Outcomes

Stanford grads entering the working world flock to three major industries in equal distribution: business/finance/consulting/retail (19 percent); computer, IT (19 percent); and public policy and service, international affairs (19 percent). Among the companies employing the largest number of recent Stanford alums are Accenture, Apple, Bain, Cisco, Facebook, Goldman Sachs, Google, McKinsey, Microsoft, and SpaceX. Other companies that employ hundreds of Cardinal alums include LinkedIn, Uber, Lyft, Salesforce, and Airbnb. California, New York, Massachusetts, Texas, DC, and Washington state were the top six destinations for recent grads. The mean salary for all Stanford graduates is a staggering $85,000; that figure is substantially higher than the national average and is usually approached only by high-end engineering schools.

Those who are graduate school bound often stay at Stanford with professors they already have a close working relationship with. The other dozen most popular universities attended by recent graduates include Oxford, Harvard, MIT, Yale, Columbia, the University of Chicago, and Johns Hopkins. You would be hard-pressed to find a top-ranked law or medical school that did not have Stanford alums among its ranks. Last year, 241 Stanford graduates applied to medical school, and acceptance rates were nearly double the national average. In sum, if you get an undergraduate degree from Stanford, your opportunities for continuing your education will be limitless.

Admission

The toughest school to get into in the United States doesn't appear to be getting less selective anytime soon. In 2018-19, a meager 4.3 percent of the 47,450 accomplished teens vying for a place in the Class of 2022 were offered admission. The profile of the average current student is about what you would expect at the university with the lowest acceptance rate in the country. The middle-50 percent SAT range for the Class of 2022 was 1420-1570 and 32-35 on the ACT. If you want to become a member of the Cardinal club, near-perfect grades are a prerequisite. Three-quarters of incoming freshmen had a GPA of a 4.0 or above in high school, although it is important to highlight that only 6 percent of applicants meeting that criterion were accepted, and only 1 percent of those with a 3.7 or lower made the cut. Almost all freshmen—96 percent—ranked in the top 10 percent of their high school class.

There are nine factors considered "very important" to the admissions office: rigor of courses, GPA, class rank, standardized test scores, essays, recommendations, extracurricular activities, talent/ability, and character/personal qualities. The last three from that list are of particular importance given that the first five will likely be similarly perfect from the bulk of those applying. First-generation status is not listed as a primary factor, but a healthy 18 percent of those admitted in 2018 are looking to become the first in their family to earn a degree. Stanford admissions has become the ultimate valedictorian meat grinder, now possessing a lower admission rate than Harvard. With so many top-shelf applicants for a limited number of spots, it helps to have a hook—an area in which you truly excel. Whether academic, athletic, or extracurricular, such a hook can help differentiate you from the throngs of other super-qualified applicants.

Worth Your Money?

An endowment of over $26 billion helps the school cover most but, surprisingly, not all of the determined need of its undergraduate students. Still, the average need-based grant is for $52k+, which helps knock the $74,570 cost of attendance down to a manageable sum for the approximately 50 percent of students who qualify. Of course, Stanford is one of those rare universities that would be worth just about any cost.

FINANCIAL
Institutional Type: Private
In-State Tuition: $52,857
Out-of-State Tuition: $52,857
Room & Board: $16,433
Required Fees: $672
Books & Supplies: $1,245

Avg. Need-Based Aid: $52,453
Avg. % of Need Met: 100%

Avg. Merit-Based Aid: $0
% Receiving Merit-Based Aid: 0%

Avg. Cumulative Debt: $21,348
% of Students Borrowing: 19%

CAREER
Who Recruits
1. Masimo
2. Wealthfront
3. Calico
4. Asurion
5. Los Angeles Dodgers

Notable Internships
1. Citadel
2. SpaceX
3. United Nations

Top Industries
1. Business
2. Engineering
3. Education
4. Research
5. Operations

Top Employers
1. Google
2. Apple
3. Facebook
4. Microsoft
5. Amazon

Where Alumni Work
1. San Francisco
2. New York City
3. Los Angeles
4. Seattle
5. Boston

Median Earnings
College Scorecard (Early Career): $94,000
EOP (Early Career): $84,800
PayScale (Mid-Career): $145,200

RANKINGS
Forbes: 2
Money: 6
U.S. News: 6 (T) National Universities
Wall Street Journal/THE: 7 (T)
Washington Monthly: 1, National Universities

#CollegesWorthYourMoney

Stevens Institute of Technology

Hoboken, New Jersey | Admissions Phone: 201-216-5194

Inside the Classroom

With the Manhattan skyline visible across the Hudson River, the Stevens Institute of Technology's Hoboken, New Jersey, campus occupies prime real estate—but the school is not merely about its breathtaking panoramic view of the Big Apple. For this small but growing private research institution with a focus on engineering and business, proximity to New York City is an asset that translates into strong corporate connections, endless internship and co-op opportunities and, ultimately, exceptional job placement rates at top companies.

There are thirty-five undergraduate majors at Stevens across four undergraduate schools: the Schaefer School of Engineering & Science, the School of Business, the College of Arts and Letters, and the School of Systems and Enterprises. There is no core curriculum at Stevens as every set of requirements is school and major dependent. The only common academic experiences for all undergrads is a sequence of two College of Arts and Letters courses that every freshman must complete—Writing and Communications and Colloquium: Knowledge, Nature, Culture. Some engineering students complete a capstone senior design project that is often conducted in coordination with an industry sponsor.

Two-thirds of course sections have an enrollment of under thirty students, and 38 percent of sections contain fewer than twenty students. The student-to-faculty ratio is 10:1 but, of course, with over 2,000 graduate students some attention is diverted in their direction. Undergraduate research possibilities are plentiful and varied. Roughly 10 percent of each freshman class are invited to become Stevens Scholars, which guarantees a paid summer research experience with a faculty member. As a research university, the school also has close ties to industry and federally run labs that can lead to many additional research opportunities. Co-op experiences that also can involve research are embarked upon by slightly less than one-third of students. A number of study abroad programs are available with some of the most popular destinations being the United Kingdom, Belgium, Jamaica, China, Spain, Thailand, and Greece.

Engineering is, by far, the most common undergraduate major, and all programs within the Schaefer School of Engineering & Science are strong. Programs in computer science, cybersecurity, and quantitative finance also receive praise. Over 80 percent of the degrees granted at Stevens are in a STEM field, and most of the remaining grads major in business, finance, and accounting. It is uncommon for Stevens grads to pursue national fellowships or scholarships as they are traditionally focused on career or graduate school as their next step after graduation.

Outside the Classroom

A relatively low 64 percent of the undergraduate student body resides on campus in college-owned housing. Greek life is a major player on campus as fraternities and sororities attract 1,100 students—37 percent of the undergrad population. Greek houses are community service oriented and work closely with charitable organizations including Big Brothers Big Sisters, the Hoboken Shelter, and the Food Bank of New Jersey. Student-athletes participate on one of twenty-six NCAA Division III varsity athletic teams known as the Ducks. There are an additional sixteen intercollegiate club sports teams and a robust intramural program featuring flag football, three-on-three basketball, and floor hockey. There are over one hundred clubs and activities to join. For the extremely adventurous, the Outdoor Adventure Program plans trips to locales like Costa Rica, Utah, and the Grand Canyon. The Stevens Honor System is taken seriously and permeates beyond academic life into the social realm. An Honor Board and Student Government Association are in place to enforce shared values and enhance the student experience. Students publish a weekly student newspaper and run campus radio and television stations. Hoboken is only one jam-packed square mile of land, making it immensely walkable. For those of age, the town holds the distinction of most bars per capita. Running alongside the Hudson is an aesthetically pleasing option and, perhaps best of all, New York City is only fifteen minutes away.

Career Services

The Stevens Career Center is made up of six professional employees who work with undergraduate students as advisors, cooperative education coordinators, or in a director/assistant director capacity; two additional members work exclusively with the university's graduate students. The student-to-advisor ratio of 572:1, which ranks in the average range when compared against other schools featured in this guide, yet Stevens' career services offerings are as strong as they come. This is a career services office that works hard to forge corporate connections and, as a result, 80 percent of seniors have secured competitive employment prior to graduation.

In the 2017-18 school year more than 300 companies recruited on campus, a phenomenal number for a school of any size, but for a small university like Stevens, that figure is astounding. It is rare for Stevens students to not complete at least one internship over their four years of study. Ninety percent of undergrads in the School of Business land internships. The co-op track is selected by 30 percent of all students, and that entails working a forty-hour paid work week beginning in the sophomore year. Three annual career fairs in September, December, and March each attract about 900 students. The March 2018 Career Fair alone attracted 125 companies, including the likes of IBM, Verizon, and JPMorgan Chase.

Professional Outcomes

The Class of 2018 found employment or graduate school homes at a 96 percent rate within six months of receiving their degree. Engineering students entered the fields of manufacturing (24 percent), engineering services (17 percent), and construction (12 percent). Bachelor of Science students most frequently entered sector was finance (42 percent) followed by technology/telecom (17 percent), and business/consulting (8 percent). Employers that hired three or more Class of 2018 Stevens grads included Google, EY, Merck, Prudential, and PwC. Massive numbers of alumni (from all graduating years) can be found at major corporations including Verizon, Citi, JPMorgan Chase, Pfizer, and Johnson & Johnson. The average starting salary was $71,400. Many alumni stay local; 53 percent of 2018 graduates remained in New Jersey, and 29 percent crossed the border to New York.

Of the 18 percent of Stevens grads who immediately enroll in graduate school, 85 percent were pursuing master's or PhDs, 11 percent entered medical school, 2 percent law school, and 2 percent dental school. Some enrolled in doctoral programs at prestigious institutions such as Carnegie Mellon, Georgia Tech, Penn, and Vanderbilt and master's programs at Imperial College London, Royal College of Art, Johns Hopkins, and Cornell. The school offers a three-three accelerated law option as well as a three-four accelerated med school program. Recent medical school acceptances include Albert Einstein College of Medicine, Mount Sanai Medical School, and New York University School of Medicine.

Admission

There were 9,265 applications submitted for the 2018-19 freshman class, an 11 percent increase from the previous year. Of those hopefuls, 41 percent received an offer of acceptance compared to 44 percent in 2017-18. However, it's important to understand that the applicant pool is relatively self-selecting and primarily comprised of strongly credentialed teens. The mid-50 percent SAT Range was 1330-1480 with an average of 1399, and the average high school GPA was 3.86. Stevens accepted and enrolled 33 percent more students in the Class of 2022 than in the previous year's class. That expansion meant that more than 1,000 freshmen enrolled while under 700 graduated in 2018.

In addition to strong grades and standardized test scores, the admissions committee at Stevens is looking for students with a track record of "ingenuity, inventiveness, and inspiration." The school does offer admissions interviews, including via Skype for those living more than 250 miles away, but although interviews are recommended, they are optional. Applying early is strongly encouraged if Stevens is your top choice; the acceptance rate for ED applicants approaches 70 percent. The acceptance rate for women is typically ten points higher than the acceptance rate for men. Women make up about 30 percent of the student body. Stevens Institute of Technology is gaining in popularity and rapidly expanding its undergraduate enrollment. Its proximity to Manhattan, corporate connections, and stellar graduate outcomes should continue to draw larger numbers of highly qualified applicants.

Worth Your Money?

Is it good news or bad news that the average graduate's starting salary and annual cost of attendance at Stevens are nearly identical? Perhaps the adage, "You have to spend money to make money," helps answer that question. With a COA of $72k and starting salaries around the same, those paying full price will be just fine, even if they have to take out substantial loans to attend. Financial aid is awarded to 65 percent of the undergraduate population, but the school only meets the full financial need of 18 percent of accepted students. The average grant is for only $12,700 per year, which barely puts a dent in the tuition bill. Again, the good news is that strong career outcomes help balance the upfront costs.

FINANCIAL
Institutional Type: Private
In-State Tuition: $54,014
Out-of-State Tuition: $54,014
Room & Board: $15,770
Required Fees: N/A
Books & Supplies: $1,200

Avg. Need-Based Aid: $35,636
Avg. % of Need Met: 73%

Avg. Merit-Based Aid: $19,632
% Receiving Merit-Based Aid: 26%

Avg. Cumulative Debt: $40,588
% of Students Borrowing: 64%

CAREER
Who Recruits
1. MThree
2. Nasdaq
3. Bristol-Meyers Squibb
4. Calgene6
5. Nielsen

Notable Internships
1. iHeartMedia
2. Merck
3. Johnson & Johnson

Top Industries
1. Engineering
2. Information Technology
3. Business
4. Operations
5. Project Management

Top Employers
1. Verizon
2. JPMorgan Chase
3. Citi
4. Johnson & JOhnson
5. Pfizer

Where Alumni Work
1. New York City
2. Philadelphia
3. San Francisco
4. Washington, DC
5. Boston

Median Earnings
College Scorecard (Early Career): $89,200
EOP (Early Career): $92,100
PayScale (Mid-Career): $139,900

RANKINGS
Forbes: 152
Money: 212
U.S. News: 74 (T), National Universities
Wall Street Journal/THE: 160 (T)
Washington Monthly: 201, National Universities

#CollegesWorthYourMoney

ADMISSION
Admission Rate: 42%
Admission Rate - Men: 41%
Admission Rate - Women: 42%
EA Admission Rate: Not Offered
ED Admission Rate: Not Offered
Admission Rate (5-Year Trend): +2%
ED Admission Rate (5-Year Trend): Not Offered
% of Admits Attending (Yield): 21%
Transfer Admission Rate: 45%

Offered Wait List: 3,828
Accepted Wait List: 1,796
Admitted Wait List: 80

SAT Reading/Writing (Middle 50%): 600-680
SAT Math (Middle 50%): 630-740
ACT Composite (Middle 50%): 26-31
Testing Policy: ACT/SAT Required
SAT Superscore: Yes
ACT Superscore: Yes

% Graduated in Top 10% of HS Class: 47%
% Graduated in Top 25% of HS Class: 80%
% Graduated in Top 50% of HS Class: 97%

ENROLLMENT
Total Undergraduate Enrollment: 17,522
% Part-Time: 7%
% Male: 52%
% Female: 48%
% Out-of-State: 6%
% Fraternity: 2%
% Sorority: 2%
% On-Campus (Freshman): 83%
% On-Campus (All Undergraduate): 53%

% African-American: 7%
% Asian: 26%
% Hispanic: 12%
% White: 32%
% Other: 3%
% Race or Ethnicity Unknown: 6%
% International: 14%
% Low-Income: 34%

ACADEMICS
Student-to-Faculty Ratio: 18:1
% of Classes Under 20: 36%
% of Classes Under 40: 69%
% Full-Time Faculty: 67%
% Full-Time Faculty w/ Terminal Degree: 91%

Top Programs
Applied Mathematics
Biomedical Engineering
Chemistry
Computer Science
Physics
Political Science
Psychology

Retention Rate: 90%
4-Year Graduation Rate: 55%
6-Year Graduation Rate: 74%

Curricular Flexibility: Less Flexible
Academic Rating: ★★★

Inside the Classroom

Like many schools within the SUNY system, Stony Brook University has quietly but steadily ascended into a different tier of public universities since the turn of the millennium. In fact, back in 1999 its acceptance rate was 58 percent, and the 25th percentile SAT score for accepted students was 1050; in recent years the acceptance rate has crept as low as the 30 percents, and the 25th percentile SAT score is now 1230. But shedding its "commuter school" status has been difficult, and 80 percent of undergrads still hail from in state, but today Stony Brook also attracts students from 110 countries, which would have been an unthinkable feat when it opened as a teacher's college in 1957. In 2018-19, Stony Brook was the undergraduate home of 17,500 students who could choose from sixty+ majors and eighty+ minors.

There are six undergraduate colleges within the university and some, like the College of Leadership and Service or the College of Global Studies are, perhaps, unexpected menu options. After a two-day compulsory orientation, the journey through the Stony Brook curriculum begins. All told, that will involve checking off double-digits worth of learning objective boxes via courses in the humanities, arts, global affairs, technology, natural science, writing, human behavior, US history, and language. Additional coursework (this can be overlapping) also must fulfill mandates related to interconnectedness, deep understanding, and lifelong learning. In sum, required coursework outside of your major will take a solid three semesters to complete but, on the plus side, there is a great deal of choice within each category for you to pursue elective areas of interest.

An 18:1 student-to-faculty ratio and 8,700 graduate students isn't exactly a recipe for small classes, but undergrads will find themselves in some first-name basis classes with 36 percent of all sections containing nineteen or fewer students. However, there also will be large numbers of face-in-the-crowd experiences because one-quarter of undergraduate sections enroll fifty or more students. That type of environment is not going to spoon feed you with one-on-one faculty mentoring or the chance to participate in undergraduate research, but such experiences are available to those who show determination. In fact, more than 1,500 students have the chance to engage in undergraduate research each year. The rate of study abroad participation is low, but exciting opportunities exist for those who choose to take advantage; the school features a winter program that whisks students to Ecuador and the Galapagos.

A popular and locally well-regarded nursing program leads to the largest number of degrees being conferred in health professions (18 percent). Strong majors in biology (13 percent), engineering (9 percent), and computer sciences (8 percent) also draw a sizable number of Seawolves (the school's mascot). The school's reputation in the hard sciences, particularly math, chemistry, and biomedical engineering, is aided by the affiliated Stony Brook University Hospital. With regard to prestigious postgraduate scholarships, Stony Brook students have really upped their game in recent years. In 2019, a record-tying eleven Stony Brook seniors earned National Science Foundation Graduate Research Fellowships. It also set an institutional record for the most Fulbright applicants (38), and a phenomenal ten seniors captured the coveted award. Between 2013 and 2018, seven students earned Goldwater Scholarships.

Outside the Classroom

No longer the commuter-heavy school it once was, 83 percent of freshmen and 53 percent of the total student population live on campus in one of thirty residence halls or twenty-three apartment-style buildings. Greek life is close-to-invisible but has a faint heartbeat as 2 percent of men and women join fraternities and sororities. There are approximately 550 student-athletes competing as the Seawolves on seven men's and nine women's NCAA Division I teams. The men's basketball team made its first March Madness tournament in 2016. There also are thirty-six club sports teams and intramural options including bowling, beach volleyball, Wiffle ball, and flag football. Over 350 clubs are on tap, including the full array of cultural, dance, charitable, and pre-professional groups. Notably strong organizations include the African Student Union, the College Democrats, and service groups like Camp Kesem and Project Sunshine. For a school without centuries of history under its belt, it does have a number of cool traditions including the annual Roth Pond Regatta where students race themed boats made of cardboard and duct tape across a campus pond. The spacious Long Island campus of 1,039 acres is located midway between Manhattan and Montauk. A train station on campus will take you the sixty miles into New York City. Parks, beaches, and shopping are all within reach, particularly for those with a car (or a friend with a car).

Career Services

The Career Center at Stony Brook University employs thirteen professional staff members who are tasked with career counseling, experiential learning, and employer relations. That translates to a 1,346:1 student-to-counselor ratio, significantly poorer than the average school featured in this guide. Fortunately, that figure does not appear to be preventing the school from reaching the entire undergraduate population. In the 2018-19 school year the center conducted 6,015 one-on-one counseling sessions, and career presentations attracted another 7,000 individuals; additionally, it facilitates 900,000 online transactions each year. It is also one of the only career centers to offer two credited courses on career development, one geared toward freshmen and sophomores and the other toward upperclassmen.

Stony Brook University (SUNY)

E-mail: enroll@stonybrook.edu | Website: www.stonybrook.edu

Stony Brook's staff helps facilitate roughly 1,200 undergraduate internships each year as well as 2,500 practicums and hundreds of clinical placements. Recently, it has adopted the practice of micro-internships, paid five- to forty-hour placements at companies ranging from Fortune 100 mega-corporations to small tech start-ups. Several job fairs take place each semester, including the Information Technology/Computer Science Job & Internship Fair, Engineering Job & Internship Fair, Business Job & Internship Fair, and the Healthcare, Research, & Human Services Job & Internship Fair. By drawing more than 400 regional and national companies to Stony Brook's campus, the Career Services Office provides ample opportunity for assertive students to make connections and land desirable jobs and internships in New York City and beyond. There were 1,224 on-campus interviews conducted at the university last year.

Professional Outcomes

Based on the most recent data available, within two years of graduation, 63 percent of Stony Brook graduates are employed, 31 percent have entered graduate/professional school, and 6 percent are presently looking for their next opportunity. Graduates of the arts and sciences, social welfare, and nursing schools had the lowest reported figures of "still searching" alumni while health tech and management students had the highest. The overall median salary was $48,470 with nursing grads earning the most ($66k), followed by those who studied engineering ($60k) and business ($52k). The organizations and companies employing the greatest number of Seawolves are Northwell Health, JPMorgan Chase, Google, Amazon, Citi, Morgan Stanley, Microsoft, Apple, Bloomberg, and Facebook. Over three-quarters of alumni are settled in the Greater New York City area; sizable pockets also can be found in San Francisco, Boston, DC, and Los Angeles.

Among those pursuing further education, common choices include Stony Brook itself, other SUNY or CUNY institutions, and NYC-based powerhouses like Columbia, Fordham, and NYU. Some recent grads also have left the region to attend some of the finest schools in the world including the London School of Economics, Oxford, Caltech, Stanford, Harvard, Duke, the University of Michigan, and Yale. Traditionally, premed students with a 3.5 GPA and an MCAT in the 67th percentile gain acceptance into medical school at a 59 percent clip. The most commonly attended medical schools include Stony Brook, Downstate, Upstate, NYMC, Albany, Buffalo, Eastern Virginia, GW, Howard, Georgetown, Penn State, and Drexel. Law schools attended by recent grads include Hofstra, Boston University, Villanova, Brooklyn Law School, Wake Forest, and the Cardozo School of Law at Yeshiva University.

Admission

Members of the Class of 2022 were admitted at a 42 percent rate, a touch higher than the 39 percent of five years ago. However, the school's popularity is definitely on the rise; it attracts double the number of applicants it did fifteen years ago. Twenty-one percent of those accepted ultimately enroll, a comparable figure to past years. The caliber of freshmen Stony Brook reels in today is higher than ever. The mid-50 percent standardized test score ranges are 1230-1420 on the SAT and 26-31 on the ACT. SAT math scores were notably strong with 46 percent of this group scoring a 700 or above. Forty-seven percent of entering 2018-19 freshmen earned a spot in the top 10 percent of their high school class; 80 percent placed in the top quartile. The average high school GPA was 3.85, and 64 percent sported at least a 3.75. Under 2 percent of entering students had less than a 3.0 GPA.

There is nothing complicated about how admissions decisions are made at Stony Brook. With such a mass of applicants, the admissions committee primarily relies on the hard facts of standardized test scores and GPA within a rigorous course load with a fair number of honors and AP selections. Recommendations and the application essay also are considered "important" to the evaluation process. The application deadline for everyone is January 15 as there are no early action or early decision options. The school does receive over 7,000 transfer applications each year and admits 45 percent of that group.

Worth Your Money?

At $7,000 in pure tuition, students living with their parents and commuting could conceivably graduate from Stony Brook for less than the cost of one semester at NYU. To top it off, 78 percent of freshmen receive financial aid. On the other hand, out-of-staters pay $25,550 in tuition and, with living and meal costs, a degree would likely cost around $170,000 total. For the 80 percent of current undergraduates hailing from the state of New York, this university is an otherworldly bargain; for international students and Americans outside the state, the value would depend on financial aid and whether the program you would pursue would be likely to yield a solid starting salary.

FINANCIAL
Institutional Type: Public
In-State Tuition: $6,870
Out-of-State Tuition: $24,540
Room & Board: $13,698
Required Fees: $2,755
Books & Supplies: $900

Avg. Need-Based Aid: $10,482
Avg. % of Need Met: 69%

Avg. Merit-Based Aid: $5,726
% Receiving Merit-Based Aid: 22%

Avg. Cumulative Debt: $28,780
% of Students Borrowing: 52%

CAREER
Who Recruits
1. Travelers
2. North Atlantic Industries
3. GEICO
4. Broadbridge
5. Canon

Notable Internships
1. Moody's Analytics
2. Bank of America
3. Northrop Grumman

Top Industries
1. Business
2. Education
3. Healthcare
4. Engineering
5. Operations

Top Employers
1. Northwell Health
2. JPMorgan Chase
3. Google
4. Citi
5. Amazon

Where Alumni Work
1. New York City
2. San Francisco
3. Boston
4. Washington, DC
5. Los Angeles

Median Earnings
College Scorecard (Early Career): $57,600
EOP (Early Career): $60,100
PayScale (Mid-Career): $107,800

RANKINGS
Forbes: 176
Money: 47
U.S. News: 91, National Universities
Wall Street Journal/THE: 105 (T)
Washington Monthly: 100, National Universities

#CollegesWorthYourMoney

Swarthmore College

Swarthmore, Pennsylvania | Admissions Phone: 610-328-8300

ADMISSION
Admission Rate: 9%
Admission Rate - Men: 11%
Admission Rate - Women: 8%
EA Admission Rate: Not Offered
ED Admission Rate: 26%
Admission Rate (5-Year Trend): -5%
ED Admission Rate (5-Year Trend): -7%
% of Admits Attending (Yield): 41%
Transfer Admission Rate: 19%

\# Offered Wait List: N/A
\# Accepted Wait List: N/A
\# Admitted Wait List: 40

SAT Reading/Writing (Middle 50%): 680-760
SAT Math (Middle 50%): 700-790
ACT Composite (Middle 50%): 31-34
Testing Policy: ACT/SAT Required
SAT Superscore: Yes
ACT Superscore: Yes

% Graduated in Top 10% of HS Class: 90%
% Graduated in Top 25% of HS Class: 99%
% Graduated in Top 50% of HS Class: 100%

ENROLLMENT
Total Undergraduate Enrollment: 1,647
% Part-Time: 0%
% Male: 49%
% Female: 51%
% Out-of-State: 88%
% Fraternity: 11%
% Sorority: 3%
% On-Campus (Freshman): 100%
% On-Campus (All Undergraduate): 96%

% African-American: 8%
% Asian: 16%
% Hispanic: 13%
% White: 39%
% Other: 7%
% Race or Ethnicity Unknown: 4%
% International: 13%
% Low-Income: 13%

ACADEMICS
Student-to-Faculty Ratio: 8:1
% of Classes Under 20: 74%
% of Classes Under 40: 95%
% Full-Time Faculty: 88%
% Full-Time Faculty w/ Terminal Degree: 100%

Top Programs
Biology
Computer Science
Economics
Educational Studies
Engineering
Mathematics
Political Science
Sociology

Retention Rate: 97%
4-Year Graduation Rate: 87%
6-Year Graduation Rate: 94%

Curricular Flexibility: Very Flexible
Academic Rating: ★★★★★

Inside the Classroom

The average person in the United States may not be fully aware that Swarthmore College, located on Philadelphia's Main Line, is one of, if not *the* finest liberal arts schools in the entire country. The good news is that top employers and grad schools know Swarthmore's quality well. The 1,647 undergraduate students who attend Swat are an exceptional group, having been among the 8.7 percent to gain acceptance. The college has never been more difficult to get into as applications have tripled since the turn of the millennium. A quick examination of the superb academics offered at this school is all it takes to fully understand the reasons for the long lines outside the gates.

Despite its small size, the college offers forty undergraduate programs and runs 600+ courses each academic year. A member of the Tri-College Consortium with fellow top institutions Haverford and Bryn Mawr, students can cross-register at those institutions as well as at the University of Pennsylvania. Unusual for a school full of perfect-SAT/valedictorian-types, Swat also offers an honors program that involves highly independent, self-directed study that culminates with a series of oral exams. All undergrads must complete at least three courses in all three divisions: Humanities, Natural Science & Engineering, and Social Sciences. Additional requirements include three courses that are designated "writing intensive," physical education, a foreign language, and one laboratory science course.

Small, seminar-style courses are the norm at Swat—an outstanding 34 percent of sections enroll fewer than ten students, and 70 percent contain a maximum of nineteen students. Overall, the average class size is sixteen. Thanks to an 8:1 student-to-faculty ratio and zero grad students, professors are extremely available in and outside the classroom. As a result, two-thirds of graduates complete at least one undergraduate research or independent creative project, and the college sets aside $800,000 in funding for that express purpose. Forty percent of students elect to study abroad for a semester in one of 300 programs in sixty countries.

Social science degrees are the most commonly conferred, accounting for 26 percent of all 2018 graduates. Future academics and researchers would do well to look at Swat—a whopping 22 percent of graduates go on to earn PhDs. Future businessmen/women, engineers, and techies are also well positioned, given Swat's incredibly strong offerings in economics, engineering, and computer science. When it comes to prestigious scholarships, Swarthmore is winning in disproportionately large numbers. In 2018, ten grads/alumni nabbed Fulbright Scholarships, four have been named Rhodes Scholars in the past decade, and undergraduates have won Gaither Fellowships, Watson Fellowships, and Luce Scholarships in recent years.

Outside the Classroom

Swarthmore is a connected and tight-knit campus community where 95 percent of students live in one of eighteen residence halls spread across the college's 425-acre grounds. Greek organizations do exist, but their presence is minor as only 11 percent of men and 3 percent of women are affiliated with a fraternity or sorority. There are twenty-two sports teams competing in the NCAA Division III ranks, and roughly 20 percent of the undergraduate student body are members of one of the varsity teams. There are also plenty of intramural and club sports options, including the uber-popular ultimate Frisbee. More than one hundred campus organizations include a number of volunteer groups that attract 60 percent of the student body. The other Tri-Co member schools, Haverford College and Bryn Mawr, are in close proximity, further expanding the social scene at Swarthmore. The town itself is located on the Main Line, which means there is plenty of dining and culture available, pretty much all of which comes at a high cost. Fortunately, everything the city of Philadelphia has to offer isn't far from campus. There is a regional rail line nearby affording students access to the entire city, and West Philadelphia and University City are only about a forty-minute bike ride.

Career Services

Career Services at Swarthmore College employs eight individuals who specialize in career education, employer relations, and internships and technology. The 204:1 student-to-advisor ratio is better than average when compared to other colleges featured in this guidebook. As a member of the Tri-College Consortium with Haverford and Bryn Mawr as well as the Fall Recruiting Consortium with schools like Brown and William & Mary, Swarthmore students are afforded innumerable opportunities to get face time with the world's leading employers; over eighty companies recruited on campus last year.

One-on-one attention is available for anyone who wishes to take advantage of it. In the 2017-18 school year Swat engaged 62 percent of the total student body, including 70 percent of seniors. The office conducted 817 counseling appointments with 373 unique individuals to address areas such as interview prep (24 percent), job search (22 percent), internship search (18 percent), and general career exploration (16 percent). A solid 70 percent of graduates completed at least one internship as part of the undergraduate experience; 42 percent completed one or more externships. Locations for those experiences included some of the most desirable organizations around including The World Bank, the FDA, and Capital One. Visitors to campus include more than one hundred alumni mentors per year and companies like Google, which spent two full days at Swat in 2018 meeting with computer science students. Offering an enviable level of service to its undergraduates and producing across-the-board positive outcomes, this career services office is held in high esteem by our staff.

Professional Outcomes

Seventy percent of Class of 2018 graduates had already entered the workforce shortly after graduation; 77 percent had secured a job prior to completing their degree. Popular industries included financial services (30 percent), research (23 percent), and technology/engineering (21 percent). Google is one of the leading employers of Swarthmore grads followed by Amazon, Goldman Sachs, IBM, and a number of the leading universities in the nation. In the last five years the cities attracting the highest percentage of Swat alumni were New York City (20 percent), Philadelphia (19 percent), DC (14 percent), Boston (8 percent), and San Francisco (6 percent). The average starting salary for 2018 graduates entering engineering jobs was $94,000. The mean figure for those in finance was $73,000, and grads working in research took home $43,000.

Over four-fifths of the 2018 senior class planned to enroll in graduate school within the next five years, and 21 percent did so directly after graduation. Among those pursuing advanced degrees the most frequently attended institutions were Harvard, Penn, Yale, Princeton, Stanford, MIT, and Cornell—not a shabby top seven. PhDs were pursued by 46 percent of this cohort while 31 percent entered master's programs, 11 percent headed to law school, and 10 percent matriculated into medical school. The medical school acceptance rate for grads and alumni typically hovers close to 85 percent, an astounding number that is roughly double the national average. The school also has an early acceptance program with Thomas Jefferson University's Sidney Kimmel Medical College. Swarthmore also sports a 97 percent acceptance rate into law schools, and the institutions attended are typically of the elite variety.

Admission

There were 11,400 applications submitted for a spot in the Class of 2023, but fewer than 1,000 were accepted for an acceptance rate of only 9 percent. While the school's acceptance rate has decreased in the last decade (it was 16 percent ten years ago), it's unlikely that anyone will mistake Swat for anything less than one of the most selective schools in the country. Ninety percent of 2018-19 freshmen placed in the top decile of their graduating high school class. Mid-50 percent standardized test scores were 1380-1550 on the SAT and 31-34 on the ACT. For perhaps a better perspective, the median SAT score was 1490 and the median ACT score was 33. An exceptional 70 percent of attending Class of 2022 students scored above a 700 on the SAT's reading section and 81 percent scored higher than 700 on the math section.

The admissions committee ranks six factors as being of paramount importance in the admissions process: rigor of secondary coursework, class rank, GPA, application essay, recommendations, and character/personal qualities. Test scores and extracurricular activities land in the second tier, but they are serious about extracurriculars, particularly those involving community service; 36 percent of those accepted into the Class of 2023 were involved with a community, national, or international service organization. In a typical year Swat enjoys a yield rate in excess of 40 percent, meaning that it has no trouble landing a sizable percentage of those offered admission. Legacy candidates make up 10 percent of the admitted Class of 2023 cohort while 27 percent are first generation. If Swarthmore is your top choice, applying early decision is wise; it fills over half of its class through ED, and the acceptance rate is a less cutthroat 26 percent. Swarthmore remains one of, if the not the best liberal arts school in the country and will continue to sport a single-digit acceptance rate well into the future.

Worth Your Money?

Swarthmore has pledged to fully meet 100 percent of student need, which helps explain why the 56 percent of undergrads who are eligible receive a sizable average grant of $53,395. That certainly makes the $73,524 cost of attendance more manageable for lower-income and middle- class families. On the flip side, Swat rarely awards any merit aid whatsoever, so if your parents earn a nice living, you will likely be paying the sticker price. Of course, for a chance to attend one of the best colleges in the world, that is hardly a bad choice.

FINANCIAL
Institutional Type: Private
In-State Tuition: $54,256
Out-of-State Tuition: $54,256
Room & Board: $16,088
Required Fees: $400
Books & Supplies: $1,400

Avg. Need-Based Aid: $53,395
Avg. % of Need Met: 100%

Avg. Merit-Based Aid: $0
% Receiving Merit-Based Aid: 0%

Avg. Cumulative Debt: $22,060
% of Students Borrowing: 24%

CAREER
Who Recruits
1. Foreseter Capital
2. The Brattle Group
3. Apogee Adventures
4. American Enterprise Institute
5. M&T Bank

Notable Internships
1. Salesforce
2. Deutsche Bank
3. Children's Hospital of Philadelphia

Top Industries
1. Education
2. Business
3. Research
4. Media
5. Social Services

Top Employers
1. Google
2. Amazon
3. Goldman Sachs
4. Apple
5. Facebook

Where Alumni Work
1. Philadelphia
2. New York City
3. San Francisco
4. Washington, DC
5. Boston

Median Earnings
College Scorecard (Early Career): $56,700
EOP (Early Career): $56,700
PayScale (Mid-Career): $123,200

RANKINGS
Forbes: 25
Money: 37
U.S. News: 3, Liberal Arts Colleges
Wall Street Journal/THE: 28
Washington Monthly: 15, Liberal Arts Colleges

#CollegesWorthYourMoney

Syracuse University

Syracuse, New York | Admissions Phone: 315-443-3611

Inside the Classroom

A private research university of over 15,000 undergraduates, Syracuse University has a reputation for more than just its instantly recognizable bright orange colors. The 'Cuse plays home to a diverse group of students, nationally-ranked sports teams, a devoted alumni network, and a broad array of academic offerings, including a number of standout programs.

In total, 200+ majors and one hundred+ minors are spread across ten undergraduate schools/colleges: The School of Architecture, the College of Arts & Sciences, the School of Education, the College of Engineering & Computer Science, the Falk College of Sport & Human Dynamics, the School of Information Studies, the Whitman School of Management, the Maxwell School of Citizenship and Public Affairs, the Newhouse School of Public Communication, and the College of Visual and Performing Arts. Required courses vary significantly by school, but some common areas include two writing-intensive courses, two classes in foreign language, and a smattering of social science, math/science, and humanities selections.

Despite a high number of graduate students also studying at SU, class sizes are kept reasonably low; 59 percent contain twenty students or fewer. A student-to-faculty ratio of 15:1 does mean you are likely to receive some instruction from graduate students/adjuncts along the way. The Undergraduate Research Program runs through the College of Arts & Sciences but is open to all SU students. Willing professors extend offers for research apprenticeships to highly motivated students. Recent student-assisted, faculty-led research projects include Community Theater in Kenya, The Internet's Role in the Political Process, and Cloning of Leukemia Cells. Syracuse Abroad, the university's office of study abroad programs, arranges for 45 percent of undergrads to spend a semester in a foreign land. There are more than a hundred programs in sixty+ countries to choose from.

The most popular majors include information technology, psychology, finance, political science, marketing, economics, and radio and television. The School of Architecture, Maxwell School of Citizenship and Public Affairs, and Newhouse are all revered names that carry a good deal of weight in their respective fields. Newhouse, in particular, is dominant in the worlds of broadcasting and television/radio/film. Students of all academic backgrounds are competitive in procuring prestigious postgraduate fellowships, albeit at a modest clip. In 2018, Orange graduates accepted at least one Fulbright, Beinecke, SMART, Luce, Mitchell, and Astronaut Scholarship; eight students took home Fulbrights in 2019.

Outside the Classroom

Frigid temperatures and snowy conditions make for long, boring winters in Upstate New York. Thus, like many other institutions in the region, Syracuse receives the designation as a top (if not *the* top) "party school" on a fair number of lists. The sixty fraternities and sororities are at the heart of the lively social scene. Roughly one-third join a Greek organization. SU offers a big-time sports program with a rabid following. Many join the sea of orange in the Carrier Dome for football and basketball games; in total, there are seven men's and eleven women's NCAA Division I teams. Non-sports activities come in the form of 300+ student-run clubs, including a wide selection of performing arts troupes (there are seven a cappella organizations), pre-professional meet-ups, or the *Daily Orange* newspaper, which is one of the more widely read campus dailies in the country and a frequent award-winner. On campus, Marshall Street is home to a number of beloved eateries and bars and is rarely quiet. Likewise, the Quad is always abuzz with activity, especially when the weather is decent. The city of Syracuse may not be the most cosmopolitan locale, but it does feature Destiny USA, the nation's sixth largest shopping/entertainment complex, and it's only a short ride from campus.

Career Services

For a school of over 15,000 undergraduates, SU's Career Services Office employs a central staff of eight career counseling professionals as well as smaller branch offices housed within the various colleges. Collectively, there are thirty-three full-time staff members working in career services, which equates to a 462:1 student-to-advisor ratio, higher than the average school featured in this guidebook but not all that concerning given the size of the university.

Flagship events include a Local Internship Fair, Fall Career Fair, and Spring Career Fair. Niche events are held year-round by the various colleges to cater to students in particular fields of study. Students can, at any time, utilize OrangeLink to view 6,000+ job and internship postings and keep abreast of on-campus recruiting/interviewing opportunities. Internship procurement varies greatly by school. The Whitman School of Management requires an internship for graduation, and three-quarters of them are paid positions. Many other undergrads must rely on the university's fervent alumni network comprised of about a quarter million people worldwide to land a position. Within Newhouse, companies recruiting on campus include CBS News, Hearst Television, McCann, Instagram, and NBCUniversal. The school does not publish the total number of one-on-one counseling sessions held or the number of on-campus interviews facilitated by career services.

Professional Outcomes

Six months after exiting the Carrier Dome for the final time, 65 percent of Orangemen and women have found employment (90 percent related to their career goals), 15 percent are continuing to graduate school, and 10 percent are either seeking employment or working part time. The companies employing the most 'Cuse grads include major media/entertainment management companies like Conde Nast, Bloomberg, and Creative Artists Agency as well as big-name corporations like GE, KPMG, EY, Lockheed Martin, and Morgan Stanley. The average starting salary for SU undergraduates across all majors is $51k. Interestingly, due to the nature of the business for which it prepares its students, Newhouse grads earn a mean starting salary of only $40k. Those who studied at the Whitman School of Management, College of Engineering & Computer Science, or School of Information Studies averaged between $59k and $66k. Over 70 percent of graduates tend to remain in the Northeast with the West Coast coming in a distant second, attracting 11 percent of grads.

A fair number of those headed to graduate school remain in New York state. NYU, Hofstra, Fordham, and the University of Buffalo are among the most popular destinations to pursue an advanced degree. Elite universities such as Yale, Johns Hopkins, Columbia, and Northwestern also make the list of most popular graduate schools attended. Examining the past several years of law school admissions data, it is fair to say that Syracuse does not send a high number of graduates to elite law schools. The university does not publish medical school acceptance data, but a review of recent acceptances indicates a strong relationship with nearby SUNY Upstate Medical School. In that time the school also has produced some acceptances into the nation's top medical institutions.

Admission

Most colleges with national name recognition on par with the 'Cuse have experienced an uptick in selectivity since the turn of the millennium. The fact that Syracuse's numbers have held steady for a couple of decades makes it a refreshing oddity. A touch over 50 percent of applicants are granted acceptance, and the academic profile of the average attendee is strong but not overly intimidating. Standardized test scores do not have to be exceptional to gain acceptance into SU. The middle-50 percent range for accepted students is 1180-1370. Last year's freshman class was comprised of 39 percent of students who finished in the top 10 percent of their high school class; 71 percent were in the top 25 percent, and 6 percent failed to crack the top 50 percent. The average GPA for all 2018-19 freshman was 3.67; 17 percent possessed less than a 3.25.

The Newhouse School of Public Communication is more selective than the university at large. The typical student admitted to Newhouse scored over 1300 on the SAT and earned a 3.8 GPA in high school. Whichever school you are applying to, early decision can work to your benefit as ED applicants got in 58 percent of the time in the most recent cycle. However, if you plan on applying ED, make sure you can afford it. While ED applicants get full consideration for financial aid, SU is on the expensive side, so having a chance to compare aid offers can be advantageous. Perfection is not expected by the SU Office of Admissions. It is a selective university that has room for those with B averages and/or non-eye-popping standardized test scores.

Worth Your Money?

With a list-price of $72,371 (annual COA), Syracuse University is not accessible to those on a budget without financial help. Forty-six percent do receive need-based with average annual grants of around $31k. The university does offer merit aid, but generally grants it to only 20 percent of the population, and those awards don't tend to be for massive sums that significantly alter the total cost of attendance. Syracuse is worth spending up for if you have the opportunity to enter a top-flight program like Newhouse, and it's a solid choice if your parents are able to pay the full bill. Those on a budget who do not receive a generous aid package may find a better value elsewhere.

FINANCIAL
Institutional Type: Private
In-State Tuition: $53,849
Out-of-State Tuition: $53,849
Room & Board: $15,910
Required Fees: $1,639
Books & Supplies: $1,536

Avg. Need-Based Aid: $42,060
Avg. % of Need Met: 94%

Avg. Merit-Based Aid: $9,830
% Receiving Merit-Based Aid: 27%

Avg. Cumulative Debt: $37,707
% of Students Borrowing: 59%

CAREER
Who Recruits
1. SmartestEnergy
2. M&T Bank
3. Oppenheimer & Co.
4. City Year
5. General Electric

Notable Internships
1. Gensler
2. WeWork
3. Berksire Hathaway

Top Industries
1. Business
2. Education
3. Operations
4. Arts & Design
5. Media

Top Employers
1. IBM
2. EY
3. Microsoft
4. JPMorgan Chase
5. Amazon

Where Alumni Work
1. New York City
2. Syracuse, NY
3. Boston
4. Washington, DC
5. Los Angeles

Median Earnings
College Scorecard (Early Career): $62,100
EOP (Early Career): $61,100
PayScale (Mid-Career): $104,800

RANKINGS
Forbes: 156
Money: 208
U.S. News: 54, National Universities
Wall Street Journal/THE: 123 (T)
Washington Monthly: 33, National Universities

#CollegesWorthYourMoney

Texas A&M University – College Station

College Station, Texas | Admissions Phone: 979-845-1060

ADMISSION
Admission Rate: 67%
Admission Rate - Men: 69%
Admission Rate - Women: 66%
EA Admission Rate: Not Offered
ED Admission Rate: Not Offered
Admission Rate (5-Year Trend): -2%
ED Admission Rate (5-Year Trend): Not Offered
% of Admits Attending (Yield): 45%
Transfer Admission Rate: 54%

Offered Wait List: Not Offered
Accepted Wait List: Not Offered
Admitted Wait List: Not Offered

SAT Reading/Writing (Middle 50%): 580-680
SAT Math (Middle 50%): 590-700
ACT Composite (Middle 50%): 25-31
Testing Policy: ACT/SAT Required
SAT Superscore: No
ACT Superscore: No

% Graduated in Top 10% of HS Class: 63%
% Graduated in Top 25% of HS Class: 92%
% Graduated in Top 50% of HS Class: 99%

ENROLLMENT
Total Undergraduate Enrollment: 53,743
% Part-Time: 12%
% Male: 53%
% Female: 47%
% Out-of-State: 4%
% Fraternity: 8%
% Sorority: 17%
% On-Campus (Freshman): 67%
% On-Campus (All Undergraduate): 22%

% African-American: 3%
% Asian: 8%
% Hispanic: 24%
% White: 60%
% Other: 3%
% Race or Ethnicity Unknown: 0%
% International: 1%
% Low-Income: 31%

ACADEMICS
Student-to-Faculty Ratio: 20:1
% of Classes Under 20: 21%
% of Classes Under 40: 64%
% Full-Time Faculty: 86%
% Full-Time Faculty w/ Terminal Degree: 86%

Top Programs
Agriculture
Architecture
Business
Communication
Engineering
Kinesiology
Political Science

Retention Rate: 92%
4-Year Graduation Rate: 55%
6-Year Graduation Rate: 82%

Curricular Flexibility: Less Flexible
Academic Rating: ★★★

Inside the Classroom

You've heard it a million times: "Everything's bigger in Texas." Perhaps the origin of that saying stems from the fact that the state is three times the size of the United Kingdom, or perhaps it was first uttered by a visitor to Texas A&M College Station's gargantuan 5,200-acre campus that is home to 54,000+ undergraduates and another 15,000 graduate and professional degree- seekers, making it one of the largest higher education operations in the United States. With nineteen schools and colleges, 130+ undergraduate degree programs, and an emphasis on agriculture, engineering, and business, this public land-grant university educates an army of future professionals who carry their Aggie pride with them for life.

The Texas Core Curriculum dictates a good amount of the coursework underclassmen must knock out, amounting to forty-two credit hours. Mandates include three classes in life and physical sciences, two classes in each of communication, mathematics, American history, government and political science, and one class in each of language philosophy and culture, creative arts, and the social and behavioral sciences. Collectively, these courses are meant to promote six key skill areas: critical thinking, communication, empirical and quantitative, teamwork, personal responsibility, and social responsibility. Students in the university Honors College are typically required to complete a senior thesis within their departmental home.

Class sizes definitely trend large, not terribly shocking considering the 20:1 student-to-faculty ratio and a graduate school population larger than many entire universities. Only 21 percent of courses enroll fewer than twenty students at A&M, and 36 percent enroll more than forty students. In order to forge personal connections with professors, the LAUNCH program encourages students to apply to participate in undergraduate research during the school year or the summer under the mentorship of a faculty member. Some majors—chemistry, for one— require all students to complete undergraduate research as part of their bachelor's program. A&M excels in facilitating study abroad experiences, sending 5,330 students to 105 countries last year, the most of any public university in the United States.

As the name of the university implies, agriculture and engineering are at the core of what A&M does. Over 19,000 students are presently enrolled in the College of Engineering and 7,700 in the College of Agriculture and Life Sciences. Yet, the College of Liberal Arts (8,500), College of Education and Human Development (6,800), and the Mays Business School (6,300) are sizable presences on campus as well. The business, agriculture, and engineering programs all place well in national rankings and garner deep respect from major national corporations and graduate/professional schools. Considering its size, A&M does not produce a large number of prestigious postgraduate scholarship winners. In 2019, it produced twelve National Science Foundation Graduate Research Fellows, seven Gilman Scholars, and two Critical Language Scholars.

Outside the Classroom

While two-thirds of freshmen live on campus, just about everyone else moves into off-campus housing by sophomore year. Housing is not guaranteed to freshmen and is awarded on a first-come, first-served basis. Fortunately, nice and affordable housing in the area is ample, and the school's database, AggieSearch, helps you locate available living spaces. There are sixty+ Greek organizations on campus with women joining sororities at a higher rate (17 percent) than men join fraternities (8 percent). Athletics are huge with 650 varsity athletes competing in twenty NCAA Division I sports, and the "Twelfth Man," the fan base, is extraordinarily passionate about its teams. For non-superstar athletes, there are thirty-four club sports squads and over 12,000 students participate in intramural sports each year, making it one of the largest programs in the country. The Student Recreation Center contains 400,000 square feet of space for fun and fitness and boasts everything from an archery room to multiple pools. Texas A&M has 1,100 student organizations, making it impossible not to find your niche. An incredible 2,600 undergrads are involved in ROTC, and the Cadet Corps is the largest such group in the country. As the name implies, College Station is a happening college town, brimming with locally famous bars and eateries, particularly within the historic Northgate District. Situated in the so-called Texas Triangle in the central part of the state, major cities like Houston or Austin can be accessed easily by car for a weekend road trip.

Career Services

The Texas A&M Career Center was established in 1939, long before the term "career services" was even a concept at most schools. Including all college-specific career advisors, employer relations, and professional school advising staff members, there are twenty-seven full-time professional staff members (not including office managers and admin assistants). That works out to a student-to-advisor ratio of 2,213:1, easily the highest in this guidebook. Irrespective of that bloated ratio, the A&M career services staff does remarkable things for the second largest undergraduate student body in the United States, and it publishes the numbers to prove it.

In the 2017-18 school year, the A&M Career Center made direct contact with 19,000 students, drew 30,000 individuals to 130 outreach events, and 37,000 to 760 workshops and other career services programs. It posted 60,000 jobs and 13,000 internship opportunities on its online database and, more importantly, it enticed a stupefying 4,000 employers to actively recruit Aggie undergrads. In total, 57 percent of students had an internship, co-op, or study abroad experience while at College Station, and interns worked with 1,000 different companies. Operating on an almost unimaginable scope, Texas A&M's Career Center gets the job done.

Professional Outcomes

On graduation day 2018, a solid 55 percent of soon-to-be degree-holders had already received at least one job offer, 24 percent were heading to graduate/professional school, and 23 percent were still searching for their next career step. Texas A&M supplies a number of major oil, tech, and consulting firms with a hard-to-fathom numbers of employees. More than 500 Aggies presently work for companies such as ExxonMobil, Halliburton, Chevron, EY, Amazon, Microsoft, Intel, Accenture, and PWC. More than 300 alumni work for Apple, Oracle, and Google. Fifty-five engineering students from the Class of 2019 alone were hired by Lockheed Martin. Starting salaries were strong with the average College of Engineering graduate making $70,500, and the average College of Liberal Arts and College of Agriculture & Life Sciences graduate netting $49,500. The vast majority of graduates remain in Texas with Houston, Dallas, College Station, Austin, and San Antonio tops in popularity. However, cities like San Fran, DC, New York, and Denver also have a notable Aggies representation.

Medical and dental school acceptance rates are far above the Texas state average. In 2018, Aggies were admitted to medical school at a 52 percent clip (state average was 28 percent) and to dental school 56 percent of the time (state average was 31 percent). Among those applicants with a 3.5 or higher GPA and a 505+ MCAT score, 91 percent were accepted to medical school. Institutions where 2018 graduates gained acceptance included Columbia, Cornell, Wake Forest, Yale, Vanderbilt, and Northwestern. Given the engineering focus at A&M, it may surprise you that the school is the eighth largest producer of law students in the entire country. The Class of 2018 collectively applied to 173 law schools and earned admission at 146 of them.

Admission

Texas A&M admitted a favorable two-thirds of those who applied for the 2018-19 freshman class. That group had a mid-50 percent SAT range of 1170-1380 and a 25-31 on the ACT. Texas A&M offers automatic admission for anyone in the top 10 percent of their high school class (public or private), and a hefty number of Class of 2022 members met that standard—63 percent. Overall, 92 percent finished at least in the top 25 percent. Five years ago, the acceptance rate was a similar 69 percent, but the average applicant had lower standardized test scores and only 78 percent of students placed in the top quartile. Simply put, you'll need better academic credentials to get into A&M today than you would have in the recent past. This is especially so for engineering and business applicants who face the toughest admission odds and who will likely need to possess grades and standardized test scores at or above the 75th percentile.

The admissions office is looking primarily at class rank, standardized test scores, rigor of courses, GPA, extracurricular activities, and talent/ability. It also looks closely at geographical residence, which translates to 94 percent of undergrads presently on the College Station campus hailing from the Lone Star State. With such a large applicant pool, there are no interviews offered. There is no early action or early decision offered either; the deadline is December 1 for every applicant. Applicants who are not admitted automatically through placing in the top 10 percent of their class have a much lower success rate of 35 percent.

Worth Your Money?

Tuition for in-state students is under $11,000, and the total cost of attendance is less than $30k. Combine those extremely fair rates with favorable return on investment figures, and A&M is clearly one of the great values in higher education. A nonresident will pay twice as much, but if you lack better in-state options close to home, a business or engineering degree from this institution will still pay for itself.

FINANCIAL
Institutional Type: Public
In-State Tuition: $7,406
Out-of-State Tuition: $33,074
Room & Board: $10,436
Required Fees: $3,562
Books & Supplies: $1,222

Avg. Need-Based Aid: $12,193
Avg. % of Need Met: 74%

Avg. Merit-Based Aid: $4,667
% Receiving Merit-Based Aid: 18%

Avg. Cumulative Debt: $24,175
% of Students Borrowing: 41%

CAREER
Who Recruits
1. Air Liquide
2. NBCUniversal
3. Ethos Group
4. Manhattan Associates
5. Nvidia

Notable Internships
1. Phillips 66
2. Novartis
3. CBRE

Top Industries
1. Business
2. Operations
3. Engineering
4. Education
5. Sales

Top Employers
1. Haliburton
2. Deloitte
3. EY
4. Amazon
5. Intel

Where Alumni Work
1. Houston
2. Dallas
3. College Station, TX
4. Austin
5. San Antonio

Median Earnings
College Scorecard (Early Career): $58,000
EOP (Early Career): $59,400
PayScale (Mid-Career): $115,700

RANKINGS
Forbes: 103
Money: 18
U.S. News: 70 (T), National Universities
Wall Street Journal/THE: 78
Washington Monthly: 10, National Universities

#CollegesWorthYourMoney

Hartford, Connecticut | Admissions Phone: 860-297-2180

ADMISSION
Admission Rate: 34%
Admission Rate - Men: 31%
Admission Rate - Women: 36%
EA Admission Rate: Not Offered
ED Admission Rate: 58%
Admission Rate (5-Year Trend): +2%
ED Admission Rate (5-Year Trend): -5%
% of Admits Attending (Yield): 28%
Transfer Admission Rate: 26%

Offered Wait List: 1,827
Accepted Wait List: 1,103
Admitted Wait List: 11

SAT Reading/Writing (Middle 50%): 630-710
SAT Math (Middle 50%): 670-750
ACT Composite (Middle 50%): 29-32
Testing Policy: Test Optional
SAT Superscore: Yes
ACT Superscore: Yes

% Graduated in Top 10% of HS Class: 46%
% Graduated in Top 25% of HS Class: 76%
% Graduated in Top 50% of HS Class: 95%

ENROLLMENT
Total Undergraduate Enrollment: 2,182
% Part-Time: 3%
% Male: 50%
% Female: 50%
% Out-of-State: 82%
% Fraternity: 29%
% Sorority: 17%
% On-Campus (Freshman): 100%
% On-Campus (All Undergraduate): 86%

% African-American: 6%
% Asian: 4%
% Hispanic: 9%
% White: 63%
% Other: 3%
% Race or Ethnicity Unknown: 3%
% International: 13%
% Low-Income: 10%

ACADEMICS
Student-to-Faculty Ratio: 9:1
% of Classes Under 20: 72%
% of Classes Under 40: 97%
% Full-Time Faculty: 74%
% Full-Time Faculty w/ Terminal Degree: 95%

Top Programs
Anthropology
Economics
Engineering
History
International Studies
Public Policy and Law
Urban Studies

Retention Rate: 91%
4-Year Graduation Rate: 78%
6-Year Graduation Rate: 84%

Curricular Flexibility: Very Flexible
Academic Rating: ★★★✔

Inside the Classroom
Established as Washington College in 1823 before being renamed in 1845, Trinity College was founded as an Episcopalian alternative to Congregationalist Yale; it is the second oldest college in the state of Connecticut. What began as a college of nine male students is today a 100-acre campus within the confines of downtown Hartford that features 2,200 full-time undergraduates, forty-one majors, and more than 900 distinct courses. Famous alumni are a disparate lot that includes both conservative voices like George Will and Tucker Carlson as well as the legendary absurdist playwright Edward Albee of *Who's Afraid of Virginia Woolf* fame.

Freshmen learn the ropes of academic reading and writing in either a first-year seminar or via the invitation-only Gateway Program. An additional course bearing the "writing intensive" designation must be completed at some point during one's undergraduate program. All students are required to demonstrate competency as writers, quantitative thinkers, and in one foreign language. Lastly, all students must either complete a course with a global focus or participate in a study abroad program. Passing one course with a C- or better in each of the arts, humanities, natural sciences, numerical and symbolic reasoning, and the social sciences are the only other requirements in what amounts to a very open curriculum.

With a total graduate student population that doesn't even hit triple digits, the bulk of the resources are directed toward Bantam undergraduates. Thus, a student/faculty ratio of 9:1 translates to 72 percent of course sections boasting an enrollment of nineteen or fewer students, and one-quarter of sections having fewer than ten; the mean number of students in a class is seventeen. Working closely with faculty is a real possibility at this school where one hundred students conduct research each year alongside faculty through the Summer Research Program, and roughly two-thirds engage in some type of undergraduate research. Greater than 60 percent of Trinity students study abroad and have access to Trinity-exclusive programs in Shanghai and Cape Town and school-run programs in Paris, Barcelona, Rome, Vienna, and Trinidad.

Trinity College is well regarded across the board with an economics department that feeds many leading investment banks and an engineering program that is among the best you will find at a small liberal arts school. Most degrees are conferred in the social sciences, biology, and psychology. While only a small percentage of graduates pursue prestigious national fellowships, a few do typically take home Fulbrights and an occasional Watson Scholarship each year, but the school has only two Rhodes Scholars in its history.

Outside the Classroom
Over 90 percent of Trinity undergraduates reside on campus, and 100 percent of freshmen are housed in one of seven first-year exclusive dorms. Greek life is more popular among men (29 percent join a fraternity) than women (17 percent join a sorority). Competing in the New England Small College Athletic Conference within NCAA Division III, the Bantams field twenty-eight varsity teams evenly split between men's and women's squads. Including club sports, over 40 percent of the student body participates in intercollegiate athletics. While sports and frats dominate the social scene, the Students Activities, Involvement, and Leadership Office (SAIL) oversees 150+ student-run clubs and organizations. While the school touts the "real-world" aspect of being located in downtown Hartford, the city presently has one of the highest per-capita crime rates in the United States. Affluent students, of whom there are many at Trinity, often prefer roads trips to Montreal, New York City, or Boston over their "home" city. However, the spirit of volunteerism is strong, and the Office of Community Service and Civic Engagement offers endless opportunities to work in areas such as hunger, housing, the homeless, and education.

Career Services
The Center for Student Success and Career Development features six full-time staff members who specialize in areas such as strategic partnerships, pre-law advising, and pre-health career advising. That equates to a student-to-advisor ratio of 370:1, in the average range when compared against other liberal arts colleges featured in this guide. The college is one of a dozen schools in the country that uses Stanford University's Designing Your Life approach that encourages undergraduates to shed rigid views and fears about career and, instead, use their passions, goals, and creative problem-solving skills to move toward a meaningful path. To pursue that aim, Trinity invites students to join one of six Career Communities designed for those who wish to take advantage of industry-specific career advice, internship opportunities, Career Treks, panel discussions, and Career Skills Labs.

Other perks include a Career Studio where students can stop by any time for help with tangible job search products like resumes, cover letters, or creating a LinkedIn profile. In addition, the Bantam Career Network functions like a private LinkedIn where current students can network with alumni in their fields of interest. The college does not host any large-scale career fairs, but the Career Connections Summit on parents' weekend affords undergraduates the chance to network with representatives from top corporations. Trinity has invested heavily in its career development in the last decade, and that financial commitment is starting to bear fruit. This forward-thinking center is innovating every year, and its efforts are reflected in career/graduate school outcomes, earning it top marks from our staff.

Professional Outcomes

Surveyed members of the Class of 2018 had found a positive outcome at a 95.2 percent clip. Those entering the world of employment landed jobs at desirable organizations like the New York City Ballet, NBC Universal, and Morgan Stanley, a company with a hefty share of alumni. A large Bantam presence also can be felt in the corporate offices of Citi, Merrill Lynch, Fidelity Investments, Google, IBM, and Goldman Sachs. Finance (17 percent), communications and media (16 percent), education (12 percent), science and health care (12 percent), and management (11 percent) are the most frequently entered fields. Starting and midcareer salaries tend to be on the higher side, ranking in the top ten among highly selective private colleges alongside many engineering-heavy schools. While a fair number of graduates remain in the Hartford area, New York City and Boston occupy the one and two slots for highest alumni concentrations.

Many Trinity grads go on to prestigious graduate schools; 60 percent of alumni have entered or completed a graduate or professional program within five years. Class of 2018 members matriculated into the likes of Yale Medical School, Cambridge University, and Columbia University. Medical or other health-related program applicants are successful 80 percent of the time and are presently enrolled at institutions such as Georgetown, Tufts, Penn, Cornell, and Boston University. Graduates eying law school earn an average LSAT of 160 (80th percentile) and enroll at a vast array of universities including Top Fourteen law schools like Duke, Cornell, Columbia, Stanford, and Northwestern.

Admission

The Class of 2023 saw 33 percent of applicants admitted, an acceptance rate identical to that of the previous three cycles. In Trinity's fourth year as a test-optional school, 58 percent of those who ultimately enrolled took advantage of the policy, not submitting an SAT or ACT score. Middle-50 percent scores of those who did submit standardized test results were 1300-1460 on the SAT and 29-32 on the ACT. Transcripts have to be strong but not immaculate as 46 percent of attendees placed in the top decile of their high school class while 76 percent were in the top quartile.

Rigor of secondary school record, GPA, and character/personal qualities constitute the triumvirate of most important factors. The committee genuinely values intangible qualities that research has shown leads to post-secondary success such as "grit, optimism, persistence, a willingness to take risks, and an ability to overcome adversity." A supplemental essay explaining why applicants wish to attend college in an urban setting also is recommended. The college fills almost half its freshman class via two early decision rounds. The 2023 cohort was comprised of 285 ED students, which included 152 varsity athletes. ED admit rates reached 58 percent in 2018-19 cycle, and those admitted via that round comprised 52 percent of the incoming class. Trinity is a more desirable destination than ever. In 2015, only 22 percent of accepted students elected to attend, but that figure has jumped to 30 percent in recent years. Applying ED or ED II is undoubtedly a wise strategic move.

Worth Your Money?

At $76,450 in annual costs, Trinity won't come cheap. It does not offer much in the way of merit aid, instead focusing its efforts on meeting all of the demonstrated need of students eligible for financial aid. In fact, the 54 percent of current undergraduates who are need-eligible receive annual grants of over $48k per year, bringing Trinity's tuition much more within reach. As a school that helps you develop professional networks and connects you to big-time employers, Trinity can be worth taking on a reasonable amount of debt in order to attend.

FINANCIAL
Institutional Type: Private
In-State Tuition: $56,380
Out-of-State Tuition: $56,380
Room & Board: $15,300
Required Fees: $2,670
Books & Supplies: $1,000

Avg. Need-Based Aid: $48,334
Avg. % of Need Met: 100%

Avg. Merit-Based Aid: $58,374
% Receiving Merit-Based Aid: 3%

Avg. Cumulative Debt: $30,893
% of Students Borrowing: 44%

CAREER
Who Recruits
1. Salesforce
2. CBRE
3. UBS
4. Accenture
5. Fidelity Investments

Notable Internships
1. WeWork
2. Wayfair
3. Boston Public Health Commission

Top Industries
1. Business
2. Education
3. Operations
4. Finance
5. Sales

Top Employers
1. Morgan Stanley
2. Google
3. Citi
4. IBM
5. Merrill Lynch

Where Alumni Work
1. New York City
2. Boston
3. Hartford
4. Washington, DC
5. San Francisco

Median Earnings
College Scorecard (Early Career): $66,100
EOP (Early Career): $67,300
PayScale (Mid-Career): $110,900

RANKINGS
Forbes: 109
Money: 163
U.S. News: 46, Liberal Arts Colleges
Wall Street Journal/THE: 89 (T)
Washington Monthly: 23, Liberal Arts Colleges

#CollegesWorthYourMoney

ADMISSION
Admission Rate: 34%
Admission Rate - Men: 35%
Admission Rate - Women: 33%
EA Admission Rate: 65%
ED Admission Rate: 79%
Admission Rate (5-Year Trend): -30%
ED Admission Rate (5-Year Trend): +22%
% of Admits Attending (Yield): 23%
Transfer Admission Rate: 30%

Offered Wait List: 876
Accepted Wait List: 455
Admitted Wait List: 7

SAT Reading/Writing (Middle 50%): 630-710
SAT Math (Middle 50%): 630-720
ACT Composite (Middle 50%): 28-32
Testing Policy: ACT/SAT Required
SAT Superscore: Yes
ACT Superscore: Yes

% Graduated in Top 10% of HS Class: 42%
% Graduated in Top 25% of HS Class: 76%
% Graduated in Top 50% of HS Class: 96%

ENROLLMENT
Total Undergraduate Enrollment: 2,477
% Part-Time: 2%
% Male: 47%
% Female: 53%
% Out-of-State: 24%
% Fraternity: 8%
% Sorority: 15%
% On-Campus (Freshman): 100%
% On-Campus (All Undergraduate): 82%

% African-American: 4%
% Asian: 7%
% Hispanic: 21%
% White: 57%
% Other: 4%
% Race or Ethnicity Unknown: 2%
% International: 5%
% Low-Income: 18%

ACADEMICS
Student-to-Faculty Ratio: 9:1
% of Classes Under 20: 62%
% of Classes Under 40: 97%
% Full-Time Faculty: 75%
% Full-Time Faculty w/ Terminal Degree: 95%

Top Programs
Accounting
Biology
Engineering Science
English
History
Mathematical Finance
Neuroscience

Retention Rate: 91%
4-Year Graduation Rate: 65%
6-Year Graduation Rate: 76%

Curricular Flexibility: Less Flexible
Academic Rating: ★★★⭒

Inside the Classroom

It is rare to see a jump in selectivity on the scale of San Antonio's top school, Trinity University, which has sliced its acceptance rate in half in only a few years. The school's meteoric rise has occurred contemporaneously with its 150th anniversary, and while the school continues to be majority Texan—two-thirds of enrollees are residents—applications from out-of-staters have risen in recent years. An increasingly gifted undergraduate student body approaching 2,500 enjoys the choice of forty-seven majors and a carefully crafted liberal arts core curriculum that is more demanding than the norm.

The distinct Pathways Program guides the educational journey at Trinity and is defined by six curricular requirements that involve an overwhelming number of manufactured terminologies. First-year experience courses, capped at sixteen students, introduce freshmen to the rigors of university-level reading and writing. In order to fulfill the Approaches to Creation and Analysis pathway, students must complete one course in the humanities, the arts and creative disciplines, social and behavioral sciences, natural sciences, and quantitative disciplines. Undergrads must also check off each of the Core Capacities: (1) written, oral, and visual communication; (2) digital literacy; and (3) engaged citizenship. All must also tackle "the Interdisciplinary Clusters," three-course groupings with themes such as ecological civilization in Asia or constructing and deconstructing language. One physical education course and one academic major round out the complex labyrinth of mandated coursework at Trinity U.

Undergraduates are the primary beneficiaries of a 9:1 student-to-faculty ratio as the university only enrolls around 140 graduate students. You won't encounter any adjuncts or teaching assistants at Trinity, and 97 percent of the 250 full-time faculty members hold terminal degrees in their fields. Sixty-three percent of courses enroll fewer than twenty students, one-quarter of sections enroll between twenty and twenty-nine, and few contain more than that. Over the summer, close to 140 students participate in intensive undergraduate research projects with faculty members. Overall, 80 percent of students engage in some type of hands-on learning, whether through research or an internship. Study abroad programs are taken advantage of by 35 percent of graduates, most of whom participate in affiliated but not Trinity-run offerings.

Trinity's well regarded School of Business attracts the greatest percentage of students as finance, accounting, and business administration degrees account for 23 percent of the total degrees conferred. Communication, biology, foreign language, and computer science also have strong representation. The university's reputation within the state of Texas is strong, and many graduates further their education or begin their careers locally, but the national prestige of the school is growing by the year. That can be seen in the procurement of highly competitive national fellowships. There were two Goldwater Scholars selected from the Class of 2018, and there were four Fulbright Scholars in the Class of 2017.

Outside the Classroom

With undergraduates required to live on campus for their first three years and 74 percent of all undergraduates residing on the 117-acre grounds, the formation of a tight-knit college community is almost unavoidable. Greek life is also alive and well with 16 percent of men pledged to fraternities and 18 percent of women members of sororities; there are sixteen total Greek organizations on campus. Nine men's and nine women's athletic teams compete at the Division III level, and they do so with intensity; they've captured four championships in recent years. The intramural programs scoop up pretty much everyone not playing a varsity sport with roughly three-fifths of the student body participating in intramural athletics. There are also ninety-seven student-run organizations, including groups devoted to animal welfare, fantasy sports and analytics, and indigenous peoples. The spirit of service is strong as 1,600 students contribute 120,000+ volunteer hours annually. Trinity's campus is only three miles from downtown San Antonio, opening possibilities for all sorts of big-city fun, but having a car is useful. Austin is a popular weekend getaway that is roughly an hour-and-a-half drive from the university.

Career Services

The newly-created Center for Experiential Learning and Career Success (CELCS) is staffed by nine full-time employees (not including administrative assistants) who specialize in areas such as career counseling, experiential learning coordination, and employer relations. That equates to a student-to-advisor ratio of 270:1, better than average when compared against other schools in this guidebook. Fall and spring career fairs were attended by fifty-one employers in the 2018-19 academic year, including top companies like KPMG, Booz Allen Hamilton, Valero Energy, and EY. It also regularly hosts smaller-scale events such as Lunch 'n Learns, employer information sessions, and workshops on topics such as networking, interviewing, and professional dining etiquette.

The school switched to the Handshake platform in 2018 and presently has opportunities from 3,600 employers posted in its database. As of the 2018-19 school year, 65 percent of Trinity students participated in at least one internship during their undergraduate education. Close to 200 on-campus interviews are conducted by employers each year. There are 29,000 actively engaged Tiger alumni, and they are more than happy to provide career advice, arrange a job-shadowing experience, or offer mentorship to current students. The office also facilitates a solid number of one-on-one counseling sessions; it held 1,058 such appointments last year. The nascent CELCS is on the rise and is quickly becoming the type of career services center that the university leadership outlined in its most recent strategic plan.

Professional Outcomes

Six months after receiving their diplomas, 45 percent of Trinity grads are employed full time, and 26 percent have matriculated into graduate school; a shade under 10 percent are still seeking employment. The companies employing the largest number of alumni include USAA (a San Antonio based financial firm), PwC, EY, Deloitte, Dell, Accenture, Morgan Stanley, and Amazon. Most Trinity grads stay in the Lone Star State with San Antonio, Houston, Dallas, and Austin being the four most common landing spots. Median salaries at midcareer are solid, ranking third in the state behind Rice and Texas A&M and just in front of UT Austin. Starting salaries are estimated at $51k while median midcareer salaries are estimated at $105,000.

Those graduating in spring 2018 were accepted into graduate school at an overall rate of 76 percent. In the last five years, acceptance rates into medical school have consistently been above national averages, hovering between 55 percent and 75 percent. Graduates have gone on to Dell Medical School (University of Texas), Harvard Medical School, and Tufts Medical School, among other less prestigious institutions. Law school rates have been within the 75-90 percent range in recent years. Among the most popular law schools attended by recent graduates are the University of Texas, Texas Tech, St. Mary's School of Law, and SMU.

Admission

Just five years ago, Trinity University received barely north of 4,500 applicants and admitted an unintimidating 64 percent; freshmen entering in 2018-19 faced an applicant pool of double that size and an acceptance rate of only 34 percent. Today, the mid-50 percent SAT score is 1260-1430 and the mid-50 percent ACT score is 28-32. A solid 42 percent of entering freshmen earned a place in the top 10 percent of their graduating classes, and 76 percent were in the top quartile; the average GPA was a 3.6 on a 4.0 scale. The average profile of a student beginning at Trinity only a few years ago was less impressive.

Trinity may be a small school that gives each application a "thorough review," yet the meat-and-potatoes factors of GPA, class rank, test scores, and engagement in a rigorous curriculum rest atop the list of most important considerations. The next tier of factors includes an interview, essays, recommendations, extracurricular activities, talent/ability, and character/personal qualities. There would have been no reason to apply early to this university in years past, but a sharp spike in competitiveness has put this strategic option firmly in play. In 2018-19, Trinity accepted 114 of 144 early applicants for a hyper-friendly 80 percent acceptance rate. Strong test scores and B+/A- average are now prerequisites for admission to Trinity, a statement that would have been hard to believe a decade ago. If you're a borderline applicant, going the ED route makes a ton of sense.

Worth Your Money?

Amazingly, given the current landscape, a list price cost of attendance of $60,780 isn't incredibly high for a private university. Yet, the truly good news is that this sticker price is rarely what undergraduates pay. Trinity awards a merit aid discount to two-thirds of current students with an average annual value of $22,000. Further, 47 percent of students meet the criteria for need-based grant eligibility, and the average annual award is $32k. With most students receiving sizable discounts, Trinity becomes a solid value, especially when you consider that its grads bring home above-average salaries at each stage of their careers.

FINANCIAL
Institutional Type: Private
In-State Tuition: $44,680
Out-of-State Tuition: $44,680
Room & Board: $13,584
Required Fees: $616
Books & Supplies: $1,000

Avg. Need-Based Aid: $32,162
Avg. % of Need Met: 98%

Avg. Merit-Based Aid: $22,102
% Receiving Merit-Based Aid: 67%

Avg. Cumulative Debt: $42,036
% of Students Borrowing: 44%

CAREER
Who Recruits
1. USAA
2. AXA Advisors
3. Dell
4. Capgemini
5. KPMG

Notable Internships
1. San Antonion Spurs
2. US State Department
3. Apple

Top Industries
1. Business
2. Education
3. Operations
4. Social Services
5. Sales

Top Employers
1. USAA
2. Deloitte
3. PwC
4. EY
5. H-E-B

Where Alumni Work
1. San Antonio
2. Houston
3. Dallas
4. Austin
5. Washington, DC

Median Earnings
College Scorecard (Early Career): $54,900
EOP (Early Career): $58,100
PayScale (Mid-Career): $102,900

RANKINGS
Forbes: 143
Money: 154
U.S. News: 1, Regional West
Wall Street Journal/THE: 111 (T)
Washington Monthly: N/A

#CollegesWorthYourMoney

Tufts University

Medford, Massachusetts | Admissions Phone: 617-627-3170

ADMISSION
Admission Rate: 15%
Admission Rate - Men: 15%
Admission Rate - Women: 14%
EA Admission Rate: Not Offered
ED Admission Rate: 42%
Admission Rate (5-Year Trend): -4%
ED Admission Rate (5-Year Trend): +7%
% of Admits Attending (Yield): 47%
Transfer Admission Rate: 14%

Offered Wait List: 1,957
Accepted Wait List: 723
Admitted Wait List: 8

SAT Reading/Writing (Middle 50%): 680-750
SAT Math (Middle 50%): 700-780
ACT Composite (Middle 50%): 31-34
Testing Policy: ACT/SAT Required
SAT Superscore: Yes
ACT Superscore: Yes

% Graduated in Top 10% of HS Class: 78%
% Graduated in Top 25% of HS Class: 93%
% Graduated in Top 50% of HS Class: 100%

ENROLLMENT
Total Undergraduate Enrollment: 5,643
% Part-Time: 2%
% Male: 48%
% Female: 52%
% Out-of-State: 76%
% Fraternity: 12%
% Sorority: 15%
% On-Campus (Freshman): 100%
% On-Campus (All Undergraduate): 65%

% African-American: 4%
% Asian: 13%
% Hispanic: 7%
% White: 55%
% Other: 5%
% Race or Ethnicity Unknown: 5%
% International: 10%
% Low-Income: 10%

ACADEMICS
Student-to-Faculty Ratio: 9:1
% of Classes Under 20: 69%
% of Classes Under 40: 89%
% Full-Time Faculty: 64%
% Full-Time Faculty w/ Terminal Degree: 94%

Top Programs
Biology
Computer Science
Economics
Engineering
English
International Relations
Quantitative Economics
Science, Technology and Society

Retention Rate: 96%
4-Year Graduation Rate: 87%
6-Year Graduation Rate: 93%

Curricular Flexibility: Very Flexible
Academic Rating: ★★★★✓

Inside the Classroom

Quite small for being one of the nation's top research universities at just over 5,600 undergraduates, Tufts excels in delivering a highly personalized educational experience that is on par with its upper-echelon liberal arts rivals Williams and Amherst. In fact, like Amherst and Brown University, the school is notable for having no core curriculum. Instead, students are "encouraged to immerse themselves in the full expanse of course offerings, deepening existing interests while discovering new areas of study."

Three schools serve Tufts' undergraduate population: The College of Arts & Sciences, the College of Engineering, and the School of the Museum of Fine Arts. The three schools combined offer more than ninety majors and minors; approximately one-third of all students double major, and half declare a minor. The school encourages freshmen and sophomores to "Go broad, then deep." Students who do not want to be tethered to a laundry list of required introductory courses will relish the freedom Tufts affords its undergrads.

The university prides itself on its undergraduate teaching, and it shows; 82 percent of the Class of 2018 reported feeling satisfied with their educational journey. Nearly every professor is willing to take on research assistants, and plenty of funding is available. In the College of Engineering, 60 percent of students have a chance to participate in a research project at some point during their collegiate experience. Classes are small, especially when considering the school's legitimate research university status. Twenty-two percent of all courses see fewer than ten students enrolled, and 69 percent have sub-twenty enrollments. The student-to-faculty ratio is 9:1. A substantial segment of the student body, 40-45 percent, study abroad at one of eighty preapproved programs in locales such as Chile, Ghana, Hong Kong, and Madrid.

Well-regarded by industry and elite graduate/professional schools, a diploma in any discipline from Tufts will get you where you want to go. The most popular majors by volume are international relations, economics, computer science, engineering, and biology—all of which receive very high marks. The university does a fantastic job helping students land nationally competitive scholarships. Tufts is a leading producer of Fulbright Scholars, hitting double digits most years, and it also has seen its fair share of Goldwater, Udall, Truman, and Astronaut Scholarships in recent memory.

Outside the Classroom

Unlike some of Tufts' graduate programs, the undergraduate schools are not located in downtown Boston. However, Medford is part of the Boston metro area and is only five miles from the city limits, which makes its location far less remote than many of its rival New England colleges. Fewer than 70 percent of students live on campus in one of forty residential options ranging from traditional dorms to shared apartments. Many upperclassmen move off campus or live in fraternity or sorority houses. Close to one-quarter of the student population has traditionally gone Greek. Yet, some recent well-publicized hazing incidents led to dissolution or suspension of many chapters that altered, at least for the time being, the influence of Greek-letter organizations on campus. Presently, only 12 percent of men and 15 percent of women are Greek affiliated. Few Tufts students are lone wolves as a staggering 94 percent join at least one of the school's 341 recognized student organizations. Opportunities for community service are plentiful. Many students are involved in athletics, whether a member of one of the twenty-nine varsity sports teams competing in NCAA Division III, twenty-two club teams, or intramural groups. Campus is attractive and full of perks, including the new 42,000-square-foot Tisch Sports & Fitness Center that features tennis courts, pools, squash courts, and dance studios. As a bonus, dining options are given rave reviews as every Tufts student has a favorite dish.

Career Services

With thirteen full-time staff members who focus on undergraduate advising, career relations, and alumni outreach, the Tufts Career Center sports a 426:1 student-to-advisor ratio, which is within the average range of schools featured in this guide. The career services staff has done an incredible job improving its outreach over the past two decades. In 1998, only 32 percent of graduates were satisfied with the university's career services, but by 2015 a healthy 83 percent expressed positive feelings, and annual interactions with students had risen to over 7,600. In 2017, they increased the number of sessions with engineering students by 41 percent from the previous year, another indicator that this is an office on the rise.

Tufts does an exceptional job of assisting undergraduates with internship procurement. A robust 66 percent of Tufts graduates completed two or more internships during their time at the university; 89 percent completed at least one. The Fall Career Fair is attended by 185+ companies, and on-campus recruiting/interviews take place throughout the academic year. Career Treks and networking events in cities like New York and San Francisco are also regular occurrences. A recent switch from the antiquated Jumbo Jobs platform to Handshake was lauded by students. As an added long-term support, alumni have lifetime access to the spectrum of career services, including one-on-one job counseling. With a solid track record in internship participation, job placement, and graduate school outcomes, Tufts career services does an exceptional job setting its undergraduates up for next level of success.

Tufts University

undergraduate.admissions@tufts.edu

Professional Outcomes

Six months after earning their diplomas, 96 percent of 2018 Tufts graduates were employed, attending graduate school, or otherwise productively engaged. The most commonly entered fields were health, life sciences, environmental (22 percent); engineering and technology (17 percent); finance, consulting, real estate (16 percent), and advocacy, education, and social services (15 percent). All of the leading finance, consulting, and technology companies sit atop the list of the most prolific employers of Tufts alums including Booz Allen Hamilton, JPMorgan, Facebook, Google, Deloitte, Amazon, Raytheon, Morgan Stanley, and BlackRock. The median salary at the start of what is considered midcareer is $73k, higher than Amherst and Boston College but lower than Bentley and Harvard. Most Tufts alumni remain in the Boston area, but many also head to New York City, San Francisco, Los Angeles, DC, and Chicago. Of the 16 percent of the Class of 2018 who went directly to graduate school, over three-quarters were accepted into their first-choice institution. Included among the ten universities enrolling the highest number of Tufts alumni were MIT, UCLA, Penn, Carnegie Mellon, and Columbia. Law school applicants routinely gain acceptance into top-tier institutions. In 2017, alumni were admitted into Harvard, Northwestern, University of Michigan, Penn, Duke, Brown, and Yale. Medical school applicants gained acceptance at a 75-90 percent rate, depending on the year. Those with at least a 3.5 undergraduate GPA find a med school home over 90 percent of the time.

Admission

The university's acceptance rate seems to have settled in the 14-15 percent range in recent years and held steady for the Class of 2022 despite an all-time record 21,502 applications. The vast majority of those applicants were for admittance into the School of Arts & Sciences followed by the School of Engineering with the smallest number applying to the fine arts programs. Overall, the mean SAT score was 1467 and the mean ACT was 33. The mid-50 percent ranges are 1380-1530 and 31-34. Last year, over 78 percent of the freshman class finished in the top 10 percent of their high school class, and 93 percent were in the top quartile.

There is nothing unexpected on the list of what factors the admissions committee considers "most important." It is looking for students who achieved top grades in AP classes, scored well on standardized tests, finished in the top 10 percent of their class, come highly recommended by their high school teachers, and are capable of composing a killer essay. Like many schools in its weight class, Tufts loves to scoop up a large portion of its freshman class in the early round—its ED acceptance rate is close to four times that of the regular round (42 percent vs. 11 percent)— and those accepted early comprise 65 percent of the incoming cohort. Even though it is no longer relegated to Ivy League safety status, Tufts is still understandably eager to lock down as many top candidates as possible via ED. Like all Ivy and Ivy-equivalent schools, Tufts is looking for the best and the brightest and is competing with even bigger names to haul in the best candidates. Therefore, demonstrating commitment through ED can pay dividends for qualified applicants.

Worth Your Money?

Boston is America's fourth-most expensive city, so perhaps it is no surprise that Tufts is on the pricey side. At $76k per year in cost of attendance, it ranks as the fifteenth most expensive school in the country. Only 37 percent of current undergrads qualify for need-based aid, and the average annual grant is for just under $49k. Of course, many in attendance don't have to worry too much about the cost because, based on historical data, a high percent of undergrads hail from wealthy families. It's no wonder that despite the high costs, graduates carry a mean amount of debt slightly lower than average (compared against all college grads). Even if you have to make an economic sacrifice to attend, Tufts is a school that will expose you to many personal and professional networks that will come in handy as you enter the world of graduate school or employment.

FINANCIAL
Institutional Type: Private
In-State Tuition: $57,324
Out-of-State Tuition: $57,324
Room & Board: $15,086
Required Fees: $1,254
Books & Supplies: $1,000

Avg. Need-Based Aid: $48,886
Avg. % of Need Met: 100%

Avg. Merit-Based Aid: $0
% Receiving Merit-Based Aid: 0%

Avg. Cumulative Debt: $28,014
% of Students Borrowing: 33%

CAREER
Who Recruits
1. Gelber Group
2. Cogo Labs
3. Amazon Robotics
4. Putnam Investments
5. Oppenheimer & Co.

Notable Internships
1. Deutsche Bank
2. UBS
3. Wayfair

Top Industries
1. Business
2. Education
3. Research
4. Engineering
5. Operations

Top Employers
1. Google
2. Amazon
3. Microsoft
4. Deloitte
5. Facebook

Where Alumni Work
1. Boston
2. New York City
3. San Francisco
4. Washington, DC
5. Los Angeles

Median Earnings
College Scorecard (Early Career): $75,800
EOP (Early Career): $73,100
PayScale (Mid-Career): $118,100

RANKINGS
Forbes: 34
Money: 90
U.S. News: 29 (T), National Universities
Wall Street Journal/THE: 30
Washington Monthly: 50, National Universities

#CollegesWorthYourMoney

Tulane University

New Orleans, Louisiana | Admissions Phone: 504-865-5731

ADMISSION

Admission Rate: 17%
Admission Rate - Men: 17%
Admission Rate - Women: 18%
EA Admission Rate: 25%
ED Admission Rate: 32%
Admission Rate (5-Year Trend): -9%
ED Admission Rate (5-Year Trend): Previously Not Offered
% of Admits Attending (Yield): 28%
Transfer Admission Rate: 38%

Offered Wait List: 10,384
Accepted Wait List: 3,111
Admitted Wait List: 2

SAT Reading/Writing (Middle 50%): 670-730
SAT Math (Middle 50%): 680-760
ACT Composite (Middle 50%): 30-33
Testing Policy: ACT/SAT Required
SAT Superscore: Yes
ACT Superscore: No

% Graduated in Top 10% of HS Class: 63%
% Graduated in Top 25% of HS Class: 88%
% Graduated in Top 50% of HS Class: 96%

ENROLLMENT

Total Undergraduate Enrollment: 6,773
% Part-Time: 0%
% Male: 40%
% Female: 60%
% Out-of-State: 79%
% Fraternity: 24%
% Sorority: 46%
% On-Campus (Freshman): 99%
% On-Campus (All Undergraduate): 48%

% African-American: 4%
% Asian: 5%
% Hispanic: 7%
% White: 73%
% Other: 4%
% Race or Ethnicity Unknown: 1%
% International: 5%
% Low-Income: 10%

ACADEMICS

Student-to-Faculty Ratio: 8:1
% of Classes Under 20: 62%
% of Classes Under 40: 88%
% Full-Time Faculty: 62%
% Full-Time Faculty w/ Terminal Degree: 95%

Top Programs
Architecture
Biology
Communication
Finance
Neuroscience
Political Science/International Relations
Sociology

Retention Rate: 94%
4-Year Graduation Rate: 75%
6-Year Graduation Rate: 85%

Curricular Flexibility: Somewhat Flexible
Academic Rating: ★★★★

Inside the Classroom

In competition with Vanderbilt and Emory for King of the Southern Ivies status, Tulane University takes the bronze; yet, that is hardly a knock on this private, midsized university in the heart of New Orleans. Home to 6,750 undergraduates, Tulane successfully combines the benefits of a renowned research university with the friendly classroom atmosphere of a liberal arts college. In the wake of Hurricane Katrina, the school dedicated itself to community service, an attribute that is now deeply woven into the fabric of the university.

Tulane offers seventy-five majors within five colleges, but all students, regardless of major, call Newcombe-Tulane College their home base. The school's core curriculum, which consists of thirty credits worth of courses, was redesigned in 2017 to "develop information literacy, critical thinking, and personal and social responsibility." As a result, coursework is required in the areas of writing skills, formal reasoning, foreign language, mathematics and natural sciences, social and behavioral sciences, textual and historical perspectives, aesthetics and the creative arts, and a first-year seminar called the Tulane Interdisciplinary Experience Seminar (TIDES). The TIDES courses center around engaging topics, many of which have to do with local New Orleans culture/history and involve one-on-one meetings with professors and a chance to connect with a student mentor.

Despite the presence of a significant number of graduate students, the university's enviable 8:1 student-to-faculty ratio can still be felt in the classroom. The average undergraduate class size is twenty-one students, and 94 percent of sections have an enrollment under fifty students. A solid 20 percent of courses have single-digit enrollments, providing a seminar-style environment. The overwhelming majority of undergraduate courses, even introductory ones, are taught by full-time professors. Exiting student surveys indicate that this focus on undergraduate education is noted as 94 percent rated their educational experience at Tulane as either "excellent" or "good." Those aiming to engage in undergraduate research at Tulane can find it; over 200 students per year land such opportunities in the School of Science and Engineering alone. An expansive study abroad program offers more than one hundred programs in forty countries, which is taken advantage of by 600 students each year.

Business/marketing, social science, biology, and health professions are the disciplines in which most degrees are conferred. The A.B. Freeman School of Business and programs in architecture, biology, and neuroscience enjoy strong national reputations. In its history, Tulane has produced eighteen Rhodes Scholars, one more than Emory. The university was a top producer of Fulbright Scholars in 2018 with fifteen graduates and recent alumni selected. Beinecke, Boren, Truman, and Marshall Scholarships also go to Green Wave alums with regularity.

Outside the Classroom

Fewer than half of the undergraduate population resides on the university's 110-acre uptown campus. Ample housing exists in the nearby community that is either within walking/biking distance of campus or accessible via the university bus system. The Greek scene is active with ten fraternities and eight sororities that collectively draw 35-40 percent of the student body. Tulane offers big-time athletics with sixteen NCAA Division I teams competing in the American Athletic Conference. The Green Wave shines brightest in baseball, men's tennis, and women's golf. An additional twenty-nine club sports teams and thirteen intramural leagues ensure that athletic participation is open to all. Over 200 student-run clubs currently are active with volunteer opportunities being among the most popular. Tulane undergrads contribute over 780,000 hours of volunteer service annually. Campus boasts thirty libraries/research centers, fifteen eateries, and the 156,000-square-foot Reily Student Recreation Center. The urban campus is located within the New Orleans city limits, only four miles from the bustling French Quarter, which provides students with all the culinary and cultural delights one can handle. The fact that classes shut down during Mardi Gras tells you all you need to know about life at Tulane.

Career Services

Tulane's Career Center is staffed by ten professionals who specialize in areas such as career advising, senior year experience coordination, pre-health advising, and pre-law advising. That works out to a 675:1 student-to-advisor ratio that is above average when compared to other schools in this guidebook. The office's strength is in organizing well-attended career and grad school fairs. The Mardi Gras Invitational Job Fair brings 145 employers to campus, the Gumbo Gathering Job Fair attracts another 134, and 118 schools are represented at the Graduate & Professional School Fair. Additionally, 11,000+ job and internship listings are posted through Tulane's Career Services Center.

E-mail: undergrad.admission@tulane.edu | Website: www.tulane.edu

A one-credit course entitled Majors, Internships, and Jobs teaches resume building, interview prep, and professional social media use. Many land internships through the UCAN Intern Consortium that Tulane belongs to alongside such schools as Harvard, Notre Dame, Swarthmore, and Washington University. A nationwide alumni network that is 140,000 members strong is another great source that current undergrads can utilize to land internships or their first paid gig. Founded in 2006, post-Hurricane Katrina, The Center for Public Service ensures that all Tulane grads engage in structured volunteer work during their four years of study. At the heart of this program is a three-credit Public Internship Program that allows students to complete sixty to seventy hours with a nonprofit organization. Thanks to an emphasis on public service and large-scale networking events, the Tulane Career Center succeeds in preparing its students for the world of work and graduate school.

Professional Outcomes

Among those receiving their diplomas in the spring of 2017, 61 percent were entering the world of gainful employment. The most popular industries were finance (17 percent), legal (17 percent), accounting (10 percent), education (6 percent), and engineering (4 percent). Significant numbers of Tulane alumni can be found working in the Louisiana-based Ochsner Health System or at corporations such as Shell, EY, Google, PwC, IBM, Morgan Stanley, Deloitte, and Accenture. Depending on the school from which one was graduating, Class of 2017 members reported median starting salaries between $37,000 and $60,000. Geographically, the most popular postgraduate move is to remain in the Greater New Orleans area although New York City, DC, Houston, San Francisco, and Los Angeles attract large numbers of Green Wave alumni as well.

Seventeen percent of Tulane grads immediately enroll in graduate or professional school. The four most commonly attended graduate schools by members of the Class of 2017 were Tulane itself, Louisiana State University, Boston University, and Johns Hopkins University. Students applying to law and medical schools, including Tulane's own institutions, fare better than the national average. Tulane undergraduates gain acceptance to medical school 58 percent of the time, and that figure rises to 93 percent for those with at least a 3.6 GPA and a score of 509 or higher on the MCAT. Recent grads have attended Columbia, Duke, and Johns Hopkins as well as the uber-selective Tulane School of Medicine. Law school hopefuls gain acceptance at an impressive 93 percent rate including roughly seventy admits annually into Tulane's own solidly ranked law school.

Admission

Tulane received 38,816 applications for its Class of 2022 but accepted only 17 percent, part of a pattern of declining admissions rates in recent years; the Class of 2021 rate was 21 percent, the Class of 2020 rate was 26 percent, and the Class of 2019 rate was 30 percent. The average accepted applicant averaged a 1456 on the SAT, and the middle 50 percent range for attending freshmen was 1350-1490. The middle 50 percent ACT composite score range is 30-33; roughly three-quarters of applicants elect to submit the ACT over the SAT. Sixty-three percent of 2018-19 freshmen had earned a place in the top decile of their high school class, and 88 percent were in the top quartile. Not everyone attending Tulane had perfect grades as 38 percent of attendees sported a high school GPA below 3.5.

With a heavy volume of applications streaming in, the Tulane Admissions Office is forced to rely on concrete factors to winnow down the pool. As a result, four factors are ranked as being most important: rigor of course-work, class rank, GPA, and standardized test scores. Essays, recommendations, and character/personal qualities receive second billing. With the school's acceptance rate in fast decline, it is not a surprise that early decision applications are increasing; ED applications rose 37.5 percent between 2017 and 2018. ED applicants to the Class of 2022 were accepted at a 32 percent clip. An institution whose heightened selectivity in recent years may go unnoticed by applicants relying on old data or the school's reputation a decade ago, Tulane has claimed its position in the realm of highly selective research universities. Successful applicants need standardized test scores above the 95th percentile to go with A's and B's in AP/honors coursework.

Worth Your Money?

Don't let the official cost of attendance of $75,000 make you think that Tulane is beyond your financial reach because a large percentage of students receive a discount in the form of merit or need-based aid that bring that sum down to a more reasonable level. Fifty-five percent of current undergrads receive an average merit aid award of $24k, and 31 percent of undergraduates are given grants averaging $34k per year. If you don't receive a sizable aid offer, the wisest move would be to evaluate (a) your other financial aid offers and (b) the amount of debt you would be likely to incur at Tulane versus the expected starting salaries for jobs related to your intended major.

FINANCIAL
Institutional Type: Private
In-State Tuition: $52,760
Out-of-State Tuition: $52,760
Room & Board: $15,774
Required Fees: $4,040
Books & Supplies: $1,200

Avg. Need-Based Aid: $34,434
Avg. % of Need Met: 96%

Avg. Merit-Based Aid: $23,983
% Receiving Merit-Based Aid: 55%

Avg. Cumulative Debt: $41,767
% of Students Borrowing: 35%

CAREER
Who Recruits
1. Facebook
2. Medtronic
3. Tesla
4. Starbucks
5. Amazon

Notable Internships
1. AIG
2. U.S. Senate
3. HBO

Top Industries
1. Business
2. Education
3. Operations
4. Healthcare
5. Social Services

Top Employers
1. Ochsner Health System
2. Shell
3. EY
4. PwC
5. Deloitte

Where Alumni Work
1. New Orleans
2. New York City
3. Washington, DC
4. Houston
5. San Francisco

Median Earnings
College Scorecard (Early Career): $61,700
EOP (Early Career): N/A
PayScale (Mid-Career): $105,300

RANKINGS
Forbes: 106
Money: 390
U.S. News: 44, National Universities
Wall Street Journal/THE: 84 (T)
Washington Monthly: 343, National Universities

#CollegesWorthYourMoney

Union College

Schenectady, New York | Admissions Phone: 518-388-6112

ADMISSION

Admission Rate: 39%
Admission Rate - Men: 37%
Admission Rate - Women: 40%
EA Admission Rate: Not Offered
ED Admission Rate: 56%
Admission Rate (5-Year Trend): +1%
ED Admission Rate (5-Year Trend): -11%
% of Admits Attending (Yield): 22%
Transfer Admission Rate: 30%

Offered Wait List: 1,045
Accepted Wait List: 516
Admitted Wait List: 13

SAT Reading/Writing (Middle 50%): 620-700
SAT Math (Middle 50%): 650-730
ACT Composite (Middle 50%): 28-32
Testing Policy: Test Optional
SAT Superscore: Yes
ACT Superscore: Yes

% Graduated in Top 10% of HS Class: 61%
% Graduated in Top 25% of HS Class: 80%
% Graduated in Top 50% of HS Class: 94%

ENROLLMENT

Total Undergraduate Enrollment: 2,206
% Part-Time: 0%
% Male: 54%
% Female: 46%
% Out-of-State: 60%
% Fraternity: 28%
% Sorority: 34%
% On-Campus (Freshman): 98%
% On-Campus (All Undergraduate): 88%

% African-American: 4%
% Asian: 5%
% Hispanic: 8%
% White: 70%
% Other: 3%
% Race or Ethnicity Unknown: 0%
% International: 9%
% Low-Income: 19%

ACADEMICS

Student-to-Faculty Ratio: 10:1
% of Classes Under 20: 58%
% of Classes Under 40: 97%
% Full-Time Faculty: 88%
% Full-Time Faculty w/ Terminal Degree: 97%

Top Programs

Biology
Economics
Engineering
History
Mathematics
Neuroscience
Political Science
Psychology

Retention Rate: 95%
4-Year Graduation Rate: 84%
6-Year Graduation Rate: 87%

Curricular Flexibility: Less Flexible
Academic Rating: ★★★★✔

Inside the Classroom

Whether intent on studying the humanities or engineering, Union College in Schenectady, New York, can perfectly meet your needs. One of the select number of schools in the country that has been in existence since the 1700s, Union, while tough to get into, has not, like many of its peer institutions, reached absurd selectivity levels in recent years. A test-optional school looking for strong but not perfect students, this rigorous, well regarded, and exclusively undergraduate institution of 2,200 students is a perfect fit for a certain subset of high schoolers. It's not a bad option considering that, in its illustrious history, Union has produced a US president, thirteen governors, 200 judges, seven cabinet secretaries, a National Book Award winner, and an Olympic Gold medalist.

Union operates on a trimester system of ten-week terms with an extended winter break. The common curriculum is both broad and highly demanding. Students begin with a First-Year Preceptorial that seeks to sharpen skills in the areas of critical reading and thinking as well as analytical writing. The Sophomore Research Seminar mandates that students participate in structured academic research early in their collegiate career. Dutchmen also must plow through requirements in literature, natural science, quantitative and mathematical reasoning, arts and humanities, science/engineering/technology, languages and cultures, and writing across the curriculum. Union is in the exclusive club of undergraduate institutions that require all graduates to complete a senior thesis.

Class sizes at Union are favorable for creating an intimate and friendly learning environment. A 10:1 student-to-faculty ratio leads to average introductory class sizes of twenty-one and average upper-level class sizes of only fourteen. Two-thirds of course sections have an enrollment of nineteen or fewer students. Faculty-mentored research is a staple of Union's undergraduate program and is experienced by 100 percent of the student body in one form or another. During the Steinmetz Symposium, hundreds of students have the chance to showcase their research. Each year, over one hundred students conduct research with a faculty member for an entire summer. The school also takes immense pride in its popular study abroad program that sees more than 60 percent of its students from all disciplines spend a semester of study in a foreign land.

Economics, mechanical engineering, political science, and psychology are the most commonly conferred degrees, and are also very stong, with Union's engineering program having perhaps the strongest national reputation. A top producer of Fulbright Scholars, the Class of 2018 produced seven winners as well as two National Science Foundation Graduate Research Fellows. Traditionally, Union is among the largest producers of Watson Fellows, but it did not have any such winners in the Class of 2018.

Outside the Classroom

Close to 90 percent of undergraduates reside in university-run dorms or one of thirteen student-run theme houses on the 120-acre grounds. The Greek influence is massive with the eighteen sororities and fraternities (ten of which are residential) attracting roughly 40 percent of the student population. Regardless of Greek affiliation, every undergrad belongs to one of seven Minerva Houses, social hubs that serve to bring students and faculty together outside the classroom for social and academic activities. On the sports front, men and women's ice hockey take center stage as each battles NCAA Division I competition; the other twenty-four squads are relegated to Division III status. In total, one-third of all Union students are members of an intercollegiate sports team. Opportunities for physical fitness also exist in the form of yoga, Pilates, dance, and aerobics classes. More than 130 student-run campus clubs are on tap, including fourteen community service groups and a number of cultural, academic, political, and performance-oriented groups. Other notables include WRUC, America's first college radio station that was founded in 1920, and the Concordiensis student newspaper that launched in 1877. Schenectady's downtown is a short car ride away, and longer road trips include Saratoga Springs, a little more than half an hour away, and New York and Boston that require three-hour trips.

Career Services

The Becker Career Center is staffed by six professionals, three of whom specialize in employer relations. That works out to a 378:1 student-to-advisor ratio that falls in the average range when compared to other institutions included this guidebook. Philosophically, the staff encourages students to follow their passions by pursuing opportunities that "pique their interest and spur their enthusiasm." The staff aims to work with students early in their undergraduate careers, regularly administering tests such as the Meyers-Briggs to freshmen. Union hosts its own career fairs but also encourages participation in larger, joint efforts with other institutions. For example, Union, Swarthmore, Bard, and Connecticut College combine for the Fall Recruiting Consortium that attracts many major companies to Times Square.

Union College

E-mail: admissions@union.edu | Website: www.union.edu

Students are encouraged to connect with alumni via the Union Career Advisory Network. Alumni are eager to help current undergrads as evidenced by participation in events such as the Walk Down Wall Street that includes representatives Goldman Sachs, Barclay's Deutsche Bank, Morgan Stanley, and CITI. On-campus recruiting has doubled in the past decade and includes visits and interview opportunities with a host of desirable employers. Roughly 60 percent of Union students complete at least one internship during their four years. Overall, thanks to strong career outcomes and an influential alumni base, Becker does well for its graduates.

Professional Outcomes

Ninety-four percent of the Class of 2018 landed at their next destination within months of completing their degree with 66 percent entering full-time employment and 21 percent matriculating into graduate school. The most popular fields were finance/banking (16 percent), engineering (14 percent), education/academia (10 percent), sales (7 percent), and research (6 percent). Of the pool of all living alumni, Union has the largest representation at IBM, GE, PwC, Morgan Stanley, Fidelity Investments, and Accenture. Location-wise, the strongest presence of Dutchmen/women can be found in New York City; Boston; Albany; Washington, DC; San Francisco; and Philadelphia. Median income figures by the start of midcareer are strong, ranking eleventh among seventy-one highly selective colleges, which is in the same range as Boston University, Trinity College, and Northeastern.

The nearly one-quarter of students who pursue further education directly out of their undergraduate experience do so at a wide range of institutions that include many elite universities. Recent graduates have gone on to advanced business degrees at Stanford, Cornell, and UVA; advanced engineering degrees at Yale, MIT, and RPI, and science degrees at Brandeis, UCLA, and WPI. Many of those headed to medical school do so through the combined BS/MD program Union offers in conjunction with Albany Medical College, but other recent grads have gone on to study medicine at the likes of Johns Hopkins, Tufts, and Dartmouth. Likewise, many pursuing a legal education do so through the combined BA/JD program with partner Albany Law School while others have entered Harvard, Boston College, and the University of Michigan.

Admission

With an acceptance rate of 39 percent for the Class of 2022, Union College, while highly selective, offers strong students better odds of success than many others of its ilk. Still, those who ultimately enroll are often toward the top of their respective high school classes with 61 percent of 2018-19 freshmen hailing from the top decile and 80 percent from the top quartile. Of those who submit test scores (more on this in a moment), the mid-50 percent standardized test ranges are 1270-1430 on the SAT and 28-32 on the ACT.

Unless you are applying to the 3+3 Accelerated Law Program, Leadership in Medicine Program, or are a homeschooled student, Union is a test-optional institution. Yet, in the most recent admissions cycle, 50 percent submitted SAT results and 29 percent included ACT scores on their applications. Atop the list of criteria deemed "very important" in evaluating an applicant are the rigor of secondary coursework, GPA, and class rank. Soft factors like talent/ability, personal qualities, volunteer work, and extracurricular activities also play a role in evaluating candidates. If you are a student on the cusp, applying early decision is absolutely the way to go as ED applicants are given a thumbs up at a 56 percent clip. You don't need perfect grades to get into Union College—the average GPA for Class of 2022 enrollees was 3.4, and only 27 percent were over a 3.75—but you do need an area of notable strength and should be engaged in a mostly AP/honors-level high school curriculum.

Worth Your Money?

Union College sports a hefty cost of attendance of $73,410 per year. One-third of undergrads receive merit aid awards that average $14,500 per student, not greatly altering the high cost of the school. Where Union truly shines is with need-based aid; like the Ivies, it meets 100 percent of demonstrated need for every single student. Half of current students meet those criteria and receive an average grant approaching $40k. Even with the high price tag, Union is a school that opens doors and sends many graduates directly into remunerative fields such as engineering and finance.

FINANCIAL
Institutional Type: Private
In-State Tuition: $56,853
Out-of-State Tuition: $56,853
Room & Board: $14,061
Required Fees: $471
Books & Supplies: $1,500

Avg. Need-Based Aid: $39,942
Avg. % of Need Met: 100%

Avg. Merit-Based Aid: $14,500
% Receiving Merit-Based Aid: 32%

Avg. Cumulative Debt: $35,388
% of Students Borrowing: 58%

CAREER
Who Recruits
1. Rapid7
2. BioSig Technologies
3. Brown Brothers Harriman
4. Northwell Health
5. Stanley Black & Decker

Notable Internships
1. Dow Jones
2. NBCUniversal
3. AIG

Top Industries
1. Business
2. Education
3. Operations
4. Engineering
5. Sales

Top Employers
1. IBM
2. GE
3. PwC
4. Morgan Stanley
5. GE Power

Where Alumni Work
1. New York City
2. Boston
3. Albany, NY
4. Washington, DC
5. San Francisco

Median Earnings
College Scorecard (Early Career): $65,400
EOP (Early Career): $66,600
PayScale (Mid-Career): $117,500

RANKINGS
Forbes: 104
Money: 58
U.S. News: 45, Liberal Arts Colleges
Wall Street Journal/THE: 115
Washington Monthly: 41, Liberal Arts Colleges

#CollegesWorthYourMoney

University at Buffalo (SUNY)

Buffalo, New York | Admissions Phone: 716-645-6900

ADMISSION
Admission Rate: 56%
Admission Rate - Men: 57%
Admission Rate - Women: 54%
EA Admission Rate: N/A
ED Admission Rate: Not Offered
Admission Rate (5-Year Trend): -1%
ED Admission Rate (5-Year Trend): Not Offered
% of Admits Attending (Yield): 24%
Transfer Admission Rate: 63%

Offered Wait List: 2,841
Accepted Wait List: 694
Admitted Wait List: 168

SAT Reading/Writing (Middle 50%): 570-650
SAT Math (Middle 50%): 590-680
ACT Composite (Middle 50%): 24-29
Testing Policy: ACT/SAT Required
SAT Superscore: Yes
ACT Superscore: No

% Graduated in Top 10% of HS Class: 35%
% Graduated in Top 25% of HS Class: 70%
% Graduated in Top 50% of HS Class: 97%

ENROLLMENT
Total Undergraduate Enrollment: 21,607
% Part-Time: 8%
% Male: 56%
% Female: 44%
% Out-of-State: 2%
% Fraternity: 2%
% Sorority: 2%
% On-Campus (Freshman): 76%
% On-Campus (All Undergraduate): 35%

% African-American: 8%
% Asian: 15%
% Hispanic: 7%
% White: 47%
% Other: 2%
% Race or Ethnicity Unknown: 5%
% International: 15%
% Low-Income: 30%

ACADEMICS
Student-to-Faculty Ratio: 14:1
% of Classes Under 20: 29%
% of Classes Under 40: 71%
% Full-Time Faculty: 72%
% Full-Time Faculty w/ Terminal Degree: 97%

Top Programs
Business
Computer Science
English
Exercise Science
Mechanical Engineering
Public Health
Speech and Hearing Science

Retention Rate: 87%
4-Year Graduation Rate: 60%
6-Year Graduation Rate: 76%

Curricular Flexibility: Less Flexible
Academic Rating: ★★★

Inside the Classroom

You can make all the jokes you want about the city of Buffalo (cold jokes from relatives never get old), and you can call the university bearing the city's name a "commuter school" if you want, but they don't care. SUNY University at Buffalo is the most popular destination within the colossal State University of New York system, boasting an undergraduate population of 20,000+. Well-regarded and highly affordable business, engineering, and computer science programs lure an increasingly more selective group of freshmen each year. It is primarily New York residents who come to Buffalo for its robust academic offerings that include 125 undergraduate degree programs. However, the university ranks in the top twenty-five for total number of international students; including graduate students, there are 4,600 foreign students from 101 countries.

Totaling forty credits, the UB curriculum will take the equivalent of almost three full semesters to complete. The program begins freshman year with a small seminar that emphasizes critical thinking and discussion. Next, students will knock out foundations courses in communication literacy, quantitative literacy, scientific literacy, and diversity learning followed by nine credits (each) from thematic and global pathways. Lastly, as a senior, students will complete a one-credit capstone course. Those in the university's Honors Program also must complete twenty-four credits in honors-only courses.

Despite a favorable 14:1 student-to-faculty ratio, undergraduate class sizes do tend to be rather large at the University at Buffalo. That is partially due to the school enrolling almost 10,000 graduate students. Only 29 percent of course sections enroll fewer than twenty students, and 23 percent of courses contain fifty or more students. The Center for Undergraduate Research and Creative Activity (CURCA) can help make a huge university feel a bit smaller by connecting students with faculty mentors for research endeavors. The center advertises that "100 percent of students have the opportunity to participate in research," thus, it is fair to say that procuring opportunities is simply a matter of being proactive. Likewise for those interested in spending a semester at a foreign university; UB offers 1,000 study abroad programs across all seven continents (Antarctica, anyone?).

A good number of Buffalo students flock to the school's strongest offerings with 18 percent of the degrees conferred coming from the School of Management and another 16 percent from the School of Engineering and Applied Sciences. Other commonly conferred degrees are in psychology (11 percent), biology (9 percent), health professions (6 percent), and communication/journalism (6 percent). There has been a slight uptick in recent years in undergraduates capturing prestigious postgraduate scholarships and fellowships. Five seniors/alumni won Fulbright Scholarships in 2019 while others netted Gilman and Critical Language Scholarships.

Outside the Classroom

Even though a sizable number of UB students commute from home or nearby rental homes/apartments, the school does bring 76 percent of freshmen to live in university-owned housing that features twelve residence halls and five apartment communities. Factoring in all undergrads, only 35 percent reside on campus. Greek life has only a faint heartbeat, attracting 2 percent of men and women. Want to see a big-name speaker live? The UB Speakers Series has enticed the likes of Hillary Clinton, Malcom Gladwell, and John Oliver to trek to Buffalo in recent years. There are 300+ student organizations to choose from at the university, and there are many campus-wide events that energize the Bulls community such as Fall Fest, Spring Fest, and Oozefest, which is the muddiest game of volleyball you will ever play. The sports scene is on the rise as the school now supports sixteen NCAA Division I athletic teams that compete in the Mid-American Conference. In the school's own words, the City of Good Neighbors is home to "a vibrant arts scene, quaint neighborhoods, remarkable restaurants, and an affordable cost of living." On campus, the Crossroads Culinary Center is rated the best in the entire SUNY system.

Career Services

The central Career Center at UB employs twelve professional staff members who hold titles such as career counselor, employer relations manager, and employer and alumni relationship associate. The Ciminelli Family Career Resource Center within the School of Management is staffed by nine full-time employees who work with or on behalf of undergraduate students. That translates to a 952:1 student-to-counselor ratio, which is significantly higher than the average school featured in this guide, but it is to be expected at a public university of Buffalo's size. The good news is that in the 2017-18 academic year, 10,896 students utilized the Career Center through attending a job fair, a workshop, or making an individual appointment for career coaching; another 15,858 students used Bullseye, the office's online networking app.

University at Buffalo (SUNY)

E-mail: ub-admissions@buffalo.edu | Website: www.buffalo.edu

Career Center staff could improve outreach efforts as only about 10 percent of the undergraduate student population seek direct career counseling services each year. However, the center did succeed in bringing many top employers to campus for expos such as for the STEAM Job + Internship Fair which draws one hundred+ employers and 2,000+ students each fall. The Spring Job + Internship Fair also brings out one hundred+ employers and around 1,300 students. Unfortunately, those efforts ultimately result in fewer than 500 on-campus interviews each year. Based on the most recent data available, close to 60 percent of students engage in at least one internship, co-op, or other experiential learning placement during their four years at the university. Like much else at the University of Buffalo, the career services spoils go to those who aggressively track down and utilize the available resources.

Professional Outcomes

Within three months of graduating, three-quarters of School of Management degree-holders in the Class of 2018 had found employment. The median base salary for those who found jobs was $48,000 (business grads only). Ten years after enrolling at the university, alumni from all majors earned a median salary of $52,600. UB graduates are well-represented in the corporate offices of many top finance, accounting, consulting, and technology companies. More than one hundred alumni of the school are currently employed at the likes of M&T Bank, Citi, Amazon, Microsoft, Google, JPMorgan Chase, PwC, Apple, Deloitte, and Cisco. The greatest number of alumni remain in the Buffalo area but many relocate to New York City, San Francisco, DC, and Boston.

There were 64 SUNY Buffalo graduates in 2018 who applied to medical school. Including those applying to osteopathic schools, a GPA of 3.5-3.7 and an MCAT score in the 505-510 range typically led to successful results. Recent graduates are currently attending medical schools at Virginia Commonwealth University and Boston University with the greatest percentage heading to the four SUNY medical training grounds at the Stony Brook, Buffalo, Upstate, and Downstate locations. Many law school attendees also stay within the SUNY system, including Buffalo's own home for legal education, but other recent grads have entered such schools as Duke, Wake Forest, and Notre Dame. That pattern is also true for those pursuing master's and doctoral degrees. Graduating with honors from UB absolutely can put elite graduate and professional schools in play, but the bulk of students select local public options.

Admission

SUNY University at Buffalo receives the largest number of applications of any school in the state system, over 31,000; the school accepted 56 percent of those aiming to join the Class of 2022. Perfect grades aren't necessary, but you need a pretty sound transcript. Over one-third of attending students placed in the top 10 percent of their high school class, and 70 percent finished in the top quartile. Forty-two percent boasted a GPA of 3.75 or greater, but giving hope to those with blemishes on their academic records, 19 percent possessed a 3.25 or under. The average SAT score for a freshman in 2018-19 was a 1242, and the average ACT score was just shy of 27. To give you a sense of the ranges of standardized test scores, the middle-50 percent scores were a 24-29 on the ACT and 1160-1330 on the SAT.

So many applicants, so little time—it's a recipe for a formulaic admissions process, and that's exactly what the University at Buffalo utilizes. At the top of the list are standardized test scores, GPA, and the rigor of one's coursework followed by the still-important factors of class rank and recommendations. State residency is not considered in the admissions process, nor is demonstrated interest. In the end, 24 percent of those admitted go on to enroll. Strangely, while a near-identical number of men and women are accepted into Buffalo, the yield rate for men is substantially higher. Roughly 350 students per year are admitted into the Honors College, and preference is given to those who apply earlier in the rolling process. For all applicants, we highly recommend meeting the priority deadline of November 15.

Worth Your Money?

Those who live with a relative can earn a four-year degree for a grand sum of $28,000, the cost of tuition alone for one semester at many private universities. Total cost of attendance for a New York resident comes to about $29,000 per year, which accounts for direct and indirect living expenses—still an excellent deal for the quality of education the school provides. For those from out of state, costs climb to $47,000 per year, making attending UB a curious choice for those with more affordable options. Over 10,000 undergraduates are determined needy each year, and the school awards an average annual need-based grant of $7,915. For New York residents, SUNY Buffalo is, unequivocally and independent of circumstance, worth your money.

FINANCIAL
Institutional Type: Public
In-State Tuition: $6,870
Out-of-State Tuition: $24,540
Room & Board: $14,213
Required Fees: $3,229
Books & Supplies: $1,203

Avg. Need-Based Aid: $7,915
Avg. % of Need Met: 45%

Avg. Merit-Based Aid: $3,869
% Receiving Merit-Based Aid: 28%

Avg. Cumulative Debt: $26,062
% of Students Borrowing: 57%

CAREER
Who Recruits
1. ACV Auctions
2. Salesforce
3. Facebook
4. PwC
5. Apple

Notable Internships
1. Walt Disney World
2. Wegmnan's Food Markets
3. HSBC

Top Industries
1. Business
2. Education
3. Operations
4. Engineering
5. Healthcare

Top Employers
1. M&T Bank
2. Citi
3. Amazon
4. Ingram Micro
5. Microsoft

Where Alumni Work
1. Buffalo, NY
2. New York City
3. Rochester, NY
4. San Francisco
5. Singapore

Median Earnings
College Scorecard (Early Career): $52,600
EOP (Early Career): $52,700
PayScale (Mid-Career): $98,000

RANKINGS
Forbes: 196
Money: 99
U.S. News: 79 (T), National Universities
Wall Street Journal/THE: 110
Washington Monthly: 114, National Universities

#CollegesWorthYourMoney

University of California, Berkeley

Berkeley, California | Admissions Phone: 510-642-6000

ADMISSION
Admission Rate: 15%
Admission Rate - Men: 13%
Admission Rate - Women: 17%
EA Admission Rate: Not Offered
ED Admission Rate: Not Offered
Admission Rate (5-Year Trend): -3%
ED Admission Rate (5-Year Trend): Not Offered
% of Admits Attending (Yield): 47%
Transfer Admission Rate: 21%

\# Offered Wait List: 7,824
\# Accepted Wait List: 4,127
\# Admitted Wait List: 1,536

SAT Reading/Writing (Middle 50%): 640-740
SAT Math (Middle 50%): 660-790
ACT Composite (Middle 50%): 28-34
Testing Policy: ACT/SAT Required
SAT Superscore: No
ACT Superscore: No

% Graduated in Top 10% of HS Class: 98%
% Graduated in Top 25% of HS Class: 100%
% Graduated in Top 50% of HS Class: 100%

ENROLLMENT
Total Undergraduate Enrollment: 30,609
% Part-Time: 4%
% Male: 47%
% Female: 53%
% Out-of-State: 16%
% Fraternity: 10%
% Sorority: 10%
% On-Campus (Freshman): 96%
% On-Campus (All Undergraduate): 27%

% African-American: 2%
% Asian: 35%
% Hispanic: 15%
% White: 25%
% Other: 6%
% Race or Ethnicity Unknown: 4%
% International: 13%
% Low-Income: 27%

ACADEMICS
Student-to-Faculty Ratio: 20:1
% of Classes Under 20: 53%
% of Classes Under 40: 77%
% Full-Time Faculty: 66%
% Full-Time Faculty w/ Terminal Degree: 99%

Top Programs
Biological Sciences
Business
Chemistry
Computer Science
Economics
Engineering
English
Psychology

Retention Rate: 97%
4-Year Graduation Rate: 75%
6-Year Graduation Rate: 91%

Curricular Flexibility: Somewhat Flexible
Academic Rating: ★★★★⌐

Inside the Classroom
The University of California, Berkeley, more commonly referred to as Berkeley or Cal, is the flagship university in the stellar and gargantuan UC system. Founded in 1868 with the motto "Fiat Lux" (Let there be light), the university today offers enlightenment to over 30,000 undergraduate and 11,000 graduate students. The name *Berkeley* likely conjures up two immediate associations—academic prestige and the protests of the 1960s. While no longer a hotbed of youth unrest on the level of the Vietnam era, Berkeley remains a bastion of liberal thought and idealism. It is fitting that the school is the number one all-time producer of Peace Corps volunteers.

More than 150 undergraduate majors and minors are available across five undergraduate schools: The College of Letters and Science, the College of Chemistry, the College of Engineering, the College of Environmental Design, and the College of Natural Resources. A sixth school, the Haas School of Business, must be applied to separately prior to one's junior year. Over two-thirds of undergrads are housed within the College of Letters and Science, which requires coursework including entry-level writing, American history and American institutions, foreign language, quantitative reasoning, and reading & composition.

Constant budget crises in the UC system haven't dented the school's reputation one iota, but the impact can be felt in measures such as student-to-faculty ratio that, at 18:1, is significantly higher than other elite flagships like UVA or Michigan. However, that doesn't translate to across-the-board large class sizes. Rather, undergrads will encounter a mix of large lectures (19 percent of sections contain more than fifty students) and tiny, single-digit enrollments in seminar-style courses (24 percent of sections contain nine or fewer students). Undergraduate research opportunities do exist despite the school's massive size; 56 percent of students assist faculty with a research project or complete a research methods course in their time at Berkeley. Study abroad opportunities are available for those who desire them, and approximately 1,800 undergrads take a semester in a foreign country each year. Locations where Berkeley faculty deliver instruction include Taiwan, Switzerland, Serbia, Peru, and the Philippines.

Thanks to its equally esteemed graduate schools, many departments have top international reputations including computer science, engineering, chemistry, English, psychology, and economics. In 2017 alone, 105 grads were awarded National Science Foundation Graduate Research Fellowships, which was more than Stanford and more than Harvard and Yale combined. In 2018, there were eleven Fulbright winners, three Schwarzman Scholars, and two alumni were awarded MacArthur Fellowships, sometimes referred to as "genius grants."

Outside the Classroom
Almost 95 percent of incoming freshmen live in university-run housing, upperclassmen are generally left to fend for themselves. Housing is a challenging issue, and while the university is building new dormitories, it presently only has the capacity to house roughly one-quarter of the undergraduate population. A prominent but far from dominant Greek life attracts 10 percent of men and women (3,600 individuals) into sixty+ active fraternities and sororities. Cal's sports program is exceptional as the Golden Bears thirty varsity teams have won a collective eighty-seven NCAA championships in the school's history; they mostly compete in the Pac-12 Conference. With 1000+ clubs and activities, there is truly somethings for everyone, including many political and public-service organizations. Roughly 5,300 undergraduate students volunteer their time to community service projects, and the campus has a genuine focus on sustainability; 87 percent of students walk, bike, or take public transit, and the school has a goal of zero non-recycled waste by 2020. Being a few miles north of Oakland and a few miles east of San Francisco, big-city fun is never far away. Berkeley itself is replete with awesome restaurants (including, of course, many vegan options), a botanical garden, a marina, an art museum, and a 2,000-acre park. Berkeley is considered one of the most socially liberal cities in the United States.

Career Services
With twenty-five full-time employees dedicated to undergraduates, the UC Berkeley Career Center has a 1,234:1 student-to-counselor ratio, much higher than most of the schools featured in this guide but comparable to the other University of California institutions. What the center lacks in its ability to connect one-on-one it makes up for by putting together large-scale events that bring 350+ employers to campus every year. There are large career fairs in the fall and spring, and many industry-specific affairs are held as well including the Social Impact Career Fair, Investment Banking Forum, Law & Graduate School Fair, and the Civil & Environmental Engineering Career Fair .

A survey of employed 2018 graduates reveals that the efforts of the career center directly contributed to their job attainment. Specifically, 17 percent found their first job through on-campus recruiting, 15 percent directly from an internship, 14 percent via a career fair or information session, and 13 percent through Cal's Handshake platform. A hard-to-beat alumni network of 493,000 individuals—100,000 are dues-paying members of the

University of California, Berkeley

E-mail: admissions.berkeley.edu/contact-us | Website: www.berkeley.edu

alumni association— can assist you throughout your career. More than 4,500 students attend webinars and in-person events hosted by alums. The average student received two job offers. Overall, despite a high counselor-to-student ratio, Cal's career services provides plenty of opportunities for undergrads to connect with top employers, resulting in students landing positions that align with their career goals while also paying the bills.

Professional Outcomes

Upon graduating, 61 percent of Cal's Class of 2018 members had already secured employment, 19 percent were headed to graduate school, and 14 percent were still seeking their first jobs. Just over three-quarters of that cohort were employed by for-profit companies, 11 percent entered the education field, 7 percent took positions at nonprofits, and 6 percent were working for government entities. Thousands of alumni can be found in the offices of Google, Apple, and Facebook, and 500+ Golden Bears are currently employed by Oracle, Amazon, and Microsoft. Most alumni are concentrated in the San Francisco Bay area with Los Angeles, New York, Seattle, DC, Boston, and the United Kingdom next in popularity. Average starting salaries vary widely by major. Computer science grads are compensated to the tune of $107k, business majors averaged $75k, biology majors made $59k, and psychology majors brought home $57k.

Because almost 8,000 students earn bachelor's degrees each year, it's hard to pinpoint the most commonly attended graduate/professional schools with literally hundreds of institutions absorbing Berkeley undergrads. They range from the most selective Ivy League universities to a host of less selective institutions. For example, political science degree-holders from the Class of 2018 attended graduate schools that included Stanford, Georgetown, San Francisco State, and Eastern Michigan University. Suffice it to say that earning strong grades at Berkeley will set you up for a successful graduate application process at the nation's most elite schools. From 2016-2018 the medical school acceptance rate has hovered in the 51-55 percent range, and law school applicants have been successful 81-89 percent of the time. Among the Class of 2018, master's degrees were the most frequently pursued degree (311) followed by PhD (170), JD (47), and MD (40).

Admission

In 2018, Berkeley received 89,615 applications for a place in the Class of 2022, but only 15 percent were offered admission. A decade prior, the university received 48,000+ applications and sported an admit rate of 22 percent. Acceptance rates fluctuate among three separate groups of candidates: California residents (17 percent), out-of-staters (15 percent), and international students (8 percent). The average SAT of an admitted resident was 1390 while the average admitted out-of-state applicant score was 1484; accepted international students had a mean of 1480. Overall, members of the Class of 2022 possessed a mid-50 percent range of 1300-1530 on the SAT and 28-34 on the ACT. An eye-popping 98 percent placed in the top decile of their high school class, and 88 percent earned a GPA of 3.75 or higher on a 4.0 scale. The average weighted GPA was an intimidating 4.45.

The committee claims that the admissions review is so holistic that it "literally hugs your application." Logistically, with nearly 90,000 applications to sift through, each embrace is surely quite short. As a result, GPA, rigor of secondary school record, and standardized test scores are among the "very important" criteria used to winnow down the initial pool; however, the application essay does rest on this same tier of importance. The next factors receiving the strongest consideration include volunteer work, work experience, extracurricular activities, and character/personal qualities. Everyone is on equal footing at Berkeley as the school does not offer early admission. Becoming a Golden Bear has been highly selective process for many decades, and now it has reached its all-time high. Flawless grades in a roster of AP and honors courses is essentially a prerequisite, but there is some wiggle-room on test scores as the committee does genuinely consider demonstrated leadership and other intangibles.

Worth Your Money?

Paying $14,000 per year in tuition to attend one of the finest institutions in the country sounds like a pipe dream, particularly considering that some private schools charge four times that. For the one-quarter or so of the undergraduate student body from out of state, the annual cost of attendance will be $65,000, a far cry from the $36,000 COA for Californians (this includes the aforementioned tuition plus all direct and indirect costs). For the 47 percent of students determined eligible for need-based aid, the average award is $23,542 per year, making Berkeley a genuinely accessible place for lower-income students to attend without incurring unhealthy student loan debt.

FINANCIAL
Institutional Type: Public
In-State Tuition: $11,442
Out-of-State Tuition: $40,434
Room & Board: $16,160
Required Fees: $2,742
Books & Supplies: $850

Avg. Need-Based Aid: $23,542
Avg. % of Need Met: 83%

Avg. Merit-Based Aid: $5,979
% Receiving Merit-Based Aid: 8%

Avg. Cumulative Debt: $18,225
% of Students Borrowing: 34%

CAREER
Who Recruits
1. AlphaSights
2. Fisher Investments
3. Navigant
4. Putnam Associates
5. Western Digital

Notable Internships
1. Lyft
2. WeWork
3. Airbnb

Top Industries
1. Business
2. Education
3. Engineering
4. Research
5. Operations

Top Employers
1. Google
2. Apple
3. Facebook
4. Amazon
5. Oracle

Where Alumni Work
1. San Francisco
2. Los Angeles
3. New York City
4. Seattle
5. Boston

Median Earnings
College Scorecard (Early Career): $64,700
EOP (Early Career): $67,900
PayScale (Mid-Career): $131,800

RANKINGS
Forbes: 13
Money: 11
U.S. News: 22, National Universities
Wall Street Journal/THE: 34
Washington Monthly: 20, National Universities

#CollegesWorthYourMoney

Davis, California | Admissions Phone: 530-752-2971

Inside the Classroom

Like so much growth in the annals of California state history, the story of UC-Davis is one of a post-World War II boom that saw the state's population increase by 53 percent from the 1940s to the 1950s. The school's rapid rise began in 1959 when Davis officially became a general campus of the University of California system. By 1962 it launched an engineering school, and its now prestigious law and medical schools opened in 1966 and 1968, respectively. One hundred years ago, Davis was known as the University Farm and offered no degree programs. Today, it is home to 30,000+ undergraduates alone and offers 102 undergraduate majors and roughly the same number of graduate programs. As with many UC campuses, the onset of the 2010s saw application numbers spike and acceptance rates plunge. The school that was once only a farm is, today, producing crops of graduates that line corporate offices at the leading tech companies in Silicon Valley.

There are four undergraduate schools at UCD: The College of Agricultural and Environmental Sciences, the College of Biological Sciences, the College of Engineering, and the College of Letters and Science. The university has two sets of core requirements—Topical Breadth, which mandates between twelve and twenty units in each of the arts and humanities, science and engineering, and the social sciences—and Core Literacies, which include English composition; writing experience; oral skills; visual literacy; American cultures, governance, and history; domestic diversity; world cultures; quantitative literacy; and scientific literacy. All told, that adds up to eighty-seven units of required coursework, but the categories are broad, and pretty much any course you could take fits at least one, making those curricular requirements less limiting than they first appear.

A 20:1 student-to-faculty ratio isn't terribly inspiring, especially with 7,500+ graduate students stealing their share of the spotlight. While class sizes aren't small, 63 percent of sections enroll fewer than thirty students, and 72 percent of classes are kept under fifty students. There are numerous opportunities for undergraduate research through programs like the McNair Scholars Program, the Biology Undergraduate Research Program, and Sponsored Undergraduate Research programs. A solid 41 percent of Davis seniors report having assisted a professor with research, and 50 percent engage in some type of research/creative project outside the classroom. Only 1,300 students choose to study abroad each year, but offerings do include fifty programs in thirty countries with courses taught by University of California professors.

The greatest number of degrees conferred are in biology (17 percent), the social sciences (17 percent), psychology (13 percent), engineering (11 percent), and agriculture (7 percent). Among the most heralded programs are those in animal science and all areas of engineering. In recent years Davis students have begun to capture a greater number of prestigious national awards. Twelve Fulbright Scholarships were awarded to grads and alumni in 2019, a Schwarzman Scholar was named in 2017, and the school has had a number of Rhodes Scholarship finalists since 2010.

Outside the Classroom

At 5,300 acres the Davis campus is one of the largest in the country, yet housing options are still expanding to keep up with enrollment increases. The housing capacity at the university is currently 11,000 students; freshmen are guaranteed on-campus housing, and 93 percent take advantage. In 2019, the school broke ground on a new housing project that will add 3,300 beds to the West Village section of the university. The gender disparity cannot be ignored at UC-Davis as women outnumber men by nearly a 60/40 ratio. A beautifully diverse student body is 33 percent Asian, 22 percent Hispanic, and 14 percent international. Roughly seventy Greek organizations attract 10 percent of the undergraduate population. There are approximately 800 student-run organizations, including award-winning academic teams that have captured the National Freescale Cup Autonomous Model Car Competition, the International Data Mining Cup, and the grand prize at the International Genetically Engineered Machines competition. On the subject of competition, the chance to participate in athletics exists no matter your level of skill. The Aggies field fourteen women's and nine men's Division I teams to go with twenty-seven intramural leagues and thirty-nine intercollegiate club squads. Volunteerism is strong with 600,000 hours donated annually by members of the UC-Davis community. Given the school's emphasis on environmental science, it should come as no shock that it is routinely voted one of the greener campuses in the United States, and 29 percent of dining hall food is sustainably grown. Sacramento is the nearest big city, only 15 miles from campus; San Francisco is a manageable hour-long car ride away.

Career Services

The UC-Davis Internship and Career Center (ICC) has eighteen professional employees who work with or on behalf of undergraduate students, many of whom specialize in a particular discipline such as engineering and physical sciences, health and biological sciences, agricultural and environmental sciences, and liberal arts and business. Others play roles in the areas of internship coordination, employer relations, and recruiting. Davis has a 1,706:1 student-to-staff ratio, which is among the poorest of any university profiled in this guidebook. While the staffing may be lacking for a school with over 30,000 undergraduates, there are plenty of encouraging statistics that indicate Aggies' career prospects are in good hands.

ADMISSION
Admission Rate: 41%
Admission Rate - Men: 36%
Admission Rate - Women: 46%
EA Admission Rate: Not Offered
ED Admission Rate: Not Offered
Admission Rate (5-Year Trend): 0%
ED Admission Rate (5-Year Trend): Not Offered
% of Admits Attending (Yield): 20%
Transfer Admission Rate: 55%

Offered Wait List: 9,213
Accepted Wait List: 3,207
Admitted Wait List: 24

SAT Reading/Writing (Middle 50%): 570-670
SAT Math (Middle 50%): 580-740
ACT Composite (Middle 50%): 25-31
Testing Policy: ACT/SAT Required
SAT Superscore: No
ACT Superscore: No

% Graduated in Top 10% of HS Class: 100%
% Graduated in Top 25% of HS Class: 100%
% Graduated in Top 50% of HS Class: 100%

ENROLLMENT
Total Undergraduate Enrollment: 30,810
% Part-Time: 2%
% Male: 39%
% Female: 61%
% Out-of-State: 5%
% Fraternity: 7%
% Sorority: 11%
% On-Campus (Freshman): 92%
% On-Campus (All Undergraduate): 75%

% African-American: 2%
% Asian: 27%
% Hispanic: 22%
% White: 24%
% Other: 5%
% Race or Ethnicity Unknown: 2%
% International: 17%
% Low-Income: 37%

ACADEMICS
Student-to-Faculty Ratio: 20:1
% of Classes Under 20: 36%
% of Classes Under 40: 68%
% Full-Time Faculty: 73%
% Full-Time Faculty w/ Terminal Degree: 94%

Top Programs
Animal Science
Biological Sciences
Communication
Computer Science
Engineering
English
Political Science
Sociology

Retention Rate: 92%
4-Year Graduation Rate: 61%
6-Year Graduation Rate: 86%

Curricular Flexibility: Less Flexible
Academic Rating: ★★★✦

University of California, Davis

E-mail: undergraduateadmissions@ucdavis.edu | Website: www.ucdavis.edu

An admirable 80 percent of undergraduates land at least one internship; 55 percent engage in two or more internships. In total, the ICC facilitates more than 10,000 internships per year. More than 500 company recruiters visit UC Davis each year looking to hire Aggies, and many major corporations attend the six large-scale career fairs that take place each year, including the Fall/Winter/Spring Internship & Career Fair, the STEM Career Fair, and the Engineering & Tech Internship & Career Fair. There are 260,000 living Aggie alumni who are embedded at many of the top companies to work for in the country. With terrific internship and recruitment statistics, the ICC overcomes its less-than-desirable staffing to be of great assistance to job-seeking graduates.

Professional Outcomes

One year after earning their BA or BS, 14 percent of Davis grads are still unemployed. Many have found homes at Silicon Valley or other California-based juggernaut employers, including about all of the world's top tech companies. The corporations employing 200 or more Aggies include Genentech, Google, Apple, Cisco, Facebook, Oracle, Amazon, Microsoft, Salesforce, Workday, and LinkedIn. More than one hundred Aggies are presently working for Adobe and rivals Uber and Lyft. The San Francisco Bay area is home to the largest concentration of Davis alumni followed by Sacramento, Los Angeles, San Diego, and Seattle. Assisted by the large number of engineering students, recent grads take home a median starting salary of $56,000 and, by midcareer, are approaching six figures.

Within one year of graduating 39 percent of Aggies elect to continue their education, and 94 percent report that their undergraduate experience prepared them somewhere between adequately and "very well" for postgraduate study. The most popular degrees pursued are masters, MDs or other health doctorates, law, and MBA/MPA. The UC Davis School of Medicine, one of the best schools for primary care training in the country, tends to favor its own graduates, filling approximately 20 percent of its cohorts with homegrown students. The average undergraduate student who gained acceptance to at least one medical school possessed a 3.58 GPA and a 512 MCAT score. The UC Davis School of Law also draws heavily from its undergraduate schools, and many grads also find homes at other University of California schools. Currently, multiple Aggie alumni are enrolled at the likes of Harvard Law School, Duke University School of Law, and a host of other top-tier institutions.

Admission

Like all schools in the University of California system the Davis branch has experienced an influx of applicants in the last several years. It set a record in 2018-19 with 95,207 applications, 76,647 of which were from freshmen; the rest were transfers. From that pool, 41 percent were welcomed aboard to form the freshman class of 2018-19. Most had near-perfect academic transcripts as 89 percent were the proud owners of a 3.75 or higher unweighted GPA. The mid-50 percent standardized test scores were in a far wider range of 1150-1410 on the SAT and 25-31 on the ACT. A decade ago, Davis admitted 52 percent of applicants and, while grades were similarly stellar to those of the Class of 2022, standardized test scores were significantly lower.

According to admissions officers, the factors most heavily weighted in the admissions process are the rigor of one's secondary courses, GPA, standardized test scores, and the application essay. The next rung of importance is made-up of softer factors like extracurricular activities, volunteer work, talent/ability, and character/personal qualities. First-generation status is listed as a "considered" factor, but the number of students who are the first in their families to enter college suggests that this is a point of emphasis for the university. In fact, an astonishing 42 percent of current students grew up in households with parents who had not completed four-year degrees. There is no early EA or ED plan at UC-Davis—all applications are due by November 30. Getting into UC-Davis is harder than it used to be and, like other University of California campuses, it requires a fairly pristine academic transcript in a rigorous curriculum, but standardized test scores can be a bit lower than at UC-San Diego and significantly lower than at Berkeley or UCLA.

Worth Your Money?

A whopping 59 percent of those attending UC Davis receive an average need-based grant of $21,402. Considering that the estimated in-state cost of attendance is just over $35,000, the majority of undergraduates are paying a reasonable price for a valuable degree. Estimated COA for nonresidents is $64k. For the 20 percent of attendees not from California, that would be an expensive venture without any financial aid, and you likely could find a better merit aid offer from a private institution.

FINANCIAL
Institutional Type: Public
In-State Tuition: $11,442
Out-of-State Tuition: $40,434
Room & Board: $15,863
Required Fees: $3,050
Books & Supplies: $1,159

Avg. Need-Based Aid: $21,402
Avg. % of Need Met: 83%

Avg. Merit-Based Aid: $6,485
% Receiving Merit-Based Aid: 5%

Avg. Cumulative Debt: $18,575
% of Students Borrowing: 48%

CAREER
Who Recruits
1. Airbnb
2. Lyft
3. Adobe
4. LinkedIn
5. Cisco

Notable Internships
1. U.S. House of Representatives
2. Adidas
3. Credit Suisse

Top Industries
1. Business
2. Education
3. Operations
4. Research
5. Engineering

Top Employers
1. Kaiser Permanente
2. Genetech
3. Google
4. Apple
5. Facebook

Where Alumni Work
1. San Francisco
2. Sacramento
3. Los Angeles
4. San Diego
5. Orange County, CA

Median Earnings
College Scorecard (Early Career): $58,200
EOP (Early Career): $61,600
PayScale (Mid-Career): $112,600

RANKINGS
Forbes: 88
Money: 5
U.S. News: 39, National Universities
Wall Street Journal/THE: 36
Washington Monthly: 11, National Universities

#CollegesWorthYourMoney

University of California, Irvine

Irvine, California | Admissions Phone: 949-824-6703

ADMISSION
Admission Rate: 29%
Admission Rate - Men: 30%
Admission Rate - Women: 28%
EA Admission Rate: Not Offered
ED Admission Rate: Not Offered
Admission Rate (5-Year Trend): -12%
ED Admission Rate (5-Year Trend): Not Offered
% of Admits Attending (Yield): 21%
Transfer Admission Rate: 42%

Offered Wait List: 12,522
Accepted Wait List: 6,428
Admitted Wait List: 136

SAT Reading/Writing (Middle 50%): 580-690
SAT Math (Middle 50%): 600-750
ACT Composite (Middle 50%): 27-33
Testing Policy: ACT/SAT Required
SAT Superscore: No
ACT Superscore: No

% Graduated in Top 10% of HS Class: 98%
% Graduated in Top 25% of HS Class: 100%
% Graduated in Top 50% of HS Class: 100%

ENROLLMENT
Total Undergraduate Enrollment: 29,736
% Part-Time: 2%
% Male: 49%
% Female: 51%
% Out-of-State: 3%
% Fraternity: 8%
% Sorority: 9%
% On-Campus (Freshman): 82%
% On-Campus (All Undergraduate): 38%

% African-American: 2%
% Asian: 36%
% Hispanic: 26%
% White: 13%
% Other: 4%
% Race or Ethnicity Unknown: 1%
% International: 17%
% Low-Income: 48%

ACADEMICS
Student-to-Faculty Ratio: 18:1
% of Classes Under 20: 53%
% of Classes Under 40: 73%
% Full-Time Faculty: 80%
% Full-Time Faculty w/ Terminal Degree: 98%

Top Programs
Biological Sciences
Chemistry
Computer Science
Criminology, Law and Society
Drama
Engineering
Engish
Public Health

Retention Rate: 93%
4-Year Graduation Rate: 68%
6-Year Graduation Rate: 83%

Curricular Flexibility: Somewhat Flexible
Academic Rating: ★★★★

Inside the Classroom

A diverse school with a strong Asian and Hispanic representation that serves a phenomenally high percentage of first-generation college students, UC-Irvine is, like the other schools in the University of California system, becoming more selective every year. On the eve of the millennium as Y2K-mania reached its crescendo, Irvine was a school that accepted roughly half of its applicants and was primarily a safety school for those applying to the more prestigious UC campuses. Today, UCI is a top-of-the-list destination for many of the 30,000 UCI undergraduate students, half of whom are California residents, and *all* of whom proudly call themselves Anteaters. As the third decade of the 2000s kicks off, freshmen flock to Orange County not just for the school's premier location but for the eighty stellar undergraduate academic programs the university offers at a bargain price.

For a school with an overwhelming number freshmen entering its gates each year, UC-Irvine takes great care to offer first-years a soft landing. The Summer Bridge Scholars Program, Freshman Edge Program, and the Freshman Seminar Series are all designed to help new students succeed, and they are effective as 92 percent of freshmen return for their sophomore year, a retention rate on par with many highly selective private institutions. All students take a liberal arts core that involves three courses in each of science and technology, arts and humanities, and the social sciences, two writing-intensive classes, and forays into foreign language, quantitative reasoning, multicultural issues, and international/global issues. Like most California publics, UCI operates on the quarter system, which means you'll need to get used to furiously paced ten-week periods of study.

At a school with an 18:1 student-to-faculty ratio and 6,300 graduate students to serve, you might expect all classes at Irvine to be held in hundred-seat lecture halls. We are pleased to report that is not the case. In fact, 53 percent of all sections enroll nineteen or fewer students, and only 23 percent of courses contain fifty+ students. The school provides a terrific number of opportunities for undergrads to participate in some type of supervised research. More than three-fifths of students have conducted a research project, and 20 percent have assisted faculty in conducting research. The Undergraduate Research Opportunities Program helps students with proposal writing, developing research plans, and presenting their results at the annual spring UCI Undergraduate Research Symposium and/or publishing their results in the *UCI Undergraduate Research Journal*. Most students remain on campus for all four years as only about 1,000 individuals study abroad each year.

The five most popular majors at Irvine are psychology, biology, business, engineering, and computer science. The Samueli School of Engineering has a solid reputation as does the Bren School, the only dedicated computer science school in the University of California system. Programs in public health and biological sciences also earn very high marks. Between two and five graduates win Fulbright Scholarships each year, and Irvine has had an occasional Goldwater, Truman, or Marshall Scholar in the last few years, but winning prestigious national postgraduate scholarships is not a primary focus of Anteater alumni.

Outside the Classroom

It's hard to think of many more desirable locations for a college setting than Orange County, California. The Pacific Ocean is only five miles from campus, including the famed Laguna and Newport beaches. Los Angeles is within an hour's drive, and San Diego is about an hour and a half and, if you have a spare twenty-five minutes, you can head over to Disneyland for the afternoon. The suburban campus covers 1,474 acres, and 38 percent of students live in university housing. Freshmen are guaranteed two full years of housing should they choose to accept it but, at present, only 82 percent of freshmen live in the dorms. Fraternities attract 9 percent of males, and 8 percent of females join sororities. There are eighteen varsity sports teams and 400 total student-athletes. All-time, the school has produced 500 All-Americans and fifty-six Olympians. Currently, there are 677 registered campus organizations representing over nineteen categories with two notables being UCI's Circle K Chapter that dedicates 35,000 hours of service annually to the surrounding community and Kababayan (Kaba), a popular Filipino-American club. Aldrich Park, modeled after Central Park, is the beautiful centerpiece to Irvine's campus and the site of an annual spring fair. Campus-wide events like Shocktoberfest and Homecoming are well attended.

Career Services

The UCI Division of Career Pathways employs fifteen professional employees who work with or on behalf of undergraduate students as career educators, internship coordinators, or employer engagement specialists. That 1,980:1 student-to-staff ratio is among the highest of any university profiled in this guidebook. Fortunately, the school still manages to reach a significant percentage of the undergraduate population through a variety of means as evidenced by numerous impressive data points.

University of California, Irvine

E-mail: admissions@uci.edu | Website: www.uci.edu

In the 2018-19 school year career counselors conducted 4,523 one-on-one counseling sessions, and 450 companies attended the school's various career fairs that drew a collective student crowd of greater than 10,000. The UCI Division of Career Pathways not only hosts general fall and spring fairs but also gatherings for STEM careers, health jobs, and law school applicants. An additional 3,000 students attended Career Pathways Panels. In 2017-18, companies conducted on-campus interviews with 1,305 undergraduate students. The list of on-campus recruiters included Deloitte, KPMG, Ernst and Young, PricewaterhouseCoopers, Google, Amazon, Northrop Grumman, and Johnson & Johnson. A total of 46 percent of students completed internships last year; half were noncredit internships while half were for credit. The job-shadowing program, now in its fifth year, attracted 268 student participants. Career services at UCI aren't perfect; it's simply too large an operation for fifteen people to handle, but the office possesses strong enough corporate connections to assist grads in achieving positive postgraduate outcomes.

Professional Outcomes

Accounting, aerospace, internet and software, K-12 education, real estate, and retail are among the industries attracting the greatest number of Anteaters. Companies employing the greatest number of Class of 2018 members include Boeing, the Walt Disney Company, Google, EY, and Microsoft. Many also end up with nonprofit organizations like Teach for America and City Year. Looking at alumni from all years, hundreds of individuals can be found at each of Kaiser Permanente, Facebook, Apple, Edwards Lifesciences, and Deloitte. The median salary within the first couple years of entering the working world, across all disciplines, is just under $40,000; five years out the median income rises to $54k, and ten years out alumni are earning a median salary of $75k. Computer science graduates earn close to $75k right off the bat. Few grads leave the state of California; Orange County, Los Angeles, San Francisco, and San Diego soak up the vast majority.

Between 75 and 80 percent of Irvine grads plan on pursuing an advanced degree within five years of earning their bachelor's. The majority of those enrolling in graduate school do so within the state of California. Many remain at Irvine or another UC campus—Berkeley, UCLA, and San Diego are among the most popular choices. Irvine also sends graduates to Stanford and USC as well as out-of-state to the University of Washington and Georgia Tech. UC-Irvine has a strong reputation for premed. In 2018-19, the university produced the twenty-fifth most medical school applicants of any institution in the country, and Anteaters possessed higher MCAT scores than the national average. The prestigious UCI School of Medicine admitted seventeen of its own alumni in 2018, which accounted for more than 15 percent of the incoming class. The UC Irvine School of Law is only a decade old but has already skyrocketed toward the top of the rankings. In addition to remaining in Irvine for law school, undergrads often gain acceptance to other excellent law schools within the UC system and also have earned acceptances to the likes of Harvard, Georgetown, and the University of Michigan.

Admission

An almost incomprehensible deluge of 117,000+ applications rained down on the UCI admissions staff in 2019, including the greatest number of high school/nontransfer students of any school in the University of California system. In 2019, its acceptance rate fell to 26.6 percent, a far cry from only five years prior when 41 percent of high school applicants were admitted. At the time the SAT mid-50 percent range was 1040-1290; today, it is 1180-1440, quite a metamorphosis in terms of selectivity. Getting into Irvine without placing in the top decile of your high school class is nearly impossible as 98 percent of 2018-19 freshmen earned that distinction. The average GPA for attending students was 4.0.

For a school receiving six-figure application numbers each year, it still professes to hold eight factors as being of the highest importance: rigor of curriculum, GPA, class rank, standardized test scores, the essay, extracurricular activities, talent/ability, work experience, and volunteer work. Interestingly, first-generation status is listed as merely "considered," yet the school's undergraduate population is comprised of an incredible 48 percent of first-generation students. While racial/ethnic status is "not considered" in admissions, 26 percent of the student population are underrepresented minorities.

Worth Your Money?

An annual tuition of under $16,000 for California residents helps explain the rising popularity of Irvine as well as the other UC campuses. No matter your intended major, this in-state rate represents a genuine bargain. Out-of-state residents without plans to pursue computer science or engineering should think twice before committing three times that amount in tuition costs alone. You would likely be better off pursuing options in your home state or private options with merit aid.

FINANCIAL
Institutional Type: Public
In-State Tuition: $11,442
Out-of-State Tuition: $40,434
Room & Board: $16,135
Required Fees: N/A
Books & Supplies: $1,390

Avg. Need-Based Aid: $19,902
Avg. % of Need Met: 83%

Avg. Merit-Based Aid: $7,771
% Receiving Merit-Based Aid: 3%

Avg. Cumulative Debt: $19,039
% of Students Borrowing: 53%

CAREER
Who Recruits
1. Pacific Life
2. Edwards Life Sciences
3. Glidewell Laboratories
4. Western Digital
5. Northwestern Mutual

Notable Internships
1. Grant Thorton LLP
2. PlayStation
3. Yelp

Top Industries
1. Business
2. Engineering
3. Education
4. Operations
5. Research

Top Employers
1. Kaiser Permanente
2. Google
3. Amazon
4. Apple
5. Microsoft

Where Alumni Work
1. Orange County, CA
2. Los Angeles
3. San Francisco
4. San Diego
5. New York City

Median Earnings
College Scorecard (Early Career): $58,400
EOP (Early Career): $60,400
PayScale (Mid-Career): $116,000

RANKINGS
Forbes: 87
Money: 1
U.S. News: 36, National Universities
Wall Street Journal/THE: 73
Washington Monthly: 18, National Universities

#CollegesWorthYourMoney

University of California, Los Angeles

Los Angeles, California | Admissions Phone: 310-825-3101

ADMISSION

Admission Rate: 14%
Admission Rate - Men: 13%
Admission Rate - Women: 15%
EA Admission Rate: Not Offered
ED Admission Rate: Not Offered
Admission Rate (5-Year Trend): -6%
ED Admission Rate (5-Year Trend): Not Offered
% of Admits Attending (Yield): 39%
Transfer Admission Rate: 24%

Offered Wait List: N/A
Accepted Wait List: N/A
Admitted Wait List: N/A

SAT Reading/Writing (Middle 50%): 630-780
SAT Math (Middle 50%): 640-740
ACT Composite (Middle 50%): 29-35
Testing Policy: ACT/SAT Required
SAT Superscore: No
ACT Superscore: No

% Graduated in Top 10% of HS Class: 97%
% Graduated in Top 25% of HS Class: 100%
% Graduated in Top 50% of HS Class: 100%

ENROLLMENT

Total Undergraduate Enrollment: 31,505
% Part-Time: 2%
% Male: 42%
% Female: 58%
% Out-of-State: 13%
% Fraternity: 11%
% Sorority: 13%
% On-Campus (Freshman): 98%
% On-Campus (All Undergraduate): 48%

% African-American: 3%
% Asian: 28%
% Hispanic: 22%
% White: 27%
% Other: 6%
% Race or Ethnicity Unknown: 2%
% International: 12%
% Low-Income: 36%

ACADEMICS

Student-to-Faculty Ratio: 18:1
% of Classes Under 20: 51%
% of Classes Under 40: 74%
% Full-Time Faculty: 71%
% Full-Time Faculty w/ Terminal Degree: 98%

Top Programs
Computer Science
Engineering
English
Fine Arts
Mathematics
Performing Arts
Political Science
Psychology

Retention Rate: 97%
4-Year Graduation Rate: 77%
6-Year Graduation Rate: 90%

Curricular Flexibility: Somewhat Flexible
Academic Rating: ★★★★✓

Inside the Classroom

Among the most selective public universities in the country, UCLA is also the most diverse campus on the planet. The undergraduate student body is 27 percent Asian, 22 percent Hispanic, and 12 percent international, not to mention 33 percent first-generation college students, making UCLA a fascinating place to pursue one of 134 majors in 109 academic departments. More than 31,500 undergraduates enjoy a whopping 3,800 course offerings that include programs in over forty languages, many of which you won't find offered at your average university such as Armenian, Old Norse, and Sanskrit.

The general education curriculum requires that every student explore three foundational areas: the arts and humanities, society and culture, and scientific inquiry. That entails completing ten courses. Additionally, in order to graduate you'll need to meet requirements in foreign language, writing, and diversity. The school's Capstone Initiative has sought to bring a culminating senior academic endeavor to as many students as possible. As of 2018, more than sixty majors at UCLA require a capstone experience that results in the creation of a tangible product under the mentorship of faculty members.

Close to half of classrooms contain fewer than twenty Bruins, but those taking introductory courses will find themselves in a fair number of lecture halls with a hundred or more students. Professors are given impressively high marks for a research university of UCLA's size. Over 90 percent of the graduates of the College of Letters and Science rate their professors as being both intellectually challenging and accessible. By senior year, 40 percent of undergraduates have participated in a research experience. There are multiple undergraduate research journals in which students can publish their original works as well as a Research Poster Day each May when students can present. Every year one-quarter of the undergraduate population elects to study abroad, a sharp increase from only a few years ago. UCLA has 115 partner universities in forty-two countries around the globe.

By volume, the most commonly conferred degrees are in the social sciences (26 percent), biology (15 percent), engineering (7 percent), mathematics (7 percent), and interdisciplinary studies (5 percent). UCLA isn't a school where one department is ranked significantly higher than any other. Departmental rankings are high across the board in areas such as computer science, engineering, film, fine and performing arts, mathematics, political science and many more. The school also produces a reasonable number of postgraduate scholarship winners—seven graduates took home Fulbright Scholarships in 2019.

Outside the Classroom

If you can't find your niche at UCLA it can hardly be blamed on the school that offers over 1,000 clubs and student organizations. There is no shortage of opportunities to volunteer in the surrounding Los Angeles community—the Volunteer Center, Center for Community Learning, and Community Programs Office offer countless avenues for civic involvement. Greek life is readily available with more than sixty fraternities and sororities on campus, but it is hardly smothering; only 11 percent of men and 13 percent of women are Greek affiliated. UCLA's sports scene boasts storied basketball and baseball teams, big-time football, and 116 all-time championships across twenty-five Division I men's and women's sports. Ninety-eight percent of freshmen reside on campus, and 52 percent of the entire student body lives in university-owned housing. As bountiful as campus life is at UCLA, the excitement that can be found in the surrounding neighborhoods is truly limitless. Within a few miles of campus undergrads can venture to Venice Beach, Santa Monica, Malibu, or Beverley Hills. In short, you won't find too many Bruins complaining of boredom.

Career Services

With twenty-three full-time employees dedicated to undergraduates, the UCLA Career Center has a 1,373:1 student-to-counselor ratio, much higher than most of the schools featured in this guide. The university does host a number of major-specific job fairs that are attended by an impressive selection of employers. In 2018, its Engineering and Technical Fair was attended by forty organizations including the CIA, Texas Instruments, Visa, and eBay. Each academic quarter the school also hosts Hire UCLA, which is well-attended by major corporations.

When it comes to finding an internship; students are not going to have their hands held throughout the entire process. The Career Center connects students with internships via Handshake, and 60 percent of undergrads do eventually land one, but the school lacks corporate partnerships that allow for a more streamlined experience. The Career Center offers services such as an online resume critique with a five-day turnaround, and students are free to schedule an appointment or drop by for career advice, a mock interview, or graduate school exploration from 9 a.m. to 4 p.m. on weekdays. Additional events are organized by the UCLA Career Center just about every day. For example, over the course of one random week in May 2019 the center hosted a resume workshop, a consulting industry meetup, a workshop on branding oneself on LinkedIn, and a recruiting visit from the Vanderbilt University School of Medicine.

University of California, Los Angeles

E-mail: ugadm@saonet.ucla.edu | Website: www.ucla.edu

Professional Outcomes

UCLA grads flow most heavily into the education, technology, and financial services sectors. The employers that snatch up the highest number of recent Bruin grads include Disney, Google (where over 1,500 alumni presently work), EY, Teach for America, Amazon, and Oracle. Hundreds also can be found in the corporate offices of Uber, Microsoft, Facebook, Netflix, Salesforce, Airbnb, and LinkedIn. Internships definitely help students land jobs; students who had at least one internship found employment at double the rate of their peers who did not have such an experience. The average starting salary for full-time employment exceeds $52,000, a solid figure considering the vast array of degrees being conferred. A good number of students stay in L.A./Orange County after graduation, but the other most popular destination points include NYC, DC, Chicago, Seattle, and Boston.

Roughly one-quarter of graduates enroll directly in a graduate/professional school. The most attended grad schools are primarily other excellent California-based institutions including Stanford, Pepperdine, USC, Berkeley, and Loyola Marymount. UCLA students applying to medical school have experienced acceptance rates varying from 51-59 percent over recent years. The most frequently attended medical schools include Duke, Boston University, Drexel, Temple, Case Western, and NYU. Over 90 percent of Bruins applying to law school garner at least one acceptance, a clip that is roughly 15 percent better than the national average. Law schools with the highest number of UCLA grads include many of the aforementioned California universities as well Georgetown, Vanderbilt, George Washington, Duke, and American.

Admission

A decade ago, 24 percent of the roughly 50,000 applicants to UCLA received acceptance letters; today, the school receives the most applications of any college in the country with 113,761 in 2018, and the acceptance rate has fallen to 14 percent. Students from out-of-state fared better than in-state applicants and international applicants by a significant margin with out-of-staters enjoying a 23 percent acceptance rate in 2017. However, the University of California Board of Regents recently passed a measure capping out-of-state/international enrollment at 18 percent moving forward, which should curb that trend.

Those accepted straight from high school are a high-achieving bunch as a hard-to-comprehend 97 percent graduated in the top 10 percent of their high school class. The SAT 25th/75th percentile breakdown is 1270-1520 and the ACT range is 28-34. For comparison, a decade ago, the average SAT score of an admitted student was 1330; the average ACT was 29. Thus, we can say that UCLA's shrinking acceptance rate is, indeed, indicative of increasing selectivity. It's important to note that there is more than one way through these heavily guarded gates. UCLA is extremely transfer friendly, offering admission to 5,770 such students in 2018 with the vast majority coming from California's system of community colleges. UCLA has joined the ranks of the uber-selective as the pool of top-of-their-class applicants continues to grow each year. While it does employ some semblance of a holistic process that considers personal qualities, likely contributions to campus life, and challenges overcome, applicants need to bring high GPAs and test scores to the table to have a genuine shot at admission.

Worth Your Money?

The average UCLA graduate has almost $10,000 less in student loan debt than the average college graduate in the country. It helps when your in-state tuition to attend one of the finest universities around is only $13k, and the total annual cost of attendance is $34,390 for a resident but $63,382 for a nonresident. Few students receive any merit-based aid, yet over half are awarded need-based grants with a mean yearly value of $20,926. While they are rarely able to meet 100 percent of a student's demonstrated financial need, the school is priced so reasonably that graduates emerge with little debt and sky-high job prospects. Depending on your intended major and/or financial situation, UCLA can be worth your money even as an out-of-stater, despite the elevated price.

FINANCIAL
Institutional Type: Public
In-State Tuition: $11,442
Out-of-State Tuition: $40,434
Room & Board: $15,902
Required Fees: $1,784
Books & Supplies: $1,464

Avg. Need-Based Aid: $20,926
Avg. % of Need Met: 81%

Avg. Merit-Based Aid: $5,763
% Receiving Merit-Based Aid: 4%

Avg. Cumulative Debt: $22,390
% of Students Borrowing: 42%

CAREER
Who Recruits
1. Bain & Company
2. Airbnb
3. Salesforce
4. Netflix
5. Oracle

Notable Internships
1. CBRE
2. Los Angeles Magazine
3. Northrop Grumman

Top Industries
1. Business
2. Education
3. Operations
4. Engineering
5. Media

Top Employers
1. Google
2. Apple
3. Amazon
4. Facebook
5. Microsoft

Where Alumni Work
1. Los Angeles
2. San Francisco
3. Orange County, CA
4. New York City
5. San Diego

Median Earnings
College Scorecard (Early Career): $60,700
EOP (Early Career): $65,800
PayScale (Mid-Career): $116,100

RANKINGS
Forbes: 38
Money: 4
U.S. News: 20, National Universities
Wall Street Journal/THE: 25 (T)
Washington Monthly: 12, National Universities

#CollegesWorthYourMoney

University of California, San Diego

La Jolla, California | Admissions Phone: 858-534-4831

ADMISSION
Admission Rate: 30%
Admission Rate - Men: 30%
Admission Rate - Women: 30%
EA Admission Rate: Not Offered
ED Admission Rate: Not Offered
Admission Rate (5-Year Trend): -7%
ED Admission Rate (5-Year Trend): Not Offered
% of Admits Attending (Yield): 23%
Transfer Admission Rate: 50%

Offered Wait List: 11,868
Accepted Wait List: 7,372
Admitted Wait List: 0

SAT Reading/Writing (Middle 50%): 620-700
SAT Math (Middle 50%): 630-770
ACT Composite (Middle 50%): 26-33
Testing Policy: ACT/SAT Required
SAT Superscore: No
ACT Superscore: No

% Graduated in Top 10% of HS Class: 100%
% Graduated in Top 25% of HS Class: 100%
% Graduated in Top 50% of HS Class: 100%

ENROLLMENT
Total Undergraduate Enrollment: 30,285
% Part-Time: 2%
% Male: 50%
% Female: 50%
% Out-of-State: 6%
% Fraternity: 14%
% Sorority: 14%
% On-Campus (Freshman): 89%
% On-Campus (All Undergraduate): 39%

% African-American: 3%
% Asian: 37%
% Hispanic: 19%
% White: 19%
% Other: N/A
% Race or Ethnicity Unknown: 3%
% International: 19%
% Low-Income: 30%

ACADEMICS
Student-to-Faculty Ratio: 19:1
% of Classes Under 20: 43%
% of Classes Under 40: 65%
% Full-Time Faculty: 84%
% Full-Time Faculty w/ Terminal Degree: 98%

Top Programs
Biological Sciences
Chemistry and Biochemistry
Cognitive Science
Communication
Computer Science
Economics
Engineering
Political Science

Retention Rate: 94%
4-Year Graduation Rate: 62%
6-Year Graduation Rate: 86%

Curricular Flexibility: Less Flexible
Academic Rating: ★★★★

Inside the Classroom

Becoming a Triton used to be a disappointing consolation prize for applicants hoping to become a Bruin or a Golden Bear. While UCLA and Berkeley remain the crème de la crème of the UC system, the gap between those uber-elite jewels and UC-San Diego has closed significantly in recent years as applications have skyrocketed to the cusp of six-figures, and the profile of the average freshman has risen commensurately. In 2003, there were fewer than 20,000 undergraduates at the university; there are now in excess of 30,000. An extremely strong academic school, UCSD offers forty-two bachelor's degrees with many concentrations as well as fifty-five minors, all available for less than $15,000 per year in tuition.

There are six undergraduate colleges at UCSD that are meant, in the Oxford and Cambridge model, not to separate by discipline but, instead, to forge flourishing small liberal arts college communities within the larger university. Core curriculum at all of the colleges includes first- year writing, advanced writing, oral communication, mathematical reasoning, quantitative reasoning, and second language. Additionally, undergrads must complete coursework in science and technological inquiry, historical inquiry, literary inquiry, social and behavioral inquiry, artistic inquiry, theological and religious inquiry, philosophical inquiry, ethical inquiry, and diversity and social justice. Two "integration" experiences in which students make connections across disciplines also must be tackled, including one during freshman year.

Over 7,600 graduate students and a 19:1 student-to-faculty ratio are two numbers that don't bode well for those hoping for an intimate classroom experience. Yet, reality is a mixed bag. While 32 percent of course sections are held in larger lecture halls and contain fifty+ students, 43 percent of undergraduate courses sport an enrollment under twenty. Sixty percent of undergrads complete at least one research project as part of their. coursework, and roughly one-quarter assist a faculty member with research outside the classroom. Study abroad numbers are approaching 1,000 undergraduates per year, which is only a sliver of the total undergraduate population. Still, opportunities in forty-two countries are available for those who desire a semester of study outside of the United States.

Altogether, the social sciences have the highest representation of all majors (29 percent) followed by biology (19 percent) and mathematics (7 percent). UCSD's computer science and engineering programs have stellar reputations in the corporate and tech communities, and programs in biology, economics, and political science are among the best anywhere. In recent years nationally competitive postgraduate fellowship programs have selected a number of Tritons, and the school has produced as many as a dozen Fulbrights per year while the Biology Department alone saw five graduates capture National Science Foundation Graduate Research Fellowships last academic year.

Outside the Classroom

Just shy of 95 percent of freshmen live on the UCSD campus, but only 44 percent of the undergraduate population live in dormitories or college-owned apartments. Fraternities and sororities have a solid but not overwhelming presence on campus, drawing 14 percent of men and women. Unlike UCLA and Berkeley, San Diego doesn't offer prime-time football or basketball teams; in fact, it hasn't fielded a football team since 1968. Rather, the twenty-three Triton squads participate in NCAA Division II and fare quite well within that less competitive environment. However, plans do exist to join Division I's Big West Conference within the next few years. A diverse student body (37 percent minority and 9 percent international) enjoy an equally diverse array of clubs. There are over 500 to choose from with many options in the areas of student government, media, and a popular intramural sports program that has a 60 percent participation rate. The 180-acre campus is situated within the wealthy beachfront town of La Jolla, a thirteen-mile highway ride from downtown San Diego. While La Jolla is not a typical college town, many students live in beachfront apartments overlooking the Pacific Ocean or Mission Bay, and few complain about the heavenly weather.

Career Services

The UC-San Diego Career Center has eighteen full-time employees who work with or on behalf of undergraduate students, many of whom specialize in a particular discipline such as pre-law, pre-health, the social sciences, the humanities, business, or engineering. UCSD's 1,683:1 student-to-counselor ratio is toward the highest of any school featured in this guide. To compensate, it puts on a multitude of annual career fairs, many of which attract 1,000+ students. Those include large-scale fairs in the fall, winter, and spring, a Graduate School Fair, an Engineering and Computing Career Fair, and an event called Impact Career Fair: Companies for a Brighter Future. Each quarter, hundreds of companies are on campus to recruit undergraduate students.

University of California, San Diego

E-mail: admissionsinfo@ucsd.edu | Website: www.ucsd.edu

In 2017-18, the school listed 8,356 jobs/internships on Handshake, and those efforts led to 79 percent of graduates having participated in an experiential learning activity—internship, research, or community service. Thirty-minute one-on-one appointments can be scheduled, but scoring one of those appointments, particularly with a "good fit" counselor can be a challenge. Students, via op-eds in the school paper, have been clamoring for an increased number of advisors to accommodate the growing number of undergraduate students at the university. Thanks to the rising prestige of the school, UCSD students have enjoyed increasingly positive post-graduation outcomes, but there is still room to increase the level of support offered.

Professional Outcomes

A healthy 92 percent of UC-San Diego graduates are employed or in graduate school within six months of receiving their diplomas. Among the 73 percent who were employed, 95 percent had one or more job offers only three months after graduation. The most commonly entered industries were marketing/sales (14 percent), finance and banking (12 percent), accounting/auditing (11 percent), technology (9 percent) and health/medical (9 percent). Employers of 2018 graduates included the Walt Disney Company, Tesla, NBC Universal, PwC, Northrup Grumman, and EY. More than 1,000 current Google employees are UC-San Diego alumni, and Qualcomm, Amazon, and Apple all employ 500+ each. The median starting salary for San Diego grads was $55,000 in 2018. Those entering the engineering field averaged $65k, those in marketing/sales averaged $51k, and those majoring in education had a mean income of $40k. The bulk of grads remain in San Diego or relocate to Los Angeles or San Francisco.

Sixteen percent of 2018 graduates moved directly into a graduate or professional program. Remaining at UC-San Diego was the most popular choice followed by USC, San Diego State, UCLA, George Washington, NYU, the University of San Francisco, Pepperdine, and Columbia. Between 400 and 500 seniors apply to medical school each year and typically experience average to slightly below average levels of success; between 34 and 40 percent of applicants have been admitted in recent years. Pre-law students most frequently head to California-based institutions such as the University of San Diego School of Law, California Western School of Law, Thomas Jefferson School of Law, and Santa Clara University School of Law. However, Class of 2018 grads also found law school homes at the University of Chicago, Pepperdine, UCLA, Notre Dame, and Fordham.

Admission

A tsunami of 97,899 applications for a place in the Class of 2018-19 flooded the inboxes of the UC-San Diego Admissions Office, more than doubling the number of applications received a decade ago. The admit rate ten years ago was only 37 percent, not all that far from today's 30 percent. Yet, the profile of the average freshman has changed drastically in that same period. Freshmen in the Class of 2022 possessed mid-50 percent standardized test scores of a 1250-1470 on the SAT, 26-32 on the ACT, and 93 percent had an unweighted GPA higher than 3.75. A decade prior, the SAT range was 1150-1380 and "only" 84 percent had GPAs in that same range. Any way you slice it, this school has become vastly more selective in the recent past.

When you are approaching 100,000 applicants, a microscopic exploration of every application is not a realistic expectation. Thus, it makes sense that three of the four "very important" factors considered by the admissions committee are cut-and-dried: level of rigor, GPA, and standardized test scores (the SAT is submitted more often than the ACT). Class rank, interestingly, is not considered. The application essay also was assigned "very important status," and extracurricular activities, state residency, volunteer work, talent/ability, and character/personal qualities earned an "important" designation. There is no early action or early decision round at this school. If the person advising you on college admissions (counselor, parent, family friend) hasn't been paying close attention to the spike in applications and selectivity, UC-San Diego can easily become an institution that should be a "reach" or "target" school, but it could be mistakenly assigned the title of "safety school." In reality, a pristine academic transcript and test scores in the 90th percentile are prerequisites for most applicants.

Worth Your Money?

For the 24 percent of undergraduates who come from outside the state, the University of California-San Diego has an annual cost of attendance of $62,000. Residents, on the other hand, enjoy a COA of $33,000. Extremely little merit aid is distributed, making grants of the need-based variety your best bet for receiving a discount. Fortunately, 56 percent of current students receive some level of financial aid; the average award is $19,366. Staying within the UC system is always an excellent choice for residents, and while the school is getting expensive for outsiders, it may still prove to be a degree that returns your investment, particularly if you aim to work in the tech industry.

FINANCIAL
Institutional Type: Public
In-State Tuition: $11,442
Out-of-State Tuition: $40,434
Room & Board: $14,286
Required Fees: $2,728
Books & Supplies: $1,127

Avg. Need-Based Aid: $19,366
Avg. % of Need Met: 85%

Avg. Merit-Based Aid: $13,933
% Receiving Merit-Based Aid: 3%

Avg. Cumulative Debt: $21,061
% of Students Borrowing: 45%

CAREER
Who Recruits
1. Nordson Corp
2. Sherwin Williams
3. IQVIA
4. Hulu
5. Netflix

Notable Internships
1. Inuit
2. Dow Jones
3. American Express

Top Industries
1. Business
2. Engineering
3. Education
4. Research
5. Operations

Top Employers
1. Google
2. Qualcomm
3. Apple
4. Amazon
5. Illumina

Where Alumni Work
1. San Diego
2. San Francisco
3. Los Angeles
4. Orange County, CA
5. New York City

Median Earnings
College Scorecard (Early Career): $59,900
EOP (Early Career): $65,300
PayScale (Mid-Career): $123,700

RANKINGS
Forbes: 79
Money: 9
U.S. News: 37, National Universities
Wall Street Journal/THE: 37
Washington Monthly: 7, National Universities

#CollegesWorthYourMoney

University of California, Santa Barbara

Santa Barbara, California | Admissions Phone: 805-893-2881

ADMISSION
Admission Rate: 32%
Admission Rate - Men: 30%
Admission Rate - Women: 34%
EA Admission Rate: Not Offered
ED Admission Rate: Not Offered
Admission Rate (5-Year Trend): -8%
ED Admission Rate (5-Year Trend): Not Offered
% of Admits Attending (Yield): 18%
Transfer Admission Rate: 57%

\# Offered Wait List: 7,856
\# Accepted Wait List: 4,883
\# Admitted Wait List: 14

SAT Reading/Writing (Middle 50%): 620-710
SAT Math (Middle 50%): 610-770
ACT Composite (Middle 50%): 26-32
Testing Policy: ACT/SAT Required
SAT Superscore: No
ACT Superscore: No

% Graduated in Top 10% of HS Class: 100%
% Graduated in Top 25% of HS Class: 100%
% Graduated in Top 50% of HS Class: 100%

ENROLLMENT
Total Undergraduate Enrollment: 23,021
% Part-Time: 2%
% Male: 45%
% Female: 55%
% Out-of-State: 5%
% Fraternity: 9%
% Sorority: 14%
% On-Campus (Freshman): 90%
% On-Campus (All Undergraduate): 38%

% African-American: 2%
% Asian: 20%
% Hispanic: 27%
% White: 32%
% Other: 6%
% Race or Ethnicity Unknown: 1%
% International: 12%
% Low-Income: 41%

ACADEMICS
Student-to-Faculty Ratio: 17:1
% of Classes Under 20: 50%
% of Classes Under 40: 78%
% Full-Time Faculty: 86%
% Full-Time Faculty w/ Terminal Degree: 100%

Top Programs
Anthropology
Communication
Computer Science
Engineering
Environmental Studies
Global and International Studies
Performing Arts
Physics

Retention Rate: 92%
4-Year Graduation Rate: 70%
6-Year Graduation Rate: 87%

Curricular Flexibility: Somewhat Flexible
Academic Rating: ★★★★↙

Inside the Classroom

When your campus is bordered on three sides by the Pacific Ocean and the weather is 70-75 degrees virtually year around, it would be easy for academics to become an afterthought. While the University of California Santa Barbara does, indeed, have a well-earned reputation as a "party school," the approximately 23,000 undergraduate majors are, today, a higher-achieving lot than ever, and they flock to UCSB for the ninety undergraduate majors and slew of top-ranked departments every bit as much as the sand and surf.

The College of Letters and Science, the College of Engineering, and the College of Creative Studies all have different core curricular requirements. There is some crossover in terms of mandated courses in all three schools that include English, reading, and composition; literature; art; social science; and culture and thought. College of Letters and Science grads also must complete classes in foreign language and science, mathematics, and technology. Classes covering the special subject areas of European traditions, ethnicity, world cultures, and quantitative relationships are also part of some academic programs.

The student-to-faculty ratio at UC Santa Barbara is a decent 17:1, and the school does an excellent job of keeping undergraduate class sizes on the small side. In fact, more than half of sections contain fewer than twenty students, and 73 percent enroll twenty-nine or fewer. Thirty-two percent of graduates stated that they often had classes where professors knew their names, and another 41 percent responded that this occurred some of the time. An even more encouraging 89 percent of respondents said there were open channels of communication with professors either "sometimes" or "often." Undergraduate research opportunities definitely exist for those willing to forge relationships with faculty outside the classroom. A solid 57 percent of graduates report engaging in some type of independent study or research. It's not as easy to inspire Gauchos to leave their campus paradise for a semester in a foreign land—only 2 percent of students per year participate in study abroad.

The social sciences are the most popular area of study accounting for 26 percent of the total degrees conferred. Biology (10 percent), interdisciplinary studies (10 percent), math (8 percent), and journalism (7 percent) are next in popularity. The school has highly regarded programs in communication, computer science, engineering, physics, environmental science, and the performing arts. Santa Barbara graduates do not tend to apply for prestigious postgraduate fellowships in overwhelming numbers, but the school did produce four Fulbright winners in 2018.

Outside the Classroom

Freshmen live on the UCSB campus at a 90 percent clip; overall, 38 percent of the undergraduate student population resides in university-owned housing. Santa Barbara's glorious 1,000-acre campus is set against the Pacific Ocean, and multiple beaches are literally in your backyard (you can actually hear the ocean while you're studying). Of course, keeping focused is a challenge with the perfect weather, beautiful surroundings, and the fact that, no matter what rankings list you check, UCSB is one of the top party schools in the entire country. The town of Isla Vista is almost exclusively a college town with a laid back vibe full of free spirits and free-flowing hard liquor. Fraternities and sororities have a presence but do not dominate the social scene; only 9 percent of men and 14 percent of women join Greek organizations. Just about everyone on campus is involved in athletics in some way as there are twenty-nine club sports teams and a stunning 18,000 intramural participants each year. Nineteen varsity teams compete in NCAA Division I's Big West Conference. The baseball program is, perhaps, the most notable making regular tournament appearances and having produced many MLB players in its almost one-hundred-year history. There are also over 500 student clubs and numerous campus-wide events, including the famous (or infamous) annual Halloween celebration on Isla Vista. Fifty-seven percent of 2018 seniors also found time to engage in community service.

Career Services

USCB Career Services is run by nineteen professional employees who function as discipline-specific career counselors, employment specialists, graduate school counselors, and internship/experience managers. That 1,211:1 student-to-staff ratio is much higher than the average school in this guidebook, but that is not particularly alarming for a public university of Santa Barbara's size. Career services certainly keeps busy, hosting 260 workshops that, collectively, draw 2,300 students each year and also meets one-on-one with 2,565 individuals through scheduled appointments and another 3,617 through drop-ins. Four job and internship fairs held over the course of the 2017-18 school year attracted 343 employers and 4,228 students. Additionally, staff posted 38,500 jobs on Handshake for undergraduate consumption.

University of California, Santa Barbara

E-mail: admissions@sa.ucsb.edu | Website: www.ucsb.edu

This office is continuing to aggressively expand the number of employers who recruit on campus. Bain & Company, Goldman Sachs, US Bank, and Kaiser Permanente all have begun visiting Santa Barbara for information sessions, career fairs, and on-campus interviews. Internship experiences are supported through programs like the Intern Scholarship Program that issues $1,500 grants to help offset the costs of unpaid placements. An encouraging 45 percent of those who land an internship end up being hired by that organization on a full-time basis. Overall, this office does a nice job of bringing top employers to campus with regularity and hosts almost daily workshops on topics such as Engineering Boot Camp, Internships 101, So You Want to be a Researcher? and Conversations about Careers in Mental Health.

Professional Outcomes

Within six months of earning their diplomas, 84 percent of Gauchos have found employment, and only 7 percent of those seeking their first jobs have yet to nail down a position. The most popular industries entered are science/research (16 percent), engineering/computer programming (14 percent), business (13 percent) finance/accounting (11 percent), and sales (10 percent). Among the top employers of recent graduates are Google, EY, KPMG, Oracle, Amazon, IBM, and Adobe. Large numbers of UCSB alumni also can be found on the payrolls of Apple, Facebook, Microsoft, Uber, Salesforce, and Lyft. A fairly even split of Gauchos can be found in the Greater Los Angeles area and San Francisco. Many also remain in Santa Barbara or head to other Golden State locales like Sacramento, Orange County, or San Diego. Average salaries vary wildly across majors. Those joining the computer science and engineering field averaged $73,000 in compensation while those in finance took home $57,000; those entering the education, health- care, and journalism fields averaged $35k-$40k.

Seventy-five percent of Santa Barbara grads stated they intend to pursue a graduate or professional degree at some point. Of those jumping directly into an advanced degree program, 9 percent are continuing at UCSB, 23 percent at a University of California location, 16 percent at a school within the California State University System, 22 percent at a private school in California, and 36 percent go out of state. In 2018-19, there were 174 applicants to medical schools from UCSB, and acceptance rates were in line with the national average. Recent acceptances included prestigious medical schools such as Harvard, Cornell, Tufts, Georgetown, Johns Hopkins, Dartmouth, Wake Forest, UVA, UNC-Chapel Hill, and Duke. Those applying to law school or other graduate programs also gained entrance to a wide range of schools, including the most prestigious in the country.

Admission

A line 92,314 students long formed for a place in the UC Santa Barbara Class of 2022; 32 percent were admitted, and 17 percent of those accepted ultimately enrolled in the university. Those entering the university in 2018-19 earned an average high school GPA of 4.12, and 92 percent had a GPA of over 3.75. The mid-50 percent standardized test scores were a 1220-1480 on the SAT, the more commonly submitted test, and a 26-32 on the ACT. A decade ago, Santa Barbara was a much easier university to get into. At that time the average SAT score was below 1200, and the acceptance rate was close to 50 percent. It's important that current applicants do not mistake the UCSB of ten years ago for the highly selective school it is today.

For a university approaching six figures worth of applicants, it is a bit surprising that it lists the application essay as being "very important," a designation only given to two other factors: GPA and standardized test scores. Rigor of one's high school course load is ranked as "important," and factors like work experience, extracurricular activities, state residency, and first-generation status are "considered." Santa Barbara does not consider recommendations, interviews, or demonstrated interest when making admissions decisions. As is the standard with schools in the University of California System, there is no early action or early decision; rather, the regular deadline is on the early side. You must submit your application by November 30. UC Santa Barbara is a transfer-friendly institution as it accepts 57 percent of those who apply.

Worth Your Money?

Cheap tuition (sub $13k) plus expensive California living brings the overall cost of attendance to a shade under $37,000 per year. As with all of the schools in the University of California System, even if you received zero aid, UC Santa Barbara would still be a solid investment. An out-of-state student would pay $66,675 per year in tuition, meaning that budget-conscious teens and families would likely have much better private or in-state options. The school caps nonresident enrollment at 18 percent (it currently sits below that mark), but that population has been rising in recent years, so there are many people willing to spend $268,000 on a public school education—a move that we do not recommend unless financial resources are unlimited and/or you happen to be majoring in engineering or computer science.

FINANCIAL
Institutional Type: Public
In-State Tuition: $11,442
Out-of-State Tuition: $40,434
Room & Board: $15,520
Required Fees: $2,949
Books & Supplies: $1,184

Avg. Need-Based Aid: $21,635
Avg. % of Need Met: 81%

Avg. Merit-Based Aid: $8,873
% Receiving Merit-Based Aid: 2%

Avg. Cumulative Debt: $20,004
% of Students Borrowing: 50%

CAREER
Who Recruits
1. Arista Networks
2. Deckers Brands
3. Peace Corps
4. Raytheon
5. West Coast Financial, LLC

Notable Internships
1. SpaceX
2. U.S. House of Representatives
3. Telsa

Top Industries
1. Business
2. Education
3. Operations
4. Sales
5. Engineering

Top Employers
1. Google
2. Apple
3. Oracle
4. Amazon
5. Microsoft

Where Alumni Work
1. Los Angeles
2. San Francisco
3. Santa Barbara, CA
4. San Diego
5. Orange County, CA

Median Earnings
College Scorecard (Early Career): $55,300
EOP (Early Career): $58,800
PayScale (Mid-Career): $116,300

RANKINGS
Forbes: 84
Money: 30
U.S. News: 34, National Universities
Wall Street Journal/THE: 71
Washington Monthly: 21, National Universities

#CollegesWorthYourMoney

University of Chicago

Chicago, Illinois | Admissions Phone: 773-702-8650

ADMISSION
Admission Rate: 7%
Admission Rate - Men: 8%
Admission Rate - Women: 7%
EA Admission Rate: N/A
ED Admission Rate: N/A
Admission Rate (5-Year Trend): -2%
ED Admission Rate (5-Year Trend): N/A
% of Admits Attending (Yield): 77%
Transfer Admission Rate: 5%

Offered Wait List: N/A
Accepted Wait List: N/A
Admitted Wait List: N/A

SAT Reading/Writing (Middle 50%): 720-770
SAT Math (Middle 50%): 750-800
ACT Composite (Middle 50%): 33-35
Testing Policy: Test Optional
SAT Superscore: Yes
ACT Superscore: Yes

% Graduated in Top 10% of HS Class: 99%
% Graduated in Top 25% of HS Class: 100%
% Graduated in Top 50% of HS Class: 100%

ENROLLMENT
Total Undergraduate Enrollment: 6,552
% Part-Time: 0%
% Male: 51%
% Female: 49%
% Out-of-State: 71%
% Fraternity: 8%
% Sorority: 12%
% On-Campus (Freshman): 100%
% On-Campus (All Undergraduate): 55%

% African-American: 6%
% Asian: 22%
% Hispanic: 16%
% White: 46%
% Other: 8%
% Race or Ethnicity Unknown: 3%
% International: 14%
% Low-Income: 11%

ACADEMICS
Student-to-Faculty Ratio: 5:1
% of Classes Under 20: 77%
% of Classes Under 40: 92%
% Full-Time Faculty: 85%
% Full-Time Faculty w/ Terminal Degree: 85%

Top Programs
Economics
English
Environmental Studies
History
International Relations
Mathematics
Psychology
Sociology

Retention Rate: 99%
4-Year Graduation Rate: 89%
6-Year Graduation Rate: 94%

Curricular Flexibility: Less Flexible
Academic Rating: ★★★★★

Inside the Classroom

Once a bastion of uncompromising intellectuals lovingly referred to as "the place where fun comes to die," the University of Chicago has undergone a transformational rebranding over the past decade. Still a destination point for an army of 6,500 brilliant young people, it now boasts an acceptance rate in the same league with Ivies like Brown and Yale (40 percent were accepted as recently as 2005) and, while still as academically rigorous as any institution in the country, it has worked to expand its previously unidimensional appeal.

There are fifty-one majors at the University of Chicago, but more than 50 percent of degrees conferred are in four concentrations: economics, biology, mathematics, and political science. Economics alone is the selection of roughly one-quarter of the undergraduate population, in large part because the university does not, for reasons of philosophy and tradition, offer a traditional business major.

The University of Chicago runs on a quarter system that equates to four ten-week sessions in which students take three or four classes at a time. Given the legendarily heavy workload at the school, the truncated terms can lead to a good deal of stress and an excessive number of all-night study sessions. All undergraduates must plow through the school's common core curriculum that requires an introduction to the tools of inquiry in every discipline: math and science (6 combined courses), humanities (6 courses), and social science (3 courses). Many elect to take nothing but core courses for their entire freshman year.

A 6:1 student-to-faculty ratio means that classrooms remain fairly intimate, and face-time with the renowned faculty is a reality. More than three-quarters of UChicago undergraduate sections have an enrollment of nineteen or fewer students. Undergraduate research opportunities are ubiquitous as 80 percent of students end up working in a research capacity alongside a faculty member. A solid 48 percent of undergrads study abroad at one of the sixty-six programs offered in thirty-two cities around the world.

No matter your area of concentration, a degree from UChicago will carry a great deal of weight in the eyes of employers and graduate/professional schools alike. All of the areas previously mentioned as the most popular majors have particularly sterling reputations with a global reach. On that topic, if you name a prestigious post-graduate award or fellowship, chances are the University of Chicago is one of the most frequent producers. In the last five years students have captured 118 Fulbright Scholarships, thirteen Goldwater Scholarships, five Marshall Scholarships, and four Rhodes Scholarships. Perhaps most astoundingly, between faculty and alumni the UChicago boasts ninety affiliated Nobel Prizes (eight are currently on faculty) over the school's illustrious history. Lastly, it also lays claim to fifty Rhodes Scholars all time, the eighth most of any university.

Outside the Classroom

With its campus based in the Hyde Park neighborhood on Chicago's South Side, students have access to a vibrant metropolis within walking distance of their dorms. Countless museums, restaurants, bookshops, parks, and theaters are never more than a stone's throw away. Given UChicago's reputation as a haven for hardcore intellectuals, it may come as a surprise that there are nineteen official Greek organizations on campus with a participation rate of 20 percent. Athletes, nicknamed the Maroons, participate in NCAA Division III. There are twenty varsity teams that are evenly split between the genders; no athletic scholarships are offered, and athletics, in general, capture a limited degree of student attention. Yet, a hard-to-comprehend 70 percent of the student body participates in the school's extensive intramural and club sports programs. Over 400 under-graduate-run clubs are active, including a number of improv and theater groups (the university is the birthplace of modern improv), community service organizations, and publications. DOC is the nation's oldest student-run film society and screens films on a daily basis. On-campus housing consists of seven residence halls divided into thirty-nine houses designed to nurture a sense of community. Freshmen are required to participate in the university housing system, but a large percentage of upperclassmen, 45 percent of the total student body, reside in off-campus housing.

Career Services

The university pours ample resources into career services, employing fifty-two full-time consultants who have highly specialized areas of expertise including business careers, law school planning, health-care careers, journalism, STEM, and start-ups. Boasting a student-to-advisor ratio of 126:1, UChicago has one of the absolute best ratios of any institution included in this book. It also puts its extensive staff to work on behalf of under-graduate students. To help quantify that statement, the staff engaged students in 12,409 one-on-one advising appointments in the 2018-19 school year.

An exceptional 80 percent of freshmen engage with the Career Advancement Office. Through the Metcalf Internship Program, massive numbers of students procure internship positions at top companies around the globe. In a given year, UChicago students secure more than 2,800 internships with more than 850 organizations. Undergraduates participate in excess of 500 employer site visits around the world that are known as Career Treks as well as 200 externships. The university forges strong connections with employers who are eager to conduct on-campus interviews with students; it currently has over one hundred full-time recruiting partners, including a laundry list of Fortune 1000 companies. Incredibly, 1,360 distinct employers recruited at the school during the 2018-19 academic year. Unmatched in terms of sheer personnel power and deeply committed to personalized, expert student counseling, UChicago Career Advancement Office is a leader in the career services realm.

Professional Outcomes

On commencement day, 93 percent of 2017 graduates already had their next step lined up, whether that involved entering the world of employment or continuing their higher education odyssey in graduate school. Business and financial services and STEM are the two sectors that scoop up the most graduates, but public policy and service and consulting also were well represented. The largest employers of 2017 grads, by volume, included Facebook, Google, JP Morgan, Goldman Sachs, McKinsey & Company, Bank of America, Citi, and Accenture. While many graduates go on to lucrative careers, the median income at age thirty-four for a UChicago alum is $62k, significantly less than graduates of many Ivy League institutions. For comparison, the median Penn grad makes $30k more.

University of Chicago grads are highly sought after by elite graduate universities. The top seven destinations for recent graduates were Yale, Columbia, Penn, MIT, Stanford, UCLA, and Johns Hopkins. Top law schools swoon at the sight of applicants from UChicago; 84 percent of applicants to Top 14 institutions gained admittance in 2017. Twenty-four grads were accepted by NYU, sixteen by UChicago itself, fourteen by Columbia, twelve by Harvard, and eight by Stanford. Med school applicants found similar success with 85 percent earning acceptance, more than double the national average. A fairly substantial 39 percent of graduates remain in the Midwest after finishing their degrees, 31 percent migrate to the Northeast, and 15 percent make the journey west.

Admission

The University of Chicago admitted a record low 7.2 percent of applicants for admission into the Class of 2022, placing the school in a selectivity stratosphere with Stanford, Yale, and Columbia. If you had predicted that figure at the turn of the millennium, sideways glances would have surely followed. In 2005 the university admitted 40 percent (not a typo) of applicants and still followed the beat of its own drummer, offering what was known as "The Uncommon App" and maintaining a reputation for welcoming waves of uber-serious bookworms. Changes in leadership and a decade of aggressive marketing practices (soliciting applications from unqualified students) led to a flood of new applicants and a sharp decline in the admit rate.

The average SAT score for admitted students is now in excess of 1500, although the school announced in 2018 that it was going test-optional. Skeptics believe that one of the motivations for the policy change was to drum up even more applicants to eventually reject, further enhancing its selectivity. Interestingly, the incoming profile of a UChicago student isn't that much different from what it was when it was "easier" to get into; the average SAT score for the Class of 2008 was in the mid-1400s, the same as a decade ago, and 99 percent of incoming students finished in the top 10 percent of their high school class. In sum, UChicago still takes similarly talented academic superstars now, accepting 7.2 percent of applicants, as it did when it accepted almost six times that figure. The difference is that instead of attracting a self-selecting pool, it now attracts hordes of applicants, the vast majority of whom are destined for rejection.

Worth Your Money?

If you are among the 43 percent of current UChicago students who qualify for financial aid, then you are in luck. The school covers 100 percent of demonstrated need, which leads to an average annual grant of $46,460. Thank goodness for that because the university has the highest cost of attendance of any school in the country at $81,531. Fortunately, if you need to pay back some epic loans, you should be able to do so by landing at one of the many top corporations to which the university funnels its graduates. If the University of Chicago is just a stop on the academic road, alumni do incredibly well in gaining acceptance into top graduate and professional schools. Either way, this school is worth your money, even at a relatively obscene price.

FINANCIAL
Institutional Type: Private
In-State Tuition: $57,642
Out-of-State Tuition: $57,642
Room & Board: $17,004
Required Fees: $1,656
Books & Supplies: $1,800

Avg. Need-Based Aid: $57,948
Avg. % of Need Met: 100%

Avg. Merit-Based Aid: N/A
% Receiving Merit-Based Aid: N/A

Avg. Cumulative Debt: $19,817
% of Students Borrowing: 29%

CAREER
Who Recruits
1. Kraft Heinz
2. Nielson
3. Boston Consulting Group
4. AQR Capital Management
5. Kaufmanm Hall & Associates

Notable Internships
1. Instagram
2. The Blackstone Group
3. Jane Street

Top Industries
1. Business
2. Education
3. Research
4. Finance
5. Media

Top Employers
1. Google
2. Goldman Sachs
3. JP Morgan
4. Facebook
5. Accenture

Where Alumni Work
1. Chicago
2. New York City
3. San Francisco
4. Washington, DC
5. Boston

Median Earnings
College Scorecard (Early Career): $68,100
EOP (Early Career): $61,700
PayScale (Mid-Career): $114,200

RANKINGS
Forbes: 16
Money: 77
U.S. News: 6 (T), National Universities
Wall Street Journal/THE: 14
Washington Monthly: 31, National Universities

#CollegesWorthYourMoney

University of Connecticut

Storrs, Connecticut | Admissions Phone: 860-486-3137

ADMISSION
Admission Rate: 49%
Admission Rate - Men: 48%
Admission Rate - Women: 50%
EA Admission Rate: Not Offered
ED Admission Rate: Not Offered
Admission Rate (5-Year Trend): -5%
ED Admission Rate (5-Year Trend): Not Offered
% of Admits Attending (Yield): 22%
Transfer Admission Rate: 61%

Offered Wait List: 2,027
Accepted Wait List: 1,249
Admitted Wait List: 502

SAT Reading/Writing (Middle 50%): 600-690
SAT Math (Middle 50%): 610-730
ACT Composite (Middle 50%): 26-31
Testing Policy: ACT/SAT Required
SAT Superscore: Yes
ACT Superscore: Yes

% Graduated in Top 10% of HS Class: 50%
% Graduated in Top 25% of HS Class: 84%
% Graduated in Top 50% of HS Class: 98%

ENROLLMENT
Total Undergraduate Enrollment: 19,133
% Part-Time: 3%
% Male: 49%
% Female: 51%
% Out-of-State: 21%
% Fraternity: 10%
% Sorority: 14%
% On-Campus (Freshman): 96%
% On-Campus (All Undergraduate): 65%

% African-American: 6%
% Asian: 11%
% Hispanic: 11%
% White: 56%
% Other: 3%
% Race or Ethnicity Unknown: 3%
% International: 10%
% Low-Income: 18%

ACADEMICS
Student-to-Faculty Ratio: 16:1
% of Classes Under 20: 52%
% of Classes Under 40: 78%
% Full-Time Faculty: 81%
% Full-Time Faculty w/ Terminal Degree: 93%

Top Programs
Accounting
Biology
Education
Exercise Science
Finance
Nursing
Pharmacy

Retention Rate: 93%
4-Year Graduation Rate: 73%
6-Year Graduation Rate: 85%

Curricular Flexibility: Somewhat Flexible
Academic Rating: ★★★✦

Inside the Classroom

New England is so overflowing with superior institutions of higher education that it is genuinely a challenge to travel more than a few miles through Massachusetts or Connecticut without accidentally bumping into one of the top colleges on the planet. However, that surplus of elite universities is balanced by a notable dearth of stellar public institutions. For applicants seeking such a school, you'll have to travel to the sleepy town of Storrs, Connecticut, a half-hour east of Hartford, where you'll find a regional giant with a national reputation. The main campus of the University of Connecticut is home to 19,000+ undergraduates, fourteen schools and colleges, and 116 undergraduate majors. While 76 percent of the student body are state residents, there are also undergraduates hailing from forty-two states and 106 countries presently enrolled, and the percentage of outsiders has been on the rise in recent years.

Whether you enter the School of Business, School of Engineering, School of Fine Arts, or other undergraduate college at Storrs you will encounter a core curriculum of basic requirements. In an effort to ensure "that a balance between professional and general education be established and maintained in which each is complementary to and compatible with the other," UConn mandates two courses in each of arts and humanities, social science, science and technology, and diversity and multiculturalism. Further, students must demonstrate competencies in information literacy, quantitative reasoning, writing, and a second language via additional coursework.

Considering the university's 16:1 student-to-faculty ratio and 8,300 graduate and professional students, one might expect all UConn courses to contain a vast sea of undergraduate faces. However, the school does a nice job of creating a balance of classroom experiences with 52 percent of sections enrolling fewer than twenty students, and only 16 percent containing more than fifty. To help forge even deeper connections with faculty, the Office of Undergraduate Research encourages students to schedule advising sessions to apply for both internal and external research posts. There are also formal programs to target including the Work-Study Research Assistant Program, the Honors Program, or the University Scholar Program that make research a centerpiece of the educational experience. Hundreds of study abroad options are on the table, and the university has taken steps to increase the rate of participation that currently sits around 15 percent.

From a sheer volume standpoint, the four most commonly conferred undergraduate degrees are in business (13 percent), health professions/nursing (12 percent), engineering (12 percent), and the social sciences (12 percent). In terms of prestige and national reputation, programs in business, pharmacy, and nursing carry a good deal of weight. Speaking of reputation, UConn's growing stature has helped its students capture an increasing number of highly competitive scholarships in 2019 including seven Fulbright Scholarships, four Goldwater Scholarships, a Udall Scholarship, and a Truman Scholarship.

Outside the Classroom

Unlike many universities of its size, a healthy 70 percent of undergraduates live on UConn's 4,100-acre campus. Freshmen are not required to live on campus, but 95 percent do. Overall, four semesters of housing are guaranteed to all entering students, and there are plenty of traditional apartments, suites, and residential learning communities available. At UConn you will be treated to one of the best college athletic programs in the country. Husky fans are a fervent bunch, and of the twenty-four varsity teams, nothing captures the attention of all of campus quite like the basketball squads. Since 1999 the men's hoops squad has captured four NCAA titles, and the women's team has won an astounding ten championships. Greek life draws 10 percent of men and 14 percent of women, adding up to 2,700 members in forty chapters. In total, there are 700 student clubs and five cultural centers. Amenities include an on-campus movie theater, ice rink, and a 191,000-square-foot recreation center that opened in 2019. Volunteer spirit is strong as students contribute a collective 1.3 million hours of community service each year. Major cities like Hartford, Providence, and Boston are close enough for a weekend jaunt.

Career Services

There are twenty-one full-time employees at the University of Connecticut Center for Career Development (CCD) who serve as career consultants, corporate relations specialists, experiential learning coordinators, and operations specialists. There are an additional six career consultants who work in the School of Business and School of Engineering, bringing the total of professional staff to twenty-seven. (That does not include the career services staff members located at UConn's branch campuses.) The CCD's 708:1 student-to-advisor ratio is higher than the average school in this guidebook, but it is fairly typical for a school with close to 20,000 undergraduates.

University of Connecticut

E-mail: beahusky@uconn.edu | Website: www.uconn.edu

Two-thirds of Huskies utilize career services at some point in their four years, and that rate is higher among students with successful postgraduate outcomes; 80 percent of 2018 graduates who found a job or graduate school within six months of receiving their diplomas had taken advantage of the CCD's services. Experiential learning—including internships—were completed by 80 percent of graduates. The school forges strong ties to national as well as local companies. In fact, the seventeen Fortune 500 companies located in Connecticut all recruit on the Storrs campus. There are number of career fairs throughout the year with the largest being the fall career fairs (All-University & STEM) that bring in 150 employers each per day and attract more than 2,000 students. Overall, the UConn CCD provides quality assistance to those it is able to reach, and its industry connections, particularly those with Connecticut-based companies, are strong.

Professional Outcomes

Eighty-eight percent of the graduating Class of 2018 had reached a positive outcome (job, grad school, military, volunteer position) within six months of earning their degrees. Among the 63 percent that had found employment, the largest numbers landed at Aetna, Cigna, Lockheed Martin, PwC, The Hartford, Travelers, and United Technologies. Historically, massive numbers of alumni also have been employed by Pratt & Whitney, Pfizer, IBM, and Deloitte. A sampling of the top job titles held by 2018 grads included financial analyst, consultant, engineer, nurse, sales consultant, and business analyst. The median midcareer salary (at age 34) is $57,000, slightly better than some higher-prestige schools within state borders like Connecticut College or Wesleyan. Huskies can be found in the largest packs in New York City and Greater Hartford—73 percent who attended a Connecticut high school remain in the state postgraduation. Boston, DC, San Francisco, and Philadelphia also have their fair share of UConn alumni.

Many of the 22 percent of 2018 graduates who immediately entered a graduate or professional program did so at their home university that caters to a total of 7,000 grad students. Based on the most recent data available, UConn grads are accepted to medical school at a 65 percent clip, a far better rate than their peers. Recent acceptances include many elite medical institutions including those at the University of Pennsylvania, Georgetown, the University of Chicago, Vanderbilt, and UVA. As many as twenty-five undergraduates per year matriculate into the University of Connecticut School of Medicine. Law acceptances in the past three years include an impressive list of the nation's top institutions such as Harvard, Yale, William & Mary, Cornell, Columbia, and Boston College.

Admission

UConn accepted 49 percent of the 34,886 Class of 2022 hopefuls, representing the lowest acceptance rate in school history and quite a departure from the UConn of a generation ago. In 2000 it received one-third as many applications and admitted more than 80 percent of in-state applicants. The mean SAT of freshmen arriving at the Storrs campus was 1306, and the mid-50 percent range was 1210-1420; a decade ago, a 1300 would have put you in the 75th percentile of attending students. Even with the changes to SAT in that time, that is still an indicator of a major jump in selectivity. Exactly half of the entering class in 2018-19 finished in the top decile of their graduating cohort, and 84 percent placed within the top quartile. That group included an astonishing 175 valedictorians and salutatorians.

For a suddenly swamped admissions office, the most important factors in evaluating applicants are the quickest to break down: standardized test scores, GPA, class rank, and the overall rigor of one's high school curriculum. First-generation status, essays, recommendations, extracurricular activities, volunteer work, character/personal qualities, and talent/ability are secondary considerations. There are no early action or early decision options at UConn; everyone faces the same January 15 deadline, but applicants should submit by the December 1 priority deadline for their best chance at merit aid offerings.

Worth Your Money?

For Constitution State residents UConn is a rock-solid deal at $13k for tuition and a total cost of attendance hovering around $30k. Those in the other New England States can attend at a discount for under $40k, but those from other states will see an annual COA of $53k. This school is a no-brainer for state residents as it's hard to get a combination of a cheaper/better education in the Northeast. For everyone else, the value of the degree would depend on the intended area of study. However, those not eligible for a discount of some kind could very likely locate better deals within their home states.

FINANCIAL
Institutional Type: Public
In-State Tuition: $13,798
Out-of-State Tuition: $36,466
Room & Board: $13,258
Required Fees: $3,428
Books & Supplies: $950

Avg. Need-Based Aid: $14,041
Avg. % of Need Met: 58%

Avg. Merit-Based Aid: $10,604
% Receiving Merit-Based Aid: 36%

Avg. Cumulative Debt: $22,208
% of Students Borrowing: 57%

CAREER
Who Recruits
1. CGI Inc.
2. ScribeAmerica
3. Mercer
4. USDA
5. Fidelity Investments

Notable Internships
1. iHeartMedia
2. UBS
3. New York Yankees

Top Industries
1. Business
2. Education
3. Operations
4. Healthcare
5. Sales

Top Employers
1. Pratt & Whitney
2. Travelers
3. The Hartford
4. Aetna
5. Cigna

Where Alumni Work
1. New York City
2. Hartford, CT
3. Boston
4. Washington, DC
5. San Francisco

Median Earnings
College Scorecard (Early Career): $58,400
EOP (Early Career): $56,700
PayScale (Mid-Career): $105,200

RANKINGS
Forbes: 130
Money: 42
U.S. News: 64, National Universities
Wall Street Journal/THE: 105 (T)
Washington Monthly: 62, National Universities

#CollegesWorthYourMoney

University of Florida

ADMISSION

Admission Rate: 39%
Admission Rate - Men: 36%
Admission Rate - Women: 41%
EA Admission Rate: Not Offered
ED Admission Rate: Not Offered
Admission Rate (5-Year Trend): -8%
ED Admission Rate (5-Year Trend): Not Offered
% of Admits Attending (Yield): 45%
Transfer Admission Rate: 47%

Offered Wait List: Not Offered
Accepted Wait List: Not Offered
Admitted Wait List: Not Offered

SAT Reading/Writing (Middle 50%): 640-710
SAT Math (Middle 50%): 640-730
ACT Composite (Middle 50%): 27-32
Testing Policy: ACT/SAT Required
SAT Superscore: Yes
ACT Superscore: Yes

% Graduated in Top 10% of HS Class: 77%
% Graduated in Top 25% of HS Class: 97%
% Graduated in Top 50% of HS Class: 100%

ENROLLMENT

Total Undergraduate Enrollment: 35,491
% Part-Time: 9%
% Male: 44%
% Female: 56%
% Out-of-State: 7%
% Fraternity: 17%
% Sorority: 22%
% On-Campus (Freshman): 78%
% On-Campus (All Undergraduate): 22%

% African-American: 6%
% Asian: 9%
% Hispanic: 22%
% White: 53%
% Other: 4%
% Race or Ethnicity Unknown: 3%
% International: 3%
% Low-Income: 30%

ACADEMICS

Student-to-Faculty Ratio: 18:1
% of Classes Under 20: 50%
% of Classes Under 40: 78%
% Full-Time Faculty: 84%
% Full-Time Faculty w/ Terminal Degree: 90%

Top Programs

Animal Science
Applied Physiology and Kinesiology
Biology
Business
Criminology
Education
Engineering
Journalism and Communication

Retention Rate: 97%
4-Year Graduation Rate: 68%
6-Year Graduation Rate: 90%

Curricular Flexibility: Somewhat Flexible
Academic Rating: ★★★★

Inside the Classroom

At a time when flagship state schools are being overrun by out-of-state and international students willing to pay full freight, the University of Florida stands strong as an almost exclusive landing spot for Sunshine State residents to the tune of 93 percent. Gator Nation could almost be its own small nation with 35,500 undergraduates, 16,800 graduate students, and roughly 400,000 living alumni. It's not hard to see why top Florida-based teens target UF as their number one choice. One of the top-ranked state universities in the United States can still be accessed by in-staters for an annual tuition under $7,000 at a time when many elite (and not so elite) schools are eight times higher in cost.

With sixteen colleges and one hundred undergraduate majors to choose from, the educational experiences of UF students are exceptionally diverse. That includes one of the country's largest honors programs at 3,400 students; classes within this program are capped at twenty-five. All Gators must chomp through a blend of state and university core academic requirements that include coursework in composition, humanities, mathematics, biological and physical sciences, social and behavioral sciences, and classes with "international" and "diversity" designations.

An 18:1 student-to-faculty ratio and a massive number of graduate students leads to some fairly large undergraduate course sections. Yet, the school impressively offers 50 percent of sections with an enrollment of fewer than twenty students, 36 percent have between twenty and forty-nine students, and the rest are fifty+. The Center for Undergraduate Research offers a University Research Scholars program, summer opportunities, and it hosts its own Undergraduate Research Symposium and publishes its own *UF Journal of Undergraduate Research*. The school offers 1,100 study abroad programs that are taken advantage of by more than 2,200 undergrads each year.

The Warrington College of Business and the Wertheim College of Engineering are highly respected, and a degree from either will yield one of the more absurd returns-on-investment in all of postsecondary education. Therefore, it's no surprise that those two programs confer the greatest percentage of degrees—13 percent and 12 percent, respectively. The social sciences (11 percent), biology (10 percent), and communications/journalism (8 percent) are next in popularity. The procurement of highly competitive fellowships and postgraduate scholarships is not a focal point of the university, but Gators do claim their fair share. Eight graduates of the Class of 2019 won a Fulbright Scholarship, and as many as twenty-seven students have won National Science Foundation Graduate Research Fellowships in recent years.

Outside the Classroom

Not leading off with a discussion of campus life at UF with football would be an egregious case of burying the lead. The 90,000 orange-and-blue adorned fans crammed into Ben Hill Griffin Stadium, more commonly referred to as "The Swamp," captures the lifeblood of the University of Florida. And it's not only football that is a point of athletic pride in Gainesville. UF is ranked alongside Stanford and UCLA as one of the best overall sports programs in the country. Twenty of the school's twenty-one teams compete in the ultra-competitive SEC Conference, and the Gators have earned an astounding thirty-six all-time national championships. Outside of varsity sports there are 1,000 student organizations, and 76 percent of students are engaged in campus activities for a minimum of an hour per week. There are sixty intramural sports leagues, two large fitness centers, and two lakes for swimming, boating, and relaxation. Due to a dearth of school-owned housing, only 22 percent of students live on campus, almost all freshmen. Many move into Greek houses as 17 percent of men and 22 percent of women enter fraternity and sorority life. Gainesville is constructed as a Southern college town-by-numbers experience with all the requisite components of beautiful weather, an overwhelming number of restaurants, bars, and shops, plenty of parties and, of course, the sports-crazed atmosphere.

Career Services

Unlike many schools of UF's size that have a network of smaller career services offices housed within various colleges, the centralized University of Florida Career Connections Center (C3) serves more than 54,000 current students and alumni. At C3 twenty-three professionals (not including accountants and HR personnel who work in the office) are available to assist you with career counseling, internship coordination, and networking. The university's overall student-to-counselor ratio of 1,678:1 is among the poorest of any school featured in this guidebook. Still, there are many positive, measurable things occurring at this career services center.

In 2017-18, almost 22,000 students engaged with C3 through workshops, virtually, or through one-on-one sessions; that figure represents more than three-fifths of UF's undergraduate population. Staff put on 341 professional development workshops, added 732 job and internship postings to Gator CareerLink each month, and attracted 1,130 employers and 13,453 students to career fairs. Most impressively, it facilitated over 4,600 on-campus interviews with 355 local, regional, and national employers. A solid 61 percent of 2018 graduates reported at least one non-academic internship experience during their four years of study. Twenty-three percent of employed grads reported a job fair as being a resource that helped them land their first jobs, and 10 percent cited the Career Connections Center. Despite limited staffing for individualized counseling to reach 35,000+ undergrads, UF does a nice job putting on large-scale events and bringing a vast array of companies onto campus to recruit and interview.

Professional Outcomes

Upon graduation, 60 percent of University of Florida grads planned on entering full-time employment, and 40 percent expected to enroll in a full-time graduate program. At the time they received their diplomas 55 percent had already procured a first job. The top occupation areas for 2018 graduates were engineering (13 percent), health care (11 percent), education (5 percent), computer science (5 percent), sales (4 percent), and finance (4 percent). Across the entirety of the alumni base, impressive numbers of Gators can be found at many of the nation's most desirable corporations. In fact, more than 200 UF grads are currently employed by Google, EY, Raymond James, Deloitte, Apple, Amazon, Microsoft, Oracle, PwC, and Facebook. Many graduates remain in the Gainesville area or spread out to other Florida cities including Miami, Tampa Bay, Orlando, Jacksonville, or West Palm Beach. However, substantial numbers of alumni also can be found in Atlanta, New York, DC, and San Francisco. As one would expect, starting salaries vary greatly by major. Grads of the College of Business Administration earn median starting salaries, including bonuses, of $65k, computer science majors earn $84k, English majors $31k, and psychology majors $27k; the average salary for all 2018 grads was $46k.

Of those seeking full-time graduate studies upon receiving their diplomas, 52 percent had already been admitted into a program at the time they were awarded their bachelor's. A master's degree was the most popular pursuit (48 percent) followed by degrees in the medical field (17 percent, including 6 percent working on MDs), law school (9 percent), and PhDs (6 percent). The pre-med program is solid as UF sends the second most undergrads to medical school of any university in the country, behind only UCLA. Students with strong GPAs and MCAT scores feed directly into the university's own highly ranked College of Medicine. In 2018, law school applicants enjoyed an 85 percent acceptance rate. The most commonly attended institution was UF's own law school where eighty-six graduates matriculated. Three students entered each of Harvard and the University of Chicago and two went to Yale while Columbia, NYU, and Penn all welcomed four Gators each into their prestigious law schools.

Admission

A record number 41,407 students submitted applications to the University of Florida for a spot in the 2019-20 freshman class; 14,136 were admitted, a 34 percent admit rate. The average Class of 2023 admitted student possessed a 4.45 GPA, SAT score of 1388, and ACT score of 31, all higher numbers than admitted applicants one year ago. Students tend to rank near the top of their high school class. The latest available data from the Class of 2022 shows that 78 percent placed in the top decile of their graduating cohort, and 97 percent finished in the top 25 percent. Five years ago, the acceptance rate was a far friendlier 47 percent, and the 75th percentile SAT score was lower than the average SAT score among 2023 admits, confirmation that the sinking acceptance rate is indicative of a genuine rise in the school's level of selectivity.

With such a mammoth pile of applications to weed through, one would expect the admissions committee to place the greatest value on hard numbers like standardized test scores, GPA, and class rank. However, of those three factors, the UF Admissions Office only rates GPA as being "very important" to the process. Other considerations listed as "very important" are more in line with those of an elite liberal arts school: rigor of secondary coursework, application essay, extracurricular activities, talent/ability, character/personal qualities, and volunteer work. The university does not offer any type of early action/decision plan, so all candidates are on equal footing in the regular cycle. Grades are king for Gainesville hopefuls; 98 percent had a GPA of 3.75 or above on a 4.0 scale. While standardized test scores are not advertised as "very important" or even "important" to the admissions process, they clearly play a role with 90 percent of students scoring above a 600 on the reading section of the SAT and 87 percent scoring above a 600 on the math portion.

Worth Your Money?

A $6,300 annual tuition cost in the modern era of universally exorbitant tuition looks like a misprint at first glance. Greater than half of current undergrads receive financial aid for an amount slightly *more* than cost of tuition, meaning that a good number of students are only paying housing and living expenses Amazingly, the University of Florida, even at full price—room and board and all fees—would only set you back $20k per year assuming, of course, that you qualify as a Florida resident. The sliver of students coming to Gainesville from out of state pay more than double that amount, but UF still ultimately proves a bargain. If you live in Florida and can get into the university, start packing your bags because you simply won't find a better value.

FINANCIAL
Institutional Type: Public
In-State Tuition: $4,477
Out-of-State Tuition: $25,694
Room & Board: $10,220
Required Fees: $1,904
Books & Supplies: $850

Avg. Need-Based Aid: $9,083
Avg. % of Need Met: 99%

Avg. Merit-Based Aid: $2,233
% Receiving Merit-Based Aid: 50%

Avg. Cumulative Debt: $21,800
% of Students Borrowing: 38%

CAREER
Who Recruits
1. L3 Harris Technologies
2. OMP
3. Citrix
4. Procter & Gamble
5. KPMG

Notable Internships
1. Jet Blue
2. The Walt Disney Company
3. Kellogg Company

Top Industries
1. Business
2. Education
3. Operations
4. Healthcare
5. Engineering

Top Employers
1. Amazon
2. Intel
3. Microsoft
4. Google
5. PwC

Where Alumni Work
1. Gainsville, FL
2. Miami
3. Tampa
4. Orlando
5. Jacksonville

Median Earnings
College Scorecard (Early Career): $56,000
EOP (Early Career): $56,700
PayScale (Mid-Career): $102,800

RANKINGS
Forbes: 70
Money: 21
U.S. News: 34, National Universities
Wall Street Journal/THE: 63 (T)
Washington Monthly: 16, National Universities

#CollegesWorthYourMoney

Athens, Georgia | Admissions Phone: 706-542-8776

ADMISSION
Admission Rate: 49%
Admission Rate - Men: 45%
Admission Rate - Women: 51%
EA Admission Rate: 54%
ED Admission Rate: Not Offered
Admission Rate (5-Year Trend): -6%
ED Admission Rate (5-Year Trend): Not Offered
% of Admits Attending (Yield): 45%
Transfer Admission Rate: 76%

Offered Wait List: 1,257
Accepted Wait List: 704
Admitted Wait List: 32

SAT Reading/Writing (Middle 50%): 630-700
SAT Math (Middle 50%): 610-710
ACT Composite (Middle 50%): 27-32
Testing Policy: ACT/SAT Required
SAT Superscore: Yes
ACT Superscore: Yes

% Graduated in Top 10% of HS Class: 60%
% Graduated in Top 25% of HS Class: 92%
% Graduated in Top 50% of HS Class: 99%

ENROLLMENT
Total Undergraduate Enrollment: 29,611
% Part-Time: 6%
% Male: 43%
% Female: 57%
% Out-of-State: 11%
% Fraternity: 20%
% Sorority: 31%
% On-Campus (Freshman): 98%
% On-Campus (All Undergraduate): 34%

% African-American: 8%
% Asian: 10%
% Hispanic: 6%
% White: 69%
% Other: 4%
% Race or Ethnicity Unknown: 1%
% International: 2%
% Low-Income: 21%

ACADEMICS
Student-to-Faculty Ratio: 17:1
% of Classes Under 20: 45%
% of Classes Under 40: 81%
% Full-Time Faculty: 88%
% Full-Time Faculty w/ Terminal Degree: 94%

Top Programs
Animal Science
Biology
Business
Exercise & Sport Science
International Affairs
Journalism & Mass Communication
Psychology
Public Health

Retention Rate: 95%
4-Year Graduation Rate: 66%
6-Year Graduation Rate: 86%

Curricular Flexibility: Somewhat Flexible
Academic Rating: ★★★⧸

Inside the Classroom
Founded in 1785 as the first state-sponsored university in the country, UGA has since grown into a vast operation that boasts seventeen distinct colleges and schools that offer 143 majors. Those who make scenic Athens their undergraduate home are free to pursue concentrations in anything from the traditional disciplines to more exotic fields such as avian biology, furnishings and interiors, and turfgrass management. Becoming a Bulldog is infinitely more difficult than a generation ago, but that's an understandable marketplace adjustment for a school that is of extraordinarily high quality, about as sports conscious as any you'll come across, and that offers as low a tuition as you can hope to find anywhere in the country.

Students cover all of the basics through the school's core curriculum that requires two or more courses in each of English, math, science, world language/culture, and social science along with one course in quantitative reasoning. Freshmen at UGA all participate in a First-Year Odyssey seminar led by a faculty member and capped at eighteen students. Within that intimate setting, students have the opportunity to explore one of 300 thought-provoking topics including Chocolate Science, Death and Dying, Pets in Modern Society, and The Psychology of Harry Potter. Freshmen also have the choice of signing up for Residential Learning Communities, a program that allows dorm residents with similar interests to take classes together. The unique academic experience does not stop as a first-year student. The University of Georgia is the largest undergraduate institution in the country to mandate hands-on learning for every single graduate. UGA students must fulfill that requirement by completing one from a lengthy menu of internships, service options, or research opportunities.

The school's student-to-faculty ratio is 17:1 and, with 9,000 graduate students to also serve, not all of your coursework will be conducted in a cozy setting. Still, 45 percent of sections enroll fewer than twenty students compared with 11 percent of sections that enroll fifty or more. No matter your major, UGA encourages you to conduct research with a member of the school's faculty. The Center for Undergraduate Research Opportunities (CURO) awards grants to 500 students per year, and in 2018-19 a robust 550 students presented at the CURO Symposium. Meanwhile, the Office of Global Engagement helps 2,000 students annually find which of the one hundred+ study abroad programs that are led by UGA faculty is right for them.

Business is the most commonly conferred undergraduate degree, accounting for 28 percent of diplomas earned. It is followed by biology (9 percent), social sciences (9 percent), mathematics (9 percent), communication/journalism (9 percent), and psychology (6 percent). Top-ranked programs include animal science, business, communications, and public and international affairs. The school has seen an increase in its number of Fulbright Scholars, producing twenty-five over the last two years. Among public institutions, UGA also has been one of the top three producers of Rhodes Scholars over the previous two decades.

Outside the Classroom
Ninety-eight percent of freshmen, but only 34 percent of the student body, reside in university-owned housing. As you would expect at a school with over 29,000 undergraduates, there is a full smorgasbord of over 800 clubs and activities from which to choose. In 2017, The Center for Leadership and Service connected 12,500 students with over 228,000 volunteer hours. Fraternities and sororities have a strong presence with sixty-two Greek-letter organizations on campus that draw 20 percent of men and 31 percent of women. If you want to follow Division I athletics, UGA's perennial powerhouse football team draws 92,746 fans to Sanford Stadium each week in autumn. The school fields competitive men's and women's teams in a variety of other sports as well as a diverse selection of over seventy club and intramural teams. For non-athletic competitors, UGA's debate team has qualified for the National Debate Tournament for twenty-five consecutive years, and its chess team routinely wins state championships. The bottom line is that no matter your passion, you'll be able to find kindred spirits at UGA.

Career Services
The University of Georgia Career Center employs twenty-one full-time staff members including administrators, career consultants, and employer relations team members. That equates to a student-to-advisor ratio of 1,410:1, well below average compared the pool of institutions included in this book. While individualized attention is a challenge, the career center does regularly host job and internship fairs, and virtual Q&A sessions with employers are hosted on Twitter. Annually, over 1,000 companies engage in on-campus recruiting through one of the university's major-specific fairs. For example, a 2018 expo for students interested in a career in insurance/risk management was attended by sixty-five major corporations including AIG, Berkshire Hathaway, Geico, and State Farm.

Students can sign up at any time for a mock interview with a career consultant. The center also offers a more formalized series of career prep events called "Arch Ready," referencing the iconic campus landmark. Those events cover topics such as major selection, career exploration, and resume writing. The career center does engage companies to become internship partners for students, but data on the percentage of UGA undergrads that land internships is unavailable; what is known is that only 27 percent of Bulldogs who secured an internship did so through the career center. A robust alumni network will help recent grads connect with other Bulldogs anywhere in the world. Each year, close to 3,000 unique employers hire UGA grads, resulting in a wide-reaching alumni presence in business, government, and educational institutions.

Professional Outcomes

UGA's career outcomes rate (the percent of students employed or continuing their education six months after graduation) is 96 percent, 11 percent above the national average. Popular employers include Amazon, PricewaterhouseCoopers, IBM, and Deloitte. Graduate schools attended by UGA grads include many elite institutions such as Duke, Emory, UVA, UNC, Penn, and Vanderbilt. While 87 percent of students hailed originally from Georgia, many migrate to metropolitan areas around the United States with Dallas, Houston, Chicago, DC, New York City, and San Francisco among the top destinations. UGA does an excellent job of tracking graduates' starting salary data by school/major. That data allows prospective students to properly calibrate their financial expectations based on area of study. For instance, engineering grads in the Class of 2017 had a median starting salary of $60k while graduates of the Grady College of Journalism and Mass Communication reported a median income of $35k.

In 2017, a solid 20 percent of graduates elected to jump directly into a full-time advanced degree program. The most commonly attended graduate/professional schools included elite institutions such as Columbia, Duke, Emory, Georgia Tech, UNC-Chapel Hill, Penn, UVA, and Vanderbilt. In a given year, roughly half of the Bulldogs applying to medical school gain acceptance. Recent graduates are currently studying medicine at local schools, such as the Mercer University School of Medicine, as well as prestigious medical training grounds like Emory, Harvard, and Washington University.

Admission

Like many flagships around the country, the University of Georgia has grown increasingly competitive in recent years. The university received 26,027 applications in 2018, more than double the number received in 2005. The acceptance rate for a place in the Class of 2022 was 49 percent. Freshmen in 2018-19 possessed an ACT mid-50 percent score of 27-32 and 1240-1410 on the SAT. Only five years ago, the mean SAT was 1280. A strong academic profile is also essential—60 percent of successful applicants were in the top 10 percent of their class, and 92 percent were in the top quartile. Perhaps the most intimidating statistic is the average GPA of 4.0 with 95 percent of freshmen earning greater than a 3.75 over their high school careers.

A scholarship program guaranteeing any valedictorian or salutatorian from a Georgia high school free tuition has led to 4 percent of the student body being comprised of students holding those illustrious distinctions. The UGA Admissions Office says, "More than any other single factor, the grades you earn in your high school courses play the most important role in determining your competitiveness for admission to UGA." A rigorous high school course load is a must as 96 percent of admitted students took at least one AP, IB, or dual enrollment class. The school has no preference between the SAT and ACT and no longer requires the essay portion of either exam. In sum, the public jewel has become a destination point for the Peach State's top high school students. Knowledgeable applicants should use caution in underestimating the level of competition for spots on the picturesque Athens campus.

Worth Your Money?

You would be hard pressed to locate a better value for a college diploma from a highly respected institution than what you would get at UGA. In-state residents pay under $10k in tuition only and, thanks to cheap living in Athens, only $26k in total cost of attendance. Out-of-staters pay a not unreasonable total annual cost of $45k. The school offers a small amount of merit aid to 14 percent of undergrads and an average need-based grant of $11k to 42 percent of current students. It's little wonder that the average amount of debt for a University of Georgia grad is well under the national average. In short, this school is worth the money for any type of degree; even nonresidents can find a solid value here.

FINANCIAL
Institutional Type: Public
In-State Tuition: $9,790
Out-of-State Tuition: $28,830
Room & Board: $10,314
Required Fees: $2,290
Books & Supplies: $990

Avg. Need-Based Aid: $11,114
Avg. % of Need Met: 79%

Avg. Merit-Based Aid: $3,799
% Receiving Merit-Based Aid: 14%

Avg. Cumulative Debt: $22,872
% of Students Borrowing: 43%

CAREER
Who Recruits
1. Mailchimp
2. State Farm
3. Yelp
4. Boston Consulting Group
5. Home Depot

Notable Internships
1. Anthropologie
2. Delta Air Lines
3. TJX Companies

Top Industries
1. Business
2. Education
3. Operations
4. Sales
5. Healthcare

Top Employers
1. Home Depot
2. Delta
3. EY
4. Coca Cola
5. Deloitte

Where Alumni Work
1. Atlanta
2. Athens, GA
3. New York City
4. Washington, DC
5. Charlotte

Median Earnings
College Scorecard (Early Career): $50,500
EOP (Early Career): $49,900
PayScale (Mid-Career): $100,700

RANKINGS
Forbes: 99
Money: 119
U.S. News: 50, National Universities
Wall Street Journal/THE: 147
Washington Monthly: 99, National Universities

#CollegesWorthYourMoney

University of Illinois at Urbana-Champaign

Champaign, Illinois | Admissions Phone: 217-333-0302

ADMISSION
Admission Rate: 62%
Admission Rate - Men: 56%
Admission Rate - Women: 70%
EA Admission Rate: N/A
ED Admission Rate: Not Offered
Admission Rate (5-Year Trend): 0%
ED Admission Rate (5-Year Trend): Not Offered
% of Admits Attending (Yield): 31%
Transfer Admission Rate: 51%

Offered Wait List: 2,178
Accepted Wait List: 1,479
Admitted Wait List: 39

SAT Reading/Writing (Middle 50%): 600-700
SAT Math (Middle 50%): 620-780
ACT Composite (Middle 50%): 26-32
Testing Policy: ACT/SAT Required
SAT Superscore: No
ACT Superscore: No

% Graduated in Top 10% of HS Class: 48%
% Graduated in Top 25% of HS Class: 81%
% Graduated in Top 50% of HS Class: 98%

ENROLLMENT
Total Undergraduate Enrollment: 33,915
% Part-Time: 3%
% Male: 54%
% Female: 46%
% Out-of-State: 12%
% Fraternity: 20%
% Sorority: 25%
% On-Campus (Freshman): 100%
% On-Campus (All Undergraduate): 50%

% African-American: 6%
% Asian: 19%
% Hispanic: 12%
% White: 44%
% Other: 3%
% Race or Ethnicity Unknown: 1%
% International: 16%
% Low-Income: 21%

ACADEMICS
Student-to-Faculty Ratio: 20:1
% of Classes Under 20: 38%
% of Classes Under 40: 73%
% Full-Time Faculty: 99%
% Full-Time Faculty w/ Terminal Degree: 93%

Top Programs
Agriculture
Business
Chemistry
Communication
Computer Science
Engineering
Information Sciences
Physics

Retention Rate: 93%
4-Year Graduation Rate: 70%
6-Year Graduation Rate: 84%

Curricular Flexibility: Less Flexible
Academic Rating: ★★★✦

Inside the Classroom

The University of Illinois at Urbana-Champlain, the mammoth, highly ranked research university with an iconic Midwestern campus, serves as the beloved home to 50,000 increasingly accomplished students, including roughly 34,000 undergraduates. The university's humble beginnings as an industrial college upon its founding in 1867 are now nothing more than a distant, long-obliterated memory. Illinois' flagship institution 135 miles south of Chicago has fifteen schools and colleges, eight of which cater to undergraduate students. There are 150 academic programs including fifteen in the acclaimed Grainger College of Engineering alone.

As at many large universities, curricular mandates vary by school. The College of Liberal Arts & Sciences, by far UIUC's largest school, has a long list of must-takes including four classes in a foreign language, two English composition courses, and two courses in each of humanities and arts, natural sciences and technology, and social and behavioral sciences. In 2019-20, three cultural studies courses were added as requirements: Western Cultures, Non-Western Cultures, and US Minority Cultures.

Illinois' student-to-faculty ratio of 20:1 is among the highest of any school in this guide, and class sizes run the gamut from single-digit (12 percent) to more than fifty students (20 percent). Still, there is plenty of personalized attention available for those bold enough to seek it. A solid 32 percent of undergraduates work with a faculty member on a research project; another 20 percent have some type of fieldwork, practicum, or clinical experience. Unique opportunities for experiential learning abound at Research Park, an on-campus technology hub that hosts more than one hundred major corporations, and 2,100 employees who use the space as an incubator of innovation and a place to collaborate with Illinois faculty and students. Also strong, particularly for a school of UIUC's size, is the 24 percent participation rate for the school's study abroad programs that offers over 350 sites in fifty countries.

In sheer volume of degrees conferred, engineering is the leader at 21 percent followed by business/marketing (14 percent), the social sciences (9 percent), and communication/journalism (6 percent). The aforementioned Grainger College of Engineering, a top-ten school on any list, has a direct pipeline to top firms and tech companies. The Gies College of Business is also strong, particularly the Accounting Department, which is also a feeder to the world's best accounting firms. Prestigious scholarship competitions are similarly fond of Illinois grads— eleven of the forty-eight Fulbright Scholarship applicants from the university won awards, a performance comparable to elites such as Berkeley, Dartmouth, and Tufts. Seven seniors in the Class of 2019 captured National Science Foundation Graduate Research Fellowships.

Outside the Classroom

The University District is one of the only campuses in the United States better measured by miles than acres. The school's 354 buildings are contained on 3.3 square miles. Everything at UIUC is massive in scale. Twenty-four residence halls are home to 8,550 undergraduates, mostly freshmen, as all first-years are required to live on campus. Including private certified housing units and frat and sorority houses, approximately half of undergrads reside on campus. Student life is dominated by ninety Greek organizations that scoop up 25 percent of female and 20 percent of male undergraduates. The twenty-one NCAA Division I sports teams are also a major focal point at this school. The Fighting Illini football team plays before crowds of 60,000+ at Memorial Stadium. An unfathomable 470,000 square feet of recreational spaces offer everything from indoor tracks to a leisure pool with slide to an inline skating rink. With roughly 1,600 student-run organizations, it's hard not to find your niche somewhere. One doesn't even have to venture off university grounds to find robust cultural opportunities as the four theaters in the Krannert Center for the Performing Arts annually host more than 350 performances by students as well as touring professionals. The Krannert Art Museum boasts 10,000 original works. Those looking to road trip to a major city can reach St. Louis, Chicago, or Indianapolis in two-to-three hours by car.

Career Services

Twenty-four professional employees staff The Career Center at Illinois (TCC) with roles such as career counselor, health-career advisor, employer relations, and professional development for international students. However, additional career services supports can be found within the Gies College of Business (three professional staff); the Grainger College of Engineering (5); the School for Information Sciences (1); the Department of Economics (1); and the College of Agricultural, Consumer & Environmental Sciences (1). All told, the University of Illinois at Urbana-Champaign possesses an overall student-to-career staff ratio of 970:1, which is higher than the average university featured in this book.

Serving 34,000 undergraduate students is a monumental task, but it's one that UIUC successfully meets by offering a wide array of services and large-group activities. The TCC served one-quarter of the student population in 2017-18; 28 percent of those utilizing the office were seniors. Almost 24,000 students used Handshake to connect with alumni and potential employers. Staff also conducted 2,629 one-on-one advising sessions, completed 4,650 resume/cover letter/LinkedIn page reviews, hosted 442 employers and graduate/professional schools at career fairs, and facilitated 808 on-campus interviews. In total, 68 percent of Class of 2018 graduates completed at least one internship while at Illinois. Job shadowing, application boot camps, career fair preparation workshops, and etiquette dinners are only a small sampling of opportunities provided by the TCC to students proactive enough to take advantage. Despite the sheer numbers challenge of serving every student, UIUC Career Services provides a number of excellent programs that lead to impressive career and graduate school outcomes.

Professional Outcomes

Ninety-one percent of the members of the graduating Class of 2018 had landed at their next destination within six months of graduation. Employed (full time) graduates represented 57 percent of the total cohort, and the most popular sectors were finance, consulting, and education. Advertising/PR/marketing, computer and electronic products, health-care services and hospitals, and manufacturing were next in line. Among the corporations that landed twenty-five or more 2018 Illini grads were KPMG, Deloitte, Epic Systems, EY, PwC, Microsoft, and Amazon. More than fifteen newly minted grads landed at companies like Facebook, Google, Northrup Grumman, PepsiCo, Allstate Insurance, and Accenture. The average salary across all majors for 2018 grads was an extremely solid $61,000. Two-thirds of graduates remained in the Land of Lincoln; California, Massachusetts, Missouri, and Washington state welcomed the greatest percentages of migrating alumni.

A notably high 34 percent of Class of 2018 graduates matriculated directly into an advanced/professional degree program with 56 percent pursuing a master's degree. More than 650 students stayed put at the University of Illinois and joined the massive group of 14,500+ graduate students currently enrolled. Over twenty Class of 2018 graduates enrolled in prestigious universities such as Columbia, NYU, Northwestern, the University of Michigan, and Washington University in St. Louis, and fifteen+ continued their studies at Carnegie Mellon, Stanford, Penn, Cornell, Johns Hopkins, and the University of Chicago. Clearly, Illinois grads are extremely competitive candidates at all of the country's elite graduate programs. Medical school applicants fare decently with acceptance rates around 10 percent higher than the national average, and recent grads have trained at Rush University Medical College, Washington University School of Medicine in St. Louis, the University of Michigan Medical School, and Johns Hopkins. Law school applicants attend many fine institutions including the University of Illinois' own highly ranked law school.

Admission

The University of Illinois at Urbana-Champaign accepted 62 percent of the 39,362 applicants battling for a place in the Class of 2022. This is one of the gentler acceptance rates of any institution featured in this book, but don't let that figure mislead you; the Illini are a high-achieving lot. Those admitted for the 2018-19 school year had mid-50 percent standardized test scores of 1220-1480 (55 percent had higher than a 700 on the math portion) on the SAT and 26-32 on the ACT. Almost half (48 percent), placed in the top decile of their graduating classes, and 81 percent hailed from the top quartile. Five years ago, the percentage of top-10 percent students was actually 55 percent, but SATs were a much lower mid-50 percent range of 1160-1350, only part of which can be explained by score inflation. Applicants to UIUC's Grainger College will need to possess grades and test scores well above the aforementioned averages. Standards for entry into a computer science major are similar to those encountered at an Ivy.

The admissions committee places greatest emphasis on the rigor of one's secondary school record and the GPA earned. Standardized test scores, essays, extracurricular activities, and talent/ability are considered "important" to the decision-making process. Interestingly, the committee does not consider class rank or recommendations in an evaluative capacity. It also states that those who submit their applications by November 1 "may [have] the best chance for being admitted to our most selective programs and special attention for admission to honors programs and for merit awards." There is no reason not to apply to UIUC by the early deadline because it is a nonbinding proposition and gives you the best odds at admission. Illinois remains primarily a university for state residents as the percentage of in-staters climbed back up to 77 percent for last year's freshman class. Strong grades and SAT scores are required for serious consideration, but the admissions process is a straightforward one.

Worth Your Money?

Three-quarters of undergraduates enrolled in this university are from within the state of Illinois, entitling them to an affordable education. One of the few American schools to charge different tuition rates to business/engineering majors than education/social work majors, residents enjoy an average cost of attendance between $31k and $36k per year. Nonresidents are offered a COA of roughly $48,000, lower than most private institutions, making the University of Illinois at Urbana-Champaign a viable option for out-of-staters, especially those planning to enter the corporate or tech world. Around half of attending undergraduates are determined eligible for need-based financial aid with an average award of $16,132.

FINANCIAL
Institutional Type: Public
In-State Tuition: $12,036
Out-of-State Tuition: $29,178
Room & Board: $11,850
Required Fees: $4,174
Books & Supplies: $1,200

Avg. Need-Based Aid: $16,132
Avg. % of Need Met: 70%

Avg. Merit-Based Aid: $5,202
% Receiving Merit-Based Aid: 20%

Avg. Cumulative Debt: $23,123
% of Students Borrowing: 43%

CAREER
Who Recruits
1. Micron
2. Crowe Horwath
3. Shell
4. Phillips 66
5. BP America

Notable Internships
1. Ford Motor Company
2. Uber
3. State Farm

Top Industries
1. Business
2. Education
3. Engineering
4. Operations
5. Research

Top Employers
1. Google
2. Microsoft
3. Amazon
4. EY
5. IBM

Where Alumni Work
1. Chicago
2. Urban-Champaign, IL
3. San Francisco
4. New York City
5. Los Angeles

Median Earnings
College Scorecard (Early Career): $61,500
EOP (Early Career): $59,700
PayScale (Mid-Career): $115,300

RANKINGS
Forbes: 68
Money: 20
U.S. News: 48 (T), National Universities
Wall Street Journal/THE: 47
Washington Monthly: 17, National Universities

#CollegesWorthYourMoney

University of Maryland, College Park

College Park, Maryland | Admissions Phone: 301-314-8385

Inside the Classroom

It's a highly affordable research university with a respected name and a big-time sports program that, oh yeah, happens to be only minutes from Washington, DC, so it's no shock that the University of Maryland-College Park has become an increasingly popular college destination. A school that has been on the rise since it became the state's flagship campus in 1988, College Park today enrolls teens from all fifty states and international students from 123 countries, although three-quarters of the undergraduate population are residents. This university enrolls 41,000 total students including 30,700 undergraduates who can select from ninety-two majors across twelve colleges. Real Terrapins may be turtles that are hyper-aggressive carriers of salmonella, but the Maryland variety is an accomplished group of young scholars who, in overwhelming numbers, go on to do great things postgraduation.

Depending on which college and program you are part of, the sequence and pace at which you will fill the school's general education requirements will vary. The requirements themselves will not. There are forty-one credits of required coursework that include twelve credits in communications, six in the arts and humanities, six in behavioral and social sciences, seven in biological and physical sciences, seven in interdisciplinary or emerging issues, and three in mathematics. Maryland offers one of the best Honors Colleges, and those more able to gain acceptance (the average SAT is 1490) must complete three honors seminars and two additional honors courses.

Despite an 18:1 student-to-faculty ratio and a heavy concentration of graduate students, many undergraduate course sections at the University of Maryland are held in intimate classroom settings. In fact, 45 percent of sections enroll fewer than twenty students. Of course, you will also have your share of packed introductory lecture courses; 17 percent of classes enroll fifty or more students. Undergraduate research opportunities are within reach as 43 percent of 2018 graduates completed one, including 9 percent who completed a summer research experience. The Maryland Center for Undergraduate Research also facilitates numerous opportunities throughout the year and hosts an annual Undergraduate Research Day at which 350+ students make presentations. A reasonable number of students also pursue a semester overseas. Over 1,500 students elect to study abroad at one of 447 destinations.

Collectively, the social sciences account for 18 percent of degrees awarded by the University of Maryland with criminology, government and politics, and economics among the most popular majors. Engineering is next with 15 percent of undergraduate degrees conferred. It is followed by business (12 percent), computer science (9 percent), biology (8 percent) and journalism (6 percent). The Robert H. Smith School of Business, the A. James Clark School of Engineering, and the Merrill College of Journalism all command respect from prospective employers and graduate schools, as do programs in computer science and criminology. Maryland's reputation also helps its graduates win highly competitive national fellowships. In 2019, that haul included ten Boren Awards, nine Fulbrights, seven Critical Language Scholarships, four Goldwater Scholars, and a Churchill Scholarship.

Outside the Classroom

Campus is home to 90 percent of Terrapin freshmen and 41 percent of the overall undergraduate student body. Only first-year students are guaranteed housing. Greek life is prominent, attracting 19 percent of women and 15 percent of men. Major sports are a thriving enterprise at the University of Maryland as the school boasts twenty Division I teams that include a basketball team that won the NCAA tournament in 2002 and is playing in March Madness pretty much every year. There are 800+ clubs, including many in the realm of improv, comedy, and pre-professional as well as an intramural program so expansive it offers both competitive and recreational levels. Also notable are The Mighty Sound of Maryland, a big-time marching band, and the strength of the volunteering spirit that sees the U of M community contribute a collective two million hours per year. Suburban Maryland isn't the most exciting place you could hope for but, fortunately, Washington, DC, is only a short Metro ride away.

Career Services

There are twenty-six full-time staff members working out of the centralized University Career Center with sixteen undergraduate-focused employees stationed in the Robert H. Smith School of Business, five in the A. James Clark School of Engineering, and another five career counselors housed within other colleges and departments. That brings the grand total of professional career services staff members at College Park to fifty-two, equating to a 590:1 student-to-counselor ratio, below average compared to the average school in this book, but strong for a school with over 30,000 undergraduates.

University of Maryland, College Park

E-mail: applymaryland@umd.edu | Website: www.umd.edu

A superb 84 percent of 2018 graduates reported completing at least one internship, and more than one was the norm with 32 percent completing two internships, and 34 percent completing three. Among those who desired to turn their internship into a full-time gig postgraduation, 79 percent received an offer of employment. The jobs landed by all graduates were closely aligned with student's career goals, another testament to the work of this office. To be precise, 93 percent of job-holders reported that their position either directly aligned with their career goals or was a proper stepping-stone toward their ultimate goal. Eleven percent of graduates landed their first job via an on-campus interview with a company arranged by the University Career Center while another 13 percent made that important connection at a school-hosted job fair. On that topic, the school puts on several career fairs, including a fall event that draws 3,500 students and a Computer Science Career & Internship Fair that, alone, brings 125 companies to campus. Additionally, you can turn to the 352,000 Terrapin alumni to help you open a door into just about any hiring organization you can conjure up. Terrific internship numbers, on-campus recruiting, and overall student outcomes make this a world-class career services outfit.

Professional Outcomes

Class of 2018 graduates from the University of Maryland had, within six months of graduating, successfully found their next life step 93.5 percent of the time. Of the 72 percent of that cohort who found employment, the companies/organizations hiring the greatest number of recent grads were Deloitte (36), KPMG (29), the National Institutes of Health (29), EY (28), Accenture (22), and PwC (22). Double-digit Terrapins were also scooped up by giants including Amazon, IBM, Northrup Grumman, Capital One, and JP Morgan Chase & Co. Taking all alumni into account, more than 200 individuals with a University of Maryland affiliation presently work for Facebook, Apple, and Google. By far the most popular landing spot for alumni is the Greater Washington, DC, area with Baltimore, New York City, San Francisco, and Philadelphia next in line. The median starting salary self-report by Class of 2018 grads was $58,703; the mid-50 percent range was $41k-$69k.

Nineteen percent of Class of 2018 members headed directly to graduate and professional school to begin work on an advanced degree. Of that contingent 9 percent entered doctoral programs, 6 percent were on the path to becoming medical doctors, and 5 percent entered law school. By a wide margin, continuing at the University of Maryland was the top choice; 280 survey respondents reported remaining at their home institution. Other popular schools were George Washington University (21), Johns Hopkins (14), the University of Pennsylvania (13), Columbia (12), Georgetown (12), NYU (12), and Boston University (11). Medical school acceptance rates for Maryland students are excellent at over 60 percent between 2015 and 2017, roughly 20 points higher than the national average. In recent years the medical schools where the largest number of alumni matriculated were the University of Maryland, George Washington University, New York Medical College, and Drexel University. In that same time, law school applicants earned seventy-seven acceptances to Georgetown, twenty-seven each to Michigan and Emory, twenty-six to Cornell, eighteen to Columbia, and seventeen to Harvard.

Admission

Applicants for a spot as a freshman at College Park in 2018-19 were accepted at a rate of 47 percent; a decade earlier the admit rate was 39 percent. The mid-50 percent standardized test scores for the Class of 2022 were 1290-1480 on the SAT and 28-33 on the ACT. Three-quarters of enrolled students earned a spot in the top 10 percent of their high school class, and 93 percent were in the top quartile. The average weighted GPA was 4.28. Those class rank and GPA numbers are similar to those of ten years ago, but SAT scores are significantly higher today, even when accounting for post-2016 score inflation.

With 33,461 applicants, this admissions committee needs to look first at cold, hard numbers, which is why GPA, standardized tests, and the presence of a rigorous course load are ranked as "very important" factors. Class rank, the essay, recommendations, state residency, first-generation status, and talent/ability make up the next rung of "important" factors. There is no binding early decision option at Maryland; the early action deadline of November 1 will get you an answer by January 31. In sum, getting into Maryland's flagship university's main campus pretty much requires a 3.75 or higher GPA and standardized test scores above the 90th percentile.

Worth Your Money?

In-state tuition is under $11,000, and the total cost of attendance for those living on campus is $27k. Out-of-staters pay three times the tuition rate, which leads to a total cost of attendance of $53k+ to become a Terrapin. Getting literally any degree at the in-state rate is a no-brainer. For nonresidents, you would have to have a compelling reason to cross state lines to pay $200,000+. However, if you are eyeing the exceptional programs in business, engineering, or computer science, that sum may be worth the education and connections you will gain.

FINANCIAL
Institutional Type: Public
In-State Tuition: $8,651
Out-of-State Tuition: $33,272
Room & Board: $12,429
Required Fees: $1,944
Books & Supplies: $1,250

Avg. Need-Based Aid: $9,980
Avg. % of Need Met: 66%

Avg. Merit-Based Aid: $4,584
% Receiving Merit-Based Aid: 36%

Avg. Cumulative Debt: $28,511
% of Students Borrowing: 41%

CAREER
Who Recruits
1. AIG Retirement Services
2. Carrier Corporation
3. Corvel Corporation
4. Federal Aviation Administration
5. Lockheed Martin

Notable Internships
1. Adobe
2. Nike
3. U.S. State Department

Top Industries
1. Business
2. Education
3. Operations
4. Engineering
5. information Technology

Top Employers
1. Booz Allen Hamilton
2. Deloitte
3. IBM
4. Capital One
5. Google

Where Alumni Work
1. Washington, DC
2. Baltimore
3. New York City
4. Philadelphia
5. San Francisco

Median Earnings
College Scorecard (Early Career): $62,900
EOP (Early Career): $53,500
PayScale (Mid-Career): $113,400

RANKINGS
Forbes: 63
Money: 43
U.S. News: 64 (T), National Universities
Wall Street Journal/THE: 75 (T)
Washington Monthly: 45, National Universities

#CollegesWorthYourMoney

Amherst, Massachusetts | Admissions Phone: 413-545-0222

ADMISSION
Admission Rate: 60%
Admission Rate - Men: 58%
Admission Rate - Women: 62%
EA Admission Rate: 74%
ED Admission Rate: Not Offered
Admission Rate (5-Year Trend): -3%
ED Admission Rate (5-Year Trend): Not Offered
% of Admits Attending (Yield): 20%
Transfer Admission Rate: 51%

Offered Wait List: 6,250
Accepted Wait List: 2,911
Admitted Wait List: 39

SAT Reading/Writing (Middle 50%): 600-680
SAT Math (Middle 50%): 600-710
ACT Composite (Middle 50%): 26-31
Testing Policy: ACT/SAT Required
SAT Superscore: Yes
ACT Superscore: Yes

% Graduated in Top 10% of HS Class: 32%
% Graduated in Top 25% of HS Class: 71%
% Graduated in Top 50% of HS Class: 97%

ENROLLMENT
Total Undergraduate Enrollment: 23,515
% Part-Time: 7%
% Male: 50%
% Female: 50%
% Out-of-State: 18%
% Fraternity: 8%
% Sorority: 8%
% On-Campus (Freshman): 99%
% On-Campus (All Undergraduate): 62%

% African-American: 5%
% Asian: 10%
% Hispanic: 7%
% White: 62%
% Other: 3%
% Race or Ethnicity Unknown: 6%
% International: 7%
% Low-Income: 22%

ACADEMICS
Student-to-Faculty Ratio: 17:1
% of Classes Under 20: 49%
% of Classes Under 40: 77%
% Full-Time Faculty: 81%
% Full-Time Faculty w/ Terminal Degree: 94%

Top Programs
Architecture
Business
Computer Science
Nursing
Psychology
Public Health Sciences
Sociology
Sport Management

Retention Rate: 91%
4-Year Graduation Rate: 71%
6-Year Graduation Rate: 80%

Curricular Flexibility: Somewhat Flexible
Academic Rating: ★★★

Inside the Classroom

Sesame Street's iconic "One of These Things (Is Not Like the Others)" song comes to mind when examining the Five College Consortium in Western Massachusetts. The group consists of tiny, elite liberal arts schools Amherst College, Mount Holyoke, Smith, Hampshire and…UMass? That's right, UMass, a school that has 23,500 undergraduate students, another 7,000 graduate students, and 109 bachelor's degree programs that are offered across eight undergraduate colleges. While UMass Amherst students are free to cross-register in any course at the affiliated liberal arts havens, there is plenty to like on the grounds of the Commonwealth's flagship campus. The home of the Minutemen and Minutewomen boasts the highly ranked and affordable Isenberg School of Management as well as revered academic programs in sports management, architecture, computer science, and nursing.

Whether you end up in the Isenberg School of Management, the College of Engineering, or the School of Public Health and Health Sciences, you will encounter the same set of general education requirements that, fortunately, are not as overbearing as at many state universities. A ten-course, thirty-credit jaunt through writing, math, analytical reasoning, the physical sciences, and social world is all it takes to knock out the full run of nonnegotiable coursework. Those in the College of Humanities and Fine Arts and the College of Natural Sciences are required to study a foreign language; those in the Isenberg School of Management or College Engineering are not required to do so. The Commonwealth Honors College at UMass Amherst has high admissions standards (average 1386 SAT and 4.23 GPA) and even higher graduation standards, requiring additional honors coursework and the completion of a senior thesis.

The student-to-faculty ratio is 17:1, leading to undergraduate class sizes that are all over the map. You will encounter a number of smaller sections during your time at UMass as 49 percent of courses enroll fewer than twenty students; 18 percent of sections contain more than fifty students, so you also will have some larger lecture hall classes. In spite of some gigantic classes where you'll feel anonymous, a stunning 96 percent of Class of 2018 graduates reported being satisfied with their academic experience. Further, a substantial and encouraging 30 percent of that cohort reported engaging in some type of undergraduate research. For a large university, UMass also enjoys fairly wide participation in its study abroad program. Every year 1,200 students spend a semester in one of more than seventy countries.

UMass has a fairly even spread of students across its various areas of concentration. Of all degrees conferred in 2018, business/marketing diplomas accounted for 14 percent. That was followed by social sciences (12 percent), biology (10 percent), health professions (9 percent), and psychology (8 percent). Those who earn high grades find a wealth of employment and graduate school options awaiting them. UMass produces an impressive number of national postgraduate scholarship winners including fourteen Fulbright Scholars in 2018, four Goldwater Scholars in 2019, and a 2019 graduate was one of only fifteen Churchill Scholars named in the nation.

Outside the Classroom

Ninety-nine percent of freshmen live on the 1,450-acre Amherst campus, and 62 percent of the entire student body lives in university-owned housing, a relatively high figure for a state university. There are fifty-two separate residence halls. Those residing off campus typically find rentals in the surrounding towns of Amherst, Hadley, and Sunderland. Men and women both join fraternities and sororities at an 8 percent clip. Twenty-one NCAA teams compete at the Division I level, mostly within the Atlantic 10 Conference. Involvement is spread around with 38 percent of students joining at least one student-run club, 24 percent playing varsity, club, or intramural sports, and 13 percent participating in community service. There are 200+ registered student organizations, and UMass students can participate in any club or activity at the other colleges within the consortium. Amherst garners consistent praise as one the top college towns in the United States because, in its own accurate words, it offers "a perfect blend of New England natural beauty and cosmopolitan culture and energy." Even on-campus dining gets rave reviews. Road trips to Boston (90 miles) or New York City (175 miles) are possible despite the somewhat remote feel of the Western Massachusetts locale.

Career Services

There are three central career service administrators at UMass Amherst, but the majority of service providers are housed within eight career service departments in the various undergraduate colleges. Obtaining an exact count of the number of advisors was, unfortunately, not possible, but to provide some reference point for counselor availability, the business school has seven advisors and a student-to-counselor ratio of 526:1, very strong compared to the other large public universities featured in this guide. Job fair offerings are plentiful, and top employers are more than willing to make the trip to Amherst to recruit top students. The College of Engineering alone hosts six annual job fairs that cater to specialty areas like biotech jobs, environmental engineering, and tech jobs.

University of Massachusetts Amherst

E-mail: mail@admissions.umass.edu | Website: www.umass.edu

Overall, Minutemen and women feel that UMass adequately prepares them for beyond graduation; 79 percent of graduates are either "very satisfied" or "somewhat satisfied" with the way the university prepared them for the world of work. Two-thirds of 2018 graduates had some type of practicum, internship, co-op experience, or clinical assignment. Routine internship and co-op placements include the Boston Red Sox, CNN, IBM, MTV, Disney World, the Boston Globe, Sheraton, and United Technologies. With 260,000 alumni heavily concentrated in the Boston and Springfield areas, it's hard to walk down a New England street without bumping into a UMass alum. This supportive network, coupled with respected academic programs, helps the career services staff succeed in opening doors for qualified graduates.

Professional Outcomes

One year after graduating, 71 percent of UMass alumni are employed full time, 11 percent are working part time, and 18 percent are attending graduate school part time. The most populated industries are health/medical professions (13 percent), K-12 or early childhood education (8 percent), information technology (7 percent), marketing/sales (7 percent), and finance (7 percent). Companies presently employing one hundred+ Minutemen and Minutewomen include Oracle, Mass Mutual, Amazon, IBM, Google, Intel, Microsoft, PwC, Wayfair, and Apple. Boston is the most popular landing spot for graduates; it's followed by Springfield, Massachusetts; New York City; San Francisco; Washington, DC; and Los Angeles. One-third of recent graduates earn between $50-75k per year, 57 percent earn less than that range, and 9 percent take home more than $75,000 in annual income.

If you achieve stellar grades while an undergraduate at UMass, you will have a full array of graduate/professional school options awaiting you. Medical school applicants with a 3.7 GPA and an MCAT score in at least the 79th percentile are admitted to medical school more than 75 percent of the time. That rate was even higher when you include the criteria of having clinical experience *and* being open to osteopathic programs. Many recent graduates have attended medical school at UMass Medical School while others have gained acceptance to medical or dental school at Harvard, the University of Chicago, the University of Michigan, and the University of Pennsylvania. Similarly, prelaw students flock to UMass' own legal training ground or other Massachusetts-based options like Suffolk Law, but recent grads also have matriculated into elite institutions like William & Mary, Northeastern, or Boston University.

Admission

Sixty-percent of the 41,000+ applicants to UMass Amherst gained entry into the Class of 2022. A popular safety school for Massachusetts residents, only 20 percent of those who were accepted ultimately enrolled in the university. Eighty-seven percent of 2018-19 freshmen had submitted an SAT score with their applications and earned mid-50 percent scores of 1200-1390; the equivalent ACT range was 26-31. Approximately one-third of students hailed from the top 10 percent of their high school class, and 71 percent were in the top quartile. Only 3 percent finished outside the top half of their graduating cohort. Two-thirds of entering students posted high school GPAs of 3.75 or better, and only 5 percent possessed a GPA under 3.5. The university received only half as many applicants at the dawn of the new millennium. The entering Class of 2000-01 had mid-50 percent SAT scores of 1010-1240, and only 52 percent were in the top quartile of their graduating class. Clearly, admissions standards are much higher now than a generation ago.

Standardized test scores, GPA, and the level of rigor of one's coursework are the three factors weighed as "very important" by the admissions committee. Also "important" are class rank, essays, recommendations, extracurricular activities, talent/ability, character/personal qualities, first-generation status, work experience, and the level of an applicant's interest. It is rare to see a large public university even consider demonstrated interest in admissions decisions, so make sure you take advantage by reaching out to a UMass admissions officer, visiting campus, or attending an admissions event in your area. There is an early action option in early November that will get you an admissions decision by mid-January at the latest. UMass does not offer binding early decision. Thousands apply for transfer to the Amherst campus each year, but the acceptance rate is lower than it is for freshmen.

Worth Your Money?

At full price, UMass Amherst will set a Massachusetts resident back $30,000 per year; an out-of-stater will pay just shy of $50,000. However, 73 percent of those applying for aid received an average discount of $11,478, and one-third of students received merit aid averaging close to $6k. Bay State residents are getting a terrific deal attending UMass and shouldn't hesitate to pull the trigger, regardless of their financial situation or intended academic path. With a bit of aid, it is possible to receive a four-year education at a solid institution for under six-figures in total cost of attendance. Those out of state will likely find better deals elsewhere unless they are eligible for the New England Regional Students Program that allows residents of other New England states to attend at a discount if their intended academic program is not offered by public colleges in their home state.

FINANCIAL
Institutional Type: Public
In-State Tuition: $15,791
Out-of-State Tuition: $35,112
Room & Board: $13,958
Required Fees: $1,083
Books & Supplies: $1,000

Avg. Need-Based Aid: $11,478
Avg. % of Need Met: 82%

Avg. Merit-Based Aid: $5,839
% Receiving Merit-Based Aid: 33%

Avg. Cumulative Debt: $31,897
% of Students Borrowing: 67%

CAREER
Who Recruits
1. HubSpot
2. Facebook
3. Salesforce
4. Wayfair
5. Apple

Notable Internships
1. PepsiCo
2. AIG
3. TJX Companies

Top Industries
1. Business
2. Education
3. Operations
4. Sales
5. Engineering

Top Employers
1. Oracle
2. MassMutual
3. IBM
4. Amazon
5. Google

Where Alumni Work
1. Boston
2. Springfield, MA
3. New York City
4. San Francisco
5. Washington, DC

Median Earnings
College Scorecard (Early Career): $51,400
EOP (Early Career): $51,700
PayScale (Mid-Career): $103,000

RANKINGS
Forbes: 155
Money: 109
U.S. News: 64 (T), National Universities
Wall Street Journal/THE: 160 (T)
Washington Monthly: 128, National Universities

#CollegesWorthYourMoney

University of Miami

Coral Gables, Florida | Admissions Phone: 305-284-4323

ADMISSION
Admission Rate: 32%
Admission Rate - Men: 34%
Admission Rate - Women: 31%
EA Admission Rate: 44%
ED Admission Rate: 56%
Admission Rate (5-Year Trend): -8%
ED Admission Rate (5-Year Trend): +32%
% of Admits Attending (Yield): 21%
Transfer Admission Rate: 53%

Offered Wait List: 10,405
Accepted Wait List: 4,041
Admitted Wait List: 30

SAT Reading/Writing (Middle 50%): 620-690
SAT Math (Middle 50%): 630-740
ACT Composite (Middle 50%): 29-32
Testing Policy: ACT/SAT Required
SAT Superscore: Yes
ACT Superscore: Yes

% Graduated in Top 10% of HS Class: 55%
% Graduated in Top 25% of HS Class: 83%
% Graduated in Top 50% of HS Class: 95%

ENROLLMENT
Total Undergraduate Enrollment: 11,117
% Part-Time: 6%
% Male: 47%
% Female: 53%
% Out-of-State: 60%
% Fraternity: 17%
% Sorority: 18%
% On-Campus (Freshman): 89%
% On-Campus (All Undergraduate): 38%

% African-American: 8%
% Asian: 5%
% Hispanic: 22%
% White: 41%
% Other: 3%
% Race or Ethnicity Unknown: 4%
% International: 15%
% Low-Income: 18%

ACADEMICS
Student-to-Faculty Ratio: 12:1
% of Classes Under 20: 50%
% of Classes Under 40: 83%
% Full-Time Faculty: 69%
% Full-Time Faculty w/ Terminal Degree: 86%

Top Programs
Architecture
Biology
Communication
Exercise Physiology
Marine Science
Music
Sport Administration

Retention Rate: 92%
4-Year Graduation Rate: 70%
6-Year Graduation Rate: 82%

Curricular Flexibility: Very Flexible
Academic Rating: ★★★✔

Inside the Classroom

The sunny paradise of Coral Gables, just south of Miami, is home to the University of Miami—commonly referred to as UM or "the U." It is easily identifiable by its team name, the Hurricanes, with its distinctive orange, green, and white colors. This large, private research institution that boasts a number of top academic programs and world-renowned faculty struggled to be taken seriously as a world-class institution for many decades. Having been dubbed "Sun Tan U" in the 1940s and suffering through revelations about its morally bereft football program of the 80s and 90s was a lot to overcome, yet Miami has finally arrived as an unquestioned member of higher education's elite. More selective than ever, Miami has more than gridiron glory to brag about as we enter the third decade of the millennium.

In an effort to ensure the acquisition of "essential intellectual skills and exposure to a range of intellectual perspectives and academic disciplines," UM mandates general education requirements via the Cognates Program. So-termed cognates are, at a minimum, three-course clusters that the faculty has determined share a focus or thematic elements. The three main areas of cognates are arts and humanities; people and society; and science, technology, engineering, and mathematics. Students fulfill one cognate through their major area of study and also must complete the other two broad areas. Hurricanes also must blow through two English composition courses and one quantitative skills class. Other than that, the core academic requirements at Miami are not prohibitive.

Students rate their teachers and their overall UM experience extremely favorably. A noteworthy 93 percent of graduates report being satisfied with their education while 83 percent were satisfied with their major, and 90 percent gained confidence in their own abilities over their four years of study. The student-to-faculty ratio is 12:1, and even though there are 6,000+ graduate students to serve, class sizes are reasonable. Exactly half of all course sections contain fewer than twenty students, and only 9 percent of sections sport enrollments of more than fifty undergrads. Study abroad opportunities are vast and include university-run programs in Rome, Shanghai, India, Paris, Prague, the Galapagos, Cape Town, and Buenos Aires. Undergraduate research posts can be had, but the onus is on the student to contact a professor directly, apply for placement through the Office of Research and Community Outreach, or apply for a summer research grant.

The University of Miami confers the greatest number of degrees in business/marketing (21 percent), biology (15 percent), engineering (10 percent), and the social sciences (10 percent). The Miami Business School and the College of Engineering enjoy solid national reputations, and programs in music, marine science, communications, and architecture sit high atop many rankings. UM graduates fared well at procuring highly competitive awards in 2018. The bounty included a Rhodes Scholarship, three National Science Foundation Graduate Research Fellowships, two Fulbright Scholarships, and two Goldwater Scholarships along with a Critical Language, Boren, and Gilman Scholarship.

Outside the Classroom

Eighty-nine percent of freshmen live on the University of Miami's 239-acre main campus in Coral Gables, but 62 percent of the total undergraduate student body live off campus. Fraternities attract 17 percent of male students, and sororities draw 18 percent of female students, creating a strong Greek presence within the social scene; there are close to three-dozen active Greek organizations. Of course, the U's most galvanizing force is its famous (and at times infamous) football team as well as sixteen other varsity sports squads that compete in the powerhouse Atlantic Coast Conference in NCAA Division I. Approximately 400 students participate in varsity athletics. The school is trying to move away from its "Sun Tan U" reputation, and it certainly has in terms of academic rankings, yet the South Beach atmosphere continues to earn Miami "top party school" status in many publication's rankings. For non-partiers, the school also offers 270+ clubs, thirty service organizations, an active student government, and an award-winning student-run cable channel. On-campus amenities border on luxurious with the Herbert Wellness Center being one of the finest collegiate gyms around. Students also enjoy an arboretum, the Lowe Art Museum, the Ring Theatre that launched stars like Sly Stallone and Ray Liotta, and close proximity to the beach.

Career Services

The Toppel Career Center is staffed by fifteen full-time professional employees (not counting admin assistants or office managers) who focus on employer relations, career counseling, and internship coordination. A student-to-advisor ratio of 722:1 is higher than average when set against the other institutions included in this book. Still, this office reaches the bulk of the population as 84 percent of graduates utilized Toppel at some point in their four years of study. The most utilized services were (1) resume and cover letter review, (2) career expo and fairs, (3) one-on-one career advising, and (4) job and internship listing search.

University of Miami

E-mail: admission@miami.edu | Website: www.miami.edu

A laundry list of impressive organizations/companies that visit Coral Gables to recruit and conduct on-campus interviews includes PepsiCo, American Airlines, Facebook, Adidas, EY, and the Miami Marlins. Last year, 175 companies attended the annual Career Expo, nearly 47,000 jobs and internships were posted to Handshake, 159 networking events were held, 2,251 students attended career fairs and workshops put on by Toppel staff, and 960 undergrads engaged in a one-on-one career counseling session. Career services also reviewed 2,200 resumes, conducted 863 practice interviews, and took 598 professional headshots for students to use in their job searches. That frenetic pace and strong outreach leads to mostly positive postgraduate outcomes for newly minted Hurricane alumni.

Professional Outcomes

The Hurricane Class of 2018 saw 81 percent of its members secure post-grad plans within six months with 55 percent employed full time and 34 percent in graduate school. Companies employing five or more 2018 graduates included ScribeAmerica, Citrix, Bloomingdale's, Bank of America Merrill Lynch, Citi, Morgan Stanley, and Insight Global. Across the entire alumni base, one hundred+ Canes also can be found in the offices of Google, IBM, PwC, Apple, and Microsoft. Average starting salaries were $51,000; those from the College of Engineering averaged $59k, business school grads took home $55k, and those from the College of Arts and Sciences enjoyed a mean income of $46k. Miami, New York, Boston, Chicago, and Los Angeles were the primary destinations of choice for 2018 grads.

The most frequently attended graduate schools included a mix of prestigious institutions, Miami itself, and other Sunshine State universities. In order, the schools of choice were Miami (146), Boston University (12), Columbia (10), Florida International (9), George Washington (9), NYU (9), University of Florida (9), and the University of Southern Florida (8). Premed students have the advantage of accumulating clinical hours within the University of Miami Health Systems or any of six other hospitals not far from campus. In a typical year the U's own Miller School of Medicine takes forty+ of its own exiting undergraduates, and over 90 percent of "highly recommended" applicants find a medical school home somewhere in the country.

Admission

Miami actually experienced a slight decline in applications in 2019 after receiving over 30,000 in 2018. However, the 32 percent acceptance rate for those jockeying for a spot in the 2018-19 freshman class was significantly lower than the 40 percent acceptance rate five years prior or the 44 percent rate a decade ago. The middle-50 percent ranges were 1250-1430 on the SAT and 29-32 on the ACT for current freshmen. Fifty-five percent of 2018-19 first-years earned a place in the top 10 percent of their high school class while 83 percent placed in the top quartile. The average high school GPA for attending students was 3.6. Those numbers are similar to those posted by incoming freshmen in the not-too-distant past.

Eight categories top the list of most important factors in making admissions decisions—GPA, rigor of coursework, class rank, standardized test scores, recommendations, application essays, extracurricular activities, and character/personal qualities. Due to the massive number of applicants, the university does not offer interviews as part of the evaluation process. The U offers an early decision round where 54 percent of applicants are let through the gates, but only about one-quarter of the freshman class is filled through ED. Aspiring Hurricanes will see their activities reviewed and their essays read carefully as part of a holistic process. Yet, at a school receiving so many applications, you will need to bring reasonably strong grades and within-range test scores. For reference, only 14-15 percent of attending students earned SAT reading or math scores under 600.

Worth Your Money?

The U's cost of attendance is approaching $70,000, over three times the in-state COA for the University of Florida or Florida State. To compete for the top students, the university dishes out merit aid to half of its attending undergrads at an annual average of $22,653. It also grants need-based aid to over two-fifths of students with an average annual award of almost $35,000. If your family has unlimited funds, or if you receive a solid aid package, Miami is definitely a school that can make a lot of sense from an investment standpoint. If you are on a budget, paying full freight could lead to an unpleasant financial situation early in one's adult life.

FINANCIAL
Institutional Type: Private
In-State Tuition: $50,400
Out-of-State Tuition: $50,400
Room & Board: $14,658
Required Fees: $1,530
Books & Supplies: $1,000

Avg. Need-Based Aid: $34,643
Avg. % of Need Met: 95%

Avg. Merit-Based Aid: $22,653
% Receiving Merit-Based Aid: 52%

Avg. Cumulative Debt: $22,000
% of Students Borrowing: 36%

CAREER
Who Recruits
1. SpaceX
2. Adidas
3. Hilton
4. Ball Aerospace
5. CIA

Notable Internships
1. Lincoln Financial Group
2. Cato Institute
3. Viacom

Top Industries
1. Business
2. Education
3. Healthcare
4. Arts & Design
5. Sales

Top Employers
1. Microsoft
2. IBM
3. Citi
4. Apple
5. PwC

Where Alumni Work
1. Miami
2. New York City
3. Los Angeles
4. West Palm Beach, FL
5. Washington, DC

Median Earnings
College Scorecard (Early Career): $60,100
EOP (Early Career): $54,800
PayScale (Mid-Career): $99,600

RANKINGS
Forbes: 90
Money: 378
U.S. News: 57, National Universities
Wall Street Journal/THE: 49
Washington Monthly: 222, National Universities

#CollegesWorthYourMoney

University of Michigan

Ann Arbor, Michigan | Admissions Phone: 734-764-7433

ADMISSION
Admission Rate: 23%
Admission Rate - Men: 21%
Admission Rate - Women: 25%
EA Admission Rate: N/A
ED Admission Rate: Not Offered
Admission Rate (5-Year Trend): -10%
ED Admission Rate (5-Year Trend): Not Offered
% of Admits Attending (Yield): 45%
Transfer Admission Rate: 39%

\# Offered Wait List: 14,783
\# Accepted Wait List: 6,000
\# Admitted Wait List: 415

SAT Reading/Writing (Middle 50%): 660-730
SAT Math (Middle 50%): 670-780
ACT Composite (Middle 50%): 30-34
Testing Policy: ACT/SAT Required
SAT Superscore: No
ACT Superscore: No

% Graduated in Top 10% of HS Class: 79%
% Graduated in Top 25% of HS Class: 96%
% Graduated in Top 50% of HS Class: 99%

ENROLLMENT
Total Undergraduate Enrollment: 30,318
% Part-Time: 4%
% Male: 50%
% Female: 50%
% Out-of-State: 41%
% Fraternity: 12%
% Sorority: 25%
% On-Campus (Freshman): 98%
% On-Campus (All Undergraduate): 31%

% African-American: 4%
% Asian: 15%
% Hispanic: 6%
% White: 58%
% Other: 4%
% Race or Ethnicity Unknown: 5%
% International: 7%
% Low-Income: 14%

ACADEMICS
Student-to-Faculty Ratio: 15:1
% of Classes Under 20: 57%
% of Classes Under 40: 78%
% Full-Time Faculty: 82%
% Full-Time Faculty w/ Terminal Degree: 91%

Top Programs
Business
Communication and Media
Computer Science
Economics
Engineering
English
Political Science
Psychology

Retention Rate: 97%
4-Year Graduation Rate: 79%
6-Year Graduation Rate: 92%

Curricular Flexibility: Somewhat Flexible
Academic Rating: ★★★★⟡

Inside the Classroom

What do you get when you combine one of the best college towns in the country, one of the premier research universities in the world, and stir in a passionate sports scene? The answer is the first public university in the Northwest Territories. Originally dubbed the "Catholepistemiad of Detroit," it is now known by the catchier name of the University of Michigan. Brilliant teens flock to Ann Arbor for 263 undergraduate degree programs across fourteen schools and colleges, and their success can be measured in countless ways, whether you look at the 97 percent freshman retention rate or the fact that more current Fortune 100 CEOs are alums of the Ross School of Business than any other school on the planet.

All applicants must apply to one of the fourteen schools right off the bat. The College of Literature, Science, and the Arts (LSA) serves the majority, and those accepted are held to school-specific rather than university-wide academic requirements. However, all Wolverines ultimately end up with broad academic requirements in the areas of English, foreign language, natural sciences, and social sciences. Freshmen in the LSA take a first-year seminar that is capped at eighteen students and affords an immediate opportunity to connect with a professor in an area of academic interest. LSAers also have the option to sign up for a "theme semester" in which major topics such as India in the World or Understanding Race are explored in-and-outside the classroom through activities such as museum visits, guest lectures, and film screenings.

With almost 46,000 students on campus, including grad students, it's not surprising that undergrads will end up sitting in some large lecture halls. Michigan sports a 15:1 student-to-faculty ratio, and 18 percent of classes contain fifty or more students, but a solid 57 percent of classes offer a more intimate experience with fewer than twenty students. Opportunities to conduct independent research or work in a laboratory beside a faculty member can be found. In the 2018-19 school year 1,300 participated in the Undergraduate Research Opportunity Program. For students in all academic programs at Michigan, study abroad opportunities are taken advantage of at high rates. In fact, the university is fifth in the nation in the number of students it sends to study in foreign lands.

In general, the faculty is exceptional and overflowing with award-winning researchers. Michigan finds itself atop any ranking of best public research universities. The Ross School of Business offers highly rated programs in entrepreneurship, management, accounting, and finance. The College of Engineering is also one of the best in the country. By sheer numbers, the school confers more engineering degrees (16 percent) than in any other discipline. The social sciences are next (12 percent), and encompass incredibly strong majors in political science, economics, and psychology. Computer science, another top-notch offering, attracts 11 percent of the student body. Graduating Wolverines are routinely awarded prestigious scholarships to continue their studies. In 2019, the school produced twenty-six Fulbright Scholars, more than any other research university in the nation.

Outside the Classroom

Ann Arbor is a prototypical college town, the type you would show to a Martian who wanted to know what a quintessential American college was like. Vibrant, stimulating, and extremely safe, the 3,200-acre campus and surrounding town are ideal places to spend four years. When your football stadium seats more than 100,000, that's a pretty solid indicator that the sports scene is thriving. Donning the iconic maize and blue jerseys, Michigan's twenty-seven Division I sports teams have enjoyed a ridiculous level of success. A substantial but not overwhelming 12 percent of men and 25 percent of women belong to one of the sixty-two fraternities and sororities on campus. A hard-to-comprehend 1,600 student organizations exist. If you can conceive it, Michigan probably already offers it, and 82 percent of the student body participates in at least one club or activity. Intramural and club sports also enjoy wide participation. The Ginsberg Center for Community and Service is popular, and 54 percent of Wolverines have engaged in volunteer experiences. Only 31 percent live on campus, almost all of whom are first-year students.

Career Services

The University of Michigan Career Center employs fourteen full-time staff members as well as seven peer advisors. Only counting the full-time employees, UM has a student-to-advisor ratio of 2,166:1, one of the highest of any school featured in this guide. Thus, hand-holding is limited, but appointments with peer advisors are available for mock interviews and resume assistance. One-on-one appointments with a professional career counselor can be scheduled to discuss finding internships and jobs. The career center reaches more students through hosting workshops, putting on more than 200 per year with a total attendance exceeding 6,000 undergrads.

Staffing may be less than desired, but on the plus side, Michigan's alumni network is one of the largest and most powerful in the nation. With over half a million loyal alums spread across one hundred countries, there is always a fellow Wolverine willing to dispense advice, facilitate a job- shadowing experience or internship, or help you get your foot in the door in the industry of your choosing. Also working in the school's favor is the fact that Michigan grads are highly sought after by major employers who are happy to travel to Ann Arbor for recruiting purposes. The Ross School of Business alone arranges for hundreds of companies to recruit on campus each year, including all of the big boys: Goldman Sachs, Deutsche Bank, EY, and Morgan Stanley. At UM counselors are not going to personally hunt you down to take personality inventories and create a killer LinkedIn profile, but large-scale resources are available that will get motivated students on the right path to their next destination.

Professional Outcomes

Within three months of exiting Ann Arbor, 93 percent of the graduates of the College of Literature, Science, and the Arts are employed full time or attending graduate school. Health care, research, nonprofit work, and consulting are the four most popular sectors in which LSA alums launch their careers. Ross School of Business graduates fare quite well on the open market; within three months, 98 percent are employed with a median salary of $72k. The companies listed above that recruit on campus are among the top employers of the Class of 2017 along with PwC, Deloitte, and Amazon. Engineering grads have similar success with 96 percent employed or in grad school within six months. Computer science/engineering students, the largest group within the School of Engineering, walk into jobs averaging close to $100k. The companies employing the greatest number of alumni across all years include General Motors, Ford, Google, Microsoft, Apple, and Facebook.

As with employers, elite graduate and professional schools also hold a Michigan diploma in high esteem. University of Michigan grads applying to law school are well prepared, averaging an LSAT score in the 80th percentile and gaining acceptance at a 92 percent clip. Those aiming for medical school average MCATs above the 85th percentile and get accepted at a 54 percent clip, a rate more than 10 percent higher than the national average. In short, if you succeed at Michigan, there isn't a graduate or professional school in existence that will be beyond your reach.

Admission

After a 10 percent increase in applications in 2018, the university now has a streak of a dozen consecutive years of breaking its own record for wanna-be Wolverines. The overall acceptance rate for a place in the Class of 2022 was 23 percent, but in-state applicants fared far better, enjoying a 41 percent rate (out-of-state was 19 percent). The SAT range of current Michigan students is 1330 to 1510, and the ACT range is 30-34. For comparison, in 2014 the SAT range was 1280-1480, and the ACT range was 29-33, which tells us that admission into this popular flagship university may be a touch more difficult now than in the recent past.

The school ranks the two most important admissions factors as "rigor of secondary school record" and "GPA." Average Michigan students earned a 3.86 GPA on a 4.0 scale in the most challenging courses available to them. Standardized test scores are listed as a secondary factor alongside recommendations, personal qualities, and first-generation status. While the University of Michigan does bring a holistic approach to the process, at the end of the day the admissions staff still needs to wade through almost 65,000 applications, which means test scores are still a major selling point. However, the office means what it says about giving preference to first-generation students. First-gens make up 13 percent of the student body, and the school does not super-score the SATs or ACTs as that practice benefits the economically advantaged. The University of Michigan has more than doubled its number of applications received in the last decade, and gaining acceptance is genuinely more challenging than ever. Top students who hail from in state will face better odds than out-of-staters who need to bring an impeccable academic record to the table to garner serious consideration.

Worth Your Money?

The average amount of debt held by a University of Michigan graduate is slightly below the national average. For residents of the Great Lakes State, the school is in the "ridiculous value" category—at least by the standards of an out-of-whack marketplace. Michigan's total cost of attendance for in-state students is $30k; the out-of-state price is over $64k. Two-fifths of undergraduates receive a merit aid award, but the average amount is under $5k and is unlikely to put a huge dent in your bill. For the 38 percent of students who qualify for need-based aid, Michigan does a phenomenal job meeting most of an individual's demonstrated financial need. In fact, 78 percent of those eligible see 100 percent of their need met. The average award is $19,145. This is truly exceptional for a public institution and is only one of the many reasons this topflight university is worth your money.

FINANCIAL
Institutional Type: Public
In-State Tuition: $14,934
Out-of-State Tuition: $49,022
Room & Board: $11,534
Required Fees: $328
Books & Supplies: $1,048

Avg. Need-Based Aid: $19,145
Avg. % of Need Met: 91%

Avg. Merit-Based Aid: $4,478
% Receiving Merit-Based Aid: 41%

Avg. Cumulative Debt: $27,224
% of Students Borrowing: 37%

CAREER
Who Recruits
1. Hudson's Bay
2. BP America
3. Bain & Company
4. United Talent
5. News America Marketing

Notable Internships
1. Uber
2. Nike
3. Lockheed Martin

Top Industries
1. Business
2. Education
3. Engineering
4. Operations
5. Research

Top Employers
1. General Motors
2. Ford Motor Company
3. Google
4. Amazon
5. Microsoft

Where Alumni Work
1. Detroit
2. New York City
3. Chicago
4. San Francisco
5. Washington, DC

Median Earnings
College Scorecard (Early Career): $63,400
EOP (Early Career): $68,700
PayScale (Mid-Career): $112,200

RANKINGS
Forbes: 20
Money: 8
U.S. News: 25, National Universities
Wall Street Journal/THE: 27
Washington Monthly: 28, National Universities

#CollegesWorthYourMoney

Minneapolis, Minnesota | Admissions Phone: 612-625-2008

ADMISSION
Admission Rate: 52%
Admission Rate - Men: 48%
Admission Rate - Women: 55%
EA Admission Rate: N/A
ED Admission Rate: Not Offered
Admission Rate (5-Year Trend): +7%
ED Admission Rate (5-Year Trend): Not Offered
% of Admits Attending (Yield): 27%
Transfer Admission Rate: 46%

Offered Wait List: N/A
Accepted Wait List: N/A
Admitted Wait List: N/A

SAT Reading/Writing (Middle 50%): 620-710
SAT Math (Middle 50%): 650-770
ACT Composite (Middle 50%): 26-31
Testing Policy: ACT/SAT Required
SAT Superscore: No
ACT Superscore: No

% Graduated in Top 10% of HS Class: 50%
% Graduated in Top 25% of HS Class: 85%
% Graduated in Top 50% of HS Class: 100%

ENROLLMENT
Total Undergraduate Enrollment: 34,633
% Part-Time: 13%
% Male: 47%
% Female: 53%
% Out-of-State: 28%
% Fraternity: 10%
% Sorority: 10%
% On-Campus (Freshman): 89%
% On-Campus (All Undergraduate): 22%

% African-American: 5%
% Asian: 10%
% Hispanic: 4%
% White: 65%
% Other: 4%
% Race or Ethnicity Unknown: 4%
% International: 8%
% Low-Income: 21%

ACADEMICS
Student-to-Faculty Ratio: 17:1
% of Classes Under 20: 37%
% of Classes Under 40: 73%
% Full-Time Faculty: 69%
% Full-Time Faculty w/ Terminal Degree: 80%

Top Programs
Business
Chemistry
Computer Science
Economics
Engineering
Mathematics
Political Science
Psychology

Retention Rate: 93%
4-Year Graduation Rate: 65%
6-Year Graduation Rate: 80%

Curricular Flexibility: Less Flexible
Academic Rating: ★★★

Inside the Classroom

Home to almost 35,000 undergraduates and another 16,000 graduate students, the University of Minnesota Twin Cities can easily be overshadowed by its neighboring flagships (Wisconsin, Michigan, and Illinois). Yet, UMTC deserves its fair share of the Midwestern limelight, thanks in part to a number of academic programs rising toward the top of national rankings and the university's positioning as a direct pipeline to the nineteen Fortune 500 companies located within state borders. While a 72 percent out-of-state tuition increase over the last seven years has slowed down the tidal wave of nonresident applicants, international students and out-of-staters still make up 35 percent of the undergraduate student body. The average Gopher today boasts significantly better academic credentials than previous generations at the university. In fact, four- year graduation rates have doubled since 1997, a testament to both the improved caliber of student as well as increased institutional support.

There are 150 majors on tap across seven freshman-admitting undergraduate colleges, but all students are subjected to the same twenty-three-credit Diversified Core as well as fifteen credits worth of Designated Themes. Those combined thirty-seven credits include forays into the art/humanities, social sciences, physical sciences, mathematics, literature, and history. More targeted topics include civic life and ethics, diversity and social justice in the US, the environment, global perspectives, and technology and society. All freshmen also must take a first-year writing course and one other course designated as "writing intensive" later in their educational journey. Students in the university's Honors Program must complete eight honors courses and a culminating senior thesis.

Despite a massive number of graduate students, this school generally keeps class sizes in check. A 17:1 student-to-faculty ratio is deployed effectively so that 64 percent of sections enroll twenty-nine or fewer students. On the other end of the spectrum, 20 percent of courses enroll fifty or more students, so you can expect some highly impersonal lecture-based introductory courses while in the Twin Cities. No matter your field of study, you can utilize UM's well-maintained database of upcoming faculty research projects as a way to connect directly with the professor of your choice. In the summer of 2018, more than 250 undergraduates participated in a campus-wide undergraduate research program. An outstanding 34 percent of UMTC students study abroad during their academic career with the most popular destinations being Spain, Italy, France, the United Kingdom, and Germany.

The most commonly conferred degrees at the university are in biology (12 percent), engineering (11 percent), social sciences (11 percent), business/marketing (10 percent), psychology (7 percent), and computer science (6 percent). The College of Science and Engineering and the Carlson School of Management have strong national reputations and offer top-ranked programs in accounting, business, and every branch of engineering. The quality of the chemistry, economics, psychology, and political science departments is also well-known by elite graduate schools. The school's reputation also helps those applying for prestigious postgraduate scholarships. Nine students won Fulbright Scholarships in 2019, and Minnesota also produced a number of Udall, Gilman, Critical Language, and Astronaut Scholars in recent years.

Outside the Classroom

Nine of every ten freshmen reside on the 1,200-acre Twin Cities campus in one of nine residence halls or eight apartment complexes; pretty much everyone else lives in off-campus housing as only 22 percent of the entire student body goes to sleep in university-owned domiciles. There are 3,400 students participating in Greek life, so fraternities and sororities play a fairly major role in social life. The Golden Gophers compete in twenty-three varsity sports; the most successful programs are the men's and women's ice hockey teams. Over 900 student organizations are active including nine student-run cultural centers, dozens of intramural sports, and a popular Outdoors Club. Arts and culture can be found right on campus at the school's own art, design, and natural history museums as well as the nearby Minneapolis Sculpture Garden, Guthrie Theater, Walker Art Center, and Minneapolis Institute of the Arts. Natural beauty also can be enjoyed on university grounds that contain 10,000 trees in the extensive Mississippi National River and Recreation Area, an area that also features miles of bike paths. For shopping or just hanging out, the famed Mall of America is only a fifteen-minute ride away. The Minneapolis and St. Paul campuses that together form UMTC are only three miles apart, and the best of both cities can be enjoyed from that advantageous central location.

Career Services

Instead of having one centralized career services office at the Twin Cities campus, the university has smaller offices housed within each of its undergraduate colleges. The College of Liberal Arts Career Services Office leads the way with eighteen full-time professional employees from the total of sixty-five across all colleges. That 538:1 ratio is within the average range when compared to other institutions profiled in this guidebook. However, for a school of UMTC's size, that level of support is exceptionally strong. Whether students are in the College of

Science and Engineering, the Carlson School of Management, or the School of Nursing, there will be a team of experts in the areas of career counseling, graduate/professional school advising, internship coordination, and employer relations ready to work directly on your behalf.

Career fairs are similarly segmented by discipline with annual offerings targeting those entering computer science, government, business, accounting, and health management. The College of Engineering (CSE) Career Fair draws around 3,500 students in the fall and 1,700 in the spring. The spring CSE event featured 175 companies such as Dell, Hewlett Packard, Tesla, Wells Fargo, and BAE Systems. A sampling of other career-related events in fall 2019 included a Harvard JD Admissions Information Session, a recruiting visit from Microsoft, and a staff-run Resume Writing Workshop. Having 225,000 working alumni, many of whom are local, is a huge advantage for carving out internships and other networking opportunities. The Carlson School of Management has a Long-Term Mentoring and Flash Mentoring program in which it will hand-pick a professional mentor from the business community to assist you. Between a sizable and friendly alumni base and a number of tight industry connections to Minnesota-based businesses, the Career Services Office at UMTC offers a wealth of opportunity to its undergraduates.

Professional Outcomes

The top seven companies snatching up the largest number of Gophers are all companies headquartered in the state of Minnesota: Medtronic (the largest medical device manufacturer in the world), Target, 3M, United Health Group, US Bank, Best Buy, and Cargill (the company with the highest revenue in the United States). Therefore, it is easy to see why roughly 70 percent of graduates remain in the Greater Minneapolis-St. Paul area. San Francisco, New York, Chicago, and Seattle also attract some graduates each year, and non-Minnesota-based companies like Intel, Microsoft, Amazon, Google, Apple, and Facebook all employ hundreds of Twin Cities alumni.

With 130 graduate programs in science, art, engineering, agriculture, medicine, and the humanities, the University of Minnesota retains many of its graduates as they pursue their next degrees. However, some of the top graduate programs in the country routinely welcome UM grads. For example, in 2017, alone seven architecture grads matriculated into Penn, Cornell, Columbia, and Yale. Future doctors benefit from the BA/MD program in conjunction with the University of Minnesota Medical School. The university produces 300+ applicants to medical school every year, and many go on to study within their home state but, in recent years, Gophers also have been accepted to prestigious medical institutions like Emory, the University of Wisconsin, and Columbia University.

Admission

UMTC saw 52 percent of those seeking a place in the Class of 2022 gain acceptance. Minnesota is predominately an ACT state, and 91 percent of the 2018-19 applicants submitted results from that exam, scoring a mid-50 percent range of 26-31. Those submitting SAT scores had mid-50 percent scores of 1270-1480. Half of those attending the university placed in the top 10 percent of their high school class, and 85 percent earned spots in the top quarter. The applicant pool here has grown stronger over the last decade, but admission is only slightly more competitive now than it was a decade ago.

The only factors rated as "very important" by the admissions committee are rigor of coursework, GPA, class rank, and standardized test scores. Essays, recommendations, and interviews are not considered in the process. Freshmen accepted into the University of Minnesota Twin Cities are admitted directly into one of seven undergraduate colleges. The schools requiring the highest grades and test scores are biological sciences, management, and science and engineering (CSE). In fact, the ACT range for those admitted into the CSE is 30-34 compared with the 23-28 mid-50th range for those admitted into the College of Education and Human Development. The school does offer an early action option with a November 1 deadline.

Worth Your Money?

In-state tuition of $15k and reasonable room-and-board fees make the list price approximately $29,000 for those from the Land of 10,000 Lakes. After financial and merit awards, even families making over $110,000 end up paying an average of $23,000. That makes UMTC a strong value for Minnesota teens no matter their area of academic/career pursuit. While out-of-state costs will run your four-year total bill to just under $200k, the return on investment numbers are the strongest of any school in Minnesota, including for nonresidents. The Carlson School of Management and the College of Science and Engineering are so highly regarded that a degree from either is worth a private university-level price tag.

FINANCIAL
Institutional Type: Public
In-State Tuition: $13,318
Out-of-State Tuition: $31,616
Room & Board: $10,358
Required Fees: $1,709
Books & Supplies: $1,000

Avg. Need-Based Aid: $11,360
Avg. % of Need Met: 76%

Avg. Merit-Based Aid: $5,058
% Receiving Merit-Based Aid: 19%

Avg. Cumulative Debt: $26,262
% of Students Borrowing: 57%

CAREER
Who Recruits
1. Enterprise Holdings
2. The Hertz Corporation
3. Aerotek
4. Thomson Reuters
5. Century Link

Notable Internships
1. Minnesota Timberwolves
2. Pratt & Whitney
3. U.S. State Department

Top Industries
1. Business
2. Education
3. Operations
4. Engineering
5. Research

Top Employers
1. Medtronic
2. Target
3. 3M
4. UnitedHealth Group
5. U.S. Bank

Where Alumni Work
1. Minneapolis
2. San Francisco
3. Chicago
4. New York City
5. Los Angeles

Median Earnings
College Scorecard (Early Career): $51,900
EOP (Early Career): $48,800
PayScale (Mid-Career): $104,000

RANKINGS
Forbes: 98
Money: 84
U.S. News: 70, National Universities
Wall Street Journal/THE: 95
Washington Monthly: 77, National Universities

#CollegesWorthYourMoney

University of North Carolina at Chapel Hill

Chapel Hill, North Carolina | Admissions Phone: 919-966-3621

ADMISSION

Admission Rate: 22%
Admission Rate - Men: 21%
Admission Rate - Women: 22%
EA Admission Rate: 31%
ED Admission Rate: Not Offered
Admission Rate (5-Year Trend): -5%
ED Admission Rate (5-Year Trend): Not Offered
% of Admits Attending (Yield): 45%
Transfer Admission Rate: 35%

Offered Wait List: 4,977
Accepted Wait List: 2,300
Admitted Wait List: 22

SAT Reading/Writing (Middle 50%): 640-720
SAT Math (Middle 50%): 630-750
ACT Composite (Middle 50%): 27-33
Testing Policy: ACT/SAT Required
SAT Superscore: Yes
ACT Superscore: Yes

% Graduated in Top 10% of HS Class: 78%
% Graduated in Top 25% of HS Class: 96%
% Graduated in Top 50% of HS Class: 99%

ENROLLMENT

Total Undergraduate Enrollment: 19,117
% Part-Time: 3%
% Male: 41%
% Female: 59%
% Out-of-State: 15%
% Fraternity: 20%
% Sorority: 20%
% On-Campus (Freshman): 100%
% On-Campus (All Undergraduate): 51%

% African-American: 8%
% Asian: 11%
% Hispanic: 8%
% White: 60%
% Other: 5%
% Race or Ethnicity Unknown: 4%
% International: 3%
% Low-Income: 20%

ACADEMICS

Student-to-Faculty Ratio: 13:1
% of Classes Under 20: 38%
% of Classes Under 40: 80%
% Full-Time Faculty: 72%
% Full-Time Faculty w/ Terminal Degree: 84%

Top Programs
Area Studies
Business
Chemistry
Environmental Science and Studies
Media and Journalism
Political Science
Psychology
Public Policy

Retention Rate: 97%
4-Year Graduation Rate: 82%
6-Year Graduation Rate: 90%

Curricular Flexibility: Somewhat Flexible
Academic Rating: ★★★★

Inside the Classroom

In 1789, a full thirty years before Thomas Jefferson founded UVA, our young nation's first public university was chartered. Four years later, the first cornerstone was laid smack dab in the middle of the new state of North Carolina, right next to a hill upon which sat New Hope Chapel. In that moment, simultaneously, the University of North Carolina and the town of Chapel Hill were born. Fast-forward 230 years and UNC Chapel Hill is one of the most prestigious flagship public schools in the country with 323,000+ proud alumni, the vast majority of whom were born and bred in the university's home state. That fact can be attributed to a thirty-year-old state law mandating that at least 82 percent of each freshman class be comprised of in-state students.

Massive in its scope, the lovely and affluent town of Chapel Hill is home to 19,117 undergraduates and 10,894 graduate/professional students. Undergraduates can choose from 77 bachelor's degree programs in a number of schools and colleges, the largest of which is the College of Arts & Sciences. The general education curriculum is called Making Connections and involves checking boxes in the areas of English composition and rhetoric, foreign language, quantitative reasoning, physical and life sciences, social and behavioral sciences, and the humanities and fine arts.

The student-faculty ratio is 13:1, and few courses are held in giant lecture halls; 88 percent of classes have fewer than fifty students. However, you won't have many intimate, seminar-style courses as part of your undergraduate education as only 38 percent of classes have a student enrollment under twenty. UNC sends more than one-third of graduates abroad to one of seventy countries at some point in their educational career. For a school of such massive size, an impressive 60 percent of students end up completing some type of research experience as undergraduates.

The social sciences (17 percent), media/journalism (9 percent), biology (9 percent), psychology (8 percent), business (7 percent), and parks and recreation (6 percent) are the areas in which the most degrees are conferred. The Kenan-Flagler Business School is internationally renowned and requires separate admission through UNC's Assured Admission program or through an application process following freshman year. Other strong programs include those in chemistry, journalism, psychology, and political science. However, an undergraduate degree of nearly any kind from UNC will open doors in the world of employment as well as for those seeking entrance into top graduate programs around the country. In its illustrious history, UNC-Chapel Hill has produced forty-nine Rhodes Scholars and thirty-eight Luce Scholars. In 2018, ten were named Fulbright Scholars, the tenth highest total among public research universities. It also has a high rate of success in helping students procure NSF Graduate Research Fellowships.

Outside the Classroom

The University of North Carolina-Chapel Hill requires that all freshmen live in one of the school's thirty-two residence halls. However, only 51 percent of the total undergraduate population lives on campus while many others live in apartments/houses in Chapel Hill or surrounding Durham or Carrboro. Still, there are many unifying experiences that bring the campus together, none more so than UNC men's basketball. Nothing short of a local religion, it sees 22,000 pack the Dean Smith Center to root for the Tar Heels; games against rival Duke are an unforgettable experience. In sum, there are twenty-eight varsity sports teams as well as a robust network of fifty club and intramural sports. One-fifth of UNC undergrads join a fraternity or sorority, but Greek life at UNC is unusually diverse, inclusive, and service oriented. On average, its students collectively contribute 35,000 hours of community service per year. More than 800 student activities are running on the Chapel Hill campus, highlighted by the popular twenty-four-hour UNC Dance Marathon fundraiser, an involved student government, a host of cultural and professional organizations, and the widely read Daily Tar Heel, which has a distribution of 20,000.

Career Services

UNC's University Career Services Office employs fifteen full-time staff members, excluding individuals who work as administrative assistants or in IT, who work with undergraduates. That equates to a student-to-advisor ratio of 1,274:1, well below average compared to the other institutions included in this book. Other schools within the larger university do have smaller career services offices, but they primarily serve graduate students. Despite less-than-ideal personnel numbers, the staff does create solid outcomes for graduates.

Career fairs draw 600+ companies to campus per year. An impressive 297 companies recruited on campus in 2017-18 and conducted 4,238 job interviews with undergraduates. Almost 200 employers held information sessions in Chapel Hill. The Carolina Career Partners Program helps connect local companies to undergraduate job candidates. Of those students directly entering the world of employment, 80 percent landed at least one internship while at UNC and, in one-third of those cases, the internship eventually led to a job with that same organization. All of the basic career services—resume assistance, practice interviews, 1:1 career counseling, and job and internship postings through Handshake—are available to undergraduates.

University of North Carolina at Chapel Hill

E-mail: unchelp@admissions.unc.edu | Website: www.unc.edu

Professional Outcomes

Six months after leaving Chapel Hill, 97 percent of the Class of 2018 had entered employment, military service, or graduate school; only 3 percent were still seeking employment. Among the for-profit companies who hire the most graduates are Wells Fargo, IBM, Cisco, Deloitte, EY, Google, Microsoft, Amazon, Oracle, Facebook, McKinsey & Company, and Goldman Sachs. In the nonprofit sector, a large number of Tar Heels are snatched up by the AmeriCorps, NIH, Teach for America, and the Peace Corps. A sizable 56 percent of 2018 graduates hung their diplomas somewhere in the state of North Carolina while 15 percent headed elsewhere in the Southeast, 12 percent to the Northeast, and 4 percent traveled to the Pacific Coast. The average starting salary for members of the Class of 2018 was $50,000, lower than the 2017 figure of $57,000. A dozen years after graduating, alumni take home the fourth-highest median salary of any North Carolina institution.

In a typical graduating class, one-quarter of students enroll directly in graduate/professional school. Some of the most commonly attended graduate schools are other Carolina-based institutions such as East Carolina University, Appalachian State, UNC-Greensboro, or—on the elite/local front—Duke and Wake Forest. Other prestigious schools frequented by UNC alums include Columbia and Harvard. UNC-Chapel Hill had 496 applicants to medical school in 2019, the eighth highest total in the nation. Recent graduates have gone on to study medicine at institutions such as Harvard Medical School, Duke University School of Medicine, UNC School of Medicine, and the Wake Forest School of Medicine.

Admission

Gaining admission into UNC-Chapel Hill is a completely different ballgame for North Carolina residents than it is for those hailing from any of the other forty-nine states or a foreign country. In-state applicants for admission into the Class of 2022 had a 41 percent success rate; all others faced harsher competition as the overall acceptance rate was only 22 percent. While many other flagship state institutions such as Michigan, Wisconsin, and UVA have substantially increased their number of non-residents in recent years, UNC has does not have the authority to follow suit as out-of-state enrollment is capped at 18 percent.

Of those who enrolled, the middle 50 percent SAT range was 1270-1470 and 27-33 on the ACT. Over three-quarters of enrolled students placed in the top 10 percent of their high school class, and 14 percent were either the valedictorian or salutatorian. In addition to high grades, test scores, and placement toward the top of your class, the UNC admissions committee considers a number of other factors to be of highest importance: test scores, essays, recommendations, extracurricular activities, talent/ability, character/personal qualities and, of course, state residency. While in-state applicants need to be strong in all of those areas, out-of-state applicants need to be exceptional, well above the mean. In sum, the fork in the residency road sends applicants down two significantly different admissions gauntlets. For out-of-staters, higher standardized test scores and/or a "hook" can help to set you apart. In-state applicants with in-range credentials have a much friendlier but still selective process awaiting them.

Worth Your Money?

One of the most incredible bargains in all of American higher education, residents of the Tar Heel State pay less than $10k in tuition and only $23,476 in annual cost of attendance. Those from out of state pay around $50k per year, not a bad price for an education at one of the premier universities in the country. UNC-Chapel Hill only grants merit aid to 6 percent of the student body, a small percentage compared to other UNC campuses (e.g., Greensboro grants aid to 62 percent). However, UNC-Chapel Hill is, by leaps and bounds, the most generous UNC school when it comes to need-based aid. The university grants an average annual award of $16,243 to those it declares eligible, meeting 100 percent of the demonstrated need for the vast majority. Whether you are headed to Chapel Hill as a resident or out-of-stater, you will get your money's worth.

FINANCIAL
Institutional Type: Public
In-State Tuition: $7,019
Out-of-State Tuition: $34,198
Room & Board: $11,526
Required Fees: $2,027
Books & Supplies: $972

Avg. Need-Based Aid: $16,243
Avg. % of Need Met: 100%

Avg. Merit-Based Aid: $10,812
% Receiving Merit-Based Aid: 6%

Avg. Cumulative Debt: $22,466
% of Students Borrowing: 40%

CAREER
Who Recruits
1. Greystar
2. Lincoln Financial Group
3. PNC Bank
4. Comcast
5. Fidus Investments

Notable Internships
1. Vanguard
2. Adobe
3. The Walt Disney Company

Top Industries
1. Business
2. Education
3. Healthcare
4. Research
5. Operations

Top Employers
1. Wells Fargo
2. IBM
3. Cisco
4. Deloitte
5. EY

Where Alumni Work
1. Raleigh-Durham, NC
2. Charlotte
3. Winston-Salem, NC
4. New York City
5. Washington, DC

Median Earnings
College Scorecard (Early Career): $55,600
EOP (Early Career): $54,200
PayScale (Mid-Career): $100,800

RANKINGS
Forbes: 45
Money: 52
U.S. News: 29 (T), National Universities
Wall Street Journal/THE: 33
Washington Monthly: 22, National Universities

#CollegesWorthYourMoney

University of Notre Dame

Notre Dame, Indiana | Admissions Phone: 574-631-7505

ADMISSION
Admission Rate: 18%
Admission Rate - Men: 18%
Admission Rate - Women: 17%
EA Admission Rate: 30%
ED Admission Rate: Not Offered
Admission Rate (5-Year Trend): -5%
ED Admission Rate (5-Year Trend): Not Offered
% of Admits Attending (Yield): 57%
Transfer Admission Rate: 23%

Offered Wait List: 1,450
Accepted Wait List: 912
Admitted Wait List: 20

SAT Reading/Writing (Middle 50%): 690-760
SAT Math (Middle 50%): 710-790
ACT Composite (Middle 50%): 33-35
Testing Policy: ACT/SAT Required
SAT Superscore: Yes
ACT Superscore: Yes

% Graduated in Top 10% of HS Class: 89%
% Graduated in Top 25% of HS Class: 98%
% Graduated in Top 50% of HS Class: 100%

ENROLLMENT
Total Undergraduate Enrollment: 8,617
% Part-Time: 0%
% Male: 52%
% Female: 48%
% Out-of-State: 92%
% Fraternity: Not Offered
% Sorority: Not Offered
% On-Campus (Freshman): 100%
% On-Campus (All Undergraduate): 78%

% African-American: 4%
% Asian: 5%
% Hispanic: 11%
% White: 68%
% Other: 5%
% Race or Ethnicity Unknown: 1%
% International: 7%
% Low-Income: 11%

ACADEMICS
Student-to-Faculty Ratio: 10:1
% of Classes Under 20: 62%
% of Classes Under 40: 85%
% Full-Time Faculty: 88%
% Full-Time Faculty w/ Terminal Degree: 91%

Top Programs
Architecture
Biological Sciences
Business
Engineering
English
Physics
Political Science
Theology

Retention Rate: 98%
4-Year Graduation Rate: 94%
6-Year Graduation Rate: 97%

Curricular Flexibility: Somewhat Flexible
Academic Rating: ★★★★★

Inside the Classroom

As iconic for its educational quality as for its storied gridiron glory, Notre Dame is the dream destination for Catholic students with Ivy-level academic qualifications. Four-fifths of the 8,400 undergraduate students possess a Catholic religious identity, reinforcing the school's values and traditions. Academically, a robust selection of seventy-five majors are offered across six undergraduate colleges: the School of Architecture, the College of Arts and Letters, the Mendoza School of Business, the College of Engineering, the Keough School of Global Affairs, and the College of Science (that includes a premed track).

Required coursework is comprehensive and includes four courses covering Catholic theology and philosophy. The Moreau First Year Experience is a two-semester course designed to help freshmen "integrate their academic, co-curricular, and residential experiences." Freshmen also take University Seminar, one of two writing-intensive courses mandated by the school. Six additional mandatory liberal arts courses assure that students at least dip their toes into the study of quantitative reasoning, science and technology, history, literature, and the social sciences.

A solid 62 percent of courses enroll fewer than twenty students, and 19 percent have single-digit numbers. Just under 10 percent of courses have an enrollment of more than fifty undergrads. A 10:1 student-to-faculty ratio is top notch and also represents an improvement over the 12:1 ratio of a decade ago. The Center for Undergraduate Scholarly Engagement offers hundreds of opportunities for conducting research, both individually and alongside faculty; one-third of graduates ultimately partake. One of the top universities for study abroad participation, 75 percent of Notre Dame undergrads select one of seventy-six programs in twenty-nine countries. The satisfaction rate for study abroad experiences is 93 percent.

The top six degrees conferred are computer science, mechanical engineering, sociology, international economics, marketing, and anthropology. Mendoza has a reputation as one of the country's best business schools and, to a slightly lesser extent, the College of Engineering often ranks highly on "best of" lists as well. Prestigious fellowships are won by the Irish in droves. After collecting twenty-six Fulbrights in 2018 and twenty-nine in 2017, it is one of the top producers in the whole United States. The National Science Foundation granted honors to twenty-three students and alumni in 2018, including twelve NSF Graduate Research Fellowships. The list goes on and on with five students winning Gilman Scholarships last year while others took home Gates Cambridge, Critical Language, and Truman Scholarships.

Outside the Classroom

Every single freshman and 80 percent of sophomores, juniors, and seniors live in one of the school's thirty residence halls. The focus of spiritual and recreational life, the residence halls serve a major role on a campus that is free of sororities and fraternities. Notre Dame also has no athletic program…just kidding! Sports are a way of life at the home of the Fighting Irish, whether you are a member or mere fan of one of the twenty-three NCAA Division I teams. Of course, the famed football program has a tradition unlike any other, and 81,000 pack the stands of Notre Dame Stadium each fall Saturday to cheer for the eleven-time national champions. One of the best intramural programs in the country and extensive recreational facilities ensure widespread athletic participation; the outdoor five-on-five basketball tournament draws 700 participating teams each year. If it's not sports, Irish men and women are engaged in some other meaningful activity; there are more than 500 student-run organizations active at the school. The 1,250-acre campus is as scenic as they come and includes two beautiful lakes, one famous golden dome, and all of the lush foliage one can absorb. South Bend is not a small college town but a city with a population of over 300,000. Within the immediate vicinity of campus are over fifty restaurants, seventy shops, and four museums. The beaches of Lake Michigan are sixty miles away, and Chicago is roughly a ninety-mile trip.

Career Services

The Center for Career Development (CCD) is staffed by twenty-six professional employees who work in career advising, employer relations, or event coordination and who impact undergraduate students (additional career services branches aimed at graduate students were not included in this figure). That equates to a 330:1 student-to-advisor ratio, which is in the average range when compared with other schools featured in this guide, but it is much stronger than most schools of Notre Dame's size. In short, this office works hard on behalf of its students, bringing to mind the classic Lou Holtz line, "No one has ever drowned in sweat."

More than three-quarters of students participate in at least one internship during their undergraduate years. Career fairs are attended by 450+ employers annually, including many major corporations known for employing large numbers of Fighting Irish alumni. Overall, more than 500 companies conduct approximately 7,000 job interviews on campus each academic year. The building in which the CCD is housed features forty-five interview/meeting rooms that have seen their fair share of "welcome aboard" handshakes. An alumni base 135,000 strong, many of whom have attained leadership positions in the field, are eagerly awaiting an opportunity to help current students and graduating seniors. Having one of the most connected, passionate, and loyal alumni networks in your corner is no small advantage. Tremendous corporate connections and graduate school/employment results for recent grads led to the Notre Dame CCD receiving high marks from our staff.

Professional Outcomes

A spectacular 98 percent of Notre Dame graduates are employed within six months of completing their degrees. Of the 65 percent who directly enter the world of employment, the most common industries are financial services (17 percent), consulting (13 percent), technology (8 percent), accounting (7 percent), and health services (6 percent). Massive numbers of alumni can be found in the offices of some of the nation's most desirable private employers including Deloitte, EY, PwC, IBM, Accenture, Booz Allen Hamilton, Google, Microsoft, Amazon, Goldman Sachs, JP Morgan, and McKinsey & Co. With so many entering the world's top finance/accounting/consulting firms, it isn't shocking that early career salaries tend to be high; as of 2018 the median figure was $59,000, a mark that is 32 percent higher than the national average for college grads. The highest concentration of alumni can be found in the Greater Chicago area followed by the Greater New York City area, South Bend itself, DC, San Francisco, and Boston.

Of the 22 percent of first-year alums who went directly into their graduate/professional studies, 23 percent were pursuing medical degrees, and 10 percent were studying law. Medical school applicants had a much higher rate of success than the national average; the Irish acceptance rate generally hovers around 80 percent. Class of 2018 members went on to attend institutions such as Harvard Medical School, Indiana University School of Medicine, Icahn School of Medicine at Mt. Sanai, Medical College of Wisconsin, and Albert Einstein Medical College. Presently, Notre Dame graduates can be found at some of the nation's top law schools such as Columbia, Duke, Harvard, Notre Dame, Boston College, UVA, and the University of Chicago. Those attending graduate schools for other fields can be found at comparably elite institutions all over the globe.

Admission

Of the 20,371 applicants to the Class of 2022 only 3,608 were accepted. The yield rate—admitted applicants who enrolled—was an impressively high 57 percent. Notre Dame hopefuls will need to finish at the very top of their high school class, and we don't just mean in the top decile. A hard-to-fathom 40 percent of accepted students hailed from the top 1 percent of the class, 50 percent were in the top 5 percent, and the median high school rank was in the top 2 percent. In total, 89 percent of accepted students placed in the top 10 percent. The SAT mid-50 percent range has reached similarly intimidating heights; it currently sits at 1400-1550. The ACT, which is submitted by 60 percent of applicants, has a mid-50 percent composite range of 33-35.

The admissions committee rates rigor of secondary coursework above all other factors. Class rank, GPA, standardized test scores, recommendations, essays, extracurricular activities, and talent/ability are all "important." Religious affiliation does matter at Notre Dame as 80 percent of admits identify as Catholic. Being a legacy applicant can help—22 percent of incoming 2018-19 freshmen were children of alumni. Both religious affiliation and legacy status are factors "considered" by the committee. The Fighting Irish do not offer early decision. Thanks to the extraordinary yield rate mentioned above, Notre Dame has no need to obtain binding commitments from prospective students. In recent years, the admissions standards at Notre Dame have approached Ivy League levels. Ten years ago, the acceptance rate was a much friendlier 27 percent, and the 25th percentile SAT mark was a full eighty points lower than it is today. Those with serious ambitions to spend four years in South Bend need to be in the top 1-2 percent in both academic performance and standardized test scores. Otherwise, you'll find yourself in the Rudy Ruettiger category as a long shot.

Worth Your Money?

Notre Dame has a high cost of attendance at over $73,000 per year. However, this is a school that funnels undergrads into high-paying jobs and top professional schools, leading to high lifetime earnings and the expansion and enhancement of one's personal and professional networks. The university does grant an average of $22k in merit aid to 17 percent of the student body and meets the full financial need of 48 percent of all undergraduates. Those receiving need-based aid receive an average annual grant of $40,098, helping to make the school a very worthy investment and accessible to students from all socioeconomic backgrounds.

FINANCIAL
Institutional Type: Private
In-State Tuition: $55,046
Out-of-State Tuition: $55,046
Room & Board: $15,640
Required Fees: $507
Books & Supplies: $1,050

Avg. Need-Based Aid: $40,098
Avg. % of Need Met: 100%

Avg. Merit-Based Aid: $21,626
% Receiving Merit-Based Aid: 17%

Avg. Cumulative Debt: $27,686
% of Students Borrowing: 42%

CAREER
Who Recruits
1. Salesforce
2. Boston Consulting Group
3. Facebook
4. JPMorgan Chase
5. McKinsey & Co.

Notable Internships
1. Saks Fifth Avenue
2. Citizens Bank
3. Citadel Securities

Top Industries
1. Business
2. Education
3. Operations
4. Finance
5. Research

Top Employers
1. Deloitte
2. EY
3. PwC
4. IBM
5. Accenture

Where Alumni Work
1. Chicago
2. New York City
3. South Bend, IN
4. Washington, DC
5. San Francisco

Median Earnings
College Scorecard (Early Career): $78,400
EOP (Early Career): $78,800
PayScale (Mid-Career): $130,500

RANKINGS
Forbes: 18
Money: 30
U.S. News: 15 (T), National Universities
Wall Street Journal/THE: 32
Washington Monthly: 30, National Universities

#CollegesWorthYourMoney

University of Pennsylvania

Philadelphia, Pennsylvania | Admissions Phone: 215-898-7507

ADMISSION
Admission Rate: 8%
Admission Rate - Men: 8%
Admission Rate - Women: 9%
EA Admission Rate: Not Offered
ED Admission Rate: 19%
Admission Rate (5-Year Trend): -4%
ED Admission Rate (5-Year Trend): -6%
% of Admits Attending (Yield): 67%
Transfer Admission Rate: 8%

Offered Wait List: 3,535
Accepted Wait List: 2,561
Admitted Wait List: 9

SAT Reading/Writing (Middle 50%): 700-760
SAT Math (Middle 50%): 740-800
ACT Composite (Middle 50%): 32-35
Testing Policy: ACT/SAT Required
SAT Superscore: Yes
ACT Superscore: Yes

% Graduated in Top 10% of HS Class: 96%
% Graduated in Top 25% of HS Class: 99%
% Graduated in Top 50% of HS Class: 100%

ENROLLMENT
Total Undergraduate Enrollment: 10,183
% Part-Time: 2%
% Male: 48%
% Female: 52%
% Out-of-State: 81%
% Fraternity: 30%
% Sorority: 28%
% On-Campus (Freshman): 100%
% On-Campus (All Undergraduate): 51%

% African-American: 9%
% Asian: 23%
% Hispanic: 11%
% White: 48%
% Other: 5%
% Race or Ethnicity Unknown: 4%
% International: 16%
% Low-Income: 15%

ACADEMICS
Student-to-Faculty Ratio: 6:1
% of Classes Under 20: 71%
% of Classes Under 40: 90%
% Full-Time Faculty: 77%
% Full-Time Faculty w/ Terminal Degree: 100%

Top Programs
Business
Cognitive Science
Communication
Computer Science
Engineering
English
Philosophy
Political Science

Retention Rate: 98%
4-Year Graduation Rate: 85%
6-Year Graduation Rate: 95%

Curricular Flexibility: Somewhat Flexible
Academic Rating: ★★★★★

Inside the Classroom

Once known for its insecurity over being frequently confused with Penn State and having a reputation in snooty circles as a "second-tier Ivy," the University of Pennsylvania in 2020 has long since brushed that dirt off its shoulders. Today, Penn boasts twice as many applicants as a decade ago and, with an 8.4 percent acceptance rate that is lower than Dartmouth's, it is now a dream destination for many of the brightest students around the world—and we mean *world*. Penn admits the highest percentage of international students of any Ivy by a wide margin. The 10,100+ Quaker undergrads on campus in 2018-19 are pursuing ninety distinct degrees across four schools: the College of Arts & Sciences, the College of Applied Science and Engineering, the College of Nursing and, of course, arguably the top business school anywhere—Wharton.

The Core Curriculum at UPenn is based on seven Sectors of Knowledge: society, history and tradition, arts and letters, humanities and social sciences, the living world, the physical world, and natural sciences and mathematics. In fulfilling those requirements students take mandatory courses in foreign language, writing (seminar), quantitative data analysis, formal reasoning, cross-cultural analysis, and diversity in the United States. The greatest number of students pursue degrees in business (20 percent), social sciences (15 percent), biology (11 percent), engineering (10 percent), and computer science (5 percent).

Penn has a 6:1 student-to-faculty ratio, but with a focus on research and 15,626 graduate students, not every undergraduate section is a tiny seminar. However, the university does boast an exceptional 30 percent of courses with an enrollment under ten and 71 percent with an enrollment under twenty—quite an achievement for a school of Penn's massive size. It also offers multiple ways for undergrads to conduct research, whether through independent studies or working side-by-side with faculty members. It is a testament to its focus in this area that the university publishes eleven distinct journals featuring original undergraduate research. Penn ranks first among Ivies and fourteenth among doctoral-granting institutions in study abroad participation rate; each year over 2,300 students head off to earn a semester's credit in one of eighty-five countries.

While Wharton is the ultimate name-drop, the Penn engineering program garners a more quiet respect. Outstanding programs abound throughout the university, in fields ranging from computer science to philosophy. Graduates of UPenn are, in general, met with high-paying jobs at desirable companies and entry into the best graduate and professional schools in existence. Prestigious national scholarship and fellowship programs adore Penn grads just the same. In 2017, two Penn grads won Rhodes Scholarships and another captured the distinguished award in 2019. Last year, the school produced thirty-four Fulbright Scholars, three Schwarzman Scholars, two Truman Scholars, and forty-one National Science Foundation Graduate Research Fellowships.

Outside the Classroom

Only 52 percent of students live in university-owned housing at Penn as 71 percent of juniors and 78 percent of seniors elect to live off campus. One reason for the lack of upperclassman interest in dorms is the popular Greek system that attracts over one-quarter of undergrads into one of fifty frat and sorority houses. The Quakers compete in thirty-three NCAA Division I sports in the Ivy League; over 1,000 members of the student body are varsity athletes. Many more participate in club and intramural athletics. There are multiple fitness centers including a 120,000-square-foot facility that includes an Olympic-size swimming pool, rock climbing wall, and sauna. The school also hosts the Penn Relays, the longest-running collegiate track meet in the country that draws 100,000 spectators annually. With 450+ student organizations active at Penn, there is a group that caters to wherever your talents and interests lie, whether that is in the performance, community service, or cultural identity realms. The school's newspaper, the Daily Pennsylvanian, has a staff of 250 students and has garnered many awards. Penn's West Philly campus is comprised of 215 buildings on 299 attached acres and contains plenty of green space. The urban setting affords students the benefits of walkability and easy trips to any part of the fifth-largest city in the United States.

Career Services

The University of Pennsylvania's Career Services Office has thirty professional staff members who are dedicated to undergraduate counseling, on-campus recruiting, and maintaining digital resources like Handshake. The 354:1 student-to-advisor ratio is average compared to other schools featured in this guide but strong for a school of Penn's size. Close to twenty annual career fairs are held, some of which are industry specific (engineering, finance, nursing) while others are themed such as the Common Good Career Fair; the Creative Career Fair; or the Startup, VC, and Data Analytics Fair.

Rising sophomores, juniors, and seniors find themselves in paid internships at some the world's top employers in droves. To quantify that, Class of 2018 members, between their junior and senior year, found positions at a 90 percent clip, including twenty-two at Goldman Sachs, twenty-one at Morgan Stanley, and nine at Google. Penn also excels at facilitating on-campus interviews; more than 300 companies conduct interviews on campus each year. Individualized attention is always available in the form of thirty-minute counseling appointments.

The office recommends a progression of exploration/involvement/experience/transition as undergraduates rise through their four years, and the university puts loads of resources into supporting all four phases. Ample support is also provided for those applying to medical, law, or graduate school. An equal emphasis on large-scale events such as industry-specific job fairs and one-on-one counseling leads to phenomenal graduate outcomes (more ahead).

Professional Outcomes

Seventy-two percent of Class of 2018 Quaker grads were employed six months following degree completion, another 18 percent were in graduate school, and 5 percent were still planning their next educational/career move. Finance was the sector attracting the highest percentage of grads (27 percent) followed by consulting (19 percent), technology (14 percent), and health care (7 percent). Employers hiring the greatest number of 2018 graduates included Goldman Sachs (27), Deloitte (26), JPMorgan (25), McKinsey & Company (23), Google (22), IBM (21), Capital One (20), Children's Hospital of Philadelphia (18), and Bain & Company (12). The median starting salary for all graduates is just shy of $75,000 plus an average sign-on bonus of $13,000. Among elite colleges, Penn alumni enjoy the highest midcareer salaries of any school except MIT. Unsurprisingly, the Philadelphia Metro area has the strongest concentration of alumni, but New York is a close second. San Francisco and DC also have a strong Quaker presence.

For those continuing their educational journeys, the most popular move is to remain at Penn—107 members of the Class of 2018 made that decision. The next most attended graduate schools were Columbia (15), Harvard (10), University of California (10), Oxford (8), and Yale (7). Students gain acceptance to medical school at a terrific rate—78 percent versus the national average of 43 percent. Medical schools that have taken more than five Penn grads since 2016-17 include Emory University, Temple University, Harvard Medical School, the Icahn School of Medicine at Mt. Sinai, and Penn's own uber-elite Perelman School of Medicine that sports a 4 percent acceptance rate. The acceptance rate into law school is 84 percent, which is made lower by the fact that the vast majority are aiming for top-tier schools. The most attended law schools is recent years are NYU School of Law, Penn Law School, Fordham University School of Law, Columbia University School of Law, and Harvard Law School.

Admission

Penn received close to 45,000 applications for a place in the Class of 2022, the second highest figure of any Ivy League university behind Cornell. In admitting only 3,731 prospective students (8.4 percent), 2018 was the most selective year in Penn history. The middle-50 percent SAT range for enrolled freshmen was 1420-1570, and the middle-50 percent ACT range was 32-35; similar numbers of students submitted results from each test. A nearly unanimous 96 percent of admitted Quakers earned a place in the top decile of their graduating high school class, and 85 percent possessed a GPA of 3.75 or higher on a 4.0 scale. In the past decade, the average admitted applicant's SAT scores have increased by around fifty points, and the grades/class rank have stayed the same. Back then, the school received half as many applications, and the acceptance rate was a far more forgiving 18 percent.

According to the admissions committee, rigor of secondary school record, GPA, standardized test scores, essays, recommendations, and character/personal qualities are deemed "very important" to the evaluative process. Factors classified as "important" are class rank, the interview, extracurricular activities, and talent/ability. One in seven 2018-19 freshmen were the first in their families to attend college. More than 1,300 students were admitted via early decision; the ED round saw an 18.5 percent acceptance rate, and more than half of the Class of 2022 was filled by those welcomed through a binding early acceptance. As is the case with so many top-shelf elite institutions, Penn rejects more students than ever, including thousands of teens who would have waltzed into the university a generation ago. Applying ED is a no-brainer if you want to gain a slight edge.

Worth Your Money?

Penn's total cost of attendance is $77,000+ per year and, unless you qualify for need-based financial aid, that is the price you will pay because the university does not award merit aid. It does, however, meet 100 percent of demonstrated need for all eligible students (46 percent of undergrads), awarding annual grants averaging $49k. Even if you are required to pay the full sticker price, Penn's starting salaries are such that even substantial loans will not be crippling to the vast majority of grads.

FINANCIAL
Institutional Type: Private
In-State Tuition: $51,156
Out-of-State Tuition: $51,156
Room & Board: $16,190
Required Fees: $6,614
Books & Supplies: $1,358

Avg. Need-Based Aid: $48,798
Avg. % of Need Met: 100%

Avg. Merit-Based Aid: $0
% Receiving Merit-Based Aid: 0%

Avg. Cumulative Debt: $22,103
% of Students Borrowing: 24%

CAREER
Who Recruits
1. Children's Hospital of Philadelphia
2. Teach for America
3. Facebook
4. Boston Consulting Group
5. JPMorgan Chase

Notable Internships
1. Pfizer
2. Gensler
3. HBO

Top Industries
1. Business
2. Education
3. Research
4. Operations
5. Social Services

Top Employers
1. Google
2. Amazon
3. Microsoft
4. Goldman Sachs
5. Facebook

Where Alumni Work
1. Philadelphia
2. New York City
3. San Francisco
4. Washington, DC
5. Boston

Median Earnings
College Scorecard (Early Career): $85,900
EOP (Early Career): $91,800
PayScale (Mid-Career): $133,900

RANKINGS
Forbes: 6
Money: 32
U.S. News: 6 (T), National Universities
Wall Street Journal/THE: 4
Washington Monthly: 6, National Universities

#CollegesWorthYourMoney

University of Pittsburgh – Pittsburgh Campus

Pittsburgh, Pennsylvania | Admissions Phone: 412-624-7488

Inside the Classroom

A generation ago you wouldn't see many teens from outside Pennsylvania clamoring to attend the University of Pittsburgh. In fact, for everyone other than western Pennsylvania residents, Penn State was the clear number one public university in the Keystone State. Fast-forwarding to today, Pitt attracts undergraduates from all fifty states and 102 countries. The home of the Panthers has ascended to the status of a premier public research university, and its 19,330 undergraduate students possess near-perfect transcripts and average standardized scores in the 90th percentile. Those in the Swanson School of Engineering sport SATs in the 97th percentile, and the top-ranked Honors College requires 99th percentile and above. In 2020, Pitt has become a true dream destination for massive numbers of high-achieving teens.

The university takes great care in welcoming new students to campus and ensuring a smooth transition. First-year mentors are available to help orient new students to campus life. Academic Foundations is a one-credit course that serves as an insiders' guide to Pitt, and first-year seminar classes are centered on a theme of interest with a capped enrollment of nineteen students. Pitt admits freshmen to the Dietrich School of Arts & Sciences, the College of Business Administration, the Swanson School of Engineering, and the School of Nursing. Across all undergraduate schools the university grants 104 distinct undergraduate degrees. Core coursework is mandated as follows: composition, two writing-intensive classes, algebra, quantitative and formal reasoning, two second language courses, and a class with a diversity designation. A total of nine courses in the humanities, social sciences, and natural sciences are required for all Dietrich School of Arts & Sciences students.

For a large public university, Pitt has a strong 14:1 student-to-faculty ratio and, as a result, it offers many smaller course sections to go along with some classes in large lecture halls. Forty-five percent of sections have an enrollment under twenty students, and 63 percent are capped at twenty-nine students. Plenty of personal connection with professors is available to those who seek it. Undergraduate research opportunities are granted to a healthy 52 percent of students. There are 350 study abroad programs in seventy-five countries, and many take advantage; the participation rate in the College of Business Administration is 55 percent.

The University of Pittsburgh is respected nationally by both top companies and prestigious graduate/professional institutions. Its engineering and business schools are rated top fifty in most rankings and are among the most commonly chosen fields of study. Pre-med offerings are also top-notch, with majors in the health professions, biology, and psychology rounding out the list of most popular majors. Pitt grads are no strangers to nationally competitive scholarships. In the last five years the school has produced forty-six Fulbright winners, seven Goldwater Scholars, two Churchill Scholars, and one Truman Scholar.

Outside the Classroom

A 132-acre urban campus houses 43 percent of the school's undergraduate student population. The Oakland neighborhood where the school is located is safe, walkable, and brimming with culture and fun. The Carnegie Museums of Art and Natural History and innumerable bars and eateries, including plenty of international options, are close by. The city, often rated as one of the "most livable in America," is truly an extension of campus, but campus itself isn't too shabby either. Pitt does guarantee housing to most students for three full years, and it is currently building dorms containing thousands of additional beds. Nine percent of men and 11 percent of women join Greek life, giving it a notable but not smothering presence. There are 400+ student organizations, and popular activities include the Pitt Dance Marathon that raised over $300,000 for the Children's Hospital of Pittsburgh. Intramural sports also are popular, and seemingly everyone participates. The university boasts an award-winning Robotics & Automation Society, Hillel Chapter, Hindu Students Council, and Society for Women Engineers. Pitt is an excellent school for sports fans as its nineteen varsity teams compete at the highest levels of NCAA Division I, and the football team shares a stadium with the Steelers and attracts over 41,000 fans per game.

Career Services

There are twenty-seven full-time employees at Pitt's Career Center, housed within the Office of Student Affairs. Members of the team serve as career consultants, employer development specialists, internship coordinators, and alumni engagement specialists. The office's 716:1 student-to-advisor ratio is greater than the average school in this guidebook but not alarming for a public university of its size. In fact, the University of Pittsburgh measures up well when it comes to the raw data in the areas of student engagement and employer relations.

In the 2018-19 school year, counselors conducted 4,573 one-on-one advising sessions and booked 402 total employers to attend their Fall Career + Internship Fair that includes separate days for engineering and computer science students. In total, 474 employers recruited at Pitt last year, and 760 on-campus interviews were held. Companies recruiting on campus include EY, Amazon, Epic Systems, Lockheed Martin, Vanguard, Cigna, and Deloitte. Tight employer partnerships led to internships being completed by 54 percent of graduates. However,

University of Pittsburgh – Pittsburgh Campus

E-mail: oafa@pitt.edu | Website: www.pitt.edu

those who complete the Internship Prep Program, a combination of workshops and individual appointments hosted by the Career Center, are guaranteed an internship or comparable experiential learning activity. With well-cultivated regional and national employer connections, Pitt students are given every opportunity to secure employment at a solid median starting salary or attend a graduate school consistent with their personal and professional goals.

Professional Outcomes

Recent grads enter full-time employment at a 50 percent clip, 27 percent enter graduate or professional school on a full-time basis, and 9 percent are both employed and beginning their graduate studies. Only 5 percent are still seeking employment within a few months of receiving their degrees. Engineering, nursing, business, and information sciences majors were the most likely to be employed full time upon graduation. Those majors had 73-86 percent employment rates while other majors tended to flock to graduate school in large numbers. The employers scooping up the highest number of 2017 graduates included the University of Pittsburgh Medical Center (92), PNC (30), PricewaterhouseCoopers (12), BNY Mellon (11), and Deloitte (11). Actual panthers may be solitary creatures, but Pitt Panthers flock in notable quantities to major corporations. More than one hundred alumni presently work for Dick's Sporting Goods, Amazon, Google, Microsoft, and Uber.

Starting salaries fluctuate across the nine undergraduate schools. The median starting salary for Class of 2017 graduates of the Swanson School of Engineering was $65,000, College of Business Administration students earned $50,000, and Dietrich School of Arts & Sciences grads were paid just shy of $37,000. Pittsburgh, Philly, New York, and DC host the most alumni.

With so many fine graduate programs at the University of Pittsburgh itself, many newly minted grads stay put to continue their education. Among the Class of 2017, Pitt was the most popular graduate location by a wide margin, attracting 211 students. Next in popularity was Penn (11), Duquesne (10), Johns Hopkins (10), Penn State (10), and Temple (10). Five or more attended Columbia, UVA, Carnegie Mellon, and Boston University. Undergraduate applicants can apply to the Guaranteed Admissions Program that earns you conditional acceptance to the University of Pittsburgh School of Medicine, one of the best medical schools in the entire U.S. Recent Pitt graduates have gone on to attend law schools at George Washington University, the University of Chicago, and UVA as well as Pennsylvania-based options like Temple, Duquesne, and Pitt itself.

Admission

Pitt received 29,857 applications to join the Class of 2022 and allowed entrance to 59 percent. However, only 23 percent of accepted applicants ultimately entered the 2018-19 freshman class as many Pennsylvania residents applying to ultra-selective schools use Pitt as a safety school. However, there is nothing that comes close to screaming "safety school" when examining the academic credentials of current undergraduates. With a mid-50 percent SAT score of 1270-1430 (42 percent had math scores above 700) and a mid-50 percent ACT range of 28-33, today's Panthers are high achievers. Not to mention that 79 percent of the 2018-19 freshman class possessed a high school GPA above a 3.75; the average was a 4.01. Fifty-five percent hailed from their graduating class' top decile, and 88 percent placed in the top quartile.

At the top of the admissions office checklist are the rigor of one's courses, GPA, and standardized test scores. The essay is the only other factor ranking at or above the "important" level. There is no early action or early decision option at Pitt, so all applicants are following the same time line. The Pitt Honors College has become one of the premier honors programs in the country. SAT scores for admitted honors students are generally in the 1450-1500 range and the average GPA is 4.39. The school accepts between 300 and 400 students each year. Prior to the turn of the new millennium, Pitt was a school that would admit "B" students. Twenty years ago, only 29 percent of the entering Arts & Sciences students were top-10 percent finishers, and the average SAT in the nursing program was a 1060. Today, Pitt takes "A" students who took AP courses and registered strong standardized test scores; getting into the Honors College is like getting into an Ivy.

Worth Your Money?

Pitt's in-state annual cost of attendance is just over $34,000 per year; out of state that number climbs to over $48,000. Families making over $75,000 a year are not going to receive much need-based aid and will pay somewhere near full price. Only a sliver of incoming Panther freshmen net any merit aid at all. Based on that data, it is fair to say that Pitt is worth the price of admission for any Keystone State resident, no matter what degree you may be pursuing. There is a lot to like about Pitt for out-of-state and international students, but the cost will be high.

FINANCIAL
Institutional Type: Public
In-State Tuition: $18,628
Out-of-State Tuition: $32,656
Room & Board: $11,250
Required Fees: $1,090
Books & Supplies: $755

Avg. Need-Based Aid: $10,512
Avg. % of Need Met: 54%

Avg. Merit-Based Aid: $10,247
% Receiving Merit-Based Aid: 13%

Avg. Cumulative Debt: $39,462
% of Students Borrowing: 60%

CAREER
Who Recruits
1. American Eagle
2. Allegheny Health Network
3. FedEx
4. EPIC Systems
5. Norfolk Southern

Notable Internships
1. Boston Consulting Group
2. NASA Jet Propulsion Laboratory
3. CVS

Top Industries
1. Business
2. Education
3. Healthcare
4. Operations
5. Engineering

Top Employers
1. PNC
2. BNY Mellon
3. Deloitte
4. Dick'sSporting Goods
5. Amazon

Where Alumni Work
1. Pittsburgh
2. Philadelphia
3. New York City
4. Washington, DC
5. San Francisco

Median Earnings
College Scorecard (Early Career): $53,900
EOP (Early Career): $48,900
PayScale (Mid-Career): $100,400

RANKINGS
Forbes: 144
Money: 294
U.S. News: 57 (T), National Universities
Wall Street Journal/THE: 96 (T)
Washington Monthly: 174, National Universities

#CollegesWorthYourMoney

University of Richmond

Richmond, Virginia | Admissions Phone: 804-289-8640

ADMISSION
Admission Rate: 30%
Admission Rate - Men: 32%
Admission Rate - Women: 28%
EA Admission Rate: N/A
ED Admission Rate: 48%
Admission Rate (5-Year Trend): -1%
ED Admission Rate (5-Year Trend): +3%
% of Admits Attending (Yield): 23%
Transfer Admission Rate: 35%

Offered Wait List: 3,653
Accepted Wait List: 1,243
Admitted Wait List: 28

SAT Reading/Writing (Middle 50%): 640-710
SAT Math (Middle 50%): 650-750
ACT Composite (Middle 50%): 30-33
Testing Policy: ACT/SAT Required
SAT Superscore: Yes
ACT Superscore: No

% Graduated in Top 10% of HS Class: 56%
% Graduated in Top 25% of HS Class: 86%
% Graduated in Top 50% of HS Class: 96%

ENROLLMENT
Total Undergraduate Enrollment: 3,227
% Part-Time: 6%
% Male: 48%
% Female: 52%
% Out-of-State: 77%
% Fraternity: 22%
% Sorority: 30%
% On-Campus (Freshman): 99%
% On-Campus (All Undergraduate): 91%

% African-American: 8%
% Asian: 7%
% Hispanic: 8%
% White: 57%
% Other: 4%
% Race or Ethnicity Unknown: 5%
% International: 11%
% Low-Income: 16%

ACADEMICS
Student-to-Faculty Ratio: 8:1
% of Classes Under 20: 70%
% of Classes Under 40: 100%
% Full-Time Faculty: 68%
% Full-Time Faculty w/ Terminal Degree: 93%

Top Programs
Accounting
Biology
Biochemistry
Business
Economics
Global Studies
Leadership Studies
Philosophy, Politics, Economics, and Law

Retention Rate: 94%
4-Year Graduation Rate: 82%
6-Year Graduation Rate: 87%

Curricular Flexibility: Somewhat Flexible
Academic Rating: ★★★★✦

Inside the Classroom

Considering that in 1861 many of the University of Richmond faculty went off to fight for the Confederacy whose capital was only miles from campus, it may come as a surprise that now the school is a diverse and progressive assemblage of young people from all fifty US states and more than seventy foreign countries. With roughly 3,200 undergraduates, the school is at once modest in size and robust in its academic and student life offerings; there are over sixty undergraduate majors at the university and many standout programs, including the one-of-a-kind Jepson School of Leadership Studies as well as a host of respected pre-professional pathways.

A distinctive general education curriculum includes a first-year seminar as well as the initial leg of a three-course wellness curriculum (the freshman course covers topics like alcohol education). From there, undergrads must demonstrate proficiency in a foreign language and then march through one course in each of historical studies, literary studies, natural sciences, social analysis, symbolic reasoning, and visual and performing arts. The list of required courses is relatively short, affording students a nice amount of academic freedom and exploration.

Don't let the "university" designation fool you; Richmond is all about undergraduate education. The student-to-faculty ratio is 8:1, the average class size is sixteen students, and not a single course is taught by a teaching assistant. Twenty-one percent of classes have single-digit enrollment numbers, and 70 percent of sections contain fewer than twenty students. Half of all Richmond students participate in an intensive research experience with a faculty member prior to graduation, and students can have those summer opportunities funded through the Richmond Guarantee that sees the university fund research apprenticeships as well as internships. More than 650 students receive such funding every summer. Going abroad is the norm at UR—59 percent take a semester or full year of study in one of seventy programs in thirty countries.

The highly regarded Robbins School of Business is responsible for granting 36 percent of the degrees conferred by the university, a staggering number that dwarfs any other field of study. The social sciences collectively attract 15 percent of the student body, and biology (premed is strong) accounts for 10 percent of degrees earned. The international relations, political science, and history departments also have excellent reputations. Applicants to prestigious fellowships fare quite well. In 2019, eight students won Fulbrights, three won Goldwater Scholarships, and one took home a Boren Scholarship.

Outside the Classroom

The University of Richmond's 350-acre campus houses 92 percent of the undergraduate population, and 97 percent live on campus all four years, creating a cohesive student body. Sixteen Greek organizations on campus rule the social scene with 30 percent of women joining sororities and 22 percent of men entering fraternity life. The Spiders compete in seventeen NCAA Division I sports within the highly competitive Atlantic Ten Conference, an astounding fact considering the size of the school's liberal arts college. There are 205 student-run organizations, including thirty club sports teams, fourteen religious groups, and seven honors societies. Intramural leagues are run out of the award-winning Weinstein Center for Recreation that contains a six-lane, twenty-five-yard swimming pool, racquetball/squash courts, and an indoor jogging track. UR's food services are regularly ranked high on lists of best college cuisine. School-run buses and shuttles make getting around a breeze. Campus is located only six miles from downtown Richmond, and longer road trips to DC (90 miles), the Atlantic Ocean, or the Blue Ridge Mountains make for an easy weekend getaway.

Career Services

The Office of Alumni and Career Services is staffed by fifteen full-time professional employees (not counting administrative coordinators) who hold positions like career advisor, employer relations coordinator, and director of experiential learning and assessment. That equates to a student-to-advisor ratio of 215:1, in the superior range when compared to the other institutions included in this book. It's no wonder that 99 percent of Richmond grads report being "generally satisfied" or "very satisfied" with their education one year after graduation, a good indicator of contentment with early career outcomes.

Richmond's career services office operates with a four-year plan that connects students to advisers during freshman year. A solid 78 percent of members of the Class of 2018 met with an advisor during their senior year. The SpiderConnect system and alumni connections help 70 percent of UR undergraduates land at least one internship during their four years of study. There are fifty+ regional alumni groups located around the United States and abroad, creating opportunities to build bridges and find mentorships in just about any major city. Career expos on campus typically attract fifty employers, and major corporations regularly travel to Richmond to recruit and interview current seniors. Spider Road Trips and Spider Shadowing are other avenues to hands-on job exploration opportunities. With strong industry connections, more-than-adequate staffing, and a number of innovative career exploration programs, the Office of Alumni and Career Services does well for its undergraduate students.

University of Richmond

E-mail: admission@richmond.edu | Website: www.richmond.edu

Professional Outcomes

One year after receiving their degrees, 95 percent of Richmond alums who are seeking employment have found jobs. The most popular sectors are financial services/insurance (13 percent), consulting (8 percent), technology (8 percent), teaching (5 percent), accounting (5 percent), and sales/business development (5 percent). Companies where you can find at least 50 Richmond alumni employed include Capital One (which employs 300+ Spiders), Deloitte, PwC, Wells Fargo, EY, Dominion Energy, Morgan Stanley, Altria, Google, and Accenture. The average salary range one year out of school is $50,000-$55,000. The majority of students remain in the Richmond area after finishing at the university, however large pockets of alumni can be found in New York City, DC, Philadelphia, and Boston. Richmond is a school with strong connections to industry in every region of the United States.

Within a year of graduation 28 percent of the Class of 2017 was already enrolled in a graduate or professional degree program. The school boasts an impressive list of recent acceptances into high-end law schools such as Harvard, Duke, the University of Chicago, Vanderbilt, Yale, UVA, and the University of Michigan. Even more notable is Richmond's success with helping students get accepted into medical school. Between 2013 and 2018 a phenomenal 73 percent of those who applied were accepted, a figure that blows away the national average. Medical schools attended by those students included Brown, Dartmouth, UNC, Stanford, Emory, and Harvard.

Admission

Of the 11,881 applicants for a place in the Class of 2022, only 3,584 were welcomed to the university, working out to an acceptance rate of 30 percent, an all-time low. The mid-50 percent standardized test scores also reached record levels of 1360-1490 on the SAT and 31-33 on the ACT. Fifty-six percent of entering freshmen hailed from the top 10 percent of their high school class, and 86 percent placed in the top quartile. Unweighted GPAs ranged from a 25th percentile 3.6 and a 75th percentile 3.96. A decade ago, 39 percent of applicants gained acceptance, and the SAT range was 1170-1370, a clear signal that Richmond has significantly increased its level of selectivity in recent years.

The admissions committee holds GPA and the rigor of one's secondary school courses as the two most important factors in evaluating an applicant. Seven categories make up the second tier of still "important" factors. Those are standardized test scores, class rank, essays, recommendations, extracurricular activities, character/personal qualities, and talent/ability. Leadership and engagement in high school is sincerely valued by this committee as the Class of 2022 included 268 athletic captains, twenty-three student government officials, and twenty-two editors-in-chief of school newspapers. Applying through early decision or early action is a good idea as the school is looking for applicants for whom Richmond is a genuine top choice. The school's yield rate is 23 percent, meaning 77 percent of admitted applicants head elsewhere. Thus, it's no wonder that 37 percent of the Class of 2022 was admitted via ED (those students enjoyed a 48 percent acceptance rate), 42 percent were admitted through nonbinding early action, and only a paltry 19 percent came through the regular cycle.

Worth Your Money?

Richmond's cost of attendance approaches $70,000, making a four-year degree list price of $280,000. Unlike many private universities, it only awards merit aid to 19 percent of the population, but those students receive a sizable discount of $30k, on average. UR focuses most of its generosity on those with true financial need, issuing average annual grants of $45,282 to 40 percent of the undergraduate student body. Further, Richmond meets 100 percent of the demonstrated need for those who qualify for financial aid. A uniquely intimate undergraduate setting and solid starting salaries (particularly for business grads) make Richmond worth your money, despite the high price tag.

FINANCIAL
Institutional Type: Private
In-State Tuition: $54,690
Out-of-State Tuition: $54,690
Room & Board: $12,900
Required Fees: $0
Books & Supplies: $1,100

Avg. Need-Based Aid: $45,282
Avg. % of Need Met: 100%

Avg. Merit-Based Aid: $30,325
% Receiving Merit-Based Aid: 19%

Avg. Cumulative Debt: $27,406
% of Students Borrowing: 43%

CAREER
Who Recruits
1. Baker Tilly
2. BB&T Corporation
3. Dominion Energy
4. John Hancock
5. MAXIMUS

Notable Internships
1. Cushman & Wakefield
2. The Cohen Group
3. Citi

Top Industries
1. Business
2. Education
3. Operations
4. Sales
5. Finance

Top Employers
1. Capital One
2. Deloitte
3. Wells Fargo
4. PwC
5. EY

Where Alumni Work
1. Richmond
2. New Yprk City
3. Washington, DC
4. Philadelphia
5. Boston

Median Earnings
College Scorecard (Early Career): $64,500
EOP (Early Career): $69,600
PayScale (Mid-Career): $107,500

RANKINGS
Forbes: 83
Money: 113
U.S. News: 23, Liberal Arts Colleges
Wall Street Journal/THE: 66
Washington Monthly: 32, Liberal Arts Colleges

#CollegesWorthYourMoney

University of Rochester

Rochester, New York | Admissions Phone: 585-275-3221

Inside the Classroom

From its founding in 1850, the University of Rochester established a national reputation as a strong research university. The adoption of its Renaissance Plan in 1995 instituted a uniquely open curriculum for a STEM-focused university, smaller class sizes, and a heavy investment in modernizing campus. Paying dividends today, those changes helped the school blossom into a world-class school that is home to over 6,500 undergraduates and another 5,000 graduate students. U of R's seventy-five undergraduate majors offer students a chance at a rigorous yet flexible educational experience at a small liberal arts college within a renowned research institution.

There are literally no required subjects at the University of Rochester's College of Arts, Sciences, and Engineering. Instead, students must, over their four years of study, take one writing-focused course of their choosing and twelve-credit clusters of courses in two of the following categories (whichever two do not encompass the student's major): humanities, social sciences, and natural sciences and engineering. Those course clusters are designed to ensure "substantive and integrated study," and there are 250+ to choose from, ensuring a high degree of autonomy in selecting one's academic path. The overarching goal of the curriculum is to best reflect the school's ideals of curiosity, competence, and community.

Rochester has maintained a 10:1 student-to-faculty ratio despite graduating 500 more undergraduate students in 2018 than a decade prior. You will encounter some large lecture halls for introductory courses, but the most common class size is ten to nineteen students; 70 percent of sections enroll fewer than twenty. An impressive 77 percent of students are involved in undergraduate research, a strong indicator that opportunities for intimate learning experiences are plentiful. Approximately one-third of students take a semester abroad in one of the forty-five+ countries the university has an affiliation with.

Excellence is everywhere you look at Rochester. The Eastman School of Music is one of the best music conservatories in the United States. The Hajim School of Engineering & Applied Sciences is a top fifty institution. Other strong majors include mathematics, economics, and political science—each will open doors in their respective fields. And graduates are no strangers to prestigious fellowship programs. From 2016 to 2018 Rochester produced twenty Fulbright Scholarship winners, sixteen National Science Foundation Graduate Research Fellowship recipients, six Gilman Scholarship winners, and four Critical Language Scholarship recipients.

Outside the Classroom

Over three-quarters of undergrads reside in university-owned housing on the school's 154-acre main campus that is nestled around a bend of the Genesee River. First-years and sophomores are required to live on campus. The school's thirty-four fraternities and sororities entice 21 percent of the undergraduate student body into joining. Most Greek participants—85 percent—also are engaged with other student organizations. Twenty one NCAA Division III sports teams play as the YellowJackets while the university also boasts one of the largest club sports systems with forty registered club sports and over 1,100 members. There are more than 300 clubs with which undergrads can become involved including the *Campus Times*, a student-run newspaper in print since 1873 and a selection of top-notch a cappella groups. There are plenty of campus-wide events such as YellowJacket Weekend, a carnival that marks the start of the academic year, and great musical acts, speakers, and activists are regularly booked to provide cultural and entertainment opportunities without straying from school grounds. Harsh weather can make for long winters, but campus is always humming with some type of appealing activity. The closest major American city is Buffalo, but for the more adventurous, Toronto, Canada, is less than three hours by car.

Career Services

The Gwen M. Green Career Center for Career Education and Connections is staffed by fourteen professionals with expertise in career education and advising, employer development, and event coordination. That number does not include the eight peer advisors or administrative assistants. The University of Rochester's 450:1 student-to-advisor ratio is higher than the average school featured in this guide. Still, it manages to mostly achieve its stated aim of assisting students "in achieving their individual career goals while providing them with the resources and tools they need to develop connections between their aspirations, academic pursuits, and co-curricular experiences."

The Greene Center engages more than 500 organizations annually in recruiting and career education programs. The Spring Career and Internship Fair draws forty+ employers to campus including the US Department of State, Epic Systems, the FBI, Citi, and Johnson & Johnson. The center also offers regular events, typically multiple workshops and information sessions per week. Events in May 2019 alone included a CV and resume workshop, a night with Kraft Heinz leadership, and a virtual career conversation about innovation in the workplace. Staff is happy to meet one-on-one to help students select and secure an internship that will be meaningful to their career development process. A near-perfect 96 percent of YellowJackets complete at least one internship during their undergraduate years; 75 percent complete two or more. You can also apply for a $1,000 to $2,500 alumni grant to help fund a summer internship that might not otherwise be possible. There are a significant number of opportunities for students to engage with UR alumni through structured programs, networking, and courses offered by the Greene Center.

Professional Outcomes

Six months after receiving their diplomas, 95 percent of Class of 2018 grads had achieved positive outcomes with 51 percent employed, and a notably high 42 percent already pursuing an advanced degree. Popular industries included higher education (15 percent), internet and software (10 percent), health care (8 percent), and manufacturing (6 percent). Top employers of 2018 grads included Deloitte (11), Epic Systems (11), EY (9), and Google (7). Looking across all graduating years, significant numbers of Rochester alumni also can be found in the offices of Amazon, IBM, Apple, and Microsoft. The average starting salary for the most recent cohort of grads was an impressive $61,776; that figure was over $75k for graduates of the Hajim School of Engineering and close to $55k for those in the School of Arts and Sciences. Upstate New York, New York City, Boston, DC, San Francisco, and Philadelphia play home to the greatest number of alumni.

With over two-fifths of grads jumping directly into a graduate program, many continue their studies at the University of Rochester (207) or at other elite East Coast institutions such as Columbia (25), NYU (15), Cornell (13), and Boston University (12). The university has an excellent premed reputation, and acceptance rates into MD programs are significantly higher than the national average. Thanks to the Rochester Early Medical Scholars program, some premed students are already on an eight-year pathway toward the completion of a medical degree at the University's School of Medicine and Dentistry. Rochester's own medical school accepted four members of the Class of 2018, neighboring SUNY Buffalo took three, and SUNY Upstate welcomed two. Students matriculated into a wide range of law schools including top tier institutions like William & Mary, Emory, Boston University, the University of Wisconsin, and Indiana University.

Admission

The fight for a place in the Class of 2022 was record setting as it was the first time in the school's history that applications exceeded 20,000 and the acceptance rate dipped below 30 percent. Those accepted possessed an average GPA of 3.8 and an SAT score slightly above 1400. The mid-50 percent range for 2018-19 freshmen was 29-33 on the ACT and 1300-1500 on the SAT. This fall (2020), the university moves from test-flexible to test-optional. Undergraduate applicants to the college may now decide which exam, if any, is an accurate representation of their ability and potential for success.

Interviews are strongly recommended as part of this holistic admissions process that seeks to "identify curious, capable, and engaged students from across the globe." In addition to stellar grades in a highly rigorous academic program, the committee wants to see evidence of leadership through extracurricular involvement as well as strong character/personal qualities. Another all-time high of 476 students who were freshmen in 2018-19 were accepted via early decision, and the ED acceptance rate hovers around 50 percent, giving early applicants far better odds than those in the regular round. Those accepted through binding ED comprise 33 percent of the overall freshman class. In sum, Rochester has never been more difficult to get into, so there is far less room for error than there was a generation ago.

Worth Your Money?

Including tuition, fees, room and board, and other estimated expenses, the total projected cost of attendance at this school is $75,186 per year. The good news is that approximately 90 percent of those who apply for need-based aid see 100 percent of their financial need met. While a $300,000 sticker price for a bachelor's degree is steep, the majority of students receive sizable discounts via need-based or merit aid. The average net price paid by families, even those in the top income bracket, is $37,900; those in the lowest brackets paid far less. Further, significant starting salaries and corporate connections allow YellowJackets to get a running start toward financial stability. For those who know what they want from their education (i.e., certain about major and career oriented), the University of Rochester is worth your money.

FINANCIAL
Institutional Type: Private
In-State Tuition: $55,040
Out-of-State Tuition: $55,040
Room & Board: $16,548
Required Fees: $990
Books & Supplies: $1,310

Avg. Need-Based Aid: $52,683
Avg. % of Need Met: 95%

Avg. Merit-Based Aid: $12,483
% Receiving Merit-Based Aid: 30%

Avg. Cumulative Debt: $29,553
% of Students Borrowing: 51%

CAREER
Who Recruits
1. Instagram
2. The Martin Agency
3. Goldman Sachs
4. CarMax
5. Citi

Notable Internships
1. Wegman's Food Markets
2. Lockheed Martin
3. SpaceX

Top Industries
1. Business
2. Education
3. Research
4. Healthcare
5. Engineering

Top Employers
1. Google
2. Apple
3. IBM
4. Amazon
5. Microsoft

Where Alumni Work
1. Rochester, NY
2. New York City
3. Boston
4. Washington, DC
5. San Francisco

Median Earnings
College Scorecard (Early Career): $61,200
EOP (Early Career): $62,000
PayScale (Mid-Career): $112,700

RANKINGS
Forbes: 82
Money: 194
U.S. News: 29 (T), National Universities
Wall Street Journal/THE: 58
Washington Monthly: 43, National Universities

#CollegesWorthYourMoney

ADMISSION
Admission Rate: 13%
Admission Rate - Men: 13%
Admission Rate - Women: 13%
EA Admission Rate: Not Offered
ED Admission Rate: Not Offered
Admission Rate (5-Year Trend): -7%
ED Admission Rate (5-Year Trend): Not Offered
% of Admits Attending (Yield): 41%
Transfer Admission Rate: 25%

\# Offered Wait List: Not Offered
\# Accepted Wait List: Not Offered
\# Admitted Wait List: Not Offered

SAT Reading/Writing (Middle 50%): 660-740
SAT Math (Middle 50%): 690-790
ACT Composite (Middle 50%): 30-34
Testing Policy: ACT/SAT Required
SAT Superscore: Yes
ACT Superscore: No

% Graduated in Top 10% of HS Class: 90%
% Graduated in Top 25% of HS Class: 97%
% Graduated in Top 50% of HS Class: 100%

ENROLLMENT
Total Undergraduate Enrollment: 19,907
% Part-Time: 4%
% Male: 49%
% Female: 51%
% Out-of-State: 35%
% Fraternity: 26%
% Sorority: 27%
% On-Campus (Freshman): 98%
% On-Campus (All Undergraduate): 30%

% African-American: 5%
% Asian: 21%
% Hispanic: 15%
% White: 39%
% Other: 6%
% Race or Ethnicity Unknown: 1%
% International: 13%
% Low-Income: 19%

ACADEMICS
Student-to-Faculty Ratio: 9:1
% of Classes Under 20: 59%
% of Classes Under 40: 79%
% Full-Time Faculty: 59%
% Full-Time Faculty w/ Terminal Degree: 92%

Top Programs
Business
Cinematic Arts
Communication
Computer Science
Design
Engineering
International Relations
Performing Arts

Retention Rate: 97%
4-Year Graduation Rate: 78%
6-Year Graduation Rate: 92%

Curricular Flexibility: Somewhat Flexible
Academic Rating: ★★★★✓

Inside the Classroom

A few decades back, if you told someone in-the-know about college admissions that the University of Southern California would eventually be in the same league with UC Berkeley, they would likely have concluded that an asteroid was headed for the San Francisco Bay area. At that time, USC was stereotyped as a lily-white school for wealthy underachievers that accepted the majority of applicants. Today, the home of the Trojans is one of the premier private research universities in the country, enriched by a diverse pool of students from around the globe and sporting a lower acceptance rate than Georgetown, Tufts, Washington University in St. Louis and—to bring things full circle—Berkeley.

There are 130 undergraduate majors and minors within the Dornslife College of Arts & Sciences alone, the University's oldest and largest school. Graduation requirements are a fairly run-of-the-mill assortment of selections across the major disciplines. By degrees conferred, the most popular areas of study are business (24 percent), social sciences (12 percent), visual and performing arts (12 percent), engineering (10 percent), and communications/journalism (9 percent).

At an institution with close to 20,000 undergraduates and 27,000 graduate students you would not expect to find many tiny seminar courses with single-digit enrollments, but 14 percent of classes at USC do, in fact, meet that standard. The bulk of courses offered are in the ten to nineteen range, but you also will find yourself in a fair share of large lecture halls in your time at USC. Still, there is little anonymity in a Trojan education. Aided by a favorable 9:1 student-to-faculty ratio, the school does an excellent job facilitating undergraduate research opportunities. Each school/college has a course entitled Directed Research 490 in which students work closely with a faculty supervisor and earn between two and eight credits as well as countless opportunities to get their hands dirty in academic research.

All programs within the Marshall School of Business and Viterbi School of Engineering are highly acclaimed and have far-reaching reputations with employers and elite grad schools (more on both later). Programs in communication, the cinematic arts, and the performing arts carry sterling reputations as well. Students are quite competitive in the race for elite postgraduate fellowships. In the last decade, the university has produced ninety-eight Fulbright Student Grant Recipients. Two alumni were awarded Rhodes Scholarships in 2017. The Class of 2019 saw four Boren winners, four Critical Language Scholarship recipients, and multiple winners of NSF awards and Gilman Scholarships.

Outside the Classroom

While most Trojans live on campus as freshmen, the majority of upperclassmen reside in the surrounding neighborhoods and commute to school. That is not entirely a matter of choice; USC offers limited university-owned housing options, only enough to accommodate 30 percent of its undergraduate population. Fortunately, the school recently opened eight new residential houses which, collectively, increased its capacity by 24 percent. Greek life is thriving at USC with a 26 percent participation rate in over sixty sororities/fraternities. The Trojans beloved football team takes center stage each fall, attracting 93,000 fans each Saturday. There are nineteen additional NCAA Division I sports teams fielded by the university as well as a massive club sports operation with 2,500+ participants. Over 1,000 student organizations are active, including popular choices like student government, cultural groups, and performance troupes. Volunteer opportunities like Alternative Breaks and Friends & Neighbors Day are favorites as well with the latter drawing more than 500 students and faculty into LA for service work. USC's LA location ensures that there is never a dearth of excitement and adventure. Within a few miles of campus are countless museums, the Staples Center, multiple theaters, and all the nightlife you could desire. Being in LA has other perks—major musical acts and guest speakers from Barack Obama to alum Will Ferrell appear at the university on a regular basis. The Visions & Voices program provides free cultural events multiple times per week that draw rave reviews from the student body.

Career Services

The University of Southern California Career Center only represents a portion of the career counseling received by Trojan undergrads as additional, more specialized experts are embedded within every undergraduate college. For example, seven professionals provide counseling only to engineering students, and six work exclusively with Annenberg students. In total, there are forty-nine full-time staff members working in counseling, employer relations, and recruiting, equating to a 407:1 student-to-counselor ratio, within the average range of institutions profiled in this book. Yet, that ratio may be the only thing that could be labelled ordinary about this highly accomplished Career Center.

On-campus recruiting at USC is extraordinary with 275 employers granting on-site interviews. In 2016-17, over 3,100 students participated in 5,357 job interviews at the university. The companies recruiting on campus make for an impressive list, even if you only highlighted those that start with "A"—Adobe Systems, Accenture, Amazon, Apple, and AT&T. Outreach efforts are successful as career services engaged with 6,430 students via 1:1 counseling appointments and had just shy of 10,000 attendees at workshops and other events. Large events include the Fall Career Fair that brings 200+ employers to campus, and every school has its own concentrated fairs in areas such as architecture, engineering, and law schools. The onlineSC system also features more than 10,000 job and internship opportunities for Trojan undergrads. A strong alumni network of more than 375,000 is another useful resource for fresh graduates. USC's recruiting, engagement, and specialized career counseling offerings earn its Career Center top grades.

Professional Outcomes

USC does not release outcomes data for its graduating classes as a whole, but an examination of school-specific destinations for the Class of 2017 reveals a rosy picture. Annenberg graduates find employment at a 96-100 percent rate within six months of graduation. Alumni at the Viterbi School of Engineering are well represented at any major technology company you can name from Apple to Yahoo! In fact, USC cracked College Transitions' list of the best engineering feeder schools, sending an extremely high percentage of graduates to the most desirable employers. USC also made our list of top feeders to the tech industry alongside institutions like Caltech, MIT, and Stanford. Presently, there are between 300 and 1,500 alumni employed at each of Google, Amazon, Apple, Microsoft, Facebook, Cisco, Netflix, and Salesforce. Median salaries at age thirty-four are comparable to graduates from the nearby UC system member schools. Half of all alumni reside in the Los Angeles area while San Francisco, Orange County, and New York City are next in popularity.

Information on the graduate schools members of recent classes have attended is not published by the university (they have only recently begun to track that information). However, what can be gleaned from other sources paints a highly positive picture. College Transitions' extensive analysis of LinkedIn data revealed that the University of Southern California is one of the most prolific producers of students accepted into the T14 Law Schools. The good news doesn't stop there; the university also ranks as one of the leading producers of students accepted into top MBA programs like Wharton, Booth, and Tuck.

Admission

USC admissions (and those at several other schools) made front-page headlines for months on end in 2019 as part of the "Varsity Blues" scandal that saw famous actresses and powerful businesspeople cheating and bribing their way into the university. Interestingly, you probably wouldn't have seen people cheating their way into USC a decade ago. Admission into USC has become significantly more challenging in recent years. Five years ago, the school accepted 20 percent of those who applied. In 2018, of 64,000 wanna-be Trojans, only 8,300 were accepted, equating to an all-time low acceptance rate of 13 percent. The SAT range of the Class of 2022 was 1350-1530, and the ACT range was 30-34. On a 4.0 scale, the average high school GPA was 3.79. Those figures are slightly higher than in previous years.

To have a legitimate chance here, being in the top 10 percent of your high school class is likely a necessity as 90 percent of those in the freshman class held that distinction; 97 percent were in the top quartile. There are no unusual factors designated as "most important" by the admissions staff, but rigor of curriculum, grades, test scores, essays, and recommendations reign supreme. USC does not have an early action/early decision option, so all candidates are in the same boat. Legacy students, called "scions," make up a significant portion of the student body—19 percent. There is definitely an edge available for those with Trojan lineage. Those from a generation ago, including USC alumni now hoping to shepherd their own children into their alma mater, may find the current level of selectivity a complete and utter shock. For additional perspective, twenty years ago, 45 percent of applicants were accepted, and the average SAT score was over 200 points lower than it is for today's enrollees. Make no mistake—getting into USC is most likely for students with standardized test scores at or above the 95th percentile and a nearly flawless high school transcript.

Worth Your Money?

At almost $75,000 there is nothing shocking about the annual cost of attendance at USC; it's pretty standard these days for a private university. Where it does seem outrageously high is when you see that amount is twice the cost of any of the elite University of California schools such as Berkley or UCLA. Still, many pay less than the list price as 53 percent of current undergraduates receive merit aid awards averaging $20k per year, and 38 percent of the student population is granted need-based aid to the tune of $40k per year. Further, many USC grads go on to lucrative careers that are enhanced by the school's employer/graduate school connections as well as those of the well-connected alumni base. Those factors make this college worth your money unless, in the words of Olivia Jade Giannulli, you "don't really care about school" but "do want the experience of, like, game days, partying…" Sorry, couldn't resist.

FINANCIAL
Institutional Type: Private
In-State Tuition: $55,320
Out-of-State Tuition: $55,320
Room & Board: $15,395
Required Fees: $1,355
Books & Supplies: $1,200

Avg. Need-Based Aid: $39,568
Avg. % of Need Met: 100%

Avg. Merit-Based Aid: $20,066
% Receiving Merit-Based Aid: 53%

Avg. Cumulative Debt: $28,228
% of Students Borrowing: 35%

CAREER
Who Recruits
1. FTI Consulting
2. Moss Adams
3. Cornerstone Research
4. Nike
5. Universal Creative

Notable Internships
1. Dow Jones
2. Tesla
3. The Blackstone Group

Top Industries
1. Business
2. Education
3. Engineering
4. Operations
5. Media

Top Employers
1. Google
2. Amazon
3. Apple
4. Microsoft
5. Facebook

Where Alumni Work
1. Los Angeles
2. San Francisco
3. Orange County, CA
4. New York City
5. San Diego

Median Earnings
College Scorecard (Early Career): $74,000
EOP (Early Career): $63,700
PayScale (Mid-Career): $120,600

RANKINGS
Forbes: 30
Money: 131
U.S. News: 22, National Universities
Wall Street Journal/THE: 18
Washington Monthly: 64, National Universities

#CollegesWorthYourMoney

The University of Texas at Austin

Austin, Texas | Admissions Phone: 512-475-7399

ADMISSION
Admission Rate: 39%
Admission Rate - Men: 35%
Admission Rate - Women: 42%
EA Admission Rate: Not Offered
ED Admission Rate: Not Offered
Admission Rate (5-Year Trend): -2%
ED Admission Rate (5-Year Trend): Not Offered
% of Admits Attending (Yield): 46%
Transfer Admission Rate: 24%

Offered Wait List: 0
Accepted Wait List: 0
Admitted Wait List: 0

SAT Reading/Writing (Middle 50%): 620-720
SAT Math (Middle 50%): 610-760
ACT Composite (Middle 50%): 27-33
Testing Policy: ACT/SAT Required
SAT Superscore: No
ACT Superscore: No

% Graduated in Top 10% of HS Class: 84%
% Graduated in Top 25% of HS Class: 95%
% Graduated in Top 50% of HS Class: 99%

ENROLLMENT
Total Undergraduate Enrollment: 40,804
% Part-Time: 7%
% Male: 46%
% Female: 54%
% Out-of-State: 6%
% Fraternity: 13%
% Sorority: 20%
% On-Campus (Freshman): 63%
% On-Campus (All Undergraduate): 18%

% African-American: 4%
% Asian: 22%
% Hispanic: 23%
% White: 40%
% Other: 4%
% Race or Ethnicity Unknown: 1%
% International: 6%
% Low-Income: 26%

ACADEMICS
Student-to-Faculty Ratio: 19:1
% of Classes Under 20: 38%
% of Classes Under 40: 68%
% Full-Time Faculty: 83%
% Full-Time Faculty w/ Terminal Degree: 91%

Top Programs
Architecture
Biochemistry
Business
Communication
Computer Science
Engineering
Geosciences
Psychology

Retention Rate: 95%
4-Year Graduation Rate: 61%
6-Year Graduation Rate: 83%

Curricular Flexibility: Somewhat Flexible
Academic Rating: ★★★↙

Inside the Classroom

A ridiculously affordable flagship university that also happens to be one of the top public schools in the United States, the University of Texas at Austin serves up a quality undergraduate education on a massive scale. The school's 40,000+ undergraduates enjoy a dizzying 156 distinct degree programs and 12,400+ annual course offerings. Austin itself is a progressive city that has wide appeal, even to coastal dwellers; however, thanks to the automatic admission granted to all Texas students in the top 6 percent of their high school class, the university remains 90 percent Texas residents.

Each year 175 freshmen are admitted into the elite Plan II Honors Program, an interdisciplinary major created in 1935. One of the best honors programs in the country, Plan II students enjoy small class sizes and are required to complete a senior thesis. The school also offers its Liberal Arts Honors Program to an additional 130 students each year. All students must complete forty-two credit hours in the statewide core curriculum. That entails a first-year Signature Course in a small seminar environment, two English composition courses, one humanities course, two classes in American and Texas government, two in US history, one in the behavioral and social sciences, one in mathematics, three in the natural sciences, and one in the visual and performing arts.

A 19:1 student-to-faculty ratio and 10,000 graduate students on campus render across-the-board tiny class sizes an impossibility. While 38 percent of course sections enroll nineteen or fewer students, more than one-quarter of classes are filled with over fifty students. Opportunities for undergraduate research vary by school. An impressive 90 percent of engineering students conduct research or intern during their four years of study; others must compete for slots in programs such as the Freshman Research Initiative, Summer Research Scholars, or use the Eureka database to find individual professors offering research assistantships. A robust study abroad program boasts 400 offerings in 103 foreign countries; 4,421 undergrads participated in 2017-18.

The Cockrell School of Engineering is one of the most heralded undergraduate engineering schools around, while The McCombs School of Business cracks just about any top ten list and dominates in the specialty areas of accounting and marketing. UT's computer science department is also top-ranked, and regularly sends graduates to the world's best tech companies (see more below). In terms of sheer volume of degrees conferred, engineering is number one (13 percent) followed by business (12 percent), social sciences (12 percent), journalism/communications (12 percent), and biology (10 percent). Prestigious fellowship organizations love UT Austin grads just as much as employers do. In its history the school has produced an impressive 112 Fulbright Scholars, thirty-one Rhodes Scholars, and twenty-three Marshall Scholars.

Outside the Classroom

You won't find many schools in this book where so few undergraduates live on campus. Only 18 percent of the total student body—63 percent of freshmen—reside on the 431-acre campus. The bulk of students live in three nearby neighborhoods: Downtown Austin, East Austin, and West Campus (which is not actually part of campus). There are more than seventy Greek organizations at UT Austin with sororities attracting 20 percent of women and fraternities enlisting 13 percent of men. Sports are a way of life at this institution. Approximately 500 student athletes compete on twenty teams in NCAA Division I competition. Since 1949 the school has captured fifty-one national championships. Texas Memorial Stadium packs in 100,000+ on football Saturdays. In excess of 1,300 student organizations includes hundreds of intramural and club sports options and a sprawling media network of newspapers, magazines, television, and radio stations to ensure that no interest goes unaccounted for. The city of Austin, a liberal enclave in a conservative state, is a perennial darling of "Best Places to Live" and "Best College Towns" lists. Few complain of boredom in a city with all the live music, good food, and culture one can handle.

Career Services

There are fifteen career centers on the UT Austin campus, eleven of which cater to undergraduate students as well as the Vick Center for Strategic Advising and Career Counseling that serves undeclared students. With fifty-two full-time employees devoted to undergrads across those eleven career centers, the university offers a 778:1 student-to-counselor ratio, higher than many of the schools featured in this guide. Some undergraduate schools offer more support than others. For example, there are twelve staff members dedicated to undergraduates in the McCombs School of Business but only two in the School of Education.

The scope of the offerings is overwhelming, as would be expected at a school with more than 40,000 undergraduates. For example, the most recent Fall Science and Technology Career Fair drew 201 employers and 2,500 students. The Spring Communication Job & Internship Fair welcomes up to eighty-five employers and 1,000 students. In 2017-18, the McCombs College of Business Career Expo featured 180+ corporations. Over one hundred employers engage in on-campus recruiting/interviewing with Texas Engineering students every year. Like many universities of its size, UT Austin cannot offer the hand-holding provided by many smaller liberal arts colleges, but it does provide plenty of on-campus networking opportunities for those bold enough to take advantage.

Professional Outcomes

Six months after graduating, 48 percent Longhorns are employed, 25 percent have entered graduate school, and 17 percent are still seeking their next opportunity. The for-profit sector attracts 68 percent of those employed, 18 percent pursue jobs at a nonprofit, and 14 percent enter public sector employment. At a school with nearly half a million living alumni, there is no shortage of major corporations that employ more than 500 UT Austin grads. In the tech realm Google, Facebook, Oracle, Microsoft, IBM, and Apple all meet that qualification, and giants such as Accenture, Amazon, and Uber also employ hundreds of Longhorns. Austin remains home for the largest number of graduates with the Houston, Dallas, and San Antonio areas next in popularity. Plenty of alumni also can be found in New York City and San Francisco. Starting salaries were solid and, as would be expected, fluctuated significantly by major. Business majors took home a median income of $76,000 while chemistry majors earned $46,000 and journalism majors had a median figure of $36,000.

University of Texas at Austin undergraduates go on to pursue advanced degrees in massive numbers with one-quarter electing to continue their educational journey right after completing their bachelor's. Many pursue advanced study at UT Austin itself, which offers more than one hundred graduate programs. Medical school acceptance rates hover around 55 percent, which is above the national average. The sheer volume of med school applicants is incredible; more than 700 seniors apply each year. The university's own Dell Medical School, founded in 2016, is a common destination as are other Texas-based institutions like UT-Houston, UT-San Antonio, and Baylor. Others land at premier medical schools, including Harvard, Georgetown, and UVA, each year. No matter what advanced degree you choose to pursue, an impressive UT Austin transcript can open doors to any institution in the country.

Admission

Longhorn hopefuls totaled 55,575 in the 2018 admissions cycle, almost 30,000 more than at the break of the new millennium. At that time the acceptance rate exceeded 60 percent; it is now only 35 percent. Among 2018-19 freshmen, the mid-50 percent standardized test scores were 1230-1480 on the SAT and 27-33 on the ACT. The vast majority were situated in the top 10 percent of their high school classes—85 percent earned such a distinction—and 95 percent were in the top quartile. The UT system has kept "outsiders" from making up a large percentage of the student body as 89 percent of current students hail from the Lone Star State. The school's policy of automatically accepting students from the top 6 percent of any Texas high school keeps quality home-grown freshmen pouring through the gates. There were an astounding 424 valedictorians and 284 salutatorians in the most recent cohort. Applicants to UT's business, computer science, and engineering majors will face the stiffest competition; earning entry typically requires Ivy-like credentials, especially if you're from out of state.

The university ranks pretty much every admissions factor as "very important," but it's safe to say that with such an onslaught of applications each year the hard numbers of standardized test scores, GPA, and class rank are most essential. There is no early round at UT Austin, so all applicants are in the same boat. The school has no interest in demonstrated interest on the part of applicants because it enjoys a relatively high yield rate approaching 50 percent. While the school accepts roughly 2,000 transfer students per year, that's only 24 percent of those who apply. That differs greatly from many other elite state universities where transferring is much easier than getting admitted directly out of high school. The University of Texas at Austin is the flagship school of the UT system and among the largest genuinely elite schools in the entire country. Texas residency, top-of-the-class academic performance, and solid test scores give you the best chance to get in.

Worth Your Money?

An annual in-state cost of attendance of $25,016 for a UT Austin degree is one of the best bargains anywhere in the country. In addition, almost 40 percent of undergrads qualify for need-based aid with average grants that are a hair over $10,000. Out of state, the sticker price for full COA is $52k, not an unreasonable sum for what you'll receive, particularly if you are majoring in business, engineering, or computer science. If you are a resident of Texas, there are no qualifiers—UT Austin is unquestionably worth every dollar.

FINANCIAL
Institutional Type: Public
In-State Tuition: $10,610
Out-of-State Tuition: $37,580
Room & Board: $10,804
Required Fees: N/A
Books & Supplies: $700

Avg. Need-Based Aid: $10,222
Avg. % of Need Met: 72%

Avg. Merit-Based Aid: $2,345
% Receiving Merit-Based Aid: 23%

Avg. Cumulative Debt: $24,244
% of Students Borrowing: 40%

CAREER
Who Recruits
1. Shell
2. General Electric
3. Affigen, LLC
4. Merck
5. SnapStream

Notable Internships
1. Visa
2. Uber
3. Boeing

Top Industries
1. Business
2. Education
3. Engineering
4. Operations
5. Sales

Top Employers
1. IBM
2. Google
3. Microsoft
4. Accenture
5. Amazon

Where Alumni Work
1. Austin
2. Houston
3. Dallas
4. San Antonio
5. San Francisco

Median Earnings
College Scorecard (Early Career): $58,200
EOP (Early Career): $57,900
PayScale (Mid-Career): $112,800

RANKINGS
Forbes: 76
Money: 28
U.S. News: 48, National Universities
Wall Street Journal/THE: 61 (T)
Washington Monthly: 61, National Universities

#CollegesWorthYourMoney

University of Virginia

Charlottesville, Virginia | Admissions Phone: 434-982-3200

ADMISSION
Admission Rate: 26%
Admission Rate - Men: 25%
Admission Rate - Women: 28%
EA Admission Rate: 28%
ED Admission Rate: New in 2019
Admission Rate (5-Year Trend): -4%
ED Admission Rate (5-Year Trend): Not Offered
% of Admits Attending (Yield): 39%
Transfer Admission Rate: 37%

Offered Wait List: 5,972
Accepted Wait List: 3,588
Admitted Wait List: 13

SAT Reading/Writing (Middle 50%): 660-730
SAT Math (Middle 50%): 670-770
ACT Composite (Middle 50%): 30-34
Testing Policy: ACT/SAT Required
SAT Superscore: Yes
ACT Superscore: Yes

% Graduated in Top 10% of HS Class: 90%
% Graduated in Top 25% of HS Class: 98%
% Graduated in Top 50% of HS Class: 100%

ENROLLMENT
Total Undergraduate Enrollment: 16,777
% Part-Time: 5%
% Male: 45%
% Female: 55%
% Out-of-State: 28%
% Fraternity: 31%
% Sorority: 31%
% On-Campus (Freshman): 100%
% On-Campus (All Undergraduate): 38%

% African-American: 7%
% Asian: 14%
% Hispanic: 6%
% White: 57%
% Other: 5%
% Race or Ethnicity Unknown: 6%
% International: 5%
% Low-Income: 13%

ACADEMICS
Student-to-Faculty Ratio: 15:1
% of Classes Under 20: 55%
% of Classes Under 40: 79%
% Full-Time Faculty: 95%
% Full-Time Faculty w/ Terminal Degree: 91%

Top Programs
Biomedical Engineering
Business
Computer Science
Economics
English
Global Studies
History
Political Philosophy, Policy, and Law

Retention Rate: 97%
4-Year Graduation Rate: 88%
6-Year Graduation Rate: 95%

Curricular Flexibility: Somewhat Flexible
Academic Rating: ★★★★✓

Inside the Classroom

When Thomas Jefferson helped to found the University of Virginia in 1819, our nation's third president did more than just assist in securing the funds—he also personally designed some of the campus' now famous architecture, planned the curriculum, and recruited the first faculty members. As the so-called "father" of the school, Jefferson would undoubtedly be thrilled with what his progeny has gone on to achieve. Two hundred years after its first cornerstone was laid, UVA has become one of the most iconic public universities in the United States where state residents can get an Ivy-level education at a bargain price.

Undergrads can study within one of seven colleges/schools: the College of Arts & Sciences, the School of Engineering and Applied Science, McIntire School of Commerce, the School of Architecture, the School of Nursing, the Batten School of Leadership & Public Policy, and the Curry School of Education. Within the College of Arts & Sciences, undergraduates must complete 30 credits worth of Area Requirements broken down as follows: Natural Science and Mathematics (12), Social Sciences (6), Humanities (6), Historical Studies (3), and Non-Western Perspectives (3). Further Competency Requirements include a First Writing Requirement, Second Writing Requirement, and a Foreign Language Requirement. The 225-250 students per freshman class who are selected for the Echols Scholars Program are not bound by any competency or area requirements.

The University of Virginia sports a 15:1 student-to-faculty ration, a very strong figure for a large public institution. As such, the school is able to offer many small classes like you would find an elite liberal arts college. In fact, 17 percent of sections boast a single-digit enrollment and 55 percent contain 19 or fewer students. There will be some large lecture courses as well—15 percent of sections contain 50 or more undergrads. Undergraduate research opportunities can be challenging to uncover at any large school where graduate students get the prime spots, yet, UVA does offer a multitude of opportunities. To cite examples, every single engineering major completes one major research project, the biology department has 230 students each semester participating research, and physics students are given the chance to get their names on published work. The classroom at UVA extends well beyond Charlottesville as one-third of the Class of 2019 took a semester abroad in one of 65 countries around the world.

The two most commonly conferred degree areas of in liberal arts/general studies (17 percent) and the social sciences (16 percent). Engineering (13 percent), business/marketing (8 percent), biology (7 percent), and psychology (5 percent) are next in sheer popularity. The McIntire School of Commerce has a glowing reputation in the finance/accounting/accounting realm and the School of Engineering and Applied Science is just as highly-respected by employers in those fields. Other notable departmental strengths include computer science, economics, and political philosophy, policy, and law. Cavaliers are extremely competitive in the pursuit of prestigious national scholarships as well. The Class of 2018 produced 12 Fulbright Scholars, five Critical Language Scholars, two Marshall Scholars, a Truman Scholar, and an Astronaut Scholar.

Outside the Classroom

Just 38 percent of all students live on UVA's campus, although 100 percent of freshman do reside on school's vast 1,682-acre grounds. Greek life is popular as an equal 31 percent of men and women sign up for fraternity and sorority life. The Cavaliers compete in 27 varsity sports teams (13 men's and 14 women's) in the Atlantic Coast Conference. Approximately 2,100 students are members of 65 club sports teams and many others participate in intramural athletics. As you would expect at such a large institution, there are 1,000+ clubs available in everything from acrobatics to high powered rocketry; the process of joining some of the more competitive clubs can be fierce (i.e. the University Judiciary Committee). A cappella is beloved pastime at the school and there are countless groups to consider. Outside of being the site of a disturbing rally in 2017, Charlottesville is generally considered to be one of the most student-friendly college towns. There is no shortage of culture, craft breweries, and outdoor recreation opportunities. Plenty of Jefferson and Madison-related history can be explored nearby and a trip to the state capital of Richmond will take you just over an hour. Those looking to fly home for the holidays will enjoy the convenience of having the Charlottesville-Albemarle Airport just eight miles from campus.

Career Services

The UVA Career Center employs 43 full-time staff members giving them a student-to-advisor ration of 390:1, which is in the average range compared to schools in this guide and a very respectable level of support for a school of the University of Virginia's size. Roles of staff members include pre-health and law advisor, career counseling for public service and government community, and director of employer relations & experiential education. This well-resourced office encourages one-on-one appointments, has ample drop-in hours, daily "Coffee Chats with Career Counselors," and hosts regular "Career Communities" that help students interested in a specific field like Business & Technology or Science and Sustainability."

University of Virginia

Of the employed members of the Class of 2018, over 20 percent were connected to their job directly by career services staff/Handshake and another 8 percent heard about the opportunity at a Career Services-sponsored career fair. The University hosts large scale general career fairs in the fall and spring as well many discipline-specific events. The Engineering, Science, and Technology Career Fair attracts over 2,000 students and 230 companies each year. According to the most recent statistics available, 40 percent of undergraduates land at least one paid internship and close to 50 percent have an unpaid workplace experience. There are close to a quarter of a million Cavalier alumni and many are happy to help current students find internships, employment, or offer some level of mentorship. Each year, more than 1,000 alums return to campus for this purpose.

Professional Outcomes

Sixty-five percent of the Class of 2018 immediately joined the workforce upon receiving their degree while 16 percent headed directly to graduate school; 17 percent of graduates were still looking for their next destination. Industries attracting the greatest number of freshly-minted graduates were Internet & Software (12 percent), Healthcare (11 percent), K-12 Education (10 percent), Management Consulting (7 percent), and Higher Education (7 percent). The companies who scooped up the greatest number of 2018 graduates were Capital One (46), Deloitte (42), Oracle (29), and Microsoft (25). The average starting salary for those finding employment was a robust $66,790. Graduates of the McIntire School of Commerce had average salaries of $75k while Arts & Sciences graduates averaged $50k. Large numbers of recent graduates migrate to Washington DC and New York City and many others head to Boston, San Francisco, Seattle, Charlotte, and Atlanta.

Among the 2018 grads who decided to continue their education, 219 enrolled in an advanced degree program at UVA—the next most popular destinations were Virginia Commonwealth University (27), Columbia University (10), the University of Michigan (10), and the College of William & Mary (8). In recent years, medical school graduation for Cavaliers have beaten national averages. In the last six years, UVA applicants to MD programs have enjoyed between a 52-60 percent acceptance rate versus the national average range of 42-45 percent. Virginia grads head to a wide range of medical colleges including the nation's best like Johns Hopkins, Emory, Cornell, Harvard, Tufts, and Georgetown.

Admission

The University of Virginia received upwards of 37,000 applications for a place in their Class of 2022, more than double the number received in 2005. Just 26 percent of this this group were welcomed into the freshman class of 2018-19. Those that went on to attend the university possessed mid-50 percent SAT scores of 1330-1500; the ACT range was 30-34. Nine out of every ten freshman earned a place in top decile of their high school class and 98 percent landed in the top quartile. A stunning 96 percent of this cohort earned better than a 3.75 GPA and only 2 percent had less than a 3.5.

Six factors are rated by the UVA committee as being "very important" to the admissions process headlined by state residency. The school offers admission to 38 percent of locals but just 21 percent hailing from outside of the state. In seeking to maintain at least a two-thirds majority of Virginians, the student body is presently comprised of 69 percent state residents. Other highly-ranked factors included: rigor of secondary school record, class rank, GPA, recommendations, and character/personal qualities. Criteria ranked as still "important" includes: standardized test scores, the application essay, extracurricular activities, and talent/ability. There are no interviews offered at UVA and they do not weight demonstrated interest into their decision-making. Early decision was just added back into the equation for the 2019-20 admissions cycle so no data is yet available on how much of an edge ED applicants might receive.

Worth Your Money?

A rare public university that meets 100 percent of all students' demonstrated financial need, UVA serves up an average of $24,608 per year to qualifying students. Merit aid only goes to a sliver of students and the amount is nominal. Roughly one-third of students take out loans and the mean amount of debt for those individuals is $24k, less than the average college graduate in the country. Residents of Virginia pay an annual cost of attendance of just $33k while out-of-state undergrads are met with a COA of almost $64,000. This school, with its sparkling national reputation and strong graduate outcomes, is worth your money either way, but the real bargain is enjoyed by those whose taxes help fund the university.

FINANCIAL
Institutional Type: Public
In-State Tuition: $14,811
Out-of-State Tuition: $45,508
Room & Board: $11,590
Required Fees: $2,842
Books & Supplies: $1,350

Avg. Need-Based Aid: $24,608
Avg. % of Need Met: 100%

Avg. Merit-Based Aid: $3,815
% Receiving Merit-Based Aid: 5%

Avg. Cumulative Debt: $24,682
% of Students Borrowing: 34%

CAREER
Who Recruits
1. Yext
2. Pariveda
3. Oak Hill Advisors
4. Altria
5. Harris Williams & Co.

Notable Internships
1. Strategic Investment Group
2. NBCUniversal
3. Proctor & Gamble

Top Industries
1. Business
2. Education
3. Operations
4. Research
5. Engineering

Top Employers
1. Capital One
2. Deloitte
3. EY
4. Google
5. Accenture

Where Alumni Work
1. Washington, DC
2. Charlottesville, VA
3. New York City
4. Richmond, VA
5. San Francisco

Median Earnings
College Scorecard (Early Career): $61,200
EOP (Early Career): $71,200
PayScale (Mid-Career): $117,500

RANKINGS
Forbes: 33
Money: 10
U.S. News: 28, National Universities
Wall Street Journal/THE: 50
Washington Monthly: 52, National Universities

#CollegesWorthYourMoney

University of Washington – Seattle

Seattle, Washington | Admissions Phone: 206-543-9686

ADMISSION
Admission Rate: 49%
Admission Rate - Men: 46%
Admission Rate - Women: 51%
EA Admission Rate: Not Offered
ED Admission Rate: Not Offered
Admission Rate (5-Year Trend): -6%
ED Admission Rate (5-Year Trend): Not Offered
% of Admits Attending (Yield): 32%
Transfer Admission Rate: 49%

Offered Wait List: Not Offered
Accepted Wait List: Not Offered
Admitted Wait List: Not Offered

SAT Reading/Writing (Middle 50%): 600-700
SAT Math (Middle 50%): 620-760
ACT Composite (Middle 50%): 27-32
Testing Policy: ACT/SAT Required
SAT Superscore: Yes
ACT Superscore: Yes

% Graduated in Top 10% of HS Class: 58%
% Graduated in Top 25% of HS Class: 88%
% Graduated in Top 50% of HS Class: 99%

ENROLLMENT
Total Undergraduate Enrollment: 32,099
% Part-Time: 8%
% Male: 47%
% Female: 53%
% Out-of-State: 19%
% Fraternity: 16%
% Sorority: 15%
% On-Campus (Freshman): 76%
% On-Campus (All Undergraduate): 29%

% African-American: 3%
% Asian: 25%
% Hispanic: 8%
% White: 38%
% Other: 7%
% Race or Ethnicity Unknown: 3%
% International: 15%
% Low-Income: 21%

ACADEMICS
Student-to-Faculty Ratio: 19:1
% of Classes Under 20: 29%
% of Classes Under 40: 67%
% Full-Time Faculty: 75%
% Full-Time Faculty w/ Terminal Degree: 80%

Top Programs
Biochemistry
Business
Communication
Computer Science
Engineering
Informatics
Psychology
Public Health

Retention Rate: 94%
4-Year Graduation Rate: 67%
6-Year Graduation Rate: 84%

Curricular Flexibility: Somewhat Flexible
Academic Rating: ★★★

Inside the Classroom

Under the perpetually rainy skies and in the birthplace of grunge, Starbucks, and modern romantic comedies rests the flagship campus of the University of Washington system, home to approximately 29,000 undergraduate students, only 63 percent of whom benefit from the uber-affordable in-state rate. International and out-of-state students have begun flocking to UW in recent years to enjoy the literally dozens of top-ranked academic programs and the deep connections to a handful of corporations located nearby that also happen to be some of the most desirable employers anywhere on the planet. With thirteen colleges/schools with undergraduate programs, 180+ majors, and 6,500 courses, UW can meet the needs of just about anyone.

UDub's quarter-based academic calendar keeps students on their toes as most students take three or four classes in each of the 10-week fall, winter, and spring quarters. A strong honors program gives students access to smaller classes, but you'll likely need a 1450+ SAT score to access the program. Core curricular requirements vary by school. Some undergraduate colleges require a foreign language, but others do not. However, all students complete coursework in three Areas of Knowledge: visual, literary, and performing arts; individual societies, and the natural world. Freshmen can enroll in First-year Interest Groups or Collegium Seminars that offer small classes and engaging topics.

The university does have a relatively high 19:1 student-to-faculty ratio that makes consistently small undergraduate class sizes a logistical impossibility. One-third of sections contain forty or more students compared to 29 percent of sections that contain fewer than twenty. Still, there are opportunities for personal connections with professors as evidenced by the fact that 55 percent of graduates complete a faculty-mentored research project. The study abroad rate of participation has climbed steadily since the turn of the millennium; roughly one-fifth now spend a semester in a foreign locale.

The most commonly earned degrees at the University of Washington are in the social sciences (15 percent), business/marketing (11 percent), biology (11 percent), engineering (9 percent), and computer science (7 percent). There are simply too many stellar majors for there to be too large a concentration in any one or two areas. The College of Engineering, which includes the revered Paul G. Allen College of Computer Science & Engineering, is one of the absolute best in the nation, but UW also boasts strong programs in everything from business to social work to environmental science. Employers adore Huskies, but so do competitive scholarship organizations. In 2019, sixteen grads and alumni were awarded Fulbrights, two won Udall Scholarships, and the school has produced thirty-five Rhodes Scholars in its illustrious history.

Outside the Classroom

A solid 83 percent of UDub students who live on campus rate the experience as "excellent." Unfortunately, only a paltry 29 percent of the undergraduate student body actually live on campus and, even among freshmen, only 68 percent reside in the dorms. Some find housing in one of the school's seventy Greek organizations that boast 4,700 members. Most live in houses and apartments in the University District of the city; downtown Seattle is a short car or bus ride away. Students come together to take part in the 850+ student organizations including the Aerial Robotics Club or the Creating a Company Club. Whatever your pleasure, the Husky Union Building (HUB) is, indeed, a great place to get involved. Heck, it even has its own bowling alley. If bowling isn't athletic enough for you, enjoy the twenty-two varsity sports teams that compete in the Pac-12 Conference. Football reigns supreme as UDub boasts the largest stadium in the Pacific Northwest, and it is known to reach deafening noise levels on fall Saturdays. Recreation is aided by state-of-the-art fitness facilities that include a pool, rock-climbing wall, driving range, and Waterfront Activities Center on Lake Washington. Gear for hiking, boating, and camping can be rented from the UWild Gear Garage.

Career Services

There are thirteen full-time employees at the Career and Internship Center that is housed within the Division of Student Life. Additional staff members serving undergraduate students can be found within the School of Engineering and School of Information Sciences to bring the total of career counselors to fifteen, a relatively small number considering that they serve more than 29,000 undergraduate students. The resulting 1933:1 student-to-advisor ratio is among the worst of any school featured in this book; however, unlike some understaffed career services offices (at schools that do make the cut for inclusion in this guide), the CIC at the University of Washington has no shortage of brag-worthy accomplishments.

UW's Career and Internship Center brings close to 400 employers to the Seattle campus each school year. In addition to the hard-to-match local corporations (chronicled in the next section), companies like Wells Fargo, Adobe Systems, Tesla, Bloomberg, Comcast, and Dell recruit and/or conduct interviews on campus. Career

University of Washington – Seattle

E-mail: admit.washington.edu/contact/ | Website: www.washington.edu

fairs are plentiful throughout the year and include specialty expos for data science, engineering, and business. In part due to the prime Seattle location, internships are not hard to locate; 55 percent of undergraduates complete at least one internship, 16 percent complete two, 10 percent complete three, and 38 percent complete a service-learning project. The average search time for UW grads to find employment was 9.1 weeks, and 83 percent of those who landed a job did so in a field related to their major. Thanks to some extremely impressive corporate connections and an alumni base that is embedded in some of the country's most desirable employers, UW's career services successfully overcomes its numbers disadvantage.

Professional Outcomes

Six months after graduation, 70 percent of Class of 2017 graduates had found employment, 19 percent had continued their education in graduate/professional school, and 10 percent were still hunting their first job. Of those employed, 65 percent entered the private sector, 18 percent took local, state, or federal government posts, and 17 percent joined nonprofit organizations. The most popular employers of the Class of 2017 included Google, Amazon, Microsoft, Boeing, and UW Medical Center. Including all living alumni, more than 6,000 Huskies currently work for Bill Gates, and more than 4,000 work for each of Boeing and Amazon. T-Mobile, Facebook, Apple, Nordstrom, Starbucks, and Tableau Software all employ at least 500 UDub alums. As you discern from the massive numbers of students employed by famous companies based in the state of Washington, most graduates stick around town. The Greater Seattle area is far and away the home of choice for UW grads, followed in popularity by San Francisco, Portland, Los Angeles, and New York. The mean salary for 2017 grads was a solid $52,000, but it is important to note that the response rate for the school-issued survey was quite low.

Of those headed to graduate school, just over half remain in state, mostly at the University of Washington itself to become one of the school's 12,000 graduate students. Sixty-two percent of graduate students were pursuing an MS/MA degree, 17 percent entered PhD programs, and 12 percent headed off to earn a professional degree. The University of Washington has one of the best medical schools in the country, and 95 percent of accepted med students come from Washington, Wyoming, Alaska, Montana, and Idaho, thus giving UW graduates an inside track. The University of Washington School of Law is a top fifty institution that gives UW undergrads an excellent at-home option for a legal education. However, multiple graduates have also gone on to study law at Stanford, Harvard, and Fordham in recent years.

Admission

UW-Seattle admitted 49 percent of the 45,000+ applicants desiring to join the Husky Class of 2022. On the SAT, by far the more commonly submitted test, the mid-50 percent range of 2018-19 freshmen was 1220-1360; the ACT range was 27-32. Math scores tended to be much higher, on average, than reading scores. An impressive 70 percent of attending undergrads sported high school GPAs of 3.75 and above, and the average GPA was a 3.8. Interestingly, the admissions standards for resident, out-of-staters, and international students are similar. However, differences do exist across desired majors, with applicants to programs in engineering, computer science facing the toughest odds. Other than a rise in SAT scores, not a ton has changed at UW admissions in the past decade. Back in 2009, the acceptance rate was a somewhat comparable 61 percent, the average GPA was almost identical, but the 25th percentile SAT score was 1100 compared to 1220 today.

Predictable factors like GPA and rigor of high school coursework are designated as "very important" by the admissions committee, but so is the application essay, a surprise given the volume of applications received. Standardized test scores occupy the realm of "important" factors alongside extracurricular activities, talent/ability, first-generation status, work experience, and volunteer experience. There are no legacy admissions, interviews, or consideration of demonstrated interest or class rank. The committee also recommends "taking full advantage of senior year, demonstrating a positive grade trend," and "exercising significant responsibility in a family, community, employment situation or through activities."

Worth Your Money?

With an annual in-state tuition of $11,500 and a direct pipeline to many of the world's top corporations that happen to have their headquarters in Washington state, UDub is a can't-miss option if you get the hometown discount. Many nonresidents, particularly those pursuing computer science, engineering, and business, also find a good value, even at a total cost of attendance for four years of about $200K. Students pursuing other majors may do better looking at other reputable yet less pricey options.

FINANCIAL
Institutional Type: Public
In-State Tuition: $10,127
Out-of-State Tuition: $35,508
Room & Board: $12,798
Required Fees: $1,080
Books & Supplies: $900

Avg. Need-Based Aid: $15,306
Avg. % of Need Met: 74%

Avg. Merit-Based Aid: $4,043
% Receiving Merit-Based Aid: 10%

Avg. Cumulative Debt: $20,094
% of Students Borrowing: 36%

CAREER
Who Recruits
1. Samsung
2. Vulcan Capital
3. Alaska Airlines
4. Liberty Mutual
5. HealthPoint

Notable Internships
1. Boeing
2. Nordstrom
3. United Nations

Top Industries
1. Business
2. Education
3. Engineering
4. Operations
5. Research

Top Employers
1. Microsoft
2. Boeing
3. Amazon
4. Google
5. T-Mobile

Where Alumni Work
1. Seattle
2. San Francisco
3. Portland, OR
4. Los Angeles
5. New York City

Median Earnings
College Scorecard (Early Career): $57,700
EOP (Early Career): $57,500
PayScale (Mid-Career): $112,300

RANKINGS
Forbes: 64
Money: 22
U.S. News: 62 (T), National Universities
Wall Street Journal/THE: 42
Washington Monthly: 19, National Universities

#CollegesWorthYourMoney

University of Wisconsin – Madison

Madison, Wisconsin | Admissions Phone: 608-262-3961

ADMISSION
Admission Rate: 52%
Admission Rate - Men: 49%
Admission Rate - Women: 54%
EA Admission Rate: N/A
ED Admission Rate: Not Offered
Admission Rate (5-Year Trend): +1%
ED Admission Rate (5-Year Trend): Not Offered
% of Admits Attending (Yield): 31%
Transfer Admission Rate: 53%

Offered Wait List: Not Offered
Accepted Wait List: Not Offered
Admitted Wait List: Not Offered

SAT Reading/Writing (Middle 50%): 630-700
SAT Math (Middle 50%): 670-780
ACT Composite (Middle 50%): 27-32
Testing Policy: ACT/SAT Required
SAT Superscore: No
ACT Superscore: No

% Graduated in Top 10% of HS Class: 54%
% Graduated in Top 25% of HS Class: 90%
% Graduated in Top 50% of HS Class: 99%

ENROLLMENT
Total Undergraduate Enrollment: 32,648
% Part-Time: 10%
% Male: 49%
% Female: 51%
% Out-of-State: 35%
% Fraternity: 8%
% Sorority: 8%
% On-Campus (Freshman): 93%
% On-Campus (All Undergraduate): 25%

% African-American: 2%
% Asian: 6%
% Hispanic: 5%
% White: 70%
% Other: 3%
% Race or Ethnicity Unknown: 2%
% International: 11%
% Low-Income: 13%

ACADEMICS
Student-to-Faculty Ratio: 17:1
% of Classes Under 20: 45%
% of Classes Under 40: 72%
% Full-Time Faculty: 84%
% Full-Time Faculty w/ Terminal Degree: 91%

Top Programs
Business
Chemistry
Communication Arts
Computer Science
Economics
Engineering
Political Science
Psychology

Retention Rate: 95%
4-Year Graduation Rate: 62%
6-Year Graduation Rate: 87%

Curricular Flexibility: Somewhat Flexible
Academic Rating: ★★★✦

Inside the Classroom

One of the country's best state institutions, the University of Wisconsin-Madison has become a coveted destination for a growing number of high-caliber teens far outside Wisconsin's seventy-two counties. In fact, the undergraduate student body of approximately 33,000 is inching toward a 50/50 split between Badger State residents and out-of-staters/foreigners. The school's over 900-acre campus is less than one mile from the Wisconsin State Capital Building and rates as one of the Midwest's most gorgeous collegiate settings. Even more attractive than the scenery are the 232+ undergraduate majors and certificates as well as 9,000 courses offered. This tough-to-match selection includes an array of renowned academic programs that rank among the best in the United States.

There are eight schools and colleges that serve undergraduates: The College of Letters and Science, the Wisconsin School of Business, the College of Engineering, the School of Nursing, the School of Education, the School of Pharmacy, the School of Human Ecology, and the College of Agricultural and Life Sciences. Regardless of your home school, breadth is the goal of the university's general education requirements that all Badgers must complete. As a result, thirteen to fifteen credits must be spread over three areas: the natural sciences, the behavioral and social sciences, and the humanities and arts. Required courses in ethnic studies, communications, and quantitative reasoning round out the mandated portion of a Badger education.

At UW-Madison undergrads can expect a mix of large and small classes; 45 percent of sections enroll fewer than twenty students, but 29 percent contain more than forty students with an average class size of thirty-one. The student-to-faculty ratio is 17:1, and roughly 9,000 graduate students suck up their share of attention. Undergraduate research opportunities exist, but the onus is on the student to show initiative and procure the placement. Overall, 15 percent of undergraduates participate in research with a faculty member during their four years of study. Participation is much higher when it comes to study abroad programs. Roughly 2,300 students participate each year, which is among the highest totals of any school in the country. Overall, there are 226 programs in sixty-nine countries to choose from.

Looking for top-ranked business or engineering programs? If so, Madison is a perfect spot for you. In terms of pure percentage of degrees conferred, biology (14 percent), business (12 percent), and engineering (12 percent) are the most popular. Programs in communication, political science, and computer science also draw a sizable number of students and are very strong. The school's guiding principal known as "The Wisconsin Idea" is that a college education should influence lives outside the confines of the classroom. Thus, it is fitting that the university is the number one producer of Peace Corps volunteers. In 2019, a phenomenal forty students earned National Science Foundation Graduate Research Fellowships, eighteen graduates captured Fulbright Scholarships, three were named Goldwater Scholars, and one received a coveted Hertz Fellowship.

Outside the Classroom

One of the best college football towns in America, it would be wrong not to lead with the rowdy, joyous atmosphere inside Camp Randall Stadium on fall Saturdays. A sea of red fills the stadium as 80,000 fans rabidly root for the Badgers and create a quintessential Midwestern college experience. Football worship, along with the other twenty-two Division I Sports teams, unite a campus that is not exactly centralized. While 93 percent of freshmen reside in university-owned housing, only one-quarter of the total undergraduate population lives on campus. Fraternities and sororities are available but hardly dominate the scene as only 8 percent of Badgers join a Greek organization; still, there are sixty Greek organizations on campus with thousands of members. In excess of 900 student-run clubs and organizations are at your disposal including near-constant events hosted by the student union such as concerts, sports viewing, guest lecturers, films, and local theater productions. The spirit of volunteerism is strong as students pledge 37,000 hours annually to local charitable causes. Nature enthusiasts don't have to travel far for hiking, boating, and birdwatching because the 300-acre Lakeshore Nature Preserve is on campus and includes four miles of shoreline along Lake Mendota. Madison is consistently ranked as one of the top college towns in the entire country because it possesses a hard-to-match combination of safety, beauty, and a booming restaurant and commercial district.

Career Services

There are ten career centers on the UW-Madison campus that, collectively, employ fifty-four professionals dedicated to career advising, internship coordination, employer relations, and other career-oriented tasks. The SuccessWorks initiative caters to students in the College of Letters & Sciences (which accounts for half of enrolled undergrads) and is the largest such office with twenty-one staff members. The Career Exploration Center (CEC) is a cross-college career services office serving those who are undecided on an area of study. Wisconsin also operates career services offices dedicated to pre-law and pre-health as well as discipline-specific offices housed in each undergraduate school and college. Wisconsin's overall 554:1 student-to-counselor ratio is higher than average compared to many schools featured in this guide, but that figure is relatively strong for a school of its size.

University of Wisconsin – Madison

E-mail: onwisconsin@admissions.wisc.edu | Website: www.wisc.edu

There are some impressive statistics that elevate UW-Madison from run-of-the-mill status with regard to career services offerings. For one, 88 percent of graduates "agreed" or "strongly agreed" that UW-Madison prepared them for the next step on their career path. More tangibly, 79 percent reported completing at least one internship during their four years of study, and a stunningly high 20 percent completed three or more. Career fairs are sweeping enough to accommodate an undergraduate population of 30,000+. The Fall Career & Internship Fair draws 320+ employers, including many top corporations and over 3,600 students annually. Other fairs include a massive Spring Career & Internship Fair, the UW-Madison STEM Fair, and the Public Service Fair (also held in the spring). Thanks to plenty of targeted and accessible career guidance within every undergrad's home college and solid employment and grad school results, UW's career services are held in high regard by our staff.

Professional Outcomes

Sixty-five percent of job-seeking 2018 University of Wisconsin-Madison grads had already received and/or accepted offers when they received their diplomas. The most commonly entered sectors were health care (11 percent), financial services (5 percent), engineering (5 percent), consulting (5 percent), retail (5 percent), technology (5 percent), and insurance (5 percent). The top five employers of Class of 2018 graduates were: UW-Madison, Epic, Kohl's, Oracle, and UW Health. However, across all graduating years corporations employing a minimum of 250 Badger alumni include Google, Target, Microsoft, Amazon, Apple, PwC, Accenture, and Facebook. The bulk of grads settle in the Madison area, Milwaukee, Chicago, or the Greater Minneapolis-St. Paul area. Those who leave the Midwest head to locations such as New York City, DC, San Francisco, Los Angeles, and Denver. Starting salaries are nothing spectacular, but that is to be expected for a large school with a wide array of offerings. Those earning a bachelor's from the Wisconsin School of Business take home $59,000 in average compensation, chemical engineering majors started at a healthy $67k, and those earning degrees in communications, social work, and philosophy earned median salaries under $35k.

Of the one-quarter of the Class of 2018 who enrolled directly in graduate/professional school, 54 percent were staying at UW-Madison; more than five members of the class headed to each of the following prestigious institutions: Columbia, Duke, USC, Northwestern, Carnegie Mellon, University of Chicago, Johns Hopkins, Emory, and Stanford. Clearly, an undergraduate degree from Wisconsin will serve you well when applying to elite graduate programs across the country. An impressive 108 members of the UW 2018 cohort matriculated in medical school, and seventy-three entered law school. The University of Wisconsin-Madison's own top-ranked medical school takes a high percentage of home-grown talent as does its top-thirty law school.

Admission

Fifty-two percent of the 42,741 applicants for the Class of 2022 gained entry into UW-Madison, but that figure hardly tells the tale of how selective this flagship university has become. Enrolled freshmen possessed mid-50 percent standardized test scores of 1300-1480 on the SAT and 27-32 on the ACT, 78 percent earned a GPA of greater than 3.75 on a 4.0 scale, 54 percent placed in the top decile of their graduating class, and 90 percent were in the top quartile. Five years ago, the SAT range was a lower 1170-1410, which is partially attributable to SAT inflation; the acceptance rate was nearly identical to the 2018-19 figure.

For a school deluged with applicants, the committee still ranks the application essay as the co-leader for most important factor considered alongside rigor of one's secondary curriculum. The second tier is highlighted by in-state residency status; 53 percent of current students are from the Badger State, but that number is down 7.5 percent from a decade ago. One's GPA, recommendations, and test scores round out the list of "important" factors. There are no admissions interviews, and demonstrated interest is not considered. It's important to point out that out-of-state applicants face significantly longer odds than in-state applicants who enjoy an acceptance rate of approximately 67 percent. The number of out-of-state applications for this university has grown rapidly in recent years. As a result, nonresidents should have test scores closer to the 75th percentile and rank in the top 10 percent of their high school classes while applicants from Wisconsin can get away with less stellar academic profiles.

Worth Your Money?

Wisconsin residents pay less than $26,000 per year total cost of attendance, an incredible bargain for such a high-quality educational experience with fantastic graduate outcomes. The growing number of students who come from other states or countries help keep the UW coffers full as such students fork over $53k annually. If you come from out of state, expect to pay full price; only 10 percent of students receive any merit aid. Over one-third of students who applied for need-based aid received an average grant of $13,556. For locals, the decision to attend Wisconsin is an easy one if you are offered admission. Outsiders still can benefit from the school's stellar reputation and vast alumni networks, but they will pay a significant sum for the privilege.

FINANCIAL
Institutional Type: Public
In-State Tuition: $10,725
Out-of-State Tuition: $37,785
Room & Board: $12,200
Required Fees: N/A
Books & Supplies: $1,150

Avg. Need-Based Aid: $13,556
Avg. % of Need Met: 76%

Avg. Merit-Based Aid: $5,039
% Receiving Merit-Based Aid: 10%

Avg. Cumulative Debt: $28,229
% of Students Borrowing: 46%

CAREER
Who Recruits
1. LinkedIn
2. Facebook
3. Goldman Sachs
4. Apple
5. Accenture

Notable Internships
1. U.S. Senate
2. Ford Motor Company
3. Hasbro

Top Industries
1. Business
2. Education
3. Operations
4. Engineering
5. Research

Top Employers
1. Google
2. Target
3. Northwestern Mutual
4. Amazon
5. Microsoft

Where Alumni Work
1. Madison, WI
2. Milwaukee
3. Chicago
4. Minneapolis
5. New York City

Median Earnings
College Scorecard (Early Career): $56,200
EOP (Early Career): $44,000
PayScale (Mid-Career): $104,400

RANKINGS
Forbes: 69
Money: 46
U.S. News: 46 (T), National Universities
Wall Street Journal/THE: 67
Washington Monthly: 23, National Universities

#CollegesWorthYourMoney

Vanderbilt University

Nashville, Tennessee | Admissions Phone: 615-322-2561

ADMISSION
Admission Rate: 10%
Admission Rate - Men: 11%
Admission Rate - Women: 9%
EA Admission Rate: Not Offered
ED Admission Rate: 21%
Admission Rate (5-Year Trend): -3%
ED Admission Rate (5-Year Trend): -1%
% of Admits Attending (Yield): 49%
Transfer Admission Rate: 25%

Offered Wait List: N/A
Accepted Wait List: N/A
Admitted Wait List: 243

SAT Reading/Writing (Middle 50%): 700-760
SAT Math (Middle 50%): 750-800
ACT Composite (Middle 50%): 33-35
Testing Policy: ACT/SAT Required
SAT Superscore: Yes
ACT Superscore: No

% Graduated in Top 10% of HS Class: 89%
% Graduated in Top 25% of HS Class: 96%
% Graduated in Top 50% of HS Class: 99%

ENROLLMENT
Total Undergraduate Enrollment: 6,861
% Part-Time: 1%
% Male: 49%
% Female: 51%
% Out-of-State: 90%
% Fraternity: 30%
% Sorority: 48%
% On-Campus (Freshman): 100%
% On-Campus (All Undergraduate): 94%

% African-American: 11%
% Asian: 14%
% Hispanic: 10%
% White: 45%
% Other: 6%
% Race or Ethnicity Unknown: 5%
% International: 9%
% Low-Income: 13%

ACADEMICS
Student-to-Faculty Ratio: 7:1
% of Classes Under 20: 66%
% of Classes Under 40: 89%
% Full-Time Faculty: 77%
% Full-Time Faculty w/ Terminal Degree: 96%

Top Programs
Biology
Economics
Education
Engineering
English
Music
Political Science
Psychology

Retention Rate: 97%
4-Year Graduation Rate: 89%
6-Year Graduation Rate: 94%

Curricular Flexibility: Less Flexible
Academic Rating: ★★★★★

Inside the Classroom

With an acceptance rate that falls between Dartmouth and Cornell, Vanderbilt University in Nashville, Tennessee, has positioned itself as not only one of the South's most selective institutions but as one of the country's ultra-elite universities. Founded in 1873 by the railroad and shipping tycoon/robber baron Cornelius Vanderbilt (who had never set foot in Tennessee), this private research university is comprised of ten schools, only four of which cater to the school's 6,700+ undergraduate students. Of the sixty-seven undergraduate majors, economics, politics and government, and neuroscience are among the most popular.

Core academic requirements known as AXLE (Achieving Excellence in Liberal Arts Education) are extensive. Those in the College of Arts and Sciences must complete three or four writing-intensive courses, including a first-year writing seminar. Thirteen additional courses are mandated in foreign language, US history, social/behavioral sciences, and mathematics and natural sciences. Juniors and seniors have the option to apply to individual department's honors programs where they are then required to produce a scholarly or creative work.

With a 7:1 student-to-faculty ratio, undergraduate class sizes are kept small. In the 2018-19 school year, 28 percent of course sections contained nine or fewer students, and close to two- thirds contained nineteen or fewer; only 7 percent were large lecture hall affairs of more than fifty students. Undergraduate research opportunities can be found as part of the classroom curriculum, capstone experiences, or through the Vanderbilt University Summer Research Program that accepted eighty-seven of the 205 applicants for its 2018 cohort. Two-fifths of Commodores are adventurous enough to study abroad, and 84 percent of those who do say the experience helped them build job skills. The university offers 120 programs in forty countries.

Vanderbilt alumni are quickly scooped up by many of the world's most desirable and highest-paying corporations. Elite graduate, law, and medical schools are equally fond of those with a Vandy diploma. The School of Engineering has a particularly strong national reputation as do offerings in biology, economics, education, and music. Vanderbilt has been named a Top Producer of Fulbright Scholars, having seen fourteen students win the award in 2018. Other 2018 graduates captured Schwarzman, Boren, Critical Language, Luce, and Marshall Scholarships.

Outside the Classroom

Vanderbilt is a cohesive campus with 90 percent of all undergraduates living in the school's twenty residence halls, ten of which are exclusively for first-year students. To support its recent switch to a residential college system the school has committed $600 million to build four new facilities by 2023. The university's seventeen fraternity and fifteen sorority chapters attract 42 percent of the undergraduate student body, making Greek life a rather dominant part of the social scene. Athletics also attract a big crowd; football games draw close to 40,000 fans, and thousands of students compete at some level. The university has ten varsity women's teams and six men's that compete in NCAA Division I. Additionally, there are more than forty intramural leagues and thirty-two club sports that offer athletic participation to all students. Overall, there are 530+ student-led organizations presently active on campus, including roughly fifty that are focused on community service. Campus is situated only a mile and a half from downtown Nashville. Music City, USA, not only offers plenty of concerts but also all of the cultural, dining, entertainment, and shopping options one could desire.

Career Services

The Vanderbilt University Career Center is staffed by fifteen full-time professionals, which equates to a student-to-advisor ratio of 453:1, in the average range compared to the liberal arts schools included in this book but stronger than that when considering the university's size. The center has career coaches who specialize in areas such as fellowships, STEM, economics, and the social sciences as well as three full-time staff members devoted exclusively to employer relations. The office received rave reviews from undergrads as 98 percent rated their interactions with career services staff positively, and there is plenty of evidence as to why.

In the 2017-18 academic year the office engaged in over 2,200 coaching sessions and 1,400+ twenty-minute walk-in sessions. It hosted 534 career programs and brought 311 employers from all over the country to Nashville to conduct 1,845 on-campus interviews. Large scale events such as the Fall Career Fair attract 2,000+ students and recruiters from 140 companies including the likes of ExxonMobil, Merck, Boeing, and Booz Allen Hamilton. An abundance of legitimate internship opportunities are posted online on two platforms, HireADore and DoreWays. With more than 136,000 living alumni, many of whom remain actively connected to the school, Vanderbilt students have success networking with former Commodores. Overall, thanks to an exceptional record of guiding students into elite graduate/professional schools and tons of industry connections that help students launch their careers, it is not difficult to see why Vanderbilt's career services efforts are viewed so favorably by its own graduates.

Vanderbilt University

E-mail: admissions@vanderbilt.edu | Website: www.vanderbilt.edu

Professional Outcomes

Six months after graduating from Vandy, 83 percent of the Class of 2018 were employed or in graduate school. That is an oddly low statistic as the Class of 2017 figure was 95 percent. The 2018 cohort saw 6 percent still seeking employment and 10 percent classified vaguely as "other." The most commonly entered industry was finance (18 percent) followed by technology (14 percent), consulting (11 percent), education (11 percent), and engineering (8 percent). Graduates landed jobs with every major financial firm, consulting company, and tech giant as well as with five NFL teams. Alumni across all graduating years can be found in droves at Deloitte, Google, Microsoft, EY, Morgan Stanley, Goldman Sachs, Citi, and Facebook. The greatest number of alumni in the Greater Nashville area but large pockets also assemble in New York City, Atlanta, DC, Chicago, San Francisco, and Dallas. Midcareer median salaries for Vanderbilt graduates are number one in the state by a wide margin and rank nationally alongside Northeastern powerhouses Boston College, Tufts, and Johns Hopkins.

Among 2018 graduates who went directly on to pursue advanced degrees, 11 percent were in medical school, 11 percent in law school, and 13 percent were beginning a PhD. Institutions where recent alumni are enrolled include Oxford, MIT, Stanford, Princeton, Columbia and just about every other elite university in the world. Vanderbilt undergraduates get into med school at a solid 66 percent clip, and 2018 acceptances included Johns Hopkins, Duke, Penn, and Yale. Those pursuing a legal education from that same graduating year landed at Vanderbilt's own excellent law school as well as UVA, Harvard, Emory, and UNC-Chapel Hill. In sum, if you succeed at Vanderbilt you will have no trouble landing at a world-class graduate or professional program.

Admission

Vanderbilt not only received a record 34,313 applications for a place in the Class of 2022 and recorded the first single-digit acceptance rate in the school's history (9.6 percent), but it also set a university-best for yield rate as 49 percent of admitted students elected to enroll. For perspective, in 2000 the school received fewer than 9,000 applications and accepted 55 percent. In the 2018-19 admissions cycle the ACT was the more frequently submitted test, and the mid-50 percent range was 33-35; the range for the SAT was 1450-1560. Just a hair under 90 percent of enrolled freshmen earned places in the top 10 percent of their high school class, and 96 percent placed in the top quartile. There were 192 National Merit Scholars entering as freshmen in 2018-19. Overall, three-quarters of enrolled students had GPAs above 3.75 on a 4.0 scale; the average was 3.83.

Seven categories are deemed "very important" by this university's admissions committee: rigor of coursework, GPA, class rank, standardized test scores, application essay, character/personal qualities, and extracurricular involvement. Vandy is serious about its emphasis on extracurriculars; 100 percent of admitted Class of 2022 students held leadership positions in high school. Recommendations and talent/ability comprise the next tier of factors that are "important" to the process. Students applying early decision were admitted at a 21 percent clip, significantly higher than those applying via the regular round. In the last twenty years, Vandy has transformed from a school that accepted more than 50 percent of applicants to a single-digit dream crusher. The regional distinction in the "Southern Ivy" label is almost irrelevant these days. Rather, Vanderbilt is an Ivy-equivalent that happens to be located in the South, and only 33 percent of the student body hails from that region.

Worth Your Money?

The full cost of attendance at Vanderbilt is $71,110, but those with financial need will pay nothing near that sum. Vandy awards an average need-based grant of $49,614 per year, putting it among the endlessly endowed Ivy League schools as one of the most generous colleges in the country. It is a rare school that can meet 100 percent of demonstrated need. Unlike the Ivies, those with exceptional credentials and special talents may actually be able to procure some level of merit aid as well. Thirteen percent of undergraduates receive an average annual merit aid award of roughly $20k. However, even if you aren't fortunate enough to be counted among this relatively small group of merit aid recipients, Vanderbilt is still worth your money.

FINANCIAL
Institutional Type: Private
In-State Tuition: $50,800
Out-of-State Tuition: $50,800
Room & Board: $16,910
Required Fees: $2,106
Books & Supplies: $1,294

Avg. Need-Based Aid: $49,614
Avg. % of Need Met: 100%

Avg. Merit-Based Aid: $19,977
% Receiving Merit-Based Aid: 13%

Avg. Cumulative Debt: $22,854
% of Students Borrowing: 21%

CAREER
Who Recruits
1. Vineyard Vines
2. ExxonMobil
3. Teach for America
4. AllianceBernstein
5. Defense Intelligence Agency

Notable Internships
1. UBS
2. Lyft
3. Spotify

Top Industries
1. Business
2. Education
3. Research
4. Operations
5. Engineering

Top Employers
1. Deloitte
2. Google
3. Microsoft
4. EY
5. Amazon

Where Alumni Work
1. Nashville
2. New York City
3. Atlanta
4. Washington, DC
5. San Francisco

Median Earnings
College Scorecard (Early Career): $69,000
EOP (Early Career): $72,800
PayScale (Mid-Career): $119,100

RANKINGS
Forbes: 27
Money: 15
U.S. News: 15 (T), National Universities
Wall Street Journal/THE: 17
Washington Monthly: 44, National Universities

#CollegesWorthYourMoney

Vassar College

Poughkeepsie, New York | Admissions Phone: 845-437-7300

ADMISSION
Admission Rate: 25%
Admission Rate - Men: 33%
Admission Rate - Women: 21%
EA Admission Rate: Not Offered
ED Admission Rate: 44%
Admission Rate (5-Year Trend): 0%
ED Admission Rate (5-Year Trend): -4%
% of Admits Attending (Yield): 34%
Transfer Admission Rate: 13%

Offered Wait List: 1,138
Accepted Wait List: 566
Admitted Wait List: 48

SAT Reading/Writing (Middle 50%): 680-740
SAT Math (Middle 50%): 690-770
ACT Composite (Middle 50%): 31-33
Testing Policy: ACT/SAT Required
SAT Superscore: Yes
ACT Superscore: Yes

% Graduated in Top 10% of HS Class: 61%
% Graduated in Top 25% of HS Class: 91%
% Graduated in Top 50% of HS Class: 98%

ENROLLMENT
Total Undergraduate Enrollment: 2,456
% Part-Time: 1%
% Male: 41%
% Female: 59%
% Out-of-State: 72%
% Fraternity: Not Offered
% Sorority: Not Offered
% On-Campus (Freshman): 99%
% On-Campus (All Undergraduate): 97%

% African-American: 4%
% Asian: 12%
% Hispanic: 11%
% White: 56%
% Other: 8%
% Race or Ethnicity Unknown: 1%
% International: 9%
% Low-Income: 29%

ACADEMICS
Student-to-Faculty Ratio: 8:1
% of Classes Under 20: 67%
% of Classes Under 40: 100%
% Full-Time Faculty: 83%
% Full-Time Faculty w/ Terminal Degree: 91%

Top Programs
Art
Biology
Drama
Film
History
International Studies
Physics
Political Science

Retention Rate: 95%
4-Year Graduation Rate: 88%
6-Year Graduation Rate: 92%

Curricular Flexibility: Very Flexible
Academic Rating: ★★★★★

Inside the Classroom

A recent three-part Malcom Gladwell podcast was full of effusive praise for one college in Poughkeepsie, New York, that puts its money where its mouth is on the subject of making college affordable for low-income and first-generation students. Vassar deserves that type of attention for its commitment to creating a more egalitarian higher education world. Yet, this original member of the Seven Sisters that became coeducational in 1969 also has a well-deserved reputation for its exceptionally flexible and high-quality liberal education.

Vassar's 2,456 undergraduate students have the choice of fifty-one majors and are not beholden to a core curriculum or a murderous series of freshman- and sophomore-year requirements; instead, there are only three mandates. All freshmen must take a first-year writing seminar capped at seventeen students. The second requirement is that all students must become proficient in a foreign language; among the languages offered are Korean, Hebrew, and Old English. The last is that students must take at least one course dealing with quantitative reasoning. Other than that and, of course, one's major, there is ample room to explore electives and burgeoning intellectual passions.

The college's 336 faculty members teach every single undergraduate course offered at Vassar. An 8:1 student-to-faculty ratio leads to an average class size of seventeen students, and 20 percent of all sections have an enrollment of nine or fewer. Professors are extremely available outside the classroom as 70 percent of the faculty live on or near campus, and faculty families also live within each residence hall. Opportunities to get involved in undergraduate research are taken advantage of by 300+ students each year who work side-by-side with professors on research in the sciences, social sciences, or arts and humanities. Roughly 500 students also engage in credited community-based learning in local organizations or agencies. Vassar's Undergraduate Research Summer Institute (URSI) has been operational since 1986 and offers a plethora of ten-week research experiences in everything from astronomy to computer science to psychology. Study abroad programs are taken advantage of by two-fifths of students.

In terms of number of degrees conferred, the most popular majors are English, political science, psychology, economics, and biology. Though slightly less popular, programs in history, physics, and the fine and performing arts also receive very high marks. The lack of a core curriculum makes it easy to double major if you desire. Many grads ultimately pursue further education and find elite graduate and professional programs that respect the rigor of a Vassar education. Over the last five years Brewers also have landed forty-four Fulbright Scholarships and nineteen National Science Foundation Graduate Research Fellowships.

Outside the Classroom

Few Vassar undergraduates are eager to flee the school's idyllic 1,000-acre campus, so 98 percent of the student body remains in the residence halls all four years. Those seeking to live off campus need to request special permission. The nine traditional houses, one cooperative house, and three school-owned apartment complexes are situated on verdant grounds that have so many different tree varieties that the campus is technically branded an arboretum. Campus cohesion is further enhanced by the absence of Greek organizations. Men make up only 43 percent of the population, which can partially be attributed to the school's history as a women's college and to the realities of the demographic make-up at most liberal arts colleges. Eighteen percent of students are varsity athletes who compete as part of twenty-three NCAA Division III athletic squads. Club and intramural teams as well as facilities that include an elevated running track, a six-lane pool, a nine-hole golf course, and thirteen tennis courts ensure that opportunities for fitness are open to all. There are 145+ student-run organizations and 1,000+ annual campus events such as concerts, guest lectures, and visiting artists/performers, so there is always something to do close to home. Weekend dance parties are popular too. Poughkeepsie offers lots of natural beauty, a mall, and an array of affordable restaurants, although it won't be mistaken for a buzzing metropolis. Those seeking big-city life will have to make the two-hour trip to New York City or the three-hour ride to Boston.

Career Services

The Career Development Office (CDO) at Vassar College is staffed by eight professionals who specialize in career counseling, employer relations, law/health professions advising, and alumni outreach. That works out to a 307:1 student-to-advisor ratio, a figure superior to many schools featured in this guide. Annual events organized by this office include Career Kickoff and First Year Friday, which are designed to give freshmen an overview of the career development services available. Sophomore Career Connections and Senior Week are class-specific events intended to focus students on tasks critical to their particular place in the career development process.

In addition to hosting its own events, Vassar is a member of the Selective Liberal Arts Consortium that sponsors recruiting trips to New York City and Washington, DC. The CDO is always happy to help you with your internship, but the majority of the resources in the area are on online platforms that include Handshake. An exceptional 87 percent of Vassar grads complete at least one internship while at the college. In the 2018-19 school year the CDO conducted 3,443 one-one-one advising appointments and invited thirty-one companies to recruit on campus including NERA Economic Consulting, Teach for America, and M&T Bank. In addition to helping students find their first jobs, the CDO should be lauded for the fantastic job it does in preparing students to continue their education in medical, law, or graduate school.

Professional Outcomes

Somewhere between twenty and fifty Vassar alums can be found at highly competitive companies including Google, Facebook, EY, Deloitte, Microsoft, Citi, EY, and Amazon. Elite universities such as Harvard, Penn, NYU, and Columbia are also among the top employers of former Vassar students, many of whom earn advanced degrees and enter academia. Large contingents of Brewers can be found in the Greater New York City area as well as Boston, DC, San Francisco, Los Angeles, and Philadelphia. Average midcareer salaries are toward the bottom-of-the-pack among elite liberal arts schools, not coincidentally, in the same range as Reed, Oberlin, and Scripps that, like Vassar, produce large numbers of advanced degree earners who do not often see high remuneration early in their careers.

Within five years of graduating, the majority of Vassar alumni pursue further education, including 20 percent who enroll directly in an advanced degree program upon completing their undergraduate studies. Over the last five years medical school applicants have been admitted at an enviable 87 percent rate, over twice the national average. The most commonly attended medical schools include Dartmouth, Tufts, Columbia, and Brown. Law school applicants experienced a superb 96 percent acceptance rate. Vassar ranks in the top fifteen in the nation in percentage of undergraduates who go on to earn a PhD. It ranks particularly well in physics, political science, and sociology.

Admission

Vassar accepted 24 percent of the 8,312 applicants seeking to join the Class of 2022. The average SAT for admitted students was 1435, and the mean ACT was 32. Thirty-eight percent of those accepted were in the top 5 percent of their high school class, 61 percent were in the top decile, and 91 percent were in the top quartile. The average GPA is in the A/A- range. The number of applications has hardly increased in the past decade, and neither has the acceptance rate. (It was 25 percent in 2008-09.)

GPA and evidence of rigorous courses rests atop the list of most important factors in the eyes of the admissions committee. Standardized test scores, essays, recommendations, extracurricular activities, talent/ability, and character/personal qualities round out a holistic process as the next most important considerations. The college is extremely committed to providing need-based aid to low-income and first-generation students, and the numbers back it up. In selecting the 2018-19 freshman class, only 7 percent were legacy admits while 13 percent were first-generation college students. In addition, 24 percent of current students are Pell Grant recipients. Despite a reasonably high yield rate of 34 percent, Vassar still treasures qualified applicants who apply on a binding early-decision basis. In the 2018-19 admissions cycle ED applicants enjoyed a 44 percent acceptance rate. Vassar deserves deep admiration for its commitment to increasing access to students from all backgrounds. It has pursued those aims at the expense of hyping application numbers and, thus, increasing the perception of selectivity. As a result, those in love with this fine liberal arts institution do not face single-digit (or close to it) odds as they would at many other schools of its quality. Of course, excellent grades and test scores are still required.

Worth Your Money?

As a result of Vassar's mission to increase access to low-income students, it does not offer any merit aid, only need-based aid, which it offers in impressively generous quantities. The blow of the list price cost of attendance of $65,240 is softened by the fact that 60 percent of the undergraduate student population qualifies for aid, and the school meets 100 percent of the demonstrated need for all students. That translates to an average grant of over $51,000, making Vassar an incredibly affordable institution for those from less advantageous economic circumstances.

FINANCIAL
Institutional Type: Private
In-State Tuition: $57,910
Out-of-State Tuition: $57,910
Room & Board: $14,220
Required Fees: $940
Books & Supplies: $900

Avg. Need-Based Aid: $51,395
Avg. % of Need Met: 100%

Avg. Merit-Based Aid: $0
% Receiving Merit-Based Aid: 0%

Avg. Cumulative Debt: $21,473
% of Students Borrowing: 49%

CAREER
Who Recruits
1. NERA Economic Consulting
2. Teach for America
3. Peace Corps
4. M&T Bank
5. Shearman and Sterling

Notable Internships
1. U.S. House of Representatives
2. Major League Baseball
3. YouTube

Top Industries
1. Business
2. Education
3. Media
4. Arts & Design
5. Social Services

Top Employers
1. Google
2. IBM
3. Morgan Stanley
4. Deloitte
5. Microsoft

Where Alumni Work
1. New York City
2. Boston
3. San Francisco
4. Washington, DC
5. Los Angeles

Median Earnings
College Scorecard (Early Career): $54,600
EOP (Early Career): $46,000
PayScale (Mid-Career): $100,100

RANKINGS
Forbes: 61
Money: 134
U.S. News: 14, Liberal Arts Colleges
Wall Street Journal/THE: 56
Washington Monthly: 7, Liberal Arts Colleges

#CollegesWorthYourMoney

Villanova University

Villanova, Pennsylvania | Admissions Phone: 610-519-4000

Inside the Classroom

Positioned twelve miles outside of Philadelphia on the swanky Main Line is Villanova University, a school that, prior to winning an NCAA basketball title in 1985, possessed only a regional reputation. Thirty years later, the prestige of its powerhouse basketball program has launched an already renowned and highly desirable school into a whole new stratosphere. Today, this midsize Catholic research university is the proud home to 6,500 enthusiastic Wildcat undergraduates. For those who can conquer the suddenly highly-selective admissions process, Nova provides a world class educational experience in a spirited collegiate atmosphere.

Students can choose one of forty-five undergraduate programs within four schools: the College of Liberal Arts & Sciences, the Villanova School of Business, the College of Engineering, and the College of Nursing. All students must conquer the school's core curriculum that is designed to ensure a "depth of study and intellectual sophistication while recognizing that learning implies different modes of inquiry." Courses in theology, ethics, and philosophy as well as the Augustine and Culture Seminar Program comprise the Core Foundational Courses. Additional requirements include all of the usual liberal arts standards (social sciences, math, foreign language, and so on) and an upper-level theology course, a writing seminar, and a senior capstone.

The university sports a 12:1 student-to-faculty ratio and offers average undergraduate classes of twenty-two students. It is possible to receive a degree from the school without ever sitting in a giant lecture hall. In fact, only 4 percent of course sections enroll forty or more students. As a consequence, professors are unusually available in and outside of the classroom. From the start of freshman year, opportunities for meaningful undergraduate research will be within your grasp. The Villanova Match Research Programs for First Year Students allows second-semester freshmen to work as research assistants alongside distinguished faculty. The Villanova Undergraduate Research Fellows Summer Program is taken advantage of by many upperclassmen. Wildcats study abroad in impressive numbers. The 42 percent participation rate places Nova among the top ten universities in the country. There is a full menu of foreign locations with semester, year-long, and summer options.

Villanova's business, accounting, and engineering programs all receive a good deal of attention from ranking publications. The school's most popular degree is business with over one-quarter of all graduates majoring in it. Engineering and nursing are the second- and third-most commonly conferred degree areas. As the school's reputation reaches new heights, more students than ever are winning prestigious national awards. In 2018 alone, Villanova graduates earned sixteen Fulbright Scholarships, five Gilman Scholarships, three Goldwater Scholarships, and multiple National Science Foundation Graduate Research Fellowships.

Outside the Classroom

Two-thirds of the undergraduate student body currently live on a 240-acre campus that is growing more beautiful and impressive by the day. Constant progress can be observed on the university's many construction projects, and we're not talking small buildings. The school is currently erecting on-campus housing for an addition 1,135 undergrads. The newly opened Finneran Pavilion and an under-construction performing arts center are emblematic of the administration's recent splurge. The school is home to twenty-four fraternities and sororities, and roughly one-third of students participate in Greek life. Athletics, particularly basketball, are a way of life at Villanova. More than 500 student-athletes compete on the Wildcats twenty-four NCCA Division I teams, and many more participate in the forty-four club and intramural sports options. In total, there are 265 active extracurricular clubs, a fair number of which are centered on community service, which is a definite point of emphasis at Nova as students contribute a quarter million service hours annually. Radnor Township isn't cheap, but it offers tons of great hangouts and places to eat. The King of Prussia Mall, the second largest in the United States, is only a few miles away. The museums, sports, restaurants, and culture of Philly are only a straight-shot, half-hour car ride away.

Career Services

The Villanova University Career Center employs fourteen individuals who specialize in career counseling, pre-law advising, employer relations, and industry advising. The center also trains seventeen career assistants who are available to support their fellow undergraduates as well. Only counting professional employees, the office has a 468:1 student-to-counselor ratio, which is within the average range of schools profiled in this guide. However, by almost every other metric, this career center, like the university's famed basketball squad, measures up well against the competition.

ADMISSION
Admission Rate: 29%
Admission Rate - Men: 28%
Admission Rate - Women: 30%
EA Admission Rate: N/A
ED Admission Rate: 41%
Admission Rate (5-Year Trend): -20%
ED Admission Rate (5-Year Trend): Not Offered
% of Admits Attending (Yield): 25%
Transfer Admission Rate: 25%

Offered Wait List: 6,321
Accepted Wait List: 2,856
Admitted Wait List: 47

SAT Reading/Writing (Middle 50%): 640-710
SAT Math (Middle 50%): 660-760
ACT Composite (Middle 50%): 30-33
Testing Policy: ACT/SAT Required
SAT Superscore: Yes
ACT Superscore: Yes

% Graduated in Top 10% of HS Class: 72%
% Graduated in Top 25% of HS Class: 93%
% Graduated in Top 50% of HS Class: 99%

ENROLLMENT
Total Undergraduate Enrollment: 6,917
% Part-Time: 5%
% Male: 47%
% Female: 53%
% Out-of-State: 79%
% Fraternity: 19%
% Sorority: 39%
% On-Campus (Freshman): 99%
% On-Campus (All Undergraduate): 67%

% African-American: 5%
% Asian: 6%
% Hispanic: 8%
% White: 75%
% Other: 3%
% Race or Ethnicity Unknown: 2%
% International: 2%
% Low-Income: 14%

ACADEMICS
Student-to-Faculty Ratio: 11:1
% of Classes Under 20: 42%
% of Classes Under 40: 95%
% Full-Time Faculty: 60%
% Full-Time Faculty w/ Terminal Degree: 88%

Top Programs
Accounting
Biology
Communication
Economics
Engineering
Finance
Nursing
Political Science

Retention Rate: 96%
4-Year Graduation Rate: 87%
6-Year Graduation Rate: 91%

Curricular Flexibility: Somewhat Flexible
Academic Rating: ★★★★

E-mail: gotovu@villanova.edu | Website: www.villanova.edu

Including graduate students, there were 7,500 visits to the career center during the 2017-18 school year. Over 35,000 job and internship opportunities were posted online for Wildcats to explore. On campus recruiting is also strong with 365 companies making the trek to Villanova's grounds last year alone. A well-connected and passionate global network of 125,000 alumni is also available to help you make connections as you search for internships and employment. Most students are successful landing an internship as 70 percent of College of Liberal Arts and Sciences students complete at least one such experience at Nova. Large events like the Fall 2018 Career Fair drew 175+ employers to the Connelly Center. With a high level of personalized support, a robust Employer Relations Department, and excellent career outcomes for graduates (more in a moment), the Villanova University Career Center continues to do excellent work on behalf of its students.

Professional Outcomes

Within six months of commencement, Class of 2018 graduates had a placement rate of 97 percent with 74 percent entering the workforce and 17 percent matriculating into graduate or professional school. The most popular employers of members of the Class of 2018 were, not coincidentally, also companies with the largest Wildcat alumni representation. That list includes Vanguard, Verizon, PwC, JP Morgan Chase, Merck, Comcast, EY, Deloitte, and Morgan Stanley. The average starting salary across all colleges within the university was $59,500. Graduates of the business, nursing, and engineering schools all earned an average salary above $63,000 while the Colleges of Liberal Arts & Sciences figure was just a hair under $50k. Remaining in the Philadelphia Metro area is the most popular move, but large numbers also migrate to New York City, DC, Boston, Chicago, San Francisco, and Los Angeles.

Class of 2018 members went on to study at a number of topflight graduate institutions. College of Engineering grads went to schools like Northwestern, the University of Notre Dame, and Georgia Institute of Technology. Liberal arts grads entered programs at Columbia, Georgetown, Tufts, UCLA, and King's College London. Nova grads enjoyed a medical school admissions rate of 70-75 percent, far above the national average. Among the fifty-three graduates applying to law school in 2018, acceptances were earned at Fordham, the University of Michigan, Northeastern, Boston College and, of course, Villanova's own Charles Widger School of Law.

Admission

The 29 percent of successful applicants who earned a place in the Class of 2022 possessed middle-50 percent results of 1380-1490 on the SAT, 31-33 on the ACT, and a 4.10-4.48 GPA. While the profile of students who actually enrolled is a bit less intimidating, the Class of 2022 cohort was still strong. Within that group the SAT range was 1300-1470, the ACT range was 30-33, and the average weighted GPA was 4.19. In terms of class rank, 69 percent of freshmen placed in their high school class' top decile, and 88 percent earned a spot in the top quartile. For perspective, in 2015 the university admitted 43 percent of its applicants, and the 25th percentile SAT score was an even 1200.

Rigor of coursework, GPA, class rank, and standardized test scores (students evenly submit the ACT and SAT) comprise the factors deemed most important by the committee. Essays, recommendations, extracurricular activities, work experience, and volunteer work are among the areas that receive secondary consideration. There is no interview offered as part of the admissions process. Those applying through binding early decision were accepted at a 41 percent rate, providing a solid advantage over those in the regular cycle. Villanova does advertise a holistic process, but with close to 23,000 applicants these days, your SATs, GPA, class rank, and other measurables need to be within range for serious consideration. Students (and their counselors) need to be aware of the year-by-year increases in selectivity as this school has transformed in the recent past.

Worth Your Money?

Villanova rarely covers a student's full amount of need, but 47 percent of current students do receive need-based aid that averages $37k per award; only 8 percent of undergraduates are presently receiving any merit aid. The total annual cost of attendance at Nova is a hair shy of $70,000, therefore, even with aid, becoming a Wildcat is not going to come cheap. It's no wonder that teens from families in the top 10 percent of income earners make up more than half of the student body. That said, starting salaries for graduates are on the higher side, making it possible to pay back the substantial loans you may need to take out in order to attend.

FINANCIAL
Institutional Type: Private
In-State Tuition: $52,578
Out-of-State Tuition: $52,578
Room & Board: $14,020
Required Fees: $820
Books & Supplies: $1,100

Avg. Need-Based Aid: $37,141
Avg. % of Need Met: 82%

Avg. Merit-Based Aid: $19,828
% Receiving Merit-Based Aid: 8%

Avg. Cumulative Debt: $35,552
% of Students Borrowing: 53%

CAREER
Who Recruits
1. CIA
2. KPMG
3. TD Securities
4. Boston Consulting Group
5. BNY Mellon

Notable Internships
1. QVC
2. NBC Universal
3. Pratt & Whitney

Top Industries
1. Business
2. Operations
3. Sales
4. Finance
5. Information Technology

Top Employers
1. Vanguard
2. Verizon
3. PwC
4. JPMorgan Chase
5. Merck

Where Alumni Work
1. Philadelphia
2. New York City
3. Washington, DC
4. Boston
5. Chicago

Median Earnings
College Scorecard (Early Career): $77,900
EOP (Early Career): $78,300
PayScale (Mid-Career): $119,500

RANKINGS
Forbes: 72
Money: 179
U.S. News: 46 (T), National Universities
Wall Street Journal/THE: 129
Washington Monthly: 87, National Universities

#CollegesWorthYourMoney

Wake Forest University

Winston-Salem, North Carolina | Admissions Phone: 336-758-5201

ADMISSION

Admission Rate: 29%
Admission Rate - Men: 33%
Admission Rate - Women: 27%
EA Admission Rate: Not Offered
ED Admission Rate: 41%
Admission Rate (5-Year Trend): -6%
ED Admission Rate (5-Year Trend): -5%
% of Admits Attending (Yield): 37%
Transfer Admission Rate: 5%

\# Offered Wait List: N/A
\# Accepted Wait List: N/A
\# Admitted Wait List: N/A

SAT Reading/Writing (Middle 50%): 650-710
SAT Math (Middle 50%): 660-760
ACT Composite (Middle 50%): 29-33
Testing Policy: Test Optional
SAT Superscore: Yes
ACT Superscore: Yes

% Graduated in Top 10% of HS Class: 76%
% Graduated in Top 25% of HS Class: 92%
% Graduated in Top 50% of HS Class: 97%

ENROLLMENT

Total Undergraduate Enrollment: 5,225
% Part-Time: 1%
% Male: 47%
% Female: 53%
% Out-of-State: 78%
% Fraternity: 33%
% Sorority: 59%
% On-Campus (Freshman): 99%
% On-Campus (All Undergraduate): 75%

% African-American: 6%
% Asian: 4%
% Hispanic: 7%
% White: 69%
% Other: 3%
% Race or Ethnicity Unknown: 0%
% International: 10%
% Low-Income: 10%

ACADEMICS

Student-to-Faculty Ratio: 10:1
% of Classes Under 20: 57%
% of Classes Under 40: 96%
% Full-Time Faculty: 69%
% Full-Time Faculty w/ Terminal Degree: 94%

Top Programs
Accountancy
Chemistry
Communication
Economics
Finance
Health and Exercise Science
Politics and International Affairs
Psychology

Retention Rate: 95%
4-Year Graduation Rate: 85%
6-Year Graduation Rate: 89%

Curricular Flexibility: Somewhat Flexible
Academic Rating: ★★★★

Inside the Classroom

Founded as the Manual Labor Institute for Baptist preachers in 1834, Wake Forest has roots that sound exaggeratedly and humorously humble. Of course, the current vibe of the university could not be further from its lowly beginnings, save the retention of its Southern charm. Today's Wake Forest is generally regarded as a bubble of conservatism and wealth—the average student's parental income is over $220k—and, from an academic standpoint, this school is viewed as one of the top private research institutions outside the Northeast.

All freshmen enter the Undergraduate College that offers forty-two majors and sixty minors. Economics, biology, psychology, finance, and communications are the areas toward which the largest number of students gravitate. Those wishing to attend the School of Business apply prior to their sophomore year. All other concentrations are open to any student. Academic requirements include a freshman seminar, a four-credit writing seminar, foreign language, physical education, and one course in both quantitative reasoning and cultural diversity.

Sporting a student-to-faculty ratio of 10:1, classes are kept on the small side with 57 percent of sections enrolling fewer than twenty students. There are a fair number of courses that have twenty to thirty-nine students, but only a minuscule number that take place in large lecture halls. Close to 60 percent of Demon Deacons have the opportunity to engage in hands-on research for academic credit. Wake's robust study abroad options feature 400 semester, summer and year-long programs in 200 cities in more than seventy countries worldwide. Undergrads participate at a 63 percent rate, good enough for the seventh highest figure among doctoral degree-granting US universities.

Wake Forest is a school with strengths across a variety of disciplines, most notably chemistry, communication, accounting, finance, and international affairs. Overall, the institution has an excellent reputation across the board in both employment and academic circles, and Wake Forest grads are always considered for prestigious postgraduate fellowships. Five members of the Class of 2018 were named Fulbright Scholars, bringing the university's all-time total to 116, and it produces a Rhodes Scholar about every other year.

Outside the Classroom

Greek life gets top billing when it comes to describing the social scene at Wake. Half the student body joins a fraternity or sorority with women joining sororities at an extraordinarily high rate (59 percent). Roughly three-quarters of students live in university-owned housing with many off-campus upperclassmen flocking to nearby apartment complexes. The Demon Deacons are a powerhouse in NCAA Division I athletics, quite an achievement considering the university's modest size. Of the sixteen varsity sports teams that compete in the vaunted ACC, men's basketball and football draw the biggest crowds. The school is brimming with less serious but still dedicated athletes as a whopping 85 percent of the student body participates in intramural athletics. Many non-sports options also are available as there are more than 240 active student organizations on campus, including a full array of political, religious, and performing arts groups. The quaint Southern charm of campus extends into the surrounding small city of Winston-Salem, which offers its fair share of cultural, culinary, and shopping pursuits. However, it is worth noting that safety can be an issue as Winston-Salem has a crime rate 57 percent higher than the national average.

Career Services

The Office of Personal and Career Development (OPCD) at Wake Forest is staffed by thirty-tree full-time professional employees who serve as career coaches, employer relations specialists, and counselors who work on personal and professional development with alumni. That equates to a student-to-advisor ratio of 158:1, which ranks among the best of the institutions included in this book. The OPCD is not only generously staffed; it also operates with the clear mission of readying every single Demon Deacon for a meaningful next step in life.

In a single year, career coaches met with over 4,000 members of the student body to engage in 1:1 career planning sessions and/or small workshops. Career treks took students to New York City, San Francisco, and DC to meet with alumni in their places of business. Perhaps the office's most unique feature is that it runs a sequence of for-credit College-to-Career courses. Having an actual academic program dedicated to career prep affords the OPCD the chance to teach large numbers of students about matching their personalities to fulfilling careers, finding internships, developing cover letters, considering cost-of-living issues postgraduation, and so much more. Almost one-quarter of graduates take at least one of those courses. Employer relations at Wake are also strong, and they host a number of well-attended job fairs. Additionally, more than 12,000 job and internship postings go up each year. All freshmen are introduced to the services offered via the OPCD Orientation that alerts students to the wealth of career-prep resources available to them from the moment they step on campus. Overall, Wake Forest's career services office is held in high regard, a view backed by the fact that almost every single graduate achieves a successful outcome within months of exiting campus.

Professional Outcomes

The members of the Class of 2018 didn't take long to arrive at their next destinations. Within six months of graduation, 98 percent had either landed their first professional job or were already matriculated into a graduate program. Employers landing the highest numbers of alumni included national and multinational corporations IBM, Siemens, Volvo, Goldman Sachs, Disney, Deloitte, Dell, Gucci, PepsiCo, EY, and Nike. Over 40 percent of graduates remain south of the Mason-Dixon Line; most of those who do exit the South head to the Mid-Atlantic region and the Northeast. By the start of midcareer Wake Forest alumni earn the second-highest median salary of any school in North Carolina, behind Duke but ahead of Davidson and UNC-Chapel Hill.

Just shy of 30 percent of graduates went directly from donning their caps and gowns to pursuing advanced degrees. Students attend a wide range of schools from a selectivity standpoint, but there is a strong representation of elite institutions. As one example, an examination of recent history majors shows acceptances at elite institutions including the University of Chicago, Emory, Duke, Georgetown, Vanderbilt, Harvard, Yale, and the London School of Economics. Many biology majors headed to PhD programs or into medical school at locations such as UNC, Duke, Johns Hopkins, Tufts, and Emory; Wake Forest's medical school takes in many of its own graduates. There were 125 medical school applicants in the Class of 2018 alone.

Admission

Applicants to the Class of 2022 were accepted at a 29 percent clip, a bit lower than five years prior when 34 percent of applicants were successful. However, the average profile of an admitted student has barely changed in that time. Applications may be on the rise, but the requirements for admission have stayed fairly constant.

Wake Forest is a test-optional school, but among those attending students who submitted scores, the middle-50 percent ranges were 1310-1470 on the SAT and 29-33 on the ACT. Over three-quarters of the freshman class finished in the top 10 percent of their high school class, and 92 percent were in the top 25 percent. Those statistics jibe with factors that the admissions office self-reports as being "most important": rigor of curriculum, GPA, class, essay, and character/personal characteristics. If being a Demon Deacon has been your lifelong dream, then you should strongly consider applying early decision to gain an edge on your competition. In 2018, Wake accepted 41 percent of ED applicants compared to 27 percent in the regular round. Further, those accepted ED comprised 56 percent of the Class of 2022. Landing a spot on this gorgeous Winston-Salem campus is a straightforward proposition that is made even simpler by the university's decision to jettison standardized testing back in 2008. Nonetheless, 41 percent of applicants still submit SAT results, and 45 percent submit ACT scores. Applicants should bring stellar grades to the table, be situated among the very best of their respective high schools, and should use their ED card to their advantage.

Worth Your Money?

Wake Forest only awards need-based aid to 30 percent of its undergraduates, a low number compared to other top schools, but when it does offer aid, it does it right. One hundred percent see their full demonstrated need met for an average annual grant of $50,422. On the flip side, the school awards massive amounts of merit aid, an unusual practice for a school of its caliber. Over one-quarter of current undergraduates are recipients of merit-based awards that average $28k. The list price cost of attendance for Wake Forest is greater than $75,000, so those packages help make the school a bit more affordable for the non-wealthy. However, Wake grads still end up with debt loads that exceed the national average. Individuals required to take out a significant amount in loans should consider their career plans and other competing offers before deciding to attend Wake.

FINANCIAL
Institutional Type: Private
In-State Tuition: $54,430
Out-of-State Tuition: $54,430
Room & Board: $16,740
Required Fees: $1,010
Books & Supplies: $1,500

Avg. Need-Based Aid: $50,422
Avg. % of Need Met: 100%

Avg. Merit-Based Aid: $28,107
% Receiving Merit-Based Aid: 27%

Avg. Cumulative Debt: $36,863
% of Students Borrowing: 30%

CAREER
Who Recruits
1. MullenLowe Mediahub
2. Gap, Inc.
3. Horizon Media
4. Gartner
5. Goldman Sachs

Notable Internships
1. Bristol-Myers Squibb
2. Aramark
3. Sotheby's

Top Industries
1. Business
2. Education
3. Finance
4. Operations
5. Sales

Top Employers
1. Wells Fargo
2. EY
3. BB&T
4. PwC
5. Deloitte

Where Alumni Work
1. Winston-Salem, NC
2. New York City
3. Charlotte
4. Washington, DC
5. Raleigh-Durham, NC

Median Earnings
College Scorecard (Early Career): $63,800
EOP (Early Career): $71,500
PayScale (Mid-Career): $114,800

RANKINGS
Forbes: 56
Money: 98
U.S. News: 27 (T), National Universities
Wall Street Journal/THE: 68 (T)
Washington Monthly: 91, National Universities

#CollegesWorthYourMoney

Washington and Lee University

Lexington, Virginia | Admissions Phone: 540-458-8710

ADMISSION
Admission Rate: 21%
Admission Rate - Men: 20%
Admission Rate - Women: 22%
EA Admission Rate: Not Offered
ED Admission Rate: 50%
Admission Rate (5-Year Trend): +3%
ED Admission Rate (5-Year Trend): +11%
% of Admits Attending (Yield): 38%
Transfer Admission Rate: 5%

Offered Wait List: 1,689
Accepted Wait List: 801
Admitted Wait List: 2

SAT Reading/Writing (Middle 50%): 670-730
SAT Math (Middle 50%): 680-760
ACT Composite (Middle 50%): 31-34
Testing Policy: ACT/SAT Required
SAT Superscore: Yes
ACT Superscore: Yes

% Graduated in Top 10% of HS Class: 83%
% Graduated in Top 25% of HS Class: 97%
% Graduated in Top 50% of HS Class: 100%

ENROLLMENT
Total Undergraduate Enrollment: 1,829
% Part-Time: 0%
% Male: 50%
% Female: 50%
% Out-of-State: 84%
% Fraternity: 75%
% Sorority: 75%
% On-Campus (Freshman): 100%
% On-Campus (All Undergraduate): 76%

% African-American: 3%
% Asian: 4%
% Hispanic: 5%
% White: 81%
% Other: 4%
% Race or Ethnicity Unknown: 1%
% International: 4%
% Low-Income: 10%

ACADEMICS
Student-to-Faculty Ratio: 8:1
% of Classes Under 20: 75%
% of Classes Under 40: 100%
% Full-Time Faculty: 78%
% Full-Time Faculty w/ Terminal Degree: 95%

Top Programs
Accounting
Biology
Business Administration
Economics
English
History
Journalism and Mass Communication
Political Science

Retention Rate: 96%
4-Year Graduation Rate: 92%
6-Year Graduation Rate: 95%

Curricular Flexibility: Less Flexible
Academic Rating: ★★★★★

Inside the Classroom

The influence of two disparate figures in American history, George Washington and Robert E. Lee, helped shape a small liberal arts school known in the eighteenth century as Liberty Hall Academy and in the nineteenth century as Washington College before it evolved into Washington and Lee University that, today, is an elite liberal arts institution home to 1,800+ undergraduates. Although dubbed a "university," the only postgraduate program is its law school. Set in the small town of Lexington, Virginia, Washington and Lee is one of the premier colleges of its modest size in all of the South, and it has remained highly selective for the entirety of the twenty-first century.

W&L demands a high number of courses to fulfill its foundational and distributional requirements that collectively will take close to three full semesters to complete. Mandated coursework includes writing, foreign language, physical education, computer science, literature, fine arts, four arts and humanities classes, and two in each of the natural and social sciences. One experiential learning course that focuses on research/presentation/cultural competence rounds out the academic requirements that apply to all undergrads. The university offers thirty-seven majors and twenty-nine minors, including a fair share of interdisciplinary programs.

With an exceptionally low 8:1 student-to-faculty ratio and no graduate students to attend to, W&L undergraduates enjoy loads of attention. Three-quarters of class sections contain nineteen or fewer students, and fewer than 2 percent of courses enroll more than thirty students. Instructors earn rave reviews as 98 percent of Class of 2018 grads were either "very satisfied" or "satisfied" by the quality of their professors. Further, 87 percent were "very satisfied" with faculty's availability outside the classroom; not a single student expressed any level of dissatisfaction. Students can participate in research via the Summer Research Scholars that allows undergrads to collaborate with faculty in the field or lab. Studying abroad is a typical part of a Washington and Lee education with 70 percent of grads spending a semester or summer in a foreign land.

Altogether the various social science disciplines account for one-quarter of the degrees conferred at Washington and Lee, business (22 percent), biology (9 percent), and foreign language (6 percent) are next in popularity. The renowned Williams School of Commerce, Politics, and Economics offers outstanding business-oriented programs that feed many of the top corporations in the world. English, history, and W&L's Department of Journalism and Mass Communication are also highly respected. Given Washington and Lee's many strengths, a healthy number of students are encouraged to apply for prestigious postgraduate fellowships, and a good number are successful. In 2018, four undergrads were awarded Fulbrights while others took home a Goldwater Scholarship and a William Jefferson Clinton Scholarship to study in Dubai.

Outside the Classroom

The main campus of Washington and Lee is concentrated on fifty acres, but it has an additional forty acres of playing fields and 215 acres of green space. All first-year students are required to reside in freshman-exclusive dormitories with twelve to twenty students per floor. Sophomores and juniors primarily live in dorms, apartments, and in Greek houses. To say the Greek scene dominates social life is to grossly understate its reach on campus. The school's eight sororities attract 75 percent of female students and an identical 75 percent of males join the thirteen fraternities on campus. The Generals play twenty-four NCAA Division III sports, which means that varsity athletes comprise a sizable 25 percent of the student body; 40 percent play a varsity sport for at least one year. Twenty-five intramural sports, from flag football to Whiffle ball, attract three-quarters of the student body as well as many faculty members who are eligible to participate. An impressive 90 percent of surveyed undergraduates were satisfied with the school's extracurricular offerings. There are 120+ clubs and organizations presently operating, including the always popular Outing Club that camps and hikes around the neighboring wilderness on weekends. Lexington is a small town with a population around 7,000, but it does have its share of bars and restaurants. Richmond is a two-hour trip by car, and DC is a three-hour drive from campus.

Career Services

The Career and Professional Development Center (CPDC) is staffed by five full-time professional employees serving as pre-law advisor, international advisor, assistant director of STEM programs, and assistant director of recruitment. That equates to a student-to-advisor ratio of 366:1, which is within the average range when compared to other institutions included in this book. Excellent personalized attention is provided to the tune of 960 unique student appointments (3.3 per participating student) per year. Each year, the center staff meets one-on-one with 52 percent of the student population, including two-thirds of seniors.

Washington and Lee University

E-mail: admissions@wlu.edu | Website: www.wlu.edu

The CPDC brought sixty employers to Lexington last year for information sessions, recruitment, and on-campus interviews. It also organized six career exploration trips to DC and New York City that focused on finance, the arts, advertising, marketing, and STEM fields. Staff also host more than sixty career exploration and skill-building workshops on topics such as social media, Excel, and how to write a personal statement. LexLink, the school's online job and internship platform, has roughly 1,000 postings for undergrads to pursue. A dazzling 85 percent of students complete at least one internship, fellowship, or practicum. Further, 94 percent of those completing such an experience found it "extremely helpful" or "somewhat helpful" in preparing for a career. With ample individualized attention and opportunity for hands-on experience, W&L's Career and Professional Development Center rates well in the eyes of our staff.

Professional Outcomes

In recent years 69-80 percent of graduates have found employment within six months of saying goodbye to Lexington. The most frequently entered industries have been financial services (12 percent), economics/finance (12 percent), education (8 percent), consulting (8 percent), and real estate (6 percent). With so many flocking to financial jobs, many top banks, accounting firms, and investment houses presently employ more than two dozen Generals including EY, Wells Fargo, Goldman Sachs, PwC, JP Morgan, Capital One, and Morgan Stanley. Washington and Lee is the rare college that sees the majority of its alumni relocate to cities in other states. DC, New York City, and Atlanta all draw more graduates than Roanoke or Richmond. Starting salaries for the Class of 2018 were solid with 57 percent of the cohort being paid $55,000 or more while 23 percent brought home in excess of $75,000.

Almost one-quarter of grads immediately matriculated into a graduate or professional program upon receiving their bachelor's degrees. Law school (29 percent), medical/health professional schools (22 percent), and engineering (12 percent) were the top three destinations. Recent physics and engineering students have gone on to graduate study at MIT, Carnegie Mellon, Stanford, and Vanderbilt. Law schools accepting recent grads included Wake Forest, Fordham, Georgetown, Vanderbilt, and W&L's own law school. Medical school acceptances included Rutgers Medical School, LSU School of Medicine in New Orleans, and University of Texas Medical Branch.

Admission

Of 5,855 applicants for a seat in the Class of 2022 only 1,239 were admitted for an acceptance rate of 21 percent; 474 ultimately enrolled. The mid-50 percent SAT score was 1360-1480, and the ACT range was 31-34. Most 2018-19 freshmen hailed from the very top of their high school class with 83 percent placing in the top decile and 97 percent in the top 25 percent. All of the admissions statistics are almost identical to those of a decade ago. In fact, the number of applicants, acceptance rate, and the achievement level of entering freshmen has remained relatively steady since the turn of the millennium.

The goal of the admissions committee is to "get to know you as well as possible through your application." The rigor of your high school curriculum is very important—96 percent of entering freshmen had an IB or AP background, and just shy of three-quarters studied four or more years of a foreign language. Only three other factors rated as "very important": class rank, extracurricular activities, and character/personal qualities. GPA, recommendations, essays, and standardized test scores also are considered as factors of importance in evaluating candidates. Applying early decision is a no-brainer for dedicated applicants as the acceptance rate hovers above 50 percent versus 18 percent for those in the regular cycle. In fact, the school locks in 58 percent of its freshman class via the ED round. Washington and Lee offers a genuinely holistic admissions process. Strong grades in highly rigorous courses are nonnegotiable, but qualities like leadership and what one brings to a student community also receive strong consideration.

Worth Your Money?

While a $70k+ price tag might make cost-conscious families aggressively scratch Washington and Lee off their child's college list, it is one of the most generous schools with merit aid for exceptional students. While only 22 percent receive that form of aid, the average amount is for a difference-making sum of $49,195, with as much as 10 percent of each entering class receiving the highly coveted Johnson Scholarship, which fully covers tuition, room, and board for chosen applicants. That generosity is only trumped by the school's dedication to meeting 100 percent of financial need for every qualifying student. Thanks to that level of financial assistance and excellent graduate outcomes, Washington and Lee is worth the money for most attendees.

FINANCIAL
Institutional Type: Private
In-State Tuition: $51,420
Out-of-State Tuition: $51,420
Room & Board: $13,925
Required Fees: $1,035
Books & Supplies: $1,950

Avg. Need-Based Aid: $49,195
Avg. % of Need Met: 100%

Avg. Merit-Based Aid: $45,742
% Receiving Merit-Based Aid: 23%

Avg. Cumulative Debt: $21,758
% of Students Borrowing: 31%

CAREER
Who Recruits
1. Walker & Dunlap
2. Citi
3. Merrill Lynch
4. Berkeley Research Group
5. Morgan Stanley

Notable Internships
1. Estee Lauder Companies
2. Twitter
3. North Carolina Museum of Art

Top Industries
1. Business
2. Finance
3. Education
4. Legal
5. Operations

Top Employers
1. EY
2. PwC
3. Morgan Stanley
4. Wells Fargo
5. JPMorgan Chase

Where Alumni Work
1. Washington, DC
2. New York City
3. Atlanta
4. Roanoke, VA
5. Richmond

Median Earnings
College Scorecard (Early Career): $76,100
EOP (Early Career): $78,200
PayScale (Mid-Career): $123,200

RANKINGS
Forbes: 42
Money: 26
U.S. News: 10, Liberal Arts Colleges
Wall Street Journal/THE: 70
Washington Monthly: 1, Liberal Arts Colleges

#CollegesWorthYourMoney

Washington University in St. Louis

St. Louis, Missouri | Admissions Phone: 314-935-6000

Inside the Classroom

Despite receiving consistently high rankings since *U.S. News* released its first college guide in 1983, Washington University in St. Louis is, perhaps, the finest institution that is not a household name across the nation. Yet, this Midwestern research and pre-professional powerhouse is one of the most respected institutions in the eyes of Fortune 500 employers and elite graduate schools alike. Catering to just over 7,700 undergraduates, WashU admits students into five schools: Arts & Sciences, the Olin School of Business, the School of Engineering & Applied Sciences, and the Art of Architecture programs housed within the Sam Fox School of Design and Visual Arts.

Arts & Sciences, which claims more than half the student body, offers more than eighty majors, and all are guided by the IQ Curriculum, the school's signature liberal arts course of study. As part of the IQ Curriculum students must take courses in applied numeracy, social contrasts, writing, and an additional course that is classified as "writing intensive." WashU students also must complete coursework in the humanities, social sciences, natural sciences/math, and foreign language along with three "integrations" that can be completed via multi-semester, cross-disciplinary coursework. Engineering students are not beholden to all of those curricular mandates. Special programs include the University Scholars Program in Medicine that allows students to apply for admission to both an undergraduate degree program and medical school before entering college as well as the Beyond Boundaries Program that allows students to implement a cross-disciplinary approach with the aim of solving major global and societal problems.

The university has an 8:1 student-faculty ratio, and 77 percent of classes have fewer than twenty-four students; close to one-quarter have single-digit enrollments. WUSTL students are known for being more collaborative than competitive and extremely hard working as evidenced by the fact that 75 percent double major or pursue multiple degrees. The Office of Undergraduate Research helps students land opportunities to research alongside faculty, primarily in the summers. A solid 59 percent of undergraduates report participating in a research endeavor. A relatively modest one-third of students study abroad.

Nationally recognized programs are numerous: the Olin Business School, the School of Engineering & Applied Sciences, and the College of Architecture are well-respected by employers. The Biology Department prepares many successful med school candidates, including for the university's own ultra-elite medical school. The most commonly conferred degrees are in business (15 percent), engineering (15 percent), social sciences (13 percent), biology (11 percent), and psychology (7 percent). Fulbright, Gilman, Luce, and Critical Language Scholarships all have been won by WashU grads in recent years, and two students were named Rhodes Scholars in 2018.

Outside the Classroom

It sounds trite, but by almost any metric one must conclude that Washington University students seem happy. Dorms, recreational facilities, and campus food are routinely rated well. The WashU atmosphere is known for being more laid-back and friendly than that at many of its elite peers. Seventy-four percent of the student body and 100 percent of freshmen reside on campus. WashU's ten fraternities and eight sororities draw roughly one-third of the student body into Greek participation. The Bears compete in NCCA Division II, fielding nine men's teams and ten women's squads. The athletically-inclined student body also have forty-one club teams, and a simply insane three-quarters of undergraduates participate in intramural sports. In excess of 380 student-run organizations are active at WUSTL, all under the purview of the Washington University Student Union, one of the most well-funded college student governments in the country. Each semester it funds a concert known as WILD (for Walk In Lay Down) that features a big-time musical act. Well-attended speaker events are also organized on a regular basis, and recent attendees include Mitt Romney, John Paul Stevens, and Ta-Nehisi Coates. The Campus YMCA connects over 800 students each year with twenty-eight service opportunities in the local community. Student media is popular, and *Student Life*, the school's independent newspaper, has won national awards on several occasions. In addition, the school's radio station, KWUR, is immensely popular, and not just on campus but across the St. Louis area. For those inclined to explore off campus, the university is located within a few miles of the St. Louis Zoo, multiple art museums, a host of great eateries, and the gorgeous Missouri Botanical Garden.

Career Services

The Washington University in St. Louis Career Center is staffed by twenty-one full-time professional employees who specialize in employer relations, career counseling, event planning, and pre-graduate school advising. With a student-to-advisor ratio of 367:1, WUSTL compares favorably to the other institutions included in this book. Having conducted 5,803 one-on-one advising sessions in the 2018-19 school year, the center staff does a superb job of engaging their undergraduate student population.

Washington University in St. Louis

E-mail: admissions@wustl.edu | Website: www.wustl.edu

Three large career fairs drew a collective audience of almost 2,000 individuals and 300 employers. The center also hosted over 280 low-key employer information sessions and a number of SLAMs, miniature career fairs for a particular industry where, in a bit of a role-reversal, employers pitch their companies to students. An almost hard-to-fathom 475 employers recruit on campus each year, and close to 1,114 on-campus interviews were conducted in 2018-19 (in 2016, the number of interviews was even higher—1,204). Thanks to the strong employer connections forged by career services staff, WashU students have no trouble landing internships at major companies like CBS News, Pfizer, and AT&T, and stipends are available through the university to help offset living expenses. All told, approximately 75 percent of students report completing at least one internship. With ample staffing, superior outreach, and positive student outcomes, WashU's Career Center could not be doing a better job.

Professional Outcomes

The Class of 2018 sent 74 percent of its exiting members into the workforce and 23 percent into graduate and professional schools. The thirty companies employing the highest number of WashU grads feature many of the most sought-after employers in the world including Amazon, Bain, Boeing, Deloitte, Google, IBM, Goldman Sachs, and Microsoft. Of the employed members of the Class of 2018 who reported their starting salaries, 70 percent were making over $50,000 and 18 percent were making more than $80k. By age thirty-four, alumni earn the highest median income of any undergraduate degree-granting institution in the state. Geographically, remaining in Missouri was the favored choice among fresh alums, but a fair number also resettled in New York and California.

The universities welcoming the largest number of Bears included the prestigious institutions of Carnegie Mellon, Columbia, Duke, Harvard, Penn, Princeton, and Stanford. Others were pursuing graduate degrees at non-elite schools including Case Western, Rutgers, Colorado State, and St. Louis University. In 2017, of 1,587 graduates, ninety were accepted into med school, including at WashU's own top-ranked medical school. Baylor College of Medicine attracted a large number of future physicians; students also enjoyed acceptances into Harvard Medical School, NYU School of Medicine, and the Icahn School of Medicine at Mt. Sinai.

Admission

WashU received over 31,000 applications for a place in the Class of 2022, but it admitted only 15 percent. Over 80 percent of attending students were in the top 10 percent of their high school class, and the middle 50 percent for SATs was 1470-1570 and 32-35 for the ACTs. For historical reference, in 2010, the university accepted 21 percent of applicants, and enrolling students possessed similar standardized test scores to those being accepted today.

Even with rising application numbers, the admissions committee carefully examines each application, granting "high importance" to soft factors including character/personal qualities, extracurricular activities, talent/ability, and volunteer/work experience. Essays also grace this list, and a new supplemental essay component was added for applicants in 2019. It behooves students seriously committed to WUSTL to give serious consideration to applying early. The admission rate is 42 percent in the early round compared to only 13 percent in the regular cycle, and ED entrants comprise 39 percent of the freshman class. For those applying in the regular cycle, demonstrating interest is critically important as the admissions staff is eager to know if WashU is truly one of your top choices or merely a safety school in case Harvard says "no." Formerly relegated to Ivy backup status, Washington University has stepped into the limelight as a destination point for the best and brightest from around the country. In fact, close to 65 percent of current students hail from over 500 miles away, including all fifty US states and one hundred countries. This Midwestern behemoth casts a wide net, but it only brings aboard the most brag-worthy high school fish it can find.

Worth Your Money?

A fairly standard (in the world of elite private colleges) $75,500 list price cost of attendance greets WashU freshmen. The 42 percent of undergrads who qualify for financial aid see 100 percent of that amount met by the university, which averages out to $49k in grant money each academic year. Roughly 14 percent of students also receive merit aid awards averaging roughly $10,500 per year. This school has one of the wealthiest groups of students in the country (rivaled by Colorado College and Colgate) so, for many, the price tag will not break the bank. Given that reality, WUSTL can make sense for students across a wide spectrum of socioeconomic backgrounds.

FINANCIAL
Institutional Type: Private
In-State Tuition: $54,250
Out-of-State Tuition: $54,250
Room & Board: $16,900
Required Fees: $1,042
Books & Supplies: $1,126

Avg. Need-Based Aid: $48,522
Avg. % of Need Met: 100%

Avg. Merit-Based Aid: $10,585
% Receiving Merit-Based Aid: 14%

Avg. Cumulative Debt: $22,555
% of Students Borrowing: 27%

CAREER
Who Recruits
1. Guggenheim Investments
2. Equifax
3. Cushman & Wakefield
4. Abercrombie & Fitch
5. Chicago Trading Company

Notable Internships
1. St. Louis Post-Dispatch
2. Uber
3. BlackRock

Top Industries
1. Business
2. Education
3. Engineering
4. Research
5. Operations

Top Employers
1. Boeing
2. Google
3. Microsoft
4. Amazon
5. Mastercard

Where Alumni Work
1. St. Louis
2. New York City
3. Chicago
4. San Francisco
5. Washington, DC

Median Earnings
College Scorecard (Early Career): $70,100
EOP (Early Career): $67,500
PayScale (Mid-Career): $114,900

RANKINGS
Forbes: 31
Money: 82
U.S. News: 19, National Universities
Wall Street Journal/THE: 19
Washington Monthly: 59, National Universities

#CollegesWorthYourMoney

Wellesley College

ADMISSION

Admission Rate: 20%
Admission Rate - Men: Not Offered
Admission Rate - Women: 20%
EA Admission Rate: Not Offered
ED Admission Rate: 31%
Admission Rate (5-Year Trend): -10%
ED Admission Rate (5-Year Trend): -5%
% of Admits Attending (Yield): 47%
Transfer Admission Rate: 16%

Offered Wait List: 1,909
Accepted Wait List: 1,245
Admitted Wait List: 36

SAT Reading/Writing (Middle 50%): 670-740
SAT Math (Middle 50%): 660-780
ACT Composite (Middle 50%): 30-34
Testing Policy: ACT/SAT Required
SAT Superscore: Yes
ACT Superscore: Yes

% Graduated in Top 10% of HS Class: 83%
% Graduated in Top 25% of HS Class: 96%
% Graduated in Top 50% of HS Class: 99%

ENROLLMENT

Total Undergraduate Enrollment: 2,534
% Part-Time: 6%
% Male: 2%
% Female: 98%
% Out-of-State: 86%
% Fraternity: Not Offered
% Sorority: Not Offered
% On-Campus (Freshman): 100%
% On-Campus (All Undergraduate): 97%

% African-American: 6%
% Asian: 21%
% Hispanic: 13%
% White: 36%
% Other: 6%
% Race or Ethnicity Unknown: 5%
% International: 14%
% Low-Income: 20%

ACADEMICS

Student-to-Faculty Ratio: 8:1
% of Classes Under 20: 67%
% of Classes Under 40: 99%
% Full-Time Faculty: 86%
% Full-Time Faculty w/ Terminal Degree: 93%

Top Programs
Area Studies
Chemistry
Computer Science
Economics
English
History
Neuroscience
Political Science

Retention Rate: 96%
4-Year Graduation Rate: 84%
6-Year Graduation Rate: 92%

Curricular Flexibility: Somewhat Flexible
Academic Rating: ★★★★★

Inside the Classroom

In 1995, the *New York Times* proclaimed, "More than any other college—large or small— Wellesley has groomed women who shatter the glass ceiling." Twenty five years later, Barnard has surpassed Wellesley for the lowest acceptance rate among women's colleges, but Wellesley's picture-perfect campus in suburban Boston remains the premier pipeline to the boardrooms of America's most powerful companies as well as to the highest levels of politics. Students are known to be a driven bunch as committed to full engagement with campus activities as they are to the exceptionally rigorous classroom experience.

The college's 2,350 undergraduate students can select from fifty departmental and interdisciplinary majors, and economics, biology, and computer science are the most frequently conferred degrees. All freshmen must complete an expository writing course, and all seniors must demonstrate foreign language proficiency. In between, students are required to complete coursework in natural and physical science, mathematical modeling and problem solving, social and behavioral analysis, language and literature, art/music/theater/film/video, epistemology and cognition, historical studies, and religion/ethics/moral philosophy. There is also a multicultural and an uncredited physical education requirement.

The student-to-faculty ratio is only 8:1, leading to average class sizes in the seventeen- to twenty-student range. Twenty percent of course sections have single-digit enrollments while two-thirds have fewer than nineteen students. With no graduate students to compete with, opportunities for participation in research with faculty members abound. The Summer Science Research Program is cited by many graduates as the most influential part of their educational experience. Wellesley students also regularly land research positions with the National Institutes of Health, Harvard Medical School, MIT, and The Children's Hospital of Philadelphia. The Office of International Studies facilitates the overseas study of hundreds of students each year with 45 percent of juniors spending a semester in one of 160 programs worldwide.

The entire undergraduate program at Wellesley is revered by top corporations and graduate schools alike. Most programs possess sterling reputations, including chemistry, computer science, neuroscience, and political science. However, the Department of Economics appears to shine most brightly, leading many into PhD programs and high-profile careers. A large number of Wellesley graduates are awarded prestigious postgraduate scholarships each year. In 2018, the school produced four Fulbright Scholars, three Gilman Scholars, three Watson Fellows, a Critical Languages Scholar, and a Princeton in Asia Fellow.

Outside the Classroom

Approximately 97 percent of undergraduates are denizens of the school's twenty-one residence halls that range in capacity from forty to 285 students. Wellesley's 500-acre campus was described by fabled architect Frederick Olmstead as possessing "a peculiar kind of intricate beauty." Thanks to Lake Waban, a golf course, an arboretum, and botanical gardens, you will never long for gorgeous landscapes and natural beauty. There are thirteen varsity athletic teams that are members of NCAA Division III as well as eight club teams in sports that include archery, equestrian, and Nordic skiing. Athletic facilities are extensive and include the Keohane Sports Center, a pool, spin rooms, dance studios, a rock climbing wall, and just about any other fitness-related amenity one can conjure up. Wellesley women have 150 student-run organizations to choose from, including a number of dance, music, and theater groups. This is a tradition-rich school with annual events like Flower Sunday and quarterly competitions like Stepsinging, a class-vs.-class singing contest on the steps of Houghton Chapel. The town of Wellesley has coffee shops, a bookstore, and a pharmacy all within a short walk. Downtown Boston is less than half an hour away by car, but most take the T, commuter trains, or a shuttle that regularly departs from campus.

Career Services

The Wellesley Career Education Office is staffed by thirty professionals working in career counseling, internships, fellowships, experiential learning, and employer relations. For a school with 2,350 students, the size and scope of this office is remarkable. The 78:1 student-to-advisor ratio is unmatched by any institution in the country. It's no wonder that the National Association of Colleges and Employers named Wellesley the 2017 winner of the Career Service Excellence Award among small colleges; the department has been similarly recognized multiple times by national organizations for its superior career service offerings. Staff members regularly present at national conferences and publish on the topic of career preparation.

Class of 2018 members had a 98 percent satisfaction rate after in-person, one-on-one appointments; that was a dramatic improvement over the Class of 2015's satisfaction rate of 45 percent. Almost 90 percent of undergraduates complete at least one internship, including so-called Signature Internships with "leading cultural, educational, and scientific institutions; international agencies; media outlets; advocacy and community organizations; and businesses" around the globe. In the 2017-18 academic year, 80 percent of the undergraduate population engaged face-to-face with career services, and 98 percent engaged digitally. Outreach begins freshman year as 82 percent of first-years meet in person with a career counselor.

Wellesley College

E-mail: admission@wellesley.edu | Website: www.wellesley.edu

The annual total of advising sessions exceeds 6,500. There were 275 events held with a total attendance of 4,690, and thirty-three employers engaged in on-campus interviews including Google, Microsoft, Citi, and the US Department of Commerce. Unlike some of the other Seven Sister institutions, opportunities at the world's premier companies are commonplace, and salaries are higher than average. With superb resources and equally strong outcomes, the Wellesley Career Education Office deserves all of the many accolades that have been heaped upon it.

Professional Outcomes

Six months after earning their degrees, 96 percent of the Wellesley College Class of 2018 had already achieved positive outcomes. Of the three-quarters of grads who were employed, 24 percent were working in the finance/consulting/business fields, 18 percent in education, 15 percent in internet and software/technology/engineering, and 13 percent in health care/life sciences. The top employers were Accenture, Google, JP Morgan, Boston Children's Hospital, Massachusetts General Hospital, and a number of top universities that included Harvard and MIT. One hundred thirty-three members of the Class of 2018 were employed in Boston, sixty-nine in New York, fifty in California, and twenty-seven in Washington, DC. The average starting salary was a solid $59,000 with an average bonus of $11,000.

Wellesley grads almost universally go on to elite graduate programs. Of the 17 percent of 2018 grads who directly entered an advanced degree program, the top dozen most common schools attended included Ivies Harvard, Columbia, Brown, Penn, and Cornell and other upper-crust institutions at Stanford, MIT, Emory, NYU, Brandeis, Boston University, and the Olin College of Engineering. Medical school applicants are generally successful; from 2008-2018 an average of 72 percent of med school hopefuls were accepted by at least one university. Three or more recent grads have been accepted into medical school at Dartmouth, Tufts, Case Western, Boston University, and Northwestern. Law school acceptance rates hover in the low-to-mid 80s, a figure that is lowered by the caliber of law schools to which Wellesley grads typically apply. Law schools that accepted a minimum of three alumni in recent years include Yale, Duke, Harvard, Georgetown, Cornell, Penn, and UC Berkeley.

Admission

The 6,488 applications received for a place in the Class of 2023 was the second highest total in school history; the acceptance rate of 20 percent was one point higher than the previous cycle. Among admitted applicants the average SAT was 1438, the average ACT was 32, and 84 percent placed in the top decile of their graduating high school class. 2018-19 freshmen possessed similar numbers. Their mid-50 percent ranges were 1330-1520 on the SAT, 30-34 on the ACT, and 83 percent were in the top 10 percent of their class. Wellesley boasts a high yield rate of 47 percent, meaning that few apply on a whim, and nearly half of all admitted students choose to enroll in the college.

As part of its holistic review process, the admissions committee seeks "people who know that we don't know everything; who have a strong voice but listen to other voices; who have big plans but are totally open to changing them; who have taken risks, failed, and figured out a better way." As such, four factors are paramount in the evaluation process: character/personal qualities, recommendations, GPA, and rigor of one's secondary school record. The second tier of factors includes test scores, class rank, essays, talent/ability, and extracurricular activities. Applying via early decision can yield a slight advantage as 31 percent of students are accepted during the ED round. In terms of pure acceptance rate, Wellesley is the second-most selective Seven Sisters school, behind only Barnard. High grades and strong test scores are required, but many softer factors weigh heavily on admissions decisions. Applicants who are involved in their high schools and communities will fare best.

Worth Your Money?

Even at a $75,198 annual cost of attendance, Wellesley is unquestionably worth the investment. You won't receive merit aid from this school, but 56 percent of the student population does receive need-based aid, and that need is met 100 percent. That translates to an average need-based grant of close to $53,000. The quality of the education, mentorship, and professional networks make Wellesley, even at full price for non-STEM/business majors, the rare school that will return your money many times over.

FINANCIAL
Institutional Type: Private
In-State Tuition: $55,728
Out-of-State Tuition: $55,728
Room & Board: $17,096
Required Fees: $324
Books & Supplies: $800

Avg. Need-Based Aid: $52,881
Avg. % of Need Met: 100%

Avg. Merit-Based Aid: $0
% Receiving Merit-Based Aid: 0%

Avg. Cumulative Debt: $16,122
% of Students Borrowing: 52%

CAREER
Who Recruits
1. Boston Consulting Group
2. Teach for America
3. U.S. Federal Reserve
4. Massachusetts General Hospital
5. State Street

Notable Internships
1. Metropolitan Museum of Art
2. American Express
3. Dick Clark Productions

Top Industries
1. Business
2. Education
3. Research
4. Media
5. Social Services

Top Employers
1. Google
2. Microsoft
3. Accenture
4. Amazon
5. Facebook

Where Alumni Work
1. Boston
2. New York City
3. San Francisco
4. Washington, DC
5. Los Angeles

Median Earnings
College Scorecard (Early Career): $60,800
EOP (Early Career): $56,300
PayScale (Mid-Career): $106,200

RANKINGS
Forbes: 44
Money: 89
U.S. News: 3, Liberal Arts Colleges
Wall Street Journal/THE: 24
Washington Monthly: 16, Liberal Arts Colleges

#CollegesWorthYourMoney

Middletown, Connecticut | Admissions Phone: 860-685-3000

ADMISSION
Admission Rate: 17%
Admission Rate - Men: 21%
Admission Rate - Women: 15%
EA Admission Rate: Not Offered
ED Admission Rate: 38%
Admission Rate (5-Year Trend): -3%
ED Admission Rate (5-Year Trend): -5%
% of Admits Attending (Yield): 36%
Transfer Admission Rate: 24%

\# Offered Wait List: 1,965
\# Accepted Wait List: 1,098
\# Admitted Wait List: 0

SAT Reading/Writing (Middle 50%): 660-740
SAT Math (Middle 50%): 660-760
ACT Composite (Middle 50%): 30-34
Testing Policy: Test Optional
SAT Superscore: Yes
ACT Superscore: Yes

% Graduated in Top 10% of HS Class: 57%
% Graduated in Top 25% of HS Class: 85%
% Graduated in Top 50% of HS Class: 98%

ENROLLMENT
Total Undergraduate Enrollment: 3,009
% Part-Time: 3%
% Male: 45%
% Female: 55%
% Out-of-State: 93%
% Fraternity: 4%
% Sorority: 1%
% On-Campus (Freshman): 100%
% On-Campus (All Undergraduate): 99%

% African-American: 7%
% Asian: 7%
% Hispanic: 12%
% White: 53%
% Other: 6%
% Race or Ethnicity Unknown: 3%
% International: 12%
% Low-Income: 18%

ACADEMICS
Student-to-Faculty Ratio: 8:1
% of Classes Under 20: 73%
% of Classes Under 40: 95%
% Full-Time Faculty: 84%
% Full-Time Faculty w/ Terminal Degree: 92%

Top Programs
Area Studies
Economics
English
Film Studies
Government
Neuroscience and Behavior
Performing Arts
Sociology

Retention Rate: 96%
4-Year Graduation Rate: 85%
6-Year Graduation Rate: 89%

Curricular Flexibility: Very Flexible
Academic Rating: ★★★★⅃

Inside the Classroom
Considered one of the "Little Ivies" and officially a member of the "Little Three" alongside Amherst and Williams, Wesleyan University in Middletown, Connecticut, has much in common with its highly selective compatriots, but it also possesses a distinctively uncompromising and independent-minded student body. One telling anecdote comes from 1998 when the administration proudly unveiled the school's new slogan, "The Independent Ivy." Many young people would love for their college to associate itself with the cache of the Ivy League, but at Wesleyan the student response was utter disgust that led to an all-out rebellion. The students launched a vocal protest, and the higher-ups quickly dropped the slogan. That's Wesleyan in a nutshell.

At 3,000 undergraduate students Wes is significantly larger than many of its elite liberal arts peers. With forty-five majors, seventeen minors, and over 1,000 classes running each academic year, the school truly has something for everyone. The academic requirements are relatively minimal, giving undergrads a high degree of intellectual freedom. There are two stages of general education courses: stage one sees students complete two courses each in the three divisions of Humanities & Arts, Social & Behavioral Sciences, and Natural Sciences & Math. Stage two is optional for most majors but may be required to receive departmental honors at graduation.

Just shy of three-quarters of class sections have fewer than twenty students, allowing for close bonds/mentorships to unfold. Students rave about the accessible faculty (the faculty-to-student ratio is 8:1), and research opportunities with professors are plentiful. The program for undergraduate Research in the Sciences funds over one hundred students per year to conduct research over the summer. The university has increased its study abroad participation in recent years to the point that almost 50 percent of students now spend a semester overseas.

There isn't one go-to major at Wes; while the social sciences (24 percent), psychology (13 percent), area/ethnic/gender studies (12 percent), and the visual and performing arts (11 percent) are the most popular, none represents a massive percentage of the total degrees conferred. Nearly every program at Wesleyan is respected in the employer/graduate school communities, with offerings in economics, English, film studies, and neuroscience receiving perhaps the most praise. Wesleyan was again named a top producer of Fulbright Scholars in 2018; six recent alums won the award after seven took home the honor in 2017.

Outside the Classroom
The unofficial but popular motto, "Keep Wes Weird," perfectly sums up this iconoclastic student body's vibe and helps describe life on campus. Those looking for wild frat parties and raucous football games would be highly disappointed (and confused) walking around the Wesleyan campus. Greek life attracts a minuscule 3 percent of students and, other than the one-quarter of undergraduates who comprise the rosters of the school's twenty-nine varsity sports teams, athletics are not a focal point for the average student. That being said, participation is high in intramural and club sports including ultimate Frisbee, kung fu, and WesClimb, which takes advantage of the schools own rock climbing wall. Wesleyan's other amenities include a 412-seat movie theater that screens films throughout the year, a fifty-meter swimming pool, a 7,500- square-foot gymnasium, and an ice skating rink. There are more than 250 active student-run groups with large numbers in the areas of activism/politics, identity, theater, comedy troupes, and a cappella. The Center for the Arts hosts more than 300 events each year from jazz concerts to one-person shows to art exhibitions. Middletown provides a nice enough small city environment with plenty of bars and restaurants to frequent, and Hartford is only a twenty-five minute drive. Just about everyone lives on campus.

Career Services
The Gordon Career Center is staffed by nine full-time staff who specialize in employer relations, general advising, health professions advising, STEM career advising, and business career advising. The 334:1 student-to-advisor ratio places it in the above-average range compared to other schools profiled in this guide. The school does not organize any large career expos/fairs; instead, it hosts events just about every day along the lines of a chat over coffee with Deloitte to a gathering entitled "Google at Wes: Laying the Foundation for Your Technical Career" featuring Wesleyan alumni who work for the tech giant.

Wes has partnered with a number of major employers to facilitate on-campus recruiting and interviews including Booz Allen, Lego (fun!), Pfizer, and Squarespace. Interested seniors participate in a job search boot camp known as Accelerate prior to engaging with those visiting companies. The WEShadow Externship programs allows current students the chance to spend anywhere from one day to one week at work with an alum. The Winter on Wyllys program is an intensive, two-week career development course available over the holidays. Data on internship participation rates and overall engagements with the career center is, at present, unavailable.

Wesleyan University

E-mail: admissions@wesleyan.edu | Website: www.wesleyan.edu

Professional Outcomes

By the end of calendar year 2018, the majority of those who received their diplomas in May had entered employment (70 percent). Graduate school was the next stop for 12 percent of new alums, and 10 percent were still seeking employment. Of those who landed jobs, the third highest number were in arts and entertainment, which isn't shocking when your school's alumni include the likes of Lin Manuel Miranda, Michael Bay, Joss Whedon, and countless Hollywood writers and producers. Tech/engineering/sciences and education took the silver and gold. The companies employing the highest numbers of Wesleyan Class of 2018 grads included Google, Epic, Analysis Group, JP Morgan Chase, Teach for America, Booz Allen Hamilton, Accenture, and Facebook. By age thirty-four Wesleyan grads have a median income of $56,500, which lags well behind the other Little Three colleges, Amherst and Williams. New York, Boston, San Francisco, and Hartford were the most popular post-college destinations.

Wes alumni are looked upon favorably by elite graduate and professional schools. From 2013-17 Wesleyan grads were accepted into medical school 55-66 percent of the time, much higher than the national average. Those with a 3.6 GPA or higher enjoyed a superior acceptance rate of 75-87 percent. In the same timespan law school applicants were successful 88-100 percent of the time and fared extremely well at the most prestigious universities. In 2016, a gasp-worthy 64 percent of law school-bound seniors found a home at a top ten law school including Yale, Harvard, Stanford, Columbia, and UChicago. Those pursuing non-professional advanced degrees enrolled in a wide range of schools from elites like MIT, Stanford, and Berkeley to state universities like Rowan, Temple, and UMass.

Admission

Wesleyan admitted 17.5 percent of its record-setting 12,788 applicants in 2018, a figure that has increased by 35 percent in the past four years. The mid-50 percent range on the SAT for members of the Class of 2022 was 1320-1500 and 30-34 on the ACT. Interestingly, this past cycle's acceptance rate was higher than 2017's 15.4 percent clip or even that of a decade ago when the university welcomed only 15 percent of applicants. Yet, somehow that is fitting because Wesleyan's admissions, like its eclectic and talented students, is not unidimensional.

Unlike some other schools of its caliber, Wesleyan does not rule out those who finished outside of the top 10 percent of their high school class. While 57 percent of the Class of 2022 earned that distinction, 85 percent finished in the top quarter, and 2 percent placed outside the top 50 percent. The No. 1 factor in admissions is the rigor of secondary school curriculum as it seeks young people who are "intellectual risk-takers" above all else. Standardized test scores have been made less important by Wesleyan's test-optional policy, but 56 percent of attending students submitted SAT scores, and 45 percent submitted ACT scores in 2018. Obviously, there's some crossover there, but we can assume the overall percentage of successful students going the test-optional route is fairly small. Applying early decision is definitely something you want to consider if Wesleyan is your top choice because it fills 51 percent of its freshman class via ED, and it has an admit rate more than double that of the regular cycle (37 percent versus 16 percent). Getting into Wesleyan is not as formulaic a process as it is at the majority of elite institutions. Essays, recommendations, first-generation status, ethnicity, personal characteristics, and performance in the classroom are all given genuine consideration. Possessing good stats is important to your admissions chances, but so is being an engaged and passionate learner.

Worth Your Money?

Wesleyan costs $75,693 annually, a price similar to its elite liberal arts kin. A tiny percentage of students receive substantial merit aid, but 97 percent receive no help of that variety. It is need-based aid that rules the day at Wes as all qualifying students (42 percent of the population) have 100 percent of their demonstrated need accounted for. The average grant for those individuals is $50,000+. Not every student who goes to this school cruises into a six-figure job, but that's the aim of a Wesleyan education. This school is worth the cost because it assists you in finding a pathway that aligns with your passions, and it makes the school affordable for those in financial need.

FINANCIAL
Institutional Type: Private
In-State Tuition: $56,704
Out-of-State Tuition: $56,704
Room & Board: $15,724
Required Fees: $300
Books & Supplies: $1,200

Avg. Need-Based Aid: $50,083
Avg. % of Need Met: 100%

Avg. Merit-Based Aid: $35,118
% Receiving Merit-Based Aid: 3%

Avg. Cumulative Debt: $23,454
% of Students Borrowing: 36%

CAREER
Who Recruits
1. MGM Resorts International
2. Pfizer
3. Analysis Group
4. McKinsey & Co.
5. Charles River Associates

Notable Internships
1. Citadel Securities
2. ABC News
3. United Nations

Top Industries
1. Business
2. Education
3. Media
4. Research
5. Social Services

Top Employers
1. Google
2. Citi
3. JPMorgan Chase
4. Accenture
5. Morgan Stanley

Where Alumni Work
1. New York City
2. Boston
3. San Francisco
4. Hartford
5. Washington, DC

Median Earnings
College Scorecard (Early Career): $54,700
EOP (Early Career): $56,500
PayScale (Mid-Career): $117,000

RANKINGS
Forbes: 40
Money: 140
U.S. News: 17, Liberal Arts Colleges
Wall Street Journal/THE: 43
Washington Monthly: 9, Liberal Arts Colleges

#CollegesWorthYourMoney

Whitman College

Walla Walla, Washington | Admissions Phone: 509-527-5176

ADMISSION
Admission Rate: 50%
Admission Rate - Men: 48%
Admission Rate - Women: 52%
EA Admission Rate: Not Offered
ED Admission Rate: N/A
Admission Rate (5-Year Trend): -7%
ED Admission Rate (5-Year Trend): N/A
% of Admits Attending (Yield): 17%
Transfer Admission Rate: 44%

Offered Wait List: N/A
Accepted Wait List: N/A
Admitted Wait List: N/A

SAT Reading/Writing (Middle 50%): 640-720
SAT Math (Middle 50%): 640-720
ACT Composite (Middle 50%): 29-32
Testing Policy: Test Optional
SAT Superscore: Yes
ACT Superscore: Yes

% Graduated in Top 10% of HS Class: 52%
% Graduated in Top 25% of HS Class: 83%
% Graduated in Top 50% of HS Class: 99%

ENROLLMENT
Total Undergraduate Enrollment: 1,475
% Part-Time: 3%
% Male: 43%
% Female: 57%
% Out-of-State: 70%
% Fraternity: 35%
% Sorority: 34%
% On-Campus (Freshman): 100%
% On-Campus (All Undergraduate): 66%

% African-American: 2%
% Asian: 6%
% Hispanic: 8%
% White: 65%
% Other: 7%
% Race or Ethnicity Unknown: 4%
% International: 8%
% Low-Income: 8%

ACADEMICS
Student-to-Faculty Ratio: 9:1
% of Classes Under 20: 68%
% of Classes Under 40: 98%
% Full-Time Faculty: 80%
% Full-Time Faculty w/ Terminal Degree: 92%

Top Programs
Art
Biology
Chemistry
Economics
Film and Media Studies
Philosophy
Politics

Retention Rate: 91%
4-Year Graduation Rate: 81%
6-Year Graduation Rate: 87%

Curricular Flexibility: Somewhat Flexible
Academic Rating: ★★★★

Inside the Classroom

Due to its location in Walla Walla, Washington, there are plenty of experienced high school guidance counselors around the country who have never even heard of Whitman College. Despite a lack of instant name recognition, you'll find Whitman side-by-side in the rankings with better-known West Coast liberal arts powerhouses like Colorado College, Pitzer, and Occidental. And there's a good reason for these accolades—few colleges in the Pacific Northwest offer the intimate and supportive academic and social environment available at Whitman. The 1,475 students at Whitman, all undergrads, are a collection of high school stars who possess a median SAT score of close to 1,400 and an A/A- average in a mostly AP slate of courses. With forty-nine majors and thirty-three minors, the academic offerings at this college are robust, particularly when considering its modest size.

The Encounters Program greets freshmen with a yearlong introduction to the liberal arts. Organized around a number of themes, those courses focus on "primary sources, discussion, writing, and the construction of knowledge across academic fields." Regardless of major, all students also must pass two courses in cultural pluralism, the humanities, the social sciences, fine arts, and the sciences as well as one course in quantitative analysis. Biology, environmental studies, geology, chemistry, economics, sociology, and politics majors are all required to complete a senior research thesis.

Whitman boasts a beautifully low 9:1 student-to-faculty ratio and hosts zero graduate students, a recipe for individualized attention. Over 90 percent of sections contain fewer than twenty-nine students. The faculty has a reputation for being extremely available, attentive, and invested in undergraduate education. Undergraduate research is so embedded into the foundation of a Whitman education that the college hosts an annual Undergraduate Conference for students to present their work. The school offers ample opportunity for students to work with faculty on research projects during the year or in the summer, and it also has forged partnerships with organizations like the Fred Hutchinson Cancer Research Center in Seattle that accepts a minimum of two Whitman students for a nine-week research endeavor each summer. Greater than 40 percent of juniors study abroad in one of eighty-eight programs in forty+ countries around the globe.

By major, the greatest number of degrees are typically conferred in the social sciences (24 percent), biology (17 percent), visual and performing arts (12 percent), physical science (9 percent), and psychology (7 percent). All degree programs have solid reputations, but the biology, politics, and economics departments all have an extra shine. Whitman also does an amazing job funneling students into the most prestigious postgraduate fellowship programs. Over the last decade Whitties have captured sixty-two Fulbright Scholarships, twenty-five National Science Foundation Fellowships, twelve Watson Fellowships, and even one Rhodes Scholarship.

Outside the Classroom

One might assume that a school with fewer than 1,500 undergraduates would house just about everyone, especially with a spacious 117-acre campus. However, only 63 percent of Whitman students reside in one of the four freshman-only dorms, four upperclassmen dorms, or the eleven Interest Houses centered around commonalities like fine arts, the environment, or Asian studies. You also might expect a West Coast liberal arts school like Whitman to be Greek free, or at least to have a minimal frat/sorority presence on campus, yet that is not at all the case. Roughly 35 percent of students join fraternities and sororities, but it is important to note that they are generally viewed as inclusive and laid-back collectives in contrast to many Greek organizations at large universities. There are fifteen varsity NCAA Division III sports teams as well as ten club and sixteen intramural squads. Forty-six percent of undergrads play intramurals, and 15 percent are varsity athletes. Of the close to one hundred student organizations on campus, the Outdoor Program is one of the most popular. Many students participate in its weekend hiking, kayaking, climbing, and skiing adventures. The school also had a run of award-winning debate teams prior to 2014, although it is presently in rebuilding mode. Walla Walla is technically a city, but it's more a of quaint and charming Pacific Northwestern small town. Seattle and Portland each are over a four-hour drive.

Career Services

The Student Engagement Center (SEC) at Whitman College employs eight professional staff members and eleven undergraduate employees, many of whom serve as peer advisors. The full-time professionals serve students through career coaching, community engagement, and internship coordination. Only counting those eight professionals, the SEC still comes out with a 184:1 student-to-advisor ratio, stronger than the vast majority of colleges profiled in this guide. Thanks to that terrific level of support, Whitties can schedule up to an hour of one-on-one career counseling whenever they like. The office lays out a Four Phase Plan that, beginning freshman year, helps students begin, develop, refine, and own their stories through job shadowing, internships, alumni networking, job fairs, community service, graduate school exploration, and professional development.

Community service is a major part of the Whitman experience, and the SEC facilitates experiential opportunities in Walla Walla for 320 students per week, and 70 percent of undergraduates participate each year. Many summer internships are arranged at local organizations like the Walla Walla Public Health Department, the Walla Walla Symphony, and a local minor league baseball team. The school is supportive of those wishing to spend their summers at nonprofits and funds more than 130 such internships per year. The Whitman Connect program helps link current students with the college's 16,000+ alumni, and seventy-five alumni and parents provide job-shadowing opportunities over spring break. The key to Whitman's career service success is its genuine ability to meaningfully connect and support every single undergraduate student. Despite a dearth of national companies visiting campus and mediocre salary statistics, this office can be counted on to provide individualized nurturing and career guidance.

Professional Outcomes

When you confer fewer than 400 degrees each year, you don't expect to have massive pockets of graduates joining major corporations. However, it is worth noting that twenty or more alumni currently work for Microsoft, Amazon, Boeing, Starbucks, T-Mobile, and Nordstrom. In the last few years, students have taken interesting first jobs including as a paralegal at the US Department of Justice-Antitrust Division, audio archivist at the Smithsonian, and marketing assistant at Oxford University Press. The largest number of Whitties settle in Seattle, but Portland, San Francisco, Los Angeles, New York, and Denver are other common destinations. Midcareer median pay is on the lower side among elite liberal arts schools, in the same range as the aforementioned Occidental and Reed as well as Kenyon, Vassar, and Macalester. Part of the lower median pay figure may be attributable to the high number of Whitman alumni who are continuing their educations well into their late twenties and early thirties.

Over 60 percent of Whitman graduates continue their educations at a wide range of graduate and professional programs. Since 2009, the school has sent graduates to law schools such as Berkeley, the University of Washington, Columbia, Georgetown, Duke, the University of Pennsylvania, and the University of Chicago. In that same time, premed students have headed to elite medical programs at Northwestern, UVA, Dartmouth, and Stanford. A significant number of Whitman grads go on to earn PhDs in the sciences; the school ranks in the top fifty nationwide in that department. While many attend elite graduate/professional programs, plenty of other grads head to West Coast publics like Colorado State University, Oregon State University, and Washington State University.

Admission

Whitman's 50 percent acceptance rate for the Class of 2022 represented an average number for the college, but it should be eye-opening for any teens looking for an elite school on the West Coast. It's important to note that this applicant pool is self-selecting; the mid-50 percent test scores of attending freshmen are 1280-1440 on the SAT and 29-32 on the ACT. Fifty-two percent hail from the top decile of their high school class, and 82 percent placed in the top quartile. The average unweighted GPA was a 3.66, and 45 percent of applicants earned above a 3.75. Whitman is the rare elite college that has become slightly easier to get into in recent years. A decade ago, the acceptance rate was 46 percent, SAT/ACT scores were comparable, 72 percent earned a GPA over 3.75, and a whopping 71 percent finished in the top 10 percent of their high school cohorts.

Rigor of academic record, GPA, and the application essay form the triumvirate of "most important" factors in the eyes of the committee. Recommendations, extracurricular activities, talent/ability, and character/personal characteristics are next in order importance followed by the merely "considered" factors of standardized test scores and class rank. In 2018, the college received 179 early decision applications and welcomed 71 percent into the fold, demonstrating a clear advantage for those willing to commit through ED. The admissions committee states that it is seeking "curious, inspired, and highly engaged students with a passion for learning and a wide and eclectic range of interests; the kind of independent-minded students who are motivated to take intellectual risks in order to become the kind of leaders who can make a difference in the world." The school's admissions practices seem to support that sentiment.

Worth Your Money?

The cost of attendance at Whitman is $69,500, not an unexpected amount for a liberal arts college with such an intimate classroom and campus environment. Fortunately, approximately half of Whitman undergrads qualify for need-based aid with an average annual award of more than $36,000. For those who receive a generous merit or need-based offer, Whitman can absolutely be worth your money; at full price, this may not be the best choice for families lacking the funds to pay the costs up front.

FINANCIAL
Institutional Type: Private
In-State Tuition: $53,820
Out-of-State Tuition: $53,820
Room & Board: $13,512
Required Fees: $400
Books & Supplies: $1,400

Avg. Need-Based Aid: $36,323
Avg. % of Need Met: 92%

Avg. Merit-Based Aid: $13,429
% Receiving Merit-Based Aid: 61%

Avg. Cumulative Debt: $25,356
% of Students Borrowing: 43%

CAREER
Who Recruits
1. The Spur Group
2. Peace Corps
3. Baker Boyer Bank
4. TFA
5. Pacific Northwest National Laboratory

Notable Internships
1. WebMD
2. U.S. House of Representatives
3. Bloomsbury USA

Top Industries
1. Business
2. Education
3. Operations
4. Social Services
5. Research

Top Employers
1. Microsoft
2. Amazon
3. Boeing
4. The Spur Group
5. T-Mobile

Where Alumni Work
1. Seattle
2. Portland, OR
3. San Francisco
4. Richland, WA
5. Los Angeles

Median Earnings
College Scorecard (Early Career): $51,300
EOP (Early Career): $48,500
PayScale (Mid-Career): $102,600

RANKINGS
Forbes: 89
Money: 545
U.S. News: 46, Liberal Arts Colleges
Wall Street Journal/THE: 101 (T)
Washington Monthly: 90, Liberal Arts Colleges

#CollegesWorthYourMoney

Williams College

Williamstown, Massachusetts | Admissions Phone: 413-597-2211

ADMISSION
Admission Rate: 13%
Admission Rate - Men: 13%
Admission Rate - Women: 13%
EA Admission Rate: Not Offered
ED Admission Rate: 34%
Admission Rate (5-Year Trend): -5%
ED Admission Rate (5-Year Trend): -6%
% of Admits Attending (Yield): 43%
Transfer Admission Rate: 3%

Offered Wait List: 1,772
Accepted Wait List: 653
Admitted Wait List: 76

SAT Reading/Writing (Middle 50%): 710-760
SAT Math (Middle 50%): 700-790
ACT Composite (Middle 50%): 32-35
Testing Policy: ACT/SAT Required
SAT Superscore: Yes
ACT Superscore: Yes

% Graduated in Top 10% of HS Class: 89%
% Graduated in Top 25% of HS Class: 97%
% Graduated in Top 50% of HS Class: 100%

ENROLLMENT
Total Undergraduate Enrollment: 2,073
% Part-Time: 3%
% Male: 52%
% Female: 48%
% Out-of-State: 86%
% Fraternity: Not Offered
% Sorority: Not Offered
% On-Campus (Freshman): 100%
% On-Campus (All Undergraduate): 93%

% African-American: 8%
% Asian: 12%
% Hispanic: 13%
% White: 51%
% Other: 5%
% Race or Ethnicity Unknown: 3%
% International: 8%
% Low-Income: 19%

ACADEMICS
Student-to-Faculty Ratio: 7:1
% of Classes Under 20: 77%
% of Classes Under 40: 95%
% Full-Time Faculty: 83%
% Full-Time Faculty w/ Terminal Degree: 97%

Top Programs
Art
Biology
Computer Science
Economics
English
History
Math
Political Science

Retention Rate: 99%
4-Year Graduation Rate: 90%
6-Year Graduation Rate: 95%

Curricular Flexibility: Very Flexible
Academic Rating: ★★★★★

Inside the Classroom

Massachusetts is home to many of the finest and most historic institutions of higher learning in the United States. Starting in Boston and traveling west you would encounter many schools featured in this book—MIT, Harvard, BU, BC, Northeastern, Tufts, Brandeis, Wellesley—and, eventually, the more remote campuses of Amherst and Mount Holyoke and, lastly, tucked in the Northwest corner of the state just below Vermont you would encounter the Bay State's second-oldest school and one of the most prestigious liberal arts schools in the entire country, Williams College. Set on 450 rural acres in the Berkshires, Williams educates just over 2,000 of the brightest and most talented undergraduates one can find. The school's twenty-five academic departments offer thirty-six majors and a number of concentrations rather than minors

Students only take thirty-two total courses—four per semester—as opposed to the standard five. A Winter Study session also runs for twenty-two days in January when students can dedicate all of their attention to one course. Prior to graduation students must complete three courses in each of three Divisions: Languages and the Arts, Social Studies, and Science and Mathematics. Additionally, two writing-intensive courses and one course in quantitative reasoning are required. Rare for a liberal arts school of this caliber, no foreign language is required. Instead, the option exists to take a class exploring how different cultures interact with one another. While not quite as open as the curriculum at Brown or Amherst, Williams certainly gives its students their fair share of autonomy when it comes to course selection.

The college possesses an excellent 7:1 student-faculty ratio, and 99 percent of professorial attention goes to undergrads (they only run two small graduate programs). An unparalleled 44 percent of courses have fewer than ten students enrolled; over three-quarters have an enrollment under twenty. Thanks to relationships built with faculty through such small classes, one Williams student said, "Students often just need to talk to a professor to find a research opportunity." However, many formal opportunities to engage in undergraduate research exist in the summer, during a semester, or as part of one's senior honors thesis. Close to 50 percent of the junior class connects with the International Education and Study Away program to pinpoint the study abroad opportunity that is right for them. Included on that menu is the opportunity to study at Oxford for an entire year.

The greatest number of degrees are conferred in the social sciences (25 percent), math and statistics (12 percent), biology (9 percent), and foreign languages (8 percent). Any degree from Williams will be viewed most favorably by graduate schools and employers, but programs in economics, English, history, math and political science are especially renowned. The college also produces a massive number of highly competitive national fellowship winners. In 2018, grads and alums won twenty Fulbright Scholarships, nine NSF Graduate Research Fellowships, and a Gates Cambridge, a Watson, and a Schwarzman. In the last five years two graduates have been named Rhodes Scholars.

Outside the Classroom

For a supremely studious, tiny liberal enclave buried in the woods, Williams is unexpectedly sports-centric within the NCAA Division III. The Ephs (a shortened version of Ephraim Williams, the school's founder) compete in thirty-two varsity sports, most of which are members of the New England Small College Athletic Conference. Overall, 35 percent of the student body competes in intercollegiate sports, and many more join intramural athletic clubs. Fraternities were banished from campus more than fifty years ago, just before the school became co-educational. In the absence of Greek life, extracurriculars take on a larger social role as 96 percent of Williams undergrads are involved in at least one of the 150 outside-the-classroom organizations. Situated in the Berkshires, there is no big city that makes an easy day trip (Boston and NYC are two or three hours away), but natural beauty is ubiquitous. The largest student-run group, the Williams Outing Club, has 750 members who engage in regular hikes, campouts, and polar bear swims in the Williamstown wilderness. The vast majority of the student body—93 percent—live on campus, making the school's breathtaking residence halls the epicenter of social activity. Freshmen live together in one of two large, nearly identical residence halls that form the bustling Frosh Quad. Upperclassmen reside in one of twenty-seven more modestly sized buildings.

Career Services

The '68 Center for Career Exploration (CCE) employs thirteen full-time staff members who focus on career advising, alumni relations, and employer relations. Specialized help is available for those eying law school, a health profession, entrepreneurship, or a career in technology. The center's 160:1 student-to-advisor ratio is one of the best of any school featured in this guide. Major events hosted by the center's crew include the Fall Job and Internship Fair that is attended by seventy employers including big names like Bain, Credit Suisse, Deloitte, Epic Systems, *The New York Times*, and T. Rowe Price. The Spring Job & Internship Fair is primarily focused on nonprofit employers.

Williams College

Williams alumni are extremely available and willing to lend a hand to current students, and 65 percent of current students report consulting with an alum to plan their next steps after college. Additionally, alumni sponsored internships provide 143 undergraduates with a $3,800 stipend to pursue non-paying summer internships. The center also has introduced a new program of winter study internships with an alum. On-campus interviews are brokered through the CCE, but no data is available on the number of interviews taking place or about on-campus recruiting, although a fair amount of both definitely occur. The college recently identified its tracking of alumni outcomes as being an area of weakness, and it has begun making strides toward remedying the situation. Thanks to its superhuman work getting students into top graduate schools, the '68 Center for Career Exploration still has a glowing reputation.

Professional Outcomes

The top three areas of gain that Williams graduates self-report are thinking critically, writing clearly and effectively, and the ability to learn on their own. It's hard to name three traits that speak more to one's employability, so it shouldn't come as a shock that the most desirable employers adore the school's alumni. Companies/organizations that consistently snatch-up Williams graduates include Apple, Google, Goldman Sachs, McKinsey & Co., the Metropolitan Museum of Art, National Institutes of Health, and the New York Times Co. A significant number of students join the Peace Corps or are accepted into Teach for America. Business and education are the industries that attract the most students. At age thirty-four Williams grads earn a median income similar to Brandeis alums but a bit less than graduates of comparable Amherst. New York City, Boston, and San Francisco are the three cities most favored by Ephs post-undergrad.

For Ephs the bachelor's degrees earned at Williams are unlikely to be their last diplomas. Approximately 75 percent pursue an advanced degree within five years of leaving the college. The most frequently attended graduate programs are a not-too-shabby trio of Harvard, Columbia, and Yale. The top business, law, and medical schools attracting grads are Harvard, Columbia, and Penn. Using LinkedIn data we were able to determine that Williams College sends one of the highest percentages of graduates to prestigious medical schools of any institution in the country. It also ranked eighth overall on our list of the top producers of future PhDs and was the second-leading producer of economics PhDs.

Admission

Williams' Class of 2022 admissions data looks extremely similar to that of rival Amherst. The acceptance rate was 13 percent, and the average standardized test scores of admitted students was a 1480 on the SAT and a 33 on the ACT. Only 6 percent of those offered admission were not in the top 10 percent of their high school class. Nothing earth-shattering has occurred in Williams' admissions standards in recent years. Like many comparably ultra-selective liberal arts colleges, the admit rate has declined. In 2011, the college accepted 17 percent of the applicant pool. The profile of the average enrollee has edged closer to perfection in that time with the median freshman in 2011 possessing a 1430 SAT score; in 2018-19, the mid-50 range was 1410-1550.

The admissions office views all of the meat-and-potatoes factors as holding the most weight: rigorous schedule, test scores, class rank, and GPA, but recommendations are carefully read as well. The next tier of criteria include race/ethnicity, legacy status (roughly 14 percent of admitted students are legacies, mostly of the primary variety), first-generation status (17 percent fit that bill), and factors like volunteer and work experience. Williams seeks a racially and socioeconomically diverse group of uniquely talented students who will thrive in a close-knit academic community. However, few Hail Mary heaves end successfully here. To quantify that point, you can count on one hand the percentage of admitted applicants who scored less than 650 on a section of the SAT. Yes, it's that competitive.

Worth Your Money?

The annual cost of attendance at Williams is, in the world of elite liberal arts schools in New England, priced at the almost-standard $75,000, but those who aren't from wealthy backgrounds will pay far less. In fact, roughly half the student population qualifies for aid, and of that group all students have 100 percent of their financial need met with the average award being $57k. For the rich, the Williams bill won't sting too badly; for those in the lower-to-middle income brackets, the school will slice the cost significantly. For those in between, Williams is the caliber of school that is worth taking on debt in order to attend. Learning in seminar-style courses from some of the brightest minds around is worth paying for, and the connections you make (to peers and faculty) will stay with you for a lifetime.

FINANCIAL
Institutional Type: Private
In-State Tuition: $56,970
Out-of-State Tuition: $56,970
Room & Board: $14,990
Required Fees: $310
Books & Supplies: $800

Avg. Need-Based Aid: $56,933
Avg. % of Need Met: 100%

Avg. Merit-Based Aid: $0
% Receiving Merit-Based Aid: 0%

Avg. Cumulative Debt: $15,496
% of Students Borrowing: 41%

CAREER
Who Recruits
1. OC&C Strategy Consultants
2. Teach for America
3. M&T Bank
4. InterSystems
5. Trinity Industries

Notable Internships
1. WeWork
2. Late Night with Seth Meyers
3. Whitney Museum of American Art

Top Industries
1. Business
2. Education
3. Research
4. Finance
5. Social Services

Top Employers
1. Google
2. Goldman Sachs
3. Morgan Stanley
4. JPMorgan Chase
5. Bain & Company

Where Alumni Work
1. New York City
2. Boston
3. San Francisco
4. Washington, DC
5. Albany, NY

Median Earnings
College Scorecard (Early Career): $59,000
EOP (Early Career): $62,600
PayScale (Mid-Career): $127,500

RANKINGS
Forbes: 19
Money: 39
U.S. News: 1, Liberal Arts Colleges
Wall Street Journal/THE: 21
Washington Monthly: 12, Liberal Arts Colleges

#CollegesWorthYourMoney

Worcester Polytechnic Institute

Worcester, Massachusetts | Admissions Phone: 508-831-5286

ADMISSION
Admission Rate: 42%
Admission Rate - Men: 38%
Admission Rate - Women: 53%
EA Admission Rate: 65%
ED Admission Rate: Not Offered
Admission Rate (5-Year Trend): -10%
ED Admission Rate (5-Year Trend): Not Offered
% of Admits Attending (Yield): 29%
Transfer Admission Rate: 37%

Offered Wait List: 3,202
Accepted Wait List: 1,092
Admitted Wait List: 153

SAT Reading/Writing (Middle 50%): 630-710
SAT Math (Middle 50%): 670-750
ACT Composite (Middle 50%): 29-33
Testing Policy: Test Optional
SAT Superscore: No
ACT Superscore: No

% Graduated in Top 10% of HS Class: 64%
% Graduated in Top 25% of HS Class: 93%
% Graduated in Top 50% of HS Class: 100%

ENROLLMENT
Total Undergraduate Enrollment: 4,668
% Part-Time: 3%
% Male: 62%
% Female: 38%
% Out-of-State: 55%
% Fraternity: 33%
% Sorority: 36%
% On-Campus (Freshman): 97%
% On-Campus (All Undergraduate): 49%

% African-American: 3%
% Asian: 5%
% Hispanic: 9%
% White: 62%
% Other: 2%
% Race or Ethnicity Unknown: 8%
% International: 9%
% Low-Income: 14%

ACADEMICS
Student-to-Faculty Ratio: 13:1
% of Classes Under 20: 64%
% of Classes Under 40: 86%
% Full-Time Faculty: 83%
% Full-Time Faculty w/ Terminal Degree: 89%

Top Programs
Aerospace Engineering
Biomedical Engineering
Chemical Engineering
Computer Science
Mathematical Sciences
Mechanical Engineering
Robotics Engineering

Retention Rate: 96%
4-Year Graduation Rate: 82%
6-Year Graduation Rate: 87%

Curricular Flexibility: Somewhat Flexible
Academic Rating: ★★★★

Inside the Classroom

Worcester Polytechnic Institute, commonly referred to as WPI, is a small-to-midsize private university that is one of the fastest-growing PhD-granting schools in the United States. More than 4,300 undergraduate students and an additional 2,000+ graduate students attend school in Worcester, a city roughly fifty miles, as the crow flies, from Boston. Working on a quarter schedule, students engage in three courses for seven-week sprints as they plow through one of fifty+ rigorous degree programs, primarily in engineering.

An education at WPI is as hands-on and innovative as you will find at any university, engineering-centric or otherwise. The Interactive Qualifying Project (IPQ), often completed off campus, features work in small teams on a project that "connects science and technology with social issues and human need." The Major Qualifying Project (MQP) is a unique capstone experience in which students must identify a real-world problem and find a novel solution. A host of industry partners work with students in the MQPs. Students can participate in a four-to-eight-month paid co-op experience as part of their undergraduate experience. Core academic requirements for all undergrads also include a foray into the humanities and arts as the school seeks to produce well-rounded, team-player engineers.

With a student-to-faculty ratio of 13:1, WPI does an exceptional job keeping undergraduate classrooms cozy. In fact, a staggering 52 percent of its classes enroll fewer than ten students, creating an incredible level of academic intimacy. There are some large lecture hall courses mixed in—11 percent of sections contain more than 50 students—but WPI's level of individualized attention and small group instruction is hard to find, even at an elite liberal arts college. All students complete a minimum of two long-term research projects that are focused on solving real-world problems. That process begins freshman year, and by senior year 72 percent have engaged in off-campus research as well. Studying abroad, like most things at WPI, is not a typical experience. Many undergrads travel to one of fifty+ project centers situated on six continents where they can engage in solving real-life problems. Beginning with the Class of 2022, the school began awarding every single student $5,000 in study abroad funding with an aim toward a 90 percent participation rate within the next few years.

The undergraduate engineering program is respected worldwide and frequently graces lists of top schools for a variety of sub-disciplines. The most popular majors are mechanical engineering (19 percent), computer science (15 percent), biomedical engineering (9 percent), robotics engineering (8 percent), and chemical engineering (8 percent). Those completing all of those programs find favorable conditions as they approach graduate schools, potential employers, and prestigious national scholarship organizations. WPI undergrads have won nineteen Gilman Scholarships in the past two years and between two and five National Science Foundation Graduate Research Fellowships per year (plus many honorable mentions).

Outside the Classroom

Housing on campus is guaranteed only to freshmen; approximately three-fifths of all undergrads live on WPI's concentrated ninety-five-acre campus. Many other students reside in one of the school's nineteen fraternities and sororities; 33 percent of men and 36 percent of women go Greek. It is worth noting that women make up only 36 percent of the undergraduate student population. Twenty varsity sports teams, evenly split between men's and women's squads, compete as the Engineers in NCAA Division III. Another forty-four combined club and intramural teams and the four-floor, state-of-the-art Sports and Recreation Center that houses a pool ensure that physical activity is accessible to all. There are 225 clubs and activities that include original offerings like underwater hockey, a Rubik's Cube club, and a lock-picking club. Hey, no one would ever argue that WPI students aren't extremely creative. Of course, there are many traditional options also on the menu, including a multitude of organizations geared toward young professionals and shared academic interests. Boston is doable day trip, but there is plenty to do right in Worcester, including bustling Shrewsbury Street, museums, theaters, and loads of eateries. A growing urban area that still possesses the charm of a small-college town, Worcester can easily be navigated via public transit.

Career Services

The Career Development Center (CDC) consists of eleven professional employees, which works out to a student-to-advisor ratio of 403:1, in the average range compared to other schools featured in this guide. The staff is comprised of career counselors, corporate relations specialists, and recruiting coordinators. Students at WPI report an exceptionally high rate of satisfaction with their school's career services offerings for reasons that are obvious when you examine the basic facts.

Worcester Polytechnic Institute

E-mail: admissions@wpi.edu | Website: www.wpi.edu

An extraordinary 80 percent of all undergraduates, including freshmen and sophomores, interact with the CDC in some capacity each year. In the 2017-18 academic year 450 companies recruited on WPI's campus at career fairs, networking events, or on-campus job interviews. Annually, hundreds of students participate in summer internships or co-op placements that help them expand their network of career resources; the school's many corporate partners are always willing to take on WPI interns. In addition to strongly encouraging one-on-one counseling appointments, the office provides services like corporate tours, an employer-in-residence program, corporate information sessions, panel discussions, and a robust online system that allows students to connect with alumni and potential employers. Considering its highly accessible and broad array of offerings as well as positive professional and graduate school outcomes for alumni, the Worcester Polytechnic Institute's Career Development Center receives high marks from our staff.

Professional Outcomes

Within six months of graduation, 93 percent of Class of 2018 members had progressed beyond the seeking phase and had landed jobs or enrolled full time in graduate school. Companies employing literally hundreds of WPI alumni of all ages include Raytheon, Pratt & Whitney, Dell, and BAE Systems. Class of 2018 graduates found jobs at companies that included Air BNB, DraftKings, Amazon Robotics, NASA, Harvard Medical School, the US Department of Defense, and SpaceX. The average starting salary crept above $69,000 and is currently among the highest of any in the country, impressive even for a school focused entirely on STEM disciplines. Within the state of Massachusetts, only MIT sports higher graduate starting salary figures. WPI graduates most frequently remain in Greater Boston, but significant numbers relocate to New York City, Hartford, San Francisco, and Providence.

Nineteen percent of recent diploma-earners elected to immediately begin work on an advanced degree. Elite graduate schools attended by Class of 2018 grads included Duke, Columbia, Carnegie Mellon, Johns Hopkins, Harvard, Brown, Stanford, and NYU. Premed students enjoy the university's early/assured acceptance arrangements with Tufts Veterinary School, Massachusetts College of Pharmacy & Health Sciences, and Lake Erie College of Osteopathic Medicine. Recent grads have been accepted into medical school at the likes of Dartmouth, Northwestern, and Cornell.

Admission

WPI became the first top engineering university to adopt a test-optional policy in 2007, and it remains a rare breed among STEM-focused institutions. That decision has contributed to the school now receiving over 10,500 applications versus roughly 7,000 one decade ago. The acceptance rate for a place in the 2018-19 freshman class was 41.5 percent. Within that cohort 64 percent finished in the top 10 percent of their high school class while 93 percent placed in the top quartile. The average GPA was 3.89, and more than four-fifths of the group possessed a GPA above a 3.75. Among those submitting standardized test scores, the mid-50 percent on the SAT was 1300-1460, and it was 29-33 on the ACT.

Rigor of secondary school record and GPA are the only two factors deemed "very important" by the Worcester Admissions Committee. Interestingly, despite being test-optional, standardized test scores are among the factors considered "important" by the school along with class rank, recommendations, extracurricular activities, and character/personal qualities. Seventy percent of enrolled members of the Class of 2022 did, in fact, submit SAT scores and 25 percent submitted ACT scores, suggesting that only a small number of test-optional candidates are successful. It is worth noting that, as at most engineering schools, women enjoy a higher acceptance rate than men. At WPI that disparity is more pronounced than is typical; female applicants gain acceptance 53 percent of the time, and men get in at a 37.5 percent clip. There is no binding early decision option at WPI, only early action. Valuing students who are "creative and curious," who "enjoy working together to get things done," and "feel pretty sure that they're leaders, not followers," the Worcester Polytechnic Institute Admissions Committee is looking for passionate candidates who possess strong grades in AP courses and, in many cases, superior test scores.

Worth Your Money?

If your family can afford WPI, you will likely recoup a sizable portion of the $70,000 cost of attendance. Just over half of accepted students do receive a merit aid package averaging $16,235 per year, which knocks the cost down a bit. Fortunately, with such high starting salaries for recent graduates, paying $200,000 plus for an undergraduate degree from this school is not at all an unwise investment. Thirty-eight percent of students who apply for need-based aid do see 100 percent of their need met. In total, 61 percent of attending undergrads receive some level of merit-based grant that averages $24,500.

FINANCIAL
Institutional Type: Private
In-State Tuition: $51,604
Out-of-State Tuition: $51,604
Room & Board: $15,292
Required Fees: $916
Books & Supplies: $1,000

Avg. Need-Based Aid: $24,500
Avg. % of Need Met: 82%

Avg. Merit-Based Aid: $16,235
% Receiving Merit-Based Aid: 52%

Avg. Cumulative Debt: $27,000
% of Students Borrowing: N/A

CAREER
Who Recruits
1. PepsiCo
2. BAE Systems
3. General Electric
4. Travelers
5. Raytheon

Notable Internships
1. ExxonMobil
2. Dell
3. State Street

Top Industries
1. Engineering
2. Operations
3. Business
4. Information Technology
5. Research

Top Employers
1. Raytheon
2. Pratt & Whitney
3. Dell
4. National Grid
5. Google

Where Alumni Work
1. Boston
2. New York City
3. Hartford, CT
4. San Francisco
5. Providence, RI

Median Earnings
College Scorecard (Early Career): $84,900
EOP (Early Career): $85,200
PayScale (Mid-Career): $135,500

RANKINGS
Forbes: 93
Money: 148
U.S. News: 64, National Universities
Wall Street Journal/THE: 119
Washington Monthly: 116, National Universities

#CollegesWorthYourMoney

Yale University

New Haven, Connecticut | Admissions Phone: 203-432-9300

ADMISSION
Admission Rate: 6%
Admission Rate - Men: 7%
Admission Rate - Women: 6%
EA Admission Rate: N/A
ED Admission Rate: Not Offered
Admission Rate (5-Year Trend): -1%
ED Admission Rate (5-Year Trend): Not Offered
% of Admits Attending (Yield): 70%
Transfer Admission Rate: 2%

Offered Wait List: N/A
Accepted Wait List: N/A
Admitted Wait List: N/A

SAT Reading/Writing (Middle 50%): 720-770
SAT Math (Middle 50%): 730-790
ACT Composite (Middle 50%): 33-35
Testing Policy: ACT/SAT Required
SAT Superscore: Yes
ACT Superscore: Yes

% Graduated in Top 10% of HS Class: 95%
% Graduated in Top 25% of HS Class: 99%
% Graduated in Top 50% of HS Class: 100%

ENROLLMENT
Total Undergraduate Enrollment: 5,964
% Part-Time: 0%
% Male: 50%
% Female: 50%
% Out-of-State: 92%
% Fraternity: 10%
% Sorority: 10%
% On-Campus (Freshman): 100%
% On-Campus (All Undergraduate): 84%

% African-American: 8%
% Asian: 19%
% Hispanic: 13%
% White: 42%
% Other: 6%
% Race or Ethnicity Unknown: 0%
% International: 11%
% Low-Income: 13%

ACADEMICS
Student-to-Faculty Ratio: 6:1
% of Classes Under 20: 73%
% of Classes Under 40: 88%
% Full-Time Faculty: 68%
% Full-Time Faculty w/ Terminal Degree: 88%

Top Programs
Biology
Computer Science
Economics
Engineering
Global Affairs
History
Political Science
Psychology

Retention Rate: 99%
4-Year Graduation Rate: 88%
6-Year Graduation Rate: 97%

Curricular Flexibility: Somewhat Flexible
Academic Rating: ★★★★★

Inside the Classroom

World leaders, Supreme Court justices, scores of famous actors, inventors, writers, Nobel Laureates, billionaire businessmen, even fictional billionaire businessmen like The Simpsons' Mr. Burns…the list of Yale alumni fills multiple volumes of history books. Founded in 1701 as a more conservative, Puritan-rooted option to Harvard, the home of the Bulldogs is today elite, even by Ivy standards, every bit as much so as its Crimson rival of over 300 years. New Haven, Connecticut, is the destination for 5,700 undergraduates and more than 6,800 graduate students yet, thanks to the nurturing Residential College housing system, the university serves as an intimate undergraduate home while still playing the role of major private research university.

There are eighty majors and 2,000 undergraduate course offerings at Yale. Economics (13 percent), political science (9 percent), history (6 percent), biology (6 percent), and psychology (5 percent) are the university's most popular areas of concentration. In aiming to strike a balance between freedom and control, the required course-work at Yale is modest and relatively broad. Students must take courses in the natural sciences, the humanities and arts, the social sciences, foreign language, quantitative reasoning, and writing. Most majors require a one-to-two semester senior capstone experience. Depending on the major, students work closely with a professor toward the completion of an essay, portfolio, or research project.

The student-to-faculty ratio of 6:1 does translate to small class sizes, even with a larger number of graduate students on campus than undergrads. Three-quarters of classes have an enrollment of fewer than twenty students, making for a perfect environment for teaching and learning. Undergraduate research is a staple of the Yale academic experience; 95 percent of science majors participate in research with faculty and, universi-ty-wide, undergraduate research fellowships are available to 90 percent of first-years who apply. In short, you'd have to try very hard to avoid engaging in research while an undergraduate at Yale. The number of Bulldogs electing to study abroad has skyrocketed in recent years, but that explosion is relative. As with most Ivies the overall percentage who take a semester abroad remains only a sliver of the student body.

Many of Yale's undergraduate programs sit atop any major rankings list. Among the crème de la crème depart-ments are biology, economics, global affairs, engineering, history, and computer science. Any degree from Yale will get your resume/application to employers or graduate schools on the top of the pile. The same goes for applications to competitive post-college scholarships, including the uber-prestigious Rhodes Scholarship. Yalies have captured the award 245 times, second only to Harvard in the all-time rankings. More than one hundred Yale students have captured Fulbright Scholarships, making it one of the leading producers in the country.

Outside the Classroom

With 319 years of history and a $29 billion endowment, Yale's 345-acre, tree-lined campus is a blend of beautiful stone edifices and modern amenities. Perhaps the most distinctive feature of life outside the classroom at Yale is the famed Residential College system that was imported from Oxford/Cambridge seventy years ago to facilitate a level of cohesiveness and connection typically only found at smaller liberal arts schools. Students are assigned to one of fourteen residential colleges that they will remain affiliated with for all four years. Each residence has two full-time, live-in faculty members. Greek life is not a dominant presence as only 10 percent of Yalies join a frat or sorority. So-called "secret societies," of which there are approximately forty, attract roughly half of seniors. Those include the famed Skull and Bones society, which has infiltrated American pop culture. Athletics are big-time at Yale as the Bulldogs field thirty-five NCAA Division I sports teams. An additional fifty club teams and thirty intramural sports are available for non-varsity athletes. Other student-run organizations include sixty cultural groups and fifty performance groups. Those seeking nature can canoe and camp on the 1,500 acres of the school's Outdoor Education Center or walk to the Yale Farm. Amenities and attractions include twelve dining halls, three on-campus museums, two theaters, and a library with 15 million holdings. Yale is situated in the middle of downtown New Haven, and the area is easily walkable. Boston and New York are each roughly a two-hour drive from New Haven.

Career Services

The Yale Office of Career Strategy (OCS) has thirteen professional staff members (excluding administrative assistants and counselors who only deal with graduate students) who are dedicated to tasks such as employer relations, career counseling, and summer funding opportunities. The 442:1 student-to-advisor ratio is within the average range when compared to other schools featured in this book. Still, the OCS has no shortage of brag-worthy statistics attached to its name.

For starters, in the 2017-18 academic year a staggering 13,062 current students and alumni engaged with the Office of Career Strategy, including over 4,300 one-on-one sessions with undergraduates. That same academic year the office hosted more than one hundred workshops and career exploration events that were attended by 6,300+ students. The OCS also hosted thirteen industry-specific career fairs that attracted 200 companies/organizations and close to 1,900 current students. Eighty-five top employers engaged in on-campus recruiting, and 500 students were granted interviews on Yale's grounds. The results are as impressive as the process—86 percent of Class of 2018 graduates reported that they were employed in an area directly related to their area of study. Yale students universally fill their summers with productive activities, often beginning immediately after their freshman year. By senior year 38 percent had spent the previous summer at a paid internship, 15 percent at an unpaid internship, 11 percent in laboratory research, 9 percent in academic study, and 5 percent in field research.

Professional Outcomes

Shortly after graduating 74 percent of the Yale Class of 2018 had entered the world of employment, 17 percent matriculated in graduate programs, and fewer than 2 percent were still looking for their next destination. The most common industries entered by the newly hired were finance (17 percent), education (16 percent), consulting (13 percent), technology (11 percent), and health care/medical/pharmaceutical (10 percent). Sixty-four percent of jobholders worked in the for-profit world while 35 percent worked in the nonprofit/government sectors. Starting salaries of more than $50,000 were earned by 67 percent of Class of 2018 grads, and 44 percent were awarded salaries of more than $70,000. The average starting salary was $64,642. Hundreds of Yale alums can be found at each of the world's top companies including Facebook, Google, Goldman Sachs, McKinsey & Company, Morgan Stanley, and Microsoft. Geographically, New York City has the highest concentration of alumni followed by San Francisco, Boston, DC, Los Angeles, and Chicago.

Using Class of 2017 data, among those pursuing graduate/professional programs 40 percent were pursuing a master's degree, 20 percent were in medical school, one-quarter started work on a PhD, and 6 percent went directly from undergraduate studies to law school. Unsurprisingly, given the quality of the minds admitted into Yale, medical school applicants traditionally find a home 90 percent of the time, exactly twice the national average; however, in 2018, that number was "only" 80 percent. Law school applicants do just fine as well; 87 percent were accepted into at least one school with a substantial number continuing at Yale Law School (YLS). Roughly 10 percent of YLS first-years attended Yale as undergraduates. For a complete list of where Yale alumni as a whole continue their educational journeys, simply consult a list of the best graduate/professional programs in the world.

Admission

Yale received over 35,000 applications for a place in the Class of 2022, but a meager 6.3 percent made it through the gates. Of those admitted, 95 percent placed in the top decile of their high school graduating class. The mid-50 percent range on the SAT was 1450-1560; the ACT span was 33-35. For an even better idea of the testing mastery required to become a Bulldog, look to the fact that 86 percent had an SAT Reading score of over 700, and 88 percent had an SAT Math score over 700.

You can bet a school that rejects nearly 94 percent of applicants relies on more than a few data points. The admissions committee ranks nine factors as being "most important": rigor of secondary record, GPA, class rank, standardized test scores (SAT Subject Test scores are recommended), application essay, recommendations, extracurricular activities, talent/ability, and character/personal qualities. The committee uses two overarching questions to guide its process: "Who is likely to make the most of Yale's resources?" and "Who will contribute most significantly to the Yale community?" Yale offers a unique single-choice early action (SCEA) option with a November 1 deadline. Those going that route are not bound to attend the university if accepted, but they cannot simultaneously apply ED or EA to any other school. Of the 6,016 SCEA applicants for the 2019-20 freshman cohort, 794 were admitted, a 13 percent success rate. More 2018-19 freshmen were first-generation students (18 percent) than legacy admits (11 percent). Getting into Yale is a hard-to-predict enterprise that sees many valedictorians and salutatorians bite the dust. Fantastic numbers along with a record of special talents and accomplishments that scream "future leader" will fare best.

Worth Your Money?

Yale is one of those rare schools where the contacts and networks you create while attending will make the education worth any cost. Fortunately, thanks to a $30 billion endowment, every single student who qualifies for need-based aid sees 100 percent of that need met by the university. The average grant is for $57,954, significantly reducing the sticker price cost of attendance of almost $76,000. There is no merit aid awarded by Yale, so those not in financial need will be paying full freight, but again, that will be money well spent.

FINANCIAL
Institutional Type: Private
In-State Tuition: $55,500
Out-of-State Tuition: $55,500
Room & Board: $16,600
Required Fees: N/A
Books & Supplies: $3,670

Avg. Need-Based Aid: $57,954
Avg. % of Need Met: 100%

Avg. Merit-Based Aid: $0
% Receiving Merit-Based Aid: 0%

Avg. Cumulative Debt: $14,575
% of Students Borrowing: 16%

CAREER
Who Recruits
1. The New York Times
2. Uber
3. Citi
4. Bain & Company
5. Boston Consulting Group

Notable Internships
1. Netflix
2. The Blackstone Group
3. United Nations

Top Industries
1. Business
2. Education
3. Research
4. Media
5. Operations

Top Employers
1. Google
2. McKinsey & Company
3. Goldman Sachs
4. Facebook
5. Morgan Stanley

Where Alumni Work
1. New York City
2. San Francisco
3. Boston
4. Washington, DC
5. Los Angeles

Median Earnings
College Scorecard (Early Career): $83,200
EOP (Early Career): $76,000
PayScale (Mid-Career): $138,300

RANKINGS
Forbes: 3
Money: 17
U.S. News: 3, National Universities
Wall Street Journal/THE: 3
Washington Monthly: 4, National Universities

#CollegesWorthYourMoney

Included in each school profile, we highlighted the academic programs that are among the very best on that particular campus. The next natural step is to look at top programs across all schools so that you can emerge with a bird's-eye picture of the premier American colleges in your major of interest. We included more than several dozen of the most popular areas of concentration in order to make these lists as useful and relevant to our audience as is possible.

For more useful lists, including a number of majors not covered in this book, we highly recommend visiting the College Transitions Dataverse at **www.collegetransitions.com/dataverse**. Please revisit the methodology section of this book (in the front) for an extensive explanation of how we selected the programs for inclusion.

And without further ado, we present College Transitions' Top Colleges for America's Top Majors:

Accounting
Baruch College (CUNY)
Binghamton University (SUNY)
Boston College
Brigham Young University
Bucknell University
Claremont McKenna College
Fordham University
Georgetown University
Indiana University Bloomington
Lehigh University
New York University
The Ohio State University – Columbus
Santa Clara University
University of Florida
University of Georgia
University of Illinois at Urbana-Champaign
University of Michigan
University of Notre Dame
University of Pennsylvania
University of Southern California
The University of Texas at Austin
Villanova University
Wake Forest University
Washington and Lee University
Washington University in St. Louis

Actuarial Science
Bentley University
Brigham Young University
Clemson University
Florida State University
Michigan State University
New York University
The Ohio State University – Columbus
Pennsylvania State University – University Park
Purdue University – West Lafayette
University of Notre Dame
University of California, Los Angeles
University of California, Santa Barbara
University of Florida
University of Georgia
University of Illinois at Urbana-Champaign
University of Michigan
University of Minnesota – Twin Cities
University of North Carolina at Chapel Hill
University of Pennsylvania
University of Wisconsin – Madison

Animal Science
California Polytechnic State University, San Luis Obispo
Clemson University
Cornell University
Michigan State University
North Carolina State University
The Ohio State University – Columbus
Pennsylvania State University – University Park
Purdue University – West Lafayette
Texas A&M University – College Station
University of California, Davis
University of Connecticut
University of Florida
University of Georgia
University of Illinois at Urbana-Champaign
University of Maryland, College Park
University of Massachusetts Amherst
University of Minnesota – Twin Cities
University of Wisconsin – Madison
Virginia Tech

Applied Mathematics
Brown University
California Institute of Technology
Carnegie Mellon University
Columbia University
Cornell University
Harvard University
Johns Hopkins University
Massachusetts Institute of Technology
New York University
Northwestern University
Princeton University
Stony Brook University (SUNY)
Texas A&M University – College Station
University of California, Berkeley
University of California, Los Angeles
University of California, San Diego
University of Pittsburgh – Pittsburgh Campus
University of Rochester
University of Washington – Seattle
Yale University

Architecture
California Polytechnic State University, San Luis Obispo
Carnegie Mellon University
Columbia University
The Cooper Union for the Advancement of Science and Art
Cornell University

Georgia Institute of Technology
Illinois Institute of Technology
Lehigh University
Northeastern University
Princeton University
Rensselaer Polytechnic Institute
Rice University
Syracuse University
Tulane University
University of California, Berkeley
University of Florida
University of Michigan
University of Minnesota – Twin Cities
University of Notre Dame
University of Pennsylvania
University of Southern California
The University of Texas at Austin
University of Virginia
Virginia Tech
Washington University in St. Louis

Art and/or Design
Arizona State University
Boston University
Carnegie Mellon
Columbia University
The Cooper Union for the Advancement of Science and Art
Cornell University
New York University
North Carolina State University
Northeastern University
Princeton University
Rochester Institute of Technology
Rutgers University – New Brunswick
Skidmore College
University of California, Los Angeles
University of California, San Diego
University of Notre Dame
University of Pennsylvania
University of Southern California
University of Washington – Seattle
University of Wisconsin – Madison
Vassar College
Washington University in St. Louis
Whitman College
Williams College
Yale University

Biology
Amherst College
Bowdoin College
Brandeis University
Brown University
California Institute of Technology
Carleton College
Colby College
Cornell University
Dartmouth College
Duke University
Emory University
Grinnell College
Harvard University
Haverford College
Johns Hopkins University
Macalester College
Massachusetts Institute of Technology

Pomona College
Princeton University
Reed College
Stanford University
Swarthmore College
University of California, Berkeley
University of California, Davis
University of California, Los Angeles
University of California, San Diego
University of Chicago
University of Pennsylvania
Washington University in St. Louis
Yale University

Biomedical Engineering
Boston University
Brown University
California Institute of Technology
Carnegie Mellon University
Case Western Reserve University
Columbia University
Cornell University
Duke University
Georgia Institute of Technology
Harvard University
Johns Hopkins University
Massachusetts Institute of Technology
Northwestern University
Purdue University – West Lafayette
Rice University
Stanford University
University of California, Berkeley
University of California, San Diego
University of Illinois at Urbana-Champaign
University of Michigan
University of Pennsylvania
University of Pittsburgh – Pittsburgh Campus
University of Rochester
The University of Texas at Austin
University of Washington – Seattle
University of Wisconsin – Madison
Vanderbilt University
Washington University in St. Louis
Worcester Polytechnic Institute
Yale University

Business Administration
Babson College
Bentley University
Boston College
Carnegie Mellon University
College of William & Mary
Cornell University
Emory University
Georgetown University
Georgia Institute of Technology
Indiana University Bloomington
Massachusetts Institute of Technology
New York University
Northeastern University
The Ohio State University – Columbus
Southern Methodist University
University of California, Berkeley
University of Illinois at Urbana-Champaign
University of Michigan
University of North Carolina at Chapel Hill

University of Notre Dame
University of Pennsylvania
University of Richmond
University of Southern California
The University of Texas at Austin
University of Virginia
University of Wisconsin – Madison
Villanova University
Wake Forest University
Washington and Lee University
Washington University in St. Louis

Chemistry
Bowdoin College
Bryn Mawr College
California Institute of Technology
Carleton College
College of the Holy Cross
College of William & Mary
Columbia University
Cornell University
Grinnell College
Harvard University
Harvey Mudd College
Haverford College
Macalester College
Massachusetts Institute of Technology
Northwestern University
Pomona College
Princeton University
Reed College
Rice University
St. Olaf College
Stanford University
University of California, Berkeley
University of California, San Diego
University of Chicago
University of Illinois at Urbana-Champaign
University of Minnesota – Twin Cities
University of North Carolina at Chapel Hill
Washington University in St. Louis
Wellesley College
Williams College

Chemical Engineering
Bucknell University
California Institute of Technology
Carnegie Mellon University
Colorado School of Mines
Columbia University
Cornell University
Georgia Institute of Technology
Johns Hopkins University
Lehigh University
Massachusetts Institute of Technology
North Carolina State University
Northwestern University
Princeton University
Purdue University – West Lafayette
Rensselaer Polytechnic Institute
Rice University
Stanford University
Tufts University
University of California, Berkeley
University of California, Santa Barbara
University of Illinois at Urbana-Champaign
University of Michigan
University of Minnesota – Twin Cities

University of Notre Dame
University of Pennsylvania
The University of Texas at Austin
University of Wisconsin – Madison
Washington University in St. Louis
Worcester Polytechnic Institute

Civil Engineering
Arizona State University
Bucknell University
California Institute of Technology
Carnegie Mellon University
Clarkson University
Columbia University
Cornell University
Georgia Institute of Technology
Johns Hopkins University
Lafayette College
Lehigh University
Massachusetts Institute of Technology
North Carolina State University
Northwestern University
The Ohio State University – Columbus
Pennsylvania State University – University Park
Princeton University
Purdue University – West Lafayette
Rose-Hulman Institute of Technology
Rice University
Stanford University
Texas A&M University – College Station
Tufts University
University of California, Berkeley
University of California, Davis
University of Illinois at Urbana-Champaign
University of Maryland, College Park
University of Michigan
The University of Texas at Austin
University of Wisconsin – Madison
Virginia Tech

Communication
American University
Boston College
Boston University
Cornell University
Fordham University
George Washington University
New York University
Northeastern University
Northwestern University
The Ohio State University – Columbus
Pennsylvania State University – University Park
Pepperdine University
Santa Clara University
Syracuse University
University of California, Berkeley
University of Florida
University of Georgia
University of Maryland, College Park
University of Miami
University of Minnesota – Twin Cities
University of North Carolina at Chapel Hill
University of Pennsylvania
University of Southern California
The University of Texas at Austin
University of Washington – Seattle
University of Wisconsin – Madison

Vanderbilt University
Villanova University
Wake Forest University
Washington and Lee University

Computer Science
California Institute of Technology
Carleton College
Carnegie Mellon University
Columbia University
Cornell University
Duke University
Georgia Institute of Technology
Harvard University
Harvey Mudd College
Massachusetts Institute of Technology
New York University
Northeastern University
Princeton University
Purdue University – West Lafayette
Rutgers University – New Brunswick
Stanford University
Swarthmore College
University of California, Berkeley
University of California, Los Angeles
University of California, San Diego
University of Illinois at Urbana-Champaign
University of Maryland, College Park
University of Massachusetts Amherst
University of Michigan
University of Pennsylvania
University of Southern California
The University of Texas at Austin
University of Washington – Seattle
University of Wisconsin – Madison
Virginia Tech

Criminology/Criminal Justice
American University
Arizona State University
Florida State University
George Mason University
George Washington University
Indiana University Bloomington
Marist College
Northeastern University
The Ohio State University – Columbus
Pennsylvania State University – University Park
Rutgers University – New Brunswick
San Diego State University
The College of New Jersey
University of California, Irvine
University of Georgia
University of Maryland, College Park
University of Miami
University of Pennsylvania
University of Pittsburgh – Pittsburgh Campus
University of Washington – Seattle

English
Amherst College
Barnard College
Bowdoin College
Brown University
Bryn Mawr College
College of the Holy Cross
Columbia University
Cornell University

Dartmouth College
Davidson College
Duke University
Harvard University
Haverford College
Johns Hopkins University
Kenyon College
Middlebury College
Northwestern University
Princeton University
Reed College
Stanford University
Swarthmore College
University of Michigan
University of California, Berkeley
University of California, Los Angeles
University of Chicago
University of Pennsylvania
University of Virginia
Vassar College
Williams College
Yale University

Economics
Amherst College
Bowdoin College
Brown University
Claremont McKenna College
Colby College
Columbia University
Cornell University
Dartmouth College
Duke University
Georgetown University
Grinnell College
Harvard University
Macalester College
Massachusetts Institute of Technology
Middlebury College
New York University
Northwestern University
Pomona College
Princeton University
Stanford University
Swarthmore College
University of California, Berkeley
University of California, San Diego
University of Chicago
University of Michigan
University of Pennsylvania
Vanderbilt University
Washington and Lee University
Williams College
Yale University

Education
Arizona State University
Boston College
Boston University
Brigham Young University
Brown University
Colgate University
College of William & Mary
Duke University
Emory University
Florida State University
Indiana University Bloomington
New York University

The Ohio State University – Columbus
Pennsylvania State University – University Park
Southern Methodist University
Swarthmore College
University of California, Irvine
University of Connecticut
University of Florida
University of Georgia
University of Illinois at Urbana-Champaign
University of Maryland, College Park
University of Michigan
University of Minnesota – Twin Cities
University of North Carolina at Chapel Hill
University of Pittsburgh – Pittsburgh Campus
The University of Texas at Austin
University of Washington – Seattle
University of Wisconsin – Madison
Vanderbilt University

Electrical Engineering
Bucknell University
California Institute of Technology
Carnegie Mellon University
Case Western Reserve University
Columbia University
Cornell University
Duke University
Franklin W. Olin College of Engineering
Georgia Institute of Technology
Illinois Institute of Technology
Massachusetts Institute of Technology
Northeastern University
Northwestern University
Princeton University
Purdue University – West Lafayette
Rensselaer Polytechnic Institute
Rice University
Stanford University
Stevens Institute of Technology
University of California, Berkeley
University of California, Los Angeles
University of California, San Diego
University of Illinois at Urbana-Champaign
University of Pennsylvania
University of Southern California
The University of Texas at Austin
University of Wisconsin – Madison
University of Michigan
University of Maryland, College Park
Virginia Tech
Worcester Polytechnic Institute

Environmental Engineering
Arizona State University
California Polytechnic State University, San Luis Obispo
California Institute of Technology
Carnegie Mellon University
Cornell University
Duke University
Georgia Institute of Technology
Johns Hopkins University
Massachusetts Institute of Technology
North Carolina State University
Pennsylvania State University – University Park
Purdue University – West Lafayette
Rice University
Stanford University

University at Buffalo (SUNY)
University of California, Berkeley
University of California, Davis
University of Florida
University of Illinois at Urbana-Champaign
University of Michigan
The University of Texas at Austin
University of Washington – Seattle
University of Wisconsin – Madison
Virginia Tech
Yale University

Environmental Studies
Amherst College
Bates College
Bowdoin College
Colby College
Colorado College
Cornell University
Dartmouth College
Dickinson College
Duke University
Hamilton College
Macalester College
Middlebury College
Mount Holyoke College
Oberlin College
Pitzer College
Pomona College
Tulane University
University of California, Berkeley
University of California, Davis
University of California, Santa Barbara
University of Chicago
University of North Carolina at Chapel Hill
University of Wisconsin – Madison
Williams College
Yale University

Film
American University
Binghamton University (SUNY)
Boston University
Chapman University
Columbia University
DePaul University
Drexel University
Emerson College
Florida State University
George Mason University
Ithaca College
Loyola Marymount University
New York University
Rochester Institute of Technology
Southern Methodist University
Stanford University
Syracuse University
Temple University
University of California, Los Angeles
University of Colorado Boulder
University of Miami
University of North Carolina at Wilmington
University of Southern California
The University of Texas at Austin
Wesleyan University

Finance
Arizona State University
Babson College
Baruch College (CUNY)
Bentley University
Boston College
Boston University
Carnegie Mellon University
Cornell University
Emory University
Fairfield University
Fordham University
George Washington University
Georgetown University
Indiana University Bloomington
Massachusetts Institute of Technology
New York University
The Ohio State University – Columbus
Pennsylvania State University – University Park
University of California, Berkeley
University of Illinois at Urbana-Champaign
University of Michigan
University of North Carolina at Chapel Hill
University of Notre Dame
University of Pennsylvania
University of Southern California
The University of Texas at Austin
University of Virginia
University of Washington – Seattle
University of Wisconsin – Madison
Washington University in St. Louis

Geology
Bowdoin College
Brown University
California Institute of Technology
Carleton College
College of William & Mary
Colorado School of Mines
Columbia University
Duke University
Lehigh University
Massachusetts Institute of Technology
Pennsylvania State University – University Park
Princeton University
Stanford University
Texas A&M University – College Station
Union College
University of California, Berkeley
University of California, Davis
University of California, Irvine
University of California, Santa Barbara
University of Florida
University of Michigan
University of Minnesota – Twin Cities
University of Pennsylvania
University of Pittsburgh – Pittsburgh Campus
The University of Texas at Austin
University of Washington – Seattle
University of Wisconsin – Madison
Whitman College
Yale University

History
Amherst College
Barnard College
Bowdoin College
Brown University

Carleton College
Colgate University
Columbia University
Cornell University
Dartmouth College
Georgetown University
Grinnell College
Harvard University
Haverford College
Johns Hopkins University
Kenyon College
Northwestern University
Oberlin College
Pomona College
Princeton University
Stanford University
Swarthmore College
University of California, Berkeley
University of California, Los Angeles
University of Chicago
University of Michigan
University of Pennsylvania
University of Wisconsin – Madison
Vanderbilt University
Williams College
Yale University

Industrial Engineering
Clarkson University
Clemson University
Columbia University
Cornell University
Georgia Institute of Technology
Lehigh University
North Carolina State University
Northeastern University
Northwestern University
The Ohio State University – Columbus
Pennsylvania State University – University Park
Purdue University – West Lafayette
Rensselaer Polytechnic Institute
Stanford University
Texas A&M University – College Station
University of California, Berkeley
University of Florida
University of Illinois at Urbana-Champaign
University of Michigan
University of Pittsburgh – Pittsburgh Campus
University of Southern California
The University of Texas at Austin
University of Wisconsin – Madison
Virginia Tech
Worcester Polytechnic Institute

Information Systems
Arizona State University
Bentley University
Carnegie Mellon University
Case Western Reserve University
Cornell University
Fairfield University
Georgetown University
Georgia Institute of Technology
Indiana University Bloomington
Massachusetts Institute of Technology
New York University
Northeastern University
The Ohio State University – Columbus

Purdue University – West Lafayette
Santa Clara University
University of Arizona
University of Georgia
University of Illinois at Urbana-Champaign
University of Maryland, College Park
University of Michigan
University of Minnesota – Twin Cities
University of Pennsylvania
The University of Texas at Austin
University of Washington – Seattle
University of Wisconsin – Madison

International Relations
American University
Boston University
Brown University
Claremont McKenna College
Colby College
Colgate University
College of William & Mary
Columbia University
Connecticut College
Cornell University
Dartmouth College
George Washington University
Georgetown University
Harvard University
Johns Hopkins University
Mount Holyoke College
Pomona College
Princeton University
Stanford University
Swarthmore College
Tufts University
University of California, Berkeley
University of California, San Diego
University of Chicago
University of Michigan
University of Pennsylvania
University of Southern California
University of Virginia
Williams College
Yale University

Kinesiology
Boston University
Brigham Young University
Indiana University Bloomington
Northeastern University
Occidental College
Pennsylvania State University – University Park
Rice University
San Diego State University
Syracuse University
Texas A&M University – College Station
University of Connecticut
University of Florida
University of Georgia
University of Illinois at Urbana-Champaign
University of Maryland, College Park
University of Massachusetts Amherst
University of Miami
University of Michigan
University of Minnesota – Twin Cities
University of North Carolina at Chapel Hill
University of Pittsburgh – Pittsburgh Campus

The University of Texas at Austin
University of Virginia
University of Wisconsin – Madison
Wake Forest University

Marketing
Arizona State University
Boston College
Cornell University
Emory University
Fordham University
George Washington University
Georgetown University
Indiana University Bloomington
New York University
Pennsylvania State University – University Park
Santa Clara University
Southern Methodist University
Tulane University
University of California, Berkeley
University of Florida
University of Illinois at Urbana-Champaign
University of Maryland, College Park
University of Michigan
University of Minnesota – Twin Cities
University of North Carolina at Chapel Hill
University of Notre Dame
University of Pennsylvania
University of Pittsburgh – Pittsburgh Campus
University of Southern California
The University of Texas at Austin
University of Virginia
University of Washington – Seattle
University of Wisconsin – Madison
Villanova University
Washington University in St. Louis

Materials Science and Engineering
California Institute of Technology
Carnegie Mellon University
Colorado School of Mines
Columbia University
Cornell University
Georgia Institute of Technology
Johns Hopkins University
Lehigh University
Massachusetts Institute of Technology
North Carolina State University
Northwestern University
The Ohio State University – Columbus
Pennsylvania State University – University Park
Purdue University – West Lafayette
Rensselaer Polytechnic Institute
Rice University
Stanford University
University of California, Berkeley
University of California, Los Angeles
University of California, Santa Barbara
University of Florida
University of Illinois at Urbana-Champaign
University of Michigan
University of Pennsylvania
The University of Texas at Austin
University of Washington – Seattle
University of Wisconsin – Madison
Virginia Tech

Mechanical Engineering

California Institute of Technology
Carnegie Mellon University
Case Western Reserve University
Columbia University
Cornell University
Duke University
Franklin W. Olin College of Engineering
Georgia Institute of Technology
Johns Hopkins University
Lehigh University
Massachusetts Institute of Technology
Northwestern University
The Ohio State University – Columbus
Pennsylvania State University – University Park
Princeton University
Purdue University – West Lafayette
Rensselaer Polytechnic Institute
Rice University
Rose-Hulman Institute of Technology
Stanford University
Stevens Institute of Technology
Texas A&M University – College Station
University of California, Berkeley
University of California, Los Angeles
University of Illinois at Urbana-Champaign
University of Michigan
University of Pennsylvania
The University of Texas at Austin
University of Wisconsin – Madison
Vanderbilt University
Virginia Tech
Worcester Polytechnic Institute

Neuroscience

Amherst College
Barnard College
Bates College
Boston University
Bowdoin College
Brandeis University
Brown University
Colgate University
College of William & Mary
Columbia University
Dartmouth College
Duke University
Emory University
Harvard University
Johns Hopkins University
Middlebury College
Northwestern University
Oberlin College
Pomona College
Princeton University
Tulane University
University of California, Los Angeles
University of Pennsylvania
University of Pittsburgh – Pittsburgh Campus
University of Rochester
University of Southern California
Vanderbilt University
Washington University in St. Louis
Wellesley College
Wesleyan University

Nursing

Binghamton University (SUNY)
Boston College
Brigham Young University
Case Western Reserve University
Clemson University
The College of New Jersey
Drexel University
Emory University
Fairfield University
Georgetown University
New York University
Northeastern University
The Ohio State University – Columbus
Pennsylvania State University – University Park
Rutgers University – New Brunswick
Stony Brook University (SUNY)
University of Connecticut
University of Florida
University of Massachusetts Amherst
University of Miami
University of Michigan
University of Minnesota – Twin Cities
University of North Carolina at Chapel Hill
University of Pennsylvania
University of Pittsburgh – Pittsburgh Campus
The University of Texas at Austin
University of Virginia
University of Washington – Seattle
University of Wisconsin – Madison
Villanova University

Physics

Brown University
California Institute of Technology
Carleton College
Carnegie Mellon University
Columbia University
Cornell University
Davidson College
Harvard University
Harvey Mudd College
Haverford College
Johns Hopkins University
Massachusetts Institute of Technology
Pomona College
Princeton University
Reed College
Rensselaer Polytechnic Institute
Rice University
Stanford University
University of California, Berkeley
University of California, Los Angeles
University of California, Santa Barbara
University of Chicago
University of Illinois at Urbana-Champaign
University of Maryland, College Park
University of Michigan
University of Notre Dame
University of Pennsylvania
University of Rochester
Yale University

Political Science

Bowdoin College
Brown University
College of William & Mary
Columbia University
Cornell University
Dartmouth College
Duke University
Georgetown University
Hamilton College
Harvard University
Haverford College
Macalester College
Middlebury College
Northwestern University
Princeton University
Stanford University
University of California, Berkeley
University of California, Los Angeles
University of Chicago
University of Michigan
University of North Carolina at Chapel Hill
University of Notre Dame
University of Pennsylvania
University of Rochester
Vanderbilt University
Vassar College
Washington and Lee University
Wesleyan University
Williams College
Yale University

Psychology

Barnard College
Bates College
Boston College
Brown University
Claremont McKenna College
Columbia University
Dartmouth College
Duke University
Harvard University
Haverford College
Northwestern University
Pomona College
Princeton University
Stanford University
Tufts University
University of California, Berkeley
University of California, Los Angeles
University of Chicago
University of Michigan
University of Minnesota – Twin Cities
University of North Carolina at Chapel Hill
University of Pennsylvania
University of Wisconsin – Madison
Vanderbilt University
Vassar College
Washington University in St. Louis
Wellesley College
Wesleyan University
Williams College
Yale University

Statistics

Brigham Young University
Carleton College
Carnegie Mellon University
Columbia University
Cornell University
Duke University
Harvard University
Johns Hopkins University
North Carolina State University
Northwestern University
Pennsylvania State University – University Park
Purdue University – West Lafayette
Rice University
Rutgers University – New Brunswick
Stanford University
Texas A&M University – College Station
University of California, Berkeley
University of California, Los Angeles
University of California, Santa Barbara
University of Chicago
University of Connecticut
University of Florida
University of Illinois at Urbana-Champaign
University of Michigan
University of Minnesota – Twin Cities
University of North Carolina at Chapel Hill
University of Pennsylvania
University of Washington – Seattle
University of Wisconsin – Madison
Virginia Tech

Theatre

Boston University
Brown University
Carnegie Mellon University
Chapman University
DePaul University
Elon University
Emerson College
Florida State University
Fordham University
The Juilliard School
Loyola Marymount University
Muhlenberg College
New York University
Northwestern University
Purchase College (SUNY)
Rutgers University – New Brunswick
Skidmore College
Syracuse University
University of California, Irvine
University of California, Los Angeles
University of California, San Diego
University of Connecticut
University of Illinois at Urbana-Champaign
University of Miami
University of Michigan
University of Minnesota – Twin Cities
University of Notre Dame
University of Southern California
Vassar College
Yale University

Andrew Belasco, Ph.D., a graduate of Georgetown University and Harvard University, is a higher education researcher, counselor, and CEO of College Transitions, an educational consulting firm. His work has been published in the nation's top higher education journals and featured in dozens of media outlets, including *The New York Times*, *Washington Post*, *Time*, *Boston Globe*, *Forbes*, *The Chronicle of Higher Education*, and NPR, among others. Andrew is also the co-author of *The Enlightened College Applicant: A New Approach to the Search and Admissions Process* (Rowman & Littlefield, 2016).

Dave Bergman, Ed.D., earned his doctoral degree from Temple University and has fifteen years of professional experience that includes work as a teacher, high school administrator, adjunct professor, researcher, and independent educational consultant. As a co-founder of College Transitions, Dave oversees the collegetransitions.com blog and Dataverse, reaching an audience in excess of one million readers annually. Dave is also the co-author of *The Enlightened College Applicant: A New Approach to the Search and Admission Process* (Rowman & Littlefield, 2016).

Michael Trivette, Ph.D., a graduate of the University of Georgia Institute of Higher Education, has over fifteen years of experience in the higher-education field, including college admissions, enrollment management, intercollegiate athletics, student support services, and student life. A co-founder of College Transitions, he also has experience working within the University of North Carolina System and the University System of Georgia. His research has been published in *Educational Policy*, *Review of Higher Education*, *The Journal of Higher Education*, and the *Journal of Education Finance*.

College Transitions is a college counseling firm that guides students through the undergraduate admissions and financial aid process, serving families in the U.S. and abroad.